P9-DNS-381

Please remember that this is a library book,
and that it belongs only temporarily to each
person who uses it. Be considerate. Do
not write in this, or any, library book.

WITHDRAWN

AAX·5110
VC Grad

COMPUTER EDUCATION
FOR TEACHERS

THIRD EDITION

VICKI SHARP
CALIFORNIA STATE UNIVERSITY, NORTHRIDGE

McGraw-Hill College

Boston   Burr Ridge, IL   Dubuque, IA   Madison, WI   New York   San Francisco
St. Louis   Bangkok   Bogotá   Caracas   Lisbon   London   Madrid   Mexico City
Milan   New Delhi   Seoul   Singapore   Sydney   Taipei   Toronto

McGraw-Hill College
A Division of The McGraw-Hill Companies

COMPUTER EDUCATION FOR TEACHERS, THIRD EDITION

Copyright © 1999 by The McGraw-Hill Companies, Inc. All rights reserved. Previous edition © 1996 by Times Mirror Higher Education Group, Inc. All rights reserved. Printed in the United States of America. Except as permitted under the United States Copyright Act of 1976, no part of this publication may be reproduced or distributed in any form or by any means, or stored in a data base or retrieval system, without the prior written permission of the publisher.

This book is printed on acid-free paper.

1 2 3 4 5 6 7 8 9 DOC/DOC 9 3 2 1 0 9 8

ISBN 0–07–292458-6

Editorial director: *Jane E. Vaicunas*
Sponsoring editor: *Beth Kaufman*
Editorial assistant: *Daniel M. Loch*
Project manager: *Janice M. Roerig-Blong*
Production supervisor: *Sandy Ludovissy*
Freelance design coordinator: *Mary L. Christianson*
Senior photo research coordinator: *Lori Hancock*
Supplement coordinator: *Tammy Juran*
Compositor: *Carlisle Communications Ltd.*
Typeface: *10/13 Palatino*
Printer: *R. R. Donnelley & Sons Company/Crawfordsville, IN*

Freelance cover designer: *Tin Box Studio, Inc.*
Cover image: © *Jose Ortega/SIS*

Library of Congress Cataloging-in-Publication Data

Sharp, Vicki F.
 Computer education for teachers / Vicki Sharp. — 3rd ed.
  p. cm.
 Includes bibliographical references and index.
 ISBN 0–07–292458-6
  1. Education—Data processing. 2. Computers—Study and teaching.
 3. Computer-assisted instruction. I. Title.
 LB1028.43.S55 1999
 370'.285—dc21   98–24365
                                CIP

www.mhhe.com

Brief Contents

Contents

Preface

Background

My first involvement with computers was in 1969 when I learned Fortran. In the early eighties, I bought pocket computers and taught programming off campus. At that time, educational software was limited and inadequate, and the focus was teaching BASIC, followed shortly thereafter by Logo.

Since the mid 1990s, there have been many technological changes, and the computer has emerged as an important tool in society. With the production of quality software, the computer's role has changed from a device used for computer programming to an instrument that can be efficiently integrated into the curriculum. Furthermore, an increasing number of teachers utilize the computer for such tasks as word processing, database management, graphics generation, desktop publishing, telecommunications, and multimedia.

With this increased interest in computers, computer literacy is becoming as necessary as reading literacy. Because computers are so commonplace, teacher education programs require students to take computer literacy courses. In order for teachers to use computers, they must acquire the skills to evaluate and use the software that is being produced and marketed.

Book Audience

Computer Education for Teachers, third edition, assumes no prior experience with computers and is designed to meet the needs of the computer novice. It is written for undergraduate and graduate students who want an up-to-date, readable, practical, concise introduction to computers. This book should help students acquire the knowledge and skills necessary to effectively integrate computers into the classroom.

Contents of the Text

The content of the text is arranged in a logical teaching order. However, the chapters are not dependent on each other and can be taught in the order the instructor requires.

This edition offers the following salient features:

▶ **Chapter objectives.** The objectives at the beginning of each chapter operate as a map of the chapter's contents, thus guiding the reader in his or her travel.

▶ **Clear illustrations.** There are more than 300 illustrations used to highlight pertinent points, facilitate understanding, and explain software.

▶ **Universal applicability.** The book discusses general concepts and principles that are applicable to any personal computer.

▶ **Chapter mastery tests.** Questions selected according to sound learning principles appear at the end of each chapter to help readers ascertain if they understand the material.

▶ **Recommended annotated software listing.** A complete, up-to-date annotated listing of software, including CD-ROM and laser discs, helps the reader make a more informed purchase decision.

▶ **Classroom activities and projects.** An assortment of learning activities and projects motivates students, enhances learning, integrates the computer in the classroom, and helps students apply the chapter concepts.

▶ **Summary of current computer research.** These summaries provide readers with an understanding of past and current research, effective and ineffective uses of the computer, and promising new directions for further research.

▶ **Exposure to state-of-the-art technology developments.** Explorations of advances in computer technology keep the student on the cutting edge of computer knowledge.

▶ **Extensive bibliography.** The reader can use the selected bibliography to investigate a wide spectrum of topics.

▶ **A chapter on desktop publishing.** The chapter on desktop publishing, which is one of the primary applications for the computer, teaches the student to create such products as newspapers, bulletins, and signs that can enrich the curriculum and enhance the classroom atmosphere.

▶ **A chapter on multimedia.** This chapter introduces the student to ways of using the computer to combine text, graphics, and sound into effective multimedia presentations.

▶ **A chapter on telecommunication, the Internet, and on-line services.** This chapter gives the student an introduction to telecommunications, the Internet, the information highway, and the various commercial services.

A chapter on the World Wide Web. This chapter gives the student an introduction to the World Wide Web, a wide array of Web sites ranging from art and computer history to science and social studies, a Web site evaluation instrument, and much more.

A teacher's manual. This manual supplies the teacher with chapter summaries, lecture outlines, answers to mastery test questions, suggested activities and projects, transparency masters, additional test items, and sample software evaluations.

New to the Third Edition

Computer Education for Teachers has been changed in numerous ways from the last edition to reflect the changes that are occurring in the computer community. All chapters have been revised and updated. The new edition offers the following features:

▶ more than 150 new illustrations;
▶ new annotated list of software (see Appendix A);
▶ an expanded and updated Internet and on-line services chapter;
▶ a new chapter on the World Wide Web including sites, evaluation instrument, and Web page creation;
▶ an expanded and updated multimedia chapter;
▶ a completely revised programming chapter that includes HTML;
▶ discussion of current topics such as *QuickTime VR,* virtual reality, morphing, warping, videoconferencing, advanced technology labs, classroom ergonomics, and distant learning; and
▶ additional chapter questions, projects, and updated bibliography.

A Message for the Readers

If you would like to see some topic in a future edition or have any comments or questions, please send your responses to one of the following addresses:

1. Internet address: vicki.sharp@csun.edu
2. America Online address: VickiFS@aol.com
3. University address: Dr. Vicki Sharp, California State University, Northridge, School of Education, 18111 Nordhoff, Northridge CA 91330-8265.

Acknowledgments

It is with great appreciation that I acknowledge the assistance of many of the people and companies who contributed to the completion of this textbook:

Abacus Concepts Inc.: Will Scoggin
Barnum Software: Christopher Wright
The Bohle Company: Cindy Monticue
Brøderbund Software: Pat Walkington, Lynette Comstock, Eric Winkler
California State University, Northridge: Dr. Bonnie Ericson, Chris Sales, Dr. Richard M. Sharp
Claris Corporation: Sue Hart
Corel: Michele Crother
Cray Research Inc.: Steve Conway
Davidson: Linda Duttenhaver

Digital Video Magazine: Peter Karnig
Don Johnson: Christine A. Filler
Dr. T's Music Software Company: John Merson
Edmark: Amy Gutmann
E.M.A.: Bob Enenstein
Equilibrium: Dave Pola
FTC Group: Mike Kessler, Morsha Kessler
Great Wave Software: Kelly Jones
Grolier Electronic Publishing
Gryphon Software Corporation
Hartley: Telaina Morse Eriksen

Hi Tech: David Summer
Ingenuity Works: David J. Young, Brian Sellstedt
Insignia Solutions: Brian Fox
Inspiration: Mark Oronzio, Susannah Sparks
Jay Klein Productions: Jay A. Klein
Knowledge Adventure: Jennifer Johnson
Lawrence Productions: Telaina Morse Eriksen
Learning Company: Evelyn Dubocq, Debbie Galdin
Logo Computer Systems Inc. (LCSI): Lea M. Laricci
MAXIS: Patrick Buechner
MECC: Patricia Kallio
Microsoft: Scott McLaughlin and Irving Kwong
Mindscape: Tracy A. Eagan
The National Center for Computer Crime: Buck BloomBecker
Optimum Resources, Inc.
Orbis Software: Gracie Pauly
The Princeton Review

Roger Wagner Inc.: Roger Wagner, Chris Saulpaugh, Sean Kelly
Sanctuary Woods: Kristy Sager, David Brooks
Scanton & Associates: Catherine L. Wambach
Scholastic Software: Ellen Margolies
Sierra On-Line: Susan Hill, Eric Twelker
SmartStuff: Rich Chapin
SoftKey: Stacy Peña
Sunburst Communication: Clair Kubasik
Terrapin Logo: Dorothy M. Fitch
TikiSoft Inc.: Marc Weiss, Michael Radonic
T/Maker: Diane La Mountaine
Time-Warner Interactive: Kim Sudhalter
Tom Snyder Productions: Christina E. McCartney
University of Washington: Terry Gray
Ventura Educational Systems: Fred Ventura, Donna Bland
Visions: Richard Otto
Xerox Imaging Software: Teri Roche

A very special thanks to **Patricia Kallio** (MECC), **Evelyn Dubocq** and **Debbie Galdin** (Learning Company), **Lynette Comstock** and **Pat Walkington** (Brøderbund), **Susan Hart** (Claris Corporation FileMaker Inc.), **Marc Weiss** and **Michael Radonic (**TikiSoft Inc.), **Dave Pola** (Equilibrium), **Roger Wagner** and **Chris Saulpaugh** (Roger Wagner Inc.), and **Clair Kubasik** (Sunburst). These individuals selflessly gave of their time and provided expert advice.

Bonnie Ericson deserves special recognition for a well-written teacher's manual, an excellent resource for the instructor. She did an outstanding job and it is greatly appreciated.

I want to express my appreciation to **Beth Kaufman** (Sponsoring Editor) and **Michele Siegal** (Editorial Assistant) at McGraw-Hill for their invaluable assistance, direction, and time. Beth and Michele were always willing listeners and supporters. Without Terry Routley and Janice Roerig this manuscript would never have been completed. They were always available, and willing to give assistance whenever needed. I also wish to thank, last but not least, the following individuals for their invaluable contributions in reviewing and critiquing my manuscript: **James Bosco** (Western Michigan University), **David Bullock** (Portland State University), **James Murphy** (Elon College), **Randy Carlson** (Georgia Southern University), **James Moseley** (Wayne State University), **Shirley Smith** (Marymount University), **John Achrazogloa** (University of Iowa), **Dr. William Michael Reed** (West Virginia University), **Tom Wilson** (Arizona USA Pacific College), and **Joan Cook** (Montana State University-Bozeman) for her extra work on my manuscript. It was greatly appreciated!

Thanks to Equilibrium for use of *DeBabelizer* to batch produce the screen shots and enhance the images, and to TikiSoft for use of *DragNet* to organize and create the bookmarks used in chapter 12.

Finally, a special thanks to **Anthony Nguyen** (Network Administrator at CSUN) for his help on the different programming languages and to my family: my husband, **Dick,** whose help on the Web site chapter and whose criticisms helped improve the manuscript, and my son, **David,** who critiqued the software. This book is dedicated to my mother Bobbie E. Friedman and the memory of my dad, Paul J. Friedman.

History of the Computer

1

Objectives

Upon completing this chapter, you will be able to:

1. Identify and place in proper sequence five of the major inventions in the history of computing;
2. Discuss succinctly each of the following six individual's contribution to the field of computing:
   a. Herman Hollerith,
   b. Joseph Marie Jacquard,
   c. Charles Babbage,
   d. John Atanasoff,
   e. Howard Aiken, and
   f. John Von Neumann; and
3. Differentiate among the generations of computers according to their technological advances.

Early Times

Primitive humans found it necessary to count and the natural instruments to use were their fingers. With their fingers, they could show how many animals they killed on a hunt or the number of people in a village. To indicate large numbers, they used all ten fingers; since humans have ten fingers, ten became the basis of our number system today.

As time passed, life became more complex, and people needed a way to keep track of their possessions. They began to use rocks as a way to store information, using one rock to represent each animal they owned, for example. Later, wanting a record of this information, they carved notches and symbols in stone or wood, an effective record-keeping method until the abacus was invented.

The Abacus

The **abacus** was different from any recording device that came before it because it allowed manipulation of data.

In 1854, at Senkereh near Babylon, archaeologists found a clay tablet resembling a primitive abacus. They believed it was nearly 4,000 years old (J.M. Pullan, 1968). The discovery of this artifact indicates that some form of calculation existed in Babylon about 3000 B.C. (The tablet now resides in the British Museum.)

Records show that ancient civilizations, such as India, China, Egypt, and Mesopotamia, were using calculating devices several thousand years ago. The Greeks in about 500 B.C. drew lines on plain boards or counters in order to perform calculations. Approximately 200 years later, the Romans developed a calculating device called the *calculi*, which consisted of a smooth board or table marked with lines. Even though no boards have survived from these times, stones have been found at many archaeological sites. The stones found in China, Japan, and Russia are similar to the stones used in the Roman bead-frame, which suggests that the use of these instruments spread from Rome to China to Japan and then to Russia, although there is no concrete evidence of this hypothesis. What is known for certain is that the Chinese devised rules for the abacus in the thirteenth century, and they are often given credit for perfecting its use.

The abacus (Fig. 1.1) user manipulates beads in a wood frame to keep track of numbers and place values. Users can perform calculations almost as quickly as people who use calculators. Of all the early aids to calculation, the abacus is the only one used today.

Figure 1.1
Abacus

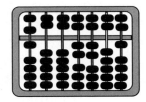

Next we will discuss the pioneers of computational devices and their inventions prior to the computer. Some of these inventions made mathematical calculation and tabulation faster and simpler, while others paved the way for inputting information into computers and controlling more complicated data processing.

The Pioneers

John Napier

John Napier, a Scottish mathematician, invented **Napier's Rods** or **Bones** in 1617. The rods, shown in Figure 1.2, were sometimes carved out of ivory in the form of an Arabian lattice. The user was able to multiply large numbers by manipulating these rods. These devices simplified tedious calculations, and they were faster and more accurate. Napier rods preceded Oughtred's slide ruler by nearly four decades.

Figure 1.2
Napier's Bones

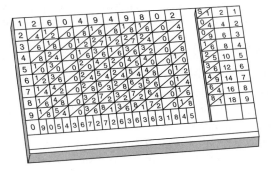

Wilhelm Schickard

Wilhelm Schickard, a German mathematician, was the first to attempt to devise a calculator. Around 1623, he built a mechanism that could add, subtract, multiply, and divide. He intended to send his friend, Johannes Kepler, a copy of his invention, but fire destroyed the parts before they could be assembled. The prototype was never found, but a rough sketch of this machine survived, and a model was built in the 1970s.

Blaise Pascal

Blaise Pascal, a child prodigy, was born in France in 1623. Before he had reached the age of thirteen, Pascal had discovered an error in Descartes's geometry. At the age of sixteen he wanted to study mathematics, but his father, a tax collector, insisted young Pascal spend his time performing additions by hand. Probably aggravated by the whole exercise, he built a calculating machine. In 1642, he built the first operating model of his calculating machine, which he called the **Pascaline** (Fig. 1.3). During the next ten years, he assembled fifty more of these machines.

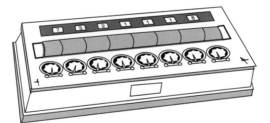

Figure 1.3
The Pascaline

The Pascaline was a shoe-sized brass box that operated with a system of gears and wheels. Since Pascal's machine was devised for English currency, the two right wheels were numbered for shillings and pence while the other wheels were numbered from 1 through 9 for pounds. The wheels could be read through holes at the top of the machine. When a wheel made a complete turn, a notch caused the next wheel to the left to move up one number, thus performing addition. By reversing the revolutions, one could subtract. Considered the first mechanical calculator, the Pascaline could handle numbers up to 999,999.99. Because of the expense to reproduce it and because people feared it would put them out of work, the Pascaline was not a commercial success.

Gottfried Wilhelm Von Leibniz

Pascal's machine was the standard until Leibniz, a German mathematician, designed an instrument called the **Stepped Reckoner,** which he completed in 1694. **Baron Gottfried Wilhelm Von Leibniz's** machine (Fig. 1.4) was more versatile than Pascal's because it could multiply and divide as well as add and subtract and it used cylinders instead of gears to do its calculations.

Unfortunately, the Stepped Reckoner and the Pascaline were not reliable machines because the technology at the time could not produce parts with the necessary precision. Leibniz's most

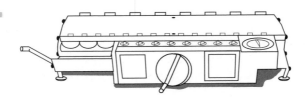

Figure 1.4
Leibniz's Stepped
Reckoner

important contribution to the computer's evolution was not his machine, but his binary arithmetic, a system of counting that uses only two digits, 0 and 1. For example, in the base 2, 0=0,
1=1, 2=10, 3=11, 4=100, and so on. In Leibniz's Universe, the symbol 1 would represent existence and the symbol 0, nonexistence.

Leibniz never completed his work on binary arithmetic.[1] It wasn't until 1854, nearly two cen-
turies later, that **George Boole** devised a system of logic based on the binary system called
Boolean Algebra. However, it wasn't until the late 1930s that inventors built a computer that used
this binary system, the standard internal language of today's digital computers.

Joseph Marie Jacquard

Though not a calculating device, Jacquard's Loom was the next invention of great significance
in the development of the computer. In 1790, **Joseph Marie Jacquard** used punched cards to create patterns on fabric woven on a loom. The hole punches directed the threads up or down, thus
producing the patterns. Jacquard's device was the forerunner of the keypunch machine (Fig. 1.5).

Figure 1.5
Jacquard's Loom

---

[1]Refer to Chapter 2 for a discussion of the binary code.

All the mechanical gadgets discussed so far could do only arithmetic. The first individual to conceptualize a real computer was Charles Babbage, a Cambridge mathematics professor.

Charles Babbage

Aggravated by the errors in the mathematical tables that were being printed, Babbage resigned his position at Cambridge to work on a machine that would solve this problem. He called this machine the *Difference Engine* because it worked on solving differential equations. Using government funds and his own resources, he labored on the computer for nineteen years but was unable to complete it. Babbage constructed only a few components, and people referred to his engine as *Babbage's Folly.*

After the government withdrew its funding, Babbage proceeded to work on another more sophisticated version of this machine, which he called the **Analytical Engine.** A close personal friend of his, **Augusta Ada Byron, Countess of Lovelace,** the only legally recognized daughter of Lord Byron, tried to help him. She raised money for his invention and wrote a demonstration program for the Analytical Engine. Because of this program, she is considered the first computer programmer, and the programming language *Ada* was named after her.

In 1835, Babbage designed a system with provision for printed data, a control unit, and an information storage unit, but the Analytical Engine (Fig. 1.6) was never completed because construction of the machine required precision tools that did not exist at the time. Babbage did not publish many details of his work, although some notes were taken of a lecture he gave at the British Association. He did leave behind enough detailed drawings with a notebook and a portion of the machine so that, in 1906, his son Henry P. Babbage was able to complete part of the engine, get it to compute, and publish samples of its work.

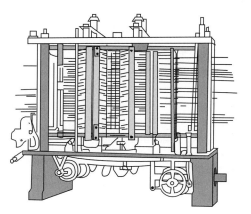

Figure 1.6
Babbage's Analytical Engine

The logic of Babbage's machine was important for other computer inventors. Babbage is responsible for the two classifications of the computer: the *store,* or memory, and the *mill,* a processing unit that carries out the arithmetic calculations for the machine. For this achievement, he is called the "father of computers," and historians have even said that all modern computers were descended directly from Babbage's Analytical Engine, ironic given that in his day Babbage was considered a failure. He died in poverty; just nineteen years later, the punched card aspect of the Analytical Engine appeared in a working machine, a tabulator built by Herman Hollerith.

Herman Hollerith

No history would be complete without discussion of the American inventor **Herman Hollerith.** When Hollerith worked at the Census Bureau in the 1880s, he met Colonel John Shaw Billings, who was the director of the division of vital statistics. They became friends, and during an evening discourse, Billings discussed the possibility of a hypothetical machine that could do the mechanical work of tabulating the population. Billings envisioned the possibility of using cards with notches punched on the edges, with the notches representing each individual's description. Hollerith was so fascinated with the idea, he decided to leave his job at the Census Bureau to go to MIT to teach and work on this Tabulating Machine. Many years later, Hollerith applied for several patents on punched-card data processing, and he devised several experimental test systems.

When Hollerith took out a patent for the first punch card calculator, he was offered a job in the Census Department by Robert Porter. He refused this offer because he was interested in winning the contract to do the 1890 census. In 1889, there was a contest held and Hollerith's system won by a landslide against two competing systems.

Hollerith's innovative Tabulating Machine (Fig. 1.7) relied heavily on Jacquard's punched card idea. Hollerith designed his machine so that it pushed pins against cards that were the size

Figure 1.7
Hollerith's
Tabulating Machine

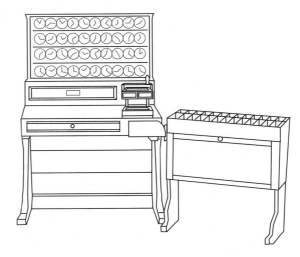

of an old-fashioned dollar bill. The holes made by the pins represented characteristics of the population, such as sex, birthplace, and number of children. If a pin went through a hole, it made contact with a metal surface below and a circuit was completed. This census item was then counted and added to the total. If there was no hole, the census item was not counted and there was nothing added to the total. The census office bought fifty-six of Hollerith's machines and commissioned him to repair them as needed. Because of Hollerith's invention, the census was completed in just two years as compared to the seven years it took for the 1880 census.

Eventually, Herman Hollerith organized his own company called the Tabulating Machine Company. In the 1900s, he rented out his more sophisticated tabulating machines for the census. His business prospered and merged with other companies. The company went through a series of name changes, and the last name change came in 1924 when it became known as International Business Machines, or IBM.

Let's conclude our discussion of these early pioneers with a summary of their achievements in Table 1.1.

Table 1.1   *Computing Devices Before the Twentieth Century*

Inventor	Invention	Year
Unknown	Abacus	3000 B.C.?
John Napier	Napier's Bones	1617
Wilhelm Schickard	Mechanical Calculator	1623
Blaise Pascal	Pascaline	1642
Gottfried Leibniz	Stepped Reckoner	1672
Joseph Marie Jacquard	Punched Card Loom	1804
Charles Babbage	Analytical Engine	1835
Herman Hollerith	Tabulating Machine	1887

In the twentieth century, the Census Bureau quit using Hollerith's machines and bought a machine designed by James Powers. Powers founded a company called Powers Accounting Machine Co., which merged with others to become known as Remington Rand and then Sperry Rand. Today, these companies are part of the conglomerate Unisys.

Hollerith's Company and Powers' Company produced machines that primarily served the business community. However, the scientific community still needed machines that could do more complex processing and therefore there was a demand for scientific data processing machines.

The Modern Computer

In 1944, the age of the modern computer began. World War II created a need for better data handling that spurred on advances in technology and the development of computers. While the war was going on, a brilliant team of scientists and engineers (among them Alan Turing, Max Newman, Ian Fleming, and Lewis Powell) gathered at Bletchley Park, north of London, to work on a machine that could solve the German secret code. They worked with electronic decoders to decipher the Germans' electromechanical teleprint, the Enigma. Much of this innovative work remains classified.

Howard Aiken

In 1937, **Howard Aiken** was working at Harvard to complete his research for his Ph.D. Because he had to do tedious calculations on nonlinear, differential equations, he decided that he needed an automatic calculating machine to make the chore less arduous. In a memo written in 1937, he proposed to create a computer. Initially, Aiken found little support at Harvard for his machine so he turned to private industry. Fortunately, IBM was taken with Aiken's idea and agreed to back him in his effort.

Aiken headed a group of scientists whose task was to build a modern equivalent to Babbage's Analytical Engine. In 1943, the **Mark I,** also called the IBM Automatic Sequence Controlled Calculator, was completed at IBM Development Laboratories at Endicott, New York. It was 51 feet long, 8 feet high, and 2 feet thick; it had 750,000 parts and 500 miles of wire; and it weighed 5 tons. Noisy, but capable of three calculations per second, it accepted information by punched cards and then stored and processed this information. The results were printed on an electric typewriter.

The first electromechanical computer was responsible for making IBM a giant in computer technology. Howard Aiken and IBM shortly afterwards parted company because of Aiken's arrogance. As documented, IBM had invested over $0.5 million in the Mark I and in return for their investment, Thomas J. Watson, who was the head of IBM, wanted the prestige of being associated with Harvard University. At the dedication ceremony for the Mark I, Dr. Howard Aiken boasted about his accomplishments without referring to IBM. This intentional oversight infuriated Watson, who shouted some blasphemies at Aiken before abruptly leaving the ceremony. Watson ended his association with Harvard. After the completion of the Mark I, IBM produced several machines that were similar to the Mark I, and Howard Aiken also built a series of machines (the Mark II, Mark III, and Mark IV).

Besides building computers, Howard Aiken had many publications in the *Annals of Harvard Computation Laboratory Series*. Perhaps his biggest contribution was the environment he helped to create at Harvard, enabling this institution to develop an illustrious program for computer scientists.

Another interesting aside on Aiken pertains to the coining of the word **debug.** In 1945, the Mark II was housed in a building without air conditioning. Because it generated tremendous heat, the windows were left open. Suddenly this giant computer stopped working, and everyone tried frantically to discover the source of the problem. Grace Hopper, a brilliant scientist, and her coworkers found the culprit: a dead moth in a relay of the computer. They removed the moth with a tweezer and placed it in the Mark II logbook. When Aiken came back to see how things were going with his associates, they told him they had to debug the machine. Today the Mark II logbook is preserved in the Naval Museum in Dahlgren, Virginia.

There was a need now for computers that would operate faster and more efficiently. After the Mark II, the computers were much faster because the moving parts were replaced by electrical circuits.

John Atanasoff

In 1939 at Iowa State University, **John Atanasoff** designed and built the first electronic digital computer while working with **Clifford Berry,** a graduate student. Atanasoff and Berry then went to work on an operational model called the ABC, the Atanasoff-Berry Computer. This computer, completed in 1942, used binary logic circuitry and had regenerative memory. No one paid much attention to Atanasoff's computer except John Mauchly, a physicist and faculty member from the University of Pennsylvania. In 1941, he took a train to Ames, Iowa, to learn more about the ABC. He stayed five days as Atanasoff's house guest where he had an opportunity to read Atanasoff's handbook explaining the electronic theories and construction plans of the ABC (Mollenhoff, 1990). Mauchly then returned home to the Moore School of Electrical Engineering at the University of Pennsylvania where he became involved in a secret military project with J. Presper Eckert, an astronomer. (He never told Eckert of his visit with Atanasoff in Ames, Iowa.)

John Mauchly and J. Presper Eckert

With the emergence of World War II, the military wanted an extremely fast computer that would be capable of doing the thousands of computations necessary for compiling ballistic tables for new Naval guns and missiles. **John Mauchly** and **J. Presper Eckert** believed the only way to solve this problem was with an electronic digital machine so they worked on this project together. In 1946, they completed an operational electronic digital computer called the **ENIAC** (Electronic Numerical Integrator and Calculator), derived from the ideas of Atanasoff's unpatented work.[2] It worked on a decimal system and had all the features of today's computers. The ENIAC, shown in Figure 1.8, was tremendous in size, filling up a very large room and weighing 30 tons. It conducted electricity through 18,000 vacuum tubes, generating tremendous heat; it had to have special air conditioning to keep it cool.

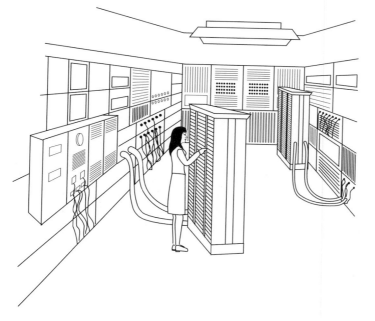

Figure 1.8
ENIAC

---

[2]Atanasoff's work was ignored for years; he was rejected by IBM, Remington Rand, and Iowa State. He was unheard of until 1973 when he received recognition as one of the fathers of computing. At this time, Sperry Rand brought a suit against Honeywell, and Federal District Judge Earl R. Larson invalidated the ENIAC Patent. Judge Larson said that Eckert and Mauchly had derived some of their ideas from Atanasoff's unpatented work.

This computer operated at a rate that was 500 times faster than any electromechanical computer of that day. A problem that took an electromechanical machine thirty to thirty-two hours to calculate, this machine solved in three minutes. The ENIAC's limitations were a small memory and a problem in shifting from one program to another. When the user wanted to shift to another program, the machine had to be rewired. These problems might have taken years to solve if it hadn't been for a meeting between Herman Goldstine, a mathematician and liaison officer for the ENIAC project, and John Von Neumann, a famous logician and mathematician. Because of that meeting, John Von Neumann joined the Moore team which was about to embark on a new computer called the **EDVAC,** the Electronic Discrete Variable Automatic Computer.

John Von Neumann

After **John Von Neumann** arrived in Philadelphia, he helped the Moore group get the contract for the EDVAC. He also assisted the group with the logical makeup of this machine. As a result of the Moore team's collaboration, a major breakthrough came in the form of the stored-program concept. Until this time, a computer stored its program externally, either on plugboards, punched tape, or cards. The ENIAC used 18,000 vacuum tubes and required a pair of these tubes joined in a particular manner to hold in memory a single bit of data.

Mauchly and Eckert discovered that one mercury delay line could replace dozens of these vacuum tubes. They figured that the delay lines would mean a gigantic savings in cost of tubes and memory space. This advance contributed to the design of the EDVAC Computer. The ED-VAC stored information in memory in the same form as data. The machine then manipulated the stored information.

Von Neumann was a member of the group that spent hours discussing the stored-program concept. Though he was not the sole creator, there is no question that it was Von Neumann's original idea to have the computer store its numbers serially and process them that way—an innovation that made the EDVAC design much faster, simpler, and smaller. However, the machine could still do only one thing at a time.

In 1945, a controversy arose involving Von Neumann and the Moore group. Von Neumann offered to write a report on EDVAC, an idea supported by the EDVAC staff. He finished the first draft, without references, and sent it to Goldstine, a member of the ENIAC group. In the report, Von Neumann did not give credit for the stored-program idea to the Moore group. Unfortunately, Goldstine, without Mauchly and Eckert's knowledge, put a cover on Von Neumann's first draft report and called it "Report on the EDVAC." Goldstine put Von Neumann's name down as the sole author and distributed it. This angered Mauchly, Eckert, and others because the paper contained almost no reference to the Moore group. They feared that credit would go completely to Von Neumann, and that it would violate their rights for a patent. Von Neumann probably never intended to take credit for what he didn't do. However, he did not try to rectify the situation by disavowing credit. This paper created a sensation, for it contained a model for computer structure and operation that was really the theoretical basis for the modern digital computer.

Although Von Neumann and his group were credited with using the stored-program concept, theirs was not the first machine. That honor goes to a group at Cambridge University who developed the **EDSAC,** Electronic Delay Storage Automatic Computer. The EDSAC and the ED-VAC computers were the first to use binary notation.

Before 1951, the computer had not been manufactured on a larger scale. In 1951, with the arrival of the UNIVAC, the era of **commercial computers** began. Only two years later, IBM started distributing its IBM 701, and other companies manufactured computers such as the Burroughs E101 and the Honeywell Datamatic 1000. The computers that were developed during the 1950s and 1960s were called *first generation computers* because they had one common feature, the vacuum tube.

Generations of Computers

Since its inception, the **computer** has gone through several stages of development. Generally writers classify these technological advances in generations, a marketing term. Even though there is some overlap, it is convenient to view the computer's technological development in this manner.

The First Generation of Computers

The **first generation** of computers began in the 1940s and extended into the 1950s. During this period, computers used **vacuum tubes,** such as the one in Figure 1.9, to conduct electricity.

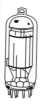

Figure 1.9
Vacuum tube

The employment of vacuum tubes made the computers big, bulky, and expensive because the tubes were continually burning out and having to be replaced. At this time, computers were classified by the main memory storage device they used. The UNIVAC I used an ingenious device called the *mercury delay line* that relied on ultrasonic pulses. Mercury delay line storage was a reliable device, but it was very slow compared to modern storage devices. Another storage device, an electrostatic one based on the Williams Tube from Manchester University in England, stored data in patterns of electric charges on the face of a cathode ray tube. There was a debate over the reliability of this storage method, causing it to disappear quickly.

During the first generation, pioneering work was done in the area of magnetic storage. Data were recorded on magnetic tapes and magnetic drums, which were used for auxiliary memory. In magnetic tape storage, the data were recorded on tapes similar to the audiocassette tapes used today. Data were held on the tapes in serial manner, which meant the user could not access the information directly, resulting in slower access time. Similar to magnetic tapes were magnetic drums. These two means of storage were important until magnetic disks appeared in the third generation.

The Second Generation of Computers

The **second generation** of computers began when the **transistor** (Fig. 1.10) replaced the vacuum tube in the late 1950s. In 1947, Bardeen, Brattain, and Shockley, a team of physicists working at Bell Labs, invented the transistor.

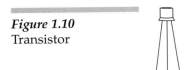

Figure 1.10
Transistor

In 1956, they shared the Nobel Prize for this invention. The transistor, an electrically operated switch similar to an old-fashioned relay, was a landmark in the development of the computer. The transistor is created by melting silicon, an element found in common sand. Transistors conduct electricity more efficiently, consume less energy, need less space, and generate less heat than vacuum tubes. In addition, they don't burn out as the tubes did. The computer with transistors became smaller, more reliable, faster, and less expensive than a computer with vacuum tubes. Small-and-medium-size businesses now found it more economical to buy computers.

A new development that started in the early 1950s came to fruition during the second generation. Magnetic-core memory was responsible for data being retrieved and stored at a millionth of a second. *Core memory* became synonymous with the main memory of the computer.

The Third Generation of Computers

The **third generation** of computers began in 1964 with the introduction of the IBM 360, the computer that pioneered the use of **integrated circuits** on a chip. In that year, computer scientists developed tiny integrated circuits and installed hundreds of these transistors on a single silicon chip, which was as small as a fingertip. The computer became smaller, more reliable, and less expensive than ever before. The integrated circuit chips made it possible for minicomputers to find their way into classrooms, homes, and businesses. They were almost a thousand times faster than the first generation of computers, and manufacturers mass produced them at a low price, making them more accessible to small companies.

The integrated circuits were now used as main memory, and magnetic disks replaced magnetic tape as auxiliary memory. These disks allowed information to be retrieved nonsequentially, speeding up access time. Computer terminals flourished, and an increasing number of individuals used them to communicate with computers at other locations. In the beginning, the terminal was like a typewriter and produced a printed output. As time went on, the video display terminals replaced the punched cards for entering data and programs into the computer. Hollerith's cards became obsolete.

The 1970s began with the development of **large-scale integration (LSI),** a method that put hundreds of thousands of transistors on a single silicon chip. The chip was as minute as a speck of dust and so delicate that miniature scientific instruments were devised to create it. The development of the LSI led to the insertion of computers in cameras, television sets, and cars. Another result of LSI was the personal computer.

The Fourth Generation of Computers

The development of microprocessor technology resulted in the **fourth generation.** The microprocessor chip (Fig. 1.11) is a central processing unit, the brains of the computer, built on a single chip. It is hard to believe, but on this single chip the processing and computing take place.

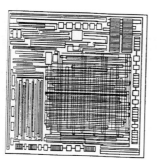

Magnified Chip

Actual Chip Size

Figure 1.11
Computer chip

In 1968, Gilbert Hyatt designed a computer to fit on a silicon microchip the size of a fingernail. Hyatt wanted the world to recognize him as the inventor who made the computer revolution occur. After a legal battle lasting twenty years, the U.S. patent and trademark office gave Hyatt patent No. 4,942.516 for a "Single Chip integrated Circuit Computer Architecture" (Takahashi, 1990).

In 1971, a group of individuals working at Intel introduced the 4004 microprocessor. They intended that this chip be used in items such as the calculator because the chip lacked the power needed to run a microcomputer. Three years later, they introduced the 8080 version that was capable of running the processing unit of a computer. *Radio Electronics,* in 1974, published an article on a home-built computer that used this technology. Subsequently, *Popular Electronics* ran a story on Altair, a computer that had the 8080 chip. In the article, the writers mentioned that Micro Instrumentation Technology Systems was selling kits for this computer. The response to this article was overwhelming, and it inspired other companies to develop new products.

Apple computers came into being in the 1970s. Steve Wozniak and Steve Jobs worked out of a garage where they began selling Apples for the price of $666.66. Figure 1.12 shows the Apple I. Wozniak and Jobs placed ads in hobbyist publications with the money that they raised from selling their personal possessions.

This duo provided software for their machines free of charge and they achieved a modicum of success. They hired professional help and support and in 1977 introduced, in what was

Figure 1.12
Apple I Computer
Courtesy of Apple
Computer, Inc.

a historic moment for computers, a new fully assembled version of their Apple machine called the Apple II. The Apple II was the first computer accepted by business users because of a spreadsheet simulation program called *VisiCalc*. It was a compact desktop computer with 4K of memory, priced at $1,298, with a clock speed of 1.0.

Four years later, IBM entered the personal computer market with the IBM PC. This computer was tremendously successful and became a best-seller. Because of IBM's successful entrance in the field, other computer makers chose to capitalize on its popularity by developing their own clones. These personal computers had many of the same features as the IBM machines and could run the same programs. Widespread use of personal computers became a reality.

The Fifth Generation of Computers

In the **fifth generation,** there are incredibly fast computer chips. Now there are computers that carry out thousands of operations simultaneously, and the execution rates of these machines are measured in **teraflops.** A teraflop is equivalent to 1 trillion floating-point operations per second (FPU).[3] A 1 teraflop machine could lead to a suitcase-size computer that is as powerful as today's fastest supercomputers. These powerful computers can solve the most complex problems in science, finance, and technology.

In the mid-1980s and early 1990s, the large Japanese firms controlled the world chip market. The dominance of Japan in this market had been a major concern among U.S. manufacturers. Since 1993, U.S. firms such as IBM, Motorola, and Intel have increased their influence in the chip market along with the Asian-Pacific companies (Helm, 1995). On March 14, 1994, Apple introduced the first Macintosh computers running on IBM/Motorola PowerPC RISC (**R**educed **I**nstruction **S**et **C**omputer) processors rather than on Motorola 680 G 0 CISC (**C**omplex **I**nstruction **S**et **C**omputer) processors (Seltzer, 1994).

In the same year, DEC's Alpha 21164 chip was the fastest in the world, able to execute 1.2 billion instructions per second at 300 MHz (Ryan, 1994). Two years later a small firm called Exponential, licensing the PowerPC design from IBM had a 533-megahertz version of the PowerPC

---

[3]"A portion of a microprocessor that handles operations in which the decimal point moves left and right to allow for very high precision when dealing with very large or very small numbers."
(Pfaffenberger, 1997)

chip which it debuted at the annual Microprocessor Forum (Morgenstern, 1997). In the next decade machines will be delivering gigahertz speeds and utilizing millions of transistors.

As the power of the computer builds, inventors will have to find new ways to deliver information to the machine. With quicker access time and lower prices, erasable optical disks will become a viable alternative to magnetic disks. Optical disks have much greater capacity for storage and greater longevity than the magnetic disk. Digital Versatile Disk (DVD), a relative of the CD-ROM, can store up to a maximum of 17 gigabytes of data (Stone, 1997). Holographic storage is still in the research laboratories, but could be another viable alternative. The data storage system will eventually come in the form of laser cards the size of a small plastic credit card that could hold terabytes of information.

The next generation of computers will be based on logical inference. There will be extensive use of **artificial intelligence (AI),** "a computer science field that tries to improve computers by endowing them with some of the characteristics associated with human intelligence, such as the capability to understand natural language and to reason under conditions of uncertainty" (Pfaffenberger, 1996). Such machines will be able to do such things as make decisions, draw conclusions, understand everyday speech, and learn from experience. There are already some accomplishments today in this area: Medical programs aid in diagnosing various diseases, and mining programs help mining companies in their explorations. AI elements already exist in educational software programs such as *Mavis Beacon Teaches Typing! for Kids* (Mindscape) and *The Time Warp of Dr. Brain* (Sierra On-Line Inc.). Artificial intelligence has been used on board games such as chess and backgammon. For example, "Deep Blue," IBM's "thinking" machine, is an attempt at artificial intelligence. Some of the chess and backgammon programs defeat the people who created them. Alan Turing proposed a test in 1950 that could determine if a computer was reasoning as a human being would. Some computers are getting close, and, who knows?—in years to come people might prefer talking to a computer rather than to a real person.

In the next generation of machines, computers will communicate in English or Chinese rather than in a computer language. They will respond to a human voice, not to a keyboard or disk drive. In Stanley Kubrick's *2001* film, the computer HAL understood every word it heard and all the subtleties of the person talking. This very thoughtful film predicted many things that are true and will become a reality. Today, the voice synthesizers that are used in computers sound more human than the ones of a few years ago. Up until very recently, only higher-end computers had voice recognition, but now many machines have this capability. In 1994, a series of IBM notebook portables having 486- and PowerPC-based chips had the ability to talk and, in some cases, answer questions. This same year, Apple's personal digital assistants (PDAs) were equipped with voice-recognition. Dr. Jim Glass, major research scientist at Massachusetts Institute of Technology's Spoken Language Systems groups, reported that his group has moved from speech recognition to speech understanding. Speech understanding lets the computer build a series of connected ideas from words it hears. Dr. Glass's group built a prototype system called Galaxy that responds to voice commands to make airline reservations or check weather (Freed, 1997).

Computers keep decreasing in size, and there seems to be no limit to how small they could become. Many systems have touch screens and handwriting recognition software that let the user employ a pencil-like stylus as the input device. HP OmniGo 120 Organizer Plus and U.S. Robotics: Pilot 5000, both Personal Data Assistants (PDAs), use Graffiti, a modified alphabet that is designed for this type of system. Graffiti is a very accurate recognition system. Although handwriting recognition seems to focus on PDAs, the desktop and laptop crowds now use these devices. Handwriter Manta by CIC is a pen-input device that translates handwriting into typed text (Freed, 1997). The notebook computer has certainly come a long way from the first active matrix, thin film transistor, color notebook computer that used Intel's 25 MHz 386SL chip set. This portable computer, introduced by NEC in 1992, is considered slow in comparison to Apple's new portable machine with 292 MHz, using up to 192 MB of Random-Access Memory (RAM)[4], a 8 GB of hard drive for storage, and the new PowerPC G3 processor.

In the future, you will be able to wear your computer, and computers, voice, and data will probably be transmitted by built-in cellular radio. Printers, projectors, and video cameras will all probably communicate through an infrared interface similar to today's television remote devices. We will have computers that answer us as well as respond to our commands in an intelligent manner. Computers will be ultra thin, weigh less than a pound, and operate on batteries that will last years. Their displays will be flat-panel, larger, in color, and detachable. These machines will come with gigabytes of RAM and huge storage capabilities. The Internet will have an even more pervasive influence on our everyday lives. Exciting new technologies will deliver huge increases in bandwidth capacity, making Internet access lighting fast at megabit-per-second speed. With these new developments come new forms of interactive content, realistic 3-D, virtual reality[5], multiplayer games, and interactive educational video forums. Teachers and students will have new ways to work from home and school. Using wireless telecommunication services, we will spend less time in the classroom and more time on the Internet via voice, data, and video conferencing. Teachers and students will use Internet's research tools and communicate through on-line courses almost exclusively. All machines will have parallel processing, that is each computer will perform more than one operation simultaneously.

Ultimately, however, we can only speculate on what other amazing innovations the fifth generation of computers will bring. After all, it took thousands of years and many inventions to arrive at the first electromechanical computer, and then, only a short time later, the UNIVAC appeared on the scene. The development of the computer has become like a stone rolling down a hill, gathering other stones and creating an explosion in technology. It is such a rapidly changing field that the computer bought today is obsolete tomorrow. The following chart highlights the major technological advances in the development of computers:

---

[4]The working memory of the computer where data and program instructions are stored (Pfaffenberger, 1997).

[5]Virtual Reality (VR) is "a computer system that can immerse the user in the illusion of a computer-generated world and permit the user to navigate throughout this world at will" (Pfaffenberger, 1997). See Chapter 10 for a further discussion.

Table 1.2   Generations of Computers

Generation of Computer	Years	Technological Advance
First	Early 1950s	Vacuum Tube
Second	Mid-1950s	Transistor
Third	Early 1960s	Integrated Circuits
Fourth	1970–Mid-1990s	Microprocessor
Fifth	Mid-1990s–2000s	AI, Internet, Parallel Processing, Virtual Reality

Summary

In the beginning, inventors who were interested in processing information wanted devices to simplify tedious arithmetic calculations. In the 1800s, Jacquard used punched cards in his loom to produce beautiful patterns, an invention that inspired Charles Babbage; Babbage used the concept of the punched card in his Analytical Engines. Babbage's work was forgotten for nearly a century. Near the end of the 1800s, Herman Hollerith improved upon Jacquard's idea and pioneered processing of statistical data in the 1890 census. Today, this is a major application for the computer. In the 1900s, inventors constructed the earliest electromechanical computer, quickly replaced by the faster electronic computer.

The machines that superseded the early experimental machines were classified in generations. In the first generation, computers used vacuum tubes to conduct electricity. In the second generation, transistors replaced tubes, followed in the 1970s by integrated circuits in the third generation. The fourth generation saw the advent of large-scale, integrated circuit chips. The fifth generation of computers will offer the development of artificial intelligence, computers based on logical inference and parallel processing, and radical changes in the Internet as we know it today.

Chapter Mastery Test

To the Professor: Refer to the Instructor's Manual for the Answers to the Mastery Questions. Furthermore, this manual has additional questions and resource materials.

Let's check for chapter comprehension with a short mastery test and some classroom activities. The activities are followed by some suggested readings and references.

1. Discuss briefly the contributions made to the computer field by the following individuals:

   a. Howard Aiken;

   b. Charles Babbage;

   c. Blaise Pascal;

   d. Herman Hollerith; and

   e. John Atanasoff.

2. Identify and place in correct order five of the major inventions in the field of computing.

3. Differentiate among the generations of computers by their technological advances.

4. Explain the significance of punched cards and vacuum tubes in the development of earlier computers.

5. Explain the importance of transistors and microprocessors in the development of modern computers.

6. What was George Boole's lasting contribution to computer history?

7. What computer opportunities would a sixth grader have in 1953 as opposed to a sixth grader in 2000?

8. Compare two early mechanical calculators and their inventors.

9. Why was Hollerith's tabulating machine for the 1890 census significant for the future of computing?

10. What was the connection between Herman Hollerith and Joseph Jacquard?

11. Explain the importance of the discovery that made personal computers possible.

12. Discuss the contribution of Dr. John Von Neumann to computer technology.

13. Explain why Charles Babbage might be considered to have been born in the wrong time.

14. What were some of the problems of first generation computers?

15. What are Steve Jobs's and Steve Wozniak's major achievements in the computer field?

16. Explain why Ada Lovelace deserves an important place in the history of computers.

17. What spearheaded the development of the electronic digital computer?

Classroom Projects

1. Prepare a paper on the 1973 court trial between Sperry Rand and Honeywell. In this case, Judge Larson ruled that, "Eckert and Mauchly did not themselves invent the electronic digital computer, but instead derived the subject matter from one John V. Atanasoff."

2. Investigate three computer magazines for recent developments in computer technology during the last five years. Write a brief summary of the findings.

3. Using a computer timeline program such as Tom Snyder's TimeLiner, list at least ten significant computer events from 1863 to 1989.

4. Prepare an in-depth research report on the life of an important inventor and his or her contribution to the history of computers.

5. What are today's schools covering in terms of computer history? What are second and seventh graders learning?

Suggested Readings and References

"1,000 MHz Chips on the Wad." *Computer Retail Week*, March 9, 1998: 35.

Asimov, Isaac. *How Did We Find out About Computers?* New York: Walker, 1984.

Aspray, William. "John Von Neumann's Contributions to Computing and Computer Science." *Annals of the History of Computing* 11, no. 3 (1989): 165.

Austrian, G. *Herman Hollerith: Forgotten Giant of Information Processing.* New York: Columbia University Press, 1982.

Barr, Christopher. "First Active-Matrix Color in a Laptop Dazzles." *PC Magazine* 11, no. 1 (January 14, 1992): 40.

Bernstein, J. *The Analytical Engine.* New York: Morrow, 1981.

Burks, A., and A. Burks, "The ENIAC: First General-Purpose Electronic Computer." *Annals of the History of Computing* (October 1981): 310–400.

Diebold, John, ed. *The World of the Computer.* New York: Random House, 1973.

Donndelinger, Peter. "Supercomputer Science." *Science Teacher* 61, no. 3 (March 1994): 16–19.

Evans, Christopher. *The Making of the Micro: A History of the Computer.* New York: Van Nostrand Reinhold, 1981.

Evans, Christopher. *The Micro Millennium.* New York: The Viking Press, 1979.

Feigenbaum, Edward A., and Pamela McCorduck. *The Fifth Generation.* Reading, Mass.: Addison-Wesley Publishing Company, 1983.

Freedman, A. *The Computer Glossary.* . New York: Amacom, 1995.

Freedman, A. *The Computer Desktop Encyclopedia.* New York: Amacom, 1996.

Freed, Les. "Recognizing The Future." *PC Magazine* 16, no. 6 (March 25, 1997): 210–213.

Gardner, David, W. "Will the Inventor of the First Digital Computer Please Stand UP?" *Datamation* 20 (February 1974): 84–90.

Gates, Bill, Myhrvold, Nathan and Peter Rinearson. *The Road Ahead.* New York: Viking Penguin, 1996.

Goldstine, H. *The Computer from Pascal to Von Neumann.* Princeton, N.J.: Princeton University Press, 1972.

Hamilton, Denise. "New Supercomputer at CalTech Ranks as the World's Fastest." *Los Angeles Times,* Business Section B2 (June 1, 1991).

Helm, Leslie. "In the Chip Business." *Los Angeles Times,* Business Section D2, (March 15, 1995).

Levy, Steven. "The Computer." *Newsweek* (February, 1998): 28–30.

Lu, Cary. "Powerbook with a Punch." *MacWorld* (April, 1997): 107–113.

Macintosh, Allan R. "Dr. Atanasoff's Computer." *Scientific American* 259, no. 2 (August 1, 1988): 90.

Magid, Lawrence J., "My MHz Is Bigger than Your MHz." *Los Angeles Times,* Business Section D2, (October 21, 1996).

Metropolis, N., J. Howlett, and G. C. Rota, eds. *A History of Computing in the Twentieth Century.* New York: Academic Press, 1980.

Miller, Greg. "Speedy Wireless Net Access is Slow to Go." *Los Angeles Times,* Business Section D5, (March 23, 1998).

Mollenhoff, Clark R. "Forgotten Father of the Computer." *The World & I* (March 1990): 319–32.

Molnar, Andrew R. " Computers in Education a Brief History." *T.H.E Journal* 24, no. 11, (June 1997): 59–62.

Moore, Johanna D. "Making Computer Tutors More Like Humans." *Journal of Artificial Intelligence in Education* 7, no. 2, (1996): 181–214.

Moreau, Rene. *The Computer Comes of Age: The People, the Hardware, and the Software.* Translated by J. Howlett. Cambridge, Mass.: MIT Press, 1984.

Morgenstern, David. "Exponential: No Fast Start for New Chips." *MacWeek* 11, no. 13 (March 31, 1997): 1.

Morrison, P., and E. Morrison, eds. *Charles Babbage and His Calculating Engines.* New York: Dover, 1961.

Naisbitt, John. *Megatrends: Ten New Directions Transforming Our Lives.* New York: Warner Books, 1982.

Naisbitt, John. *Megatrends 2000: Ten New Directions for the 1990s.* New York: Morrow, 1990.

Niemiec, Richard P., and Richard J. Walberg. "From Teaching Machines to Microcomputers: Some Milestones in the History of Computer-Based Instruction." *Journal of Research on Computing in Education* 21, no. 3 (Spring 1989): 263.

Norr, Henry. "MacHandwriter Puts Pen on Desktop." *MacWeek* 8, no. 5 (January 31, 1994): 1.

Pfaffenberger, Bruce. *Webster's New World Dictionary of Computer Terms.* 6th ed. New York: MacMillan General Reference, 1997.

Pfaffenberger, Bruce. *Dictionary of Computer Terms.* 6th ed. California: Que Corporation, 1996.

Piller, Charles. "Blindingly Fast Chips." MacWorld, (November 1996).

Pullan, J. M. *A History of the Abacus.* New York: Praeger Publishers, 1968.

Quain, John R. "Going Mainstream." *PC Magazine* 13, no. 4 (February 22, 1994): 110.

Ralston, Anthon, and C. L. Meek, eds. *Encyclopedia of Computer Science.* New York: Petrocelli, 1976.

Ritchie, David. *The Computer Pioneers: The Making of the Modern Computer.* New York: Simon and Schuster, 1986.

Rochester, J., and J. Gantz. *The Naked Computer.* New York: Morrow, 1983.

Slater, Michael. "PowerPC Steps into Right with Pentium." *MacWEEK* 8, no. 11 (March 14, 1994): 1.

Smarte, Gene, and Andrew Reinhardt. "15 Years of Bits, Bytes and Other Great Moments: A Look at Key Events in Byte, the Computer Industry." *Byte* 15, no. 9 (September 1, 1990): 369–400.

Stone, David, M. "Even Faster and Smaller." *PC Magazine* 16, no. 6 (March 25, 1997): 186–189.

Takahashi, D. "A Dogged Inventor Makes the Computer Industry Say: Hello, Mr. Chip." *Los Angeles Times*, Business Section (October 21, 1990).

Zilber, Jon. "Why 2004 Won't Be Like 1994." *MacUser* 8, no. 1 (January 1, 1994): 92.

Zorpette, Glen. "Science and Medicine." *Los Angeles Times*, Business Section B5 (December 30, 1991).

Getting Started on the Computer

2

Objectives

Upon completing this chapter, you will be able to:

1. Discuss how the basic components of a computer system operate;
2. Explain the following terms:
   a. Random Access Memory (RAM),
   b. Read Only Memory (ROM),
   c. bit,
   d. byte,
   e. kilobyte, and
   f. American Standard Code for Information Interchange (ASCII);
3. Discuss the unique characteristics of the Macintosh and Windows operating systems;
4. List three precautions the user should follow when handling floppy disks;
5. Give an explanation of the following terms:
   a. formatting or initializing a disk,
   b. making a backup copy of a disk, and
   c. copying or deleting a file; and
6. List the differences and similarities between a mainframe, minicomputer, and microcomputer.

Computer Classification

Computers are frequently divided into categories: mainframes, minicomputers, and microcomputers. In the past, there was a technical distinction among these computers, but today the differences are in terms of cost and speed. These categories have become blurred because many new microcomputers have the same capabilities of the old mainframes.

In the early 1960s, all computers were called **mainframes** in reference to the cabinet that held the central processing unit. As time progressed, very large computers began to be called mainframe computers. Mainframes cost thousands of dollars, had enormous memory and speed, and took up the space of a standard-size classroom. Because of the machine's memory, it could dispatch complex programs very quickly and it could execute these programs while many individuals utilized the computer simultaneously. A team of specialists usually managed the machine at a prepared site for the large corporations or financial institutions that used it. Mainframes were usually connected to terminals that resembled small computers. These terminals relayed information to and from the mainframe housed in the same building or even in another city. If the terminals were in another city, they communicated with the mainframe via telephone.

The largest and fastest of the mainframe computers are called **supercomputers.** These state-of-the-art machines, produced by the United States and Japan and costing millions of dollars, have the most advanced processing abilities and are now able to execute 1 trillion calculations per second. In the early days, government laboratories developed these computers under top secrecy. For years the U.S. government was the only market for these supercomputers; only a few scientists had access to these machines, and they did not develop the computers' capabilities aggressively because the government did not allow it. In the 1980s, access to the supercomputers increased, and today they are used worldwide. In the near future, this processing speed will be trillions of calculations per second (Michael Conway, Cray Research Incorporated, 1996).

Cray Computers, founded by Seymour Cray, was the only American company to manufacture supercomputers until this company divided into two corporations in May of 1989 to become Cray Research Incorporated and Cray Computer Corporation. Because of the supercomputers' high cost, the Aerospace industry, the military, the National Weather Service, and oil conglomerates at one time were the primary users. Now, there is a merging of business and technical, and companies such as Cray and Sun are producing lower-cost machines for commercial usage.

In 1965, Digital Equipment Corporation (DEC) introduced the **minicomputer.** Universities and large companies needed a machine that did not require a staff of professionals or large storage space, and the minicomputer met this need. This machine was smaller and less costly than the mainframes and usually fit in a large cabinet in a corner of a room. Usually, its terminals were housed in the same building or room. The minicomputer did not have the diversified input/output devices of the mainframe or its memory capacity. However, like the mainframe, the minicomputer could handle more than one task at a time. The minicomputer was still too expensive and too sophisticated for most individuals, but it was used in small businesses and by school districts. Because it cost less than the mainframe, this computer was prevalent until the microcomputer came on the scene in the mid-1970s.

The **microcomputer** came into being because computer engineers were able to etch many circuits on a single chip. This advance in computer technology produced a computer that was less costly, more powerful, and smaller than the minicomputer. Today, the microcomputer is a powerful piece of equipment, small enough to sit on a desk or fit in a briefcase.

Microcomputers originally were differentiated as either *personal computers* or *business computers.* Most software developed for personal machines, such as the Apple II series, was educational or had applications in the home: home management, computer literacy, and word processing. Most software developed for business machines, IBM, PC compatibles, and the Macintosh, consisted of complex spreadsheets, elaborate databases, professional word processing programs, statistical applications, scientific programs, and desktop publishing programs. Now, these distinctions among microcomputers are not clear-cut, and educational software and business software are developed for all machines.

To appreciate the beauty and sophistication of these machines, let's spend a little time exploring what a computer is and how it operates.

What Is a Computer?

A computer is a machine that can handle huge amounts of information at an incredible speed. Computers do not have brains, feelings, or the ability to solve their own problems; they can only solve problems they have been programmed to solve. A typical computer system might have a monitor, keyboard, mouse, printer, internal disk drive, hard disk drive, CD-ROM drive, modem, and speakers. Figure 2.1 is an example of a computer and its components.

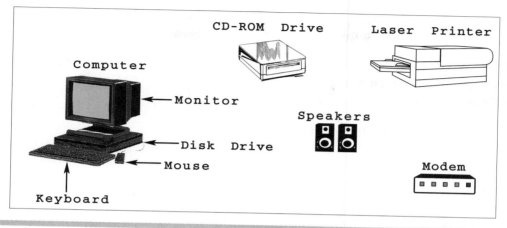

Figure 2.1
Computer and its components
ClickArt Images © T/Maker Company and © Corel, Mega Gallery, 1996.

A computer performs four tasks

1. receiving input such as figures, facts, or sets of instructions;
2. storing information by placing it in its memory;
3. processing the data by acting on the information; and
4. outputting the information by generating the results of the processing.

Professor Friedman's research study serves as a hypothetical example of how the computer performs the preceding four tasks. The professor is conducting a research study. She has collected her data carefully and now wants the computer to do some statistical analysis on it. She installs her statistical program onto the hard drive of her computer. Next, using the keyboard, she enters her data into the spreadsheet of the statistical program and chooses analysis of variance from the statistical procedures. The computer stores the data she enters in memory and then processes this information by performing the necessary statistical calculations in its central processing unit of the computer, discussed later in this chapter. The professor sees the results of the analysis on the screen or as a printout from the printer.

This example sheds some light on how the computer works. Let's continue by examining the computer in more detail. A computer system consists of a central processing unit and the peripheral devices connected to it, along with the computer's operating system. The central processor, or CPU, is contained on one single chip called a **microprocessor.** The memory, RAM (Random Access Memory) and ROM (Read Only Memory), of the computer is also contained on computer chips. Before discussing these various chips, let's define the term computer **chip.**

The Computer Chip

A computer chip is a silicon wafer, approximately 1/16 inch wide and 1/30th of an inch thick, that holds from a couple dozen to millions of electronic components. The term *chip* is synonymous with *integrated circuit*. Computer chips are encased in plastic to protect them, and metal pins enable these chips to be plugged into a computer circuit board. Figure 2.2 shows a chip encased in its plastic protection.

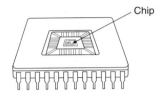

Figure 2.2
Computer chip encased in plastic

Chip

If you look carefully at this chip, you can see tiny circuits etched on the metal. The process of putting these circuits on one chip and connecting them together is called *Large Scale Integration (LSI)* or *Very Large Scale Integration (VLSI)*. This complex procedure, which involves engineering, plotting, photography, baking, and magnetism, permits silicon chips to be produced in large quantities at a very low cost. Today, there are millions of transistors on a single chip, and with wafer scale integration, eventually these circuits will be built in overlapping layers and there will be billions of transistors.

In the microcomputer, the RAM chips, ROM chips, CPU chips, and other components are plugged into a flat board called a printed circuit board (Fig. 2.3).

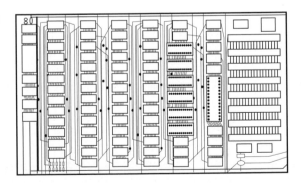

Figure 2.3
Printed circuit board

The other side of this board is printed with electrical conductive pathways between the components. A circuit board in 1960 connected discrete components together, while the boards in the 1990s connect chips that each contain hundreds of thousands and millions of elementary components (Freedman, 1996).

Computer systems have different components on their boards and there is no standard way of designing them. Nevertheless, the main component of any computer system is the central processing unit, the brain of the computer.

Central Processing Unit

The **central processor,** also called the processor, is the computing part of the computer. A personal computer's central processor, or CPU, is contained on one single chip called a microprocessor, which is smaller than a fingernail. This unit is essential because it controls the way the computer operates. Whenever a programmer gives instructions to the computer, the processor executes these instructions. The central processor gets instructions from memory and either carries out the instructions or tells other components to follow the instructions. Then it goes back to get the next set of instructions. This procedure is repeated until the task is completed.

The central processing unit (Fig. 2.4) consists of three components: the control unit, the arithmetic unit, and the logic unit. In most microcomputers, the arithmetic unit and the logic unit are combined and are referred to as the **arithmetic logic unit (ALU).**

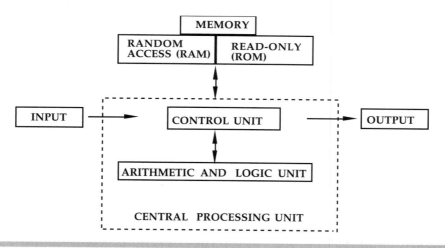

Figure 2.4
Central processing unit

The control unit verifies that the computer carries out instructions, transfers instructions to the main memory for storage, and relays information back and forth between the main memory and the ALU. The arithmetic logic unit carries out all the arithmetic operations and logical decisions. Since the central processing unit can work only on small amounts of information at a time, it needs a way to store information while it is not being processed. It needs memory.

Memory

There are two types of chips that take care of the computer's internal memory: **read only memory chips (ROM)** and **random access memory chips (RAM).**

ROM chips store information permanently in the computer's memory, and this memory supplies the computer with a list of operating instructions. These instructions are burnt into the computer during the manufacturing process. ROM is called *nonvolatile memory* because it does not disappear when the computer is turned off. There is nothing an ordinary computer user can do to remove or replace the instructions of ROM because the computer can only read information burned onto these ROM chips. Most computers have a program in ROM that puts on the screen symbols, such as a cursor (usually in the form of a blinking square or line). BASIC was stored in the ROM of the Apple II line of computers, and today there are ROM chips in microwave ovens, watches, and calculators.

The information on RAM chips, however, can be modified; users can write, read, and erase its information. The problem with this type of memory is that it needs a constant power supply so that the data are not lost. RAM is referred to as *volatile memory* because of its temporary nature. Whenever an individual turns off the computer, he or she loses whatever information is in RAM. The basic unit for RAM storage is a **byte,** the space available to hold letters, numbers, and special characters.[1] Because a computer user normally manipulates thousands of characters at a time, the RAM size is usually measured in **kilobytes,** or thousands of bytes (the symbol for kilobytes is K). For example, a computer that has 512K is capable of holding approximately 512,000 numbers, symbols, and letters.[2]

The amount of RAM chips a computer has determines the amount of information that can be retained in memory, the size and number of programs that can be run simultaneously, and the number of data that will be processed immediately. Programs vary in their memory requirements; for example, *ClarisWorks* needs 2 MB (million bytes or **megabytes**) of RAM memory to run on a Macintosh with System 7, while 16 MB of RAM is required for the Windows version of *DeBabelizer.* Fortunately, the RAM size of most computers can be expanded by adding RAM chips. In the early 1980s, computers usually had a memory size of 64K, then considered more than adequate for a personal computer. Today, the RAM size of a computer is usually described in terms of *megabytes.* Tomorrow, the RAM size will be in trillions of bytes, or **terabytes.**

So now we know about the physical properties of memory, but how does the computer store this information since it cannot store it as a printed page? What does it use to translate information? The fundamental principle behind digital computers' storage is binary notation.

Binary Notation

All computer input is converted into binary numbers consisting of two digits, 0 and 1. An instruction that is read as a 1 tells the computer to turn on a circuit, and an instruction read as a 0 tells the computer to turn off the circuit. The digits 0 and 1 are called **bits,** short for *binary* dig*its.* The computer can represent letters, numbers, and symbols by combining these individual bits into a **binary code.** The most common binary codes use eight-bit combinations, and each eight-bit combination is called a *byte.* Each character or letter typed is translated into a byte by turning circuits off and on. This whole procedure happens at lightning speed whenever a user hits a key on the computer keyboard. For example, when the user types the letter Z, the computer translates

---

[1]Byte is discussed in more detail in the Binary Notation section of this chapter.
[2]The accurate number is 524,288(512 × 1024) because the computer uses powers of 2, and 2^{10} is 1,024. A kilobyte then represents 1,024, or approximately, 1,000 bytes.

it into 01011010. When the user types the number 1, it is translated into 00110001. Every character on the keyboard has a different eight-bit combination or special code.

There are several coding systems, but the most commonly used one is the **American Standard Code for Information Interchange** (ASCII—pronounced *ask-ee*). This coding system uses seven bits as one byte, with one bit unused. It represents each character 2^7 times, so it has 128 possible codes. These codes represent the uppercase and lowercase letters of the alphabet, the digits, the most-used punctuation marks, math signs, and control characters, such as carriage return and line feed. The letter A is the ASCII code 65 (the ASCII code 66 represents the letter B, 67 represents the letter C, 48 represents 0, 49 represents 1, etc.)[3] or the binary notation 01000001. Table 2.1 shows a partial listing of the ASCII Code and corresponding binary notation.

Table 2.1   *ASCII Code (Partial Listing)*

Character	Binary Notation	ASCII Code
A	01000001	65
B	01000010	66
0	00110000	48
a	01100001	97
b	01100010	98
?	00111111	63
>	00111110	62

Before leaving memory, let's look briefly at how the computer user stores his or her data permanently.

Disks

The most prevalent method of storage is still the disk. In the early 1990s, one of the most used methods of storage was the 5 1/4-inch disk, but it has disappeared like the dinosaur. The manufacturers are producing disks in increasingly smaller sizes. For example, Integral Peripherals manufactured a subminiature hard disk that weighed only 3.3 ounces and was only 1.8 inches long when it was introduced in 1992 (Barr, 1992). There are four commonly used storage devices, pictured in Figure 2.5: the Optical Disk, information stored in the form of tiny pits and read by laser beam; the 3 1/2-inch disk, and Zip disk, flexible tapelike material encased in a firm plastic cover; and the hard disk, positioned in a sealed unit. The 3 1/2-inch disk, the Zip disk, and the hard disk store data in the same way: The disk spins on a surface that can be magnetized or demagnetized.

---

[3]The letter A represented by 65, would have circuits 7 and 1 turned on and the rest of the circuits turned off.

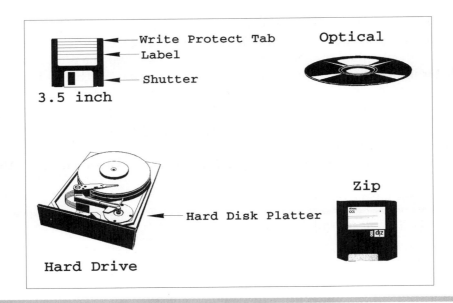

Figure 2.5
Four commonly used storage methods
ClickArt Images © T/Maker Company and © Corel, Mega Gallery, 1996.

The number of tracks that are on a disk is a function of how accurately the disk is constructed, how fast the disk spins, how sensitive the disk is to magnetization, and so forth. It is for this reason that the Zip disk holds more information than the 3 1/2-inch disk, and the hard disk is capable of holding more information than either one.

The hard disk is made of metal and covered with a magnetic recording surface. The read/write head, an electronic device that electromagnetically records and reads the information from the disk, travels across this surface via an air cushion, without touching the disk. This disk is fixed or removable and can hold anywhere from 160 megabytes to 9 gigabytes of information. This is a much greater storage capacity than a 3 1/2-inch floppy disk that holds anywhere from 800 kilobytes to 2 megabytes of information. Hard disk storage capacity is the amount of room on the hard disk and should not be confused with RAM, the amount of memory necessary to run a program. Presently, the 5 gigabyte hard disk is commonplace, and by the year 2002, you will see drives that are ten times this amount (Stone, 1997) .

Covered with a magnetic coating, such as iron oxide, a floppy disk (or diskette) looks like a small phonograph record divided into tracks invisible to the human eye. The information is sorted on the cylindrical tracks on the disk's surface. Whenever the computer records or reads from the disk, the disk revolves at a constant speed inside its disk drive and the slightest separation between the drive head(s) and the disk surface can lead to the loss of data. The storage capacity of this disk depends on whether data can be stored on both sides of the diskette and on the storage density on each side of the disk. A floppy disk is delicate, and a user should protect this disk from damage by adhering to the following eight suggestions:

1. Always hold a disk by its label and refrain from touching the shutter (refer to Fig. 2.5).
2. Never store 3 1/2-inch disks in plastic envelopes because of the static thus created.
3. When the red in-use light is on or the disk drive is working, *do not* remove or insert a disk.
4. Never bend the disk or use rubber bands or paper clips on it.
5. Keep the disk away from television, magnets, or severe heat.
6. Do not smoke, eat, or drink near a disk.
7. Do not write on the disk label with a ball point because it will leave impressions. Always use a felt tip pen.
8. Stand the disks up in their storage container.

Optical Disk.   An optical disk holds a huge capacity of information that is stored at high density in the form of small pits that are read by a laser beam. There are a variety of optical disks such as CD-ROM (Compact **D**isc **R**ead **O**nly **M**emory) , DVD-ROM disks (Digital Versatile Disk or Digital Videodisk) , WORM (write once, read many) and the erasable optical disks. The CD-ROM disks are an economical means for storing read only programs and data; they hold 650MB of data. The DVD-ROM disks are a step beyond the CD-ROM; they can hold up to 17 gigabytes of data and have a faster access time than the CD-ROM disks. The WORM disk lets the user write information to this optical disk once, but the disk can be read repeatedly by the user. This disk cannot be erased and reused. On the other hand, the erasable optical can be erased and reused over and over. These removable optical disks give more storage than the magnetic disks, are not as vulnerable to cold and heat, and have a longer life expectancy. Expect optical disk storage to play a major role in data storage technology.

Zip Disk.   With the advent of Iomega's Zip disk, the disk storage media has changed forever. People now have an alternative to the floppy disk which holds only 2 MB of data. The Zip stores 100 MB, is small, and is removable (refer to Fig. 2.5). These disks use a flexible disk material that is enclosed in a plastic case. (See Chapter 12 for a discussion of other storage disks.) Because of the popularity of this storage device, other companies, such as Syquest, produce competitive disks.

Formatting or Initializing a Disk

If a disk is not formatted, it cannot save or store data. Formatting a disk prepares the disk to store information by instructing the computer to record some magnetic reference marks on the disk. These reference marks define the number and size of the sectors on a soft-sectored disk. The storage layout of the disk is determined by the computer operating system's access method. Disks must be initialized with the particular operating system of the computer; operating system A cannot use a disk from operating system B. Each disk is formatted only once unless the user wants to erase everything on the disk. Disks are presently sold unformatted or formatted; the formatted ones are more expensive but they save time and effort.

Operating Systems

In the early days of computing, a person controlled the operation of a computer by using an elaborate control panel. Later, computer programmers designed a program that would allow the computer to control its own operation. This control program is the operating system of the computer, and its major task is to handle the transfer of data and programs to and from the computer's disks. The operating system can display a directory showing the names of programs stored on the disk; it can copy a program from one disk to another; it can display and print the contents of any file on the screen. The operating system controls the computer components and allows them to communicate with each other. (The term *DOS* is an abbreviation for *disk operating system*.) There are many other functions that an operating system performs; the computer's system manual enumerates them.

Different computers have different operating systems. The same computer, moreover, may have more than one operating system available to it. For example, the old Apple II computers used DOS 3.3, ProDOS, and OS/GS operating systems. Some other well-known operating systems are MS-DOS, PC-DOS, Microsoft Windows 95, Microsoft Windows NT, Microsoft UNIX, OS/2, Macintosh System 6 and System 7, and Mac OS 8. Rhapsody is the most recent Apple OS (operating system), and Windows 98 is the most recent Microsoft operating system. In Appendix B, there is a brief step-by-step summary of the following operating systems: Windows 3.1, Windows 95, and Apple Macintosh's System 8.1. Lacking a single standard operating system, all computers are not compatible. However, many companies are seeking a solution to this incompatibility problem. *SoftWindows 95* (Insignia Solutions) and *Virtual PC* (Connectix) are software programs that let your Macintosh computer run Windows 95 programs. These economical software products require plenty of memory and a fast computer to run effectively. The IBM 615-based system runs X86, Macintosh, Unix, and OS/2 software. There are other manufacturers, such as Orange Micro and Daystar, that produce cards that can be placed inside computers to allow them to run more than one system. Apple-IBM subnotebook portable runs both the Windows and Macintosh software on a 4-pound computer (Poultney, 1997). In the past, different models of computers varied in the way the operating system was supplied to the computer. Some computers had the entire operating system built into the ROM of the machine, while others had their operating systems placed on separate floppy disks. Presently, the majority of computers have hard disk drives, and their operating systems are installed from floppies or CD-ROM onto the hard disks.

When the operating system was stored on a disk, the computer, when turned on, would run a small program usually stored in the ROM of the computer. This program's purpose was to load the operating system into the main memory of the computer and then turn over its authority to the operating system. The procedure of starting the computer so that it could load its operating system became known as **booting** the system, a term that has interesting origins. In the past, when the computer first loaded the operating system into main memory, the small program that helped it do this was called a *bootstrap loader* because the initial loading was analogous to "lifting yourself by your own bootstraps." As time went on, computer experts began referring to the procedure of starting the computer system as "booting the system."

How does one physically boot a system? If the operating system was on a disk, the user simply put the disk in a disk drive, turned on the machine, and waited for it to boot. Some computer's operating systems requested that the user supply information, such as date or time of day, before the operating system would respond to the person's commands. Currently, the operating system is on the hard disk and the user simply turns on the computer.

Since its inception, the Macintosh's trademark has been its ease of use. It had the most workable operating system, a characteristic that distinguished it from other systems. Practically every Macintosh application program used the same user interface so the user did not have to relearn commands each time he or she used a different application. The success of the Macintosh interface led Microsoft to introduce Windows for the IBM, which has an interface that is similar to the Macintosh. Before proceeding to the next chapter, let's get acquainted with these two very popular operating systems. Both Apple Macintosh OS 8.1 and Microsoft's Windows 95 feature graphical user interfaces (GUIs) in which the user points to a picture or icon to select a program instead of typing commands.

Getting Started on the Computer

Before you turn on the computer, familiarize yourself with the following accepted sequence for turning most computers on and off. This sequence provides a safeguard against electrical problems. Computer Checklist

1. Turn on the printer.
2. Turn on the monitor.
3. Turn on any other peripherals.
4. Turn on the computer.
5. When finished working, remove the disk from the disk drive.
6. Turn off the computer.
7. Turn off the printer, monitor, and peripherals.[4]

Even though this sequence is very common, some computers require a different sequence. Check in the manual or consult the *read me first* document before proceeding.

Now that we're aware of the suggested order for turning on the equipment, let's acquaint ourselves with the Macintosh and Windows operating systems.

Macintosh Opening Screen

The opening screen, Figure 2.6, consists of several components with a menu bar located at the top. An icon representing the hard disk is located at the top right side of the screen, and icons representing the Mac OS Info Center, Browse the Internet, Mail, Personal Laser Writer NTR, Games, and the trash are located on the right side. The screen represents the desktop that, in turn, represents the working memory (RAM) of the computer.

---

[4]Use a power strip to safeguard your equipment from power surges.

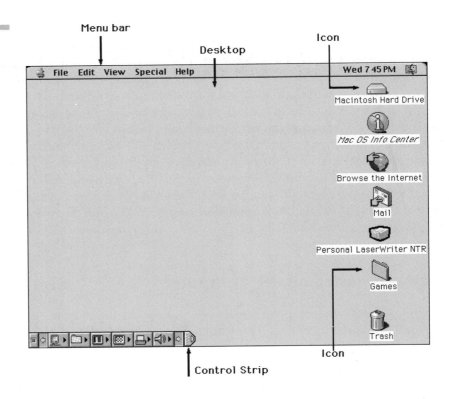

Figure 2.6
Macintosh Opening
Screen
© Apple Computer, Inc.
Used with permission.

Each title in the menu bar is a pull-down menu consisting of different commands. If you want to see some of the commands that are available under *File*'s pull-down menu, open the menu title *File* by positioning the pointer over the word *File* and then holding down the mouse button while dragging it down. The menu in Figure 2.7 appears.

Figure 2.7
Macintosh File menu
©Apple Computer, Inc.
Used with permission.

The boldfaced commands, such as *New Folder, Open, Print, Move to Trash, Get Info,* are the ones that are currently available; the dimmed commands *Close Window, Sharing . . ., Show Original* are not usable.

Windows Opening Screen

The desktop for Windows 95 is the opening screen consisting of objects, a start button, a taskbar (Fig. 2.8). For this discussion, objects represent the items that a person uses when working with the computer system, such as *My Computer* or the *Recycle Bin.* The *Start* button located at the end of the taskbar opens a Start menu where the user chooses menus and launches programs. Finally, the taskbar is used to start programs and switch between tasks.

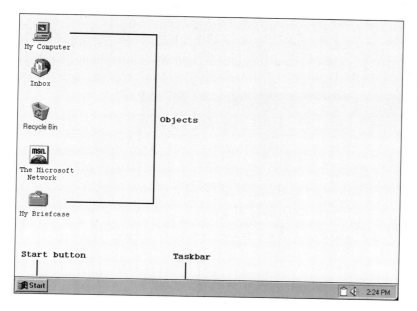

Figure 2.8
Windows opening screen
Screen shot reprinted with permission from Microsoft Corporation.

Macintosh Hard Drive Directory

To view the contents of the Macintosh hard disk, either use the keyboard shortcut command (0-0) or use the mouse to double click it. The hard disk icon opens and displays the contents of the disk. Figure 2.9 shows the names of the files; their size, kind, and date; and the time each file was modified. By selecting *View* from the menu bar, you can view the hard drive by large or small icon, date, size, or name. Figure 2.9 displays the names of the files in alphabetical order.

Macintosh HD			
29 items, 3.2 GB available			
Name	Date Modified	Size	Kind
▷ 🗀 Adobe Acrobat 3.0	Sat, Dec 27, 1997, 11:50 AM	—	folder
▷ 🗀 Adobe PhotoShop3.05	Yesterday, 11:09 AM	—	folder
▷ 🗀 Adobe® PageMill™ 2.0	Fri, Dec 26, 1997, 6:07 PM	—	folder
▷ 🗀 Apple Extras	Mon, Dec 22, 1997, 6:44 PM	—	folder
▷ 🗀 Applications	Mon, Dec 22, 1997, 6:35 PM	—	folder
▷ 🗀 Assistants	Mon, Dec 22, 1997, 6:39 PM	—	folder
▷ 🗀 Claris Emailer Folder	Tue, Dec 23, 1997, 10:20 PM	—	folder
▷ 🗀 Fetch 3.0.3 Folder	Mon, Dec 29, 1997, 11:57 PM	—	folder

Figure 2.9
Mcintosh hard drive directory
©Apple Company, Inc. Used with permission.

Windows Directory

Windows 95 uses the Windows Explorer to view the contents of the Windows hard disk (Fig. 2.10).

Figure 2.10
Windows Contents
Screen shot reprinted with
permission from Microsoft
Corporation.

The left side contains a graphical representation of the disk or folders. The right side of this window contains a list of files that are in the selected directory.

Basic System Utilities

During a normal session of computing, several utility functions are usually requested. The following four functions will illustrate the concept:

- formatting,
- copying disks,
- copying files, and
- deleting files.

Formatting lets the user store data on a disk. Copying disks makes backup copies of data files or applications; this is imperative because original disks can become defective or accidentally erased. Copying files copies a few files instead of the whole disk. Finally, deleting files removes unwanted files from a disk.

Although the Macintosh and Windows systems are both graphical interfaces, which rely heavily on icons or pictures, their respective systems handle their basic functions in unique ways. For example, the Macintosh computer automatically gives the user the option to format or initialize the disk the minute you introduce a blank disk through the disk drive (Fig. 2.11).

Figure 2.11
Initialization screen
©Apple Computer, Inc.
Used with permission.

In Windows, the user inserts the disk in the disk drive first, then opens the *My Computer* icon, selects the disk for formatting, and uses the *Format* command found under the *File* menu (Fig. 2.12).

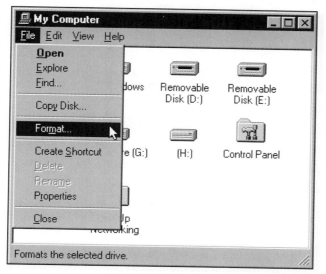

Figure 2.12
Windows format
Box shots reprinted with permission from
© Microsoft Corporation

The Macintosh makes a copy of a floppy disk if the user moves the icon of the disk on top of the hard disk's icon (Fig. 2.13). On the other hand, the Windows user starts either

Step 1	Step 2	Step 3

Figure 2.13
Copying a floppy disk—
©Apple Computer, Inc. Used with permission.

My Computer or *Explorer,* then selects a floppy disk to copy. The user clicks on the right mouse button and Windows brings up a pop-up dialog where the necessary choices are made (Fig. 2.14).

Figure 2.14
Creating a floppy disk—Windows
Box shots reprinted with permission from © Microsoft Corporation

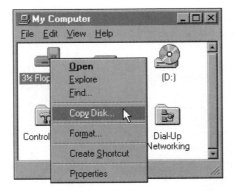

Macintosh and Windows copy files and folders in identical manners. Both copy the items the user selects with the mouse and drags to the appropriate location. Windows also lets you make a copy with the menu.

To rid yourself of unwanted files and folders using a Macintosh computer, select the file and then drag the file to the trash can (Fig. 2.15). Delete or "take out" your trash by choosing *Empty Trash* from *The Special Menu.*

Before   **After**

Figure 2.15
Taking out the trash
©Apple Computer, Inc.
Used with permission.

Windows, similar to the Macintosh, lets you delete files and folders by dragging them, in this instance to the *Recycle Bin,* and then emptying it. Furthermore, Windows lets the user delete files with the menu.

For further discussion of the Macintosh and Microsoft Windows operating systems, consult Appendix B. Let's conclude this chapter with a summary, chapter mastery test, classroom projects, and suggested readings and references.

Summary

Even though advances in technology have blurred the distinctions, computers are classified by memory capacity, speed, capability, price range, and size. The three classifications are mainframe, minicomputer, and microcomputer. In education, the student uses the computer to perform three functions: logic comparisons, arithmetic operations, and storage and retrieval. The computer accomplishes these functions at high speed, storing huge amounts of data in a binary format. The central processing unit, the brain of the computer, consists of a control unit that controls what is happening; an arithmetic/logic unit (ALU) that does the arithmetic and logic operations; and primary memory, ROM and RAM that store all data and instructions necessary for operation. ROM, read only memory, cannot be changed and is hard wired into the machine. RAM, random access memory, is temporary memory that stores data and programs that need processing. Because of its erasable characteristics, RAM allows a program to be executed as many times as the user needs. Since RAM is temporary, disks are very important permanent storage media. The floppy disk is delicate and requires special handling. The operating system, the control program that handles the transfer of data and programs to and from computer disks, makes it possible to enter and run programs. The Macintosh and Windows operating systems illustrate how a computer's operating system displays the hard drive, formats a disk, makes a backup copy of a disk, and copies and deletes files.

Chapter Mastery Test

1. What are the major differences among these categories of computers: mainframe, minicomputer, and microcomputer?

2. Give some pointers on how to protect a floppy disk from harm and discuss why a disk can easily be damaged.

3. Compare and contrast RAM and ROM.

4. Explain how the different components of a central processing unit work.

5. What is an operating system and what function does it perform?

6. What is the purpose of the ASCII code and what is its relationship to the binary code?

7. Discuss the microprocessor, the CPU, and memory and explain how they function independently and as a complete unit.

8. Explain what K is and why it is important to have enough K in RAM.

9. Why is it necessary to initialize or format a disk?

10. Define and explain the following terms: bit, byte, kilobytes, and megabytes.

11. What does it mean "to boot a computer"?
12. Explain the following terms: formatting or initializing, copying disks, copying files, and deleting files.
13. Explain what an optical disk is and what distinguishes it from a floppy disk?
14. Why are erasable optical disks the wave of the future?

Classroom Projects

Lab Activities

1. Boot the computer.
2. Initialize or format a disk.
3. Make a backup copy of a system disk.
4. Copy a file.
5. Delete a file.

Classroom Activities

1. Write a paper on the history of computer memory and in this paper explain the following:
     a. how data is stored in the computer,
     b. the speed and cost of memory, and
     c. the limitations and advantages of the system used.
2. At the library, find a recent article on microchips and discuss recent developments in this technology.
3. Compare and contrast two operating systems.

Suggested Readings and References

American National Standards Institute. *American National Standard Code for Information Interchange.* New York: 1986.

Alessi, S.M., and S.R. Trollip. *Computer-Based Instruction: Methods and Development.* Englewood Cliffs, N.J.: Prentice-Hall, 1985.

Barr, Christopher. "First Sub-Mini Hard Disk." *PC Magazine* 11, no. 1 (January 14, 1992): 30.

Bott, Ed. "The Top Secret Windows: Memphis." *PC Computing,* (August 1997): 154–182

Brown, Margaret. *Learning Windows 95.* New York: DDC Publishing, 1995.

DeVoney, Chris. *PCDos User's Guide.* Indianapolis: Que Corporation, 1984.

Eoyang, Christopher. "The Second Generation of Japanese Computers." *SuperComputer Review.*

San Diego, Calif.: Myrias Research Corporation, 1988, 26;nf27.

Freedman, Alan. *The Computer Glossary,* 5th ed. New York: Amacom, 1995.

Freedman, Alan. *The Computer Desktop Encyclopedia.* New York: Amacom, 1996.

Godman, A. *The Color-Coded Guide to Microcomputers.* New York: Barnes and Noble, 1983.

Harold, Fred G. *Introduction to Computers.* St. Paul, Minn.: West Publishing Company, 1984.

Langer, Maria. MAC OS 8 Visual QuickStart Guide. Berkeley, Calif., Peachpit Press,1997.

Laurie, Peter. *The Joy of Computers.* Boston: Little, Brown, 1983.

Lechner, Pieter, and Don Worth. *Beneath Apple DOS*. Chatsworth, Calif.: Quality Software, 1985.

Long, Larry E. *Computers,* 2d ed. Englewood Cliffs, N.J.: Prentice Hall, 1990.

Maran, Ruth. *Windows 95 Visual Pocket Guide*. California: IDG Books , Worldwide, Inc., 1995.

Matthews Carol and Martin. *Windows 95 Instant Reference*. California: Sybex, 1995.

Mello, Adrian. "Into the Next Decade." *Macworld* (February 1994): 21–22.

Norr, Henry. "Rhapsody Tunes Up." *MacUser* (September 1997): 76–77.

Patton, Peter. "Survey Forecasts Super Computer Market Growth at 35% to 40%." *SuperComputer Review*. San Diego, Calif.: Myrias Research Corporation, (1988): 28–29.

Poultney, John. "Apple-IBM subnotebook due to hit U.S. in summer." *MacWeek* 11, no. 12 (March 24, 1997): 1.

Richman, Ellen. *Spotlight on Computer Literacy,* rev. ed. New York: Random House, 1982, 27.

Rollwagen, John A. "Cray Research Inc. Annual Report." Eagan, Minn.: Cray Research Inc., 1997.

Stone, David. "Future Mass Storage." PCMagazine 16, no. 6 (March 25, 1997): 182–184.

Taub, Eric A. "Multimedia Users Awaiting Rhapsody." *MacWeek* 11, no. 42 (November 3, 1997): S10.

Waite, Mitchell, John Angermeyer, and Mark Noble. *DOS Primer for the IBM PC and XT*. New York: Plume/Waite Books, 1984.

Zorpette, Glenn. "Science and Medicine." *Los Angeles Times* (December 30, 1991): B–5.

Word Processing

3

Objectives

Upon completing this chapter, you will be able to:

1. Define the term **word processor;**
2. Describe the features and functions of a word processor;
3. Demonstrate how a word processing program operates;

4. Evaluate word processing software based on standard criteria;
5. Utilize and create a repertoire of word processing activities for the classroom; and
6. Evaluate a word processing program utilizing the criteria given in this book.

Historical Background

How did word processing evolve? At the onset, there were simple typewriters, eventually followed by more sophisticated ones. In 1961, IBM introduced the elite Selectric typewriter, a fast electric model with changeable print balls, typefaces, and type sizes. Ten years later, Wang Laboratories inaugurated its Wang 1200, a small-screen typing workstation capable of reading output and storing information on a cassette tape. System users could retrieve documents whenever needed and could edit text. Several years later, Wang expanded and improved the 1200 by developing a disk storage system that could store approximately 4,200 pages.

Altair 8800, a microcomputer kit introduced in 1974, was the first commercially successful microcomputer. This computer could store a small amount of data in memory; however, it had neither a keyboard nor a monitor screen. The user entered data and programs by flipping small toggle switches. The microcomputer did not have disks as a workable storage medium until 1976 when Digital Research Corporation introduced the Computer Program Management (CP/M) operating system. Three years later, Seymour Rubenstein created *WordStar,* a word processor for the CP/M operating system, and in 1980, Alan Ashton and Bruce Bastian produced *WordPerfect,* another word processor for the Data General minicomputer. Dedicated word processors, machines designed solely for word processing, soon dominated the office market.

This situation changed in 1981, when IBM introduced its personal computer, the PC. Simultaneously, Unlimited Software announced the first piece of software to run on this new machine: a word processor program called *EasyWriter.* A few months before the announcement, Lifetree Software developed a program called *Volkswriter.*[1] From 1981 to 1985, word processing programs,

---

[1] Lifetree is now called Writing Tools Groups, a subsidiary of Wordstar International.

such as *MacWrite* (Apple), *Microsoft Word* (Microsoft Corporation), *Bank Street Writer* (Scholastic), *PFS Write* (Software Inc.), and *Appleworks* (Apple), flourished. *Appleworks,* introduced in 1983, was an integrated program combining word processor, database, and spreadsheet. In the 1980's, there were helpful features introduced such as spell checker, mail merge, font capabilities, and electronic thesaurus. Because of the popularity of the **graphical user interface(GUI)** systems, such as Macintosh and personal computers that ran Windows, programs could now display different types of fonts and font size choices on the screen as well as handle simple desktop publishing functions such as newsletters. Today, the computer field has hundreds of word processing programs, the most widely used computer application in the office, classroom, and home (Pfaffenberger, 1996). In a 1991 study of teacher's perceptions, word processing was ranked as the primary need for students and teachers (Woodrow, 1991). Now that we have some background for the evolution of word processing, we need to define the term *word processing* and see what it involves.

What Is a Word Processor?

A word processor is a software program designed to make the computer a useful electronic writing tool that can edit, store, and print documents. Before the computer, the typewriter was the principle means of writing reports, and a typist took great pains not to make mistakes because correcting and revising were tedious tasks. Word processing changed all that because the user could make changes quickly and efficiently simply by pressing a few keys on the keyboard. He or she could easily save a document on a disk, make multiple copies, and put the disks away for safekeeping.

In the past, businesses used computers that were designed primarily for word processing (dedicated word processors). They had a special keyboard where the keys were programmed to perform such tasks as underline and change to italics. These machines were inexpensive and perfectly adequate for typing projects only. Now, the microcomputer, packaged with sophisticated word processing software, is found in the office. The majority of these computers are networked so that programs and correspondence can be handled electronically.

Today, when writers discuss word processing they usually are talking about personal computers with word processing software. Such software programs are for sale at local software stores in 3 1/2-inch floppy disk format or CD-ROM disk. The buyer loads the program onto a computer. Then, after opening the program, he or she can create a document, edit text, underline, delete, and add and remove words.

Components of Word Processing

A word processor usually involves the interaction of the components pictured in Figure 3.1. Through the software, the user enters the text using the keyboard, views it on the monitor, changes it as necessary, saves the document on disk, and prints it on the printer.

Since word processing is a primary use for a personal computer, you should exercise care in choosing the right package. The next section explains the factors you should consider before purchasing word processing software. However, before continuing on to the next section, experiment with a word processor package. After you're comfortable with the software, you'll be ready to learn how to select a word processor for the classroom.

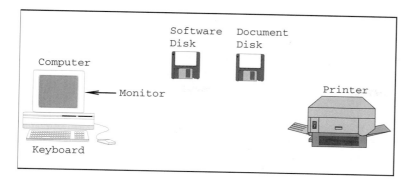

Figure 3.1
Word processing
components
ClickArt Images
© T/Maker Company.

How to Select a Word Processor for the Classroom

There are hundreds of word processing packages on the market today, complete with every imaginable feature. Among these hundreds of programs are word processors well-suited for classroom use. Some word processing programs that fit into this category are *Write:OutLoud, Paint, Write & Play!, Kid Works Deluxe, Storybook Weaver Deluxe, Bank Street Writer, ClarisWorks,* and *Microsoft Works. ClarisWorks, WordPerfect, Bank Street Writer,* and *Microsoft Word* are for the advanced junior high, high school and college student. The software reviewers recommend programs such as *Write:OutLoud, Paint, Write & Play!* and *Storybook Weaver Deluxe* for elementary school since they have fewer features and are easier to use. The features included in most programs are the ones that will help students the most, such as delete, which removes unwanted text, and insert, which inserts lines or passages. The word processors for the upper grades have become more complicated, offer multiple features, and occupy more disk space and memory. A case in point is the *Microsoft Word* 6.0 for the Macintosh. When this program is fully installed, it occupies 19.4 MB of hard disk space, and the suggested RAM partition for the application is 3 MB, but 5 MB is preferred (Staten, 1994). The program contains many desktop publishing features, charting tools, and custom tool bars.

Choosing software for the classroom consists of the following five-step process: (1) determine the hardware compatibility; (2) study the program's general features; (3) examine its standard editing features; (4) review formatting functions; (5) consider instructional design, cost effectiveness, and technical support.

Hardware Compatibility

Check out a computer available at your school: old Apple IIe, Power Macintosh, an IBM PC, or an IBM compatible, for example. How much memory does it have: 128K, 1 MB, or 64 MB of RAM? How much storage space does the hard disk drive contain? What other peripherals or external devices connected to the computer's CPU are available? For instance, does the school district have a CD-ROM player or a laser disc player ?

General Features

Most word processors have cursor control, word wrap, and page break. Since cursor control is an important feature, it warrants discussion first.

Cursor Control.   A cursor (Fig. 3.2) is usually a blinking white block of light that shows the position of a character. It is a place marker that lets the computer user quickly find the place to correct or enter data. The equivalent on a typewriter is the place on the paper where the next keystroke will strike.

Figure 3.2
Cursor

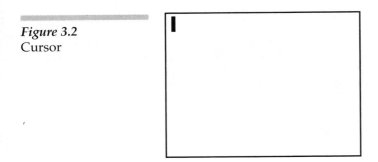

You use the cursor to move within the text and handle editing functions faster than you could with keystrokes. As you type, the cursor moves ahead or under each character that is on the screen. The cursor can move one character at a time, line by line, or over a block of text. You can also move it with the mouse.

Word Wrap.   Word wrap lets you type as much as you want without paying attention to the end of lines; when you reach the right hand margin, the cursor automatically moves to the beginning of the next line, without your having to hit the return key. If the word does not fit on a line, it automatically moves to the next line. You hit the return key only to show a new paragraph or to move down a line.

Page Breaks.   Most word processors display some mark on the screen that tells where the pages in the document break. Before printing your document you can thus check to make sure there are no bad breaks.

Standard Editing Features of a Word Processor

Word processors vary in their editing capabilities because some are more powerful than others. However, they all usually have the same basic editing features: insert, delete, find and replace, and block operations.

Insert.   The **insert** function allows you to insert lines of text, words, and paragraphs anywhere in the document, without retyping any information preceding or following the inserted material.

Delete.   The **delete** function allows you to erase words, lines, or paragraphs of text. After you delete the material, the remaining text arranges itself so that the layout is proper.

Find and Replace.   The **replace** function (Fig. 3.3) in *Microsoft Word* allows you to search a document for a word or phrase and then to replace it. For example, if you misuse the word *their,*

Figure 3.3
Replace function
Box shots reprinted with
permission from ©
Microsoft Corporation

you can later instruct the computer to find every incident of *their* so you can replace it with *there.* This function also allows you to conduct a global search. So, in the example, you can tell the computer to automatically change all entries of *their* to *there.* This particular function is extremely useful for editing a manuscript because it makes locating corrections a simple matter.

Block Operations.   A block is a part of text found between two marked points. The advantage of working with blocks is that they allow you instead of deleting, inserting, or copying one word or line at a time to perform these operations on large blocks of text. To delete a block of text, apply the **cut** function by highlighting the block of text or paragraph that will be cut and then instructing the computer to cut. In the past, if you wanted to change the order of paragraphs, you had to cut the original typewritten sheet of paper and paste the sections into the new sequence. Today, thanks to modern technology, you can use the **cut and paste** function by following these steps:

1. Highlight the block of text that will be moved.

2. Using the cut function, remove the specified portion of text.
3. Position the cursor where you want the material to be placed and then instruct the computer to paste or insert. The text will arrange itself automatically with the proper spacing.

Today, many word processors have **drag-and-drop** text editing. With the mouse, select a small block of text. Then, while pressing the mouse button, drag the text to a new location. This function is very handy for moving text short distances within a document.

The **copy** function works similarly. Choose some text or a picture by highlighting it. Use the copy function to copy it. Once you've copied it, you can paste or insert it in a new location in the document or even in another document.

Standard Formatting Functions

Besides editing features, word processors offer numerous formatting functions. We'll examine only a few of the more pertinent ones such as spacing, justification, and margins. Formatting is the process of making the text appear a certain way on the printed page. First, we'll consider the formatting functions concerned with space, and second, we'll consider those concerned with form.

Space Functions.   The most common space functions are margins, tabs, justification, centering, headers and footers, and line spacing.

Margins.   The margin is the spacing between the edge of the page and the main text area. A margin is set for the entire document whereas an indent is set for individual paragraphs. Margins can be adjusted easily to meet your needs.

Tabs.   Tabs are similar to the tabs on a typewriter which position text precisely within a line in a document or within a column in a table. When you press the tab key, you move the cursor across the page quickly to a predetermined point. These points are adjustable.

A. Left-Justified Text

Suddenly this giant computer stopped working, and everyone was frantically attempting to discover the source of the problem.   Grace Hooper and her coworkers found the culprit was a dead moth in a relay of the computer. They removed the moth with a tweezer and placed it in the Mark II logbook.

B. Right-Justified Text

Suddenly this giant computer stopped working, and everyone was frantically attempting to discover the source of the problem.   Grace Hooper and her coworkers found the culprit was a dead moth in a relay of the computer. They removed the moth with a tweezer and placed it in the Mark II logbook.

C. Full-Justified Text

Suddenly this giant computer stopped working, and everyone was frantically attempting to discover the source of the problem.   Grace Hooper and her coworkers found the culprit was a dead moth in a relay of the computer. They removed the moth with a tweezer and placed it in the Mark II logbook.

D. Center-Justified Text

Suddenly this giant computer stopped working, and everyone was frantically attempting to discover the source of the problem.   Grace Hooper and her coworkers found the culprit was a dead moth in a relay of the computer. They removed the moth with a tweezer and placed it in the
Mark II logbook.

Figure 3.4
Justification Types

Justification.   Justification aligns the margins of text. Text can be aligned along the left side, it can be aligned along the right side, it can fill the type space to align both left and right, or it can be centered. In left-justified text (Fig. 3.4A), the left margin is aligned and the right margin is uneven. This is the most common type of justification, and word processing programs usually have this as their default. In right-justified text (Fig. 3.4B), the right margin is aligned and the left margin is uneven. Full-justified text (Fig. 3.4C) is aligned along both margins. The computer achieves this alignment by adding space between words in a line of text to extend it. In center-justified text (Fig. 3.4D), all the lines of text are aligned in the center of the page. This type of justification is often used to make headings more attractive on a page.

The *Microsoft Word* word processing program uses icons identical to the ones shown in Figure 3.5 for the different types of justification. For example, for full-justified text, select the icon on the extreme right.

Figure 3.5
Justification icons
Screen shot Microsoft ®
Word © 1984–1989
Microsoft Corporation.
Reprinted with permission
from Microsoft
Corporation.

Headers and Footers.   A **header** is text that appears at the top margin of each page of manuscript, while a **footer** is text that prints in the bottom margin of a page of manuscript. Headers and footers usually include descriptive text, such as page numbers, titles, and dates.

Line Spacing.   **Line spacing** is the amount of space between lines of text. You can single- one and one-half- or double-space text in the document with the line spacing function.

Form Functions.   The form functions include boldface, underlining, superscripts, subscripts, fonts, and numbering.

Boldface.   Boldfacing darkens words or sentences and slightly enlarges the text in a document. **This sentence is an example of bold-faced text.** Some programs show actual boldfacing on the screen, while others indicate with special characters what words are to be boldfaced. When a program shows boldfacing with special characters, the selected words are not seen as boldface until printed.

Underlining.   Underlining is simply putting a <u>line</u> under a word or sentence. Some software programs will show the word underlined; other programs will indicate the underlining with special characters.

Superscripts and Subscripts.   Superscripts and subscripts are used in mathematical formulas and with footnote markers. The 8 in 2^8 is a superscript while the 1 in A_1 is a subscript.

Font.   Font refers to the physical characteristics of a typed character. These characteristics include typeface, spacing, pitch, point size, and style. *Typeface* refers to the design of the characters, such as 𝕷𝖔𝖓𝖉𝖔𝖓 𝕿𝖊𝖝𝖙; *pitch* represents characters per inch; *point size* is the height of characters; *style* includes italicizing and boldfacing. Programs vary in the number of fonts that can be used. Figure 3.6 shows examples of different fonts, sizes, and styles that can be generated on a Macintosh computer. Fonts can be printed either as bit map, in a pattern of dots, or as outlines defined by a mathematical formula.

Figure 3.6
Font styles and sizes

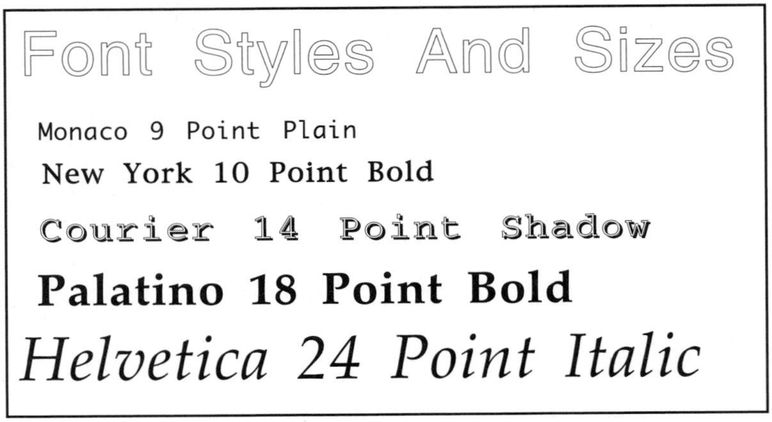

Font Styles And Sizes

Monaco 9 Point Plain

New York 10 Point Bold

Courier 14 Point Shadow

Palatino 18 Point Bold

Helvetica 24 Point Italic

Numbering.   Many word processors offer automatic **numbering** functions. These number the pages in a document.

After examining formatting functions, look carefully at the instructional design and features of your program. The next few pages should give you an idea of what to scrutinize.

Instructional Design and Features

For the lowest grade levels, a word processor should offer at least the following functions: insert, delete, center, underline, double space, save text, and print. A word processor program should be easy for the student to learn and not require hours of instruction.

Write:OutLoud is a talking word processor that provides auditory feedback for students with or without learning disabilities. Students hear the words, letters, or sentences as they are typed. There is a talking spelling checker and a toolbar. The word processor also has large font sizes to make the letters easier to read. *Write:OutLoud* has its functions displayed at the top of the screen (Fig. 3.7). This is ideal for beginners because it saves them from having to remember the functions. For example, to print a document, the user chooses the printer icon on the toolbar, and to save the work, he or she chooses the floppy disk icon on the toolbar. This word processor is a perfect example of a picture or icon-based application.

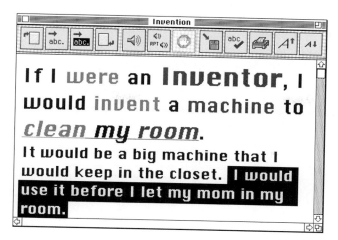

Figure 3.7
Write:OutLoud
Used with permission of
Don Johnston, Inc.

Bank Street Writer has always been popular because it has on-screen prompts and a tutorial disk. The most recent Macintosh version (Fig. 3.8) has a spelling checker, a thesaurus, hypermedia functions, and desktop capabilities. In this version of *Bank Street Writer,* the major functions appear at the top of the screen. When you pull down a menu, you get a list of options. Figure 3.9

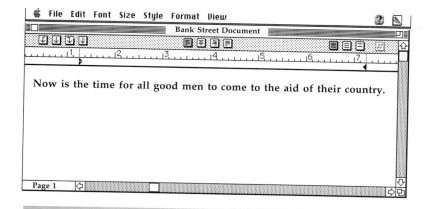

Figure 3.8
Bank Street Writer
Figure reproduced by permission of Scholastic, Inc.

Edit	
Can't Undo	⌘Z
Cut	⌘X
Copy	⌘C
Paste	⌘V
Clear	
Select All	⌘A
Find/Replace...	⌘F
Check Spelling...	⌘K
Search Dictionary	
Find Synonyms...	⌘Y
Preferences...	

Figure 3.9
Bank Street Writer
edit menu options
Figures reproduced by
permission of Scholastic Inc.

shows the list of options that are available under the *Edit* menu. Since these are editing functions, the list includes such items as *Cut, Paste,* and *Copy.*

In your search for a word processor, examine only those that have easy-to-remember keys for functions. Find out how the word processor carries out simple functions such as underlining or boldfacing.

In the higher grade levels, students make considerable use of word processing, so they need a word processor like *WordPerfect* (Corel Corp.) This program has many advanced features but it still retains its simplicity. At this upper grade level, a word processor should have features such as the following:

Table 3.1 Advanced Word Processor Features

Feature	Description
Charts	Insert and create charts in document.
Equation Editor	Builds complex equations using special math symbols. $$\dfrac{-b \pm \sqrt{b^2 - 4ac}}{2a}$$
Footnotes	Reserves space at the bottom of each page for footnote[1] text like the following: ————————————— [1]A footnote is a reference at the bottom of a page.
Glossary Creation	Helps create a list of technical words and definitions for the end of the textbook such as **ABC** An abbreviation for the Atanasoff-Berry-Computer, the first electronic digital computer. **Access time** The time a computer needs from the instant it asks for information until it receives it.
Index	A list of key words in a document along with page numbers that the reader can use to find information. An example follows: QuickTime movie 179–186 Creating 183–186 Playing 179–181 Quit HyperStudio 33, 46, 61, 72,

Table 3.1 Advanced Word Processor Features

Feature	Description
Mail Merge	Creates a personalized document by inserting information such as the person's name and address into a form letter.
Outlining	Creates headings for key ideas.
Picture Insertion	Using the word processor, the user inserts images with different types of graphic format such as PICT, GIF, PCX, BMP, EPS, etc.
Style Sheets	Once a document is created its format can be used repeatedly. Fonts, tabs, margins etc., can be stored in a style sheet file and applied to a new document.
Table of Contents	Using codes that are assigned to words in the document, the word processor generates a list of major headings.
Tables	By simply typing in the number of rows and columns, the word processor creates a table like this one for advanced features.
Voice Annotation	Adds sound comments to explain the text.

An instructor must know what the students' requirements are and what word processing features are available.

Safety Features.   Are there safety devices that prevent a student from making a mistake? If the student is about to format a disk and wipe out all data, is there a screen that cautions the student not to proceed? *Bank Street Writer* (Macintosh version) handles problems such as this by asking questions: ARE YOU SURE YOU WANT TO CONTINUE? DO YOU WANT TO CLEAR ALL OF YOUR TEXT (Y/N)? These types of queries warn both the novice and advanced user that they may be making errors. Many word processing programs try to protect against data loss by automatically saving material intermittently. Other programs remind the user to save the document. *Bank Street Writer* displays the screen in Figure 3.10 when the user is about to quit an application without saving the changes. He or she then has three options: not to save, to cancel, or to save.

Figure 3.10
Bank Street Writer
dialog box
Figure reproduced by
permission of Scholastic,
Inc.

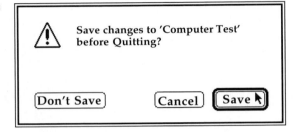

Most word processing programs have undo features that reverse the last action performed on the document. *Nisus,* an advanced-level word processor program designed for the Macintosh, has unlimited undos. It is important to have as many of these safeguards as possible, especially when you are about to format a disk, delete a file, or save material.

Screen Display.   When it comes to screen displays, there are two primary concerns: What You See Is What You Get (WYSIWYG) and column size. WYSIWYG is a feature that is commonplace in most word processors. It means text and graphics appear on screen the same as they will appear when printed. To have WYSIWYG text, a matching screen font must be installed for each printer font. It is a rare occurrence to get 100% exact representation because printer resolution and screen resolution rarely match. For example, the Apple Macintosh displays font size and graphic images that only approximate the printed copy. Column size is very important when it comes to the page layout of your document. Can you make a large number of columns and easily adjust their width?

Consumer Value.   Software is expensive, and for teachers, cost is often a consideration. Any public domain software package that can be purchased for a minimal price and duplicated as often as needed would be very advantageous for the teacher if the package is good. There is one catch: The program cannot be sold to anyone. Usually, commercial software is more expensive, but there are exceptions. Be sure to find out if the software comes with a backup copy or allows you to make a backup. If the software is copy protected, make sure to buy a backup copy for a minimum charge.

Ease of Use.   A major consideration when buying a word processor is how easy is it to learn the program. It is immaterial what features the program has if it is difficult to learn. Ask the following questions:

1. Can a person in a reasonable amount of time learn to use this program? *Paint, Write and Play!* for grades K-2 (Learning Co., Fig. 3.11) is exceptionally easy to use. The majority of instructions appear on the right side of the screen so teachers do not have to read a large manual. There are icons every step of the way to remind you what each function does. For example, choose the printer picture to print the document, and the **crocodile** to dispose of the unwanted document.

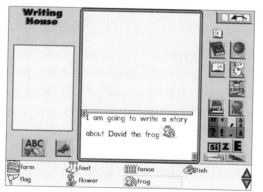

Figure 3.11
Paint, Write and Play!
© The Learning Company.
All rights reserved.

2. Are there help screens that tell the student what to do each step of the way?
3. Is there a tutorial disk or manual that takes the user through the program?
4. Can you set up the printer easily and is it ready to print immediately?
5. Is there a spelling checker, grammar checker, or thesaurus?

Even the more advanced word processors (Fig. 3.12) such as *Microsoft Word* (Windows version) have icons at the top of the screen so you can just click on them.

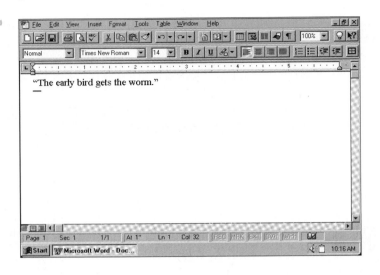

Figure 3.12
Microsoft Word
(Windows version)
Box shots reprinted with
permission from ©
Microsoft Corporation

Support.   Support refers to personal as well as written help from the software company. Can you call a technician at the software company to get immediate help or must you sift through a series of messages and wait an unbearable amount of time? Is the technical support toll free or is it a pay call? Are you charged for the amount of time you're on the telephone with the technician? Is there a yearly fee for unlimited support and is it reasonable? Is the manual readable with activities and lesson plans and an index? The new and revised advanced programs are packaged with all three.

Spelling Checkers.   The **spelling checker** is commonplace in the majority of word processors. It can come as an add-on package, or it can be built into the word processing program. The spelling checker looks for spelling and typing errors by checking the spelling of the words in your document against a dictionary that is stored on the hard disk drive. If a word in the document does not appear in the dictionary, the spelling checker will display the word in question and give you the opportunity to override the query or select an alternative. In *Microsoft Word* (Windows version, Fig. 3.13), the word *looks* is misspelled; the spelling checker suggests many alternatives and highlights the most likely. You can add any words you wish to the spelling checker's dictionary. Once you've added a word, the spelling checker will no longer question that particular spelling. The good spelling checker lets you see the misspelled word in context.

Grammar Checkers.   Because of the rapidly increasing demand for grammar checkers, these programs are widely available. Grammar checkers help with grammar, style, punctuation, and even spelling errors. The grammar checker identifies problems such as inconsistencies, awkward phrases, clichés, and wordiness. After it identifies the problem, it makes suggestions on how to correct it and provides an on-line tutorial explaining the grammar rule that applies. Usually, you make the correc-

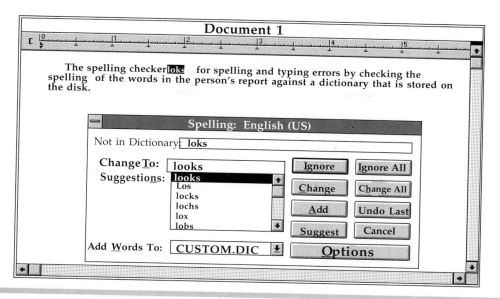

Figure 3.13
Microsoft Word spelling checker
Screen shot reprinted with permission from Microsoft Corporation.

tion with a click of the mouse. You also have the option of rewriting the incorrect sentence or leaving it just as it is. The screen from *Correct Grammar* (Softkey International, Inc.), a stand-alone grammar checker, in Figure 3.14 shows a dialog box that offers a correction or suggestion to the writer. The top

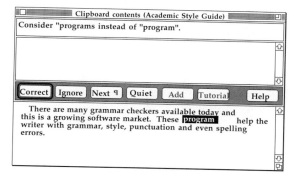

Figure 3.14
Correct Grammar
Correct Grammar, used with permission of Softkey International, Inc.
Copyright © 1994.

of this display offers a suggestion when an error is found. In this case, it tells the writer that the sentence should have *programs* instead of *program.* The middle portion of the box displays buttons. Only the highlighted buttons are available to handle this particular problem. The *Correct* button lets the program correct the sentence, and the *Ignore* button ignores the suggestions. The *Next* button lets the writer skip the paragraph entirely, and the *Quiet* button turns off the rule that was used for the current suggestion. The *Help* button explains procedure. The bottom of the dialog box displays the pertinent part of the writer's document and lets him or her type in the corrections directly.

Early grammar checkers were limited because of their emphasis on mechanical and stylistic errors, but the new programs like the Grammarian (Casady & Green) are more versatile. The grammar checkers do not restrict the writer to one writing style but offer a choice, depending on the writer's purpose. For example, *Correct Grammar* gives the choice of ten different writing styles, from *Academic* to *Technical*. This program also compares the readability of the writing, sentence by sentence, to the educational level of the audience. If a particular sentence is too difficult for the selected audience to understand, the checker tells the writer immediately.

Grammar checkers that are integrated into word processors are becoming as common as spelling checkers. A few accompany the word processing packages, some are sold as Sound-a-lone packages, while others are built into the word processing software. For example, *Microsoft Word* and its IBM counterpart as well as *WordPerfect* (Corel Corp.) both have grammar checkers built into their programs. Even though there have been advances in the last two years, the grammar checkers are still in the process of evolving.

Thesaurus.   The thesaurus has the capacity to generate synonyms for any word that it has in its dictionary. For example, if you want a different word for *peculiar, Word Perfect's Thesaurus* lists such words as: *characteristic, distinctive, idiosyncratic, unique* and *bizarre.* Figure 3.15 shows the *Word Perfect's Thesaurus* screen. Select the synonym you want and click on *Replace,* and the program automatically substitutes the new word.

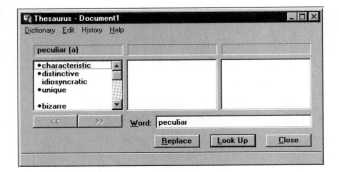

Figure 3.15
WordPerfect Thesaurus
© Corel Corporation.
Reprinted by permission.

The previous description of available features shows that word processing has come a long way from the *Wang 1200.* A teacher looking for a classroom word processing program now must weigh many factors. **Be sure to review the award-winning annotated word processing list in Appendix A.** Next, examine any one of these programs by using the following checklist and evaluation rating instrument.

WORD PROCESSOR CHECKLIST

Directions: Examine the following items and determine which ones you feel are important for your class situation. Evaluate your word processor and place an X on each line where the software meets your needs.

Product Name _____   Manufacturer _____   Grade Level _____

A. Hardware
___ 1. Memory Needed
___ 2. Computer compatibility
___ 3. Printer compatibility
___ 4. Hard disk space required
___ 5. CD-ROM Drive

B. Standard Editing Features
___ 1. Cursor control
___ 2. Insert and delete
___ 3. Find/replace
___ 4. Block operations
   ___a. Delete block
   ___b. Copy block
   ___c. Drag-and-drop

C. Standard Formatting Functions
___ 1. Margins
___ 2. Tabs
___ 3. Justification
___ 4. Centering
___ 5. Headers and footers
___ 6. Line spacing
___ 7. Boldfacing
___ 8. Underlining
___ 9. Superscripts and subscripts
___ 10. Automatic numbering

D. Advanced Features
___ 1. Split screen
___ 2. Footnoting
___ 3. Automatic indexing
___ 4. Outlining
___ 5. Glossary
___ 6. Mail merge
___ 7. Equation editor
___ 8. Charting

___ 9. Table of contents
___ 10. Voice annotation
___ 11. Ability to import different graphic file formats

E. Safety Features
___ 1. Undo last move(s)
___ 2. Undo last erase(s)
___ 3. Warning questions
___ 4. Automatic save
___ 5. Formats disk anytime

F. Screen Display
___ 1. WYSIWYG
___ 2. 20-40-80 columns

G. Ease of Use
___ 1. Help screens
___ 2. Tutorial disk
___ 3. Printer setup
___ 4. Talking processor

H. Support Features
___ 1. Technical support
___ 2. Tutorial material
___ 3. Readable manual
   ___a. Activities and lesson plans
   ___b. Tutorial
   ___c. Index
___ 4. Spelling checker
___ 5. Grammar checker
___ 6. Thesaurus

I. Consumer Value
___ 1. Cost
___ 2. Free backup disk
___ 3. Guarantees

Rating Scale

Rate the Word Processor by placing a check on the appropriate line.

Excellent ___   Very Good ___   Good ___   Fair ___ Poor ___

Comments

Learning to Use a Word Processor

The following exercises are meant to be used in conjunction with any word processor. If a computer lab is not available, just follow this section to get a feel for what is involved in using a word processor.

Begin by loading a word processing program into the computer. Be sure to format one or more data disks with the word processing program so that the floppy disk can store files.

Now you're ready to begin writing on the word processor. The cursor shows where the next letter or number will appear. The *delete* key will move the cursor to the left and delete letters. The *return* key operates like the carriage return on a typewriter. After working through the following preliminary exercises, you will be ready to handle the six subsequent classroom activities.

Type the following jumbled sentence[2] as it appears:

"LIS NOT THERE PRIZES HARD DIFFICULT WORK."

Do *not* press the *return* key because it will move the cursor down a line.

1. Use the delete key in this instance to (a) delete the *L* in *LIS,* (b) the *T* in *NOT,* and (c) the word *DIFFICULT.* The delete key deletes characters, words, or paragraphs, depending on the writer's purpose.
2. Now insert the word *FOR* between *prizes* and *hard.*
3. Next, learn to use the move function and position the word *THERE* at the beginning of the sentence.
4. Use the find/replace function to replace the word *PRIZES* with *SUBSTITUTE.* If you completed the word processing task correctly, the following quotation should appear:

"THERE IS NO SUBSTITUTE FOR HARD WORK."

Before continuing with the next exercise, learn how to save the material you just typed and how to erase the screen.

In order to practice some basic word processing functions, let's unscramble a famous poem. First, type the following poem exactly as it appears:

> Bananas
> Stories are made by fools like me,
> But only God can make a flea.
>
> A flea whose hungry mouth is prest;
> Against the earth's sweet flowing breaset;

---

[2]This quotation by Alva Edison appeared in *Life.*

A flea that looks at God all day,
And lifts his strong arms to pray;

A flea wear

A nest of robins in his hair;

Upon whose boosom snow has lain;
Who intimately lives with rain.

My love he is the one for me;
He is bound to me for eternity.

I think that I shall neever see
A poem lovely as a flea.

1. Use the find/replace option to exchange the word *Bananas* with the word *Trees*. Now exchange the word *strong* with the word *leafy,* and the word *Stories* with the word *Poems*. Use this option to exchange every instance of the word *flea* with the word *tree* and the word *his* with the word *her.*
2. Center the word *Trees* as the title of the poem.
3. Use the cut and paste option to exchange lines 1 and 2 of the poem with lines 13 and 14. Proceed by cutting lines 1 and 2 and moving them to the very end of the poem. Cut and move lines 13 and 14 to the top of the poem. These lines will fill the empty spaces left.
4. Use the delete option to delete lines 11 and 12. Now there are two blank lines, so hit the delete key twice to get rid of them. Next insert four words in the poem by putting the cursor on line seven, after the word *tree* and before the word *wear,* and then typing the following words:

> that may in Summer

Use the spacebar to create a space where one is needed.
5. Use the spelling checker to find any spelling errors in the poem. The first word the spelling checker finds is *neever*. Change it to *never*. The second word the checker finds is *prest*; this word exists, so don't change it but do add the word to the dictionary. The next word is *breaset*; correct it by typing *breast*. The last word the checker finds is *boosom*. Correct it by typing *bosom*.
6. Now save the poem on the formatted disk.
7. As a final activity print the poem. The printout is the poem *Trees,* by Sergeant Joyce Kilmer:[3]

---

[3] Reprinted from *Trees and Other Poems* by Sergeant Joyce Kilmer. George H. Doran Company, 1914.

Trees

I think that I shall never see
A poem lovely as a tree.

A tree whose hungry mouth is prest
Against the earth's sweet flowing breast;

A tree that looks at God all day,
And lifts her leafy arms to pray;

A tree that may in Summer wear
A nest of robins in her hair;

Upon whose bosom snow has lain;
Who intimately lives with rain.

Poems are made by fools like me,
But only God can make a tree.

8. To finish this exercise, learn how to retrieve a saved file and then reboot the computer and retrieve the poem that was just saved. Finally, learn how to boldface and underline the poem.

The following six ready-to-use classroom activities test your students' ability to use successfully the different features of the word processor.

Classroom Applications

▼   I. Math Race   ▼

Objective
Students will improve their math skills and, in the process, practice editing on the word processor.

Procedure

1. Create a list of math problems from the work that the class is currently doing.
2. Develop a race sheet similar to the following:

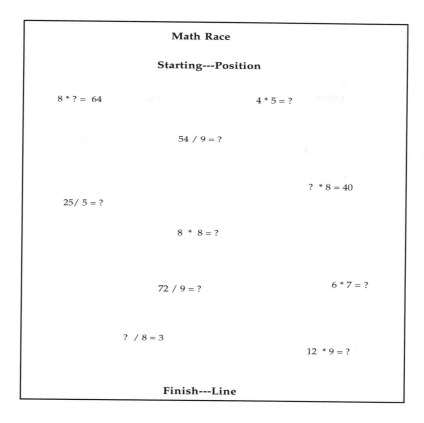

Math Race

Starting---Position

8 * ? = 64   4 * 5 = ?

54 / 9 = ?

? * 8 = 40

25/ 5 = ?

8 * 8 = ?

72 / 9 = ?   6 * 7 = ?

? / 8 = 3

12 * 9 = ?

Finish---Line

3. On this race sheet, vary the horizontal distance and the vertical spaces between the problems and diversify the missing parts of the problems.
4. Save the race sheet on the disk under the name *Math Race.*
5. Next, have the students load this program into their computers.
6. When you give the signal, the students race to solve the problems. They must use their arrow keys to reach each problem, delete the question mark, replace it with the correct response, and then cross the finish line. The student who has the fastest time and most correct answers wins the race.
7. Record a time after each student's name and check each problem, taking 10 percent off for each problem not solved correctly.

Variation

You can make this a group activity by dividing the class in half and creating two competing teams, Team A and Team B. Follow the same procedures as before and record the time score for each student. Next, compute Team A's score by adding together all the individual scores for

Team A and deducting 10% for each problem not solved correctly. Then compute Team B's score in the same manner. The winning team is the one with the lowest combined time with the most correct answers.

▼   II. Unscramble the Story   ▼

Objective
Students will improve reading comprehension and learn how to use the word processor's move/block function.

Procedure
1. Choose a story that the students are currently reading.
2. Type the story or part of the story into the computer. For example, type "The Hare and the Tortoise,"[4] one of Aesop's Fables.

The Hare and the Tortoise

A hare was once boasting about how fast he could run when a tortoise, overhearing him, said, "I'll run you a race." "Done," said the hare and laughed to himself, "but let's get the fox for a judge." The fox consented and the two started. The hare quickly outran the tortoise, and knowing he was far ahead, lay down to take a nap. "I can soon pass the tortoise whenever I awaken." But, unfortunately, the hare overslept himself; therefore when he awoke, though he ran his best, he found the tortoise was already at the goal.
 Slow and steady wins the race.

---

3. Save this story under *Hare/Tortoise.*
4. Now scramble the story on the computer screen and use the Cut/Paste functions on the word processor to rearrange the story. The scrambled Tortoise and Hare story could look like this:

The Scrambled Hare and the Tortoise

 The hare quickly outran the tortoise, and knowing he was far ahead, lay down to take a nap. "Done," said the hare and laughed to himself, "but let's get the fox for a judge." The fox consented and the two started. But, unfortunately, the hare overslept himself; therefore, when he awoke, though he ran his best, he found the tortoise was

---

[4]From *The Children's Treasury,* Paula S. Goepfert, ed. New York: Gallery Books, 1987, p. 229.

already at the goal. A hare was once boasting about how fast he could run when a tortoise, overhearing him, said, "I'll run you a race." "I can soon pass the tortoise whenever I awaken."

5. Save this scrambled fable under *AERH*—*Hare* scrambled.
6. Load *AERH* into each student's computer.
7. The students must use their word processors to rearrange the story correctly.
8. Record each student's score by writing down the time taken to complete the activity and the number of sentences arranged correctly.
9. The winner is the student who finishes first and arranges all the sentences correctly.

Variation

1. Divide the class into two teams, Team A and Team B.
2. Instruct Team A to scramble a story.
3. Instruct Team B to rearrange the story.
4. Determine Team B's score by calculating the time it takes the team to rearrange the story and the number of sentences correct on completion.
5. Then have the teams swap roles.

▼   III. The Editor   ▼

Objective

Students will gain practice in basic word processing skills and in using the spelling checker.

Procedure

Enter into the computer two or three paragraphs from a story the students have been reading in class. Deliberately make four or five spelling errors. For purposes of illustration, let us use the following paragraphs[5]:

Programming the Calculator

Most people regard the calculator as an electrenic marvel, yet the principle on which it works is relativly simple. The heart of the calculator is an arithmetic and logical unit (which adds, subtracts, multiplies, divides, and compares numbers at highe speed by electronic means) and a memory unit, in which many thousands of numbers can be electornically stored

---

[5] Mitchell, James, ed. "How Computers Work." *The Random House Encyclopedia.* New York: Random House, 1977, p. 1672.

How Calculators Work

The value of the calculator over the human being lies in its ability to work without error and at immense speed; it can carry out hundreds of thousands of calculations every second, storing intermediate results in its memory and recalling them instantly when required. The various instrucitons for the stages in the program are stored in the computer memory in numerical form for instant access. The use of the calculator is based on the technique known as programming—the conversion of the problem the calculator is to solve, or the tasks it is to perform, into the simple steps the calculator can carry out. The computer is a very useful device.

Save these paragraphs under the name *Editor.* Now create five or six editing activities. An activity sheet sample follows:

1. Find and replace the word *calculator* with the word *computer.*
2. In paragraph 2 in the second line, insert the sentence, "A programmer defines precisely what has to be done in each succeeding step."
3. Delete the last sentence in paragraph 2.
4. In the last sentence of paragraph 1 after the word *stored,* insert, "and recalled on command."
5. In paragraph 2, make the last sentence the first sentence.
6. Switch the titles of the paragraphs.
7. Use the spelling checker to correct the five spelling errors.

Have the students compete with each other and record the time it takes each of them to complete the editing activities. The numerical score is the time it takes each student to complete all six directions, plus a penalty for any incorrect items. The student with the fastest time and the most correct items wins.

Variation

The teacher can design this activity for two groups by dividing the class in half. Team A would design a paragraph and create a set of directions. Team B would take Team A's paragraph and follow the directions. Team A would time Team B. Then the teams would switch roles. The team with the fastest time and the most correct responses would win.

▼   IV. Punctuation Exercise   ▼

Objective

Students will improve punctuation skills and practice using the find/replace function.

Procedure

1. Design an activity sheet for the students. Type six to ten sentences, eliminating all punctuation marks and putting in asterisks instead. A sample sheet follows:
    1. The sun is shining*
    2. I bought a computer* a monitor* a printer* and a modem at the computer store*

3. Mom asked* *When will you clean your room*
4. I have to teach a class at 1*30 this afternoon*
5. "I am going to lunch*" said Dick
6. The computer cost $3*700*

2. Save the punctuation exercise under *Punct* and load this file into each student's computer and save.
3. Have the students use their FIND/REPLACE function to find each asterisk and replace each with the correct punctuation mark.
4. When the students finish, have them save their corrected work under their initials.
5. Correct the exercises and return the results.

▼   V. Insert the Adjectives   ▼

Objective

Students will improve their ability to recognize adjectives and practice using the FIND/REPLACE function of the word processor.

Procedure

1. Design an activity sheet, eliminating adjectives. A sample sheet follows:

    1. The * mansion sat on top of the hill in a remote end of the forest.
    2. The * professor gave a very * lecture to the class.
    3. Jim flew the * plane into the sunset.
    4. The * horses raced to the end of the glen to see the * man.
    5. An * individual visited the classroom yesterday.
    6. She was a * * woman with * blue eyes.

2. Save this file under the name *Adj.* and load it into each student's computer and save.
3. Have students search for the asterisk before each noun by using the FIND/REPLACE function of the word processor and replace each asterisk with an adjective.
4. When the students finish, have them save the work under their initials.
5. Correct the exercises and return the results.

▼   VI. Replace the Sentences   ▼

Objective

Students will improve their writing skills and, in the process, use the CUT/PASTE and FIND/REPLACE functions.

Procedure

1. Have students independently create random sentences for a story file.
2. Instruct each student to write his or her sentence on a piece of paper. Ask the class to examine the sentences of two classmates, correcting grammar errors.

3. Next instruct the students to enter, one at a time, their sentences into the computer.
4. When the sentences are entered, separate them by a line and number them in the order they are entered.
5. The last student to enter his or her sentence should save the entire file of sentences under a name such as *Story 1.*
6. Go around the room asking students to call out random numbers no higher than the number of sentences that were recorded for *Story 1.*
7. Call up *Story 1* on the computer and record the random sequence of numbers the students gave at the top of the screen.
8. Have the students take turns using the FIND/REPLACE function to locate the sentences in the random sequence and using the CUT/PASTE function to move the sentences into the order of the random sequence.
9. Print out a copy of the ordered sentences for each student. During independent work time, ask the students to make stories out of their sentences, without changing the order of sentences, by adding sentences or words.
10. Ask students to share their finished stories.

An example follows:

Story 1

Use the find/replace and move/block functions to create a story from the sentences that follow. Arrange the sentences in the following sequence:

1 4 8 2 3 5 6 9 7

1. Do not judge food on calories alone.
2. The professor was frustrated with the paperwork he had to turn in next week.
3. The student was eagerly awaiting an exciting lecture on computers.
4. The wind blew a bee into the room.
5. "Don't forget to pick up the groceries at the store," said Paul.
6. "Did the emergency rations arrive?" asked Maria.
7. There were many children on the playground.
8. The center fielder could not catch the ball.
9. The sound came from another room.

One Student's Story:

Do not judge food on calories alone. This is what the professor was saying as the wind blew a bee into the classroom. I was daydreaming as usual, watching the baseball team. The center fielder could not catch the ball. The professor banged on the board. I looked up. He seemed crabby. I think he was frustrated with the paperwork he had to turn in next week. He called on Dewayne. The student was eagerly awaiting an exciting lecture on computers but instead he was invited up to the board to solve a complicated problem. I went back to daydreaming. There was something I was supposed to do after class. Suddenly I remembered. While I was brushing my teeth that morning, my roommate made a grocery list. "Don't forget to pick up the groceries at the store," said Paul as I ran out the door. Then at the bus stop, I ran into my friend Maria, who was heading up an earthquake disaster team. She was talking to someone else on the disaster team. "Did the emergency rations arrive?" asked Maria. As Dewayne tried to solve the problem, I decided I would donate some of my groceries to Maria's earthquake relief efforts. My daydreaming was interrupted by an explosion. The sound came from another room, the chemistry lab. Dewayne still wasn't finished. I looked back out the window. There were many children on the playground.

Summary

This chapter traced the historical beginnings of word processing. We examined the merits of the word processor over the standard typewriter. We discovered how easy it is for users to change and edit documents by using word processors. We became familiar with the basic features of word processing and gained insight into what features to consider when selecting a word processor. The chapter presented a checklist and evaluation scale to facilitate this decision-making process, along with specific ideas on how to incorporate the word processor into the classroom. Six word processing activities featured covered a range of curriculum areas.

Let's continue with the mastery test and the suggested readings and references. Be sure to review the award-winning annotated word processing list in Appendix A.

Chapter Mastery Test

1. What is word processing and why is it important in education?

2. What distinguishes a typewriter from a word processor?

3. Identify and describe five features that are common to all word processors.

4. Discuss three different ways a word processor would be useful in the classroom.

5. Distinguish among a thesaurus, a spelling checker, and a grammar checker and explain which a sixth grader and a tenth grader would prefer.

6. Select two standard editing features and justify their use.

7. Explain the concept of line justification as it relates to the computer and give two examples.

8. Discuss the factors involved in selecting a word processor for a school district. Use Appendix A for an annotated list of word processing software.

9. Define the following terms:
   a. font,
   b. cut,
   c. block function,
   d. text insertion, and
   e. find and replace.

10. What safety features should be included in a word processor and why?

11. Evaluate a real or hypothetical word processing software program based on the criteria used in this chapter.

12. What is a dedicated word processor and how is it used?

13. Choose three advance word processing features and explain how you would use them in a high school classroom.

14. If you were buying a word processing program for the elementary school, what three features would be essential and why?

Classroom Projects

1. Create a word processing activity for any grade level.

2. Use a word processor with a thesaurus and develop a classroom activity for this feature.

3. Write a story with misspelled words and use the spelling checker to find the words that are incorrectly spelled.

4. Compare two word processors on the basis of their features; then review each one separately.

Suggested Readings and References

Abbott, Chris. "Microcomputers' Software Word Processing for All." *British Journal of Special Education* 18, no. 1 (March 1, 1991): 8.

Allen, Philip A. "Adult Age Difference in Letter-Level and Word-Level Processing." *Psychology and Aging* 6, no. 2 (June 1, 1991): 261.

Anderson, Cindy, ed. "CompuKids, 1996." *CompuKids* 2, no. 1–6 (January-December, 1996).

Balajthy, E. "Keyboarding, Language Arts, and the Elementary School Child." *The Computing Teacher* (February 1988): 40–43.

Bahr, Christine M., and others. "The Effects of Text-Based and Graphics-Based Software Tools on Planning and Organizing of Stories." *Journal of Learning Disabilities* 29, no. 4 (July 1996): 355–370.

Boone, R. *Teaching Process Writing with Computers.* Eugene, Ore.: ISTE, 1991.

Braun, Ellen. "Word Processing. Desktop Publishing Share Features." *The Office* 117, no. 5 (May 1, 1993): 9.

Cerrito, Patricia. "Writing Technology and Experimentation to Explore the Concepts of Elementary Statistics." *Mathematics and Computer Education* 28, no. 2 (Spring 1994): 141.

"Coats, Kaye et. al. "Ideas from Teachers!; Writing Notebook." *Creative Word Processing in the Classroom* 7, no. 4 (April-May, 1990): 40–41.

Cochran-Smith, Marilyn. "Writing Processing and Writing in Elementary Classrooms: A Critical Review of Related Literature." *Review of Educational Research* 61, no. 1 (Spring 1991): 107.

Daiute, C. *Writing and Computers.* Reading, Mass.: Addison-Wesley, 1985.

Greenleaf, Cynthia. "Technological Indeterminacy: The Role of Classroom Writing Practices and Pedagogy in Shaping Student Use of the Computer." *Written Communication* 11, no. 11 (January 1, 1994): 85.

Howell, R., and P. Scott. *Microcomputer Applications for Teachers.* Scottsdale, Ariz.: Gorsuch, 1985.

Howie, S.H. *Reading, Writing, and Computers: Planning for Integration.* Needham Heights, Mass.: Allyn & Bacon, Longwood Division, 1989.

Jarchow, E. "Computers and Computing: The Pros and Cons." *Electronic Education* (June 1984): 38.

Joslin, E. "Welcome to Word Processing." *The Computing Teacher* (March 1986): 16–19.

Laframboise, Kathryn L. "The Facilitative Effects of Word Processing on Sentence-Combining Tasks with At-Risk Fourth Graders." *Journal of Research and Development in Education* 24, no. 2 (Winter 1991): 1.

Land, Michael and Sandra Turner. *Tools for Schools,* 2nd ed. New York: Wadsworth Publishing Company, 1996.

Langone, John, and others. "The Differential Effects of a Typing Tutor and Microcomputer-Based Word Processing on the Writing Samples of Elementary Students with

Behavior Disorders." *Journal of Research on Computing in Education* 29, no. 2 (Winter 1996):141–158.

Levy, Michael C., and S. Ransdell. "Computer-Aided Protocol Analysis of Writing Processes." *Behavior Research Methods, Instruments, & Computing* 26, no. 2 (May 1, 1994): 219.

Marcus, Stephen. "Word Processing: Transforming Students' Potential to Write." *Media and Methods* 27, no. 5 (May 1, 1991): 8.

MacArthur, Charles A. "Using Technology to Enhance the Writing Processes of Students with Learning Disabilities." *Journal of Learning Disabilities* 29, no. 4 (July 1996): 334–354.

Microsoft Word Reference to Microsoft Word. Redmond, Wash.: Microsoft Corporation, 1992.

Milone, Michael N. *Every Teacher's Guide to Word Processing: 101 Classroom Computer.* Englewood Cliffs, N.J.: Prentice-Hall, 1985.

Montague, Marjorie and Fionelle Fonseca. "Using Computers to Improve Story Writing." *Teaching Exceptional Children* 25, no. 4 (Summer 1993): 46–49.

Morton, L.L. "Lab-Based Word Processing for the Learning-Disabled." *Computers in the Schools* 8, no. 1/3 (1991): 225.

Nichols, Lois Mayer. "Pencil and Paper Versus Word Processing: A Comparative Study of Creative Writing in the Elementary School." *Journal of Research on Computing in Education* 29, no. 2 (Winter 1996): 159–166.

Owen, Trevor. "Poems That Change the World: Canada's Wired Writers." *English Journal* 84, no. 6 (October 1995): 48–52.

Poulsen, Erik. "Writing Processes with Word Processing in Teaching English as a Foreign Language." *Computers & Education* 16, no. 1 (1991): 77.

Pfaffenberger, Bryan. *Que's Computer User's Dictionary,* 5th ed. Indianapolis, Indiana: Que Corporation, 1996, 531–532.

Robinette, Michelle. "Top 10 Uses for ClarisWorks in the One-Computer Classroom." *Learning and Leading with Technology* 24, no. 2 (October 1996): 37–40.

Roblyer, M.D. "The Effectiveness of Microcomputers in Education: A Review of the Research from 1980-1987." *T.H.E. Journal* (September 1988): 85–89.

Schramm, Robert M. "The Effects of Using Word Processing Equipment in Writing Instruction." *Business Education Forum* 45, no. 5 (February 1, 1991): 7.

Smith, Frank E. *Bank Street Writer Plus.* San Rafael, Calif.: Bank Street College of Education, International Education, Inc., Brøderbund Software, 1986.

Staten, James. "Word to Bulk Up in Version 6; New Tricks Weigh Down System." *Macweek* 8, no. 20 (June 1994): 1.

Varblow, Judy. "Reading, Writing, and Word Processing: An Interdisciplinary Approach." *The Balance Sheet* 72, no. 2 (Winter 1990): 22.

Watt, D. "Tools for Writing." *Popular Computing* (January 1984): 75–78.

Woodrow, Janice F.J. "Teachers' Perceptions of Computer Needs." *Journal of Research on Computing in Education* 23, no. 4 (Summer 1991): 475–93.

Zorko, Leslie J. "Creative Writing: A Comparison Using the Computer Vs. Handwriting." *National Association of Laboratory Schools Journal* 18, no. 2 (Winter 1993): 28.

Desktop Publishing

4

Objectives

Upon completing this chapter, you will be able to:

1. Explain what desktop publishing is;
2. Describe the features of desktop publishing;
3. Operate a desktop publishing program;
4. Evaluate different desktop publishing packages using standard criteria;
5. Create and apply a repertoire of desktop publishing activities for the classroom; and
6. Discuss three guidelines for desktop publishing.

Historical Background

In Europe, before the 1400s, information was transmitted orally by troubadours who traveled from place to place. They would sing ballads or recite poems concerning the news or gossip of the day. Few people could read or write, and books were scarce because they had to be hand-written. Reading was mainly for religious instruction or entertainment.

Then around 1450, Johann Gutenberg revolutionized communication with the invention of moveable type. Modifying a wine makers' press to hold type, he poured hot metal into molds from which he created letters, numbers, and symbols. He placed his type and engravings on the bed of the press, inked the surface, and covered it with a sheet of paper. When he cranked the handle of the press, the pressure of the plate created an image on the paper (Fig. 4.1).

Figure 4.1
Early printing press
Dubl-Click Software, Inc.
© Dubl-Click Software, Inc.

Gutenberg's printing innovation gave more people the opportunity to read by making books more available. Even though Gutenberg's methods were refined over time, his basic concept remained unchanged for 400 years.

In the late 1880s, Ottmar Mergenthaler invented Linotype, the first successful automated typecasting machine. This mechanical type-composing machine let the operator cast an entire line of type at once by using a keyboard. It was first used to typeset the *New York Tribune* in 1886. A year later, Tolbert Lanston invented the Monotype machine that produced three characters of set type a second and was widely used for books.

The Linotype and Monotype, along with hand-set type, dominated typesetting until Intertype introduced the first phototypesetting machine in 1950. Phototypesetting replaced cast type because of its low cost, faster speed, and flexibility. Phototypesetting used film to reproduce type and images on metal plates that could then be inked for reproduction on paper.

The search for higher typesetting speeds resulted in the development of a method that would dispense with phototypesetting altogether by storing characters in electronic digital format. However, it wasn't until the mid-1960s that digital typesetting came into existence. Today, it coexists with phototypesetting as the standards for setting type. Digital type uses computer typesetting equipment to describe letter forms as nearly invisible dots. This invention led the way for desktop publishing (DTP), a term coined by Paul Brainward of Aldus Software.

What Is Desktop Publishing?

Desktop publishing (DTP) is probably the second most popular use of computers in the school next to word processing (Kearsley, Hunter, Furlong, 1992). Desktop publishing uses the personal computer (in conjunction with specialized software) to combine text and graphics to produce high quality output on either a laser printer or a typesetting machine. This multistep process, which involves different types of software and equipment, is illustrated in Figure 4.2.

Your first step is to create and/or edit text using the word processor and to produce illustrations using a drawing, CAD, or painting program or to reproduce illustrations with a scanner. Desktop publishing programs are not generally used for original creation of a document. DTP's major purpose is to provide the ultimate in page-layout capabilities. For this reason, many programs lack a fully functioning word processor or graphics program. After text and art have been gathered, you turn to the DTP and

1. Input your material using the keyboard, a scanner, a floppy disk, or a video digitizer. Also input illustrations from clip art, from a drawing or painting program, or a program such as *Captivate* (Mainstay) that captures images on the computer screen.
2. Lay out the text and graphics on the screen, revising and refining the material using the DTP's capabilities.
3. At this point, you have two choices: printing the finished document on a laser printer or, for better quality, printing it on a typesetting machine.
4. After obtaining proofs, make further changes and corrections and ready the final copy for printing or instruct the typesetter to do so.

Desktop publishing has become an all-encompassing term: It can refer to fourteen Macintosh computers connected to a magazine's editorial and design departments; to an IBM user running Print Shop PressWriter (Brøderbund) to produce a newsletter on a ink-jet printer; or to an

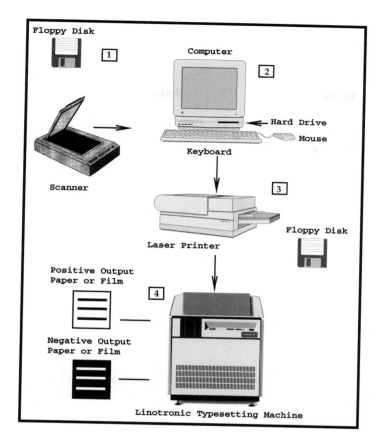

Figure 4.2
Desktop publishing
process
Modified from Desktop
Design by Laura Lamar,
Crisp Publications, 1990
ClickArt Images ©
T/Maker Company and
Que.

eight-year-old creating a sign to find a lost pet. DTP is no longer the exclusive property of the skilled technician or computer programmer. With a desktop publishing program, you can design a business newsletter, create a banner, or produce a school newspaper.

In the past each student working on the high school or college newspaper was assigned a different task. Typically, there was a designer, a writer, an illustrator, a typesetter, and a pasteup artist. Now DTP makes it possible for one person to perform all these functions. DTP permits the student to

1. create on-screen layouts,
2. use different typefaces or fonts,
3. right-justify text and lay out multiple columns,
4. insert and print art and text on the same page, and
5. print camera-ready copy.

The student can easily change the images, enlarge or shrink them, save them on a disk for later revision, and view the finished product early in the process.

There are many advantages to preparing student publications this way. DTP offers greater flexibility in designing graphics and headlines and gives more control over the final product than ever before. DTP is a more versatile, faster, and less expensive way to produce publications than the traditional methods because fewer people are involved and fewer revisions are necessary. It is a natural outgrowth of word processing programs such as *Bank Street Writer* (Scholastic) (Macintosh version), *The Student Writing Center* (The Learning Company) (Windows version), and *The Writing Center* (The Learning Company) (Macintosh version) that have limited desktop features.

As recently as 1985, there were few DTP programs, and the available ones were *PageMaker* (Adobe) and *Ready Set Go* (Manhattan Graphics),[1] programs designed only for the Macintosh computer. Today, there are many programs to choose from, and they exist for all computers. The software and hardware that the student needs for DTP range in price from inexpensive to very expensive. If you want to print an informal newsletter, you might use a program such as *The Student Writing Center* or *Print Shop PressWriter* (Brøderbund) and a simple color ink-jet printer. If you are responsible for a business presentation, you might use expensive scanning equipment, programs such as *PageMaker* or *QuarkXPress* (Quark) and a full-fledged word processor. Although the resolution from a laser printer would not be as high as that from professional typesetting equipment, the resulting copy would be quite exceptional.

Desktop programs differ in degree of complexity and features. Let's explore some of the basic characteristics of these programs.

The Basic Desktop Publishing Features

Some of the features included in desktop publishing programs are a spelling checker, a thesaurus, a fully integrated word processor, text rotation, and various graphics tools. Although the desktop programs differ in their sophistication, all of them offer (1) page layout, (2) word processing, (3) style sheets and templates, (4) graphics, and (5) page view.

Page Layout

Page layout is the process of arranging the various elements on the page. During the process, you set the page margins, the number and width of the columns for regular text, and the position of the graphics and text. The most powerful programs, such as *Adobe PageMaker* and *QuarkXPress*, allow greatest control in page design; however, these programs are sophisticated and demand a steep learning curve. There are less powerful programs such as *Print Shop PressWriter* and *Microsoft Publisher* (Windows version) that offer a wide variety of options but require less learning time. *Microsoft Publisher* (Windows version) offers the choices shown in Figure 4.3. You select a business card, a flyer, a newsletter, or some other publication format. Then you answer a series of questions; based on your answers, the program builds the publication. The program also lets you work from scratch. It is more complicated than *The Ultimate Writing and Creativity Center* or *Young Authors* (ESL). Nevertheless, it does not have all the features of *PageMaker* or *QuarkXPress*.

In addition to these programs, there are word processing programs such as *The Student Writing Center, Bilingual Writing Center* (Learning Company), *Bank Street Writer,* and *Print Shop Press-*

---

[1]This product is currently produced by Letraset USA.

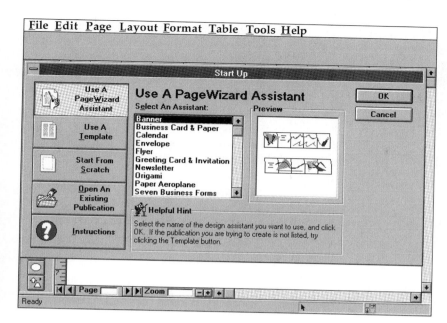

Figure 4.3
Microsoft Publisher
(Windows version)
Screen shot reprinted with
permission from Microsoft
Corporation.

Writer that have sufficient desktop capabilities to fulfill the desktop publishing needs of students from ages ten and up. Finally, there are for the young user programs such as *Young Authors* and *The Ultimate Writing and Creativity Center. Young Authors* produces twenty-four different books in English and Spanish and lets you create flyers, greeting cards, and banners. *The Ultimate Writing and Creativity Center,* for users ages six to ten, creates reports, signs, journals, storybooks, and newsletters. Reports are limited to one-column pages, and newsletters have two or three fixed columns of text and a heading region that extends across the full width of the page. This program has the ability to have documents read aloud and can add animation.

In *PageMaker,* you determine the page size, set the margins, and choose the number of columns and the width of each column. This program has master pages, or templates, that allow you to design a template for the document with measuring rulers and guides to help with the placement of graphics and text on the page. The majority of DTP programs show an overview of the page to help you decide if the final design meets your approval. Many present programs can resize, reshape, and reposition text or graphics, and they all have automatic page numbering.

Most page-layout programs are based on frames. If you want to put text into a document, you either place it on the base page, an immovable frame that covers the entire page, or draw a frame and enter or import text or graphics into it. With the help of a screen ruler, you define the shape of a text block or the size of a graphic by drawing a box or frame on the page. Once the frame is defined, you can import the text or graphic to fill the space. The user can stack frames or create captions that overlay illustrations. The desktop publishing program should let you create as many frames as you want and put them anywhere on the page, stacking them and adjusting them as necessary. Using this type of frame-based page, you are able to more easily design a page visually to achieve a desired effect.

PageMaker, the program that set the standard for desktop publishing, originally was a variation on this frame-based model. The latest version, now uses frames, similar to its rival *QuarkXPress.*

Word Processing

The power of the word processor varies with the desktop publishing program, but all DTPs can edit and format text to some degree.

Editing.   The majority of these packages allow you to enter text, edit it, and import documents from other programs. The typical word processing functions are delete, insert, and copy. The majority of DTP programs have spelling checkers and thesauruses. For the high school student, it is important that there are move, search, and replace functions.

Formatting Text.   The formatting features, such as type size, font, and typeface, determine how the page will look. The more control you have over the text, the more professional the document will appear. Many DTP programs let you center or align text, which makes uniform margins, and some programs let you define the space between letters, words, and lines, which improves the readability and appearance of the document.

Style Sheets and Templates

A style sheet is a format that you can repeat throughout the paper. For example, you might design a style sheet with page numbers in the right corner, two inches from the top of the page. Once you've created the style sheet, all pages in your document will automatically have page numbers in the right corner. On your style sheet, you can set the margins, type style, line spacing, headers, footers, and quotations for your entire document. Figure 4.4 shows the dialog box

Figure 4.4
PageMaker
Used with express permission. Adobe and Adobe Pagemaker and Adobe Illustrator are trademarks of Adobe Systems Incorporated or its subsidiaries and are registered in certain jurisdictions.

you would use to define a style. In this example, the style selected is *Body text,* and it is defined as Times at 12 points, with automatic leading, flush left justification, a 0.333 first indent, and automatic hyphenation. To apply this style you would select the text and click on *Body text* in the *Style* dialog box. The style sheet then automatically would be applied to the selected text. It would look like this:

> "The longest running-computer crime. Double-entry inventory control at Saxon Industries. A Fortune 500 company that reported profits of $7.1 million and $5.3 million in 1979 and 1980, respectively, it went bankrupt in 1982. A bogus inventory record was maintained by computer by Saxon's Business Products Division. It was used to inflate the company's annual revenues. The double books were kept for thirteen years, and the crime might never have been revealed if the company had been profitable. Saxon was $53 million in the hole when it went under" (Rochester and Gantz, 1983, p. 117).

Quite a few DTP programs contain their own style sheets and others let you import style sheets into their word processors. Many DTPs provide templates—guides already set up—and some companies let you create your own templates. The templates are time-savers because the user has a professionally designed document and does not have to worry about placement of text or pictures. The classroom template in Figure 4.5 is from *Print Shop PressWriter.* This program is packaged with a multitude of templates covering different subject areas.

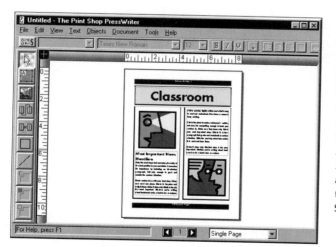

Figure 4.5
Print Shop
PressWriter
Screen shot courtesy of *The Print Shop® Press Writer* ™ © Broderbund Software, Inc. All rights reserved. Used by Permission. *The Print Shop, Press Writer and Broderbund* are trademarks and/or registered trademarks of Broderbund Software, Inc.

Graphics

Desktop publishing programs permit you to add different types of pictures or graphics to text either by drawing them or by importing them. Even though graphics can be created in the DTP program, these programs rarely have full-featured graphic capabilities. Typically the graphic is created in a draw or paint program and then imported into the publishing program. A desktop program usually has a variety of tools similar to *QuarkXPress,* Figure 4.6.

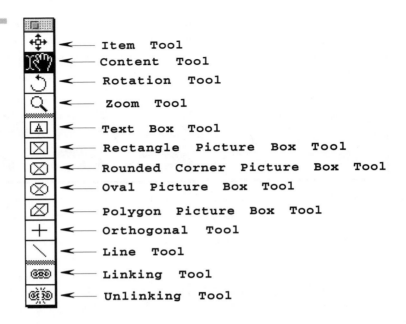

Figure 4.6
Tools from
QuarkXPress
© QuarkXPress™ is a
registered trademark of
Quark, Inc.

Each tool serves a different function. Let us look at these tools. The Item Tool ⊕ moves the boxes, items, or lines on the page, the Content Tool 🖑 manipulates the content within the box, the Rotation tool ↺ rotates the item, the Zoom Tool 🔍 lets you get a closer look at the item. The middle set of tools on the palette are called creation tools because they are used to create text boxes, picture boxes, and lines. The Text Box Tool 🅰 draws the text frames that are used to hold the text as illustrated by the following heading:

THE NEWS

The Rectangle Picture Box Tool ⊠ creates a rectangle box, whereas the Rounded Corner Picture Box Tool ⊠ creates a rounded corner picture box. The Oval Picture Box Tool ⊗ creates an oval box and the Polygon Picture Box Tool ⊠ creates a polygon box. The Orthogonal Tool ⊞ draws vertical as well as horizontal lines, while the Line Tool ⟍ draws lines at any angle. The two bottom tools are used for linking and unlinking text. The linking tool connects text boxes, permitting the flow of text from one box to another. The unlinking tool breaks the connection between these text boxes.

Generally, DTPs offer features that customize artwork; reduce, enlarge, rotate, or flip a drawing; zoom in for detail; and edit, pixel by pixel.[2] Some programs can trace edges and change per-

---

[2] A **pixel** is a small element that in combination with others creates an image on the screen. It is the smallest manipulatable element in an image.

spective, useful in producing halo effects around graphics, in outlining type, or even in converting silhouettes to simple outline form. With a DTP, you can crop or trim away part of an image and use it as a separate graphic. You can also repeat or duplicate an image. Figure 4.7 shows the

Figure 4.7
Dolphin border pattern
ClickArt images © T/Maker Company.

same dolphin image duplicated in a regular border pattern. A student who can't draw to his or her own satisfaction can import artwork from other places, creating in the process artistic layouts or designs. Make sure you have a text wrap feature to take care of any graphic overlay problems caused by importing.

Page View.   After the page layout is completed, you invariably want to see how it looks before printing out the document. *The Writing Center* (Macintosh) and *The Student Writing Center* (MS-DOS) show what the layout will actually look like on the page or at least in a reduced size. Programs like *QuarkXPress* and *Pagemaker* gives you a full range of page view magnifications.

Now that you have some idea of DTP features, let us look at some ways to select a good program that will meet your students' needs.

How to Choose a Good Desktop Publishing Program

Many desktop publishing packages are on the market today, and they come with every imaginable feature. Among these are DTP programs that lend themselves easily to classroom use, such as *Storybook Weaver Deluxe* (MECC) (Macintosh and IBM versions), (*Print Shop PressWriter,* (IBM and Macintosh versions, *Bank Street Writer* (Macintosh and IBM versions), *The Ultimate Writing and Creativity Center* (IBM, Macintosh version), *The Writing Center* (Macintosh version), *The Student Writing Center* (IBM version), *Microsoft Publisher* (Windows version), *Kid Works 2* (Davidson) (IBM and Macintosh), and *Young Authors* (Macintosh version).

To choose a DTP program for the classroom, (1) examine the hardware compatibility of the program; (2) look at the program's general features; (3) study the program's instructional design; (4) find out how easy it is to use the package; (5) check out the program's cost effectiveness; and (6) check out the program's technical support.

Hardware Compatibility

Find out what computers are available at your school: Window-based PCs, Macintoshes, or old Apple IIGS's? How much memory does each machine have: 64K, 8 MB, 64 MB, or more? How many disk drives are available for each machine and what kind? What is the size of these drives: 3-1/2-inch floppy, a 4 gigabyte hard drive, or a 100 kilobyte Zip drive? What other equipment is available: video digitizers, printers, multipage monitors, modems, or scanners?

General Features

How many columns can you create for a document? (*PageMaker* creates twenty columns, *The Writing Center* creates a maximum of nine columns, and *The Ultimate Writing and Creativity Center* creates only two or three fixed columns.) Is the program a What You See Is What You Get (WYSIWYG) program? Can you enlarge or shrink the graphics you import? If you make a mistake, can you easily change it? When you load a program into the computer, what is displayed on the screen? Is there an untitled document with tools or an endless series of screens? How difficult is it to change the fonts and italicize or boldface the text? How many fonts are included, and can you mix type and font styles and sizes anywhere on the page? How easy is it to insert art in the document? What graphic formats does the program handle? What graphics tools are supplied to change the artwork that was imported or created? How extensive are the word processing features? Does the program have a find and replace feature; the ability to copy, cut, and paste text; and a spelling checker and thesaurus?

There are a myriad of features to consider, but the most important question to ask is, "Which features are necessary?" For the elementary school child, the major concern should be a product that produces pleasant results. The high school student or novice should have a program that has more features and, thus, more versatility.

Instructional Design

A desktop publishing program design should be straightforward. Programs with a menu bar displayed at the top of the screen are ideal for beginners who do not then have to memorize the different functions. *The Ultimate Writing and Creativity Center* (Fig. 4.8) has such a menu bar. It clearly displays the choices that are available in this program.

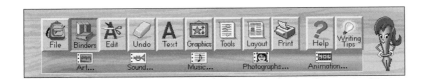

Figure 4.8
The Ultimate Writing and Creativity Center™ menu bar
© The Learning Company. All rights reserved.

Any novice can change the font, add a picture, or use the printer by selecting the proper icon in the menu bar. The keys to programs such as *Print Shop PressWriter* and *Microsoft Publisher* are the flexibility of their design and the many options available for the user. *Print Shop PressWriter* has an excellent manual and is easy to learn. *Microsoft Publisher* has a great on-screen tutorial that guides users step by step.

In looking at instructional design, you should ask the following questions: Is it a simple matter to make changes? Can you easily delete, add, or insert text? How fast is the general performance? (A program that is very slow can waste time if you are in a hurry to complete a job. For example, *Newsroom,* one of the first DTP programs for the elementary school, was a slow and cumbersome program.) How quickly can you change fonts, font style, character, line spacing, and paragraph justification? What flexibility does the program have in printing the newspaper? How easy is it to access the program functions? (Some programs, such as *Microsoft Publisher,* have keyboard shortcuts for many of their functions, so it is not necessary to use their pull-down menus.)

Ease of Use

The program must be easy to learn and must use simple English commands. Ask the following questions: Can a student in approximately sixty minutes learn to use this program? Are there help screens that inform users what to do each step of the way, and are they easily accessible? Is there a menu bar across the screen so users do not have to memorize the different functions? Is there a tutorial disk or manual that takes students through the program? How difficult is it to figure out how to print a document? Can the printer be set up quickly? Is the program tedious to use because of too many help prompts and safety questions? Is there an automatic save feature?

Consumer Value

Cost has to be a major consideration in choosing a program for the classroom. *The Ultimate Writing and Creativity Center* can be purchased for under $50 (consumer edition), whereas programs such as *PageMaker* and *QuarkXPress* cost hundreds of dollars. Ask the following questions: If the software is protected, does the software company provide a free backup copy? Does the program include templates and graphic art? (*The Writing Center, Print Shop PressWriter, Young Authors,* and *Microsoft Publisher* have templates and art included, which makes these programs better value for the money.) Are there on-site licenses, lab packs, or networked versions available? (Software companies, at a special price, offer on-site licenses so that you can freely copy the software for in-house use. Other manufacturers distribute lab packs that let you purchase software at a reduced price. Finally, many manufacturers offer networked versions of the software so that a set of software can be shared among many computers.)

Support

Is the documentation sent with the program helpful or bulky and unreadable? Can you call someone immediately to get help on the telephone, or must you wade through a series of messages and wait an unbearable amount of time? (Many software companies now tell you how many customers are in "line" before you and how long the wait is. When the wait is too long, some manufacturers have you leave your number and they call you back.) Do you have to pay a yearly fee or a fee per incident to get technical support? Is customer support available toll free or through a pay call? Is there a tutorial with the software package? Is the tutorial in the form of a manual, disk, or both? (Many manufacturers provide both to simplify learning of their programs.) Is the manual readable, with activities, lesson plans, and an index? How easy is it to get a refund if the disk is defective?

Before selecting a desktop publishing program, look at the pupils' needs in the classroom. Determine what features meet these needs.

Refer now to Appendix A for an annotated bibliography of highly rated DTP programs for the classroom. Next, examine one of these programs using the sample checklist and evaluation rating instrument on page 83.

After using this checklist a couple of times, you should be able to make a more informed decision on how to select software. Now let us explore how to use a desktop publishing program.

Learning to Use a Desktop Publishing Program

This section gives an overview of how a desktop program operates. It should not serve as a substitute for the program's operational manual. For illustrative purposes, let's use *The Writing Center,* a word processing program with some desktop capabilities. This program has many more advanced features than *The Children's Writing and Creativity Center,* The Learning Company's first DTP for the schools. We'll consider how *The Writing Center* creates a layout, adds text and graphics, and refines the product to produce a printout.

When you open *The Writing Center,* you see the screen in Figure 4.9, which offers three page layout options. You have the option of creating a report or letter, a newsletter, or a custom document.

Figure 4.9
The Writing Center
opening screen
"The Writing Company™"
© 1991–The Learning
Company. Permission to
use granted by The
Learning Company. The
Writing Center is a
trademark of The Learning
Company. All rights
reserved.

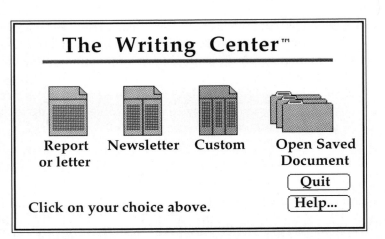

DESKTOP PUBLISHING CHECKLIST

Directions: Examine the following items and determine which ones you feel are important for your class situation. Evaluate your desktop publishing program and place an X on each line where the software meets your needs.

Product Name_____ Manufacturer_____ Grade Level_____

A. Hardware
__ 1. Memory needed
__ 2. Computer compatibility
__ 3. Printer compatibility
__ 4. disk drive type

B. Features
__ 1. Comprehensive undo
__ 2. Page size selection
__ 3. Adjustable column size
__ 4. Page preview
__ 5. Graphics
__   a. Ruler guides
__   b. Resize, position, crop
__   c. Flip, slip, invert
__   d. Graphic importing
__   e. File formats, EPS, Pict, GIF, JPEG, etc.
__ 6. Wraparound graphics
__ 7. Word processing
__   a. Insert/delete
__   b. Search/replace
__   c. Copy/paste
__   d. Spelling checker
__   e. Thesaurus
__   f. Tabs
__   g. Automatic pagination
__   h. Hyphenation
__ 8. Typesetting
__   a. Variety of type sizes
__   b. Different type styles
__   c. Variety of fonts
__   d. Kerning
__   e. Margin setting
__ 9. Drawing/painting tools

C. Design
__ 1. Speed of execution
__ 2. Ease of graphics insertion
__ 3. Simple saving function
__ 4. Easy printing procedure
__ 5. Number of columns possible
__ 6. Type of page layout
__ 7. Method of graphic importing
__ 8. Formatting within program

D. Ease of Use
__ 1. On-screen help
__ 2. Tutorial disk
__ 3. Easy printer setup
__ 4. Minimal learning time
__ 5. Automatic save

E. Consumer Value
__ 1. Cost
__ 2. Unprotected software
__ 3. Backup
__ 4. Templates
__ 5. Clip art included
__ 6. Lab packs
__ 7. Networked version
__ 8. On-site license

F. Support Features
__ 1. Technical
__ 2. Tutorial material
__ 3. Readable manual
__   a. Activities
__   b. Lesson plans
__   c. Index
__ 4. Money back guarantee

Rating Scale
Rate the Desktop Publishing Program by placing a check on the appropriate line.
Excellent ___ Very Good ___ Good ___ Fair ___ Poor ___

Comments

Choose the *Custom* option when you want a different column size or formatting. Next, you'll be asked to make a series of decisions about the page layout. Let's assume you selected *Newsletter.* Figure 4.10 shows the screen that would next appear.

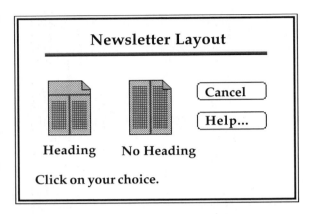

Figure 4.10
The Writing Center
newsletter screen
"The Writing Center™"
© 1991–The Learning
Company. Permission to
use granted by The
Learning Company. The
Writing Center is a
trademark of The Learning
Company. All rights
reserved.

If you choose *Heading,* a screen displays a heading and body. During the process, you can change the margins, column size, page numbers, and border lines. After determining these layout issues, you're ready to write or import text and pictures into the document. In many DTP programs, it is easier to edit text and graphics in your word processing program and import them into the DTP program only when they're close to finished. *The Writing Center* and *The Student Writing Center* import text from word processing documents in a text only format, which means the imported text loses its formatting. In many DTP programs, such as *Microsoft Publisher,* the text is imported in the form of text frames that can be moved as a complete unit. *The Writing Center* lets you add text by simply positioning the insertion point. You can then make any adjustments, such as justification, spacing, bordering, or font changes. You can spell check the document and use the thesaurus to find alternate words.

Occasionally, you'll want to import graphics to illustrate a story; this usually means defining spaces or frames in which the graphics will fit. In *The Writing Center,* you choose the picture you want by selecting it and then placing it in the document. The picture then will appear in a frame with eight "edit handles" around it. After the picture is placed, you can resize it, move it, rotate it, or turn it sideways by using the edit handles. *The Writing Center* has 200 importable pictures that cover a range of subjects; you can also import pictures from clip art collections and pictures that you created with paint programs (unlike *PageMaker* or *Microsoft Publisher,* this particular program has no painting or graphics tools of its own).

As you experiment with layout and importing of art, you frequently need to view the entire page. Activate the page preview function to display the document in a reduced size that fits on-screen, as shown in Figure 4.11. Many DTP programs have a zoom feature that lets you see a close-up of small sections of the document.

The last step is printing the document either on a dot matrix, ink-jet, or laser printer. The laser printer produces a very professional quality copy; Figure 4.12 shows a sample newsletter

Preview of "Le Tigre NEwsletter"- Page 1

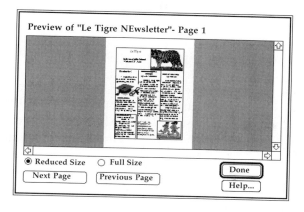

○ Reduced Size   ○ Full Size

Next Page   Previous Page

Done

Help...

Figure 4.11
The Writing Center
page preview function
"The Writing Center™"
© 1991–The Learning
Company. Permission to use
granted by The Learning
Company. The Writing
Center is a trademark of The
Learning Company. All
rights reserved.

Le Tigre

Sullivan Middle School
Volume IX - June

Graduation !

Congratulations to all those in our newest

graduating class. Our commencement exercises will begin on Sunday, June 23rd at 2 p.m. in Eisenhower Auditorium. See Mrs. Sanchez in Room 110 for your cap and gown!

Mr. Rizzo Retiring!
Please join us in the cafeteria on Friday, June 14th to say good-bye to Mr. Thomas Rizzo who has taught Science at Sullivan M.S. since 1973. He will be sadly missed by all of us and

we wish him well.

Summer Support Groups:
by Mrs. Weisenfeld

In support groups, kids can discuss their problems or they can pass and just listen to the other kids and what they have to say. Sometimes, it is a great way to solve your problems. On CNN Newsroom, we saw how kids have learned to settle their own battles. They had a "Conflict Manager" who acted as a mediator to help solve the problems. It's a cool thing to try at home or at school.

The "Kids with Single Parents" Group meets the second and fourth Wednesday of every

month in the library at 3:15 p.m.

Sullivan Field Day!
by Kim Lee

Our annual event offered stiff competition in both the girls and boys track events. Sally Mueller, an 8th grader, broke the school record of 1:33 in the 300-meter fun run. "I really wanted to win this event. It is good practice for me," said Sally. "I hope to make to make the track team next year."
Billy Fitts led the medley relay team to a big win. Once Billy got

Figure 4.12
The Writing Center
sample newsletter
"The Wrinting Center™"
© 1991–The Learning
Company. Permission to
use granted by The
Learning Company. The
Writing Company is a
trademark of The Learning
Company. All rights
reserved.

from *The Writing Center.* However, this output does not approach the resolution of a professional typesetting machine.

As you can see, using a program like *The Writing Center* takes you through step by step. There are limited choices, but this program is more appropriate for elementary school and junior high school students. A program like *QuarkXPress* is more suitable for high school and college students. *QuarkXPress's* introductory screen is simply a tool palette (Figure 4.13). When

Figure 4.13
QuarkXPress Tool
Palette
QuarkXPress™ is a
registered trademark of
Quark, Inc.

you choose to create a new document, the following dialog box (Figure 4.14) appears.

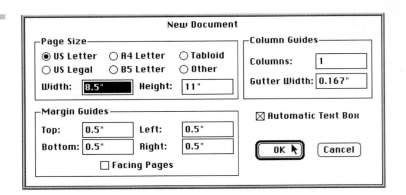

Figure 4.14
QuarkXPress Dialog
Box
QuarkXPress™ is a
registered trademark of
Quark, Inc.

At this point, you have to be knowledgeable enough to make choices about such items as number of columns, gutter width, and page size. Working on a blank document, you then bring in text and graphics. After you are finished creating your document, you can view it in different ways such as a thumbnail sketch, 50%, or 200% or in a prearranged window (Figure 4.15).

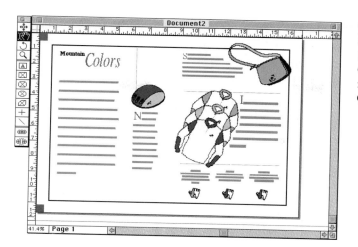

Figure 4.15
QuarkXPress Preview
QuarkXPress™ is a
registered trademark of
Quark, Inc.

Although using a DTP seems like a straightforward process, there always are compatibility problems between programs since different programs have different features and capabilities. Some are much easier to use and import graphics easily, while others offer more flexibility, include painting and drawing tools, but are more difficult to use.

Desktop Publishing Programs for the Classroom

Appendix A features an annotated listing of highly rated desktop publishing programs. Let us quickly review a few of these programs in terms of age-level suitability. *Storybook Weaver Deluxe,The Ultimate Writing and Creativity Center* (Learning Company), and *Kid Works 2* are early-grade programs with desktop publishing features. *Storybook Weaver Deluxe* lets children design and publish their own illustrated books. The children can choose from hundreds of graphics to illustrate their books. *The Ultimate Writing and Creativity Center* lets children produce reports, newsletter, storybooks, and signs. The children can add animations to their stories and the program has the ability to have documents read aloud. With *Kid Works 2,* the child creates stories combining text with graphics. These programs have very limited word processing and picture handling features, but they are superior programs for the primary grades because of their low learning curve.

Imagination Express Series (Edmark) and *Young Authors* are more advanced and suitable for the middle grades because of their better picture handling and increased word processing capabilities. Although these programs offer improved features, they are by no means fully functioning desktop publishing programs. *Young Authors* has basic word processing features with a spelling checker. It lets students combine graphics and text to produce twenty-four different sizes of books in Spanish and English. The *Imagination! Express Series* has rudimentary word processing features, bare-bones page-layout capabilities. Nevertheless, it lets the children create interactive stories by selecting background, scenery, and characters, by recording dialogue, and by adding text and sound effects. When students graduate from this type of program, they might try *Bank Street Writer* or *The Writing Center* or *The Student Writing Center*. These programs have better word processing features and more desktop publishing capabilities, but they lack graphics tools. Programs such as *Print Shop PressWriter* and *Microsoft Publisher* fill this void by providing drawing tools and additional word processing and page-layout features that are useful for the junior high school student.

Finally, at the high school level, advanced professional programs such as *PageMaker*, or *QuarkXPress* are suitable because they possess a multitude of features, file handling capabilities, and flexibility.

Guidelines for Desktop Publishing

1. Spend time planning ahead and collect the items that will be included in the proposed paper or newsletter. Make a sketch or a rough layout. Review what will be communicated. Who is the audience? What approach will be best for communicating the message? Be flexible and willing to experiment. Look for consistency on each page of the document and check for balance of design. Add interest when it is needed. Organize a page around a dominant visual.
2. Determine the format of the publication. Pay close attention to borders and margins. Provide a dramatic graphic for the front page. Make headlines forceful to organize the writing.
3. Add emphasis to the work. For example, use a large type size to emphasize important ideas when needed. When necessary, vary the type style by using boldface or italics. Use blank spaces to make the designs stand out. Highlight the ideas with artwork, but do not overdo it. Let the reader's eyes focus on a particular part of the page.
4. Be careful not to clutter the page with too many elements. At the same time, use a variety of items so as not to bore the audience.
5. Do not use too many typefaces because it detracts from the general feeling of the writing.
6. Select typefaces that are easy to read, like COURIER; avoid typefaces like *KOPPEL*.
7. Try to avoid white space, the part of the page where nothing appears. If blank space is unavoidable, make it gray or black.
8. Make the design fit the content of the document.
9. Make sure the information is easy to find and not buried. Have it flow from the upper left corner to the right following a logical sequence.
10. Use page and column balance. Make sure that the facing pages and columns are aligned within approximately one or two lines of each other.
11. Make the size of the components on the page consistent with the surrounding components.
12. Have the artwork face into the text.
13. Check the work thoroughly before printing out copies, and look at the printout again to apply finishing touches.
14. When possible, place titles below your illustrations and guide the reader with your headings.

There are many activities a teacher can use to motivate students to write with a DTP program. What follows are five such activities.

Classroom Applications

▼   I. Preliminary Language Arts Skills   ▼

Objectives

Students will learn some preliminary organizational skills and produce a simple picture with a few lines of text.

Procedure

1. Have the students bring in newsletters, newspapers, and magazines. Distribute these items around the class.
2. Divide the class into groups of five and have each group clip out text and pictures from the newspapers and magazines.
3. Next, instruct each group to choose a picture and a line or two of text and put them together to communicate a message. Students might choose a headline from an article, a graphic from an advertisement, and a line of text from the front page, for example.
4. Now have each group use the desktop publishing program to translate its pasteup representation into print. Students will have to make some substitutions depending on the graphics available from their desktop publishing program.
5. End the process by having each group display its final design and discuss it with the entire class.

▼   II. Language Arts   ▼

Objective

Students will learn some preliminary DTP skills.

Procedure

1. Have each student in the class write a story.
2. Discuss each story with the student and as a class and make recommendations on how to improve it.
3. Have the students use their scissors to revise their stories.
4. Next, instruct each student to use the DTP program to enter his or her story.
5. Print out copies of each child's story for the entire class.
6. Divide the class in groups and have them read and discuss the stories.

▼   III. Math Stories   ▼

Objective
Students will learn how to write math word problems using their DTP program.

Procedure
1. Distribute a math story similar to the one shown in Figure 4.16.

Figure 4.16
Math story
© Dubl-Click Software Inc.

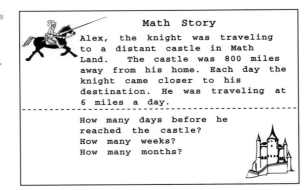

```
              Math Story
Alex,  the  knight  was  traveling
to  a  distant  castle  in  Math
Land.    The  castle  was  800  miles
away  from  his  home.  Each  day  the
knight  came  closer  to  his
destination.  He  was  traveling  at
6  miles  a  day.
- - - - - - - - - - - - - - - - - - - - - - - -
How  many  days  before  he
reached  the  castle?
How  many  weeks?
How  many  months?
```

2. Ask the students to read and solve the word problems found on this sheet.
3. Next, have the students write their own stories and related word problems.
4. After the students have finished writing their story problems, they should take turns entering these stories into the computer.
5. Have the students lay out and illustrate their stories with clip art, scanned images, or their own art created in a drawing program.
6. Use the printed stories as a math test for class.

IV. Science Activity

Objective
Students will design their own science lab sheet and experiment.

Procedure
1. Help the students design individual experiments related to an overall classroom science topic.
2. Show students some sample lab sheets similar to the one in Figure 4.17.
3. Ask students to design with the DTP lab report forms for their experiments.
4. Have students conduct their experiments using their own lab reports. After the experiments, discuss how the students would modify their reports for the next experiment.

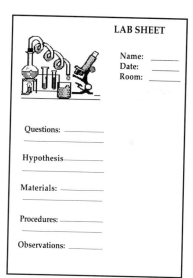

LAB SHEET

Name: _____
Date: _____
Room: _____

Questions: _____

Hypothesis _____

Materials: _____

Procedures: _____

Observations: _____

Figure 4.17
The Student Writing Center
"Student Writing Center™" © 1993, 1995–The Learning Company. Permission to use granted by The Learning Company. The Student Writing Center is a trademark of The Learning Company. All rights reserved.

▼   **V. Newsletter Production**   ▼

Objective

Students will be able to produce a newsletter for the class using word processing, page-layout, and graphics programs.

Procedure

1. Bring in sample newspapers and newsletters and distribute them to everyone.
2. Divide the students into work groups and assign each group a different writing task. For example, one group might write a news article on dolphins while another group might write an editorial on a controversial issue and third group might be responsible for a gossip column or movie reviews. Discuss with the students the process followed by journalists. Instruct them to determine who, what, why, where, and when in their reporting.
3. Have each work group write and revise its story.
4. Next, have the students write headlines and choose the pictures they want to use. Talk about the importance of visual appeal. Discuss how to be bold with headlines and how to place pictures effectively. The students should plan their placement of articles early in the process. Check their work for grammar and spelling errors. Use the sample from *PageMaker* in Figure 4.18 as a model.
5. Ask students to use the DTP program to enter their articles for the paper. Make sure students view the entire document repeatedly to check its visual appeal.
6. After everyone is satisfied with the product, print out a copy. For later editions of the paper, rotate the tasks of the different groups in the class.

Figure 4.18
Sample from
PageMaker
Used with express
permission. Adobe and
AdobePagemaker and
Adobe Illustrator are
trademarks of Adobe
Systems Incorporated or
its subsidiaries and are
registered in certain
jurisdictions.

WEEKENDER

Volume 2 Number 15 • April 25, 1992

Hill Resort to Open in Early May

Smooth Hill Resort, Hilson Properties' latest in a collection of comfortable family vacation spots, will open its doors in May of this year. Located in the Mustang River Valley, the resort is surrounded by the Hoosik Hills, which offer a variety of vacation activities year-round.

Smooth Hill Resort is reminiscent of a southern mansion, with tall white columns and gingerbread eaves, surrounded by manicured lawns and graceful willows. The resort features 180 spacious one- and two-bedroom units. Each unit sports 1-1/2 baths, 2 closets, cable TV, and a fully-equipped kitchen with dishwasher and full-sized refrigerator. Extra beds are available. Four restaurants offer variety: The Hilltop, for gourmet dining, The Captain's Table for family dining, and two snack bars, one at poolside. The resort offers child care references all year round. A small shopping arcade will meet the needs of most vacationers, including a drug store, clothing stores, and gift shop.

In the summer, vacationers can walk along 8 miles of marked nature trails that offer valley views. Nearby streams offer trout fishing with equipment rental available at the main lodge. Swimmers will find Smooth Hill's 2 swimming pools suitable for all family members, the olympic-sized pool for adults, and a smaller pool for children.

In the winter, the hiking trails become cross-country

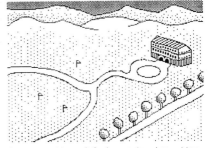

An entrance reminiscent of a Southern mansion welcomes visitors to Smooth Hill.

skiing routes with three levels of difficulty clearly marked. Activities for children include cross-country ski lessons, and the annual Snow Castle Contest. Smooth Hill is located within an hour's drive a 2 major downhill ski areas.

For reservations at Smooth Hill, call Getaway at (555) 555-5555. Special introductory vacation packages available.

Weekend Scuba Diving in Niagara Falls

Fred and Harriet Brown were a just another professional couple until a recent vacation experience transformed their lives. "We had fallen into the patterns of suburban life—the same schedule, day in and day out; housework on the weekends. . .we never envisioned the impact this experience would have upon our lives," they told us excitedly.

Waterfall Scuba Diving is not new to the sporting world, although recent technological breakthroughs, such as oxygen tanks and diving helmets, have propelled the sport into an entirely new dimension. Early, more primitive,

forms involved holding one's breath while plunging over the falls in a wooden barrel reinforced with steel rings. Although a favorite activity among thrillseekers, this version of the sport soon lost popularity, probably due to a steady decrease in the number of available participants.

The recent fitness craze has transformed the tourist of the past, who was satisfied at merely gazing at the falls from a safe distance or remaining sedentary on a tour boat, into an active participant. Fred and Harriet now claim, "You haven't seen the falls until you've seen them from inside."

Weekend packages are available through the Great Adventure Travel Agency, including weekend accommodations for two, a hearty meal plan, scuba gear rental, and a hospitalization plan. For more information on this new sport, please contact Getaway at (555) 555-5555.

Students can write historical, autobiographical, art, sports, or science newsletters. Find out where your students' interest is and capitalize on that interest.

Additional Activities

The list of DTP activities is almost endless. Students can design awards, flyers, progress reports, questionnaires, and outlines for book reports. A sample award sheet created with *Print Artist* (Sierra) is shown in Figure 4.19.

Figure 4.19
Sample from *Print ©
Artist* (Sierra Home)
© Sierra On-Line, Inc.

Summary

The computer has changed the steps involved in publishing a newsletter, magazine, or book. What was done mechanically is now handled electronically. Desktop publishing has altered the way school newspapers, business newsletters, and advertisements are produced.

This chapter traced the historical beginnings of desktop publishing. In the process, we considered the merits of desktop publishing. We discovered how easy it is for a user to produce a newsletter or lab report with one of these programs. We became familiar with the basic features of desktop publishing and gained insight into what features to consider when selecting a program. A checklist and evaluation scale presented in this chapter facilitates this decision-making process. The chapter also offered specific ideas on how to incorporate DTPs into the classroom. Five DTP activities that cover a range of curriculum areas were outlined.

Let's continue with the mastery test, some classroom projects, and suggested readings and references.

Be sure to review the annotated list of award-winning desktop publishing programs listed in Appendix A.

Chapter Mastery Test

1. Explain the difference between a word processor and a desktop publishing program.
2. What is desktop publishing? Explain its importance in education.
3. Name and describe three features of a desktop publishing program.
4. Discuss a few general rules to follow when creating a newsletter or advertisement using desktop publishing software.
5. Which five DTP features are critical in producing a school publication? Explain your reasons.
6. Discuss three uses of DTP programs in the classroom.
7. Does DTP software make the traditional methods of producing newsletter and books obsolete? Justify your answer.
8. What is a layout? Briefly discuss why it is important to take considerable time when creating a layout.
9. Explain in general terms the way a newsletter might be produced with a DTP program.
10. Briefly trace the history of DTP from inception to the present.
11. What are some of the software, hardware, and design requirements of a typical DTP program?
12. Develop a lesson plan using a DTP program.

Classroom Projects

1. Design the following with a DTP program:
   a. a two-page newsletter
   b. an advertisement for a product
   c. an award
   d. a science experiment sheet
2. Describe one DTP activity and show how a teacher can use it in a classroom situation.
3. Examine two DTP programs and compare their strengths and weaknesses.

4. Learn more about DTP by interviewing someone who uses a program. Have the individual demonstrate three or four features of the program. Identify any feature that is too complicated and then discuss some way of reducing the difficulty.
5. Read two articles about a DTP program and then use it. Next, prepare a report that might persuade a school district to buy this program. In the presentation, discuss the benefits of using a DTP program.

Suggested Readings and References

Beasley, Augie E. "Spreading the News with Desktop Publishing." *Media and Methods* 27, no. 4 (March 1, 1991): 15.

Braun, Ellen. "Word Processing, Desktop, Publishing Share Features." *The Office* 117, no. 5 (May 1, 1993).

"Buyer's Guide: Desktop Publishing Software." *Home Office Computing* 15, no. 4 (April 1, 1997): 77.

Clark, Sandra. "Desktop Publishing: Alive, Well & Growing." *Media and Methods* 27, no. 3 (January 1, 1991): 42.

Crawford, Walt. "Pages from the Desktop: Desktop Publishing Today." *Library Hi Tech* 12, no. 3 (1994): 101–19.

Dennis, Anita. "Seven Ways to Build a Page." *Publish!* 10, no. 10 (fall 1995): 43.

Desktop Art for the Macintosh. Peoria, Ill.: Dynamic Graphics, 1986.

"Desktop Publishing/Graphics—Corel DRAW 6.0, Fractal Painter, 4.0, FreeHand 5.5, Micrografx Designer 4.1, Microsoft Publisher 95, PageMaker 6.0, PhotoShop 3.0, QuarkXPress 3.22." *Windows Magazine* (special edition 1997): 116.

Ekhaml, Leticia. "Creating Better Newsletters." *School Library Media Activities Monthly* 12, no. 9 (May 1996): 36–38.

Ellis, Robert. "Creating a Studio Newsletter." *Clavier* 35, no. 3 (March 1, 1996): 27.

Freedman, Alan. *The Computer Desktop Encyclopedia.* New York: Amacom, 1996.

Guthrie, Jim. "Designing Design into an Advanced Desktop Publishing Course (A Teaching Tip)." *Technical Communication: Journal of the Society for Technical Communication* 42, no. 2 (May 1995): 319–21.

Hartley, James. "Thomas Jefferson, Page Design, and Desktop Publishing." *Educational Technology* 31, no. 1 (January 1, 1991): 54.

Hedley, Carolyn N., and Nancy J. Ellsworth. "What's New in Software? Mastery of the Computer through Desktop Publishing." *Reading and Writing Quarterly: Overcoming Learning Difficulties* 9, no. 3 (July–September 1993)" 279–82.

Kearsley, G., B. Hunter, and M. Furlong. *We teach with Technology.* Wilsonville, Oreg.: Franklin, Beedle, and Associates, 1992.

Kramer, Robert, and Stephen A. Bernhardt. "Teaching Text Design." *Technical Communication Quarterly* 5, no. 1 (winter 1996): 35–60.

Lamar, Laura. *Desktop Design.* Los Altos, Calif.: Crisp Publications, 1990.

Maxymuk, John. "Using Desktop Publishing to Create Newsletters, Handouts, and Web Pages: A How-To-Do-It Manual." *How-To-Do-It Manuals for Librarians* 74 (1997).

Min, Zheng, and Roy Rada. "MUCH Electronic Publishing Environment: Principles and Practices." *Journal of the American Society for Information Science* 45, no. 5 (June 1994): 300–309.

Parker, R. *Aldus Guide to Basic Design.* Seattle, Wash.: Aldus Corporation, 1987.

Perreault, Heidi, and Lun Wasson. "Desktop Publishing: Considerations for Curriculum Design." *Business Education Forum* 45, no. 4 (January 1, 1991): 23.

Popyk, Marilyn K. "If Gutenberg Could See Us Now: Teaching Desktop Publishing." *The Balance Sheet* 71, no. 3 (spring 1990): 5.

Reganick, Karol A. "Using Computers to Initiate Active Learning for Students with Severe Behavior Problems." *T.H.E. Journal* 21, no. 11 (June 1994): 72–74.

Roth, Evan. "Designs on Desktop." *Museum News* 70, no. 4 (July 1991): 59.

Sutton, Jayne O. "Stepping Up to Desktop Publishing." *The Secretary* 57, no. 3 (March 1, 1997): 14.

Thompson, James A. "Producing an Institutional Fact Book: Layout and Design for a User-Friendly Product." *New Directions for Institutional Research* 91 (fall 1996): 49–62.

Thompson, Patricia A. "Promises and Realities of Desktop Publishing." *The Journalism Educator* 46, no. 1 (spring 1991): 22.

Wasson, Gregory. "Layout for Less." *MacUser* 7, no. 7 (July 1, 1991): 110–21.

Databases

5

Objectives

Upon completing this chapter, you will be able to:

1. Explain what a database is and name its basic components;
2. Describe the basic features of a database;
3. Evaluate database software based on standard criteria;
4. Create and utilize a repertoire of database activities for the classroom;
5. Explain three methods of organizing data within a database; and
6. Describe three different types of databases.

What Is a Database?

We are constantly bombarded by information in the workplace, at home, or at school. John Naisbitt, in his book *Megatrends,* writes, "We are drowning in information but starved for knowledge" (1982, p. 24). Since teachers cannot possibly retain all this data in memory, it is imperative that they develop skills in finding and interpreting the required information. Students also must master skills of organizing, retrieving, manipulating, and evaluating the information available.

Whenever there is a large amount of information to be managed, there is a need for **database management system** software that controls the storage and organization of data in a database. A **database** is a collection of information organized according to some structure or purpose. An all-encompassing term, database describes anything from an address book, recipe box, dictionary, or file cabinet to a set of computerized data files with sophisticated data relationships. In order to understand what a database is, you must be familiar with three terms: **file, record,** and **field.**

File

A file is a collection of information on some subject. For example, a class studying birds may place all its information on this topic in a folder labeled *birds.*

Record

A record contains the information about one entry in the file. In our example on birds, a record would be information about a particular bird, say the *hummingbird.*

Field

Within a record there exist fields or spaces for specific information. The fields set aside for the hummingbird might include *beak type, scientific name, habitat,* and *migration patterns.*

The file cabinet, or database, in Figure 5.1 contains related files that store information in a

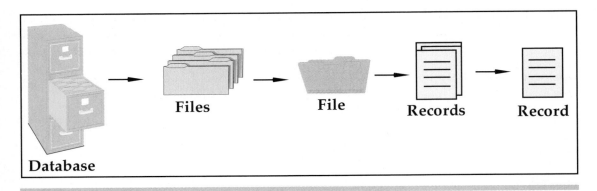

Files   **File**   **Records**   **Record**

Database

Figure 5.1
How a database works
ClickArt images © T/Maker Company.

systematic way. A principal using this file cabinet at Clayton High School might take a stack of folders out of the personal information drawer. She searches through the files for John Doe's file. This file contains a number of records, including a personal information record. She scans the information record for John Doe's address. The record is organized into five fields, or categories of information (Fig. 5.2): name, address, telephone number, birthdate, and social security number.

Figure 5.2
Fields

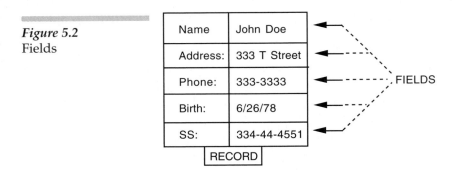

Name	John Doe
Address:	333 T Street
Phone:	333-3333
Birth:	6/26/78
SS:	334-44-4551

FIELDS

RECORD

When the principal wants John Doe's phone number, she gets it from the telephone field. In an electronic database, the information is stored on a disk. Figure 5.3 shows six individual student records in *Microsoft Works* (Macintosh version).

Name	Address	Phone	Birth	SS
Adams, James	628 Elm Street	555-4807	6/10/63	485-66-5643
Barris, Bill	456 St. Dennis	213-1261	5/17/25	187-94-1776
Clinton, George	369 Dayton	222-2222	12/14/71	805-69-1555
Devlin, Michael	260 Laguna	708-4952	5/11/77	415-82-1661
Doe, John	333 T Street	333-3333	6/26/70	334-33-4551
Elliot, Vicki	888 Valencia	243-2020	1/8/52	660-16-1492

AddressFile (DB)

Figure 5.3
Sample database
Screen shot from Microsoft® Works © 1986–1990 Microsoft Corporation. Reprinted with permission from Microsoft Corporation.

Advantages of an Electronic Database

The computerized database has many advantages over the file cabinet. Every database has a method of organization that lets a person retrieve information using some key word. For example, Figure 5.3 has the address file arranged alphabetically. The problem with the nonelectronic listing of this information is it cannot be easily modified; after too many changes, the sheets of paper become unreadable and need retyping. This is not the case with an electronic database where the information is stored on disk. The computer database also minimizes data redundancy, that is, the same information being automatically available in different files. When a clerk searches through a file cabinet, he uses his fingers to locate key files, which can take a long time. The electronic database user can generate reports, retrieve files almost instantaneously, sort data in a variety of ways, edit, and print information with more flexibility and at faster speeds than the file clerk can. Furthermore, electronic files cannot easily be misplaced, and data can be shared easily among individuals. In addition, a user can execute a file search with incomplete information. With only the first half of a name and a brief description, for example, the police can search for a suspect. The only disadvantages to using a database are its expense and the fact that existing written files must first be converted into the database format.

Computerized databases are used daily in government, occupational, and professional agencies. There are virtually thousands of repositories of information, such as Educational Resources Information Clearinghouse (ERIC), that students utilize for their research work. ERIC, the primary database for teachers, is the basic indexing and abstracting source for information about education. For example, a student searching for *problem solving* in *primary math* would input these key words to locate abstracts on the recent research articles on this topic.

How a Database Operates

In this section, we'll use *ClarisWorks* as an example of how an electronic database operates, but this discussion is not a substitute for Claris's documentation. Let's imagine that a teacher needs to keep track of the software she has accumulated haphazardly in a closet. The teacher wants to create a database to make order out of this chaos. This particular database has one file simply labeled Software that represents the software collection. The teacher must first determine the number of fields for the record. She designs a record based on library referencing techniques that includes five fields: Title, Subject, Company, Copies, and Grade Level. In this example, the first field the teacher creates is *Title* (Fig. 5.4).

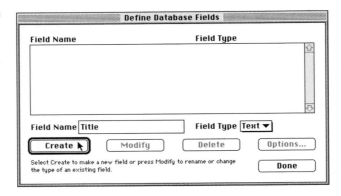

Figure 5.4
Selecting a field
Courtesy of FileMaker, Inc.

After she designs the format, or template, the record is automatically saved. An example of her record is shown in Figure 5.5.

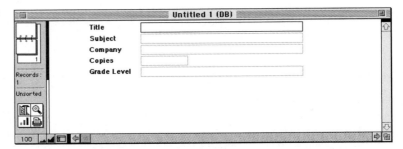

Figure 5.5
Sample record
Courtesy of FileMaker, Inc.

The next step is to enter the record data for each piece of software in the closet. A completed software file record is shown in Figure 5.6.

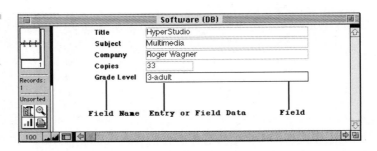

Figure 5.6
Software file record
Courtesy of FileMaker, Inc.

The field *Title* has the entry *HyperStudio*, the field *Subject* has *Multimedia,* and the field *Company* has Roger Wagner. As the teacher enters the information, she has the option of adding or changing it. When one record is completed, she generates another. The teacher continues filling in records until she decides to stop or reaches the storage capacity of the particular database file program. When the task is finished, she has a database file that lists ten records for the software file (Fig. 5.7).

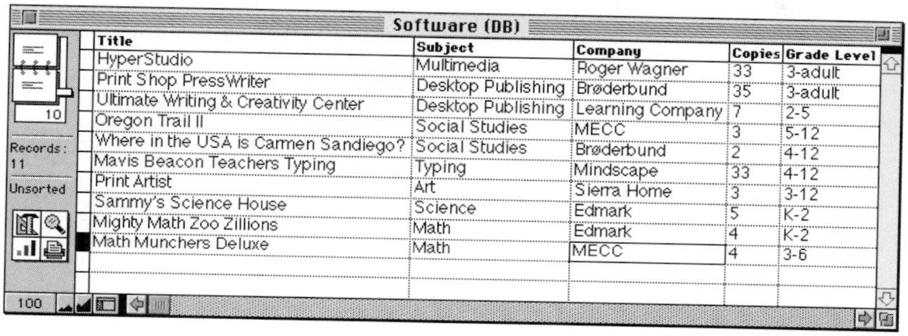

Title	Subject	Company	Copies	Grade Level
HyperStudio	Multimedia	Roger Wagner	33	3-adult
Print Shop PressWriter	Desktop Publishing	Brøderbund	35	3-adult
Ultimate Writing & Creativity Center	Desktop Publishing	Learning Company	7	2-5
Oregon Trail II	Social Studies	MECC	3	5-12
Where in the USA is Carmen Sandiego?	Social Studies	Brøderbund	2	4-12
Mavis Beacon Teachers Typing	Typing	Mindscape	33	4-12
Print Artist	Art	Sierra Home	3	3-12
Sammy's Science House	Science	Edmark	5	K-2
Mighty Math Zoo Zillions	Math	Edmark	4	K-2
Math Munchers Deluxe	Math	MECC	4	3-6

Figure 5.7
Records from software file
Courtesy of FileMaker, Inc.

Functions of a Database

Now that the database is completed, the teacher can select or retrieve a file and sort the records. One of the major tasks of any database is to retrieve information, and there are a variety of ways of retrieving this information:

1. Retrieve an entire file as shown by listing this file on the screen or printing it out.
2. Retrieve only a few field headings, such as *Title* and *Subject* (Fig. 5.8).

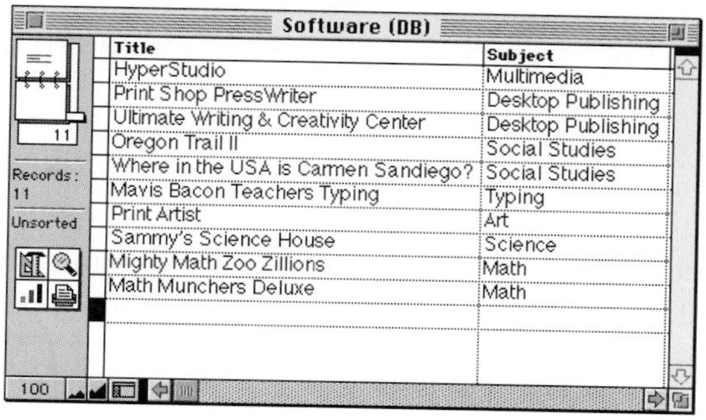

Title	Subject
HyperStudio	Multimedia
Print Shop PressWriter	Desktop Publishing
Ultimate Writing & Creativity Center	Desktop Publishing
Oregon Trail II	Social Studies
Where in the USA is Carmen Sandiego?	Social Studies
Mavis Bacon Teachers Typing	Typing
Print Artist	Art
Sammy's Science House	Science
Mighty Math Zoo Zillions	Math
Math Munchers Deluxe	Math

Figure 5.8
Two field headings
Courtesy of FileMaker, Inc.

3. Use a field to search for one record in the database. For example, the teacher might type *Ultimate Writing & Creativity Center* in the *Title* field. The teacher must type the title as it was originally entered or it will not be retrieved. Figure 5.9 shows this retrieved record.

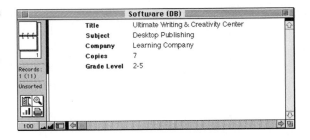

Figure 5.9
Retrieved record
Courtesy of FileMaker, Inc.

4. Retrieve a record using more than one criterion, such as the company name and the grade level. Use **Boolean operators** such as *and* and *or* to search for more than one record.[1] For example, in this next search, the teacher uses the Boolean operator *and* to search for software that meets two criteria: (1) is a desktop publishing program and (2) has at least two copies available. The result of this search (Fig. 5.10) generates two programs: *Print Shop PressWriter* and *The Ultimate Writing and Creativity Center.*

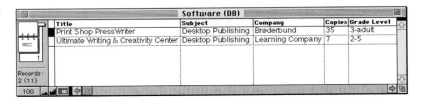

Figure 5.10
Result of a search
Courtesy of FileMaker, Inc.

The Boolean operator *or* lets the teacher find records that meet the requirements of either criterion. In this instance, either a desktop publishing program or software with at least two copies available is acceptable.

5. Search for a record with data strings. There are times when the database user wants to search for a record and is not sure how to find it. For instance, suppose the teacher cannot remember the name of a publisher but recalls that it begins with *Sun.* A **data string** is a subset of the characters within a field. *Sun* and *burst* are data strings for the publisher Sunburst. To find the Sunburst publisher, the teacher need only type *Sun* as the field name to distinguish the choice from information in other records. This type of search is often called a **wildcard search.** The search usually uses symbols to represent any value. For example an asterisk (*) will act as a wildcard character and the word *Sun** will return documents with the words *Sunburst, Sunfield,* or *Sunland* depending what publishers are in the database. This type of wildcard usage is the most common and is known as right-hand truncation.

---

[1]In arithmetic, the primary operations are add, subtract, multiply, and divide, but in Boolean logic, the primary operations are *and, or,* and *not.*

The other important function of a database program is sorting, the ability to arrange the records in a file so that the values in a field are sorted either in alphabetical, numerical, or chronological order. Any field can be sorted, and sorting is done by field type. If the field has characters in it, it is sorted alphabetically, *A* to *Z* or *Z* to *A*. If the field is numeric, it is sorted lowest to highest or highest to lowest. An example of a numeric sort would be the number of copies from lowest to highest. Finally, a user can sort a field chronologically by date or time.

Types of Databases

Hundreds of database programs are available. These programs vary in price and capabilities. Some database programs are single purpose while others are integrated. The single-purpose program performs database functions exclusively. It is primarily used in business situations that require a database that is powerful and can hold many records. *FileMaker Pro* (Now FileMaker, Inc.) (Macintosh and IBM) is a good example of this type of program. The integrated program offers other capabilities such as telecommunication, charting, word processing, and spreadsheet. A good example of this type of database is *ClarisWorks* (Macintosh and IBM). Chapter 7 discusses integrated programs more thoroughly.

Database software employs different methods of data organization. These include hierarchical, network, *HyperCard* (Apple), free-form or encyclopedia, relational, and flat-file databases.

The hierarchical database was one of the first methods of database organization developed for the computer. The majority of operating systems, including DOS, Windows, NT Windows 98, and the Macintosh OS, use this file system to store data and programs. This database stores information in a top-to-bottom organizational structure. Access of data through this database is done sequentially. In other words, you start at the top and proceed through the hierarchical levels. The database organizes data into a series, with the most general grouping first and the subgroups next. Each subgroup branches downward and can only link to the parent group. For example, a professor who wants to access a student's record must move first through the university, then the college, and then the departmental data before accessing the record of the particular student. There are two disadvantages to this database. First, you cannot easily locate records in different sections or subgroups of the database. In the example just given, if you wanted to access another student's record, you would have to start all over again by moving first to the university level; there are no shortcuts. This method can be inefficient and time consuming when a user wants to access data from multiple groups and redefine part of the database. Second, the hierarchical database requires a complete restructuring each time the user adds a new field. On the positive side, once the data is set up, searching is fast and efficient because you don't have to search through all the records, you just search through specific groups.

The network database works the same as a hierarchical database except that a record can belong to more than one main group. This database is superior to the hierarchical database because it allows the user access to multiple data sets. Data can be accessed with speed and ease through different types of sources. Regardless, networked databases still require every relationship to be predefined and the addition of any new field requires a complete redefinition of the database.

Hierarchical and network databases enter data in a structured format. Free-form, or encyclopedia, databases let the user access data without specifying data type or data size. In this type of database, the user does not search for data in a field but instead uses a keyword or keywords. The software then searches all its text entries for matches. The advantage of this encyclopedia database is that if you forgot the exact title of an article, you could find it using a keyword search. Many of the Internet search engines use keyword searches. The main application of the free-form database is the on-line encyclopedia. There is an example of this type of database in Chapter 11. The encyclopedia database maintains a large collection of information that is subject oriented. For example, an education database may group files according to different issues in education. You can then search by categories. Many times these databases are collections of data from other large free-form databases, which lets you locate vast amounts of information. Typically these databases include such topics as news, microcomputer information, magazines articles, and medical information. *News* would let you access current news articles, newspapers, and information from news wire services. *Microcomputer information* would contain data from popular computing magazines. *Magazine articles* would let you access thousands of periodicals that focus on specialized areas such as medicine, education, and business. *Medical information* would give you access to medical journals.

HyperCard has played an important role in changing the way databases are used in education. *HyperCard* integrates data organization with graphics. Using *HyperCard*, the teacher and student can create individual cards or screens of data with both text and graphics. They can then link these cards to produce a stack, or group of cards. The *HyperCard* stack is equivalent to a database. In education, the ability to create cards, link these cards, and produce instructional data is a very potent tool. *HyperCard*, (Apple) along with other programs of this nature such as *LinkWay Live!* (IBM) and *HyperStudio* (Roger Wagner), are explored further in Chapter 10.

Relational databases let the user work with more than one file at a time and help with data redundancy. For example, a department chair might need several different files, such as test scores and transcript data on a particular student. If each of these files is a separate electronic file, he would have to duplicate information for each file to make it understandable. The relational database removes this problem by linking separate files or even entire databases through a common key field such as the student's social security number. The chair then can retrieve the data from any file by identifying the social security number of the student. In relational databases, changes made in one file are automatically reflected in the other files of the record. The product *visual dBase* (Borland International) is a classic example of this type of database. This database is very useful for the administration of elementary, high school, and college records. However, the majority of classroom teachers have little need for this type of data analysis.

Classroom teachers want a simple, straightforward way of entering their data, and the flat-file database fulfills this requirement. It works with only one data file at a time, and there is no linking to other data files. This database does not permit multiple access to data files or advanced questioning techniques. There is variation among flat-file databases, but generally they do not allow merging with other application programs.

Why Use a Database in the Classroom?

In the past, the administrative office of a school district was the only place in the district that needed a database; the office is where student records, personnel files, and school resources were kept. Recently, however, classroom teachers are using computerized databases to keep track of students' progress and to store anecdotal comments on individual students. Furthermore, pupils are creating their own databases and using prepared databases such as *3D Atlas* (Electronic Arts) and *World GeoGraph* and *USA GeoGraph II* (MECC).

These databases provide users with a vast amount of information. *USA GeoGraph II* lets students link maps with a database containing more than 124 categories. The database is considered a "living map" because it is interactive; users can zoom in on different places, they can use electronic map overlays to see places from various thematic perspectives, and the map changes as the user explores with the database. In Figure 5.11, the user wanted to see the borders of the states, the major urban areas, and the major rivers and lakes.

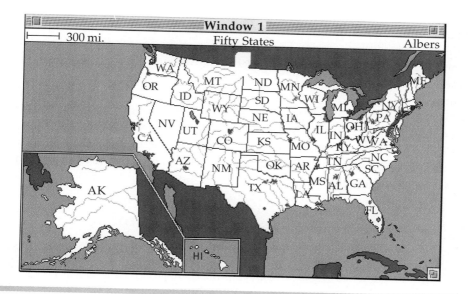

Figure 5.11
USA GeoGraph II
Used with permission of MECC. All rights reserved. *USA GeoGraph* is a trademark of MECC.

The database is the perfect tool for teaching higher level critical thinking skills, such as the ability to hypothesize, draw inferences, and use Boolean logic. Here's an example. Imagine that students in a class are instructed to search a hypothetical database for the names of students who took Dr. Gallio's computer class. After the students develop a strategy, they perform the search and find out who the students are. The teacher then asks them to hypothesize how many females received *A*s in the computer class. This time their strategy is more complex as they are looking for names of people who meet two criteria: (1) students who are female and (2) students who received an *A*. Following this search, the students are asked to draw inferences about the results of the search and conduct further searches to see if there is any correlation among other items.

Besides helping with higher level thinking, a database can help students learn content material in any of the curriculum areas. Many databases are being commercially developed in association with specific academic areas. These databases have informational files on topics ranging from animals to countries. If students understand how to manipulate a database, they can gain deeper insight into any field of study; they can find patterns, draw relationships, or identify trends.

Today, students can use database files that they created themselves or files prepared by teachers or software houses. It is often more beneficial for students to enter their research into a design created by their teacher. The mastery of databases takes longer than the mastery of word processing because to learn databases, students must be given more experience and different types of assignments.

The manuals supplied with databases include instructions on how to manipulate the data, student worksheets, and suggested activities. The database programs that exist for the lower grades should be used only on an elementary level because schoolchildren cannot understand the logic behind database programs. They can, however, understand some essential concepts such as record, field, and search. It may be wise to save the complex searching for the junior high school students.

There are different questions to ask when choosing a database program: How limited is the program in its ability to search? Can you easily add or change the data in the files? Are there multiple copies of the program available? If there is a prepared database with the product, is the content proper for the students? Is the information accurate? What is the quality of the documentation? How easy is the program to use? Let us examine these factors more closely for the purpose of making a more informed decision.

How to Select a Good Database for the Classroom

There are quite a few database packages on the market today with every imaginable feature, some more appropriate for classroom use than others. The more popular programs for the schools include *ClarisWorks for Kids, Microsoft Works,* and *ClarisWorks.* Generally, these classroom-appropriate databases have fewer features and are easier to use than business programs such as *FileMaker Pro.* Choosing a database program for the classroom is a six-step process; consider the following: (1) hardware compatibility; (2) general features; (3) instructional design; (4) ease of use; (5) consumer value; and (6) support.

Hardware Compatibility

Check out the computer that your school is using. Is it an old Apple IIe, an IBM with a Pentium II chip, or a Macintosh with a PowerPC chip? How much memory does it have: 64K, 512K, or 4 MB of memory? (Some database programs need a huge amount of computer memory. You may have to extend the memory of the computer you choose by adding RAM chips.) How many disk drives are available for each machine? (Generally, most computer applications need two disk drives: a floppy drive and a hard drive.) What printers will work with this database program?

General Features

The most common functions provided by database programs are (1) sorting data; (2) changing or updating data; (3) searching for specific information; (4) deleting and adding information in the file; and (5) printing.

Sorting.   In review, sorting is the ability to arrange the records in different ways. Programs should allow you to name the field type easily and to do the sort quickly. At the very least, the program should do the following: (1) an alphabetical sort from *A* to *Z* or *Z* to *A,* in any appropriate character field; (2) a numeric sort from lowest to highest and highest to lowest, in any numeric field. No matter what program you choose, you should be able to sort to the screen and the printer.

Changing and Updating.   Every database can update and change a file. The questions that must be asked are the following: How difficult is it to accomplish this task? Is it easy to find the record and change it? How hard is it to add a record to the file, and is it a drawn-out procedure?

Searching or Retrieving.   Database programs vary in the type of search criteria used to find forms in a file. For instance, there may be exact matches, partial matches, numeric matches, and numeric range matches. In an exact match, the program looks for the forms that exactly match the search criteria. An exact match for Florence Singer would be Florence Singer or FLORENCE SINGER; Mrs. Florence Singer; Singer, Florence; or FlorenceSinger would not be matches.

All database programs have exact matches, and many database programs have partial matches. You would use a partial match when you are unsure of how the information was entered into the database or when you are interested in locating different records with the same information. For instance, you might be able to find Florence Singer's file by just typing in *Florence* or *Singer.* You would use a partial match to find the records of students who have computer experience.

The more advanced the database, the more exotic the features. *Professional File* (Software Publishing Corporation), an advanced program for the IBM, does quite a few numeric searches. This program lets you look for items less than, greater than, or equal to a given number. If you want to find the records for all children who were born later than 1982, you would enter *Year: >1982.* This program also has a numeric range match feature that allows you to search for numbers within a certain range. For instance, you might search for dates with the range of 1988 to 2000.

The database program should let you search using multiple criteria as well. For instance, you might want to search for the students eligible to take your advanced computer course. You would use two criteria: (1) students who are in eleventh grade and (2) students who have computer experience. At the end of your search, the computer would generate the names of students who fit these qualifications.

Searching a file in some database programs can change the file if you're not careful. Because of this problem, it is desirable to choose a program in which the search feature is separate from the add feature. The ideal program has a way to lock files so they will not be accidentally erased.

Deleting and Adding.   The database program should allow you to add information to or delete it from a record or field with minimum trouble. When you add a new field to one record, you want the new field to be added to all the records.

Printing.   Your program should allow you to print a neat report. The instructions for this task should be easy to follow and the printout should show the data fields that you want in the report.

Advanced Features.   Some programs let you design the way the data will be displayed and others perform mathematical calculations on the data. These programs do not perform the complex functions of a spreadsheet, but they let you total simple columns of numbers or compute student averages. Most database programs show the final list or report on the screen before it is printed. *FileMaker Pro, ClarisWorks, Microsoft Works,* and *FoxPro* (Microsoft) let you select fields for different records and display them on the screen all at once. Some databases can store a picture with each record. The advanced programs such as *Professional File, Access* (Microsoft), and *FoxPro* can merge data from a database document with a word processing document to produce a customized letter or report. With the mail merge function, you can send out form letters to parents or students, each letter with a different name, address, and grade. The mail merge function automatically places the name, address, and grade from the data base into the word processing document's form letter. To produce a mail merge document, you start by writing a basic form letter, the general text you want to send each person on your mailing list. In this letter you do not include the names, address or grades because these items will be inserted automatically from a mailing list. In their place you insert place holders, or merge fields, that tell your word processor where to put the names, addresses, and grades. Next, you click on a mail merge tool. You select the list you want to merge and the word processor prints one personalized letter for each record received from your mailing list.

Instructional Design

A database program should require minimum learning time. The program that has a menu bar displayed at the top of the screen is ideal for beginners because users do not have to memorize the different functions. *FileMaker Pro* (Figure 5.12) is very popular because of its design and its collection of templates that help you use the product quickly. The templates can be easily modified to suit your own needs. Just add or modify fields, layouts, or text when necessary.

The key to the success of database programs is their flexibility of design. How easy is it to make changes and how easy is it to add a field or add information to a field in the data-

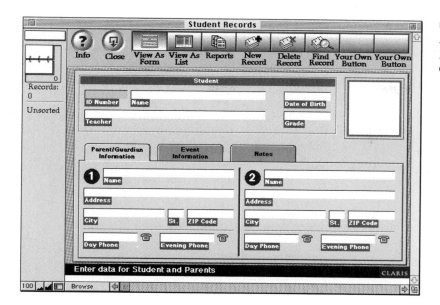

Figure 5.12
FileMaker Pro
Courtesy of FileMaker, Inc.

base program? When you do, do you lose the information that already exists in the field? Does the database program make you start again when you want to make changes? What is the search speed of the program? What flexibility is there in printing a report? Can you be selective in printing certain columns or are you forced to print all the items as shown on the screen? What is the size limit of the database? *Professional File* theoretically can have 100 fields on a page and a file size of eight megabytes. Is there a size limitation for the information in each field? *Professional File* allows 4,000 characters per page or field, while *ClarisWorks* allows a total of 63 characters, including the field name. Database programs vary in the kinds of searches they are capable of accomplishing—what type of searches do you require? Can you conduct Boolean searches? Does the searching technique fit the skills you are emphasizing in the classroom?

Ease of Use

A major concern when buying a database program is how easy the program is to learn. It is immaterial what features it has if it is difficult to comprehend. Ask the following questions: Can you learn in a reasonable amount of time to use this program? Is there a tutorial disk that takes the user through the program? (*ClarisWorks* uses simple English commands and has on-line help to teach you the program step by step.) Are there help screens that tell the user what to do each step of the way? Can you access these help screens whenever you need them? Are there menu bars across the screens so users do not have to memorize the different functions? Is the printer set up easily, and can you be ready to print immediately? Are there too many help prompts and safety questions?

Consumer Value

Because software is expensive, cost is a major consideration. Since public domain software costs very little, it is a natural alternative to commercial software. For example, there is free software available in California through the California State Department of Education. Commercial software is more expensive, but there are many programs worth the cost. Be sure to find out if the software comes with a backup copy. If the software publisher does not supply a disk, how much money will it cost to purchase one? Many software companies let you use one disk to load the software on all your computers. Other companies offer an inexpensive on-site license that enables you to make as many copies as you need. Some companies have lab packs that let you purchase a large quantity of software at a reduced price.

Support

Ask these questions: Can you call someone on the telephone at the software company and get immediate help, or must you wade through a series of messages and wait an unbearable amount of time? (As mentioned previously, many houses will tell you how many customers are in line before you and how long you must wait.) Is the technical support available toll free? (Many companies are charging a fee for technical support.) Does the software package have tutorial lessons to help the beginner learn the program? Is the manual readable and does it have an index? Does the program have templates or computer-based files? Do the software producers have data files for various content areas? (For example, MECC has a collection of prepared databases for U.S. geography and world geography.)

Before selecting the software, decide which features are important for your particular class.

Refer now to Appendix A for an annotated bibliography of highly rated database programs for the classroom. Next, examine one of these programs using the sample checklist and evaluation rating instrument on page 111.

Teacher Practice

The following exercises are meant to be used in conjunction with any database. If a computer lab is not available, just follow this section to get an idea of what kinds of activities can be used in the classroom. The first exercise is a step-by-step introduction to a database program. You will need two disks: a program disk and a newly formatted disk to store your file with records.

A. Database 1

1. Load the program disk into the computer and boot the machine.
2. From the main menu, select the option that creates a file and gives the file a name, such as *Class.*
3. Type in the following field names: *Teacher, Students, Room, Grade,* and *Sex.* Correct any mistakes made.

DATABASE CHECKLIST

Directions: Examine the following items and determine which ones you feel are important for your class situation. Evaluate your database and place an X on each line where the software meets your needs.

Product Name_____   Manufacturer_____   Appropriate Grade Level_____

A. Hardware
— 1. Memory needed
— 2. Computer compatibility
— 3. Printer compatibility
— 4. Types of disk drives

B. Features
— 1. Selection of field types
— 2. Sort
—   a. Alphabetic
—   b. Numeric
—   c. Chronological
—   d. Reverse order
—   e. To screen and printer
— 3. Deleting and adding fields
— 4. Search
—   a. Alphabetic
—   b. Numeric
—   c. And-or
—   d. Using multiple criteria
— 5. Mathematical calculation of data
— 6. Mail merge
— 7. Display
—   a. Printout—screen or printer
—   b. Can display selected fields
—   c. 40–80 column display
— 8. Copy and paste
— 9. Capacity to create reports

C. Design
— 1. Speed of search
— 2. Ease of changing fields

— 3. Ease of adding new fields
— 4. Size requirements
—   a. field size
—   b. characters per field
—   c. no. of records in a file

D. Ease of Use
— 1. Help screens
— 2. Tutorial disk
— 3. Easy printer setup
— 4. Disk formatting within program
— 5. Automatic save
— 6. Warning questions

E. Consumer Value
— 1. Cost
— 2. Lab packs or on-site licensing
— 3. Backup disk

F. Support
— 1. Technical
— 2. Tutorial material
— 3. Readable manual
— 4. Lab packs
— 5. Templates
— 6. Prepared software
— 7. Readable manual
—   a. Activities
—   b. Lesson plans
—   c. Tutorial
—   d. Index

Rating Scale

Rate the Database Program by placing a check in the appropriate box.

Excellent ___   Very Good ___   Good ___   Fair ___   Poor ___

Comments

4. Using the add-a-record function, type the following information for each record:

TEACHER	STUDENTS	ROOM	GRADE	SEX
Smith	23	21	K	Male
Adams	16	14	4	Female
Gramacy	17	25	3	Female
Witham	33	29	1	Female
Youngblood	21	24	K	Male

5. Add another record to the list: *Teacher,* Sharp; *Students,* 20; *Room,* 12; *Grade,* 3; and *Sex,* Female.

6. Change (a) the name Smith to Small and his room number 21 to 24 and (b) the name Adams to Allen and the number of students she has from 16 to 28.

7. Next, delete the Gramacy record.

8. Alphabetize the list of records *A* to *Z* in the teacher's name field. The list should now look like this:

TEACHER	STUDENTS	ROOM	GRADE	SEX
Allen	28	14	4	Female
Sharp	20	12	3	Female
Small	23	24	K	Male
Witham	33	29	1	Female
Youngblood	21	24	K	Male

9. Print out the results.

10. Next, numerically sort the field *Grade* from highest to lowest:

TEACHER	GRADE
Allen	4
Sharp	3
Witham	1
Small	K
Youngblood	K

11. Search for the following records:
    a. Youngblood (type the name Youngblood in the *Teacher* field);
    b. Allen; and
    c. the kindergarten records (type *K* in the field *Grade*). The program should find Small and Youngblood. The database shows the records that match the specifications you type. If there is no record, the program usually displays a 0. You also get a 0 if you spell the record name differently from the way it was spelled in the original entry in the database.

12. Search for records using two criteria: (1) teachers who are male, and (2) teachers who have exactly twenty-one students. Type 21 for the *Students* field and male for the *Sex* field. For this search, there is only one record: Youngblood.

13. Let's find the male kindergarten teachers records. Type *K* for the *grade* and male for the *sex.* In this case, there are two teachers that fit these criteria: Small and Youngblood.

14. If the database program has a greater than (>) or less than (<) feature, find the following records:
    a. all the teachers that have a class size greater than twenty;
    b. the male teachers who have twenty-three or more students; and
    c. the female teachers who have eighteen or more students.

B. Database 2

For practice, create another database. Type in the following field names: *Student, Sex, Hair Color,* and *Birth Date.*

1. Using the add function, type the following information for each record:

Student Data Sheet

Pupil: Smith, Joan
Sex: Female
Hair Color: Brown
Birth Date: 1975

Pupil: Lorenzo, Max
Sex: Male
Hair Color: Black
Birth Date: 1977

Pupil: Chen, Mark
Sex: Male
Hair Color: Black
Birth Date: 1978

Pupil: Sharp, David
Sex: Male
Hair Color: Brown
Birth Date: 1977

Pupil: Schainker, Nancy
Sex: Female
Hair Color: Red
Birth Date: 1976

Pupil: Edwards, Bobbie
Sex: Female
Hair Color: Blond
Birth Date: 1979

Pupil: Lopez, Mary
Sex: Female
Hair Color: Black
Birth Date: 1980

Pupil: Jefferson, LeMar
Sex: Male
Hair Color: Black
Birth Date: 1979

Pupil: Jung, Nicky
Sex: Female
Hair Color: Red
Birth Date: 1979

2. Change the field name *Pupil* to *Student.*
3. Next, change David Sharp's birth date to 1950, Nicky Jung's description to a male with black hair, and Bobbie Edwards's hair color to red.
4. Add the following file: *Student,* Lee, Bessie; *Hair Color,* Brown; *Sex,* Female; *Birth Date,* 1980.

5. Alphabetize the list *A* to *Z* in the *Student* field and print out the list.
6. Find the following files:
   a. David Sharp;
   b. all students who are female;
   c. students who have red hair;
   d. students born after 1950;
   e. students born before 1977; and
   f. all students who are female and have red hair.

Classroom Applications

▼   I. General Database   ▼

Materials
You will need the personal data sheet, a database program (*FileMaker Pro, ClarisWorks, Microsoft Works*, etc.), and one computer or more.

Objective
Students will use the Boolean operators *and* and *or.*

Procedure

1. Discuss the use of *and* and *or* to connect two fields.
2. Have the students write personal data sheets about themselves using Figure 5.13 as a model.

Figure 5.13
Personal data sheet

PERSONAL DATA SHEET
1. YOUR LAST NAME
2. YOUR FIRST NAME
3. YOUR BIRTH MONTH
4. NUMBER OF BROTHERS
5. NUMBER OF SISTERS
6. FAVORITE SPORT
7. NUMBER OF PETS

3. Collect the data sheets from the students.
4. Enter the data into the computer database.

5. Have the students do the following tasks:
   a. Find every student whose first name starts with *A* or *C*.
   b. Sort the sheets by birth month.
   c. Print a list of students who have two pets and whose last names begin with *S*.
   d. Print out the names of students whose birth month is August and who have one brother.
   e. Find out which students have two brothers.
   f. Find out who has the most sisters.
   g. Find out how many students have one brother and one sister.
   h. Sort by the *Last Name* field.
   i. Find out how many people were born in April.
   j. Find out whose favorite sport is baseball.

▼   II. Science Database   ▼

Materials

You will need the dinosaur database form, a database program (*FileMaker Pro, ClarisWorks, Microsoft Works*, etc.) and one computer or more.

Objectives

Students will create a dinosaur database, learn about dinosaurs, sort alphabetically, practice using Boolean operators, and sort by number.

Procedure

1. Have each student read about a dinosaur.
2. After the reading assignment is completed, have each student fill out the dinosaur database form (Fig. 5.14).

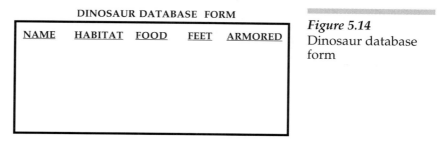

DINOSAUR DATABASE FORM

NAME	HABITAT	FOOD	FEET	ARMORED

Figure 5.14
Dinosaur database form

3. Instruct each student to enter his or her information on the same data file disk.

4. Following are sample data for this database:

Dinosaur Database

Name	Habitat	Food	Feet	Armored
Ankylosaurus	Land	Plants	4	Yes
Tryannosaurus	Land	Meat	2	No
Brachiosaurus	Water-Swamp	Plants	4	No
Brontosaurus	Water-Swamp	Plants	4	No
Corythosaurs	Water-Swamp	Plants	2	No
Diplodocus	Water-Swamp	Plants	4	No
Iguanodon	Land	Plants	2	No
Proceratops	Land	Plants	4	Yes
Stegosaurus	Land	Plants	4	Yes
Coelophysis	Land	Meat	2	No

5. After this task has been completed, have the students do the following:
   a. Sort the file by the number of feet in the field, highest to lowest.
   b. Using the Boolean operator *and,* find out if there are any two-legged plant eaters and any four-legged meat eaters.
   c. Sort alphabetically by name and print out the list.

Additional Suggestions

Have students add fields such as *weight, height,* and *nickname* and sort the fields by (1) length (lowest to highest); (2) weight; (3) characteristics.

▼ III. Language Arts Database ▼

Materials

You will need the book report form, a database program (*MyDataBase,* [My Software Co.] *File-Maker Pro, ClarisWorks, Microsoft Works,* etc.), and one computer or more.

Objectives

Students will create a database book report file, learn to sort alphabetically, and read a book.

Procedure

1. Have each student read a book.

2. After the reading assignment is finished, have each student complete the book report form (Fig. 5.15).

BOOK REPORT FORM

STUDENT'S NAME _____

1. **AUTHOR:**

2. **TITLE:**

3. **TYPE OF BOOK:**

4. **SETTING:**

5. **MAIN CHARACTER OF THE STORY:**

6. **SUMMARY OF THE STORY:**

Figure 5.15
Book report form

3. Instruct students to input their information under each field name on the same data file disk. This activity requires a database program that has a comment field. If the database program does not have this feature, eliminate this field name.

4. After this task has been completed, have the students do the following:
   a. Search for books they might like to read, using the search function.
   b. Print out a list of all the books in the database.
   c. Sort the database alphabetically by title and print out the list.
   d. Sort the database file alphabetically by author and print out the list.
   e. Find out how many students read baseball stories or biographies by using the Find function of the database program.

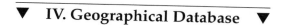

▼ IV. Geographical Database ▼

Materials

You will need the state geographical sheet, a database program (*FileMaker Pro, ClarisWorks, Microsoft Works,* etc.), and one computer or more.

Objectives

Students will create a geographical data file for each state, learn geographical information about each state, sort alphabetically, and search using the Boolean operators *and* and *or*.

Procedure

1. Have each student in the class choose a state to research.
2. Have the students use reference books to complete the state geographical sheet (Fig. 5.16).

Figure 5.16
State geographical
sheet

State Geographical Sheet	
FIELD NAME	DATA
1. LOCATION (Midwest, Northeast, etc.)	
2. SIZE (Square Miles)	
3. NATURAL RESOURCES	
4. CLIMATE	
5. TERRAIN (Desert, Mountains, etc.)	

3. Have the students enter the proper information under each field name on the data file disk.
4. After this task has been completed, have the student independently use the search function to answer *Who Am I?* questions (Fig. 5.17).

Figure 5.17
Who am I? questions

WHO AM I?
1. I am a small state
2. I am known for my mountains.
3. I have red clover flowers.

▼   V. Math Database   ▼

Materials
You will need the state data sheet, a database program (*MyDataBase, FileMaker Pro, ClarisWorks, Microsoft Works,* etc.), and one computer or more.

Objectives
Students will create a state data file, learn statistical information about the United States, sort alphabetically, and search using the Boolean operators *and* and *or.*

Procedure

1. Have each student in the class choose a state to research.
2. Have the students use encyclopedias to complete the state data sheet (Fig. 5.18).

STATE DATA SHEET	
FIELD NAME	DATA
1. CAPITAL	
2. POPULATION	
3. NUMBER OF REPRESENTATIVES IN CONGRESS	
4. YEAR OF STATEHOOD	

Figure 5.18
State data sheet

3. Tell students to complete the proper information under each field name on the same data file disk.
4. After this task has been completed, have the students independently use the search function to carry out the following tasks:
   a. Search for the states that have populations over two million.
   b. Find the last state that was added to the United States.
   c. Sort the records according to population from lowest to highest.
   d. Sort the records alphabetically by the name of the state and print out a list.
   e. Sort the states by population and print out a list.
5. Next, divide the class into two teams and collect each team's state data sheets.
6. Read aloud one of the state data sheets without revealing the name of the state.
7. Ask Team One to try to figure out what state the data sheet describes.
8. Ask Team Two to check Team One's answer by using the computer. If Team One has answered correctly, it scores a point.
9. Read another data sheet.
10. Ask Team Two to try to identify the state and Team One to check Team Two's answer. The first team to achieve ten points wins.
    Here is a list of additional database ideas: (1) scheduling, (2) hobbies, (3) opinion survey, (4) dictionary of spelling words, (5) planets, (6) presidents, (7) world events, (8) whales, (9) animal groups, (10) plants, (11) rocks, and (12) minerals.

Summary

The database is an effective manager of information and a powerful tool for learning in the classroom. With a database, students can look for relationships among data, test hypotheses, and draw conclusions.

This chapter discussed the merits of an electronic database and its basic features. We examined a database checklist evaluation form and learned how to introduce the database to the class. Classroom activities presented covered a range of curriculum areas. A mastery test, classroom projects, and suggested readings and references follow.

Be sure to review the award-winning, highly rated database programs listed in Appendix A.

Chapter Mastery Test

1. What is a database and how can it be used in the classroom?
2. Define the following: file, record, and field.
3. Name and describe two ways of sorting data.
4. What differentiates a file cabinet from a database?
5. Discuss the advantages of using a computerized database.
6. Discuss the factors involved in selecting a database for a school district.
7. Name and describe three ways of searching for a file.
8. When should a student use a wild card search?
9. Explain three methods of organizing data within a database.
10. What is a relational database?
11. Name two common functions of a database.
12. Why has *HyperCard* played an important role in changing the way databases are used in education?

Classroom Projects

1. Create a prepared database file. Using this file, do the following:
   a. Sort alphabetically from *A* to *Z*.
   b. Sort alphabetically from *Z* to *A*.
   c. Sort numerically from lowest to highest.
   d. Sort numerically from highest to lowest.
   e. Use the Boolean operators *and* and *or* to find an entry on your database.
   f. Print a listing of the database file.
   g. Add fields to the database.
   h. Add information to the fields in the database.
   i. Delete information or fields from the database.
   j. Save a file.
   k. Retrieve a saved file.
   l. Print a file.
   m. Examine three databases and compare their different features.
   n. Choose a grade level and create a database activity for it.

Suggested Readings and References

Anders, Vicki, and Kathy M. Jackson. "Online vs. CD-ROM—The Impact of CD-ROM Databases upon a Large Online Searching Program." *Online* 12, no. 6 (November 1, 1988): 24.

Antonoff, Michael. "Using a Spreadsheet as a Database." *Personal Computing* (1986): 65–71.

Bachor, D. G. "Toward Improving Assessment of Students with Special Needs: Expanding the Database to Include Classroom Performance." *Alberta Journal of Educational Research* 36, no. 1 (March 1, 1990): 65.

Barbour, A. "A Cemetery Database Makes Math Come Alive." *Electronic Learning* (February 1988): 12–13.

Bensu, Janet. "Use Your Database in New Ways." *HR Magazine* 35, no. 3 (March 1, 1990): 33.

Bock, Douglas B. "Solving Crime with Database Technology." *Journal of Systems Management* 39, no. 10 (October 1, 1988): 16.

Braun, Ellen. "Word Processing: Desktop Publishing Share Features." *The Office* 117, no. 5 (May 1, 1993): 9.

Caughlin, Janet. *Claris Workshop for Teachers.* Eugene, Oreg.: Visons, 1995.

Caughlin, Janet. *Claris Workshop for Students Secondary 7–12.* Eugene, Oreg.: Visons, 1997.

Coe, Michael. "Keeping up with Technology." *The Computing Teacher* 18, no. 5 (February 1991): 14–15.

Coulson, C. J. "Creation of Inhouse Database." *Transactions* 17, no. 5 (October 1, 1989): 838.

Davey, Claire, and Adrian S. Jarvis. "Microcomputers for Microhistory: A Database Approach to the Reconstitution of Small English Populations." *History & Computing* 2, no. 3 (1990): 187.

Dunfey, J. "Using a Database in an English Classroom." *The Computing Teacher* 12, no. 8 (1984): 26–27.

Ennis, Demetria. "Interdisciplinary Database Activities for Fifth Graders at Tomas Rivera." *Journal of Computing in Childhood Education* 8, no. 1 (1997): 83–88.

Epler, D. M. *Online Searching Goes to School.* Phoenix, Ariz.: Oryx Press, 1989.

Fagan, Patsy J., and Ann D. Thompson. "Using a Database to Aid in Learning the Meanings and Purposes of Math Notations and Symbols." *The Journal of Computers in Mathematics and Science* 8, no. 4 (summer 1989): 26.

MacUser. *FileMaker Pro 3.0* 12, no. 5 (1996): 47.

Flynn, Marilyn L. "Using Computer-Assisted Instruction to Increase Organizational Effectiveness." *Administration in Social Work* 14, no. 1 (winter 1990): 103.

Hannah, L. "The Database: Getting to Know You." *The Computing Teacher* (June 1987): 16–23.

Harris, Richard. *Understanding Desktop Publishing.* San Francisco, Calif.: Sybex, 1990.

Hodson, Yvonne D., and David Leibelshon. "Creating Databases with Students." *School Library Journal* 32, (May 1986): 12–15.

Hunter, Beverly. "Problem Solving with Databases." *The Computing Teacher* 12 (1985): 20–27.

Kearsley, G., B. Hunter, and M. Furlong. *We Teach with Technology.* Wilsonville, Oreg.: Franklin, Beedle, & Associates, 1992.

Kramer, Felix. "Warm Hearts/Cold Type: Desktop Publishing Arrives." *Computers in Human Services* 8, no. 1 (1991): 119.

Lathrop, Ann. "*Online and CD-ROM Databases in School Libraries:* Readings." *Libraries Unlimited, Database Searching Series* no. 2 (1989): 361–66.

Lynch, George. *ClarisWorks Step by Step: Windows Version 4.0 Word Processing, Databases, Spreadsheets, Graphics.* Gilroy, Calif.: Computer Literacy Press, 1997.

Marschalek, Douglas. "The National Gallery of Art Laserdisk and Accompanying Database: A Means to Enhance Art Instruction." *Art Education* 44, no. 3 (May 1, 1991): 48.

McIntyre, D. R.; Hao-Che, Pu; and Francis G. Wolff. "Use of Software Tools in Teaching

Relational Database Design." *Computers & Education* 24, no. 4 (1995): 279.

Mittlefehlt, Bill. "Social Studies: Problem Solving with Databases." *The Computing Teacher* 18, no. 5 (February 1991): 54–55.

Mohan, C., and H. Pirahesh. "Parallelism in Relational Database Management Systems." *IBM Systems Journal* 33, no. 2 (1994): 2.

Naisbitt, J. *Megatrends.* New York: Warner, 1982.

O'Leary, Mick. "Online Comes of Age." *Online* 21, no. 1 (January–February 1997): 10–14, 16–20.

Peck, Jacqueline K. and Sharon V. Hughes. "So Much Success. . . from a First-Grade Database Project!" *Computers in the Schools* 13, no. 1–2 (1997): 109–16.

PC/Computing. *Microsoft Office 97* 10, no. 1 (1997): 87.

Pfaffenberger, Bryan. *Democratizing Information: Online Databases and Rise of End-User Searching.* Boston, Mass.: G.K. Hall, 1990.

Pierman, Dennis F. "Myths and Realities of Desktop Publishing. *"Association Management* 45, no. 10 (October 1, 1993): 105.

Rae, John. "Getting to Grips with Database Design: A Step-By-Step Approach." *Computers & Education* 14, no. 6 (1990): 281.

Rather, Stephen. "The Database Dilemma. Flat-file or Relational Database—Which One Is Right for You?" *Direct Marketing* 54, no. 11 (March 1, 1992): 16.

Robinette, Michelle. "Top 10 Uses for ClarisWorks in the One-Computer Classroom." *Learning and Leading with Technology* 24, no. 2 (October 1996): 37–40.

Seiter, Charles. "Databases That Work." *Macworld* 11, no. 1 (January 1, 1994): 140.

Stewart, Dorothy. "Materials on Reform of Teacher Education in the ERIC Database." *Journal of Teacher Education* 41, no. 2 (March 1, 1990): 63.

Townsend, J. J. *Introduction to Databases.* Carmel, Ind.: Que Corporation, 1992.

Wakerfield, A. P. "Creating and Using a Database of Children's Literature." *Reading Teacher* 48, no. 4 (December/January 1994–1995): 366–367.

Watson, J. *Teaching Thinking Skills with Databases.* Eugene, Oreg.: International Society for Technology in Education, 1991.

Watts, William. "The Brave New World of Desktop Publishing." *Computers and the Humanities* 26, no. 5/6 (December 1, 1992): 457.

Weib, J. H. "Teaching Mathematics with Technology: Data Base Programs in Mathematics Classroom." *Arithmetic Teacher* 37, no. 5 (January 1990): 38–40.

White, Charles S. "Developing Information-Processing Skills through Structured Activities with a Computerized File-Management Program." *Journal of Educational Computing Research* 3 (1987): 355–75.

Yu, Clement, and Weiyi Meng. "Confronting Database Complexities." *IEEE Software* 11, no. 3 (May 1, 1994): 6.

Spreadsheets and Integrated Programs

6

Objectives

Upon completing this chapter, you will be able to:

1. Define spreadsheet, integrated software, cell, windowing, macro, mail merge, and logical functions;
2. Describe the basic features and functions of spreadsheets and integrated programs;
3. Explain how spreadsheets and integrated programs operate;
4. Evaluate different spreadsheet software and integrated programs based on standard criteria; and
5. Utilize and create a repertoire of spreadsheet activities for the classroom.

Historical Overview

In this chapter, we examine the spreadsheet, one of the earliest applications of the microcomputer. We start with a short historical discussion and then explore what a spreadsheet is and how it operates.

In the early 1970s, the microcomputer was used primarily by hackers and hobbyists. This all changed when Dan Bricklin, a Harvard student, and Robert Frankston, an MIT student, combined efforts to create the first spreadsheet, *VisiCalc*, introduced in 1979. *VisiCalc*, primarily designed for microcomputers, had a small grid size and limited features. Because the Apple Computer was the only computer that could run *VisiCalc*, it became the first computer to be accepted by business users. *VisiCalc* served as a prototype for many other programs, such as *LogicCalc* and *Plannercalc*, designed for microcomputers. Within a decade, the spreadsheets improved vastly, offering more features (such as the ability to create graphic displays), faster execution speeds, and a larger grid size.

In 1982, *Lotus 1-2-3*, Lotus Development, initiated a new generation and became the leading spreadsheet. It was the first integrated spreadsheet, meaning that it combined several different programs so that information could be presented in different formats. Later versions of spreadsheets had extended capabilities: a communication component, expanded spreadsheet size, and word processing. The word processor feature let the user easily explain the figures presented in the spreadsheet, while the communication component let computers communicate with each other over telephone lines.

Spreadsheets

Every year people across the United States prepare their income tax forms. College students request government loans and families determine their budgets based on their income in order to predict their annual expenses. The businessperson keeps a record of transactions to determine profits and liabilities, while the scientist performs mathematical calculations on experimental data. A teacher enters pupils' test scores and assignments, performs calculations, and makes inferences about the numerical data. To accomplish their various tasks, these people use worksheets or electronic spreadsheets. A spreadsheet is "a graphical representation of an accountant's worksheet, replete with rows and columns for recording labels (headings and subheadings) and values (Pfaffenberger, 1997).

Components of a Spreadsheet

Every electronic spreadsheet is organized in a similar manner with two axes, rows, and columns. Figure 6.1 shows *Microsoft Excel*'s blank spreadsheet (Windows version).

Figure 6.1
Spreadsheet from
Microsoft Excel
(Windows version)
Box shots reprinted with
permission from
© Microsoft Corporation

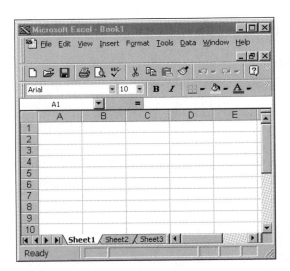

The letters across the top are used to identify the columns and the numbers along the side identify the rows.[1] The intersection of each row and column forms a box, called a **cell.** A cell is identified by its column letter and row number. For example, in Figure 6.2, cell A1 is in the top left corner, and cell B1 is one cell to the right. To locate cell D4, you would count over to column D and then count down four cells to row 4. You would select cell D4 by clicking the cursor in its box. When selected, a cell shows a heavy border and its name appears in the indicator box above the A label.

---

[1]Spreadsheets can differ in the system used to label these rows and columns.

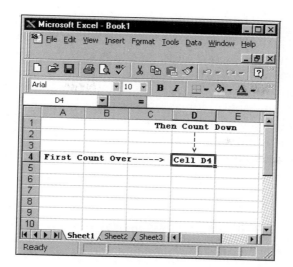

Figure 6.2
Spreadsheet cells
from *Microsoft Excel*
Box shots reprinted with
permission from
© Microsoft Corporation

Three types of information can be entered into any single cell: number, text, or formula. The ability to enter formulas onto the spreadsheet makes it a powerful tool for business, science, and education.

How a Spreadsheet Operates

This section will explain how an electronic spreadsheet operates. For illustrative purposes, let's use *Microsoft Excel* (Windows version) and a grade book example, a popular educational usage of the spreadsheet.

To use a *manual* spreadsheet for grade records, you would enter the students' names and their quiz scores. Let's say there are eight students and three quiz scores (Fig. 6.3). Next, using

Name	Quiz 1	Quiz 2	Quiz 3	Total	Average
1. Apple, Richard	99	97	86	282	94
2. Berger, Karen	85	82	76	243	81
3. Collins, Nancy	78	65	67	210	70
4. Diaz, Robert	88	85	79	252	84
5. Frank, Scott	98	88	81	267	89
6. O'Brien, Jeff	99	96	78	273	91
7. Sharp, David	99	94	95	288	96
8. Winters, Philip	88	87	83	258	86

Figure 6.3
Teacher's grade roster

paper, pencil, and a calculator, you would add Richard Apple's scores, obtaining a total of 282. You would record the answer in the total column and then divide this total by 3 for an average of 94. You would continue this manual procedure for each subsequent student. If you made an error or changed a score, you would have to recalculate everything. An electronic spreadsheet offers many advantages over a manual one. Let's open *Microsoft Excel.* You see a blank spreadsheet (Fig. 6.1). You enter the same headings—Name, Quiz 1, Quiz 2, Quiz 3, and Average.[2] Then you type the eight pupils' names, name first, and their respective quiz scores. While entering this information, you can easily make changes, corrections, deletions, or additions. You also can use the sort function to alphabetize the list of students by last names. When you're finished, your screen resembles the one in Figure 6.4.

Figure 6.4
Grade book roster in
Microsoft Excel.
Box shots reprinted with
permission from
© Microsoft Corporation

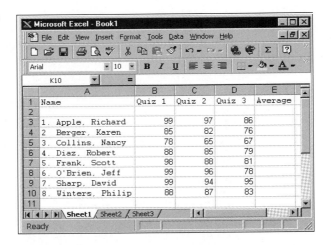

The beauty of any spreadsheet is that each cell serves as an individual calculator that does computations quickly and accurately. For example, to determine each student's average score, select cell E3 and type in *Microsoft Excel*'s formula tool bar: =(B3+C3+D3)/3. The spreadsheet calculates the mean for numbers 99, 97, and 86 and records the answer 94 instantaneously in cell E3. (The = sign that begins the formula (B3+C3+D3)/3 tells the computer to compute an average from cell B3 to D3; see Fig. 6.5.)

---

[2]It is unnecessary to have a total column in this electronic spreadsheet.

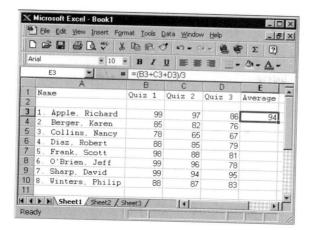

Figure 6.5
Grade book roster
with average
Box shots reprinted with
permission from
© Microsoft Corporation

To calculate the averages for the remaining pupils, you would not have to rewrite the formula, since every spreadsheet has a way of copying the original formula. In *Microsoft Excel*, you could use the Fill handle to select cells E3 through E10. The rest of the students' averages would be automatically displayed in the appropriate cells as shown in the highlighted cells in column E of Figure 6.6.

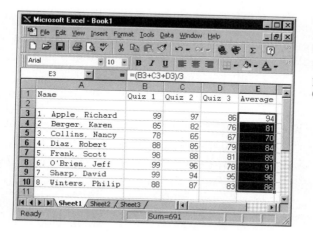

Figure 6.6
Completed roster
Box shots reprinted with
permission from
© Microsoft Corporation

Furthermore, *Microsoft Excel* has more than 100 functions, or shortcuts, that save you from typing in formulas. A function is a built-in software routine that performs a task in the program. To apply the average function, click on Edit formula (=) in the formula tool bar and then select the average function from the pull-down menu that appears (Fig. 6.7).

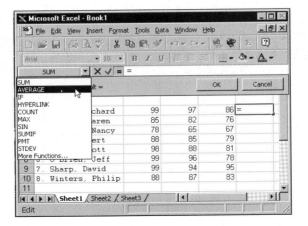

Figure 6.7
Average function
(Windows version)
Box shots reprinted with
permission from
© Microsoft Corporation

Every spreadsheet has its own collection of built-in functions, ranging from *sum* to *average* to *sine*. These functions make the use and application of formulas very quick and easy. You simply select the function and it is pasted into the spreadsheet. *ClarisWorks* has more than ninety built-in functions, while *The Cruncher* (Davidson) has twenty-three. Generally, the more built-in or pre-determined functions, the more versatile the spreadsheet.

Why Use an Electronic Spreadsheet?

There are many reasons for a teacher to choose a computerized spreadsheet over a manual worksheet. The electronic spreadsheet is faster and more flexible than the traditional methods of numerical calculation and data prediction, permitting you to change the information on the screen as often as you want. A noncomputerized spreadsheet with a matrix of more than twenty-five rows and columns is cumbersome, whereas a computerized spreadsheet with a matrix of thousands of data entries performs instant calculations. Furthermore, on a computerized spreadsheet, you can access any number instantaneously, simply by pressing a key or two. Another major feature of a spreadsheet is its ability to recalculate; that is, when you change the number in a cell, the spreadsheet automatically recalculates the other values. The recalculation feature of an electronic spreadsheet lets you employ what-if analysis strategies, used to answer questions such as "What would happen if Elena scored a 90 on this exam instead of a 60?" Another question commonly asked by students is, "What grade will I achieve in the course if I earn an 80 on the final exam?" Most homeowners ask, "If the interest rates drop from 8 to 7 percent, what will my mortgage payments be?" As a spreadsheet user, you would only have to enter the score or rate and see the effects or answers immediately.

There are still more advantages to the electronic spreadsheet. It lets you display and print the output in many visually appealing ways. Also, as long as you enter the formula correctly, your data will be accurate. Spreadsheets have the invaluable copy function that lets you effortlessly repeat a formula once it's been defined. Needless to say, the electronic spreadsheet has enormous advantage over a manual spreadsheet in terms of saving time and increasing productivity.

Now let's look at some of the basic features of the spreadsheet to see which ones would be most useful for the classroom teacher.

Basic Features of a Spreadsheet

Protected and Hidden Cells

Many spreadsheets have safeguards built into the program that protect a group of cells from being altered or erased. For example, you may have a formula that you want to keep safe from accidental erasure or deletion. Even when you remove this cell protection so that you can view the data, there may be a command you can give to prevent accidental erasure of data. In addition to this option, some spreadsheets allow you to take confidential information and hide it from view, even blocking it out in your printed reports. On a good spreadsheet, you should be able to retrieve easily the information from these hidden cells. Some spreadsheets require users to employ a secret password to access data.

Logical Functions

Powerful spreadsheets have logical functions that evaluate whether a statement is true or false. For example, let's say a teacher created a grade book spreadsheet with four exam grades and an average score for each student. He now wants to invite into honors math only those students who received averages of 97 or above. Since the first average is in cell F4, he would enter a formula in G4 and repeat this formula for every student's score. With the spreadsheet program *Lotus 1-2-3*, this formula would read as follows: @If(F4>96,100,0).

The formula lets a 100 represent the honors class and a 0 represent the standard class. When the spreadsheet does its calculation, it checks to see whether the value entered (F4) is greater than 96, and if it is, the spreadsheet will print the first option (100) in cell G4. If the average in F4 is lower than 97, the spreadsheet will print the second option (0) in G4. All the students with 100s meet the requirements for honors class.

Date and Time Function

The date and time function is another advanced feature. It automatically calculates how many days have elapsed between two dates in spreadsheet cells.

Macros

Macros are a group of routines or commands combined into one or two keystrokes. You can play these routines back at the touch of a key or two. This is how it works. First, you determine what keys you want to use, such as key F12. Then, you decide what the key will generate; for instance, F12 could generate a name, address, and telephone number. Finally, you program the macro so that when F12 is pressed, it automatically enters the name, address, and telephone number in the chosen cell. Some macros execute their commands to a certain point, wait for the input, and then continue with the command execution.

Graphing

Many spreadsheets generate bar or pie graphs based on the information contained in the spreadsheet. These graphs are great visual aids because as the data changes, you can see the corresponding changes in the graphs.

Memory

When you enter data into a spreadsheet, you want to know how much memory remains so that you don't run out at a crucial point. A spreadsheet that has a running indicator of the memory available is better than one that simply flashes a message once the program is out of memory.

Cell Names

Some programs let you label the cells with words instead of the short cell address. For instance, if you record profit in Column C, Rows 3 through 15, you can tell the program to call these cells *Profit*. Then you can use the name *Profit* in any formula that refers to this range.

Windows

When you work on a large spreadsheet, you cannot see the whole spreadsheet on the screen but must use the cursor to scroll between sections. If you need to compare figures on different screens, it is helpful to be able to split the screen into two or three sections, each windowing a different part of the work, so that you can see your current location in the spreadsheet, see the effect your work has on cells in different locations, and easily compare figures from different sections. If the spreadsheet does not have a split-screen option, an alternative feature is a spreadsheet with the ability to set fixed titles. A fixed title option lets you keep designated rows and columns permanently on the screen, even as you scroll through sections.

Attached Notes

Some spreadsheets can attach notes, much as you would attach Post-it notes to your written work.

Editing and Sorting

When you make a mistake, the spreadsheet should offer a simple way of correcting the error. You should be able to insert and delete rows and columns. You should be able to quickly widen or narrow the spreadsheet's columns to meet your entry requirements. After the information is edited to your satisfaction, you should be able to sort it alphabetically and numerically.

Templates

It is very useful to have a spreadsheet that offers ready-to-use templates. A template is simply a spreadsheet that contains no data but has selected functions chosen for certain cells. You fill the appropriate cells of this spreadsheet with your own data. When you enter data in cells for which formulas are selected, the computer makes the calculations and the results are displayed in the appropriate cells. When you are finished, you save this altered spreadsheet under another name so that the template can be used for another spreadsheet. You can also create your own templates.

On-Line Help

On-line help allows you to get help from the computer while using the program.

Advanced Features of a Spreadsheet

The more powerful spreadsheets can link other spreadsheets, have database capabilities, can chart or graph, and can print sideways. Linking spreadsheets allows you to get information from one spreadsheet and pull this information directly into your current sheet (this complicated feature is not meant for novices). *Lotus 1-2-3* has database capabilities, but these functions are not comparable to those of a database program; what they offer is a spreadsheet approach to dealing with database functions. Generally, printing is limited to 80 columns, or 136 if you use compressed type, but sometimes you need more room to fit all the columns on one sheet of paper. The best way to accomplish this is by using a utility program that turns the printout on its side. A few spreadsheet programs offer this convenience. The most advanced spreadsheets offer special fonts, multiple dimensions, sound, and add-on software.

Copying Command

The copying command on a spreadsheet copies the contents of a group of cells from one column to another, replicating formulas, values, and labels. The ability to copy and move from one location to another saves time on data entry. For instance, instead of retyping a formula, you quickly can copy it from one cell in the spreadsheet and then paste it into any other cells in which you need to use the same formula (Fig. 6.6).

How to Select a Good Spreadsheet for the Classroom

The spreadsheet is not only a management tool; it's also a tool for learning in the classroom. Not only can you use it as a grade book, but you can also use it to help students explore mathematical relationships and formulas, improve their problem solving, and delve into social studies or scientific investigation. It can keep track of money from fund-raising activities such as magazine drives. It can be used to calculate sports statistics and do comparison shopping. Classroom surveys can be recorded and calculated using a spreadsheet. The students can test various hypotheses and do what-if analyses. You can teach the class about stocks and have the students keep track of their portfolio's performance. The students can learn about the weather and use the spreadsheet to store data about such items as temperature, precipitation, and barometer reading. In reality, you can use the spreadsheet to do activities that range from statistics to energy consumption to simple science experiments.

Spreadsheets were originally designed for adults, but a handful of programs are suitable for the classroom. *ClarisWorks for Kids* is devised specifically for the elementary school child grades K–5 and *The Cruncher* is for grades 3 and up, while the high schools utilize *Microsoft Works, ClarisWorks, Microsoft Excel,* and *Quattro Pro 7* (Corel).

Choosing spreadsheet software for the classroom is a six-step process: (1) determine the hardware compatibility; (2) study the program's features; (3) test how easy it is to use the program; (4) examine the program's built-in functions; (5) investigate the program's consumer value; and (6) check out the technical support.

Hardware Compatibility

What computers are available in the school: old Apple IIGS, Windows-based machines or power Macintoshs? How much memory do these machines have? Is there enough memory to accommodate the spreadsheets the students are using? How many disk drives are available for each machine? (Generally, spreadsheet programs need a hard drive and a floppy disk drive.)

General Features

Ask these questions: How is the labeling done on the spreadsheet? Can you easily center the labels or move them to the left or right? How does the spreadsheet handle decimal points and dollar signs? If you make a mistake, can you effortlessly modify the cell or cells? Can the width of the columns be easily adjusted? Can you protect the cells from being accidentally erased? Can you hide certain cells and not print them out? How does the spreadsheet show negative values? How many logical functions does the spreadsheet have? Does it have a date and time function? Can you easily calculate how many days have passed between two dates entered in the spreadsheet? Does the spreadsheet have macros? Can you generate bar or pie graphs? How does the spreadsheet indicate how much memory it has left? Does the spreadsheet have windows so that you can split the screen into two or three sections, each displaying a different part of the work? Can you link this spreadsheet with other spreadsheets or arrange the information in the spreadsheet alphabetically or numerically? Does the spreadsheet have enough columns and rows to meet the classroom needs?

Ease of Use

The spreadsheet is much more difficult to use than a database program because it involves working with numbers and formulas. Therefore, it is imperative that you choose a spreadsheet program that gives on-line help that can be accessed quickly. *The Cruncher* fits these criteria with a step-by-step tutorial and on-line help. Figure 6.8 shows a screen from this tutorial.

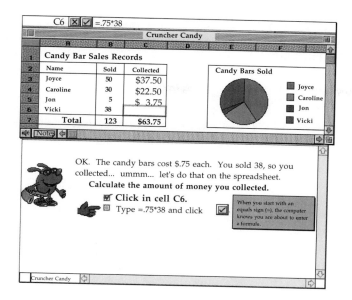

Figure 6.8
The Cruncher
Reprinted with permission
of Davidson and
Associates.

ClarisWorks for Kids, designed specifically for grades K–5, has a word processor, spreadsheet, and a painting component. The program lets the child quickly build graphs, slide shows, and pictures. It is packaged with clip art images, sounds, movies and templates that duplicate what the children are learning in school. This program offers simplicity for the younger child, and it has text-to-speech functions, which aid the user (Fig. 6.9).

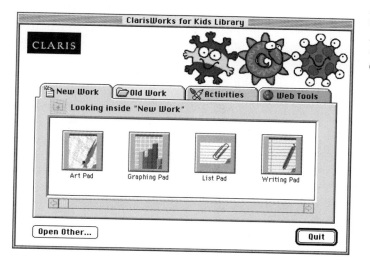

Figure 6.9
ClarisWorks for Kids
Courtesy of FileMaker, Inc.

Ask these questions: How fast can you edit the cells and enter the data? Can you smoothly delete and insert rows or columns? Is it hard to copy formulas from one row to another? How do you move the cursor from one cell to another?

Built-in Functions

What special functions do the students need to use in the class? For example, when students use the spreadsheet, is it to calculate sums, averages, or standard deviations?

Consumer Value

Software is expensive, so cost is an important consideration. *The Cruncher* costs under $100, while *Microsoft Excel* sells for more than $250. Does the software company let you make a backup copy. Some software companies offer on-site licenses so that you can freely make copies of the software for in-house use. Other manufacturers distribute lab packs that let you purchase software at a reduced price.)

Support

The software company's willingness to support its product is an extremely important factor. Ask these questions: Can you call someone on the telephone at the company and get immediate help? Do you have to spend excessive time waiting on the phone? Is the technical support toll free or are you charged by the minute? Do you have to pay a yearly fee to receive any type of assistance? Does the software package come with a tutorial? Is the manual readable—with an index? Does the program have templates?

Use the checklist on the following page when selecting a spreadsheet.

Teacher Practice

The following exercises are meant to be used in conjunction with any spreadsheet. If a computer lab is not available, simply read through this section to get an idea of how you would set up a spreadsheet. The first exercise introduces you step by step to a spreadsheet program. You will need two disks: a program disk and a formatted disk to store the information.

1. Load the spreadsheet program into the computer.
2. Format a blank disk with the operating system that the spreadsheet program accepts.
3. Create a new file and give it the name *Grade Book.*
4. Begin by entering labels across the first row of the spreadsheet. Starting at cell B1, type the following labels: *Exam 1, Exam 2, Exam 3, Exam 4, Exam 5.* Place the label *Exam 1* in cell B1, *Exam 2* in C1, *Exam 3* in D1, *Exam 4* in E1, and *Exam 5* in F1. Leaving cells A1 and A2 empty,

SPREADSHEET CHECKLIST

Directions: Examine the following items and determine which ones you feel are important for your class situation. Evaluate your Spreadsheet and place an X on each line where the software meets your needs.

Program Name ————————   **Manufacturer** ——————   **Grade Level** ————

A. Hardware
 __ 1. Memory needed
 __ 2. Computer compatibility
 __ 3. Printer compatibility
 __ 4. Hard disk space

B. Features
 __ 1. Protected cells
 __ 2. Hidden cells
 __ 3. Sorting
      __a. Alphabetical
      __b. Numerical
 __ 4. Windowing
 __ 5. Macros
 __ 6. Formulas
 __ 7. Logical operators
 __ 8. Fixed titles
 __ 9. Transfer to word processing
 __ 10. Link to other spreadsheets
 __ 11. Integration with database
 __ 12. Name ranges
 __ 13. Graphing
 __ 14. Flexibility of printing
 __ 15. Manual recalculation
 __ 16. Sound

C. Editing
 __ 1. Deleting and adding columns
 __ 2. Changing column width
 __ 3. Copying labels and formulas
 __ 4. Formatting of cells
 __ 5. Erasure

D. Ease of Use
 __ 1. Help screens
 __ 2. Tutorial disks
 __ 3. Quick printer setup
 __ 4. Easy editing of cells
 __ 5. Simple command names
 __ 6. Quick cell movement
 __ 7. Warning questions

E. Consumer Value
 __ 1. Cost
 __ 2. On-site license
 __ 3. Lab packs

F. Support
 __ 1. Technical
 __ 2. Tutorial material
 __ 3. Readable manual
 __ 4. Templates

Rating Scale

Rate the spreadsheet program by placing a check in the appropriate box

Excellent ___   Very Good ___   Good ___   Fair ___   Poor ___

Comments

put the label *Pupils* in Cell A3. These labels will describe the contents of the cells. The spreadsheet should look similar to the one in Figure 6.10, which is in *Microsoft Excel.*

5. Starting at A5, enter the pupils' last names: Smith; A6, Sharp; A7, Garcia; A8, Raj; A9, Friedman; A10, Washington; A11, Reilly; A12, Hughes; A13, Sherrin; and A14, Jones.

Figure 6.10
Microsoft Excel
spreadsheet
Screen shot from Microsoft
Excel reprinted with
permission from Microsoft
Corporation.

	A	B	C	D	E	F
1		EXAM 1	EXAM 2	EXAM 3	EXAM 4	EXAM 5
2						
3	PUPILS					
4						

6. Using the sort or arrange function, alphabetize the names and align each name on the left side of the cell.

7. Now enter the data in the grade book. Enter Friedman's Exam 1 score as 89 in cell B5, his Exam 2 score as 46 in cell C5, Exam 3 as 69 in D5, Exam 4 as 74 in cell E5, and Exam 5 as 35 in cell F5. Now continue entering the exam scores for the remaining students; the spreadsheet should look like the one in Figure 6.11.

	A	B	C	D	E	F
1		EXAM 1	EXAM 2	EXAM 3	EXAM 4	EXAM 5
2						
3	PUPILS					
4						
5	FRIEDMAN	89	46	69	74	35
6	GARCIA	45	23	75	75	34
7	HUGHES	89	43	67	67	34
8	JONES	99	45	75	75	40
9	RAJ	98	50	73	73	39
10	REILLY	56	50	67	67	32
11	SHARP	98	45	72	71	39
12	SHERRIN	78	46	73	72	34
13	SMITH	99	45	74	74	40
14	WASHINGTON	87	45	72	72	34
15						

Figure 6.11
Microsoft Excel spreadsheet with grades
Screen shot from Microsoft Excel reprinted with permission from Microsoft Corporation.

8. Next, type the label *AVERAGE* in cell G1. You want to enter a formula to calculate the average score for Friedman's five exams. Begin by putting the cursor on cell G5 and write the formula. There will be a variation in these formulas; for instance, if you are using *Claris-Works*, the formula is =AVERAGE(B5..F5). In *Microsoft Excel*, the formula is =AVERAGE(B5:F5). After you enter the formula, the average (62.6) should appear instantaneously in cell G5.

9. Next, use the copy function to calculate the averages for the remaining students (Fig. 6.12).
10. Learn how to save the data on the formatted disk and print it out for inspection. What follows are four ready-to-use classroom activities that test the students' ability to use successfully the different features of the spreadsheet.

	A		G
1			AVERAGE
2			
3	PUPILS		
4			
5	FRIEDMAN		62.6
6	GARCIA		50.4
7	HUGHES		60
8	JONES		66.8
9	RAJ		66.6
10	REILLY		54.4
11	SHARP		65
12	SHERRIN		60.6
13	SMITH		66.4
14	WASHINGTON		62
15			

Figure 6.12
Calculating averages
Screen shot from Microsoft Excel reprinted with permission from Microsoft Corporation.

Classroom Applications

▼   I. Math/Science   ▼

Objectives
Students will learn about speed and how to use a spreadsheet to do simple calculations.

Procedure
1. Discuss how fast an automobile can travel and the relationship between distance, miles, and time.
2. Have the students create a spreadsheet similar to the one in Figure 6.13.
3. Next, pose the following question: What is the distance covered when traveling so many hours at a given speed?
4. Have the students type a formula in cell C2 that multiplies cell A2 by cell B2. Then copy this formula for cells C3 to C11.
5. After the students have accomplished this, have them examine the results and determine the answers to questions that you and they pose. If there are not enough computers, let the students use their calculators and a pencil and paper to complete this task.

Figure 6.13
Speed spreadsheet
Screen shot from Microsoft
Excel reprinted with
permission from Microsoft
Corporation.

	A	B	C
1	RATE	TIME	DISTANCE
2	25	0.5	
3	30	1	
4	35	2	
5	40	2	
6	45	3	
7	50	3	
8	55	4	
9	60	5	
10	65	6	
11	70	7	

Variations

You can generate other spreadsheets that would enable students to answer the following questions:

1. How much time does it take to travel a specified number of miles at a certain speed?
2. How much distance is covered when traveling so many hours at a given speed?

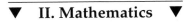

▼ II. Mathematics ▼

Objective

Students will use a spreadsheet to keep track of expenses.

Procedure

1. Discuss the following problem with the students: The $10 Computer Club is having a fundraiser to buy software for its club. The cost of the software is $700 and the club members expect to sell three raffle tickets apiece. They are selling these tickets for $3 each. Figure 6.14 shows how many tickets each student in the club sells.
2. Have each student create the same spreadsheet and then finish this table by calculating the average for each student.
3. Tell the students to use the logical function to determine how many club members sold six or more tickets on a daily basis. Was the $10 Computer Club able to buy its software?

Variation

1. Change the totals in the spreadsheet for any two students not selling at least three raffle tickets daily to three raffle tickets and record the value the spreadsheet recalculates.
2. Have the students compute the averages again if the raffle ticket price were raised to $5.

Figure 6.14
Ticket sales
spreadsheet

$10 CLUB	\multicolumn{7}{c}{DAYS OF THE WEEK}	AVERAGE
	1	2	3	4	5	6	7	
1. Adams	6	4	6	2	3	4	5	
2. Barrett	5	4	4	5	0	0	3	
3. Devlin	5	2	6	2	6	1	2	
4. Johnson	2	1	4	4	2	1	3	
5. Mason	3	0	0	0	10	0	2	
6. Garcia	1	2	3	4	3	2	1	
7. Youngblood	2	3	4	5	5	7	8	
8. Sands	1	3	2	5	0	4	3	

▼   III. Home Economics   ▼

Objective

Students will use a spreadsheet to keep track of their expenditures for six months.

Procedure

1. Have each student record in a spreadsheet expenditures for the ten items shown in Figure 6.15 during a six-month period.

EXPENSES	JAN.	FEB.	MARCH	APRIL	MAY	JUNE
Food						
Telephone						
Utilites						
Rent						
Automobile Loan						
Insurance						
Entertainment						
Clothes						
Medical Bills						
Savings						

Figure 6.15
Expenditures spreadsheet

2. Have students use the sum formula to total each column.
3. Ask them to add an additional column to keep track of six-month totals.

4. Change values in the completed table so that the students can answer "what if" questions such as "If I cut down on my entertainment, how much more can I save a year?"

Variation

From the savings row, create a spreadsheet that shows how much an initial deposit of $200 would grow at different interest rates and at different intervals of time.

▼   IV. The Pendulum   ▼

Objectives

Students will practice predicting, changing variables, and estimating and learn how to use a formula in a spreadsheet.

Materials

You will need string, thumbtacks, and weights.

Procedure

Before beginning, students must understand how the pendulum works.

1. Have each student enter different weights, lengths, and amplitude values. The objective is to determine what affects the pendulum's period. A period is simply the time it takes the pendulum to swing from point A to point B and then back to point A again.
2. Ask each student to create a table like the one in Figure 6.16.

Pendulum Investigations			
Length	Weight	Amplitude	Period

Figure 6.16
Pendulum spreadsheet

3. Have students use a formula to figure each period for the pendulum.

Spreadsheet Versatility

There are numerous ways to use a spreadsheet in everyday life: comparison shopping, calorie counting, calculating income tax returns, figuring baseball statistics, and budgeting. The teacher can use a spreadsheet for a grade book and as a study aid for history, for physics experiments, and for accounting problems. The students can calculate averages and standard deviations for statistics problems and even keep track of their own grades.

Since you now have a background in spreadsheets, let's turn our attention to the integrated program.

Integrated Programs

Previously, we discussed three popular applications of the computer: the word processor, the database, and the spreadsheet. Each application was dedicated to a separate task: The word processor created and edited documents, the database organized information, and the spreadsheet worked with numerical data.

Once you are comfortable with these individual programs, you may require software that allows for the free interchange of data among programs. For example, you may need to take budget information stored in the spreadsheet and transfer it to a letter that you're writing on the word processor. Regardless of the software you have, you can accomplish this task by going through seven laborious steps: (1) write the report on the word processor, leaving space for the spreadsheet table; (2) print a hard copy of the report; (3) close the word processing application and open the spreadsheet; (4) enter data into the spreadsheet's cells and manipulate it; (5) generate a printout of this spreadsheet; (6) use actual scissors to cut the spreadsheet printout and paste the results onto the word processor hard copy; (7) photocopy the report. However, cutting and pasting among applications in this way is a time-consuming chore.

Stand-alone programs are generally not capable of communicating with other applications. There are many aspects of programming that limit the ability of these programs to address one another, and one important limitation is the differences among their command structures. For example, *The Cruncher* spreadsheet cannot electronically transfer information into the *Bank Street Writer* word processor because of their different commands.

The integrated program, on the other hand, includes in its most common configuration a word processor, a database, and a spreadsheet that can communicate with one another. *Lotus 1-2-3*, a pioneer in its field, was developed in the early 1980s as a spreadsheet. It was one of the first programs to offer as a part of its design a database with some graphics capabilities. After the success of *Lotus 1-2-3*, many programs followed its example. *SuperCalc 3* integrated database, spreadsheet, and graphics. *Microsoft Works* combined spreadsheet with file management and word processing. Integrated programs, such as *Microsoft Works*, expanded to include more applications such as telecommunications and graphics. *ClarisWorks* Figure 6.17, another popular integrated program, offers word processor, spreadsheet, database, manager, communications, painting and drawing, presentation, Internet access and Web design capabilities.

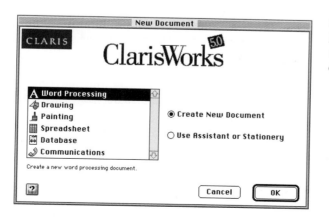

Figure 6.17
ClarisWorks
Courtesy of FileMaker, Inc.

The integrated program is a single program with applications that share a similar command structure. Because of similarity of command structure across the various applications, the program is easy to learn. Since each module is a component of one program, data is transferred seamlessly. You can effortlessly combine tables with text, for example. Finally, integrated programs cost much less than the several stand-alone programs that would offer similar applications. Nevertheless, this type of program does have two disadvantages: The integrated program typically needs more memory and has a weaker module than the stand-alone program. For example, the word processing application in an integrated program could have more limited functions than those in the stand-alone word processing package.

How Does an Integrated Program Work?

Let's use the *Microsoft Works* tutorial example, which creates a financial report on *Pie-in-the-Sky Bakers*, to examine how the components of an integrated program work together.

1. The tutorial creates a database that records pies ordered and delivered as shown in Figure 6.18.

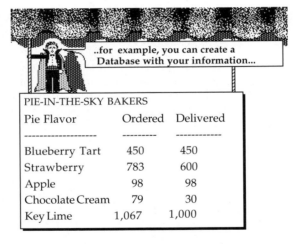

Figure 6.18
Microsoft Works tutorial
Screen shot from Microsoft ® Works © 1986–1990 Microsoft Corporation. Reprinted with permission from Microsoft Corporation.

2. The program copies the number of pies delivered and transfers these data into the spreadsheet for manipulation. Next, the program calculates the total sales for each type of pie sold, and the report appears on the next screen (Fig. 6.19).

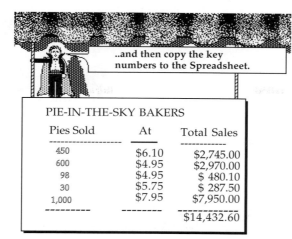

Figure 6.19
Calculating total
sales
Screen shot with Microsoft
® Works © 1986–1990
Microsoft Corporation.
Reprinted with permission
from Microsoft
Corporation.

3. Using the chart function of the integrated package, the tutorial represents the data graphically as shown in Figure 6.20.

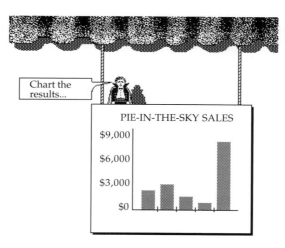

Figure 6.20
Charting the results
Screen shot from Microsoft
® Works © 1986–1990
Microsoft Corporation.
Reprinted with permission
from Microsoft
Corporation.

4. Next, the tutorial uses the word processing program to write a letter about the August sales. This report highlights the Key Lime pie sales and illustrates these sales with the chart created in step 3 (Fig. 6.21).

Figure 6.21
Writing the sales report

Screen shot from Microsoft ® Works © 1986–1990 Microsoft Corporation. Reprinted with permission from Microsoft Corporation.

5. The report is printed or sent by modem to another microcomputer (Fig. 6.22) or mainframe.[3] The recipient of the report can print it or just look at it on the screen.

Figure 6.22
Modeming the report

Screen shot from Microsoft ® Works © 1986–1990 Microsoft Corporation. Reprinted with permission from Microsoft Corporation.

Alternatives to an Integrated Program

What are the alternatives to integrated programs?

1. You can use the stand-alone program as it is and cut and paste when necessary. If you are fortunate, your stand-alone program may have all the database or word processing capabilities that you require, even if they are limited.
2. You can retype your data into the separate applications. This sounds like a reasonable alternative, but it requires much typing and opens your data to errors since it is very easy to make a typo. Also, any time you change a number in one application, you will have to retype it in the other applications.

---

[3] A modem is a device that attaches to the computer and sends its output over the telephone lines (see Chapter 11).

3. You can file share, which permits access to the files of the other programs. Because there is little standardization among the files of programs, these files cannot be directly read. If you want to read them, you need a special translator program like *MacLink Plus* (DataViz), which lets you input a file of one type, make it conform to the file structure of another type, and then output this transformed file. Unfortunately, these translator programs are not available for all software programs, and sometimes in the process of tranforming the data it may lose its formatting.

In conclusion, if you do not need to transfer data among applications, a basic stand-alone application that fits your computer needs should suffice. However, if you are going to do work in which you need to transfer information from one application to another, you should buy an integrated software package or perhaps try a software suite.

Software Suites

In the 1990s the software companies started a new trend with the introduction of software suites. A software suite is a package of individual programs designed to work together to share data easily and quickly. The suite consists of stand-alone applications that are sold individually. Each application works together through special links that create a mock integration. Three popular examples of suites are: *Corel WordPerfect Suite 7, Microsoft Office 97, Microsoft Office 98,* and *Lotus SmartSuite*. A suite costs less than the individual pieces of software and they offer more features. For example, *Corel WordPerfect Suite 7* includes the following software: *WordPerfect, Quattro Pro, Corel Presentations, Sidekick, Dashboard,* and *Envoy* as well as 150 fonts and 10,000 clip art images. You can install the entire suite or only the programs that you want.

Similarities and Differences

There are many similarities between an integrated package and a suite. They both enable you to run many programs at once and they are designed to work together. An integrated program and a suite feature a clipboard, a place to store text, graphic, audio, and video clips. You use this clipboard to move data among the suite or integrated programs applications. You copy the data to the clipboard and then paste it into the other applications. Both integrated programs and suites let you write more sophisticated reports and papers because you have access to a variety of programs.

The main difference between a software suite and an integrated program is that the suite's components are full-featured programs and not limited versions. These applications usually started as independent programs that were popular before being combined in a suite. In most cases, a suite is very economical, because the software vendor uses it as an inducement for people to buy their products. It serves as a marketing strategy preventing the user from switching to a new product.

On the negative side, the various components in a suite do not work as smoothly as do those in an integrated program. There are very high hardware requirements to run a suite. The hard disk space, the memory, and the speed of the computer should all be taken into consideration. A suite like *Microsoft Office 97* requires more than 120 MB of hard disk space to install its different components. Additionally, the memory or RAM requirements for smooth running is 16 MB. It is preferable to have a powerful computer with a Pentium chip to take full advantage of the programs' capabilities. Mastering a suite is definitely harder than mastering an integrated program. Expect to spend considerable time and effort if you want to learn more than just the basics.

Features

When you scrutinize an integrated program or suite you are concerned with the same features that you would be when considering separate applications. You should consider the same questions: How rapidly does the database sort? How much time is needed to load a file? How quickly does the spreadsheet calculate? How many columns and rows can you create using the spreadsheet document? Does the word processor have a thesaurus or grammar checker? You should find out how quickly and easily each module in the integrated package or software suite shares data and if the program has mail merge and windowing capabilities.

Mail Merge.   Mail merge, as previously discussed in Chapter 5, gives you the ability to combine the database information with the word processing documents to produce a customized letter or report. In an integrated program, you may have a list of names and addresses in the database and a form letter in the word processor. The integrated program or suite merges the information from these applications to produce a customized letter.

Windowing.   Windowing is the ability to display different parts of a worksheet on the screen so that you can work within each module window simultaneously. For example, one window might display a spreadsheet while another window might display a graph being generated from the spreadsheet. With windowing, you can change numbers in the spreadsheet and watch the effect on the graph as it is redrawn with the new values.

Summary

The electronic spreadsheet, which consists of a matrix of rows and columns intersecting at cells, was developed to handle complicated and tedious calculations. In this chapter, we became familiar with the basic features of a spreadsheet and discussed which features to consider when buying a spreadsheet program for the classroom. We also explored activities for introducing the spreadsheet to students.

In addition, we examined the integrated software package, a group of programs that freely exchange data with each other. In its most common configuration today, these integrated programs include a word processor, database, spreadsheet, telecommunication module, drawing module, and graphics module. Additionally, we discussed the software suite, a bundling of linked stand-alone programs. A mastery test, classroom projects, and suggested readings and references follow. **Be sure to review the annotated list of award-winning spreadsheet and integrated programs in Appendix A.**

Chapter Mastery Test

1. What is a spreadsheet?
2. Give an example of each of the following terms: (a) macro, (b) cell, (c) logical functions, (d) predefined functions, (e) windows.
3. What is the advantage of being able to copy a formula in a spreadsheet?
4. Explain how a spreadsheet can be useful in determining a classroom budget.

5. Describe five features of a spreadsheet and their functions.

6. Choose two important features of a spreadsheet and show how they can be utilized in the classroom.

7. Discuss the factors involved in selecting a spreadsheet for a school district.

8. Explain the advantage of a spreadsheet over a calculator.

9. Give an example of a situation in which an integrated software program has an advantage over a stand-alone program.

10. Explain how an integrated program works.

11. Define windowing and mail merge, and give an example of each.

12. Describe the advantage of using "What if" analysis with a spreadsheet. Give some applications in which this type of comparison would be important.

13. Explain the popularity of software suites. Give your reasons.

14. If you were buying an integrated program, what are some features you would look at before buying?

Classroom Projects

1. Develop a spreadsheet activity for the classroom.

2. Create a spreadsheet similar to the grade book example given in this chapter, but for this example have twelve students take three exams and a final. Calculate the final exam as 40 percent of the grade and the other three exams as 20 percent each.

3. Prepare a review comparing three spreadsheets.

4. Use a spreadsheet to compare the expenses with a devised budget.

5. Outline in a lesson plan format three different ways a spreadsheet would be useful in the classroom.

6. Prepare a report on the integrated programs, comparing their strengths and weaknesses.

7. List the different ways an integrated program would be useful in the school district office.

Suggested Readings and References

Abramovich, Sergei, and Wanda Nabors. "Spreadsheets as Generators of New Meanings in Middle School Algebra." *Computers in the Schools* 13, no. 1–2 (1997): 13–25.

Anderson, Wynema. *Lotus 1-2-3 5.0 for Windows: Applications for Reinforcement.* Cincinnati, Ohio: South-Western Educational Publishing, 1997.

Arad, O. S. "The Spreadsheet Solving Word Problems." *The Computing Teacher* 14, no. 4 (December/January 1986–1987): 13–15, 45.

Aranbright, Deane E. "Mathematical Applications of an Electronic Spreadsheet." *Computers in Mathematics Education.* Reston, Va.: NCTM 1984 Yearbook, 1984.

Baras, E. M. *Guide Using Lotus 1-2-3.* 2d ed. Berkeley, Calif: McGraw-Hill, 1986.

Berit Fuglestad, Anne. "Spreadsheets as Support for Understanding Decimal Numbers." *Micromath* 13, no. 1 (1997): 6.

Bowman, C. "Integrated Software Solves Scheduling Problems." *Electronic Learning* (April 1985): 22–24.

Brooks, Lloyd D. *101 Spreadsheet Exercises for Lotus 1-2-3 and Other Spreadsheet Software.* 2d ed. New York: Glencoe, Macmillan/McGraw-Hill, 1992.

Brown, J. M. "Spreadsheets in the Classroom." *The Computing Teacher* 14, no. 3 (1987): 8–12.

Brown, J. M. "Spreadsheets in the Classroom Part II." *The Computing Teacher* 14, no. 4 (February 1987): 9–12.

Cooke, B. A. "Some Ideas for Using Spreadsheets in Physics." *Physics Education* 32, no. 2 (March 1997): 80–87.

Duncan, Judy. "PFS: WindowWorks Is a Smooth Integrator." *InfoWorld* 13, no. 29 (July 20, 1991): 63–64.

Holmes, Elizabeth. "The Spreadsheet—Absolutely Elementary!" *Learning and Leading with Technology* 24, no. 8 (May 1997): 6–12.

Hunt, William J. "Technology Tips: Spreadsheets—a Tool for the Mathematics Classroom." *Mathematics Teacher* 88, no. 9 (1995): 774–77.

Joshi, B. D. "Lotus 1-2-3: A Tool for Scientific Problem Solving." *Journal of Computers in Mathematics and Science Teaching* 10, no. 8 (1986–1987): 25–38.

Karlin, M. "Beyond Distance-Rate/Time." The Computing Teacher (February 1988): 20–23.

Koselka, Rita. "The Game of Life in Bits and Bytes—Spreadsheets Can't Solve All Problems. That's Why You Need Virtual People." Forbes 159, no. 7 (1997): 100.

Lacher, John. Journal of Accountancy 183, no. 5 (1997):66.

Luehrmann, Arthur. "Spreadsheets: More Than Just Finance." *The Computing Teacher* 13 (1986): 24–28.

Luthy, David H. "CPA 2000." *Journal of Accountancy* 178, no. 1 (July 1, 1994): 57.

Lynch, George. *ClarisWorks Step by Step: Windows Version 4.0: Word Processing, Databases, Spreadsheets, Graphics.* Gilroy, Calif.: Computer Literacy Press, 1997.

Manouchehri, Azita. "Exploring Number Structures with Spreadsheets." *Learning and Leading with Technology* 24, no. 8 (May 1997): 32–36.

McDowell, Monica. *Getting Started with Microsoft Excel 7.0 for Windows.* Chichester: Liberty Hall, 1997.

Miller, Michael J. "Microsoft Improves Works, Its Low-End Integrated Package." *InfoWorld* (October 16, 1989): 78.

Nelson, Stephen L. *Excel for Windows.* Microsoft Press, 1994.

Nelson, Stephen L. *Office 97: The Complete Reference.* Berkeley, Calif.: Osborne, 1997.

Parker, J. "Using Spreadsheets to Encourage Critical Thinking." *The Computing Teacher* 16, no. 6 (1989): 27–28.

Parker, O. J. *Spreadsheet Chemistry.* Englewood Cliffs, N.J.: Prentice Hall, 1991.

Pfaffenberger, Bryan. *Que's Computer User's Dictionary.* 4th ed. Indianapolis: Que, 1993.

Pfaffenberger, Bryan. *Webster's New World Computer User's Dictionary.* 6th ed. New York: Macmillan, 1997.

Robinette, Michelle. "Top Ten Uses for ClarisWorks in the One-Computer Classroom." *Learning and Leading with Technology* 24, no. 2 (October 1996): 37–40.

Rubin, Ross Scott. "Integrated Software." *Incider A+* (February 1991): 28–34.

Russell, J. C. "Probability Modeling with a Spreadsheet." *The Computing Teacher* 14 (November 1987): 58–60.

Sloan, Michael L. *Working with Works.* Glenview, Ill.: Scott, Foresman, 1990.

Smith-Gratto, Karen, and Marcy A. Blackburn. "The Computer as a Scientific Tool: Integrating Spreadsheets into the Elementary Science Curriculum." *Computers in the Schools* 13, no. 1–2 (1997): 125–31.

"The Spreadsheet Tips." *PC World* 12, no. 3 (March 1, 1994): 180.

Stang, A., and M. Levinson. "Spreadsheets Come to School." *Media and Methods* (September 1984): 28–29.

Using Microsoft Works. Microsoft Corporation, 1989. Redmond, Washington.

Weitzel, Keith. *Microsoft Works for the Macintosh—A Workbook for Educators.* ISTE, 1992. Eugene, Oregon.

Wilcox, W. Joseph. *Excel 97 for Windows: Step by Step.* Terra Cotta, Ont.: Norbry Publishing, 1997.

Software Integration and Evaluation

7

Objectives

Upon completing this chapter, you will be able to:

1. Differentiate between computer-assisted instruction and computer-managed instruction;
2. Define these software terms: public domain, shareware, drill and practice, problem solving, simulation, and games;
3. Name and discuss the criteria for selecting quality software;

4. Evaluate a piece of software based on standard criteria;
5. Create a plan for organizing a software library; and
6. Distinguish between the constructivist learning model and the teacher-directed learning model.

Introduction

In previous chapters, we considered the computer as a productivity tool in the classroom—its uses as a word processor, database, spreadsheet, and desktop publisher. This chapter will focus on the computer as an instructional tool or tutor.

The computer has many purposes in the classroom, and it can be utilized to help a student in all areas of the curriculum. **Computer-assisted instruction (CAI)** refers to the use of the computer as a tool to facilitate and improve instruction. CAI programs use tutorials, drill and practice, simulation, and problem solving approaches to present topics, and they test the student's understanding. These programs let students progress at their own pace, assisting them in learning the material. The subject matter taught through CAI can range from basic math facts to more complex concepts in math, history, science, social studies, and language arts.

In 1950, MIT scientists designed a flight simulator program for combat pilots, the first example of CAI. Nine years later, IBM developed its CAI technology for elementary schools and Florida State University offered CAI courses in statistics and physics. About the same time, John Kemeny and Thomas Kurtz created BASIC, Beginner's All-purpose Symbolic Instruction Code, at Dartmouth College, which provided a programming language for devising CAI programs.

In the early 1960s, CAI programs ran on large mainframe computers and were primarily used in reading and mathematics instruction. Computer programmers also produced simulation programs, modeled after real-life situations. Unfortunately, most of this early software was tedious, long on theory and short on imagination, lacking motivation, sound, and graphics.

The invention of the microcomputer led to the development of improved instructional software and, indirectly, to the resurgence of interest in classroom computer usage because of public demand and the competition among companies. Today, software companies employ teams of educators to enhance their products, and many textbook publishers are involved in producing software.

Computer-Assisted Instruction

Computer-assisted instruction facilitates student learning through various methods. CAI can provide the student with practice in problem solving in math; it can also serve as a tutorial in history and provide further drill and practice in English. Let us look at the different types of CAI: (1) tutorial, (2) simulation, (3) drill and practice, (4) problem solving, and (5) games.

Tutorial Programs

A tutorial's job is to tutor by interactive means—in other words, by having a dialogue with the student. The tutorial presents information, asks questions, and makes decisions based on the student's responses. Like a good teacher, the computer decides whether to move on to new material, review past information, or provide remediation. The computer can serve as the teacher's assistant by helping the learner with special needs or the student who has missed a few days of school. The computer tutorial is very efficient, because it gives individual attention to the student who needs it. In addition the student can progress at his or her own pace. A good tutorial is interesting, easy to follow, and enhances learning with sound and graphics. It has sound educational objectives, is able to regulate the instructional pace, and provides tests to measure the student's progress.

CAI tutorials are based on the principles of programmed learning: The student responds to each bit of information presented by answering questions about the material and then gets immediate feedback on each response. Each tutorial lesson has a series of frames. Each frame poses a question to the student. If the student answers correctly, the next frame appears on screen. There is disagreement among educators on how these frames should be arranged. Some educators are proponents of the linear tutorial, while others prefer the branching tutorial.

The linear tutorial presents the student with a series of frames, each of which supplies new information or reinforces the information learned in previous frames. The student has to respond to every frame in the exact order presented, and there is no deviation from this presentation, but the student does have the freedom to work through the material at his or her own speed.

The branching tutorial allows more flexibility in the way the material is covered. The computer decides what material to present to each student. The pupil's responses to the questions determine whether the computer will review the previous material or skip to more advanced work.

There are many tutorial programs, spanning the gamut of software. Media Quest has an excellent tutorial program called *Algebra Quest* (Fig. 7.1) that teaches the students how to master the challenges of algebra instruction. The *Algebra Quest* CD-ROM tutorial series is powerful and easy to use, with a personal guide called Ali Gebra who motivates students with friendly, corrective feedback.

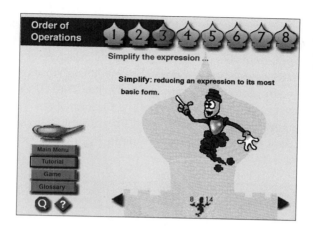

Figure 7.1
Algebra Quest
© Media Quest

Another example of a good tutorial is *Success Builder Math Library-TRIGONOME-TRY* (The Learning Company). This tutorial is a fun and easy way to learn trigonometry. It offers step-by-step learning with animated visuals and concise audio. Figure 7.2 shows a screen from trigonometry that discusses how to find the remaining angle and two unknown sides in the sample triangle.

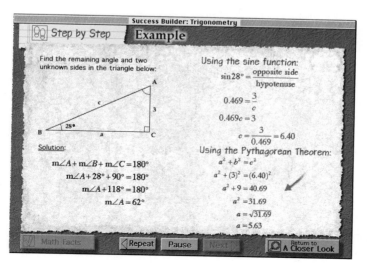

Figure 7.2
Success Builder Math Library-Trigonometry
Used with permission of The Learning Company, Inc. All rights reserved. Success Builder Math Library-Trigonometry™ is a ® trademark of Learning Company Properties, Inc.

Simulation Programs

In simulation programs, students take risks as if they were confronted with real-life situations without having to suffer the consequences of failure. Students can experiment with dangerous chemicals on the computer screen, for example, and not be in danger from the actual chemicals. With laboratory simulations, there is no expensive lab equipment to buy and students do not have to wait a long period of time for the effects of experimental conditions before they can observe the results. Moreover, students can repeat experiments easily as often as they wish. Simulations save time and money, reduce risks, and work well in decision-making situations. Many educators feel that a well-designed simulation software affords students the opportunity to apply classroom knowledge in more realistic situations than can otherwise be set up in a classroom, which enhances students' learning.

A classic example of a simulation program is *The Oregon Trail* III (The Learning Company, Inc.) Students use these program (Fig. 7.3) to travel the Oregon, California, and Mormon Trails as an emigrant facing dangers in the 1840s. The goal for students is to survive the various conditions and hardships as they travel across the continent.

Figure 7.3
*The Oregon Trail III
3rd Edition: Pioneer
Adventures*
Used with permission of
The Learning Company,
Inc. All rights reserved.
The Oregon Trail™ is a ®
trademark of Learning
Company Properties, Inc.

Students make significant decisions before leaving on the trip: A student can travel as a banker with $1,600, a carpenter with $800, or a farmer with $400. (The more money, and therefore the more supplies and services, the student has, the harder it is to earn points.) Before embarking on the journey, students must purchase food, ammunition, clothing, and oxen and decide in which month to start. Along the trail, the class makes decisions about resting, hunting, fighting, crossing rivers, and protecting themselves from Indian attacks in order to avoid starvation, exposure, and death. In the process, the class gains an understanding of what it was like to be a settler of European descent during the pre–gold rush years between 1840 and 1848.

In The Learning Company's *The Amazon Trail* simulation, students travel along the Amazon River, experience hardships, and risk possible death on a mission for the Inca King. *Africa Trail* (MECC) transports students to Africa for a bicycle trek based on the historic 1992 transcontinental expedition of Dan Buettner, the world famous bicyclist.

SimSafari lets students from ages 8 and above explore and manage their own African Safari park and camp, while *SimPark* (Maxis) lets students manage and design their own nature park. Once the students learn how the program works, there is plenty of action to keep them occupied for weeks. In the example shown from SimPark Figure 7.4, the students begin by choosing the geographical location for their park.

Figure 7.4
SimPark
Screenshot from
SimPark™ © 1996
Electronic Arts, Inc.
SimPark is a trademark or
registered trademark of
Electronic Arts in the U.S.
and/or other countries. All
rights reserved. Maxis is a
division of Electronic Arts.

SimCity 2000 for the upper grades and *SimTown* for the lower grades (Maxis) are simulations designed to teach students about critical issues involved in building and managing a city. In *SimCity 2000*, the user becomes the mayor of the city and can approve a new solar power system, raise taxes, read two local newspapers, build a zoo, and deal with an earthquake or an alien invasion. All the mayor's actions are followed by corresponding jumps or falls in the ratings.

The *Decisions, Decisions* series (Tom Snyder) offers well-executed simulation social studies software programs. The series includes titles such as *Colonization, Revolutionary Wars, Immigrants,* and *Substance Abuse.*

Drill and Practice Programs

In 1963, Patrick Suppes and Richard Atkinson produced drill and practice software on a mainframe computer. The computer screen displayed a problem, the student responded, and the computer provided immediate feedback. The learner stayed with the problems until reaching a certain level of proficiency and then moved on to a more difficult level. With the arrival of the microcomputer in the 1970s, this drill and practice software began to be widely produced in all subject areas. It was so popular that 75 percent of the educational software developed at this time was drill and practice. In the 1980s, many educators argued that drill and practice software was being overused. They believed that the computer should be used to encourage higher-level thinking and not as an electronic workbook. Today's drill and practice programs are more sophisticated, offer greater capabilities, and are accepted in the schools. Most educators see the value of a good individualized drill and practice program; this software frees the students and the teacher to do more creative work in the classroom. Many of these programs serve as diagnostic tools, giving the teacher relevant data on how well the students are doing and what they need to work on. The programs also provide immediate feedback for students, allowing them to progress at their own speed and motivating them to continue.

Drill and practice software differs from tutorial software in a key way: It helps students remember and utilize skills they have previously been taught, whereas a tutorial teaches new material. Students must be familiar with certain concepts prior to working drill and practice programs in order to understand the contents.

The typical drill and practice program design includes four steps: (1) the computer screen presents the student with questions to respond to or problems to solve; (2) the student responds; (3) the computer informs the student whether the answer is correct; and (4) if the student is right, he or she is given another problem to solve, but if the student responds with a wrong answer, he or she is corrected by the computer. Figure 7.5 illustrates the four steps.

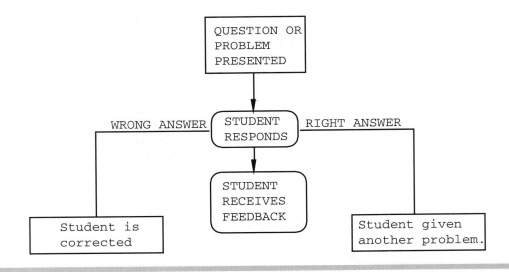

Figure 7.5
Drill and practice program steps

The computer program can handle incorrect responses in several different ways. The computer display might tell students to try the problem again. If they keep giving the wrong answer, the computer gives the right answer and then proceeds to the next problem. The computer might ignore all keys pressed except the right one or even beep when students try to type another response. It might display the answer that should have been typed. It might give students a hint when they respond incorrectly and a better hint if they miss the answer again. After three or four hints, it shows the right answer. Finally, it might give students additional information to help them respond to a question. This type of program is similar to a tutorial program.

Many drill and practice programs motivate students with their ingenious use of graphics and sound. Some programs are games in which players are rewarded points for the correct answers. *Zip Zap Map* (National Geographic Software) is a social studies drill and practice program. It tests students' knowledge and physical dexterity by having them correctly place all fifty states and their capitals, major cities, and significant physical features on a U.S. map. The students earn points by placing the geographical pieces as they fall from the top of the screen.

Math Blaster: Ages 6–9 (Davidson) is a very popular math program that uses points, certificates, and animation for reinforcement. The program has five activities including an older but very popular *Math Blaster* game. The *Math Blaster* activity is an arcadelike game in which students try to improve their speed and accuracy in solving basic math facts. The object of the activity is to help the Blasternaut solve the math problem that appears on Gelator's spaceship. Shoot the guard pod with the correct answer on it and at the same time avoid the ooze on the Blasternaut. To further motivate the student, the pods drop items like pacifiers, and bananas, which the Blasternaut moves over to pick up to earn points. As you can see in Figure 7.6, the student has shot the correct answer and the guard pod has disintegrated.

Figure 7.6
Math Blaster: Ages 6–9
Courtesy of Davidson & Associates, Inc., Copyright 1996.

Reading Blaster (Davidson) offers five different activities including vocabulary development, antonyms and synonyms, spelling, following instructions, and alphabetizing. This program features a multimedia adventure with dazzling graphics, animation, and sound effects. In the Word Zapper activity a word is typed in the word tray at the top of the screen and the student has to grab the letter group that completes that word. Typed clues about the words help the student accomplish this task.

Problem-Solving Programs

Problem-solving skills are necessary in a complex world, and a good way to develop these skills is to practice solving problems. The critical thinking needed for problem solving can be practiced in any content area. Problem-solving programs emphasize cooperation and are suitable for small groups or individual students.

A variety of computer programs focus on higher level thinking. Some of the better programs are *Math Keys* (Houghton Mifflin/MECC); *The King's Rule, The Factory, Deluxe Safari Search, SemCalc,* and *The Geometric SuperSupposer* (Sunburst); *Super Solvers Midnight Rescue! Super Solvers Gizmos & Gadgets!* and *Super Solvers OutNumbered!* (The Learning Company); *Where in the World Is Carmen Sandiego? Where in Time Is Carmen Sandiego?; Where in America's Past Is Carmen Sandiego?* and *Where in the World is Carmen Sandiego? Jr.* (Brøderbund), *Widget Workshop: School Edition* (Maxis); and *Big Science Comics* (Theatrix).

The new version of *Where in the World Is Carmen Sandiego?* asks students to search for a criminal who is hiding out in one of sixty countries. Students discover clues (Fig. 7.7) as they track the culprit's whereabouts and log these clues into the crime computer.

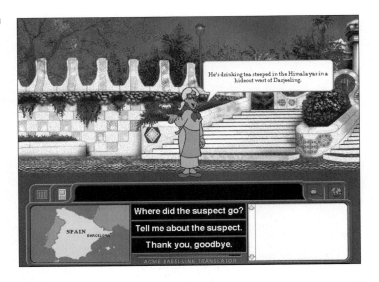

Figure 7.7
Where in the World Is Carmen Sandiego?
Screen shot courtesy of *Where in the World is Carmen Sandiego®* © 1991, 1992, 1994 Brøderbund Software, Inc. All rights reserved. Used by Permission. *Where in the World is Carmen Sandiego* and *Brøderbund* are trademarks and/or registered trademarks of Brøderbund Software, Inc.

Students also use a world almanac for help. When students are able to find out the identity of the criminal, they issue a warrant for the person's arrest. There are forty possible suspects, and Carmen Sandiego is the most difficult one to find. Students begin at the rookie level but advance as cases are solved. The higher a student's rank is, the harder is the case that is assigned to the student.

Another example of problem-solving software is *Big Science Comics*. In this program the student escapes from Bette's basement and leads a bunch of shipwrecked "Bumptz" back to their spaceship. On the way, the student creates simple machines out of everyday objects, experiments with gravity-defying contraptions, and develops thinking skills. Users compare Bumptz, learn about equivalence, and create a standard for measuring the Bumptz weight. With the aid of a hanger (Fig. 7.8), students answer questions such as "Can a small Bumptz weigh more than a large one?"

Figure 7.8
Big Science Comics
© Theatrix. Reprinted by permission.

Presently, there is a keen interest in problem-solving software as evidenced by the number of entries in the commercial software catalogs. Teachers like this type of software because it helps students with hypothesis testing and taking notes. Similar to simulation, problem-solving programs easily can be used with only one computer and as many as thirty students. The whole class can be involved in critical thinking and making inferences. This type of software gives students more freedom to explore than drill and practice software does.

Game Programs

Game programs for the computer usually involve fantasy situations with some sort of competition. Game programs are classified as either entertainment or educational software. The educational programs have specific learning objectives, with the game serving as a motivational device, whereas the major goal of the entertainment programs is playing the game. Educational software offers a range of learning outcomes; entertainment software has little academic value except in learning game strategy.

Most CAI programs use a game format that ranges from drill and practice to logic. For example, in *Spell It Deluxe* (Davidson), a drill and practice spelling program, a frog swallows correct answers. *Reader Rabbit 1* (The Learning Company), a language arts program, consists of four games that build reading skills and improve children's letter recognition, memory, vocabulary, and concentration. In Reader Rabbit's Sorter Game, students find all the words that start, for example with the letter S; if they are successful, the rabbit does a jig.

The program *Muncher Trivia Deluxe CD* (The Learning Company Inc.) helps students master history, science, social studies, general knowledge, and music facts. Figure 7.9 shows a muncher trying to eat all the words that are dinosaurs before the troggle (with teeth) disposes of him.

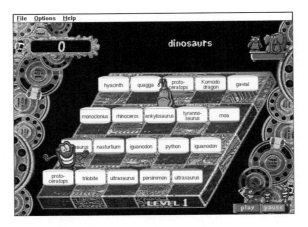

Figure 7.9
Muncher Trivia Deluxe
Used with permission of The Learning Company, Inc. All rights reserved. Trivia Munchers Deluxe™ is a ® trademark of Learning Company Properties, Inc.

Finally, *Math Heads* (Theatrix) helps students develop prealgebra skills; solve word problems; make mental calculations; compute fractions, decimals, percentages, and equivalencies; build estimation skills; and use logical thinking skills. In the Face the Music section (Fig. 7.10),

Figure 7.10
Math Heads
© Theatrix. Reprinted by permission.

students must click on all the fractions symbols that are equivalent to one-half. Students improve their understanding of equivalencies, proportions, and geometry while collecting cool graphics to make a movie video.

Because computer games are very popular, many educators think that CAI programs should be designed as games. A good educational game involves the active physical and mental participation of the players. Graphics, fast motion, and sound effects are used to enhance the program, not to distract from its educational value.

Most CAI programs incorporate more than one type of software in their design. For example, a program that is a tutorial may have a drill and practice element, while a simulation may have a game as an integral part of its program. The main element of *The Oregon Trail* is simulation; its game component is a hunting game.

Applications for Students with Special Needs

Much of the software that has been reviewed can be used with the student who has special needs. The computer is patient, always waits for a response, and repeatedly gives the same explanation, and so it is an ideal tool for individualization and remediation. Furthermore, the teacher can add special hardware devices to the computer to overcome the physical limitations of the learning disabled child. For example, the instructor can install a special communication board that will respond to the student's spoken command. Students who have to stay at home can enjoy all the benefits of CAI with a terminal or modem connected to the school computer.

Computer-Managed Instruction

We just explored CAI and how it focuses on the learner. In this section we'll examine **computer-managed instruction (CMI).** CMI differs from CAI in that it focuses on the needs of the teacher, helping him or her manage the learning of students.

The computer in CMI manages instruction; keeps track of student test scores, attendance records, and schedules; and offers diagnostic-perspective instruction in all curricular areas. CMI makes the teaching environment more organized and productive, allowing the teacher to individualize instruction. It directs students so that they can proceed at their own pace, and it supervises instruction by telling the students to read certain books and listen to particular tapes. When the students finish their work, the computer tests them and gives further assignments. The computer grades the tests and records scores so that the teacher can see and evaluate the students' progress.

CMI is based on the underlying concept that all children can learn if they proceed at their own pace and are given the proper instructions and materials. CMI can be a comprehensive program for one or more areas of the curriculum. Many computer-managed instruction programs are based on pretest, diagnosis, prescription, instruction, and posttest. The results of the testing are then used by the instructor to determine the materials that are best for the individual student.

An example of a complex management system is *Classroom Management System—Mathematics* (SRA). This particular system is designed for pupils in the primary grades. It manages math work on such topics as whole numbers, addition, subtraction, problem solving, measurement, time, geometry, and money. It helps the teacher test, evaluate student progress, and prescribe remedial work. In addition, it gives the teacher a record of the students' progress. The suggestions for activities are keyed to six of the important basal math textbooks and a few SRA programs. Teachers type in their name, class, and a code word that allows them to access the necessary information on the class. The teacher then makes the choice of which textbooks and materials to suggest. The teacher can also add activities and materials to the list.

At the beginning of the CMI program, the student takes a pretest on the computer. If the computer survey indicates an area of need, the student is given the appropriate test to pinpoint the area of weakness. If questions are missed on this exam, a prescription is given. If the student fails again, he or she must see the teacher. The teacher can customize the program, omitting tests for individuals in the class. The teacher also selects remediation assignments and decides when the testing ends. The instructor can call up records, class lists, tests, status reports on individuals, class reports, group reports, and graph reports.

Many CMI packages are stand-alone packages, but some elements of CMI are being incorporated into tutorial and drill and practice software. For example, *Math Blaster: In Search of Spot* (Davidson) has a test maker that lets the teacher create and print a math test. If the teacher then wants students to work on specific problems, he or she can use the editor and enter a set of problems. The program also has a record-keeping device that lets the teacher keep track of every student's score. There are many utility programs that are available to help teachers in the task of recording grades and taking attendance. A superior program is *Grade Busters Mac: Making the Grade* and *Grade Busters IBM: Record Breaker* (Jay Klein Productions), a state-of-the-art grade book and user-defined attendance categories program. Teacher utility software packages aid the teacher in producing materials for the classroom. *Teacher's Toolkit* (Hi Tech) is an award-winning program that produces word searches, word scrambles, word matches, and multiple choice questions.

In theory, CMI is sound, but in practice, it poses some real problems. A common complaint is the difficulty of setting up the management module for students. It takes time to enter each student's name and define tasks, a job that normally would occur over a span of months but that with CMI has to be accomplished immediately. The CMI systems are moving toward more user-friendly software, but most programs still are quite difficult to use. Some researchers feel CMI results in a decrease in the interaction between the student and teacher when this system is used (Coburn, et al. 1982, p. 48). Another frequent teacher complaint is the quality of the software.

CMI only tests basic skills, using such instruments as multiple choice and true/false questions. Another complaint is the cost, which can be quite exorbitant for the integrated learning systems and may require considerable access to computers. Finally, there is some question about the capability of the computer to truly assess the students' performance and provide the appropriate prescription for learning. Unfortunately, CMI has not been adequately researched and its results are inconclusive (Clements, 1989).

Public Domain/Shareware

Most software programs discussed in this book are commercial. The commercial programs are expensive, especially in multiple copies. Fortunately, there is an alternative to commercial software: public domain software. Public domain software can be legally copied and shared with other users with no restrictions on use. Public domain is not copyrighted, and its authors choose not to seek formal rights or royalties. Users pay a one-time postage and handling fee. The software is distributed by electronic **bulletin board** services (BBSs) and software vendors, downloaded through a commercial service such as America Online (AOL) or from the Internet. User groups pass around public domain software to their members. The quality of this software varies considerably. There are very useful public domain programs, but you have to choose carefully and wisely; professional programmers and teachers write these programs in their free time.

Shareware is software that is distributed using the honor system. It is inexpensive software that may or may not be copyrighted. Its authors send their products directly to users. Usually, authors do not have to worry about marketing or promotion cost. The software is distributed on a trial basis through BBSs, on-line services, mail-order vendors, and user groups. Users examine the program to see if it fits their needs. They also may give the software to friends for examination purposes. If, after looking over the software, the parties involved wish to use the product, they must register with the owner of the product and pay a fee. A shareware fee to an author may be as low as $5 and as high as $50. The author's name and address are always on the disk. In return for the fee, the user usually gets documentation, technical support, and free updates. If the shareware is sold through the software vendors, the software buyer must pay an additional fee to the vendor for distributing the shareware. There are tens of thousands of shareware programs; some are terrific, while others are mediocre.

Software Selection: A General Guide

In prior chapters, we examined different application software such as word processing and desktop publishing and learned how to evaluate these programs by using appropriate criteria. Now let's look at some general principles that apply to evaluating any software.

Choosing good software is an eight-step process: (1) know the specific software needs of your population; (2) locate the software; (3) research hardware compatibility; (4) examine the program's contents; (5) look at instructional design; (6) check out how easy the program is to learn; (7) evaluate the program in terms of consumer value; and (8) investigate the technical support and cost.

Specific Software Needs

To make a wise decision, it is essential to know the needs of your classroom. After you have determined the specific requirements, you can ask the following questions: What is the grade level and ability level? For what purpose will the software be used? Does the class need a math drill and practice program to reinforce some math skill? Does the group need a word processor or a remediation program to help the students learn something already taught? What type of software should you select? How sophisticated should this software be? For example, should the program be a simple word processor for letter writing or a heavy-duty word processor for book writing? After making these decisions, list the features the classroom requires. If you are teaching first grade, you might want a word processor that produces a nice assortment of interesting large letter fonts. If you are working with eighth graders, you might want a word processor that has an outliner.

Locating Software

The major sources of software information are journals, indexes, educational organizations, magazines, software house catalogs, and the Internet.

A fast way to locate software is through catalogs such as *Learning Services* (1-800-877-9378 [West] or 1-800-877-3278 [East]), Educational Resources (1-800-624-2926), Technology Resource Center (1-800-517-2320), and Educational Software Institute (1-800-955-5570). These catalogs include program descriptions and often tell you the names of the company's best-selling programs. The companies operate via mail order and have discounted prices. **See Appendix E for a listing of recommended mail-order software sources.** There are numerous published reviews from professional journals and periodicals in the field. For example, the *Arithmetic Teacher* publishes reviews on math software, the *Journal of Learning Disabilities* prints occasional reviews for learning disabled individuals. Additional magazines like *T.H.E. Journal, Electronic Learning, Learning and Leading With Technology,* and *Journal of Special Education* all review software. Furthermore, there are many specialized resources such as *Only the Best Educational Software and Multimedia,* published by the Association for Supervising and Curriculum Development (1-800-933-2723), the *Elementary Teacher's SourceBook on Children's Software* (1-908-284-0404), and the *Educational Software Preview Guide,* published by the International Society for Technology in Education (1-800-336-5191). On the Internet there are sites that focus on reviewing software such as Software Publishers Association, Newsweek *Parents Guide to Children's Software 97,* and Family PC. At the end of this chapter are eleven Internet Sites that rate software.

Regardless of what source you use, you should read several reviews of the software to get different perspectives. Often there is disagreement among reviewers on what constitutes "good" software because every reviewer has a priority. For example, Reviewer A may feel that ease of use is the most important factor, while Reviewer B might be concerned with features. Also, look at advertisements for new products. You can see what new products are available just by scanning the magazine ads or asking the manufacturers to send a more detailed list. You might want to call the producers of the product directly to find out about some features. Software developers such as Sunburst send preview copies if you guarantee their safe return. Many software publishers let you download from the Internet or order by phone demonstration versions of their software programs. There are other sources for previewing software: university software libraries, state departments of education, and software clearinghouses. An additional avenue is to seek out a computer enthusiast or a friend who has used the product. *Microsoft Word* may be a hot-selling program, but by talking to a friend who is actually using it, you might learn it's not right for your particular situation. Computer user groups recommend good software, demonstrate it at their meetings, and answer questions. At the very least, these groups put you in touch with people who have the software, and they generally keep abreast of new developments in the field.

After you have properly researched the types of software, you'll be ready to enter the computer store and look at the software package. Make sure the store is reputable and reliable and find out what its policy is on defective disks and returns. When examining a program, check the version number to be sure it's not an old version that has been lying around the store. Also, inspect the package to see if it is a teacher's version or a consumer version. The consumer edition will be less expensive, but it usually does not have a backup disk or an activity book.

Hardware Compatibility

Ask the following questions: Do the computers at the school have enough memory to run this program? How many disk drives does each machine have and what size are they? How fast is the CD-ROM drive? Most software programs today are in the CD-ROM format. Does the software program need more RAM to run faster and more efficiently? What are the video RAM requirements? What equipment is necessary? Does the program require a mouse, a joystick, or a color monitor? What type of printers does the program support?

Program Content

First, ask these questions: What are the objectives of this program? Are these objectives clearly stated? Does the program meet these objectives? (Many programs are not logically organized and lack a theoretical base. The objectives do not have to be seen on the computer screen. However, they should be found in the documentation that accompanies this software package.)

Next ask these questions: How appropriate is the program for the students? What knowledge or skills must a student possess to utilize this software program? Are the graphics and skills required reasonable for this grade level? (Be careful not to buy a program that is too easy or hard for the class.) Is the vocabulary appropriate for the grade level? (Many publishers supply readability scores that can serve as a benchmark.) How accurate is the material presented in the program? Is the program free of unnecessary computer jargon, and are the spelling and grammar correct? If it is a historical program, are the data accurate? How much time is needed to run the program? What about the program's transmitted values? Is the program free from prejudices or stereotypes? Is the program violent in nature?

Instructional Design

Many important factors relate to program design, such as (a) learner control, (b) reinforcement, (c) sequencing, (d) flexibility, and (e) appearance.

Learner Control.   Who controls the software program, the student or the computer? Can the student move back and forth in the lesson easily? Can the student quickly return to the previous frame? Can the student escape to the menu whenever he or she wants? Can the student control the speed of the program? Does the program move the academically bright students forward to more difficult problems, or is the level of difficulty the same? (It is important to be able to use the program at more than one ability level.) How easy is it for the student to exit the program or to restart an activity?

Reinforcement.   How are the students reinforced? (The reinforcement should be delivered in a positive way. The software should be encouraging and not degrading. There should be little reinforcement for inappropriate responses. Some programs have reinforcement for wrong answers that is more rewarding than the reinforcement for right answers.) Does the program vary the reinforcement? Is the feedback active, passive, or interactive? (A student receives passive feedback when the program simply states that the answer is wrong or right. The student receives active feedback when animation appears on the screen, such as Reader Rabbit's jig. A program that is interactive rewards the student with a game or something extra.

Sequencing.   Is the instructional sequence appropriate? Does it start from the simple idea and move to the complex?

Flexibility.   You should be able to adapt the program to small and large groups. You also should be able to modify the program to meet the individual needs of the students in the classroom. For example, *Spell It 3* enables you to add spelling words to the program. Does the program provide a record of the student's progress?

Program Appearance.   Does the program have colorful graphics, animation, and sound? Does the sound motivate the students or does it interfere with their learning? Are the graphics distracting or helpful? How is the screen laid out? Is it crowded or well organized? Is the full power of the computer being used? Are there too many instructions on the screen?

Ease of Use

Is the program easy to learn? Can the student immediately load the program and use it? Does the program use simple English commands? Can the student access a help screen whenever it is needed? Does a tutorial disk or manual take the user through the program? Is the printer easy to set? Can the student answer a few questions and then be ready to print immediately? Are there help prompts and safety questions? Is there an automatic save feature? What happens when the student hits a wrong key? Must the student reload the program or does the software crash? Does the program have error messages so that the student can correct problems? Are the directions clear and concise? Can the student follow the directions on the screen without going to the documentation that accompanies the software? Are the instructions brief and to the point?

Consumer Value

Cost is a concern because some software can run into the thousands. You have to decide whether that $395 word processor is really better than the $65 one: Are all the features found in that $395 package worth the cost? (Find out if a discount house or mail-order firm carries the software at a considerable saving; **see Appendix E for a list of recommended mail-order sources.** Is the software protected? Do you have to type in a serial number or find a code word in the manual or use the original disk to install? Are lab packs available? (Lab packs are multiple copies of a program with one set of documentation, sold at a substantial discount.)

Support

How is the technical support? Can you call someone immediately to get help or must you wait forever on the telephone? Do you have to make five or six menu choices and then get a recorded message that sends you on-line? Is the telephone call toll free or is it a long distance call? Does the company charge by the minute for technical help? Is there a tutorial with the software package? Is the tutorial on a disk or in book form? (Many manufacturers provide both to simplify learning their program.) Is the manual readable, with activities and lesson plans? (The documentation should be written for the target audience.) Is this publisher reputable? Will the company still be in business when you're having trouble with the software product? If you happen to get a defective disk, will the publisher replace it?

Shopping for software is an involved process. Using the software checklist on p.166 should simplify this task.

Software and Hardware Quality

Hardware manufacturers frequently rush out their new products while the products are still unfinished and bug ridden. For example, computers with Intel's Pentium chip had a flaw that resulted in inaccurate calculations. The Power Macintosh would at first not support many peripheral devices. Software quality varies as well. In the past, a lack of sophistication in software development frequently led to errors in programs. Today, the most common reasons for poor quality software are greed, technical incompetence, and lack of instructional design.

Greed

Some computer developers deliberately turn out products prematurely to keep up with the competition or beat it into the marketplace. They rely on clever advertising, catchy titles, and deceptive marketing to get the public to buy their products, which are so faulty that they need many revisions to run properly.

SOFTWARE EVALUATION CHECKLIST

Directions: Examine the following items and determine which ones you feel are important for your class situation. Evaluate your program and place an X on each line where the software meets your needs.

Program Name_____   Manufacturer_____   Grade Level_____

Subject Area _____   Skill Level _____   Time _____

A. Program Type
___ 1. Drill and practice
___ 2. Tutorial
___ 3. Simulation
___ 4. Educational game
___ 5. Problem solving
___ 6. Teacher management
___ 7. Other _____

B. Hardware
___ 1. Memory needed
___ 2. Computer compatibility
___ 3. Printer compatibility
___ 4. Hard disk space
___ 5. CD-ROM drive speed
___ 6. Periperhals

C. Program Content
___ 1. Objectives met
___ 2. Vocabulary appropriate
___ 3. Material accurate
___ 4. Free of bias or stereotype
___ 5. Motivational
___ 6. Grade appropriate skills

D. Instructional Design
___ 1. Learner control
     ___ a. Speed control
     ___ b. Program movement
___ 2. Proper reinforcement
___ 3. Self-directed program
___ 4. Appropriate sequencing
___ 5. Student record keeping
___ 6. Disk crash safeguards

___ 7. Appropriate learning theory
___ 8. Wide range of abilities

E. Program Appearance
___ 1. No distracting sound/visuals
___ 2. Animation/sound/graphics
___ 3. Uncluttered screen
___ 4. Material clearly presented
___ 5. Product reliability

F. Ease of Use
___ 1. Easy program installation
___ 2. Simple screen directions
___ 3. On-screen help
___ 4. Tutorial manual
___ 5. Easy printer setup
___ 6. Students can use without help
___ 7. Students can review directions on
     demand

G. Consumer Value
___ 1. Cost
___ 2. Backup disk policy
___ 3. Lab packs
___ 4. Network version

H. Support
___ 1. Free technical help
___ 2. Toll free number
___ 3. Readable manual
     ___ a. Activities
     ___ b. Lesson plans
     ___ c. Tutorial
     ___ d. Index
___ 4. Money-back guarantee
___ 5. Defective disk policy

Rating Scale

Rate the program by placing a check in the appropriate box.

Excellent ____Very Good____ Good___ Fair___ Poor___

Comments

Technical Incompetence

Because hardware manufacturers are constantly turning out new machines, software manufacturers expend a great amount of effort just keeping up. Many of the new machines are not compatible with the current software. (The manufacturer usually makes some minor modification that prevents the existing software from working on the machine.) The software developer is then faced with angry customers who cannot understand why their programs are not working. The developer has to make modifications and send out revised versions to all customers, an expensive proposition.

Lack of Instructional Design

Many programs have good graphics and sound and are attractive. However, despite their slick appearance, these programs often have little value because they are not based on sound educational theory. It is, therefore, important that educators become involved in the process of software development. Incorporating learning theory is a crucial part of the instructional design of any first-rate classroom software package. Many educational programs are no different from what might be found in a workbook. Why spend thousands of dollars producing a software program when all a teacher has to do is buy a workbook? The software program should offer much more than a standard textbook or workbook.

Once you have the software, the most important job still remains ahead. Every teacher needs guidelines on how to organize a software collection. What follows is one approach to software organization.

Guidelines for Setting Up a Software Library

1. Consult your school librarian for knowledge on cataloging and advice on time-saving techniques.
2. Choose the location for the collection wisely. It could be a classroom, library, or media center. The more central the location, the easier the access.
3. Use a database software program to keep a record of the software. Alphabetize the software by title and subject, and simultaneously, make an annotated listing of the software.
4. Catalog the software. There is no standardized procedure, but one of the simplest and most effective ways is to color code the software and documentation by subject area. For example, math software would be labeled with blue stickers or kept in blue folders. If you have a large software collection, use the Dewey Decimal System and the Sears List of Subject Headings.
5. Decide how the software is to be stored. Will you use hanging file folders, file cabinets, or disk boxes?
6. Protect the collection. Make security arrangements and store disks vertically in disk boxes. Protect disks from dust, dirt, and strong magnetic fields.
7. Separate the disks from the documentation for security reasons.
8. Devise a set of rules for software use. For example, forbid food or drinks in any of the computer labs. Place diskettes in their designated containers.

9. Create a policy and procedures manual that handles the following issues: (a) Who is responsible for this collection? (b) What procedures will be used to evaluate, select, and catalog this software? (c) How will the software be checked out? (d) How does a teacher verify that the software is workable? (e) How will the teacher report technical problems? Organizing and maintaining a software library is a monumental task that requires someone to be in charge of it on a full-time basis. After this library is established, schools can benefit by devising a review procedure so that a continually growing library of software reviews can be developed and made available to all teachers.

Learning Theories and Technology Integration

Before 1980, educators debated whether to use the computer as a tool, as a teaching aid or tutor, or as a programming device. There was an absence of software and technology was limited. As different types of technologies have become available, choices have increased. In order to take advantage of these advances in technology, educators agree there has to be a change in education to help individuals achieve optimal learning.

Learning theories attempt to explain how an individual acquires knowledge and what factors contribute to this learning. The teaching that takes place in the classroom is often based on one or more learning theories. Using teaching strategies that have a solid theoretical base makes the computer a more effective tool. When evaluating software, it is important that the software includes elements of one or more learning theories. Jonassen (1988) discusses learning theories and their application to microcomputer courseware.

Theories such as behaviorism, cognitive theory, constructivism, and situated cognition have been used to investigate the effect of the computer on teaching and learning. Learning theorists have disagreed on what strategies would be most useful in achieving educational goals. From this disagreement has evolved a recent interest in two different approaches, teacher directed and constructivism (Roblyer, Edwards, & Havriluk, 1997). The teacher-directed approach is based on the behaviorism learning theory, while the constructivism approach comes from other branches of cognitive learning theory. (Since this textbook is not an instructional theory textbook, we will not cover this topic in great depth.)

Teacher Directed

The teacher-directed approach is derived from the behavioral theories of B. F. Skinner, Edward Thorndike, Richard Atkinson, David Ausubel, Robert Gagne, and Lee Cronbach. The teacher is seen as the manipulator of the classroom environment and the student is the receptacle. Famous for his work in behavior modification, B. F. Skinner favored programmed instruction. The lessons and drills are planned in small incremental steps to lessen the chance of incorrect responses on the part of the student. The idea is that the student can learn by tightly structuring the environment. The teacher focuses on teaching skills that begin at a lower level and build to higher skills, a systematic approach. There are clearly stated objectives, with test items that coincide. This approach stresses individual work and emphasizes the traditional teaching and assessment methods, such as lectures, worksheets, and so on.

During the 1970s and 1980s when computers first appeared in the classroom, the behavioral theories were very popular. The software then was based on programmed instruction. Today thousands of educational software programs—such as *Math Munchers Deluxe* (MECC), *Quarter Mile* (Barnum Software), *Math Blaster; Ages 6–9* (Davidson), *Algebra Quest* (Media Quest), *Mavis Beacon Teaches Typing* (Mindscape), and *Inside the SAT & ACT* (Princeton Review)—are based on the behavioral models of instructions. The programs are associated with drill and practice and tutorial software applications. They diagnose student skills, monitor student performance, and make changes in instruction when necessary. The software program usually generates student and class performance information for teacher use. The advocates of this approach praise the software for its individual pacing, self-instructional sequences, and remediation when the teacher's time is limited. The software generally makes learning faster especially for instruction in skills that are necessary for higher level skills. This software performs time-consuming tasks and frees the teacher for more complex student needs.

Opponents of this type of software criticize its lack of flexibility because it comes with a predefined curricula. They say it uses only one type of educational technology, while other approaches use problem solving, multimedia, telecommunication, and cooperative problem solving.

Constructivism

The constructivist models have evolved from the work of developmental theorists such as Jerome Bruner, Jean Piaget, Lev Vygotosk, and Seymour Papert (See chapter 15). The constructivist feels that learning occurs when the learner controls his or her own knowledge. These models focus on posing problems and searching for answers. Constructivism emphasizes exploration or discovery learning. Constructivism uses assessment by student portfolios, performance checklists, and tests with open-ended questions and narratives. It differs from the teacher-directed model because of its emphasis on group work as opposed to individual work. Students play an active role rather than passive, and they work to solve problems through cooperative learning activities. Even though the constructivist instructional theories and simulations have been around for years, the strategies used, such as annotated movies and hypertext, are recent innovations.

The application of simulations can be traced to seventeenth-century war games used to simulate the battles between opposite sides. In the mid 1950s, simulations were introduced in business training, and in the 1970s the popular simulation program *Lemonade Stand* by Minnesota Educational Computing Corporation (MECC) was introduced and ran on the Apple II computer. Today programs such as *Hot Dog Stand* (Sunburst) and the Sim series— *SimCity 2000, SimPark, SimSafari* and others—are created to teach the concepts of supply and demand. Players make decisions about cost, production, price structure, and advertising. A further innovation in this field is virtual reality, in which the student feels a part of the environment, and programs like *Riven* and *Myst* by Brøderbund (see chapter 10) have come into their own. The advocates of constructivism say that it makes skills more relevant to students' experiences and that tasks are anchored in real-life visual situations. The students address problems through interactive situations and play active rather than passive roles. They work together in groups to solve problems through cooperative learning activities. This software emphasizes motivational activities that require high-level as well as low-level skills at the same time.

Both approaches attempt to identify what Gagné (1985) calls the "conditions of learning" or the circumstances that influence learning. Both approaches are based on work done by respected psychologists and learning theorists and the approaches differ only in the way they describe the environment in which learning occurs.

Table 7.1 compares the characteristics of the teacher directed model with the constructivist model.

Table 7.1   *Comparison of Teacher Directed Versus Constructivist Instructional Models*

Teacher Directed	Constructivist
Worksheet & Textbook based	Manipulatives, primary sources
Curriculum Fixed	Curriculum Flexible
Teaches Basic Skills	Concept Development
Teacher Transmits Knowledge	Student explores and discovers Knowledge
Teaches Basic Skills	Large Concepts
Didactic Instruction	Interactive Activities
Results in a correct answer	Concern with the process of learning
Assessment-Testing	Assessment-student products & student observation
Stresses Individualized work	Stresses Cooperative Group Work

Let's briefly review what has previously been discussed and then work through some questions about the material, consider some classroom projects, and examine the suggested readings and references.

Summary

The computer has many invaluable uses in all areas of the curriculum. Computer-assisted instruction (CAI) software uses the computer as a tool to improve instruction, provide the student with practice in problem solving, serve as a tutor, and supply drill and practice. CAI directly involves the learner, whereas computer-managed instruction (CMI) assists the teacher in managing learning. We considered eight criteria to apply when choosing software. We examined a software evaluation form (checklist) to aid in software selection. Following this discussion was a brief discourse on software quality, followed by guidelines for setting up a software library. The chapter concluded with a discussion of teacher-directed and constructivist approaches to learning.

Chapter Mastery Test

1. What is the most critical step in the evaluation of software? Explain its importance.

2. Discuss three criteria that a teacher should consider when choosing software for the classroom.

3. What is the main difference between shareware and public domain software?

4. Why is feedback a crucial element to consider when evaluating software?

5. Should the student or the computer control the direction of the program? Explain.

6. What is the major difference between a drill and practice program and a tutorial program?

7. Define *simulation program* and give an example.

8. Can a problem-solving program also be a simulation program? Explain in detail.

9. Give the paradigm for the typical drill and practice program design.

10. What is the major difference between computer-managed instruction and computer-assisted instruction?

11. Discuss two reasons for poor quality software.

12. What are important considerations for setting up a software library?

13. As a student, are you more comfortable with teacher-directed or constructivist strategies? Explain your answer.

14. Name three characteristics associated with the constructivist learning model and three characteristics associated with the teacher-directed model.

Classroom Projects

1. Review a piece of software using the guidelines that were given in this chapter.

2. The software evaluation form that was used in this chapter was of a general nature. Develop a software checklist for a drill and practice software program in the area of math or science.

3. Go to the library and find three or four software review forms. Write a paper comparing these forms, discussing their similarities and differences.

4. Visit a high school or elementary school software library, and write a paper discussing its cataloging system.

5. Examine a software program that runs on two types of machines. See if there are any differences in how the software works on each machine.

6. Visit the library to research a public domain software program. Write a review. What are the advantages and disadvantages of using this type of software program?

7. Use Appendix A or a software directory to locate several math software packages for an eighth-grade class. Make a list.

8. Find a published review on a piece of software in the school's collection. Test out the product to determine the validity of the review. Write your own review.

9. Form small groups in the class; in each group develop a common evaluation form no more than three pages long. Make sure there is a consensus on all items and discuss the areas in which the group did not reach a consensus.

Suggest Readings and References

Alperson, J. R., and D. H. O'Neil. "The Boxscore: Tutorials 2, Simulation O." *Academic Computing* (February 1990): 18–19, 47–49.

Anders CD-ROM Guide, 1997. 2d ed. Brooklings, Mass.: Andiron Press. 1997.

Armstrong, Timothy, and Russell F. Loane. "Educational Software: A Developer's Perspective. *Techtrends* 39, no. 1 (January 1, 1994): 20.

Berlin, D., and A. Wite. "Computer Simulations and the Transition from Concrete Manipulation of Objects to Abstract Thinking in Elementary School Mathematics." *School Science and Mathematics* 86, no. 6 (1986): 468–79.

Buckleitner, Warren, ed. "The Elementary Teacher's Sourcebook on Children's Software." *Children's Software Revue* 5 (winter 1998). Published by Active Learning Associates, Flemington, N.J.

Carlson, Kurt, and Valle Dwight *The Family PC Software Buyer's Guide*. New York: Hyperion, 1996.

"Child Education." *Children's Software Revue 74*, no. 6 (1997): 59.

Clements, F. H. *Computers in Elementary Mathematics*. Englewood Cliffs, N. J.: Prentice-Hall, 1989.

Cohen, Steve, Richard Chechile, and George Smith. "A Method for Evaluating the Effectiveness of Educational Software." *Behavior Research Methods, Instruments, & Computing* 26, no. 2 (May 1, 1994): 236.

Collis, B. *The Best of Research Windows: Trends and Issues in Educational Computing*. Eugene, Oreg.: International Society for Technology in Education, 1990.

Collopy, D. "Software Documentation: Reading a Package by Its Cover." *Personal Computing* (February 1983): 134–44.

"Computer Education." *Children's Software Revue* Volume 7 no. 2 (1997): 30.

Dede, C. "A Review and Synthesis of Recent Research in Intelligent Computer-Assisted Instruction." *International Journal of Man Machines Studies* 24, no. 4 (1986): 329–53.

DeMillo, Richard A. *Software Testing and Evaluation*. Menlo Park, Calif.: Benjamin/Cummings, 1987.

Edward, C. "Project MICRO." *The Computing Teacher* 16, no. 5 (1989): 11–13.

Flynn, Marilyn L. "Using Computer-Assisted Instruction to Increase Organizational Effectiveness." *Administration in Social Work* 14, no. 1 (1990): 103.

Gagné, R. *The Conditions of Learning*. New York: Holt, Rinehart and Winston, 1985.

Haugland, Susan W. *Developmental Evaluations of Software for Young Children*. Albany, N.Y.: Delmar Publishers, 1990.

Helm, Leslie. "Standards for Quality May Be Computers' Next Advances." *Los Angeles Times* (December 14, 1994): D1.

Hooper, Mary E. "Usable Software in Advanced Educational Computing Projects." *Computer Graphics* 28, no. 1 (February 1, 1994): 46.

"Information Technology and Libraries." *Children's Software Revue* 16, no. 1 (1997): 45.

Johnson, Judi Mathis. "Software for an Evaluation Workshop." *Learning and Leading with Technology* 24, no. 4 (December-January 1996–1997): 48–50.

Jonassen, D. H. *Instructional Designs for Microcomputer Courseware*. Hillsdale, N.J.: Lawrence Erlbaum Associates, 1988.

Kalmon, Ted. *Microcomputer Software: Step by Step*. Englewood Cliffs, N.J.: Prentice-Hall, 1990.

Martin, J. H. "Developing More Powerful Educational Software." *Educational Leadership* (March 1986): 32–34.

McLester, Susan "Presenting the 1997–98 Technology & Learning Software Awards." *Technology & Learning* 18, no. 4 (November/December 1997): 23–46

Miranker, Cathy. "Smart Software." *Parents* 72, no. 3 (March 1, 1997): 65.

Morgan, Bill, ed. "101 Things You Want To Know About Computers." *Educational Technology* 10, no. 8 (May/June 1991): 25–38.

Morenstern, Steve. "Computer Reviews & News." *Parents* 72, no. 6 (June 1, 1997): 194.

Neuman, Delia. "Computer Equity: A Model for the Library Media Specialist." *The Computing Teacher* 18, no. 8 (May 1991): 35–37.

Norales, Francisca O. "Students' Evaluation of Microcomputer Software." *Interface* 13, no. 2 (summer 1991): 45.

Noss, Richard. "The Rebirth of Educational Software." *Micromath* 9, no. 3 (fall 1993): 13.

Only the Best Educational News Service, Association for Supervising and Curriculum Development 1-800-933-272, 31250 N. Pitt Street, Alexandria Virginia 22314-1453.

Pollack, Rachel H. "The Road to Software-Buying Success." *Currents* 23, no. 5 (May 1997): 36–40.

Pride, Mary. "Virtual Education: Educational Software Explodes." *The World & I* 9, no. 4 (April 1, 1994): 166.

Roblyer, M. D. "When Is It Good Courseware? Problems in Developing Standards for Microcomputer Courseware." *Educational Technology* (October 1981): 47–54.

Roblyer, M. D., Jack Edwards, and Mary Anne Havriluk. *Integrating Educational Technology into Teaching.* New York: Merrill–Prentice Hall, 1997.

Rockwell, Sarah F. "Computers Serious Fun." *Atlantic Monthly* 273, no. 4 (April 1, 1993): 115.

Schank, Roger C. "Active Learning through Multimedia." *IEEE Multimedia* 1, no. 1 (Spring 1994): 69.

"Science and Children." *Children's Software Revue* 34, no. 7 (1997): 50.

"Science and Children's." *Software Revue* 34, no. 8 (1997): 56.

Skinner, B. F. *The Technology of Teaching.* New York: Appleton, 1968.

"Software At-a-Glance." *Electronic Learning* 13, no. 5 (February 1, 1994): 36.

Starfield, A. M. *"How to Model It: Problem Solving for the Computer Age.* New York: McGraw-Hill, 1990.

TechTrends Media Reviews columns that have in-depth evaluations of educational multimedia. Published by Association for Educational Communications and Technology, 1 (202) 347-7834.

Thomas, Rex, and Elizabeth Hooper. "Simulations: An Opportunity We Are Missing." *Journal of Research on Computing in Education* 23, no. 4 (Summer 1991): 497–511.

Titus, Richard. "Finding Good Educational Software: Where to Begin." *Learning* (October 1985): 15.

Vargus, Julie S. "Instructional Design Found in Computer Assisted Instruction." *Phi Delta Kappan* (June 1986): 738–44.

White, James A., and Stephanie S. VanDeventer. "A Successful Model for Software Evaluation." *Computers in the Schools* 8, no. 1/3 (1991): 323.

Software Reviews on the Internet

California Instructional Technology Clearninghouse

http://tic.stan-co.k12.ca.us/

At this site you can access the Technology in Curriculum Evaluations database with more than 2000 reviews of educational products

Children's Software Revue

http://www2.childrenssoftware.com/childrenssoftware/

Children's Software Revue contains All-Star lists of software and articles from past issues of this magazine.

Family PC

http://zdnet.com/familypc/

At this location, you will find information on late-breaking hardware and software reviews.

HomePC

http://www.techweb.com/hpc/

A good review source that covers games, learning, lifestyles and more.

Kids Domain

http://www.kidsdomain.com

Kids Domain contains hundreds of reviews of software, informative articles, downloads, and online activities for kids.

Newsweek Parents Guide to Children's Software 97

http://www.newsweekparentsguide.com

This site offers illustrated reviews with ratings of more than 250 titles. The site also contains bulletin board discussions with *Newsweek* columnists on software and a variety of other issues.

Software Publishers Association

http://www.spa.org/project/resource.htm

Software Publishers Association contains a listing of educational software review sources as well as a database of software companies.

Superkids

http://www.superkids.com

Superkids contains software reviews with ratings.

Technology & Learning

http://www.techlearning.com

The Technology & Learning site offers a searchable database from past issues of the magazine.

Worldvillage

http://worldvillage.com/

Worldvillage contains illustrated reviews from forty different U. S. reviewers. The reviews cover everything from games to education.

Ziff Davis Software Library

http://www.hotfiles.com/index.html

This software library contains shareware ratings and software demos that can be downloaded immediately.

Using the Computer in All Curriculum Areas

8

Objectives

Upon completing this chapter, you will be able to:

1. List strategies for using one computer with thirty or more children in the math, science, social studies, and language arts areas;

2. Describe examples of the major software in four curricular areas;

3. List two major advantages for using CD-ROM software;

4. Distinguish between CD-ROM, DVD-ROM and laserDisc, or videodisc, technology; and

5. Explain why DVD-ROM is the wave of the future.

One Computer in the Classroom

The typical classroom used to have one computer for thirty or more children, but a recent survey now shows seven students per computer (Market Data Retrieval, 1997). Regardless, most of the time these computers reside in a lab and the teacher only has access to one in the classroom. Some teachers store the computer encased in plastic wrap with strict rules to govern its use, and others, afraid to use the computer, let it gather dust in a remote corner of the room. In either situation, the computer is not being used to its potential. Here are seven suggestions that will help you better capitalize on the computer's capabilities: (1) select the software according to needs of the students; (2) collect the appropriate equipment; (3) organize the classroom; (4) use the team approach; (5) know the software's time factor; (6) encourage group participation; and (7) integrate the computer

Selection of Software

In any good instruction, you adapt the material to the students' needs. This principle holds for software as well. Students have varied abilities, interests, and preferences that warrant different teaching considerations and strategies. For example, if a student does not know how to type, he or she will have to search for the keys on the keyboard, thus becoming easily frustrated with the computer. At a third grade level, a teacher's first strategy may be to instruct the students in keyboarding skills, starting with the return, escape, and arrow keys.[1] Create a large keyboard and

---

[1] Dr. Olsen, a Research Scientist at SRI International does not recommend keyboarding to be formally introduced until third grade (Buckleitner, 1998).

place it in front of the room. Next, arrange the students in pairs to practice the letter and number locations on a seat copy of the larger-size keyboard. After the students have had the experience of helping each other explore the keyboard, direct the whole class in finding designated keys. Eventually, have the children close their eyes while continuing this activity. Once the children are skillful in locating keys, they are ready to work with a typing program such as *Stickybear Typing* (Optimum Resource), *Mario Teaches Typing* (InterPlay), *Kid's Typing* (Sierra), *Mavis Beacon Teaches Typing! For Kids, Mavis Beacon Teaches Typing!* (Mindscape), *All the Right Type* (Didatech, now Ingenuity Works) and *Kid Keys* (Davidson).

Stickybear Typing has bold graphics and three activities that use jokes, riddles, and action games to sharpen the beginner's skills in typing and keyboard mastery. For example, in the Thump game, the user challenges the robot and tries to save Stickybear from being bumped by the blocks the robot is tossing. If the user types fast enough, Stickybear blocks a cube from hitting the user.

Mario Teaches Typing is a delightful program with all the Mario characters and scenes. Users begin by choosing Mario, the Princess, Luigi, or a made-up identity. Players progress at their own pace through each adventure-filled level.

Kid's Typing has a friendly ghost named Spooky who teaches the students their home keys and tracks their progress in typing. The ghost is charming and has a remark for every student action, including posture, slowness, and quitting the program. In the practice mode, the keyboard remains displayed on the screen to aid the child in correct finger placement. The program also includes a library of actual stories to type and bonus rounds in which the child helps Spooky haunt the house.

All the Right Type (Fig. 8.1) is an easy-to-use typing program that links the keyboarding program with a word processor. It includes a record keeping feature, and the lessons are customized for the student's use in a classroom setting.

The software has a motivating rowing game that pits the student against the computer.

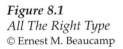

Figure 8.1
All The Right Type
© Ernest M. Beaucamp

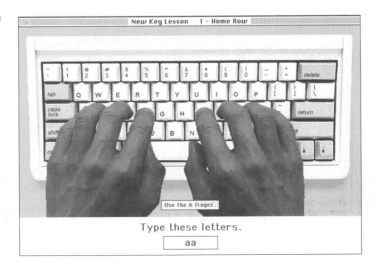

Once the students have achieved keyboard mastery, they can spend more time working with programs instead of working on the mechanics of finding keys.

If the students in the class need to improve their problem-solving abilities, a large range of programs are available. For example, problem-solving software such as *Where in the World Is Carmen Sandiego?* (Brøderbund) could work effectively for middle grade students in the social studies area, while *Science in Your Ear* (The Learning Company, Inc.) could work well for the same students in the science area. Using these programs, students can collectively improve their critical thinking skills by taking notes, manipulating variables, analyzing the results, drawing conclusions, and offering solutions to problems (Fig. 8.2).

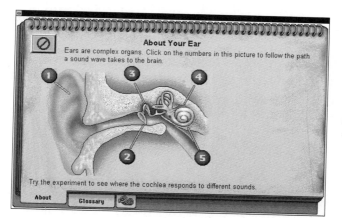

Figure 8.2
Science in Your Ear
Used with permission of The Learning Company, Inc. All rights reserved. Science in Your Ear™ is a ® trademark of Learning Company Properties, Inc.

If the class needs to study and research information about the United States, you can use a database software program such as *ClarisWorks for Kids* or *ClarisWorks*. The students create information sheets, compose questionnaires, and collect appropriate data for computer entry. Each student might research two states and input information about each state's population, capital, number of representatives, and main crop. After information is entered into the database, students might search for a state in which the main crop is corn. When the state appears on the screen, the student at the computer calls out its name and the other students shade the state on a blank seat map. After the students find all the applicable states and shade them, you could study the maps and discuss where the corn-producing states are located. From this class discussion, the students could learn about the corn belt and why this region produces the most corn.

Collection of Equipment

When there is only one computer in the classroom, you need additional equipment to make the computer screen visible to the whole class. Very expensive projectors like the LitePro display enlarged images from a personal computer onto a wall screen. Another alternative is a portable liquid crystal display (LCD) projection panel and an overhead projector that uses the personal computer to display enlarged images on a screen. If the district cannot afford a projector or projection panel, there is a less expensive alternative: the "T" or "Y" adapter. You use this device to split the signal coming from the class computer in order to display it on a larger television or monitor.

Many Macintosh computers have television ports; you simply plug into that particular port for large-screen television reception. The Macintosh AV models also have this capability and are ready for use with an additional monitor. However, the IBM and IBM compatibles and older Macintosh computers require additional hardware devices such as Micropresenter or Focus to provide high quality television display.

When you are cramped for space, you can improve the situation by elevating a large television or monitor to increase visibility. You also can tape a transparency on the TV screen and use a grease pencil to write on the screen to illustrate a point. Furthermore, you can create practice sheets that duplicate a screen from a computer program so that students can work along with the presentation.

Classroom Organization

Ask yourself questions to determine the best seating arrangement for viewing the computer. Are the students going to be in their seats or on the floor? Will the pupils be placed in small groups for discussion purposes? Will they be traveling to different learning stations in the room as they use manipulatives? Are they using an instrument such as a thermistor[2] to collect temperature data in different sections of the room?

Team Approach

Many classrooms have two or three students who have been using computers since they were very young. If you have enough pupils who are familiar with the computer, organize them into a team. Under your tutelage, the team can practice giving directions, solving problems, and introducing new software. After the team is experienced, give the members identification badges and have them walk around the room answering questions on the current program. In addition to reducing the number of questions you'll receive, this team method reaches a larger number of pupils and gets them involved in helping each other.

Software Time Factor

For the computer program to be a success, you need not only to select the appropriate program for the situation, but also to know the program's time constraints. For instance, when the time frame is short, don't choose open-ended software, because the students will be unhappy when they have to stop prematurely. *The Oregon Trail III* (MECC) takes at least thirty-five minutes to complete, and the students will object to quitting even though the program has a save function. *The Louvre Museum* (Voyager), on the other hand, is not as goal oriented and therefore is easier to stop and start with a class. Additionally, in selecting a program, check whether it saves the game or activity instantaneously or at the end of a level. Software programs that require fifteen or twenty minutes to finish a level might be inappropriate for a particular classroom situation.

---

[2] A thermistor is a sensoring device that converts temperature into electrical impulses.

Group Involvement

Your interactions with a class are very important and will determine how free your students feel to participate in class lessons involving computers. At the introduction of a lesson, explain that there are many acceptable answers and that there is no one solution to a problem. Try to reduce the pupils' anxiety about evaluation. At first, involve the whole class in discussion; later, break the class up into smaller groups. Ask probing questions and ask students for their next move. Search for the reasons behind their answers and give them time to think. You should be a facilitator, letting the students do most of the talking and never imposing ideas on the class discussion. Try not to be judgmental in responding to the students; they will pick up on your nonverbal body language. Encourage the students to cooperate in order to promote learning and social skills. Advance the students' thinking by making comments such as, "That seems like a good idea, but expand on it."

Let the students practice problem solving by having them solve the same problem again, checking out their hypotheses and recording their collective answers. Give the students objects to manipulate at their desks to help them answer the questions that the software is posing. For example, *Puzzle Tanks* (Sunburst), a classic program, poses problems that involve filling tanks with Wonder Juice, Odd Oil, or Gummy Glue and moving this liquid over to a storage tank. At the simplest level, the program might ask the students to move fourteen grams of Gummy Glue to a storage tank. For this problem, students are shown on screen a tank that can hold seven grams and another tank that can hold one gram. You can involve the whole class in this activity by distributing measuring cups and beans at the students' desks. A favorite ploy is to divide the class into small groups that challenge each other to see which group gets the most problems correct. At the end of the day, have the students work on the computer in pairs, one partner using the computer and the other coaching and recording. This pairing encourages students to develop strategies for handling the problems inherent in the software. Organize the time the students spend at the computer with a schedule similar to the one in Figure 8.3. The students should work on a program for a designated time interval. When their time is up, the next pair of pupils listed in the chart take a turn. If a team is absent or busy, the next available partnership fills the void. This way the computer can be used by everyone in the class.

PROGRAM: WHERE IN THE WORLD IS CARMEN SANDIEGO		
TIME	TEAMS	FINISHED
8:30-8:50	David Scott	✓
8:50-9:10	Bobbie Florence	✓
9:10-9:30	Jill Judy	☐

Figure 8.3
Computer-use chart

Integrating the Computer in the Classroom

How do you make the computer an integral part of the core curriculum? The software should not substitute for the standard curriculum but rather should complement it on a regular basis. Let's look at four different software programs and how these programs can be included in classroom instruction.

If you want to improve students' writing skills, you might use a program such as *Hollywood High* (Theatrix) that encourages creative writing and provides an opportunity for students to listen to their own written work and make revisions. When students use *Hollywood High* (Fig. 8.4), they choose characters, expressions, and scenery for their play. They write scripts, add actions, edit these scripts, and then listen to and watch the characters perform.

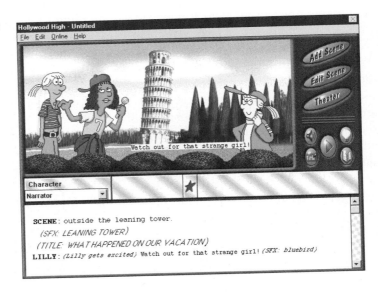

Figure 8.4
Hollywood High
© Theatrix. Reprinted by
permission

You can make suggestions for scripts that include recent events, historical occurrences, stories read, or class science experiments. Each student can work at his or her own desk to develop ideas for scripts, and the class can collectively brainstorm these ideas. Then, you and the class can discuss the characters, plot, purpose, and climax. The class then can form small groups to write their own scripts, and these scripts can be translated to the computer and viewed by the whole class.

In math, you can use a simulation program such as *Mighty Math Calculating Crew* (Edmark) to help students improve their math problem solving skills. This program invites students into an animated world of math adventure. They are given practice in handling topics such as multiplication, division, number lines, money, and 3-D geometry. Many of the activities contain virtual manipulatives, which help students make connections between concrete and abstract math.

Using this program, the students experiment with geometry by rotating a 3-D solid or by changing a 2-D net to see the effect on the corresponding solid. They build spatial orientation skills, which let them recognize the same object when viewed from different angles, and spatial visualization skills, which allow them to mentally rotate a 3-D solid or imagine it in different configurations.

For social studies, there is a truck-driving simulation series entitled *Crosscountry* (Didatech now Ingenuity Works) that includes such titles as *USA, Texas, Canada,* and *California.* These programs are very interactive: They "understand" about 250 different English words and respond to sentences, shortened instructions, and phrases. For example, if the user tries to drive the truck without starting the engine, the program responds with, "The truck is not turned on. You can't go that way" (Fig. 8.5).

Figure 8.5
Crosscountry USA
Reprinted by permission of Ingenuity Works.

The *Crosscountry* programs are effective for teaching map reading, geography, spatial relationships, and critical thinking skills. In *Crosscountry USA,* students discover the geography of the United States by driving trucks to pick up commodities that the teacher or computer has selected from a list of fifty-two possibilities. These commodities are located in cities all over the United States. You could divide the class into two competing trucking companies and set them on their missions. (If one trucking company chooses to pick up only four commodities, its mission will require about forty minutes.) You can customize the operation of the program so that both companies have to travel the same distance. Each team decides when to eat, sleep, and get gas; which cities to travel to; and how to get to the final destination. Obviously, each team's objective is to pick up and deliver its loads before the other team does. Members of the teams can record the trip routes, cities visited, population, county locations, and other features. A winning team's strategy can be discussed, and each team can keep a journal of the journey.

Sierra's School House - Science (Sierra On-Line) is a learning lab that includes a couple hundred exercises in science. Students learn about earth science, life science, and physical science (Fig. 8.6).

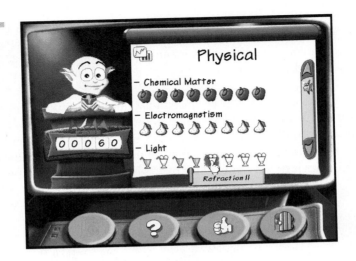

Figure 8.6
Sierra's School House
© Sierra On-Line, Inc.

Students develop and strengthen skills appropriate to their grade and age group. The program is designed to be a comprehensive course of study paralleling the curriculum presently taught in elementary schools throughout the United States. Students learn about life as they look at the workings of the human respiratory system and discover where air goes when a person breathes. They create color masterpieces and put on their own multimedia presentation. They explore the wonders of the earth and visit the stars and planets and are rewarded by solving puzzles and playing collective games. The teacher can generate progress reports as the students complete lessons in the program. At each level, the students face a different challenge and must use a unique set of strategies. The teacher can lead interesting discussions on the different topics covered by the program. At the same time, members of the class can be encouraged to take notes by writing in their computer notebook and then sharing their notes with the class.

In summation, you should select software that best satisfies the students' needs. You should also take time to collect the appropriate equipment, organize the room, and put the student experts to work. Learn the software, be aware of its time limitations, know how to integrate it into the classroom curriculum, and always encourage student participation by asking appropriate questions.

Now that we're acquainted with how to integrate the computer into the classroom, let's turn our attention to the way the software comes packaged today. The majority of software is shipped as CD-ROM discs, floppy disks, or to a lesser extent, Laserdiscs.

CD-ROM Discs

The **CD-ROM** disc drive looks like a compact disc (CD) player (Fig. 8.7), but it utilizes a CD-ROM compact disc format that holds text, graphics, and hi-fi stereo sound. The CD-ROM drive contains circuitry that can access data at high speeds, whereas a CD player only needs to access the beginning of an audio track quickly. The CD-ROM disc is similar to a music CD except that

Figure 8.7
CD-ROM drive

it uses different tracks for data storage. The disc is circular, is 4.75 inches in diameter, writes only one time, and reads numerous times. It also stores immense amounts of information, up to 680 MB of information on a single disc. For example, a CD-ROM can store all the volumes of an encyclopedia set with room to spare. One single CD-ROM is equivalent to roughly four hundred 3-inch floppy disks and 250,000 pages of text.

Growth of CD-ROM

CD-ROM software sales increased approximately 350 percent between June 1993 and June 1994. In fact, about 43 percent of all software sold in 1994 was CD-ROM, according to PC Data (PC Novice, 1994). In 1997, approximately 50 percent of the software purchases planned by schools were CD-ROM titles. According to a 1996-1997 survey done by Technology and Learning, all educational software producers are creating CD-ROMs. In fact 63 percent said that every single title being produced was in CD-ROM format, while 10 percent only have the floppy disk option, and 64 percent have stopped making floppy versions (Salpeter, 1997). Not very long ago, CD-ROM discs hardly occupied any shelf space in software stores; now they are in almost every software package sold. Besides the huge storage capabilities, there are other reasons for the increasing popularity of CD-ROM software in the schools.

Advantages of the CD-ROM

These reasons are related to the introduction of cheaper computers, the advent of sound computers, and the lower costs of the CD-ROM drives and discs. Due to technological advances, you can now retrieve vast amounts of information by hooking up a microcomputer and a compact disc drive. Most significant are the massive amounts of information that can be duplicated on a single CD-ROM disc. The fact that manufacturers can use existing CD audio technology with some modifications to produce these discs is another advantage because production costs remain relatively low. In addition, the CD-ROM is easy to use. All you have to do is insert a disk in the drive and follow some simple installation instructions. Many times the software runs from the CD-ROM so that only a few files need to be stored permanently on the hard disk. As a result, students do not have to swap multiple floppy disks in and out of their computer to copy a large program on their hard disk drive. Even though most software is packaged on a CD-ROM, there is still a need for the floppy disk. Manufacturers of small programs still use floppies, and many other companies still include a floppy or two with their CD for components that need frequent updating. For example, Roger Wagner, creator of *HyperStudio*, uses a floppy for his *HyperStudio* application so that it can be easily updated, while his CD-ROM disk remains the same.

Our discussion of software makes no distinction between a floppy disk program or a CD-ROM. The next step up from CD-ROM discs are DVD-ROM discs, the wave of the future.

DVD-ROM Discs

DVD (Digital VideoDisc or Digital Versatile Disc) is the next generation of video CD and high-storage CD-ROM. It is an optical disc format that is similar to CD-ROM, with greater storage capacity. DVD's storage capacity ranges between 9 and 18 GB and it uses MPEG-2 compression. The visual quality of DVD's images is between LaserDisc and VHS tape. The drive reads standard CDs as well as standard CD-ROMs and audio CDs. DVD will make LaserDiscs and VHS videotape obsolete because of its ability to hold video length of 135 minutes, which is what most movies are. Furthermore, the smallness of this medium and its hardware make it a very attractive product. DVDs show digital images, which is important for distribution of data over networks. With decreasing DVD drive prices, software will be packaged using DVD-ROM discs instead of CD-ROM discs or videodiscs. There are still companies active in publishing videodiscs, but videodisc development has decreased 20 percent (Salpeter, 1997). In the next few paragraphs, we discuss some of the software that is available on videodiscs or LaserDiscs.[3]

LaserDiscs

The **LaserDisc** is similar to a large CD and is approximately the size of an old 8-inch vinyl record. It has a huge storage capacity that allows the user to access as many as 110,000 visual images. With a bar code reader, a LaserDisc player, and a television, students can explore pictures, text, and simulations. If a computer is attached to the LaserDisc player, students can transfer images and text, music, or full-motion video from the disc into a multimedia format to be used on the computer at some future date. Using a program like *Media Max* (Videodiscovery) makes assessing a LaserDisc an easy task. Chapter 12 gives a more complete description of the LaserDisc technology. Regardless of the attractiveness of CD-ROM, the LaserDisc, or videodisc, is presently the choice for accessing premier quality motion video.

LaserDisc Software

Tom Snyder Productions has produced a unique interactive LaserDisc called *The Great Ocean Rescue* (Fig. 8.8). Instead of passively watching a database of photos, students work in teams to analyze information from this videodisc, and then they share their knowledge and ideas to solve different problems. The disc covers three areas: Ocean Basics, with movies and stills that show the basic features of the ocean; The Living Seas, with movies that show the types of life found in the ocean; and Protecting Our Oceans, with stills and movies on the pollution threat and possible

---

[3]The terms Videodiscs and LaserDiscs are used interchangeably.

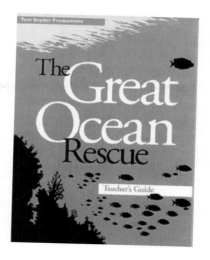

Figure 8.8
The Great Ocean Rescue
Reprinted by permission of Tom Snyder Productions.

solutions. Tom Snyder also distributes *The Great Solar System Rescue,* in which students search for lost probes in our solar system.

Another excellent disc with a similar focus is *Race to Save the Planet* (Scholastic), which lets students learn how humans damage air, land, and water; how different species are affected by pollution; and what can be done to effect change (Fig. 8.9). This disc contains sound tracks in both English and Spanish; all the user has to do is select the appropriate channel to hear one or

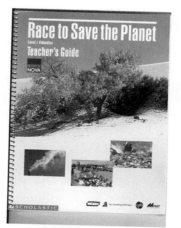

Figure 8.9
Race to Save the Planet
Figure reproduced by permission of Scholastic, Inc.

the other. Video footage of authentic case studies teach about topics such as the greenhouse effect, water and air pollution, and waste disposal. Scholastic distributes two other Interactive Nova videodiscs: *The Miracle of Life,* which lets the students explore human reproduction and sexuality, and *Animal Pathfinders,* which brings into the classroom hundreds of animals, their habitats, and behaviors. *Math Sleuths* (Videodiscovery) challenges students to apply varied problem-solving strategies. Ten different episodes that mirror the real world are included.

In addition to these LaserDiscs, other popular sellers cover a range of topics from solar systems to dinosaurs. For example, *The Solar System* (National Geographic Society) explores the planets in our solar system. *An American Portfolio* (D. C. Heath) examines European explorations in America with map animations. *The Encyclopedia of Animals* (Pioneer New Media Technologies) has a collection of discs on animals and their behaviors, diets, and habitats. *National Gallery of Art* (Voyager) includes more than 1,600 images with documentary clippings on the museum. The *1st National Kids Disc* (Voyager) includes activities, projects, and games. Students can learn to communicate in sign language, learn hundreds of jokes, or solve secret messages. *Regard for the Planet* (Voyager) invites the user to take a journey to distant cultures and continents, with more than 50,000 photographs of world events and daily life. *The Visual Almanac* (Voyager) contains more than 7,000 different images, resources, movies, picture sequences, still images, and sounds. Furthermore, Voyager has the following movies on LaserDisc: *Richard II, Hamlet, Henry V,* and *Othello.* Finally, *Dinosaurs: Fantastic Creatures* (Lumivision) explores the world of dinosaurs, and *Ancient Egypt* (Voyager) is an hour-long documentary that features walking tours of tombs and temples of Egypt. **See Appendix A for an annotated listing of LaserDisc titles.**

Subject Area Software

Now that we're acquainted with some LaserDisc programs, let's examine software in four different curricular areas.

Mathematics Programs

Since most computer scientists have training in mathematics, the computer is usually associated with this field. The research literature offers no apparent agreement on how best to use computer software for improving math skills or for developing higher order thinking. You must decide how to use this math software according to your own classroom needs. Math software is grouped as follows: drill and practice, simulation, problem solving, and tutorial.

Drill and Practice Programs.   Drill and practice math programs help students become more proficient in their math skills and concepts. These programs give students the needed practice in a highly motivating format and assist the less academically adept child in mastering the concepts. Programs such as *Fraction Attraction* (Sunburst) focus on ordering, relative size, addition and subtraction, equivalence, counting, and relative distance. The program helps students acquire an understanding of fractions by using four different activities. For example, the Whack-a-Frac game uses an arcade format to motivate the learners to improve their fraction skills. Each Frac-Mole stays on its hole until the student hits the Yes or No sign. As you can see in Figure 8.10, 9/11 is not equivalent to the target of 1/4, so the user's mallet is on the No sign. Every correct answer counts as a hit. The student must score enough hits to reach the goal, shown at the bottom of the screen.

Figure 8.10
Fraction Attraction
Sunburst (800) 321-7511

The game automatically advances to the next level after the student successfully clears the screen of all the target values. On the program's next screen appears another set of equivalent fractions and target values. *Fraction Attraction* is a good drill and practice math program because the Frac-Moles are motivating and the user can control the level of difficulty and speed.

A classic example of an addictive drill and practice program is the *Quarter Mile* (Fig. 8.11). Barnum Software produces a series of these math programs that cover whole numbers, fractions, decimals, percents, integers, equations, estimation, and math tricks. The *Quarter Mile* is designed so that users are in a competitive drag race with themselves. (Students can opt to race "wild running horses" instead of cars.) When they answer a problem correctly, the car leaves the starting line at 55 miles per hour. Thereafter, the car accelerates by 5 mph with each correct answer, racing against an exact video replay of their own five best previous races. The car goes faster and

Figure 8.11
The Quarter Mile
Used with permission of
Barnum Software.

faster as the racer accelerates to the accompanying sound effects, giving users the thrill of watching their improvement. The program features an excellent teacher management component. This particular program produces great results for the average or needier student.

Finally, there is the exciting *Stickybear's Math Splash* (Optimum Resource), which guides students ages five to ten on a water-filled wacky adventure. The software contains four inventive drill and practice activities, one of which is the arcade game *Rapid Fire*. The student is given an arithmetic problem at the top of the screen, and each correct answer moves the shark toward the finish line. *StickyBear's Math Splash* has more than 60 different mathematics skills in addition, subtraction, multiplication, and division.

Appendix A has a selection of popular drill and practice programs such as *Fractions Munchers* (MECC), *Math Blaster: Ages 6–9* (Davidson), *Hop to It!* (Sunburst), *Math Blaster: Algebra* and *Math Blaster: Geometry* (Davidson), and *Super Solvers OutNumbered!* (Learning Company).

Simulation Programs.   In the past, mathematics was often taught as an abstract concept devoid of any real meaning, but today there are math simulation programs modeled after daily real-life situations.

For example, *Mathville VIP* (Coursewares Solutions) is a simulation of a village in which students use math skills to solve problems that they encounter, such as buying food, earning money, buying clothes. In Figure 8.12, the student chooses to buy a shirt and pants and must figure out what is owed by taking into account the 1/4 off sale.

Figure 8.12
Mathville
© Courseware Solutions

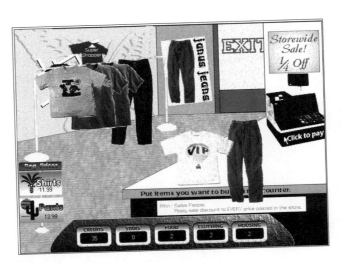

This program spans a variety of topics and difficulty levels. *Mathville VIP* is targeted for sixth grade and up, while *Mathville 1,2,3!* covers grades one to three; *Mathville Jr.*, grades four to six; and *Mathville*, grades seven to nine.

Major League Math (Sanctuary Woods) is a simulation math program in which students assume the role of a baseball player on a team. Students pick what kind of pitch to throw or what kind of hit to make and then answer math questions. The program contains realistic animations, real teams, real statistics, and math workshops. This program has several difficulty levels and 4,000 well-designed math questions that let teachers add more questions about their favorite professional team. Sanctuary Woods also produces *Real World Math: Adventures in Flight,* in which students assume the role of airport workers to apply math concepts in realistic settings. For instance, a student using the program might be asked to determine the length of the runway needed for an airplane to take off. Students who solve the problems correctly earn "Air Time." Students who master the math skill get to print, color and fly their own paper airplane.

Problem-Solving Programs.   Problem-solving software promotes critical thinking skills. Most problem-solving software is similar to simulation software in that users are placed in situations in which they manipulate variables and receive information on the results.

For example, the *Lost Mind of Dr. Brain* (Sierra Discovery Series) is a combination logic, language, spatial reasoning, memory, and music program for ages twelve and up. There are nine unique puzzles that expand thinking, and they are at different levels of difficulty. Dr. Elaina Brain, Dr. Brain's niece, is their guide as students explore and repair the demented region of Dr. Brain's brain. In Figure 8.13, Train of Thought, students must sort out Dr. Brain's scrabbled ideas

Figure 8.13
Lost Mind of Dr. Brain
© Sierra On-Line, Inc.

by docking the right colored ball in the right order. The *Lost Mind of Dr. Brain* has humor and wonderful graphics. The sequel to this series is the *Time Warp of Dr. Brain,* which includes a set of ten multilevel puzzles to help Dr. Brain figure out how to get back to the present time warp.

Edmark's *Thinkin' Things Collection 3,* a delightful program for seven- to thirteen-year-olds, teaches problem solving, introduces computer programming, utilizes inductive and deductive reasoning, identifies relevant information, and predicts a series of outcomes.

What's My Logic? (Critical Thinking Press & Software) is a program for older students and adults (Fig. 8.14). It contains a series of mind-stretching games. Students have to discover what

Figure 8.14
What's My Logic?
Used with permission of
Critical Thinking Press.

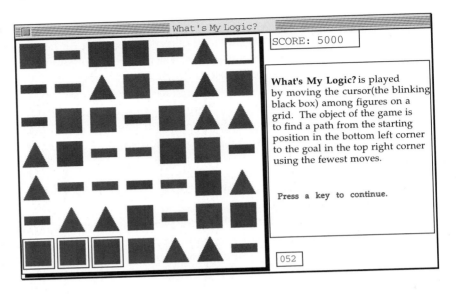

What's My Logic?

SCORE: 5000

What's My Logic? is played by moving the cursor(the blinking black box) among figures on a grid. The object of the game is to find a path from the starting position in the bottom left corner to the goal in the top right corner using the fewest moves.

Press a key to continue.

052

the fundamental rule of logic is that will let them travel through a maze to the end. There are thirty different fascinating mazes. This company produces many logic programs, including *Math Mind Benders, Memory Challenge,* and *Riddle Mysteries.*

Optimum Resource has created an excellent program for English-speaking and Spanish-speaking children ages five to ten called *Stickybear's Math Town.* In this adventure math program, students choose one of several unique locations as the site for engaging in real-life word problems. *Stickybear's Math Town* gives both verbal and visual reinforcement in the form of animations to reward the users' efforts. The program has six levels of difficulty, great graphics, and speech, and it develops math excellence in both English and Spanish.

Tutorial Programs.   A tutorial program gives students instruction in a particular subject and serves as a well-organized private teacher for the learner. A good tutorial usually starts with an overview of the subject matter and then checks the student for understanding. The student can move through the material, answering questions posed by the software. The program provides feedback for correct and incorrect responses, positive reinforcement, and a record of the student's performance. Math is a logical curriculum area for a tutorial because it lends itself to small-step sequencing of material. *Algebra Smart* (Princeton Review) is an interactive tutorial that covers a full year of Algebra I. The program has more than 500 practice problems with step-by-step solutions, algebra games, and 130 videos that take students through twelve key lessons. For example, Figure 8.15 (see page 191) has a live video introducing the student to equations.

Boxer Trigonometry (Brøderbund), a high school program developed by Boxer Inc., is a self-paced, comprehensive mathematics program that teaches fundamental concepts of trigonometry. Students manipulate angles and triangles to see how measurements and ratios change or remain the same. Each lesson has an example of how trigonometry is used in everyday life.

Coordinate Geometry (Ventura Educational Systems) is a tutorial that introduces students to Cartesian plane geometry and leads them to an exploration of coordinate geometry. Some of

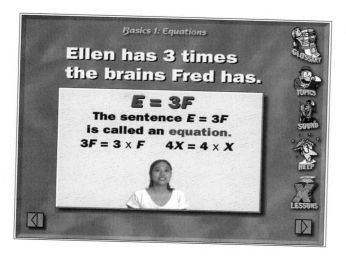

Figure 8.15
Algebra Smart
© Princeton Review.

the main topics handled by this program are locating points on the Cartesian plane, defining a locus, using set notation, and the concept of a y-intercept. The material is presented in a step-by-step manner in a leisurely paced format. With *Coordinate Geometry's* graphic equation processor (Fig. 8.16), students can define an equation that the computer will automatically graph.

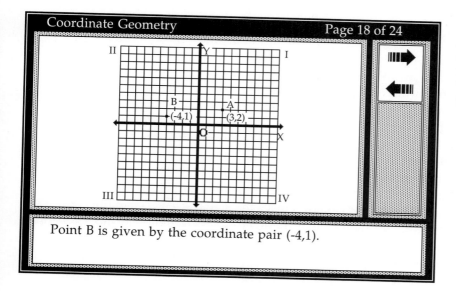

Figure 8.16
Coordinate Geometry
Used with permission of
Ventura Educational
Systems.

A quiz component can randomly generate problems, and the package includes a teacher's guide with reproducible worksheets. The beauty of *Coordinate Geometry* is its close adherence to the geometry curriculum taught at the majority of high schools.

Geometer's Sketchpad (Key Curriculum Press) is not a true tutorial, but it is an exploratory program that teaches geometry in an unusual way. Using Sketchpad 3 (Fig. 8.17), students manipulate and create geometric figures. They are able to explore freely or use the program as a tool to do assigned problems. The program comes with a user manual and sample activities.

Figure 8.17
Geometer's Sketchpad
The Geometer's Sketchpad®,
Key Curriculum Press,
P. O. Box 2304, Berkeley,
CA 94702, 1-800-995-
MATH.

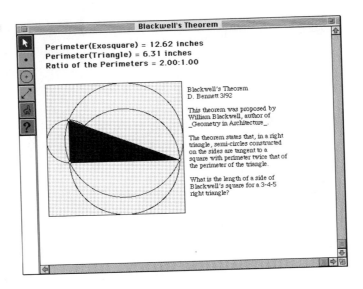

Science Programs

In many elementary schools, science programs have been limited to memorization of textbook facts; teachers have not had the time or money to collect the necessary materials for an exciting hands-on science lesson. Furthermore, the breadth of the science class has depended on the teacher's interests and specific areas of expertise. Because of their general lack of knowledge in science, teachers have ignored many science topics and most elementary students have received very little science education. Experimentation has occurred primarily in the high school science lab, an experience usually reserved for college-bound students.

The computer has begun to change this unfortunate situation. The science investigation skills of classifying, synthesizing, analyzing, and summarizing data are skills that the computer is designed to reinforce. The computer cannot replace the actual science laboratory, but it can simulate complex, expensive, and dangerous experiments, saving time and money. Because there is a renewed interest in science education, more schools are incorporating the computer into the science curriculum and science software is flourishing. Publishers such as MECC are producing exciting interactive programs such as *Explore Yellowstone, Science in Your Ear, Big Science Ideas: Systems, Science Sleuths 1 & 2,* and *Odell Down Under.* Brøderbund has a delightful exploratory science program called *Spelunx and the Caves of Mr. Seudo.* In this program, students, while learning about astronomy and cause and effect, explore the caves built by Professor

Spelunx. Knowledge Adventures produces a series of animated interactive science programs that include *Dinosaurs, Kid's Zoo, Undersea, Space Adventure, 3-D Body*, and *Science Adventure*, and Times Warner Interactive has produced the *Body Voyage: A 3-D Tour of the Human Body*. The graphics were created from a combination of computer imaging and medical photography and were based on a real human who donated his body to science.

Sunburst Communications has a rich and vast assortment of science programs including *Learn about Dinosaurs, Learn about the Human Body, Learn about Plants, Message in a Fossil, A Field Trip to the Rain Forest, Chemistry Explorer Series, Biology Explorer Series*, and *Genetics*. These programs range from elementary to adult levels. The series of early learning programs teaches students about dinosaurs, the human body, plants, fossils, animals; the programs for older students or adults instruct them in chemistry, biology, and genetics.

Drill and Practice Programs.   Today, quite a few superior science software programs offer drill and practice components. An example is *BodyScope* (MECC), which teaches the names of the organs and bones, the organ functions, and the systems. This program features on-screen diagrams of the human body systems and regions and different difficulty levels. The *BodyScope* screen in Figure 8.18 shows the user matching the word *clavicle* with its correct location in the body.

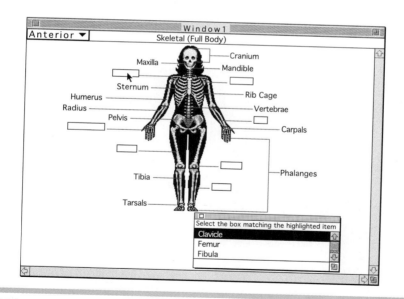

Figure 8.18
BodyScope
Used with permission of MECC. All rights reserved. *BodyScope* is a trademark of MECC.

GeoSafari Animals (Educational Insights Interactive) is a program that uses a game show format with questions based on animal trivia. The question categories include: Dog Show, Animal Tracks, Bird Call, Name That, and so on.

Senses (Ventura Educational Systems) utilizes outstanding graphics to help students identify the names of sense organs. Students are challenged to identify and spell the names of the basic parts of the ear, eye, nose, skin, and tongue. After users have correctly identified the part, they are provided with relevant facts about it.

Simulation Programs.   Science simulation programs such as *Operation Frog* (Scholastic) are designed for repeated use. This program simulates a frog dissection (without blood) and can be used as a prelude or alternative to a real dissection in the classroom. Students divide the organism into parts and then use a magnifying glass to examine closely each part of the frog's body. During the dissection, students can reconstruct the frog, part by part, reinforcing their knowledge of anatomy and biology, and can access essential information on frogs. A whole collection of dissection programs by Digital Imaging Associates includes the frog, crayfish, perch, grasshopper, starfish, and earthworm.

BodyWorks (Softkey International) (Fig. 8.19) makes students feel as if they are actually traveling in the human body and not just exploring a database. The program inspires students to learn the different functions of the systems of the human body. It contains a complete health section that includes information on such topics as first aid, fitness, common illness, and nutrition. *BodyWorks* has colorful photographic graphics on more than 100 glossary entries, detailed movie clips, and sound. Additionally, lesson plans and quizzes improve students' knowledge of human anatomy.

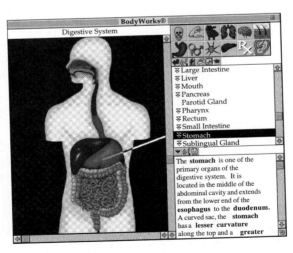

Figure 8.19
BodyWorks
BodyWorks used with
permission of Softkey
International Inc.
Copyright © 1994.

EyeWitness Virtual Reality: Dinosaur (Dorling Kindersley Multimedia) lets students enter the virtual reality of a dinosaur museum. In this program, students go to a simulated excavation site where they rebuild a dinosaur skeleton by finding just the right missing bones inside the earth.

Students can climb stairs to view models of different dinosaurs and can take mini quizzes as they travel around the museum.

Finally, *Physics Lab Simulator* (Visual Touch of America) is a tool designed to help physics teachers demonstrate experiments that ordinarily would need expensive equipment such as a cyclotron or mass spectrometer. Students can examine Einstein's theory of relativity, Rutherford's gold foil experiment, elastic collision, and other phenomena (Fig. 8.20).

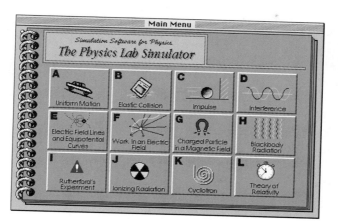

Figure 8.20
Physics Lab Simulator
© Visual Systems

Problem-Solving Programs.   The rapidly increasing collection of problem-solving and critical thinking programs serves as evidence of the emphasis on problem solving in science. An excellent example of a science problem-solving program and simulation combination is the classic *Botanical Gardens* (Sunburst), which challenges students to grow a variety of plants in a controlled environment. Through trial and error, students discover the effect of each variable on the plants. During the experiment, students adjust variables such as light, temperature, water, and music and monitor the resulting height of each plant.

The Incredible Machine 3 (Sierra) has 160 mind-melting, unusual puzzles with 100 animated parts. Students build trip-lever contraptions by placing parts such as trampolines and monkey motors on the screen. When these parts are combined correctly, the machine is able to complete its task. In the example in Figure 8.21 (see page 196), solving the puzzles lets the user put the bowling balls onto a large column box in the center. This program is meant for the bright middle schooler and for any adult brave enough to try it!

A wonderful program by Edmark, *Sammy's Science House,* is intended for the primary grades. With its appealing characters and animation, captivating voice, and charming music, this program makes a child curious about science. *Sammy's Science House* has five activities that help the student with sorting, sequencing, observing, predicting, and constructing. Students learn simple scientific classification painlessly. Students use logical thinking for building toys and machines, classifying plants, and sequencing movies. There are two modes to every activity: a discover mode and a question and answer mode.

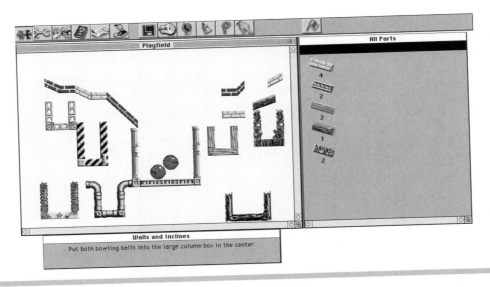

Figure 8.21
The Incredible Machine 3
© Sierra On-Line, Inc.

Tutorial Programs.   Good science tutorials are readily available, especially at the upper elementary, high school, and college levels. For example, *Science Smart* (Princeton Review) reviews all major topics covered in high school science. It uses more than seventy animations to explain key concepts in biology, chemistry, and physics and has more than 600 practice problems. Figure 8.22 shows an explanation of Newton's Law with film clips and sound.

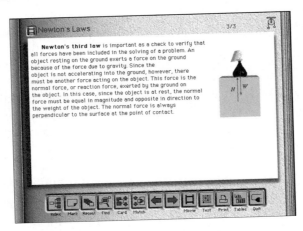

Figure 8.22
Science Smart
© Princeton Review

Cliff Study Ware (Cliff Study Ware) covers thirty topics from vectors and kinematics to waves and sound, to atomic, nuclear, and particle physics.

SuperTutor Chemistry (Stanford Multimedia) is a self-paced chemistry tutorial that covers hundreds of topics step by step with animation, voice lectures, exercises, and examples. This software covers one year of high school chemistry. Tutorial software on subjects of current health interest such as drugs and AIDS is also available. *Cocaine and Crack* (SAE Software) is a tutorial that reviews the physical and psychological effects of cocaine and crack, reasons for using it and not using it, and forms of cocaine. The program provides a list of objectives, tutorial lessons, and a self-test with multiple-choice questions. *AIDS* (SAE Software) is an interactive tutorial that provides up-to-date factual information about AIDS. It discusses the history of AIDS, how AIDS spreads, risk factors, current treatments, effects on the body, and resources.

In the past, science tutorial software has been limited to high-school and college level. However, software publishers are beginning to see the potential for science software development in the lower grades. Tutorial programs for the elementary level include the *Science for Kids* series (Science for Kids) This software is interactive English/Spanish courseware. The students have guided lessons and hands on activities. There is full motion video, wonderful pictures, sound, original art, and great instructional materials. The programs in the series are: "Cell"ebration for grades K–3; Forces & Motions, grades 3–6; and Simple Machines, grades 4–9. **Appendix A provides an annotated list of commendable science software for classroom use.**

Social Studies Programs

Social studies software excels at presenting current and historical events that foster class discussion and decision making. Students make decisions and then examine the consequences of those decisions. For instance, students can experience indirectly the results of a poorly planned presidential campaign, gaining perspective on political and social realities. Social studies programs are divided into two main categories: application software and computer-assisted instruction.

Application Programs.   With application software, a teacher can integrate other information into the social studies program. Students can use word processors to write about any subject, spreadsheet and graphics programs to analyze statistical data and to display pertinent information, and database programs to retrieve data and analyze the information. For example, students using the social studies program *Compton's 3 D World Atlas Deluxe* (The Learning Company) gain access to detailed maps and comprehensive statistics and information of 250 countries and 10,000 cities. Students can use the software to form patterns and see relationships. *3-D Atlas 98* (Creative Wonders) is a similar program that lets the student zoom in on the planet earth at nine different levels. This particular version has an on-line component, photographs of each country with their statistics, time-lapse depiction of the effects of pollution and deforestation, and an option to select city maps.

Teachers can use programs like *TimeLiner 4.0* (Tom Snyder Productions) to create time lines for any subject. There are disks available for different subject areas.

Computer-Assisted Instruction.   A teacher can integrate computer-assisted instruction programs into the social studies curriculum. To do so, the teacher should examine the purpose of instruction before selecting the software. Teacher A may need only a drill and practice program to reinforce the simple recall of the states and their capitals. Teacher B may need a simulation program to help students study the causes of the Civil War. In social studies, there are many excellent drill and practice and simulation programs that could meet the needs of both teachers.

Drill and Practice Programs.   Drill and practice social studies programs are easy to use, help in the retention of factual material, are fun because they use a game format, and require minimal teacher supervision. *World Discovery Deluxe* (Great Wave) is an inventive drill and practice program that contains twelve games. In Map Match, one of the activities, students place the puzzle pieces, each in the shape of a country or state, in their appropriate positions on the map. If students do this correctly, the state or country changes color and a cheery sound plays. The quicker the students find the correct answer, the more points earned. Whenever students answer incorrectly, the program makes a different sound, the puzzle piece slides away, and the number missed is recorded. Figure 8.23 shows a student earning 114 points by locat-

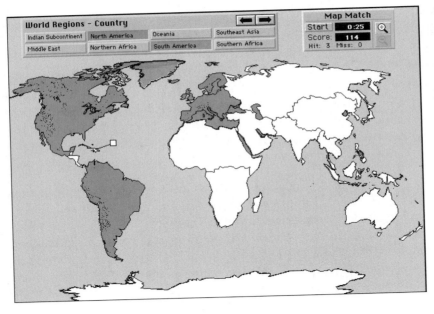

Figure 8.23
World Discovery Deluxe
Software designed by Mason Day. *World Discovery* is a trademark of Great Wave Software. Great Wave Software, 5353 Scotts Valley Drive, Scotts Valley, CA 95066 (800) 423-1144 Fax: (408) 438-7171 info@greatwave.com www.greatwave.com

ing three of the world's regions. Anyone can become a geography expert with award-winning *World Discovery Deluxe.* Designed for grades three through twelve, students build knowledge of countries, states, cities, and more, and answer questions about historical people, places, and events. The puzzle-like interface provides self-paced learning, with seventy-five maps from around the world, native greetings, national anthems, flags, and more. Students can print maps, save games, and challenge each other to exciting tournaments and relays. Teachers can create their own questions and customize *World Discovery Deluxe* for individual or whole-class learning.

Another drill and practice program is *GeoBee* (National Geographic Society). This program contains 3,000 multiple-choice questions. Students race a clock to score points in three rounds of play. *GeoSafari Multimedia,* (Educational Insights Interactive) teaches geography, history, and science facts. This program contains multiple-choice quizzes that cover geography, science, and history facts. For example, the student has to match a country with its respective flag. This program keeps track of correct answers and the student's progress.

Simulation Programs.   A well-designed social studies simulation challenges students to make difficult decisions concerning money, politics, or some other important factor. The *Carmen Sandiego* series (Brøderbund); *The Oregon Trail, The Amazon Trail, Africa Trail, The Yukon Trail,* and the *Maya Quest Trail* (The Learning Company, Inc.); the *Crosscountry* series (Didatech now Ingenuity Works); and *Decisions, Decisions* series (Tom Snyder Productions) all help students gain a better understanding of different people, places, and ideas in the present or past. Students learn to use the study of history as a basis for decision making and to distinguish between fact and opinion. In the Tom Snyder program *Cultural Debates* (Fig. 8.24), students view one of twelve short video clips together. This video clip inspires different questions, allowing students to debate, for example, whether this remote village should use technology. Afterward, the students use a worksheet to construct their debate questions.

Figure 8.24
Cultural Debates
Used with permission of
Tom Snyder Productions.

The *Carmen Sandiego* series has students travel around the world, the United States, Europe, and the American continent through time. *Where in Time Is Carmen Sandiego?* covers history from the year 400 to the 1950s as Carmen and her gang travel through time to steal a valuable resource. Student detectives track the thief and in the process learn about scientific inventions, famous individuals, important historical facts, and different cultures.

Language Arts Programs

Language arts programs are subdivided into the categories of writing, foreign language, vocabulary, spelling, grammar, and reading including reference tools. Because of the multitude of good language arts programs, it is often easier to integrate language arts programs into the curriculum than it is other types of programs.

Writing Programs.   The computer is an effective tool for motivating and reinforcing the necessary skills to improve a student's writing by linking the various processes involved in writing. We'll discuss both word processing and story writing programs.

We learned in Chapter 3 how word processors can help students save time and reduce effort by moving paragraphs, deleting sentences, and checking spelling. The word processor not only increases students' productivity, but also gives students extra time to think about content. We discussed word processors such as *Microsoft Word, WordPerfect* (Corel Corp.), *Bank Street Writer* (Scholastic), *Write: OutLoud* (Don Johnson), and ClarisWorks.

Other programs go beyond word processing, such as *Dr. Peet's Talk/Writer* (Hartley), which has a voice synthesizer pronouncing words as they are typed. This program is useful for students with special needs, ESL students, and young students. *MicroWorlds Project Builder Writer* combines word processing with Logo and *MicroWorlds Language* (Logo Computer Systems), a creative learning tool for exploring language and image. *My Words* (Hartley), a writing tool for children and adults, can be used by readers and nonreaders. It has been designed for the reluctant writer, offering features such as synthesized speech, sound effects, color, and word banks. *Write This Way* (Hartley) is a special writing program designed for the special needs student. It highlights spelling and grammatical errors and helps students solve their writing problems. The program has full voice so that students can hear their errors and expand their vocabularies.

In addition to these word processors are story writing programs such as *Storybook Weaver Deluxe* (MECC), *Stanley Sticker Stories* (Edmark), *Imagination Express* (Edmark), and the *Ultimate Writing & Creativity Center* (The Learning Company).

In the program *Storybook Weaver Deluxe*, students from grade level one to six can have the thrill of creating their own printed and illustrated stories by placing, moving, and sizing different pictures on the screen. Figure 8.25 illustrates a story written by an eleven-year-old. Students can write in Spanish or English with a bilingual spell checker and a flexible text-to-speech component that reads aloud in either language.

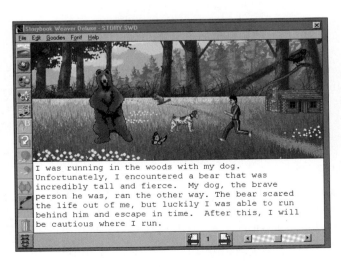

Figure 8.25
StoryBook Weaver Deluxe
Used with permission of The Learning Company, Inc. All rights reserved. StoryBook Weaver Deluxe™ is a ® trademark of Learning Company Properties, Inc.

Stanley Sticker Stories introduces children from ages three to six to story telling and story writing. The students create stories using 300 stickers and thirty different background scenes. The majority of the stickers are animated and they automatically resize in relationship to their placement on the background.

Imagination Express, for ages five and up, is a story construction kit that lets the child combine realistic background scenes with resizable figures or stickers, music, and word processing to make their own electronic books. The backgrounds and stickers are sold in different theme packs such as rain forest, oceans, and so on.

Finally, *The Ultimate Writing and Creativity Center* (The Learning Company, Inc.) combines graphics and word processing. The software contains ideas for more than 1,000 writing projects. There is a dictionary, thesaurus, spell checker, and text-to-speech capacity that reads the story out loud. Students can even transform their documents into multimedia presentations with music and animation. With this program, students are able to create reports, storybooks, journals, newsletters, and signs.

Foreign Language Programs.   Using state-of-the-art technology, the *Learn to Speak* series (The Learning Company) provides tutorial programs in Spanish (Fig. 8.26), English, French, and German. These programs let the students record their own speech and compare it with one of the twenty native speakers. The lessons have high quality sound, pictures, and video. The instructions are in writing, reading, grammar, and cultural information.

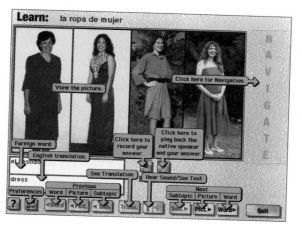

Figure 8.26
Learn to Speak Spanish
HyperGlot Software/©
The Learning Company.
All rights reserved.

Vocabulary Programs.   *Word Attack 3* (Davidson), *The Mind Castle* (Lawrence Productions), *Word City* (Magic Quest), and *Word Smart* (Princeton Review) are fun-filled programs that are more appealing than ordinary vocabulary work sheets. In *The Mind Castle's* Spell of the Word Wizard, students work their way through five challenging floors, racing against time to solve the puzzles in each room of the castle. There are 200 vocabulary-building puzzles on more than 600 words and definitions at all grade levels.

Word Smart is a program for grades six and up. Students explore a movie studio in which they find new words in different movie scripts. This program has eight levels of difficulty and covers 1,600 words. There are quizzes, rewards, a say-it feature, and a glossary (Fig. 8.27).

Figure 8.27
Word Smart
© Princeton Review

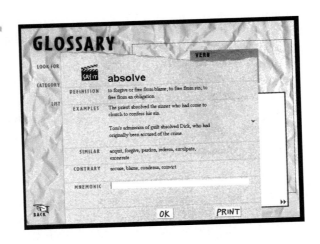

Spelling Programs.   The many spelling programs involve everyone and everything from sea animals, magic castles, and gulping frogs to jungle adventures and penny arcade activities. In *Spell It 3* (Davidson), which contains five spelling activities, an animated frog devours words for the correct responses. This program is suitable for middle grades to high school.

I Hate Love Spelling (Dorling Kindersley Multimedia) for ages seven to eleven is a collection of classic spelling games such as spelling bee, hangman, and anagrams that are packaged in a cartoon format.

Tomorrow's Promise Spelling series (Hartley) is written for grades one and two. These programs cover a full years' spelling curriculum with thirty spelling lists. There are fourteen activities, three games, and an assessment test for each list. *Tomorrow's Promise Spelling* has a story creator, a practice dictionary with pictures, and a tool to create custom word lists.

How Do You Spell Adventure? (Sanctuary Woods) is an unusual spelling program. This program is a combination adventure game, arcade game, and education program. Students help Robert Ripley collect artifacts, battle snakes, and gather gold while answering spelling questions that take the form of word jumbles, text passages, and hangman puzzles. There are many levels of play and 4,000 words.

Grammar Programs.   In the beginning, the grammar programs covered a range of skills from subject-verb agreement to recognition of the parts of speech through drill and practice activities. Today, grammar programs are not only drill and practice but are tutorials and simulations.

Grammar Rock (Creative Wonders) for ages six to ten contains videos on grammar from the ABC television program. Students complete nineteen multilevel activities and practice grammar concepts. The correct answers win coins that are used to play arcade games. An example of a good grammar tutorial for grades seven to adult is *Phrase Maze: Grammar through Phrases* (My Word Associates). This program teaches grammar while covering different types of phrases and their application in sentences. The tutorial component gives an explanation for every answer that a student chooses.

Grammar Games (Davidson) helps students enjoy their study of grammar skills such as subject-verb agreement, punctuation, and identification of sentence fragments. Set in a rain forest, it includes forty-two original stories, musical sound effects, and interesting rain forest facts.

Reading Programs.   Many simulations, drill and practice programs, and tutorial programs provide reading instruction. For the elementary schools there is a rich assortment to choose from including *New Katie's Farm* and *McGee's School Days* (Lawrence Productions), *The Playroom* and *The Treehouse* (Brøderbund), the *JumpStart* series (Knowledge Adventure) and the *Living Books* series. The Lawrence Productions programs tell stories without words in a *HyperCard* environment that lets students click on objects to produce sound and movement, encouraging them to share thoughts and feelings about each story. *The Playroom* and *The Treehouse* are interactive programs with elements of strategic thinking, simulation, and discovery.

The *JumpStart* series of interactive award-winning programs range from toddlers to fifth grade. The students learn to navigate through a schoolhouse full of interactive educational songs, puzzles, and games with a friendly host. *JumpStart Kindergarten* includes interactive modules that teach more than twenty-eight appropriate skills such as uppercase and lowercase letters, sorting, and more. After signing in on a board posted in the classroom, the student can click on the objects in this classroom scene to launch an activity (Fig. 8.28).

Figure 8.28
JumpStart
Kindergarten
JumpStart Kindergarten,
courtesy of Knowledge
Adventure, Inc., Copyright
1997.

For the high school level there are titles that range from Shakespeare to Dickens to Steinbeck. Creative Multimedia produces *Shakespeare—The Complete Works*. This single CD-ROM contains the complete works of William Shakespeare: his 37 plays and 159 sonnets and poems. Not only does the disk have the American English version, but it also has the Queen's English version. The

Literature: The Time, Life, and Works Series (Clearvue/eav) has such titles as *Chaucer, Thomas Hardy, Wordsworth, Dickens,* and *Shakespeare. MacBeth* by William Shakespeare, produced by Voyager,[4] gives an in-depth analysis, reference tools, a full reading of the play, video clips from three film versions of *MacBeth,* and a karaoke that lets you perform scenes from the play (Fig. 8.29). Along the same lines, Voyager has *American Poetry: 19th Century.*

Figure 8.29
MacBeth
© Voyager/Learn
Technologies Interactive

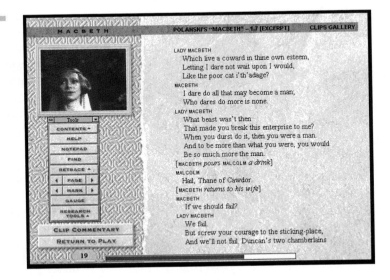

Romeo and Juliet (Cambrix Publishing) has students read and listen to the play, which is enhanced by synchronized on-screen text presented with hypertext study notes. This CD-ROM would be very helpful for the special needs student. *John Steinbeck Library: Of Mice and Men* by Mindscape/Penguin Books tells the classic tale of two men trying to find their niche in the world. The students learn about the history of the early 1900s in California. The CD-ROM contains film footage, archival photos, maps, and period music.

The *Living Books* series are unique clickable storybooks that offer such titles as *Arthur's Reading Race,* a story about Arthur's bet that his sister can't read ten words, *New Kid on the Block,* a humorous introduction to poetry, *Stellaluna,* a charming story of a little bat (Stellaluna) who is separated from her mother and falls into a bird's nest, and *Green Eggs & Ham,* which presents the classic Dr. Seuss tale with word and letter games.

Stickybear's Reading Room is a reading and thinking skills program that has won the hearts of many young children. The program offers four fun-filled activities with animation and human speech in both English and Spanish. Another reading program featuring Stickybear is *Stickybear's Reading Fun Park* (ages five to ten), which has a fun park setting and drills the child on phonics using four delightful activities. The level of difficulty is adjusted as the child progresses.

---

[4]Voyager sold their CD-ROM division to Learn Technologies.

Word Munchers (MECC), a drill and practice program, helps students master vowel sounds in a Pacman game format. In this program, the munchers try to eat words that have the correct vowel sound before the troggle disposes of them.

Optimum Resource's Stickybear Reading Comprehension Series is a series of high-interest programs, including *Sports, Science,* and *Geography,* that improve reading comprehension skills. These programs feature multilevel stories of interest to children in second through fifth grades. The geography stories address everything from caves to rain forests, the science stories cover the range from snakes to plants, and the sports stories discuss everything from superstars to sports facts.

Great Wave software has two reading comprehension programs that are quite useful to the classroom teacher. *Reading Search,* which is for grades two to six, has the students read folktales and answer questions. The *Reading Mansion* is for students in kindergarten through second grade and has the students visit fifty different mansions in which they answer all kinds of questions. It is a very flexible program that allows teachers to set options in order to give remedial help to each and every student.

Hartley has produced some programs for grades four to six with colorful graphics and sound capabilities that teach comprehension and the ability to draw conclusions. The titles in the series are: *Read to Think, Read to Image* (Fig. 8.30), *Read for Meaning,* and *Reading All around You.* These interactive lessons offer motivating reading material, including folktales and adventure stories in science and the humanities.

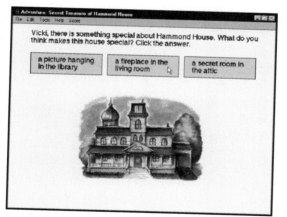

Figure 8.30
Read to Image
Screen courtesy of Hartley Courseware, a division of Jostens Learning.

Other excellent reading comprehension programs are *Major League Reading* (Sanctuary Woods), the *Reading Success* series by Pixel Genius Entertainment, and *NFL Reading* (Sanctuary Woods). *Major League Reading* for ages eight to eleven contains 1,500 baseball articles and 2,500 questions. The articles are very interesting because they contain the inside scoop on all the pro teams and players. These articles are the basis for seven critical activities that help students sharpen their reading skills. The *Reading Success* series consists of electronic books for five-to-ten year-olds with clickable vocabulary words and comprehension exercises. Finally, *NFL Reading,* for ages eight to twelve, is packed with passages featuring true pro football facts and statistics.

Inside the SAT (Princeton Review) is a tutorial program that uses a step-by-step approach to help secondary students master the strategies for dealing with material found on the SAT in all pertinent subject areas (Fig. 8.31) The program's instructor reviews basic skills using multimedia lesson topics. Students are able to see their scores improve and track their progress against last year's freshman class. Furthermore, students can research more than 1,200 colleges, including financial aid information, and contact the home pages of these institutions on the World Wide Web. This program covers every type of test question and offers test-taking tips as well as 1,700 sample questions.

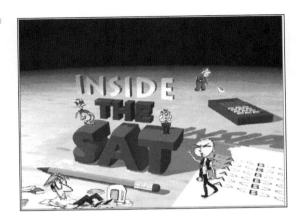

Figure 8.31
Inside the SAT
© Princeton Review

Reference Tools. Examples of some of Microsoft's exciting reference programs are *1998 Microsoft Bookshelf* and *Encarta. Microsoft Bookshelf* is the best all-around reference tool available because it combines a dictionary, *Bartlett's Quotations,* an encyclopedia, a thesaurus, a world atlas, and a world almanac. *Encarta* is a multimedia encyclopedia. *3-D Atlas 98* (Creative Wonders), lets the user zoom in on the planet earth from nine levels with an updated 3-D atlas. There are photographs of each country and updated statistics.

IVI Publishing manufactures the *Mayo Clinic Learning Series: An Adventure in Anatomy, The Human Body,* and *What Is a Bellybutton?* Both *An Adventure in Anatomy* and *The Human Body* teach the fundamentals of anatomy, biology, and logic. *What Is a Bellybutton?* is about an inquisitive girl named Elizabeth who likes to ask all sorts of questions.

Mindscape has produced among its many winners *The San Diego Zoo Presents . . . The Animals!* This program introduces the sights and sounds of the well-known San Diego Zoo, including more than 200 exotic reptiles, birds, and mammals.

Macmillan's *Dictionary for Children* defines and pronounces each word in its dictionary. The definitions are illustrated, and 400 sound effects make the dictionary come alive.

In the 1960s, there wasn't a literate child who hadn't heard of the Golden books. Hartley's *First Connections: The Golden Book Encyclopedia* brings the Golden books to computer. This program is designed for students in kindergarten through grade three, but it definitely can be utilized at other grade levels, particularly by reluctant readers. Students can read or listen to articles and stories that they can locate in a variety of ways. The program contains more than 1,500 articles, 200 tables, and 2,700 pictures.

Hartley produces another fine program disc called *Community Exploration* (Fig. 8.32) for students of all ages who are learning English as a second language. Community Exploration lets students explore and learn about different places in towns and cities. For example, students can

Figure 8.32
Community Exploration
Screen courtesy of Hartley Courseware, a division of Jostens Learning.

travel to hospitals, shopping centers, airports, police stations, and supermarkets. Students point and click to get information at these different locales. There is an abundance of language arts software. **Appendix A offers a comprehensive and annotated list of award-winning language arts programs.** Following is a chapter summary, a chapter mastery test, and a list of suggested readings and references.

Summary

In this chapter, we explored how to integrate the computer into the curriculum, select software according to the needs of pupils, collect the appropriate equipment, organize the classroom, and utilize the team approach. Next, we reviewed a variety of programs that are available on floppy disk, CD-ROM, and LaserDisc in math, science, social studies, and language arts.

Chapter Mastery Test

1. Give three suggestions for using one computer with thirty students and explain each suggestion thoroughly.

2. Name two advantages of using drill and practice software to learn mathematics.

3. Give two suggestions on how social studies software can be used to teach U.S. history.

4. Should the teacher use language arts software to improve writing skills? Give reasons to support your position.

5. Using one computer, how can the teacher increase group involvement in the learning process?

6. How can the teacher teach keyboarding skills more effectively to young children?

7. What methods can a teacher use to improve problem-solving skills on the computer?

8. How can the computer enhance the development of reading skills?

9. Explain how students might use the computer in gathering, organizing, and displaying social studies information. Include two titles of exemplary software.

10. How can the teacher utilize the computer to report scientific information?

11. What procedures can a teacher use to incorporate a variety of math software into the classroom?

12. What are the advantages of using computer math manipulatives over traditional math manipulators?

13. Explain why CD-ROM software has grown in the last three years.

14. Give two major advantages of using CD-ROM software.

15. What is a LaserDisc and how can it be used in the classroom?

16. What is DVD-ROM and why will it eventually replace the LaserDisc?

Classroom Projects

1. Visit a school that uses computers and a variety of computer programs. Write a brief report on the criteria used by the school in selecting its software.

2. Devise an organizational schedule for a classroom with only one computer.

3. Discuss the problems inherent in language arts software given the existing curriculum.

Research the topic to support your discussion.

4. Using the form in Chapter 7, review five software programs on the annotated list in Appendix A.

5. How does the school work with the media librarian to store, disseminate, and evaluate computer courseware?

Suggested Readings and References

Adams, Richard C. "Sometimes the Heat Drives You Nuts." *The Computing Teacher* 18, no. 7 (April 1991): 43–44.

Allen, Denise. "On-Screen Writing. Teaching with Technology." *Teaching Pre K–8* 27, no. 5 (Feb 1997): 18, 23–24.

Anderson, Kimberley; and Cay Evans. "The Development of the Canonical Story Grammar Model and Its Use in the Analysis of Beginning Reading Computer Stories." *Reading Improvement* 33, no. 1 (Spring 1996): 2–15.

Bearden, Donna, and Kathleen Martin. "My Make Believe Castle." *Learning & Leading With Technology* 25, no. 5 (February 1998): 21–25.

Bishop, Philip. "Build the Ultimate Software Library." *FamilyPC* (September 1996): 96–112.

Bigelow, Bill. "On the Road to Cultural Bias: A Critique of 'The Oregon Trail' CD-ROM." *Language Arts* 74, no. 2 (February 1997): 84–93.

Blanchard, Jay S., and George E. Mason. "Using Computers in Content Area Reading Instruction." *Journal of Reading* (November 1985): 112–17.

Brandt, D. Scott. "Tutorial, or Not Tutorial, That Is the Question . . ." *Computers in Libraries* 17, no. 5 (May 1997): 44–46.

Bratt, M. "Microcomputers in Elementary Science Education." *School Science and Mathematics* 83, no. 4 (1983): 333–37.

Brumfit, Christopher, Martin Phillips, and Peter Skeham, eds. *Computers in English Language Teaching: A View from the Classroom.* New York: Pergamon Press, 1985.

Buckleitner, Warren, ed. "The Elementary Teacher's Sourcebook of Children's Software." New Jersey: *Active Learning Associates.* Volume 4, (June 7, 1997).

Buckleitner, Warren, ed. "The Elementary Teacher's Sourcebook of Children's Software." New Jersey: *Active Learning Associates.* Volume 5, winter 1998 page 31.

Buckleitner, Warren, ed. *Children's Software Revue* (June/July 1997): entire issue.

Cappo, Marge, and Gail Osterman. "Math: Teach Students to Communicate Mathematically." *The Computing Teacher* 18, no. 5 (February 1991): 34–39.

Carlson, Kurt, and Valle Dwight. *The FamilyPC Software Buyer's Guide.* New York: Hyperion Press, 1996.

Cassidy, Jacquelyn A. "Computer-Assisted Language Arts Instruction for the ESL Learner." *English Journal* 85, no. 8 (December 1996): 55–57.

Cherry, Joan M., et al. "Evaluating the Effectiveness of a Concept-Based Computer

Tutorial for OPAC Users." *College and Research Libraries* 55, no. 4 (July 1994): 355–64.

Clements, Douglas H. *Computers in Elementary Mathematics Education.* Englewood Cliffs, N.J.: Prentice-Hall, 1989.

Collis, S., and M. Newman. *Computer Technology in Curriculum: An Instructional Handbook: Courseware Evaluation.* Olympia, Wash.: Washington Office of the State Superintendent of Public Instruction, 1982.

Dinkheller, Ann. *The Computer in the Mathematics Curriculum.* Santa Cruz, Calif.: Mitchell Publishing, 1989.

Eiser, L. "Problem-Solving Software; What It Really Teaches." *Classroom Computer Learning* (March 1986): 42–45.

Ellis, James D. "Preparing Science Teachers for the Information Age." *The Journal of Computers in Mathematics and Science* 9, no. 4 (summer 1990): 55.

"Top 50 Products." *FamilyPC* (July/August 1997): 61–70.

Field, Cynthia. "The Lighter Side of Education." *Incider A+* (September 1991): 34–39.

Gonce-Winder, C., and H. H. Walbesser. "Toward Quality Software." *Contemporary Educational Psychology* 12, no. 10 (July 1987): 19–25.

Hatfield, L. L. "Towards Comprehensive Instructional Computing in Mathematics." *Computers in Mathematics Education, NCTM Yearbook* (1984): 1–10.

Harrison, Nancy, and Evelyn M. Van Devender. "The Effects of Drill-and-Practice Computer Instruction on Learning Basic Mathematics Facts." *Journal of Computing in Childhood Education* 3, no. 3–4 (1992): 349–56.

Hodges, Bob. "Task Computing." *Learning and Leading with Technology* 25, no. 2 (October 1997): 6–8.

Howie, Sherry Hill. *Reading, Writing, and Computers: Planning for Integration.* Boston, Mass.: Allyn and Bacon, 1989.

Ignatz, M. E. "Suggestions for Selecting Science Education Software." *Journal of Computers in Mathematics and Science Teaching* (fall 1985): 27–29.

Ivers, Karen S. "Desktop Adventures: Building Problem-Solving and Computer Skills." *Learning and Leading with Technology* 24 no. 4 (December–January 1996-97): 6–11.

Johnson, Judi Mathis, ed. *Educational Software Preview Guide 1997.* Eugene, Oreg.: International Society for Technology (ISTE), 1997.

Kujubu, Laura. "Vendors End 56Kbps modem war." *InfoWorld* 19 (December 15, 1997): Volume 50, 51.

Lake, Daniel T. "Language Arts: Two Steps Beyond Word Processing." *The Computing Teacher* 18, no. 8 (May 1991): 30–32.

Mann, William P. *Edutainment Comes Alive!* Indianapolis: SAMS Publishing, 1994.

Margalit, Malka. *Effective Technology Integration for Disabled Children: The Family.* New York: Springer, 1990.

McMillen, Linda, et al. "Integrating Technology in the Classroom." *Language Arts* 74, no. 2 (February 1997): 137–49.

McLester, Susan. "Presenting the 1997–98 'Technology & Learning' Software Awards." *Technology & Learning* 18 no. 4 (November–December 1997): 23–28, 30–46.

McGinnis, J. Randy, et al. "Beliefs and Perceived Needs of Rural K-12 Teachers of Science toward the Uses of Computing Technologies." *Journal of Science Education and Technology* 5, no. 2 (June 1996): 111–20.

Myers, Lee. *Educational Software Institute 1997 Resource Guide.* Omaha, Nebr.: 1998.

"Microsoft Sits Atop Heap." *PC Novice* (1995): 10.

Mittlefehlt, Bill. "Social Studies Problem Solving with Databases." *The Computing Teacher* 18, no. 5 (February 1991): 54–56.

Nash, James, and Lawrence Schwartz. "Making Computers Work in the Writing Class." *Educational Technology* (May 1985): 19–26.

Pescovitz, David. "DVD Certainly Dazzles, but High Cost Is Stalling Its Acceptance." *Los Angeles Times* (July 21, 1997): D 10.

Reed, W. Michael. "Assessing the Impact of Computer-Based Writing Instruction." *Journal of Research on Computing in Education* 28, no. 4 (summer 1996): 418–37.

Salpeter, Judy. "Industry Snapshot. Where are we Headed?" *Technology & Learning* 17, no. 6 (March 1997): 21–30.

Schlenker, Richard M., and Sara J. Yoshida. "Integrating Computers into Elementary School Science Using Toothpicks to Generate Data." *Science Activities* 27, no. 4 (winter 1990): 13.

Smiddie, Laura. "ERIC Resources on Using Computers to Teach the Social Studies." *The International Journal of Social Education* 5, no. 1 (spring 1990): 85.

Solomon, G. "Writing with Computers." *Electronic Learning* (November/December 1985): 39–43.

Starfield, A. M. *How to Model It: Problem Solving for the Computer Age.* New York: McGraw-Hill, 1990.

Swanson, John, ed. *Anders CD-ROM Guide 97, 2d ed.* (Andrion Press/Penguin Books), 1997.

Tan, Soo Boo. "Making One-Computer Teaching Fun!" *Learning & Leading with Technology* 25, no. 5 (February 1998): 6–10.

Vockell, Edward, and Robert M. Deusen. *The Computer and Higher-Order Thinking Skills.* Watsonville, Calif.: Mitchell Publishing, 1989.

Wainwright, Camille L. "The Effectiveness of a Computer-Assisted Instruction Package in High School Chemistry." *Journal of Research in Science Teaching* 26, no. 4 (April 1989): 275.

Wepner, Shelley B. "Holistic Computer Applications in Literature-Based Classrooms." *The Reading Teacher* 44, no. 1 (September 1, 1990): 12.

Wilson, Timothy L.Y., and Kathy Fite. "Integrating the Language Arts Curriculum with Computer Applications in Mathematics." *Reading Improvement* 34, no. 2 (summer 1997): 66–70.

Teacher Tool
Software, Graphics,
Art, and Music

9

Objectives

Upon completing this chapter, you will be able to:

1. Discuss the features of a variety of teacher utility software;

2. Describe four types of graphics software programs;

3. Discuss the features of an assortment of art and music programs; and

4. Integrate art and music programs into the classroom.

Teacher Tool Software

Teacher support tools increase the classroom teacher's effectiveness. These programs are not meant for the student but for the teacher—to help in such tasks as grade keeping, test generating, flashcard makers, puzzle and work sheet generating, and statistic analysis. These programs reduce time and improve accuracy by assisting the teacher in chores that cannot easily be done in a traditional manner. For example, a grade book program can quickly weigh the students' grades, calculate the means and standard deviations, assign grades, and alphabetize the student list. When shopping for a utility program, you should determine whether the program fits your needs, saves time, and results in a more effective output. In the following section, we'll examine a variety of teacher support tools.

Grade Books

An old-fashioned grade book is useful, but an electronic one is more advantageous. Why spend hours recording and averaging grades when numerous grade book programs on the market today can do this burdensome task for you? Programs that are effective for the classroom teacher are *Grade Busters 1/2/3, Grade Busters Mac: Making the Grade,* and *Grade Busters IBM: Record Breaker* (Jay Klein Productions); *Easy Grade Pro 3.0* (ORBIS Software); *Gradebook Plus*(E.M.A. Software); *Grade Machine* (Misty City); and *Grade Quick* (Jackson Software). **Appendix A gives an annotated list of these grade book programs.**

A good grade book should let you enter students' names easily and correct any errors. Once you have typed in the students' names, there should be an option for sorting the names alphabetically, numerically, or by class standing. The grade book should let you enter a large number of students for each class, record a sufficient number of grades, record absences, and flag students with problems. For each score you enter, there should be a scaling factor to ensure that appropriate scores are figured in the students' or class averages. Furthermore, you should be able to assign weights according to the value of the class assignments. The program should calculate pertinent statistics—such as the range, mean, and medium scores—and should be able to save test information and produce a hard copy. Additionally, you should be able to easily print out copies of graphs and tables depicting the performance of the students and showing comparisons with other class averages.

Gradebook Plus 6.1 (E.M.A.) is very easy to use. The program gives oral reminders such as "Don't forget to back up." Figure 9.1 shows the program's screen with student names alphabetized, letter grades assigned, and averages calculated for each test and each individual. With this program, you can create form letters, choose fifteen user-definable comments, and annotate sound to student reports. You can use on-screen editing and a mini word processor to create the reports and letters. This grade program keeps track of eight classes with forty-five students and sixty entries per student. If you want to do any elaborate graphing, you can export to *Excel* or *Word*. Despite its many attributes, *Gradebook Plus* is not as feature laden as the more advanced programs, nor does it have a large number of entries, assignment allocations, grading scales, or weighing factors.

Figure 9.1
Gradebook Plus 6.1
© 1994, E.M.A. Software.

Name	1	2	3	Total	Pct.	Grade
EED 613						
Alt, Sue	98	88	95	281	93.7	A
Devlin, Mike	91	87	91	269	89.7	B
Feathers, John	65	78	87	280	76.7	C
Friedman, Bobbie	98	93	95	286	95.5	A
Jimenez, Felix	95	93	89	277	92.3	A
Johnson, Bill	77	79	83	239	79.9	C
Randall, Collen	78	84	87	249	83.0	B
Riley, Holly	89	87	88	264	88.0	B
Sharp, David	88	92	99	279	93.0	A
Washington, Morgan	78	90	93	261	87.0	B
Average:	85.7	87.1	90.7	263.5	87.8	
Possible:	100	100	100	300		

The more elaborate grade books display data as histograms or line graphs, report a wider range of statistics, and have a variety of templates in English and Spanish for parent correspondence. An example is *Grade Busters Mac: Making the Grade,* which records eighty students per class, 320 assignments, ten assignment categories, and five grading scales per class and displays the results graphically. Furthermore, it allows you to generate reports in English and Spanish. *Easy Grade Pro 3.0* offers grading, attendance, seating analysis, and reporting tools. A single grade book contains unlimited classes, students, and assignments.

An obvious advantage of an electronic grade book is its potential for helping teachers quickly inform students, parents, and administrators about pupil performance in the classroom.

However, many teachers feel that they need to maintain a pencil and paper grade book in addition to an electronic one, which requires double entry, because computers are not always accessible.

Test Generators

A test-generating program resembles a word processor in that it has standard editing capabilities such as deletion and insertion. Many of these programs have font libraries from which you can select different typefaces. There are various test formats including true or false, multiple choice, fill in the blank, short answer, essay, and matching. Some programs have graphics editors to help you integrate diagrams and pictures into your document. After entering your test questions, you can save them as a database file that can be retrieved on demand. Many programs let you randomize the order of the test questions and the arrangement of the possible responses to multiple choice questions for makeup tests or alternate tests. The majority of programs let you print final copies of the tests along with answer sheets.

Suitable test-making programs are *Test Designer Plus* (Superschool Software), *Teacher's Tool Kit* (Hi Tech), *Teacher's Helper Plus* (Visions), and *Test Quick* (Jackson Software).

Test Designer Plus combines test creation, test taking, sound, graphics, and foreign languages. This program lets you insert questions from a database and use an overhead projector to give students a timed test on the computer. In addition, you can choose the test format you want and integrate graphics into it. *Test Designer Plus* was one of the first programs to integrate graphics into a test. Programs such as *Teacher's Helper Plus* also integrate graphics and offer a wide selection of options.

Teacher's Helper Plus has an easy-to-use interface that many developers are following. This program has a variety of graphics options. Figure 9.2 shows a half-page fill-in graphic exam. You can use this program in all subject areas including special education, ESL, foreign language, and geography. With *Teacher's Helper Plus,* you can create tests, quizzes, activity sheets, and curriculum packages in a wide variety of formats including word searches, multiple choice, matching, true or false, and short essay.

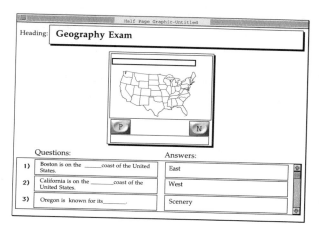

Figure 9.2
Teacher's Helper Plus
Teacher's Helper Plus™
© Arnie Vretsky 1993.
Publisher: Visions
Technology in
Education.™

Puzzle Makers

Puzzle makers motivate pupils studying potentially unexciting topics such as state capitals and parts of the body. You can use such programs to develop a crossword puzzle for reviewing Spanish, generate a geographical crossword for studying Europe, or create a math quiz in which equations are clues to a mystery. There are many noteworthy puzzle generators for the classroom including *Crossword Companion* (Visions), *Friday Afternoon* (Hartley), *Word Bingo* and *Word Cross* (Hi Tech), and *Crossword Creator* and *Puzzle Power* (Centron).

Figure 9.3 is a sample crossword puzzle generated from *Word Cross*. This crossword puzzle maker is simple to use. It lets you create your own crossword puzzles, and it automatically generates a variety of puzzles from the same word list. You can customize the puzzle maker to help your students learn new vocabulary words, or you can design a study guide for a test.

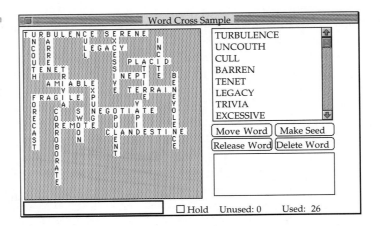

Figure 9.3
Word Cross
© Hi Tech of Santa Cruz

Drill Sheet Generators and Organizers

Some programs, such as *Worksheet Magic* (Teacher Support Software) and *Math Companion* (Visions), produce worksheets in a variety of formats. Other programs, such as *Make-A-Flash* (Teacher Support Software), make flash cards with vocabulary generated by the word processor. Profile tools such as Scholastic's *Electronic Portfolio* and *Grady's Profile* (Aurbach & Associates) assist teachers in the design and management of performance-based portfolios. *Electronic Portfolio* is a multimedia tool in which, teachers can create, manage, and present multimedia student portfolios using scanned images, sounds, full motion video, graphics, and textual data. *Grady's Profile*, a *HyperCard* application, keeps student work samples with assessment and narration. With this tool, the teacher can record students reading, talking, singing, and playing music, and can even make QuickTime videos of performances and print progress reports through any word processor.

Some programs produce labels, time lines, attendance charts, flowcharts, and lesson plans. *Bilingual Timeliner* (Tom Snyder Productions) lets you design and print out time lines of any length in Spanish or English. There are data disks available for the different curriculum areas. *Lesson Plan Helper* (FTC Publishing), written by former teacher Marsha Lifter (Fig. 9.4), generates 350 "tried and true" lesson plans for all elementary subject areas. In addition, this program lets you enter your own lessons and has a search feature to find the lesson plan you need.

Figure 9.4
Lesson Plan Helper
Author: Marsha Lifter and Marion Adams Publisher: FTC Publishing. Reprinted by permission.

Daily Plan-It Lesson Planner (FoolProof Security) is a lesson planner/calendar designed for teachers. It provides day, week, month, and year views, and it contains an outliner for organizing curriculum. *Inspiration* (Inspiration Software), a powerful visual thinking tool, helps organize students' ideas and information (Fig. 9.5). This program assists students in developing visual diagrams, flowcharts, and knowledge maps. It has an integrated outline view that helps create concise written proposals and reports.

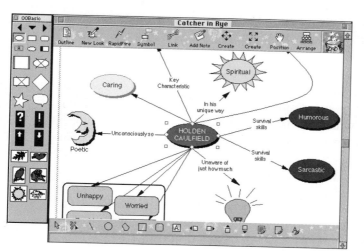

Figure 9.5
Inspiration
Reprinted with permission of Inspiration Software Inc.

Statistical Programs

In the past, if you wanted to do statistical analysis, you had to do the work by hand or on a mainframe at a university. Today, many microcomputer programs help the classroom teacher make calculations and analyze statistics. Most of these programs handle the simplest statistics such as mean and standard deviation, while the more complex programs handle multilinear regression and factor/time series analysis. In a matter of seconds, you can compute a regression, an analysis of variance, or an unpaired t-test. Figure 9.6 from *StatView 4.0* (Abacus Concepts) shows the

Figure 9.6
StatView 4.0
Abacus Concepts Statview,
Abacus Concepts, Inc.,
Berkeley, CA, 1992.

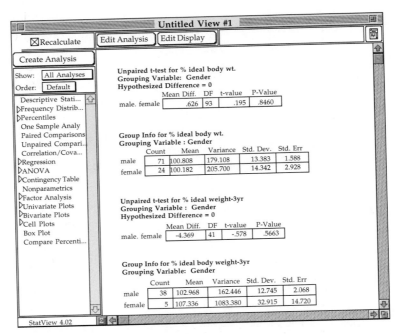

calculation of an unpaired t-test, performed simply by double clicking. *StatView 4.0* offers all the tools needed to analyze and present data in one application. Years ago, you had to enter data in a spreadsheet, perform manipulations, and then import this data into a statistical package for analysis. Next, you had to use another program to create graphs. Finally, you had to use a draw program to prepare tables and graphs for presentation. *StatView 4.0* seamlessly integrates its data analysis into one well-designed package. There are many other statistical packages, including *GB Stat* (Dynamic Micro Systems), *Fastat and Systat* (Systat), and *SPSS* (SPSS).

In most cases, you won't need this type of package because many grade book programs have sufficient statistics capabilities. However, if you are doing research or if your grade management program does not provide statistics, then you'll need this type of program.

Graphics Software

Just as utility programs are beneficial for the teacher, graphics are beneficial for the classroom. Pictures shape our perceptions and help us to communicate. When children first begin to read, they are always fascinated by illustrations. When a biology instructor discusses the anatomy of the body, he or she finds it beneficial to show a labeled drawing. The businessperson uses graphics to make important presentational points. The artist draws beautiful landscapes to make a statement. The engineer creates a scale drawing to construct a bridge, and the architect uses graphics to design a building. The statistician creates charts from tables. In our society, people use pictures to educate, to communicate, to express emotions, to build, and to persuade. A picture is indeed worth a thousand words.

The term *graphics* refers to the representation of images on a two-dimensional surface. Graphics can be as simple as a pie graph or as elaborate as a detailed anatomical painting of the human body. When discussing computer graphics, we are referring to computer-generated pictures on a screen, paper, or film. Let's divide our discussion of graphics into four categories: design, presentation, productivity, and art software.

Computer-Aided Design (CAD)

Computer-aided design (CAD) assists in the design of objects such as machine parts, of homes, or of anatomical drawings. You must have the proper CAD program to accomplish such tasks. With CAD software, you can easily change or modify designs without having to create actual models, saving time, money, and effort. *Claris CAD* can be used by students from grades ten and up to create any two-dimensional geometric designs, lines, arcs, and spline curves. It is a complete CAD program that supports American and International design standards and facilitates drawing with a Graphic Guide System that locates an important geometric point automatically. *Generic CAD 2.0* (Autodesk), a good mid-level 2-D drafting program, offers a fine complement of tools and some high-end features such as floating point precision. Finally, *Key CAD Complete* (Softkey) is an inexpensive CAD that turns the computer into a design and drafting tool. Users can produce drawings, plans, and layouts to scale. This program lets users add to or renovate homes and schools, create school projects, or design furniture.

Many of the programs in this field are simulations that let users create models and show their use. For instance, CAD software allows an engineer to design a car, test it, and even rotate it to gain perspectives. *Car Builder* (Optimum Resource/Weekly Reader Software) is a simulation for education that lets students construct, modify, and test a car. In the process of constructing the car, students design the inside of the car and select the chassis length, the fuel tank, and the tires. When the mechanical selection is complete, students modify the body with data generated through a testing procedure that includes a wind tunnel and a test track. At the end of this testing session, students can save the specifications of the designed car on a disk.

Kid CAD (Davidson) is a three-dimensional kit with which students build houses with electronic building blocks and click them into position. Students can paint, decorate with anything displayed on the screen, and fill the house with pets, furniture, and even a dinosaur. The program creates a realistic environment with full view; students can change the perspective from a view of the house from the backyard to a view through the front door (Fig. 9.7). *Kid Cad* is a creative and innovative program that comes with sound effects and is designed for students from seven years old to adult.

Figure 9.7
Kid CAD
Reprinted with permission of Davidson and Associates.

SimTown and *SimCity 2000* are two popular simulation programs designed by Maxis. *SimTown* is for younger students and *SimCity 2000* (Fig. 9.8) is for older students. Both programs are building games in which students create cities and then try to increase their size. In *SimCity 2000*, students become planners, designers, and mayors of an unlimited number of cities.

Figure 9.8
SimCity 2000
SimCity 2000 by MAXIS, Orinda, CA.

When using any type of simulation, students engage in problem solving. For example, in *SimCity 2000* the students have to consider the consequences of placing police and fire protection in the wrong locations.

Finally, *Design Your Own Railroad, Design Your Own Train,* and *Run Your Own Train* (Abracadata) provide students with model railroad programs. With *Design Your Own Railroad,* students can draw layouts to scale of model railroads, which they can save or print. *Design Your Own Train* lets users create model trains, subways, buses, or trolley layouts. *Run Your Own Train* lets students in the role of engineers traverse each layout from the top view to the inside of the locomotive.

Presentation Graphics in Business and Education

In Chapters 5 and 6, we learned about databases and spreadsheets and about how useful these application programs are. It is not difficult to create graphs from such databases and spreadsheets to illustrate presentations. These types of illustrations are called **presentation graphics,** and business people use them all the time to illustrate salary distribution, inventory fluctuation, and monthly profitability. The images can take many forms, such as the exploded pie chart in Figure 9.9 from *CA-Cricket Graph III* (Computer Associates). The section that represents 1973 is separated from the pie for emphasis.

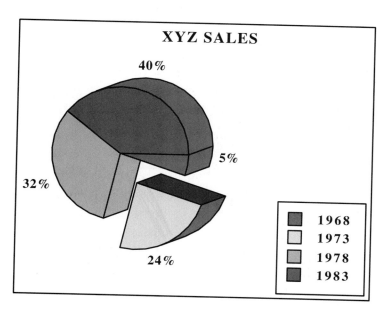

Figure 9.9
Exploded pie chart
Reprinted courtesy of Computer Associates International, Inc. © Copyright Computer Associates International, Inc. All Rights Reserved. Cricket is a registered trademark and Cricket Graph is a trademark of Computer Associates International, Inc.

Graphs show a relationship among categories of data. The exploded pie chart compares the results in four different years, with each slice representing a year. Other types of graphs could have illustrated the same data in different ways. Figure 9.10 shows a sample bar graph.

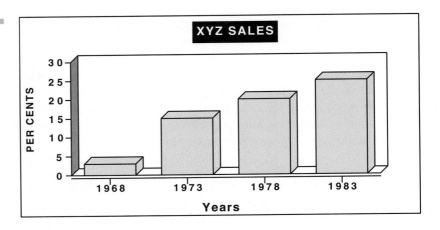

Figure 9.10
Bar graph
Reprinted courtesy of
Computer Associates
International, Inc.
© Copyright Computer
Associates International,
Inc. All Rights Reserved.
Cricket is a registered
trademark and Cricket
Graph is a trademark of
Computer Associates
International, Inc.

You can use graphics to better understand a student's performance on a series of exams. In Figure 9.11, the teacher charts Jane Smith's scores on six math tests to quickly grasp the effect of an extreme score (65) on this student's performance.

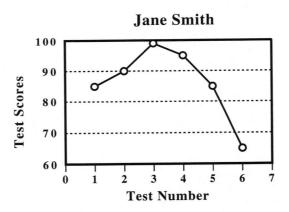

Figure 9.11
Line graph
Reprinted courtesy of
Computer Associates
International, Inc.
© Copyright Computer
Associates International,
Inc. All Rights Reserved.
Cricket is a registered
trademark and Cricket
Graph is a trademark of
Computer Associates
International, Inc.

Graphing is a means of getting a clearer picture of what the data represent. In education, graphing possibilities are unlimited. In science, students can graph the results of a series of plant experiments in which they alter variables such as temperature and water. In economics or social studies, the teacher might want the class to chart a stock's progress for a year or to graph voting trends. In English, the teacher can chart the incidences of certain words used in student writing to make a point about vocabulary.

Graphic programs such as *Graphics at Your Fingertips* (Vicki Legue) and *GraphPower* (Ventura Educational Systems) are suitable for classroom use. Additionally, if teachers do not want to buy a separate graphing program, they can use an integrated program like *ClarisWorks*, which has a graphing component in the spreadsheet. With *GraphPower* (Fig. 9.12), you can create a bar graph of the area of the continents, one example of the use of graphs to develop skills for analyzing and interpreting data. In addition to bar graphs, the program can create pictographs, line graphs, circle graphs, and box graphs. To use this program, you simply enter data in the Data Center and click on a graph icon to instantaneously create a graph. After creating a graph, you can export it to word processing or desktop publishing programs. Furthermore, an on-line tutorial called the Graph Tutor helps you overcome problems. *GraphPower* not only shows how to read graphs but also teaches the different functions of various graphs.

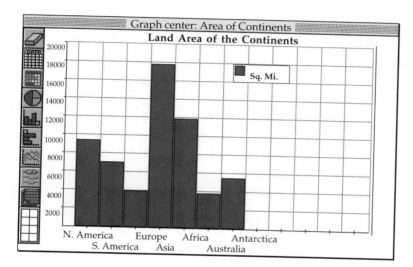

Figure 9.12
GraphPower
Used with permission of Ventura Educational Systems.

Classroom Applications

▼   I. Pet Data Sheet   ▼

Materials
You will need a program that does graphics like *GraphPower* or *ClarisWorks* and one or more computers.

Objectives
Students will learn how to do a survey and how to graph their survey using a bar graph and a pie graph.

Procedure
1. Have each student survey seven other students to find out how many family pets they have.
2. Ask each student to create a bar graph on the computer.

3. Instruct students to survey their seven students again to find out what kinds of animals they have and how many of each.
4. Have students create a pie graph and a bar graph showing this new information.

▼ II. State Data Sheet ▼

Materials
You will need a program like *GraphPower* and one or more computers.

Objectives
Students will read an almanac for information and learn how to graph their information using a bar graph and a line graph.

Procedure
1. Have each student select three states and research the annual rainfall of those states.
2. Ask the students to create bar graphs on the computer comparing the statistics.
3. Have the students track down state rainfall statistics for three specific dates in the past.
4. Instruct students to construct line graphs showing the changes in the data for each state over a period of time.

Productivity Graphics

To create an award, a poster, a banner, a greeting card, or a certificate, you use productivity graphics software. The best known is *The Print Shop* (Brøderbund), which lets you create a wide assortment of multicolored graphics. This classic program has won countless awards because it is easy to use and it saves hours of time and effort. Figure 9.13 shows a ready-made sign from the newest version, *The Print Shop Deluxe*. Since the introduction of the original *Print*

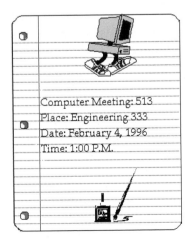

Figure 9.13
The Print Shop Deluxe
From Print Shop Deluxe.
Copyright © Broderbund
Software, Inc. Reprinted
by permission.

Shop, several versions have been produced. Although the concept remains the same, these programs vary in their capacity to produce color and graphics and use a laser printer.

There are dozens of programs that can be used for productivity graphics. Some of the more popular are Scholastic's *SuperPrint II,* which comes in a bilingual version; *Print Artist* (Sierra); *Kid Pix Studio* (Brøderbund); *PrintMaster Gold Deluxe* (Mindscape); and *Disney Print Kits* (Walt Disney Buena Vista). These programs produce attractive flyers, banners, and awards. *KidCulture* (Pierian Spring Publishing) lets children explore history, myth, art, tradition, and daily life in an interactive environment. Each culture offers printable art with which students can construct authentic headdresses, masks, (see Fig. 9.14), castles, entire 3-D villages, skyscrapers, trains, cars, boats, animals, people, and more.

Figure 9.14
KidCulture
Used with permission of
Pierian Spring Software.

Productivity programs offer different templates, fonts, border designs, and clip art. These enhancement programs, designed for users with limited artistic talent, have far-reaching educational benefits. The teacher can produce attractive and interesting bulletin boards, announcements, awards, work sheets, and even transparency masters. The students can design their own letterhead stationery to use in communicating with each other by classroom mailbox.

Classroom Applications

▼   I. Educational Sign   ▼

Materials
You will need *Print Shop Deluxe* or *SuperPrint II* and one or more computers.

Objectives
Students will use a productivity graphics program to design a sign, learn about design and placement of objects, and discuss the reasons for not taking drugs.

Procedure

1. Talk about placement and design with the students.
2. Instruct pupils to use the productivity graphics program to design a sign warning people not to take drugs.
3. After all students have designed signs, discuss what makes certain signs more appealing than others.
4. Discuss the reasons students should not take drugs.

▼   II. Math Riddle Card   ▼

Materials

You will need *Print Shop Deluxe* or *SuperPrint II* and one or more computers.

Objectives

Students will use a productivity graphics program to design a greeting card and practice solving math riddles.

Procedure

1. Give each child a riddle or have children find riddles in books.
2. Tell the pupils to design a greeting card, putting the riddle on the cover and the answer on the inside of the card.
3. An example is shown in Figure 9.15.

A train left Chicago at 1:00 P.M. A second train left New York at 3:00 P.M. The train from Chicago traveled toward New York at 40 miles per hour. The train from New York traveled toward Chicago at 50 miles per hour. If the distance from Chicago to New York is 1,000 miles, which train was farthest from Chicago when they met?

They are the same distance from Chicago.

Figure 9.15
Greeting card cover in *Print Shop Deluxe*
From Print Shop Deluxe. Copyright © Broderbund Software, Inc. Reprinted by permission.

4. Now distribute the greeting cards and have the students solve the riddles.

Art Software

Paint programs are art oriented rather than design oriented, giving the user tools to draw and paint computerized pictures. There are significant advantages to using the computers for drawing and painting. If the artist makes a mistake, she or he can easily correct it because there are no real paints or water colors to spill, drip, or smear. The painter simply clicks the mouse and instantaneously changes the picture or color, enlarges an image, or moves an object.

The majority of paint programs mentioned in this text offer coloring and texturing capabilities. Most paint programs also have brushes of different widths and shapes, drawing tools, a mirror image function, different fonts, and an undo function. Furthermore, the programs enable the artist to cut and paste images in any location in the document and to import images from other programs.

With paint programs, students can draw geometric shapes, create designs, and construct miniature cities. To create images, students can use an input device, such as the keyboard, a mouse, a light pen with a graphics tablet, or a digitizer. The light pen (Fig. 9.16), which handles exactly like a pencil, translates the students' drawings from the tablet into the computer program so that the drawings instantly appear on-screen. The digitizer converts the shades of an image into a digital representation for the computer. A digitizer can be in the form of a scanner or camera; this equipment will be discussed in Chapter 13.

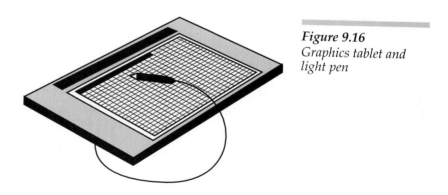

Figure 9.16
Graphics tablet and light pen

There are many good paint programs available today including *Canvas* (Deneba Software), *Dabbler 2.0* and *Fractal Design Painter* (Fractal Design), *Kid Pix Deluxe* (Brøderbund), and *EA Kids Art Center* (EA Kids). An example of a paint program that is especially appropriate for elementary school children is *EA Kids Art Center*. Students use a paint box loaded with colors, funny paintbrushes, and a collection of different tools, each with its own sound. The program includes a talking alphabet, stickers, a coloring book, and block art. Students learn shapes and practice motor skills by creating block art. The costume activity lets students mix and match outfits and color them (Fig. 9.17). *EA Kids Art Center* comes with forty colorful projects that foster creative talents.

Figure 9.17
EA Kids Art Center
Used with permission of EA Kids.

An example of a first-rate program for older students is *Dabbler* (Fractal Design). This program (Fig. 9.18) offers an art tutorial that follows Walter Foster's step-by-step drawing lessons. *Dabbler* plays back many of the printed lessons that are in Foster's book. The program lets students work

Figure 9.18
Dabbler
Used with permission of Fractal Design.

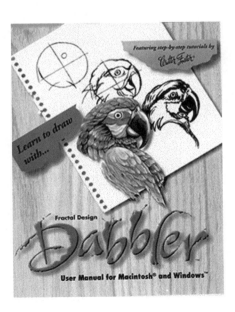

through a lesson one stroke at a time with the customary tools and textures. Special *Dabbler* sound effects add some spice to the program and tell the user what actions are taking place. For example, opening a drawer is accompanied by animation and drawer-opening sounds.

Classroom Applications

▼   I. Math   ▼

Materials
You will need a program like *Dabbler* or *Kid Pix Deluxe* and one or more computers.

Objectives
Students will use the paint program to make various geometric shapes, and they will learn about shapes.

Procedure
1. Teach the students about different geometric shapes as they learn to recognize each shape.
2. Show the students how to use the paint program to create these shapes. Figure 9.19 shows an example.

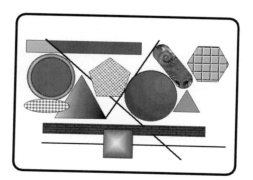

Figure 9.19
Shapes in a draw program

3. Explain how to fill the shapes with color and how to copy and paste shapes.
4. Have the students use the paint program to make abstract drawings without a fill pattern.
5. When they are finished, have them print out their shapes and color them, making sure all shapes of the same type have the same color.
6. Display these drawings on the bulletin board.
7. As a follow-up activity, have the students make collages with shapes.

▼ II. Science—Cells ▼

Materials
You will need a program like *Dabbler* or *ClarisWorks* and one or more computers.

Objectives
Students will use a productivity graphics program to illustrate the parts of an animal or plant cell and paste it in their report.

Procedure
1. Students should draw the cell on paper, labeling its parts.
2. Students then take turns using the computer to create their plant or animal cell.
3. Have the student use a text tool to label each part of the cell, for example, the cell membrane, nucleus, and so on.
4. Save this picture to disk.
5. Tell the students to prepare a report about animal cells or plant cells on the computer.
6. Have the students insert their picture in their report.
7. As a related activity, have the students draw the human body and label its parts.

Music Software

Music education software is scarce because of a lack of interest in using the computer for teaching music. However, recently there has been a resurgence in music programs. Current programs give instruction in playing music, in composition and music theory, and in music appreciation. Some programs provide specific practice in music skills. *Piano Discovery System* (Jump! Music) and *Musicware Piano* (Musicware Piano) offer comprehensive, self-guided piano instruction. The *Piano Discovery System* comes with a MIDI keyboard and has arcade-style games and tutorials. *Musicware Piano* is adult oriented, taking students step by step from basics to playing complete songs. The tutorial provides in-depth interactive lessons on basic notation, theory, and playing techniques .

ConcertWare Pro (Jump! Music) is one of the best programs for teaching students music notation. This theory program has a simple interface and professional capabilities. *ConcertWare Pro* supports editing, printing, and playback of musical pieces and arrangements.

Another music theory program, *Anatomy of Music* (Tom Snyder Productions), explains the structure of classical music. Students access different musical passages by clicking on the mouse. Students listen to different musical selections and study their structure on the computer screen in order to analyze the different parts and their relationship to the whole piece. *Anatomy of Music* presents the different classical forms: minuet, rondo, sonata, concerto, and symphony. This program includes seven compact discs that feature recordings of such composers as Bach and Mozart.

Numerous software programs analyze a specific composition. Voyager/Learn Technologies, a pioneer in the music CD area, offers some comprehensive music CD-ROMs on different composers:

Ludwig van Beethoven: Symphony No. 9, Wolfgang Amadeus Mozart: "Dissonant" Quartet, Antonín Dvořák: Symphony No. 9 "From the New World" (Fig. 9.20).

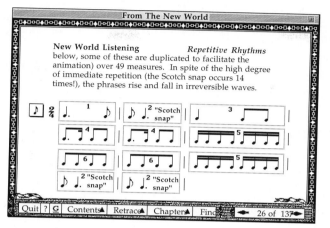

Figure 9.20
Dvorak: The Ninth Symphony.
"From the New World,"
by author Robert Winter,
developed by Voyager
Company, now Learn
Technologies.

The *Antonín Dvořák* CD-ROM contains the entire score of his Symphony No. 9, expert commentary and musical analysis, glossary definitions, and musical examples. It also has an illustrated section on the instruments of the orchestra as well as an in-depth historical essay on Dvořák's life and times. Anytime during the program, students can choose to play a board game that tests their knowledge.

Still other music programs are sing-a-long adventures, let students experiment with music, teach musical elements, and teach about musical instruments. *Dr. T's Sing-A-Long Around the World* (Dr. T's Music Software) has the students star in a sing-along adventure (Fig. 9.21). The

Figure 9.21
Dr. T's Sing-A-Long Around the World
Used with permission of
Dr. T's Music Software,
Johnmerson @aol.com.

students learn about different cultures by visiting with animated characters from twenty-two countries. Students select the songs, and then they sing as the words scroll across the screen. They can mix and choose from different sound sources, customize their own list of songs to play, and choose to read and hear lyrics in English or the original language.

In *Rock and Bach Studio* (Brøderbund), users learn about famous classical music composers and listen to some of their compositions. Additionally, the program lets students produce their own action-packed music video. They are able to assemble a group of musicians from a cast of characters and teach them their own songs or songs from a collection of programmed selections.

Making Music (Forest Technologies) allows children to experiment with the elements of music. This program contains games and open-ended creativity activities.

Microsoft Musical Instruments teaches students about different musical instruments around the world. Students click on an instrument to see its description, learn about its components, or listen to its sound. This multimedia delight covers more than 200 musical instruments.

Classroom Applications

▼   I. Music   ▼

Materials
You will need a program like *Rock and Bach Studio* (Brøderbund) and one or more computers.

Objective
Students will identify musical notes.

Procedure
1. Draw eight bars on the board to represent a scale.
2. Turn the computer monitor away from the students and have a student play six random notes.
3. Ask the students to listen carefully to the sounds and draw the bars and notes that represent the sound patterns.
4. Do this two more times so that the students can check their work.
5. Now turn the monitor toward the class and play the pattern. Have them compare their patterns to the ones that are being played.

▼   II. "Mother, May I?" Adaptation   ▼

Materials
You will need *ConcertWare Pro* (Jump! Music) or *Anatomy of Music* and one or more computers.

Objective
Students will improve musical comprehension and increase their knowledge of music theory.

Procedure
1. Have the students stand in a straight line in the back of the classroom.
2. Select students at random to answer questions such as, "How many beats does a quarter note have?"
3. Instruct the student to advance one step if he or she answers the question correctly and to move back one step if not.
4. The first student to make it to the front of the room wins.

Appendix A offers an annotated list of award-winning teacher utility, graphics, art, and music programs. A summary, a mastery test, classroom projects, and selected readings and references conclude this chapter.

Summary

Teacher support tools can make a teacher more effective. One of the most popular tools is the grade book, which lessens the time a teacher spends entering grades, computing averages, and informing parents about students' progress. Other tools that save time and reduce effort are test and work sheet generators, puzzle makers, and statistical packages.

A good paint program lets the user draw without the fear of making a mistake, and a productivity program enables those who are not artistically inclined to create any graphic from an award to a poster. CAD programs are useful in designing room layouts, machine parts, and cars; presentation graphics produce charts and graphs that show relationships within categories of data; and music programs are an effective aide in practicing music skills and theory. We examined eight activities for integrating graphics, art, and music programs into the classroom.

Chapter Mastery Test

1. Discuss two examples of music software and how each one can help the student in a different phase of the music curriculum.

2. What is the difference between a presentation graphics program and a paint program? Describe the major features of each.

3. How has the availability of paint programs on the computer affected the traditional way of drawing and painting?

4. Define *CAD* and discuss its primary use.

5. What is a teacher tool program? Explain how it can provide individualized instruction for a class.

6. What is a productivity graphics program? Discuss two uses for this program in the school curriculum.

7. Define *computer graphics* and explain its importance in today's world.

8. What are the advantages and disadvantages of using a grade book program?

9. What is an exploded pie chart? How can a teacher use it in the classroom?

10. Explain how graphics programs can be beneficial for the classroom.

Classroom Projects

1. Prepare a report showing why it is important that your school use productivity graphics.

2. Use a presentation graphics program to graphically represent Jane Smith's grades of 50, 60, 70, 88, 97, and 100.

3. Use a productivity graphics program to produce (a) a riddle card, (b) a poster, (c) a calendar, and (d) letterhead stationery. Explain the educational value of each product.

4. Pretend your school will let you purchase only one graphics program. Will you choose a productivity graphics, presentation graphics, paint, or computer-aided design (CAD) package? Explain and justify your selection.

5. Create a test for the class using a test-making program.

6. Evaluate three test-making programs, discussing their strengths and weaknesses.

7. Use one of the many puzzle utilities to create a product for class consumption.

8. Review three grade book programs and talk about their differences and similarities. Explain why you would choose one over the others.

Suggested Readings and References

Beamer, Scott. "10 Reasons Why You Need a Charting Program." *MacUser* (June 1990): 126–38.

Benton, R., and Mary Balcer. *The Official Print Shop Handbook.* New York: Bantam Books, 1987.

Bunescu, Marci. "Turn Your Computer into a Music Workstation." *Electronic Learning* 9, no. 5 (February 1990): 7–39.

Eiser, L. "Print It! 101 Things to Print with Your Computer." *Classroom Computer Learning* (April 1988): 76, 77.

Field, Cynthia. "The Electronic Palette." *Incider A+* (August 1991): 33–39.

Greh, Deborah. "Graphics Gallery 6: Is It Art Yet?" *Incider A+* (September 1991): 46–48.

Harris, Judith B. "What Do Freehand and Computer-Facilitated Drawings Tell Teachers about the Children Who Drew Them?" *Journal of Research on Computing in Education* 29, no. 4 (summer 1997): 351–69.

Holzberg, Carol. "Print Creativity Packages." *Techology & Learning* 17, no. 7 (April 1997): 8–12.

Keizer, Gregg. "Command Performance." *Incider A+* (August 1991): 41–43.

Klinger, Mike. "The One-Computer Music Classroom." *Teaching Music* 3, no. 3 (December 1995): 34–35.

Lifter, Marsha, and Marian E. Adams. *Make and Take Technology.* Gresham, Oreg.: Visions Technology in Education, 1997.

Larking, Conal L. "The New Print Shop." *Home Office Computing* (April 1990): 77.

Mack, Warren E. "Computer-Aided Design Training and Spatial Visualization Ability in Gifted Adolescents." *Journal of Technology Studies* 21, no. 2 (summer–fall 1995): 57–63.

Martin, Joan, Mei-Hung Chiu, and Anne Dailey. "Science: Graphing in the Second Grade." *The Computing Teacher* (November 1990): 28–32.

Mathis, J. "Personal Tools for Administrators." *The Computing Teacher* 19, no. 4 (December/January 1991–92): 44–50.

Mathis, Judi, and Cathy Carney. "Easy Color Paint." *The Computing Teacher* 45 (April 1991): 46.

McLester, Susan. "Presenting the 1996–97 'Technology & Learning' Software Awards." *Technology & Learning* 17, no. 3 (November–December 1996): 36–38, 40, 42–43, 46–48.

McLester, Susan. "Presenting the 1997–98 'Technology & Learning' Software Awards." *Technology & Learning* 18, no. 4 (November–December 1997): 23–28, 30–46.

Mendrinos, R. "Computers as Curriculum Tools: Exceeding Expectations." *Media and Methods* (January/February 1988).

"Microsoft Sits Atop Heap." *PC Novice* (1995): 10.

Rogers, Laurence T. "Computer as an Aid for Exploring Graphs." *School Science Review* 76, no. 276 (March 1995): 31–39.

Sigesmund, B. J. "The Top 50." *Newsweek Extra Computers & the Family* (winter 1997): 26–50.

Ursyn, Anna. "Computer Art Graphics Integration of Art and Science." *Learning and Instruction* 7, no. 1 (March 1997): 65–86.

Wempen, Faithe. *PowerPoint 97.* Indianapolis, Ind.: QUE Corporation, 1996.

Stafford, Deborah J. "PowerPointing the Way." *Technology Connection* 4, no. 1 (March 1997): 16–17.

Woestman, Kelly A. "Test Generators: The Next Generation." *History Microcomputer Review* 11, no. 1 (spring 1995): 26–37.

Vockel, Edward L., and Douglas J. Fiore. "Electronic Gradebooks: What Current Programs Can Do for Teachers." *ERIC Clearinghouse* 66, no. 3 (January–February 1993): 141–45.

Multimedia

10

Objectives

Upon completing this chapter, you will be able to:

1. Define *multimedia*;
2. Explain the terms *hypermedia* and *hypertext*;
3. Discuss the origins of hypermedia;
4. Identify several major contributors to the field of hypermedia;

5. Explain the basic features of hypermedia programs such as *HyperCard*, *HyperStudio*, *Digital Chisel*, and *LinkWay Live!*;
6. Describe some ways that hypermedia can be incorporated into teaching;
7. Discuss some of the issues surrounding hypermedia; and
8. Describe *QuickTime*, morphing, warping, and virtual reality (VR).

What Is Multimedia?

We are bombarded with the term **multimedia** everywhere we travel: on television, at the shopping mall, in newspapers, and in educational circles. What does this ubiquitous and elusive term really imply? Is it just a catchword tossed about, or does it have a specific meaning? In general and in this textbook, *multimedia* refers to communication from more than one media source such as text, audio, graphics, animated graphics, and full-motion video.

The concept of multimedia is not new. For years, teachers have made presentations using different kinds of media. Traditionally, they have used slides, movies, cassette players, and overhead projectors to enrich lessons. Now, however, teachers may employ a personal computer and hard disk storage to combine these different media sources in their teaching. A computer-based method of presenting information, multimedia emphasizes interactivity (Pfaffenberger, 1994). Computers offer input and output devices such as laser discs, CD-ROM, and stereo sound.

Historical Perspective

In the professional literature, the words closely related to multimedia are **hypertext** and **hypermedia.** Hypertext originated more than fifty years ago with Vannevar Bush. An electrical engineer and Franklin Delano Roosevelt's first director of the Office of Scientific Research and Development, Bush is given credit for first proposing the idea of a hypothetical machine, predating computers, that would mimic the mind's associative process. In 1945, Bush described a work station called a *memex,* that imitated the linking and retrieval of the human mind. Influenced by

233

Bush's associative linking and browsing concepts, Douglas Engelbard conducted research at the Stanford Research Institute in 1960 that led to several significant inventions including the mouse, an on-line work environment now named *Augment,* and the concept of a "viewing filter." With a viewing filter, users could quickly view an abstract of a document or file, thus being able to scan a database for important information (Fiderio, 1988).

These developments were important, but it was Ted Nelson who made the most critical step in the development of multimedia. Around 1965, he coined the term *hypertext,* meaning nonsequential writing, and he developed the writing environment called *Xanadu* that lets a user create electronic documents and interconnect them with other text information. Through this endeavor, Nelson was attempting to make literary works available electronically. (Each time a user accessed text on this system, Nelson was paid a royalty.)

In hypertext, text, images, sound, and actions are linked together in nonsequential associations that let the user browse through related topics in any order. At the center of this system is linking. No document or bit of information exists alone; each document contains links to other related documents. Figure 10.1 illustrates the nonlinearity of hypertext.

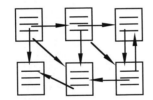

Figure 10.1
The nonlinearity of hypertext

An example of hypertext is a computer glossary from which a user can select a word and retrieve its definition. This definition is linked to other words and the user can move from it on to other related terms.

Hypermedia is nearly synonymous with *hypertext;* however, it emphasizes the nontextual components of hypertext. Hypermedia uses the computer to input, manipulate and output graphics, sound, text, and video as part of a hypertext system. The different forms of information are linked together so that the user can move from one to another. When a teacher uses hypermedia, the computer directs the action of devices such as a video camera, videodisc player, CD-ROM player, tape recorder, VCR tape deck, scanner, video digitizer, audio digitizer, or musical keyboard. Figure 10.2 shows an example of a hypermedia workstation.

A computer and a monitor are the basic equipment necessary for a hypermedia presentation, with the computer acting as a controller and the monitor displaying images. Depending on the sophistication of their equipment, teachers can add a variety of devices and software programs to enhance the hypermedia creation. For example, they can use the video camera to film a scene while the videocassette player records a television program, the audio digitizer transfers sounds, the scanner adds graphics or text, and the video digitizer transfers noncomputer media such as

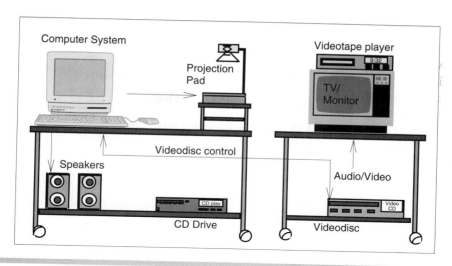

Figure 10.2
Using technology in the classroom—hypermedia workstation
ClickArt images © T/Maker Company and Corel Draw 3.0

photos or videotape. Furthermore, teachers can use art programs such as *Corel Draw* or *Kid Pix Deluxe* (Brøderbund) to enhance artwork, a musical keyboard to provide customized musical accompaniment, and a laser printer to produce high-quality images. Hypermedia components range from sound-enhanced documents that will play on any computer to a *HyperCard* or *HyperStudio* stack that offers sound, animation, and color.

Hypermedia Authoring Tools

One objective of this chapter is to provide an overview of hypermedia authoring tools and programs and how they operate. While you cannot expect to become hypermedia programming experts based on the information in this chapter, you will be introduced to the *possibilities* of hypermedia.

HyperCard

One of the first implementations of hypermedia and the best known one is *HyperCard*, developed by Bill Atkinson at Apple Computer. Atkinson created **HyperCard** in 1987 to run on the Macintosh computer. Since then, *HyperCard* has become almost synonymous with hypermedia, although it is important to remember that not all hypermedia use *HyperCard*.

   HyperCard is an authoring tool that lets you organize information, browse through it, and retrieve it. Information is stored in the form of on-screen *cards* (rectangular boxes on your screen) that contain text, graphics, sound, and animation. You can browse through the cards with the help of *buttons* that you click (Fig. 10.3). The cards are organized in *stacks,* much in the same way

Figure 10.3
Elements of a card
HyperCard 2.2 © 1987-1993 Apple Computer, Inc. All rights reserved. Used with permission.

you would organize index cards. *HyperCard* comes with ready-made stacks but the program also enables you to create your own. One of the program's unique features is its simplicity, enabling nonprogrammers to create their own applications without having to master a complicated programming language.

Let's examine how *HyperCard* works. When you first open *HyperCard,* you access the home stack of cards.[1] In the 2.2 version of *HyperCard,* this stack has five cards. The first card is the home card (Fig. 10.4), which essentially welcomes you to the program and serves as a visual directory

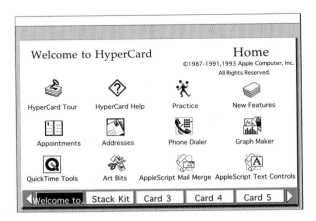

Figure 10.4
HyperCard home card
© Apple Computer, Inc. Used with permission.

---

[1]Even if you do not start *Hypercard* with home stack, you need to have a home stack on the disk to run the program.

of the elements in the program. The second card is the stack kit card, which transports you to advanced stacks. Cards 3, 4, and 5 allow you to create your own stacks. No matter where you are in *HyperCard*, you can usually return to the home card of the home stack by simply clicking the home button, as shown in Figure 10.5.

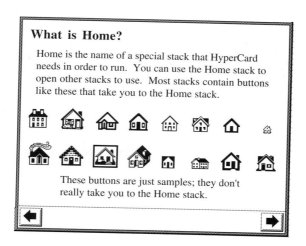

What is Home?

Home is the name of a special stack that HyperCard needs in order to run. You can use the Home stack to open other stacks to use. Most stacks contain buttons like these that take you to the Home stack.

These buttons are just samples; they don't really take you to the Home stack.

Figure 10.5
HyperCard home
stack buttons
© Apple Computer, Inc.
Used with permission.

From the home card, you can embark on a stack-creating journey, designing stacks on any topic imaginable. For example, you might create a stack that teaches a foreign language, takes the user on a tour of a foreign city, tells an interactive story, or describes an historical event. You might create a stack on endangered animals, a schedule stack, or an address stack. Figure 10.6

Figure 10.6
HyperCard 2.2
address card
© Apple Computer, Inc.
Used with permission.

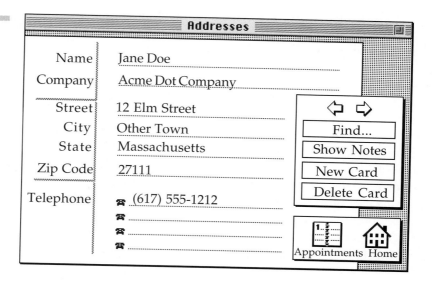

Addresses

Name	Jane Doe
Company	Acme Dot Company
Street	12 Elm Street
City	Other Town
State	Massachusetts
Zip Code	27111
Telephone	☎ (617) 555-1212

Find...
Show Notes
New Card
Delete Card

Appointments Home

shows one card in a stack of addresses. On this card, the telephone and address of Jane Doe are recorded in *fields*, similar to those found in a database record. Each card in this stack will have the same fields but different information for each individual.

When you create a stack, you determine what appears on the cards. You will probably want to include the home icon so that users can easily return home. You will include buttons that enable the user to browse through the cards in the stack. The user can simply click the buttons with the hand browse tool 🖐 to move in a variety of directions through the stack. There are several other ways to browse through a stack—by choosing commands from the menu, typing commands in the message box, or using the arrow keys on the keyboard—but the buttons are usually the most straightforward way (Fig. 10.7). Each button that you create has a script written in

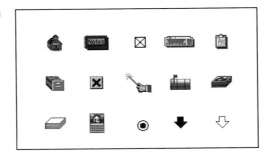

Figure 10.7
HyperCard buttons
© Apple Computer, Inc.
Used with permission.

the programming language **HyperTalk;** when the button is activated, the computer follows the procedure outlined in the script. You may choose your buttons from a variety of types including pop-up text, video, text entry, sound, and multibuttons.

A *pop-up text button* pops up a small window with text. This text adds information, definitions, or instructions to the screen without cluttering it.

A *video button* sends a command to a videodisc player, causing it to display a single, still video image or a complex sequence of images. The video can appear on a separate monitor, or if you're using a video overlay card, the images can replace or be integrated with the computer screen images.

A *text entry button* lets you type a free response to a question instead of selecting an option. If your entry matches the pattern supplied by the program, you receive positive feedback on the screen; however, if you give an incorrect response, you are told your answer is not correct.

A *sound button* plays a sound clip when it is clicked; the sounds played may range from musical selections to sound effects such as rain falling or digitized sounds such as speech in English or Spanish. In the *HyperCard* example in Figure 10.8, pressing the horn button makes a moo sound; the user must respond by pressing the cow button.

A multibutton activates a list of buttons in a special order. Clicking one of these buttons might give a message, change disks, and link a card stack with a new card stack.

To clarify even more how *HyperCard* works, let's consider a specific example. Imagine that you have created a stack to enable students to browse through the permanent collection

Figure 10.8
HyperCard 2.2 sound
buttons
© Apple Computer, Inc.
Used with permission.

of the National Gallery of Art in Washington, D.C. You have imported color images of the different works of art from the gallery onto the cards in the stack. Students in your class move through the gallery at their leisure, clicking buttons to move on to new paintings or to return to ones they have already seen. They also can click on buttons to take a tour through the French countryside that inspired Monet's work or to listen to a concert of the music of composers, such as Debussy, who were contemporaries of some of the artists represented in the gallery. If students run out of class time, by clicking on the home button they can return to the opening screen from where they can embark again on a new tour of the gallery the next day.

HyperCard clearly is a user-friendly program, although it requires considerable work to construct a stack. Many other authoring tools for hypermedia perform the same functions as *Hyper-Card.* Another example of this type of program is *HyperStudio.*

HyperStudio

While *HyperStudio* originated on the Apple II series of computers, it now has a Macintosh version and a Windows version for the IBM and its compatibles. *HyperStudio* has many of the *Hy-perCard* features and functions, but *HyperStudio's* simplicity makes it more suitable for most teachers and students. *HyperStudio* does not require scripting (programming) because all its major functions are already built into the program. Nevertheless, programming is available for the advanced user in the form of a scripting language called *HyperLogo. HyperStudio* has many built-in features and functions, including color, videodisc, and CD-ROM support, animation, and scrolling. By examining *HyperStudio* more closely, you'll gain an understanding of what is involved in working with an authoring tool.

When you first open *HyperStudio,* you open to the home stack (Fig. 10.9).

The home stack is the guide to the other stacks included in *HyperStudio.* It serves as a visual directory of the different elements in the program. For example, if you click on the "Sample Projects" button, you will be asked to choose either home, school, or kid projects stacks. To create a stack, you click on the *New Stack* button. A blank card will appear. On that blank card, you can

Figure 10.9
HyperStudio home
stack
Used with permission of
Roger Wagner Publishing,
Inc.

begin to design your new stack. Let's say you decide to create an African stack. On your first card (Fig. 10.10), you introduce users to Africa.

Figure 10.10
HyperStudio stack
card 1
© Roger Wagner
Publishing, Inc.

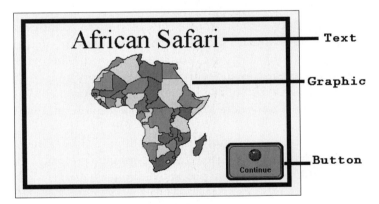

You add the text "African Safari," a map graphic, and two buttons—one visible and one invisible. The invisible button is superimposed over the map graphic. When users press it, it makes a roaring sound. The visible button, Continue, plays music and provides a nice transition to Card 2 (Fig. 10.11).

Figure 10.11
HyperStudio stack
card 2
© Roger Wagner
Publishing, Inc.

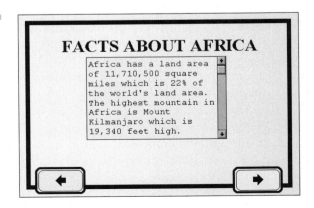

Card 2, your sound card, contains a box with text, an invisible button, and two arrow buttons. When users show this card, a voice reads the text enclosed in the box. The left arrow button takes users to Card 1, while the right arrow button plays a sound clip and then takes users to Card 3. When users open Card 3 (Fig. 10.12), a self-activating invisible button uses animation to send the elephant down a hill.

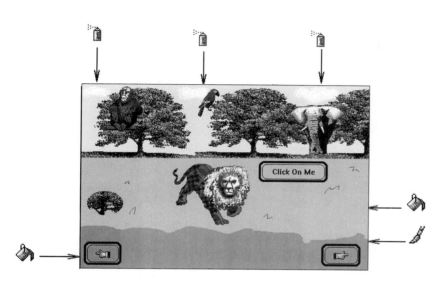

Figure 10.12
HyperStudio stack
card 3
© Roger Wagner
Publishing, Inc.

The Click On Me button lets the lion run to the bottom of the card. You would have drawn this card with the *HyperStudio* paint tools shown on the outside of the card in Figure 10.12. The left arrow sends users back to Card 2, and the right arrow takes users forward to Card 4 with accompanying sound effects.

Finally, Card 4 (Fig. 10.13) has a self-activated scrolling text button. The information enclosed in the rectangular box scrolls the way credits on a movie screen do. The home button returns users to Card 1 to start the stack again.

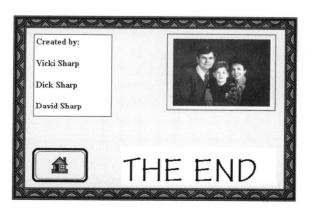

Figure 10.13
HyperStudio stack
card 4
© Roger Wagner
Publishing, Inc.

From this example, you can envision the amount of time, effort, and creativity involved in only a four-card stack. *HyperStudio* is a versatile product, and the kinds of stacks a teacher and student can create are endless. Because of *HyperStudio's* popularity, a whole collection of software materials has sprung up to accommodate it. For example, *Sound Companion* (FTC Publishing) lets students place sounds in *HyperStudio* stacks by recording directly through their computer microphone (Fig. 10.14). Students can change the sound tempo and pitch, add

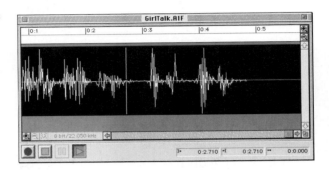

Figure 10.14
Sound Companion
Developer: Jeff Patterson
Publisher: FTC Publishing.
Reprinted by permission.

echo, and play backwards. Bill Lynn's multimedia electronic *HyperStudio Journal* gives clever *HyperStudio* ideas and tips, while Dave Cochran's *HyperStudio Network* has interesting articles about *HyperStudio* along with products. These products range from Karl Bunker and Bill Lynn's *HS Icon Librarian Maker,* a utility that lets you create an icon library for use with *HyperStudio* to Ann Brundige's collection of creative stacks. There are books like *HyperStudio in an Hour* (Sharp, 1998), a tutorial that takes the student through the program step by step, and *Help! I have HyperStudio. . . Now What Do I Do?*(McBride and Luntz, 1996) that helps the students design multimedia projects with *HyperStudio*. In the references section of this chapter are some *HyperStudio* resources.

Other Hypermedia Authoring Tools

The various hypermedia programs have different skill levels and traits. Advanced programs, like Macromedia's *MacroMind Director,* can run on both Apple and Intel-based platforms and are more appropriate for business applications. Besides *HyperCard 2* (Apple) and *HyperStudio* (Roger Wagner), there are other programs found in educational circles like *LinkWay Live!* (IBM), and *Digital Chisel* (Pierian Spring Software).

LinkWay Live!

LinkWay Live! is an authoring tool similar to *HyperCard.* However, *LinkWay Live!* is devised exclusively for IBM and IBM-compatible computers requiring DOS 4.0 or higher. A relatively inexpensive piece of software, it comes with considerable documentation, including a comic book instruction manual (Fig. 10.15) and a tutorial that is loaded when the program is installed.

Figure 10.15
LinkWay Live!
Reprinted with permission
of LinkWay Live, 1992 by
International Business
Machines Corporation.

LinkWay Live! organizes information into folders that resemble file folders. You put pages of information into a folder, and then you can link these pages to related pages in the same folder or a different folder. This procedure resembles the way *HyperCard* uses cards in a stack. In *LinkWay,* the equivalent of the *HyperCard* home stack is the main folder. Each folder has a base page and may or may not have additional pages. On a page, items of information can be stored as objects. Each page can contain five types of objects: fields, pictures, buttons, lists, and media. *Fields* display text information such as titles or sentences. Pictures are drawing or graphic objects from video capture or *LinkWay Live!* paint documents. Buttons are active spots that perform different actions when clicked. Lists display text. Media let you control audio, animation, or video.

LinkWay Live! is a very powerful tool. Like *HyperCard,* it is effective with junior high students and up. Another program for ages twelve through adult is *Digital Chisel,* which is easier to use than *HyperCard* and *LinkWay Live!* because it has many more built-in functions.

Digital Chisel

With *Digital Chisel,* students can create captivating interactive presentations, storybooks, lessons, or reports with graphics (Fig. 10.16). Instead of pages in a folder or cards in a stack, *Digital Chisel*

Figure 10.16
Digital Chisel
Used with permission of
Pierian Spring Software.

features screens. Each screen may contain text, pictures, movies, sounds, and animation. On every screen appears a navigator palette, which allows users to progress from one screen to the next. Of special interest to teachers is *Digital Chisel*'s ability to create tests in a variety of formats, including multiple choice, essay, fill in, true/false, and matching. *Digital Chisel* even has a database so that teachers may record the answers to test questions and then automatically score students' answers. The program also has a full selection of paint and draw tools. It is designed to run on the Macintosh and Windows operating systems. *Digital Chisel*, along with *HyperCard*, *HyperStudio*, and *LinkWay Live!*, are designed for the older child or adult. Later in this chapter we discuss multimedia programs that are more appropriate for the beginner and young child.

Classroom Suggestions for Using Hypermedia

Teachers and students clearly have a rich selection of software and hardware to choose from in order to develop first-class hypermedia presentations. Students can use a desktop publishing package such as *The Children's Writing and Publishing Center* and *The Writing Center* (Learning Company) to write and illustrate stories that combine text with graphics. They can also create their own motion pictures with sight and sound by using a videodisc player or by inventing their own interactive, branching stories. Teachers can generate slide shows that explain a range of topics from Beethoven to cell mitosis and are accompanied by canned music, sound effects, and digitized human voices. Students can use tape recorders to record interviews on the overcrowding of schools and then turn the interviews into presentations by adding background sounds, such as the noise of children in an overcrowded classroom and sound effects synchronized with words from their scripts.

Numerous other possibilities exist for hypermedia use in classrooms. Teachers can prepare interesting film clips of field trips or school events with video cameras, and camcorders. A video camera presentation can be combined with computer graphics, photographs, animation, sound, and music. Teachers or students can then add computer titles and credits to their videotapes.

A teacher could prepare, for example, a presentation on the different types of clouds. To make this report more interesting, the teacher could record video shots of actual clouds. A program such as *ClarisDraw* would allow graphic screen illustrations to be added. In the finished hypermedia presentation, each type of cloud would have a text explanation, sound effects, and music.

Before concluding our exploration of hypermedia authoring tools, let's consider some of the benefits and drawbacks of this technology.

Pros and Cons of Hypermedia

Hypermedia is entertainment that may effectively mesmerize its audience with spectacular presentations. A student viewing a hypermedia presentation that has text, graphics, film clips, still photographs, sound effects, and moving maps is very likely to be an involved student! One of the teacher's first responsibilities is to motivate students to learn, and the hypermedia presentation addresses this concern. Using hypermedia products, students are not passive receptacles of knowledge; rather, they are actively engaged in their learning, making decisions about how to proceed. The technology facilitates the development of research skills and encourages cooperative learning and problem solving. Reluctant readers are motivated to read, and inquisitive students have the freedom to explore topics independently. All students are able to acquire depth of knowledge on whatever stack, folder, or assortment of screens they are using. Dede (1994) sees this tool as beyond simple presentations, offering new methods of structured discovery, addressing varied learning styles, motivating students, and in the future applying pattern recognition techniques to help students master higher order thinking skills. Turner and Dipinto (1992) discuss how the hypermedia environment encourages students to be introspective and imaginative. According to Bill Gates (1995), hypermedia authoring may play a major role in preparing students for the intensive information world of the future.

Researchers such as Marchionini (1988) feel there are important contributions that hypermedia systems offer for educators. First, students have quick and easy access to large amounts of information in a variety of formats. Learners can easily use this diverse material stored in a compact form to follow paths that point out relationships between items, or they may create their own interpretations. Second, the environment offers a high level of learner control because users may choose predetermined paths through the lesson or paths that suit individual interests and abilities. Third, hypermedia gives teachers and students an opportunity to change roles, in that students can use the technology to make presentations and teach one another and in that teachers can learn from the technologys offerings about students' interests and abilities.

While it is obvious that hypermedia has great potential, there are also problems that must be addressed. One key question concerns the overburdened teacher's responsibility in this process: How is a teacher going to find the time to master hypermedia and devise hypermedia presentations? The average time required to put together a quality hypermedia presentation is between 20 and 40 hours. Who is going to train these teachers to use hypermedia programs? Training requires funds and a commitment from the school districts. While there is general agreement that this media stimulates in-depth knowledge, whether it fosters breadth of knowledge is yet to be determined. Also unclear are the implications of random learning, possible when students determine their own programs. Another problem according to Roblyer, Edward, and Havriluk (1997) is that students need sufficient on-line time, and their computers must be configured for hypermedia authoring, that is, have the capacity for digitized sound or input video. Finally, some critics question the value of hypermedia, claiming that it is all form and little substance. Teachers who prepare these presentations do spend inordinate amounts of time and energy so that their presentations will look professional on the screen, but perhaps this time is being diverted from substantive learning. A presentation ending with a barrage of images that have a limited connection with a topic may be a way of ensuring emotional involvement, but the cost may be a loss of real learning.

Fiderio (1988), Stanton and Baber (1992, 1994), and Roblyer, Edward, and Havriluk (1997) describe some of the negatives of hypermedia as a technology: (1) users need guidance because they can become lost in obscure links when they explore various databases; (2) students may be attracted to tangential topics and be diverted away from subject matter that is relevant; (3) teachers also may have difficulty breaking the information into smaller, more organized components; and (4) the cost of hardware and the large memory requirements of hypermedia may make hypermedia prohibitively expensive for many schools. Other critics caution us not to substitute hypermedia for books and the library.

In conclusion, hypermedia is so embryonic a technology that research on its roles in classrooms is inconclusive (Bruder, 1991) and not yet extensive (Toomey and Ketterer, 1995). Do the benefits outweigh the problems? In the end, each individual educator must decide whether to embrace the technology of the 1990s, adopt selected hypermedia software, or cautiously await further developments.

MP EXPRESS (Bytes of Learning) is the easiest-of-all multimedia presentation tools for Macintosh and Windows. Its streamlined design and simplified user interface let beginners and advanced users produce high quality presentations in minutes. All the tools and page control information needed to produce effective, professional looking multimedia are provided on two simple, intuitive floating palettes. Beginners need use nothing more. Advanced users can find customizing options in pull down menus. The interface and software appear and perform identically on both Macintosh and Windows platforms.

The publishers also provide collections of award-winning multimedia resources that they bundle and integrate with MP Express in what they call Multimedia Production Kits. The first of these bundled production kits, released in 1997, is the multiple award winning product MP EXPRESS: ON THE BRINK that combines MP Express with over 700 pictures, movies, sounds and music tracks focusing on 56 endangered mammal and bird species of North America, including their habitats. This production kit develops awareness of endangered species and environmental issues. A second production kit called MP: EXPRESS: LIVING DESERTS & RAIN FORESTS (Figure 10.17) was also released in 1997 and features MP:

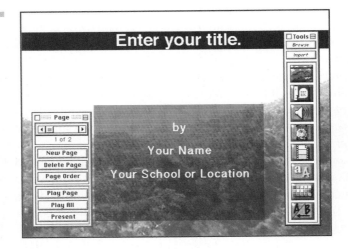

Figure 10.17
MP: Express: Living Deserts & Rain Forests.
Used with permission of Bytes of Learning Inc.

Express: Living Deserts & Rain Forest. Stunning images and movies from award winning BBC wildlife documentaries. With each MP Express Production Kit, students can readily research, write, create and present multimedia presentations, electronic projects or show and tell for the next millenium.

Additional Software for Multimedia Presentations

As was discussed earlier in this chapter, preparing stacks can be a complicated and time-consuming task; unfortunately, providing a complete explanation of this involved process is beyond the scope of the chapter. In response to the time-consuming nature of hypermedia presentations, software has been developed that could be used in conjunction with authoring systems and without authoring systems to alleviate this problem.

Modern Learning Aids (MPG), one of the first programs of its kind, has a multimedia presentation generator that helps produce hypermedia presentations on the computer as easily as operating a VCR remote control. A typical MPG presentation is a lesson on environmental problems caused by clearing the rain forests in Brazil. A VCR is used to present a newscast on these issues, a videodisc of an expedition down the Amazon river depicts forests, inhabitants, and sounds; digitized satellite images and text can be added; and, finally, the additional sound of jungle music can come from a CD-ROM player. Such a system would allow you to play segments of the presentation in a user-paced mode or in an automatically sequenced video presentation.

The Multimedia Workshop

The Multimedia Workshop (Davidson) is a tool that creates printed documents and video presentations. Users may elect to work in any of three workshops: Writing Workshop, Paint Workshop, and Video Workshop. The Writing Workshop offers a word processor with desktop publishing capabilities and includes a spelling checker and thesaurus. It also lets users add pictures and color to their documents. The Paint Workshop creates custom drawings and photographs. Powerful paint tools produce special effects and color gradations. Finally, the Video Workshop allows users to pick a background, insert a video clip or picture, and record a narration. The scenes and sounds are laid out on a storyboard grid and can be viewed on the computer screen. This program comes with a CD-ROM that includes more than 300 photographs, 400 pieces of clip art, 75 *QuickTime* movie clips, 200 sound effects, and 35 music clips. (*QuickTime* movies are used by hypermedia authoring tools and multimedia software.)

mPower

mPower(Multimedia Design Corporation) is a multimedia presentation tool that uses a push button interface. This product creates and edits *QuickTime* movies, links to the Internet, and controls hardware peripherals. With a touch of a button, users can add digital images, video, audio, charts, and Internet content to classroom presentations. Users can create *QuickTime* movies from laser disc, videotapes, digital cameras, and camcorders.

Power Point 97

Finally, *PowerPoint 97* (Microsoft), a more advanced presentation tool for high school to adult levels, lets users turn ideas into powerful presentations. The program has instant layouts, on-screen directions, and tool tips that let users make compelling multimedia presentations. With

PowerPoint, users can create overheads for class presentations (Fig. 10.18), slides for a meeting, or dazzling effects for an on-screen presentation. Furthermore, a complete set of easy-to-use

Figure 10.18
PowerPoint 97
Box shots reprinted with
permission from
© Microsoft Corporation

tools help with the creations. To learn it quickly, the product offers prompts, tips, and cue cards along with wizards, templates, and autolayouts. An alternative to buying a separate program like *mPower* or *PowerPoint* is to purchase an integrated package like *ClarisWorks. ClarisWorks* not only has a word processor, database, spreadsheet, and drawing and painting modules, but its slide show feature allows users to create electronic presentations.

Multimedia Features: QuickTime, Morphing, and Warping

All the popular computer magazines mention the term *QuickTime* or *QuickTime Virtual Reality (VR)* as important features of multimedia. Other recent and key features include morphing and warping.

QuickTime

QuickTime is an extension of the Macintosh system software that lets an application display miniature motion picture sequences in a screen window. *QuickTime* is an expandable file folder for all kinds of digital media. You can stuff large digital audio and video files into *QuickTime* and use that data in various applications, moving from one to another. Any application that is compatible with *QuickTime* can play video, sound, and animation within its program. Apple became the leader in this field by first integrating motion video into its operating system. The MS-DOS options are called *Audio Video Interleaved (AVI), QuickTime for Windows*, and IBM's *PhotoMotion* (Freedman, 1997).

The major advantage of these digital files is that no special hardware is required to play the videos for any of these formats. However, there are problems with this software solution. The video quality is low resolution and the viewing window is small. Additionally, the quickness of video playback is dependent on the computer used. Generally, the playback occurs at only about one-half of the normal speed of the computer. Another drawback is the large video file size required to transport and store these files. Presently, a huge amount of hard disk storage space is required to accommodate these large file sizes, although the software developers are working to improve compression ratios to produce a file size more reasonable for typical hard disk capacities. Many users are purchasing Zip and Jazz drives to hold their work in order to have enough space. Many of these criticisms may be answered by QuickTime 3(Apple) which improves the compression rate of these multimedia files has superb-quality video and audio, and has quick playback (Stafford, 1998).

QuickTime VR

QuickTime VR, an extension of *QuickTime 2.0,* lets the user view on-screen in 3-D space. The scenes are created from renderings or multiple still shots taken at all sides. *QuickTime VR* has pushed technology to new heights. Using this extension, the developer can create photorealistic 3-D shots based not on video clips, but on images that are fastened together into one continuous file. Thus, computer users are able to see 360 degrees around an object, with seamless pan and zoom abilities. Users are able to designate an item or items in a scene as buttons that invite interactivity. The first product that used this technology was *Star Trek: The Next Generation Interactive Technical Manual.* Some current program that use *QuickTime VR* are: *Myst* and *Riven* (Brøderbund); *An Odyssey of Discovery: Science, and Continent Explorer World Geography* (Pierian Spring Software); *Oregon Trail III* (Learning Company); and *HyperStudio* (Roger Wagner).

Morphing

Morphing programs animate a picture sequence by gradually blending one image into another. An example of morphing is the shape-shifting security guard in *Star Trek: Deep Space Nine* or the evil terminator in *Terminator 2: Judgment Day.* I used *Morph Version 2.5,* a program by Gryphon, to morph a picture of my son, David, at five years old into a picture of him at ten years old. This five-second video clip shows his transformation over the five-year period. Figure 10.19 shows four still pictures from this transition.

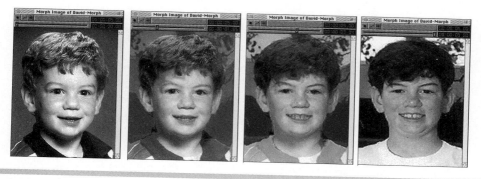

Figure 10.19
Morph Version 2.5
Used with permission of Gryphon Software Corporation.

The morphing software accomplishes the smooth transformation by matching a series of central points set in the beginning image to the ending image. In my short film, I selected the nose in the first image as a central point to be matched to the location of the nose in the last image. I kept adding these central points until the important features such as the mouth, eyes, ears, and head shape were charted. When the points are established, the morphing software sends the dots that are charted in the beginning image to their final location in the ending image, blending their shapes and colors.

The more points you add in morphing, the smoother the transition from one figure to the other. The traditional animation techniques that were perfected in the 1940s required thirty to thirty-five hand-drawn images to animate a figure for a single second on the screen. Today, a morphing program relieves artists from performing this type of tedious detailed work and also generates a remarkable effect.

Warping

Warping is a completely different type of special effect from morphing. In warping, the key points of one image are used to create an effect that does not involve the blending of two images. By adjusting these main points, you push the selected points of the original image into a different shape. The final production stretches the shape into an image that is completely different from the original one. For example, a rounded human face could be stretched into a narrow face, pointed jaw, and bulging eyes. In the movie *The Mask*, warping was used to stretch Jim Carey's face whenever he put on the mask.

The Mona Lisa's face in Figure 10.20 is warped using *Kai's Power Goo* (Metatools). This program lets the user create liquid images and manipulate them by smearing, smudging, stretching, and fusing them. You can superimpose these images and blend parts of one image with another to create a third image.

Figure 10.20
Kai's Power Goo
Used with permission
from MetaCreations
Corporation, formerly
Metatools.

As motivational devices, morphing and warping have some practical classroom applications. Students can experiment with different images and then copy and paste them to illustrate a story or report. They can create a morphed movie or warped picture for a hypermedia presentation. For example, students might show cell division or plant growth by morphing different pictures together.

Virtual Reality

The ultimate achievement in multimedia is **virtual reality** (VR). Many authorities in the field consider William Gibson's depiction of cyberspace in his book *Neuromancer* to be the ultimate example of VR. In this book, cyberspace is described as the sum of all interconnected telecommunication networks in this future world (Gibson, 1984). A more down-to-earth explanation of VR is a three-dimensional, interactive simulation. Participants in a computer-generated VR environment can manipulate what they see all around them.

Historical Perspective

The predecessor of virtual reality was Edward Link's flight simulator. In 1929, he built a carnival ride that enabled passengers to feel as if they were flying a real airplane. This particular ride developed into the flight simulators that are currently used for training aviators. In the 1960s, Morton Heilig created the Sensorama arcade simulator, another predecessor of VR. The Sensorama arcade simulator used sound, motion, images, and even smell to give spectators in this motorcycle ride the feeling that they were experiencing a ride through Brooklyn, New York. In 1965, Ivan Sutherland created a head-mounted computer graphics display that tracked the head movements of the user. The person wearing this device could view simulations shown in graphic frames. Two years later, Frederick Brooks explored force feedback, which "directs physical pressure or force through a user interface to the user so that he or she can feel computer-simulated forces" (Eddings, 1994). In the early 1970s, Nolan Bushnell introduced the popular electronic arcade game *Pong*, in which players played Ping-Pong against each other or against the game. Although the game seems incredibly simple today, its interactivity was an important development in the field of virtual reality. Finally, Ames Research Center at NASA developed low-cost VR equipment. Because of this development, VR companies such as VPL Research began the ongoing commercial production of virtual reality hardware and software.

How Virtual Reality Works

In VR, users are electronically immersed in a simulated environment, in which they use their sight, hearing, and touch in all three dimensions. The purpose is not only to enter this world but to manipulate it. Participants wear headgear in which computer-generated images are sent to small screens placed before their eyes and to headphones in their ears. The headgear permits users to block out all actual stimuli to concentrate solely on the simulated stimuli. Participants also wear gloves or bodysuits equipped with sensors that communicate changes in body position to the computer, which then communicates the changes to the headgear (Fig. 10.21).

Figure 10.21
Virtual reality equip-
ment

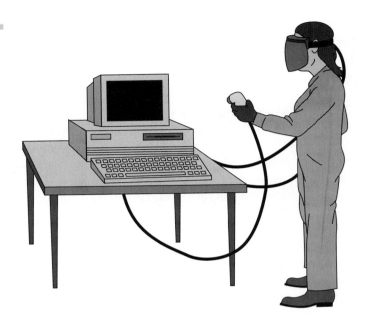

Let's consider an example. Imagine that you are entering a simulation of the Tate Gallery. You look into one of the exhibit rooms. All around you are paintings and sculptures. As you turn your head, the screens in your headgear adjust to show you what you would be seeing in the actual gallery. If you walk forward, the screens will change again to simulate your movement. As you approach the security guard to ask her a question, her voice becomes louder and louder in your headphones. When you raise your hand to point at one of the paintings, you see a simulated hand on your headgear screen. When you pick up one of the sculptures to examine it from different angles, the screen shows your hands and the different views of the sculpture, and your headphones transmit the angry voice of the security guard.

Virtual reality has found its way into research labs, business, the military, and video arcade games. In some video games, you direct the action of the game with the movements of your own body, wearing headgear, gloves, and a bodysuit. In 1994, the first virtual reality wedding took place in a computer simulation of the lost city of Atlantis. The couple, Monika Liston and Hugh Jo, was married at the CyberMind Virtual Reality Center in San Francisco where Liston works. The bridegroom, bride, and minister wore helmets with small built-in eye-level monitors; hand-held controllers allowed them to move their virtual reality parts. Guests could view the ceremony on three large TV screens (Snider, 1994).

In education, virtual reality's potential has yet to be explored. What is certain is that this potential is tremendously exciting; virtual reality technology will let students more fully interact with information being presented in all subject areas. Physically disabled students would benefit from VR by being able to immerse themselves physically in different environments. Students and teachers would be able to conduct experiments and experience situations that otherwise might be too costly or dangerous. Imagine networking an educational virtual reality system worldwide in real time. It would be a wonderful way to foster positive interaction among people of different cultures. Consider the usefulness of a virtual reality tour of London. Or, your students could don helmets and fly the first spaceship to the moon or enter the human blood stream to look at the heart.

In a physical education class, students could use a simulation to practice baseball against an all-star baseball player. In a science class, they could explore the laws of physics in a virtual world by testing how changes in gravitational forces affect virtual objects. In a language arts class, students could be visited by a virtual Mark Twain who could talk to them about his books and even answer the students' questions. A student violinist might even practice with the world's finest virtual orchestra and receive individualized tutoring. These are but a few of the options that will be available to educators in the near future. The biggest impediment to this advancement in technology is cost. A smaller concern is the problematic weight of the necessary equipment. Still, a future with virtual reality holds much promise for educators.

Multimedia Software

Floppy disk programs are the technology of the past; most software now is packaged in the form of CD-ROMs that hold 650 MB or more of data. Now that we are used to 650 MB on a single disk, be prepared to see it be replaced by the DVD-ROM a CD-ROM, cousin (see chapter 8). This disc is capable of storing 17 GB, the equivalent of twenty-five CD-ROM discs.

Almost all recent software programs are multimedia, and there is a definite trend toward surrealistic adventures or virtual reality adventures such as *Myst* and *Riven* (Brøderbund). Programs such as *American Girls Premiere* (Learning Company) let you choose characters that walk, dance, or curtsy. After you set the stage, you can then direct them to frown, laugh, or act surprised. *Collier's Encyclopedia* (Sierra), with thousands of multimedia elements and interactive simulations, can display advanced full-motion videos. As evidenced by the software catalogs, developers are rapidly producing software that incorporates multimedia into all areas of the curriculum. With thousands of programs currently available, we only have space to mention a few. One of the easiest multimedia undertakings is to connect the computer to a laser disc player. Regardless of the attractiveness of CD-ROM, the laser disc, or videodisc, presently is the choice for accessing premier quality motion video. Many well-known laser discs are appropriate for classrooms, such as *Miracle of Life, Dream Machine, Regard for the Planet, First National Kids Disc and, National Gallery of Art* (Voyager) and *Interactive Nova* (Scholastic). (Chapter 8 has a review of some of the more popular videodiscs.)

This current software can be divided into many different categories, including application programs with multimedia components, social studies, language development and art, mathematics, general reference, music, and science and within these categories are programs especially applicable to special needs. Let us examine some of these diverse programs and discover what makes them particularly useful in a classroom setting. **Chapter 8 and Appendix A feature additional multimedia software.**

Word Processing

Bank Street Writer (Macintosh Version) has a hypertext button feature that allows users to turn text into a multimedia document. Users can insert buttons (such as the note button in Figure 10.22) into the document and link these buttons to text, picture, sound, or voice annotation.

Figure 10.22
Bank Street Writer
Figure reproduced by permission of Scholastic, Inc.

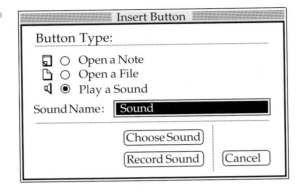

Special Needs. A couple of relevant programs for students struggling with writing due to physical challenges, language delays, or learning disabilities are *Write: Outloud* and *Co:Writer* (Don Johnson). *Write: Outloud* is a talking word processor with a talking spell checker that offers multi-sensory learning. *Co:Writer* is an intelligent word prediction program that works with any word processor to decrease the number of keystrokes to complete an intended word.

Social Studies

Point of View (Scholastic), a classic multimedia program, provides users with information about topics from different points of view. Students using the program analyze historical events and write their own opinions about these events. They can examine original documents and see or hear eyewitness testimony, essays, pictures, statistics, video, sound, and even animation. Each point of view includes information about politics, government, art, music, literature, daily life, science, and technology. Students view charts, maps, and text that can be cut and pasted into a word processing program to produce elegant reports. This program is useful to the student who wants to conduct historical research and to the researcher who wishes to offer his or her own point of view in an exciting hypermedia presentation. The program integrates computer graphics, text, charts, animation, videodisc footage, and sound.

Students can view the historical information in ten ways. For example, imagine that students are studying the Kennedy administration. In Picture View, they see a likeness of JFK. In Sound View, they listen to a recording of JFK's inaugural address. Document View presents copies of JFK's speeches. Milestone View reveals a time line of events from the period (Fig. 10.23). In the Chart and Map views, students examine data from the 1960s in different configurations. Essay View is a simple word processor enabling students to compose title pages or short responses to the information. Presentation View is a slide show feature.

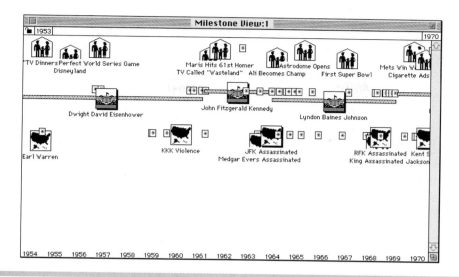

Figure 10.23
Point of View
Figure reproduced by permission of Scholastic, Inc.

Another inventive program in the social studies area is the deluxe edition of *Where in the World Is Carmen Sandiego?* The IBM and Macintosh versions have Carmen and her gang of ten villains and new recruits stealing treasures in forty-five countries all over the world. This edition features sixty-two animations, more than 2,500 clues, digitized location graphics originating from National Geographic Society slides, digitized sound, and composed music. Users learn about world geography, study facts, and acquire research skills. This program offers a higher level of difficulty than the original version because it has been expanded to include three world map representations and a 1,300-page encyclopedia of American culture and history covering such topics as science, art, music, and philosophy.

Language Arts

Lawrence Productions' *McGee, McGee Visits Katie's Farm* and *McGee at the Fun Fair* and Brøderbund's *The Playroom, The Treehouse,* and *The Backyard* are examples of quality language arts multimedia programs. In fact, *The Playroom,* with its interactive and multimedia features, was one of the first of this genre.

The *McGee* series consists of early learning programs in which students click on various objects on the screen and the objects respond with speech and movement. These programs let students make decisions about real-life situations. For example, in the first program of the series, McGee completes ordinary morning tasks: He brushes his teeth and goes to the bathroom. Some of the other programs are *Katie's Farm, Fun Fair,* and *McGee's School Days.* These programs are engaging introductions to the computer for young children and non-English-speaking children, and they encourage communication skills by asking users to discuss what is happening on the screen.

The Playroom, The Treehouse, and *The Backyard* go a step farther. *The Playroom* and *The Backyard* are directed at five- and six-year-olds, while *The Treehouse* is meant for the six- to nine-year-old age group. Using these programs, students can spend many hours exploring games, toys, and surprises, each of which has something to teach; these programs skillfully use animation, sound, music, and graphics to accomplish this task.

The *JumpStart* series (Knowledge Adventure) for prekindergarten through fifth grades are interactive award-winning programs that teach many different skills. These programs are designed for the impatient attention spans, with puzzles, games, music, curriculum-based activities, and much more.

A very popular genre these days is the CD-ROM interactive book. In the *Living Books Children's Series, Just Grandma and Me,* a picture book by Mercer Mayer, presents the illustrations of the original book. The program expands on the book by offering users the option to read the story in English, Spanish, or Japanese, by adding clever quips and dialogue, and by animating the characters that fill the pages. There are hidden buttons; if users click the same objects in different places, various performances occur. Young readers who work through the book several times will discover something different each time.

The New Kid on the Block is a *Living Books* program for children in kindergarten through sixth grade. Students are encouraged to learn the meaning of words by exploring a collection of poems with appealing topics and themes. Figure 10.24 invites students to explore the poem "I Spied My Shadow Slinking." Students are given the option of having the poem read to them or of playing with the different figures in the poem.

Figure 10.24
The New Kid on the Block
The New Kid on the Block
copyright ©1984 William
Morrow. All software
copyrights are jointly
owned by Living Books
and their respective
authors.

Sanctuary Woods programs require users to do more than just "turn" the pages of an electronic book. The first program they produced in their series was a CD-ROM called *Sitting on the Farm.* This program is a musical storybook in French and English. Students use the read, sing, listen, and write along modes to learn language arts, music, vocabulary, and creative writing. *Sitting on the Farm* integrates multimedia features such as animation and sound. Students can record and play back their voices, publish related stories, or print text, among other activities. Sanctuary Woods produces many delightful programs for varying age groups; among them are *The Cat Came Back; Hawaii High: The Mystery of Tiki; Victor Vector & Yondo: The Hypnotic Harp;* and *Oscar Wilde's The Selfish Giant.*

Myst, a program mentioned earlier, is an advanced problem-solving program for junior high and older students. This discovery program involves students in reading for information. The program's *QuickTime* movies are quite unusual and the music has an eerie quality that draws students into a surrealistic setting. *Myst* is not linear, it is not shallow, and it has remarkable depth of detail. *Myst* presents many realistic dilemmas about which students must plan preferable courses of action. Most situations are not dead ends, but offer a complexity of involvement. Students must pay attention to detail and collect information needed to uncover the secrets of *Myst* (Fig. 10.25).

Riven, the sequel to *Myst,* is the latest virtual reality program from Brøderbund. This program has greater graphic detail, full-motion video, and puzzles that are more integrated into the story line.

Figure 10.25
Myst
Screen shot from Myst. Copyright © Brøderbund Software, Inc. Reprinted by permission.

Art

Kid Pix 2 (new version *Kid Pix Deluxe*) (Brøderbund) is one of the most celebrated of the multimedia art programs for a wide range of users, from age three to adult. This program is a combination of the original *Kid Pix,* an art program, and *Kid Pix Companion,* a slide show program. Each paint tool in *Kid Pix 2* makes a sound: the pencil scratches, the brush "bloops," and the moving tool "vrooms" like a truck's engine. The color paint program contains soda pop bubbles and wacky brushes that drip paint. Many of these brushes are animated and grow into different objects. Electric mixer tools splash or drop big blobs of paint on the students' creations. There are eighty images that kids can "stamp" onto their drawings, and there are also unusual erasers, such as a firecracker eraser that blows drawings to bits. Users can even record personal messages that play every time they open a drawing (if the computer has a microphone). *Kid Pix 2* (for the Macintosh and Windows operating systems) comes with hidden pictures (Fig. 10.26) that students may uncover by selecting the question mark option and using the eraser.

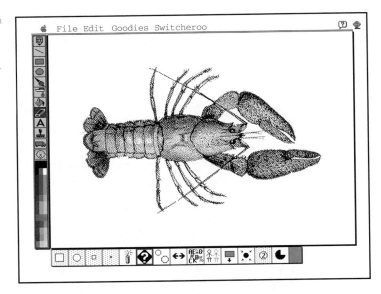

Figure 10.26
Kid Pix 2
Screen shot from Kid Pix 2. Copyright © Brøderbund Software, Inc. Reprinted by permission.

Additionally, students can import a variety of computer-generated images from clip art, digitized photos, *Print Shop* graphics, or pictures created with other paint program such as Dabbler. After users have created four or five individual screens, they can combine them into a slide show.

Special Needs.   Two excellent programs for students with special needs are *Knowledge Adventure Bricks* (Knowledge Adventure, Inc.) and *Blocks in Motion* (Don Johnson). These programs give students a sense of confidence and help them handle problem-solving tasks and practice their manual dexterity. *Knowledge Adventure Bricks* lets the user click on more than 300 brick styles to build objects that range from cars and boats to dinosaurs. There is an adult version as well as a child's version integrated into the program. The child's version has a friendly interface with larger, easy-to-click buttons, automatic saving, and a single view. The adult version has sophisticated design tools. Users can animate their creations or automatically build models brick by brick. They can even view their masterpiece at different angles (Fig. 10.27).

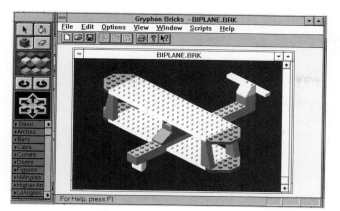

Figure 10.27
Knowledge Adventure Bricks
Knowledge Adventure Bricks, courtesy of Knowledge Adventure, Inc., © 1996.

Blocks in Motion lets users create, manipulate, and animate their blocks. This paint and motion program has multiple tools, sound effects, and many programmable options to bring forth the student's creativity. Users can create or import backgrounds, paint pictures, and create scenes with different types of blocks. Motion controllers can assign movement and animation to the created object so the user can explore concepts such as gravity, cause and effect, and much more (Fig. 10.28).

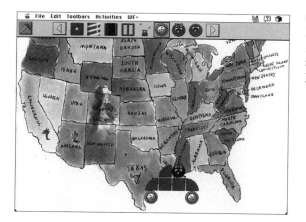

Figure 10.28
Blocks in Motion
Screen shot courtesy Don Johnston, Inc.

Mathematics and Logical Thinking

Millie's Math House (Edmark) is an award-winning multimedia program that teaches beginning math skills. Children learn about numbers, patterns, sizes, and shapes. There are six interactive activities with animated characters, colorful graphics, and lively music. In Figure 10.29, the cookie-making machine puts the selected number of chips on the cookie, and then the cookie travels along the conveyer belt into the horse's mouth. Other equally enchanting programs by Edmark were discussed in chapter 8.

Figure 10.29
Millie's Math House
Used by permission of
Edmark.

The Castle of Dr. Brain is just one in a series of programs developed by Sierra On-Line. These programs, intended for students who are ages twelve or older, have strong math and logical thinking elements. *The Castle of Dr. Brain* is filled with puzzles for students to solve. The goal in Figure 10.30 is to enter the correct numbers in the magic square to make both the columns and rows add up to eight.

Figure 10.30
The Castle of Dr. Brain
Reprinted by permission
of Sierra On-Line, Inc.

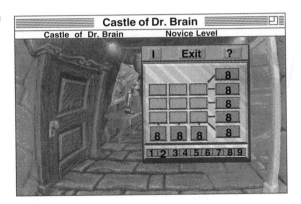

Students employ different strategies to solve the puzzles that Dr. Brain has set up to test job applicants. Many of these problems require that students plan ahead, others require pattern recognition, and still others require logical thinking. *The Island of Dr. Brain,* a sequel to *The Castle of Dr. Brain,* tests students' problem-solving skills and knowledge of math, language, chemistry, art history, physics, logic, mechanics, music, genetics, literature, navigation, and even more. *The Lost Mind of Dr. Brain* goes farther into the world of Dr. Brain; in this program, students experience outrageous 3-D graphics, animation, and addicting puzzles. Finally, in *The Time Warp of Dr. Brain* students rescue Dr. Brain, who is trapped in the space time discontinuum.

Special Needs.   *Big:Calc* (Don Johnson) is a talking calculator program that can be used alone or with other databases, spreadsheets, and number programs. Especially useful for special need students, this program gives instant auditory feedback on information that is inputted, has large number keys, and provides excellent quality speech with a variety of voices.

General Reference

Another very important category of multimedia programs is the general reference tool, which can address any area of the curriculum. An award-winning example of a reference program is *The 1998 Grolier Multimedia Encyclopedia,* which gives users access to such items as multimedia maps, pictures, videos, animation, sounds, and time lines. Users are able to access audiovisual essays that combine photos, music, and narration to give a comprehensive overview of subjects such as the human body or space exploration (Fig. 10.31). The motion videos feature sequences

Figure 10.31
*The 1998 Grolier
Multimedia*
© Groler Interactive, Inc.
Reprinted by permission.

of memorable events such as Dr. Martin Luther King Jr.'s "I Have a Dream" speech. A time line lets students travel along a continuum from prehistoric times to the present. There are thousands of pictures, sounds, full-color maps, and updated encyclopedia text entries. Step-by-step animated sequences make it easy to understand a topic such as how the human eye works. Another multimedia reference is *Collier's Encyclopedia* (Sierra Home), containing twenty-four volumes of information, thousands of multimedia elements, and interactive simulations and activities.

Music

Microsoft Musical Instruments (Microsoft and Dorling Kindersley) cleverly brings to life more than 200 instruments that are found around the world. By simply clicking on an instrument, users can learn how it works and can hear a classical, rock, or jazz sample. The program has an impressive collection of more than 500 photographs of musical instruments and ensembles and more than 1,500 sound clips recorded live by professional musicians. The table of contents

(Fig. 10.32) offers four overall topics: Families of Instruments, Musical Ensembles, Instruments of the World, and A–Z of Instruments. Music software has recently become much more excit-

Figure 10.32
Microsoft Musical
Instruments
Reprinted with permission
of Dorling Kindersley
Multimedia.

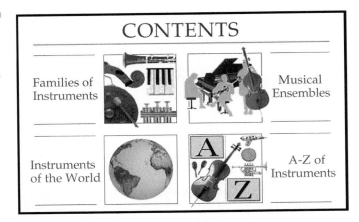

ing because of publishers such as Voyager who have developed a series of discs on composers such as Mozart, Beethoven, and Dvořák. **See chapter 9 and Appendix A for a description of these programs.**

Science

Science software has become increasingly popular. One reason is the effectiveness of this media in explaining difficult scientific topics. A well-done CD-ROM disc with step-by-step video clips facilitates students' understanding of a complex scientific subject such as the circulatory system.

Medical book companies are beginning to publish high-quality CD-ROM discs on different types of surgical operations. A pioneer in this field is Quality Medical Books, which publishes discs for medical schools and doctors. Using their CD-ROM discs, students or doctors can view an operational procedure carried out step-by-step.

Another example of a quality multimedia science program is *Interactive NOVA Animal Pathfinders* (Scholastic). Using a Macintosh computer and videodisc player, the program links full-motion videos and slides from the award-winning *NOVA* television series to a database of text and graphics cards. Students can work alone or in small groups to probe the science information, sights, and sounds; in the process they learn important science content and develop critical thinking skills. This program addresses topics such as animal classification, migration, adaptation, evolution, and behavior. *Animal Pathfinders* (Fig. 10.33) is accessed through point- and-click icons and menus. Students view informative text or graphics on the computer screen and the related video clip or slide on the color monitor simultaneously. Other programs in the series focus on human reproductive biology and environmental and ecological issues.

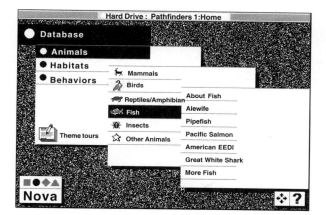

Figure 10.33
*Interactive NOVA
Animal Pathfinders*
Figure reproduced by
permission of Scholastic,
Inc.

Pierian Spring Software has produced *An Odyssey of Discovery Science* with eight real-life adventures that teach the wonders of life, earth/space, and physical science. This program has 3-D graphics, and animation. Users are drawn into a multimedia world with endless scientific interactions. The program is perfect for individual investigation, small group studies, or whole class projects (Fig. 10.34).

Figure 10.34
Odyssey of Discovery
Used with permission of
Pierian Spring Software.

DK Multimedia is known for its collection of interactive science software. Their *Eyewitness Encyclopedias* series transport students to virtual worlds from rain forests to the inside of the earth. *My Amazing Human Body* features interactive games and activities with more than 200 animated sequences. *The Way Things Work* features animations and audio. The machines actually function, and users can see and hear for themselves how the machines work.

You can see from this discussion that current computer programs have come a very long way from the static drill and practice programs of the 1970s. These new programs push technology to new heights with their multimedia features and their lifelike animations.

Summary

We discussed the origins of hypermedia and defined *hypermedia* as use of a computer to input, manipulate, and output graphics, sound, text, and audio in the presentation of information. We learned how hypermedia authoring tools such as *HyperCard, HyperStudio,* and *Linkway Live!* operate and how they may be used as tools for instruction. We examined some of the unique multimedia software, the special effects that are available for the classroom, and some suggested activities for multimedia software.

Following are a mastery test, teacher projects, and suggested readings and references. **Appendix A features an annotated list of multimedia software.**

Chapter Mastery Test

1. What is hypermedia?

2. What are two advantages of using your own authoring tool for a hypermedia presentation?

3. Who invented *HyperCard* and why was it so revolutionary?

4. Define the following hypermedia terms: cards, stacks, and buttons. Give an example of each.

5. What is the major disadvantage of using programs such as *Digital Chisel, HyperCard,* and *HyperStudio?*

6. *HyperCard* has been characterized as being similar to a database. Explain this statement.

7. Discuss how you would use the button function in a *HyperCard* or HyperStudio program. Name at least three types of buttons and give examples of each one.

8. Describe a multimedia program available in each of the following subject areas: social studies, language arts, science, music, and mathematics.

9. If you were to buy two multimedia programs, which two would you choose? What are the reasons for your choices?

10. Discuss the advantages and disadvantages of multimedia productions in the school setting.

11. Define *virtual reality* and discuss some of its implications.

12. Explain how morphing and warping work.

Teacher Projects

1. Learn a hypermedia application (such as *HyperStudio, HyperCard,* or *MP Express*) and write a short report describing its strengths and weaknesses.

2. Explain a mathematical concept by generating your own slide show, using software such as *Kid's Pix Deluxe.*

3. Tape record an interview on some important topic. Write a script using the speaker's words and add your own synchronized sound effects.

4. Record an interesting event or trip with a camcorder and combine this with animation, speech, and music, using one or more of the software programs discussed in this chapter.

Suggested Readings and References

Adams P. E. "Hypermedia in the Cassroom Using Earth and Space Science CD-ROMs." *Journal of Computers in Mathematics and Science Teaching* 15, no. 1–2 (1996): 19–34.

Arnett, Nick. "Multimedia on the Macintosh." *InfoWorld* (April 9, 1990): 79–80.

Bornman, H., and S. H. von Solms. "Hypermedia, Multimedia, and Hypertext—Definitions and Overview." *Electronic Library* 11, no. 4–5 (1993): 259–68.

Brownstein, Mark. "Batter Up for Broadband." *Byte Special Report,* (October 1997): 71–74.

Bruder, Isabelle. "Multimedia—How It Changes the Way We Teach and Learn." *Electronic Learning* 11, no. 1 (September 1991): 22–26.

Brundige, Ann. *Nifty Animation Tips.* HyperStudio Network, 1997. (609)466-3196

Bull, Glen, Gina Bull, and Aileen Nonis. "Intent Scripting With HyperStudio." *Learning & Leading with Technology* 24, no. 8 (May 1997) 40–43.

Cates, Ward Mitchell and Susan C. Goodling. "The Relative Effectiveness of Learning Options in Multimedia Computer-Based Fifth-Grade Spelling Instruction." *Educational Technology Research and Development* 45 no. 2 (1997): 27–46.

Dede, Christopher J: "The Future of Multimedia. Bridging to Virtual World." Educational Technology; v. 32 n. 5 p. 54–60, May, 1992.

Dede, Christopher "Making the Most of Multimedia." Multimedia and Learning: A School Leaders Guide. Alexandria, VA: NSBA, 1994.

D'Ignazio, Fred. "A New Curriculum Paradigm: The Fusion of Technology, the Arts, and Classroom Instruction." *The Computing Teacher* (April 1991): 45–48.

D'Ignazio, and Joanne Davis. "What I Did Last Summer 21st Century Style." *Learning & Leading With Technology* 24, no. 8. (May 1997): 44–47.

Eddings, Joshua. *How Virtual Reality Works.* Emeryville, Calif.: Ziff-Davis Press, 1994.

Fiderio, Janet. "Grand Vision." *Byte* 13, no. 10 (October 1, 1988): 237–42.

Field, Cynthia E. "Exploring Hypermedia." *Incider A+* (November 1990): 36–44.

Finkel, LeRoy. *Technology Tools in the Information Age Classroom.* Wilsonville, Oreg.: Franklin Beedle and Associates, 1991.

Florio, Chris and Michael Murie. "Authoritative Authoring: Software That Makes Multimedia Happen." *NewMedia* 6 no.12 (September 9, 1996): 67–70, 72–75.

Gates, Bill. "Multimedia revolution is here. Life On-Line." *Gainesville(Florida) Sun* (May 15, 1995): 7.

Gibson, William. *Neuromancer.* New York: Ace Books, 1984.

Goodman, Danny. *The Complete HyperCard Handbook 2.0.* New York: Bantam, 1990.

Guglielmo, Connie. "Multimedia Makers Get Point, Click." *Macweek* 5, no. 18 (May 1991): 22.

Holsinger, Erik. *How Multimedia Works.* Emeryville, Calif.: Ziff-Davis Press, 1994.

Hoffman, Joseph L., and David J. Lyons. "Evaluating Instructional Software." *Learning & Leading with Technology* 25, no. 2 (October 1997) 52–53.

HyperStudio Multimedia Journal, Simtech, Inc. (HyperStudio Network)

Jensen, Eric. "HyperCard and AppleShare Help At-Risk Students." *The Computing Teacher* (March 1991): 26–30.

Johnson, Stuart J. "Multimedia: Myth vs. Reality." *InfoWorld* 12, no. 8 (February 19, 1990): 47–52.

Malnig, Anita. "New Chapter for Electronic Books." *Macweek* 6, no. 2 (January 13, 1992): 42, 47.

Marchionini, G. "Hypermedia and Learning: Freedom and Chaos." *Educational Technology* 28, no. 11 (1988): 8–12.

McBride, Karen, and Elizabeth DeBoer Luntz. *Help I have HyperStudio . . . Now What Do I Do?* HyperStudio Network.

Milligan, Patrick, and Chris Okon. "Mastering Multimedia." *MacUser* (October 1994): 82–88.

Milheim, William D. "Virtual Reality and Its Potential Application in Education and Training." *Machine-Mediated Learning* 5, no. 1 (1995): 43–55.

Milton, Karen, and Pattie Spradley. "A Renaissance of the Renaissance—Using HyperStudio for Research Projects." *Learning & Leading with Technology* 23, no. 6 (March 1996): 20–22.

Monahan, Susan, and Dee Susong. "Author Slide Shows and Texas Wildlife: Thematic Multimedia Projects." *Learning & Leading with Technology* 24, no. 2 (October 1996): 6–11.

Moran, Tom. "QuickTime VR: A New Spin." *MacWorld* (October 1994): 34–35.

Needleman, Raphael. "'Action' Takes the Pain Out of Creating Presentations." *InfoWorld* 13, no. 32 (August 12, 1991): 1, 91.

Nelson, Theodore H. *Dream Machines: New Freedoms through Computer Screens—A Minority Report.* Chicago: Hugo Books Service, 1974.

Pfaffenberger, Bryan. *Que's Computer User's Dictionary,* 4th ed. Indianapolis, Ind.: Que, 1994.

Pfiffner, Pamela. "Welcome to QuickTime's Virtual Reality." *MacUser* (September 1994): 31.

Porter, Anne E. "Scavenged Idea and Virtual Hypermedia." *The Computing Teacher* (May 1991): 38–40.

Roblyer, M. D., J. Edward and Mary Anne Havriluk. "Integrating Educational Technology into Teaching." Merrill, New Jersey: 1997.

Sharp, Vicki. *HyperStudio 3.0 in an Hour* (Windows Version). Eugene, Oreg.: ISTE, 1997.

Sharp, Vicki. *HyperStudio 3.1 in an Hour* (Macintosh Version). Eugene, Oreg.: ISTE, 1997.

Smith, Irene, and Sharon Yoder. *Inside HyperStudio: Scripting with HyperLogo.* Eugene, Oreg.: ISTE, 1997.

Snider, Mike. "In the Heart of Cyberspace." *USA Today* (August 19, 1994): 1.

Stamp, Dave, Bernie Roehl, and John Eagan. *Virtual Reality Creations.* Corte Madera, Calif.: Waite Group Press, 1994.

Stanford, Alan. "It's time for Quicktime." *MacHome,* (May 1998): 18–20.

Stanton, Neville; Baber, Chris;. "An Investigation of Styles and Strategies in Self-Directed Learning."; *Journal of Educational Multimedia and Hypermedia;* v1 n2 p147–67 1992.

Stefananc, S., and L. Weiman. "Macworld Multimedia: Is It Real?" *MacWorld* (April 1990): 116–23.

Swartz, James D. and Tim Hatcher. "Virtual Experience: The Impact of Mediated Communication in a Democratic Society." *Educational Technology* 36, no. 6 (November–December 1996): 40–44.

Toomey, R., and K. Ketterer. "Using Multimedia as a Cognitive Tool." *Journal of Research on Computing in Education.* 27, no. 4 (summer 1995): 472–83.

Turner, S. V., and V. H. Dipinto. "Students as Hypermedia Author: Themes Emerging from a Qualitative Study." *Journal of Research on Computing Education* 25 no. 2 (1992): 187–99.

Telecommunications, The Internet, and On-Line Services

11

Objectives

Upon completing this chapter, you will be able to:

1. Define *telecommunications*;
2. Describe the hardware and software involved in telecommunications;
3. Identify and discuss two popular on-line services;
4. Discuss the Internet and its history;
5. Describe networking and explain how it operates; and
6. Discuss distant learning and its implications for education.

Telecommunications

Telecommunications is the electronic transmission of information including data, television pictures, sound, and facsimiles. It usually involves a computer, a modem, software, and a printer. With this equipment, you can communicate with a friend in St. Louis, Missouri, or Paris, France, sending and receiving anything from a manuscript to a simple message over the telephone lines. Using the same method, a homebound child can interact with a teacher in the classroom, an office worker can work at home, and a doctor can access a remote computer for research data.

The reasons for using telecommunications are convincing:

1. It is expedient and efficient;
2. It decreases car pollution;
3. It saves time and money;
4. It allows the home to serve as an office; and
5. It promotes distant learning in which students can share information and computer research findings.

When you connect one computer to another, you use hardware and software. In the majority of cases, the hardware consists of equipment that sends the data over some type of communications line, such as a telephone line. The software controls the flow of this data. The necessary hardware consists of a modem, telephone lines, and computer.

The **modem** lets two computers communicate with each other. There are two types of modems: internal and external. Internal modems reside in the computer and are plugged into an open slot. They do not require any special cabling, nor do they take up any extra desk space. External modems (Fig. 11.1) are separate units that sit outside the computer; the modem is connected to the telephone

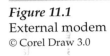

Figure 11.1
External modem
© Corel Draw 3.0

jack with a telephone cable. External modems usually have diagnostic lights so users can monitor what is transpiring. This type of modem is portable and easily accessible for repair.

Modem comes from *MOdulator/DEModulator*. The modem **modulates** the computer output to an acceptable signal for transmission and then **demodulates** the signal back for computer input. The modem on the transmitting computer converts the digital signals to modulated, analog signal tones and transmits them over the telephone lines. The receiving computer's modem transforms the incoming analog signals back to their digital equivalents in order to understand them. Figure 11.2 illustrates this modem-to-modem transmission.

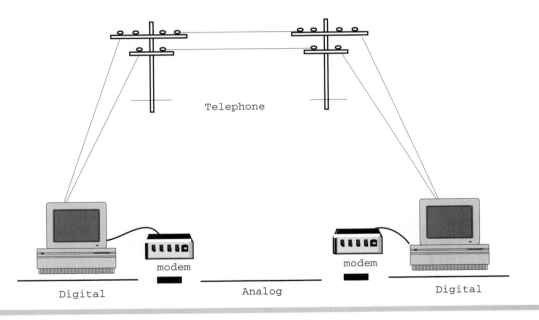

Figure 11.2
Modem-to-modem transmission
© Corel Draw 3.0

To use a modem, both the sending and receiving computers need communications software such as *Z-term* (a shareware product, written by David P. Alverson), *ClarisWorks*, *MicroPhone II*, or *Microsoft Works*, Software Ventures Corp. Communications software programs differ in their levels of complexity, features offered, cost, and difficulty. You should choose the simplest and least expensive package that offers the features that you need. As a rule, the more complicated software is harder to learn and more expensive. The majority of electronic information services require communications software that has been designed for their particular service.

To use telecommunications software, load the software, make the correct settings, dial the other modem, and wait for the connection to be made; only then is data transferal possible. Make certain the settings for both computers are the same for communication to take place; if you are using a computer service, you must change your computer modem settings to match the computer service's settings.

How Telecommunications Software Works

To demonstrate how communications software works, let's use *ClarisWorks,* one of the more prevalent programs in schools. *ClarisWorks,* previously discussed in chapter 6, is an integrated package with a communications module. Each time you connect with another computer or an on-line service, you begin what is called a computer session. To begin this session in *ClarisWorks,* open up the communications document.

Before attempting to send data over the phone lines, choose Connections from the Setting menu. Figure 11.3 shows the *ClarisWorks* communication settings dialog box. Select the method of communicating (in the example, Apple Modem), provide the telephone number to be dialed (here, 1-818-885-3333), select the dialing method (Touch Tone), and supply the other information requested.

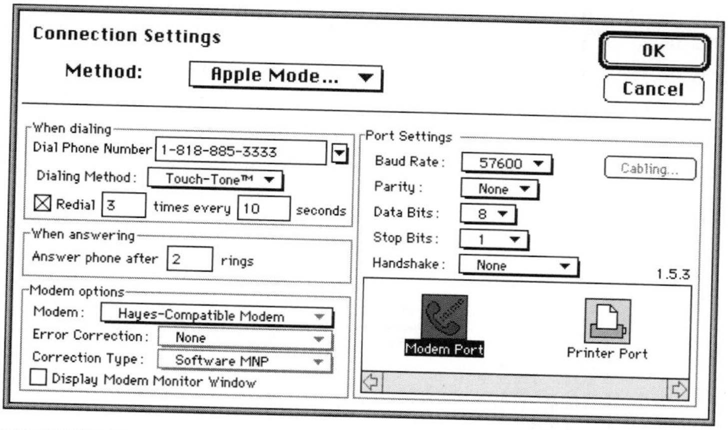

Figure 11.3
ClarisWorks communication settings
Used with permission of FileMaker, Inc.

As for the Port Settings, the first consideration is the **baud rate.** A baud is the unit of measure used for the modem's speed of transmission.[1] A 300-baud modem transmits 300 bits per

---

[1]The technical definition is "a variation or change in a signal in a communications channel." (Pfaffenberger, 1997).

second. Since there are ten bits in a telecommunication byte, this baud rate means that the modem transmits at thirty bytes, or characters, per second.[2] This speed is very slow, since for most human beings 1,200 bytes is a good reading speed. The modem's speed is especially important when you are sending large files, because the faster the modem, the less time it takes to send a file. For example, a 560K file might take fifty minutes to **download,** or receive, on a 2,400-baud modem but only four minutes to download on a 28,800-baud modem. Years ago, the common baud rate was 300. Currently, 56 **Kbps** is the standard for the majority of on-line services, more than 200 times the old 300 rate. Most people are buying modems with 56 Kbps capabilities. In Figure 11.3 a baud rate of 57,600 has been selected to match the recipient's setting.

The next setting, **Parity,** is the method the modem uses to check to see that data isn't garbled during its transmission. You can choose None, Odd, or Even. Since the data are sent one byte at a time, you must decide first how many data bits will make up a byte—the setting is usually seven or eight data bits per byte. After this selection, you should specify when the data has been sent. The stop bit is a bit inserted in the data transmission that informs the receiving computer that the byte of data is concluded. **HandShake** regulates the flow of data between your computer and the other location.

Data can be relayed in three ways: **simplex, half-duplex,** and **full-duplex.** A simplex channel sends data in one direction only. For example, on such a channel, a computer would be able to send data to a printer but would be unable to receive information. Half-duplex, synonymous with *local echo,* is a protocol that lets data be sent in both directions but in only one direction at a time. A walkie talkie in which only one user can talk at a time is a good example. Lastly, full-duplex sends data in both directions simultaneously. A telephone in which both parties can listen and talk at once is a good example.

In the *ClarisWorks* Terminal dialog box (Fig. 11.4), Local Echo (or half-duplex) has been selected. With this selection, the characters that you type appear on your computer screen as well

Figure 11.4
ClarisWorks terminal settings
Courtesy of FileMaker, Inc.

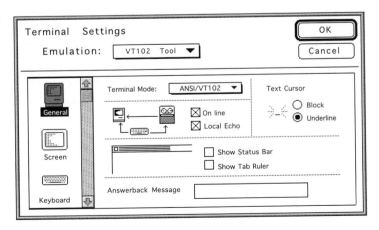

---

[2]A 300-baud modem equals 300 bits per second, but when the rate is higher, the bits per second transmitted are higher because one change can represent more than one bit of data.

as on the screen of the receiving computer. However, most host computers show the characters as the person types, so Local Echo is unselected. If for any reason, you are not able to see the characters on the screen, select Local Echo or half-duplex. However, if you see duplication of the characters, turn off Local Echo, which switches the channel to full-duplex.

Many other choices can be made from this Terminal dialog box. Since the purpose of this book is to give you an overview, we'll only discuss the most common settings. For more information about telecommunication parameters, refer to a technical manual.

Fax/Modem

Besides sending and receiving data, many modems today can answer the telephone like an answering machine does and can store the message on the hard disk. Some modems even have comprehensive voice-mail capabilities similar to business voice-mail systems. Furthermore, the majority of modems have facsimile (fax) capabilities; that is, they can send graphic images and text between distant locations. Such modems emulate fax machines, allowing you to receive and send fax transmissions directly via your computer. A fax/modem is different from a standard fax machine in the way it handles documents. The fax/modem can only send documents that are already in the computer; they can display the documents on the computer screen or print them when they receive them. How does the fax/modem user fax documents not inputted into the computer? One way is to use a scanner to scan documents into the computer. Nevertheless, the traditional fax machine is more versatile than the fax/modem. It is also more expensive.

Fax Machine

The dedicated **fax machine** (Fig. 11.5) is a combination scanner, fax/modem, and printer. This machine scans a piece of paper and converts its image into coded form for transmission over

Figure 11.5
Fax machine
ClickArt Images ©
T/Maker Company.

the telephone system. On the other end, a fax machine reconverts the transmitted code and prints out a facsimile of the original sheet of paper. In the 1970s, the fax transmitted pages slowly, but today it is fast enough to serve as one of the most popular devices for transmitting mail electronically.

Electronic Mail

Electronic mail, or **e-mail,** can send messages to individuals at local or distant locations in a matter of seconds. What makes this system unique is the fact that the message recipient does not have to be present to receive a message. The computer stores in memory any messages received;

when the recipient logs on the system, the screen displays a message informing him or her about the mail. There are many additional advantages to e-mail. You can quickly address an issue via e-mail without time-consuming social interaction. E-mail also conquers the problems of long-distance communication. People all over the world can easily communicate with each other instantly. E-mail can generate answers quickly and inexpensively. Figure 11.6 shows an electronic mail message sent via *Eudora Light,* a freeware product from Qualcomm.

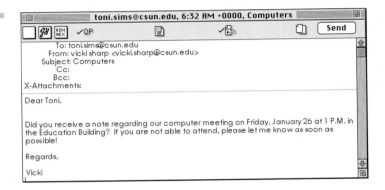

Figure 11.6
Eudora Light
Eudora ® is a registered
trademark of
QUALCOMM
Incorporated.

At one time, experts predicted that e-mail could replace the postal service. Not wanting to be consigned to the dead-letter heap, the U.S. Postal Service developed its own e-mail service, E-Comm, in the early 1980s. This e-mail attempt failed miserably in 1984, and the Post Office has not tried again. Nevertheless, electronic mail did not develop as rapidly as everyone thought it would. There were two impediments to quick development: (1) The traditional fax machine did not require a computer or special knowledge in order for people to exchange information quickly, and (2) there were many incompatible electronic mail systems inadequately connected. It seems likely that the competition between e-mail, fax, and the postal service will always exist.

However, the Internet has solved the incompatibility problems of electronic mail systems. The **Internet,** a worldwide system of computer linkage, is becoming the world forum for electronic mail and communications. This development has resulted in a remarkable explosion of electronic mail. Before discussing the Internet and its historical origins, let's first examine networking.

Networking

Networking is another way that computers communicate with each other. In a **network,** numerous computers are connected together. To have a computer network, you need to have the computers to connect, or network; these computers can be of any type. A network system generally includes a file server, which is a computer with a large data capacity that serves as a repository for information. The file server directs the flow of information to and from the computers in the network. You need a network card if the networking capabilities are not built or plugged into the computer; you also need cables, wires, hookups, and operating system software—available from companies such as Novell, Apple, and LAN Techs—that gives access to the file server. Besides this special software and equipment, you need *networkable* software that runs on the network.

A network can have a temporary connection made through the telephone or other communication device or a permanent connection such as a cable. According to Chris Saulpaugh, a computer expert with Roger Wagner Inc., "infrared transmission has become very popular for small networks in one room or room to room. This type of transmission is very easy to install and all the user has to worry about is blocking or deflecting the signal to the computers." The current portable computers have infrared transceivers so they can send files to their printer, computer or handheld computers. Furthermore, the computer's network cable connection can be either copper or fiber optic. The more expensive fiber optic cables, a transmission medium consisting of glass fibers, transmits digital signals in the form of pulses of light produced by a laser. Using this type of cabling, the user can send more messages simultaneously than by using copper wiring or coaxial cable. "For example, two glass optical fibers can handle 6,000 telephone conversations at a time, a task that would take 250 copper wires" (Heinich, Molenda, and Russell, 1993).

The three most commonly known network arrangements are the ring, the star, and the shared-bus. The **ring network** does not rely on a file server, and if one computer goes down in the system, the others still operate (Fig. 11.7). This configuration is found in university administrative offices in which each computer performs when needed and each computer has its own software.

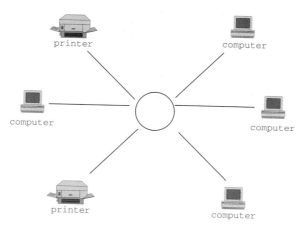

Figure 11.7
Ring network
ClickArt Images ©
T/Maker Company.

In the second arrangement, the **star network** (Fig. 11.8, page 274), a central computer or file server is connected with several computers or terminals. The star network becomes inoperable if the file server fails because it has in its memory all the data that the other computers use for processing. A school computer center might use this type of network for its card catalog.

In the third arrangement, the **shared-bus network** (Fig. 11.9, page 274), a single bidirectional cable acts as a "bus line" to carry messages to and from devices. "Each node on the network has a unique address and failure at a single node will not disrupt the rest of the network" (Pfaffenberger, 1993). Information is stored in a central computer, but complicated communication

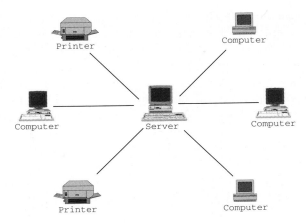

Figure 11.8
Star network
ClickArt Images ©
T/Maker Company.

Figure 11.9
Shared-bus network
ClickArt Images ©
T/Maker Company.

protocols are required to avoid data collision. Small local area networks use this configuration because it is an easy system to set up and use.

Local area networks (LAN), wide area networks (WAN), and telephones are three types of networks. LANs provide communication within a local area, usually within 200 or 300 feet, such as in an office building. A school might have its card catalog stored on a file server's hard disk, accessible by other computers throughout the building through a LAN. WANs provide communication for a larger area that requires miles of communication linkage. A telephone network connects computers via telephone. The only difference between a WAN and a telephone network is the fact that the telephone's communication is intermittent, while the wide area network communicates all the time.

Let us consider the pros and cons of this fast-growing networking industry.

Advantages. Networking establishes communication among computers and is especially helpful when people work on different floors or in different buildings. This system improves the speed and accuracy of communication, preventing messages from being misplaced and automatically ensuring total distribution of key information. Networks let users share software and equipment such as word processing programs and laser printers. Not only do users save on hardware, they save on software as well. A network allows users to share files with one another, which makes it suitable for class research.

Disadvantages. The cost of networking depends on the computer hardware, number of users, and networking software. The price can be high for hardware, computer training, and maintenance. Networking requires expertise that may not always be readily available, and it is difficult to find competent technicians to repair this equipment. A school district must consider the frustration level of teachers given the extra burden of learning a new system. Another disadvantage is "computer dependency"; teachers who come to rely on their computers may be at a loss if the system crashes. Furthermore, the necessary networking software is not always available. A final disadvantage is system security; an unauthorized individual can access all information if the network is unprotected. In fact, it was the issue of security that led to the creation of the Internet, the mother of all networks.

The Internet

The Internet provides many services to millions of people. Having access to the Internet means that you can tap into thousands of databases and talk electronically with experts worldwide on any subject. You can find jobs, communicate with customers, work out technical problems, sell products, and conduct research. Just how did this remarkable technology develop in such a relatively short time span?

Historical Background

In 1969, the Department of Defense created the Internet for military research purposes. The Department's major concerns were to ensure mass communication of information while providing for maximum security. It wanted to connect the Pentagon with defense researchers in academia and business. The original network was called ARPAnet because the Advanced Research Projects Agency designed it. The goal was to build a decentralized network that would run even if nuclear war destroyed a portion of it. This network would continue to function during a disaster because it didn't rely on a single pathway for data transmission. The Department of Defense experimented with different ways of sending the data efficiently. Eventually, researchers devised a protocol that they called the Internet Protocol, or IP, to be used along with Transmission Control Protocol, or TCP.

In its first few years, this electronic highway provided a way of exchanging electronic mail service and linking on-line libraries to government agencies and universities. These agencies served as testers for the network's integrity. In the early 1980s, the original ARPAnet network divided into two networks, ARPAnet and Milnet. The connection between the networks was called the Defense Advanced Research Projects Agency, or DARPA Internet. In a short time, the name was shortened to the Internet.

In 1986, the National Science Foundation encouraged nondefense use of the Internet by creating a special network called NSFNet, which connected five new supercomputing centers across the country. Universities all over the country then started connecting into NSFNet. As the United States continued to develop its national and local networks during the 1980s, other countries did the same. This gave rise to connections among different national networks. As time passed, more countries joined the Internet to share its rich resources. By the late 1980s, students gained Internet access when they registered at their colleges. Since the Internet has become easier to use, more individuals and businesses have accessed it. In 1991, only 376,000 computers were registered on the Internet, but a year later this number had increased to 727,000 (Badgett and Sandler, 1993). In 1994, the Internet was a "global web of 30,000 computer networks, at least 2.2 million computers, and 20 million people in more than 70 countries" (Wiseman, 1994). In 1997, the number of users on the Internet numbered more than 50 million, which is still only a little more than 20 percent of the population (Chapman, 1997). This figure could surge to 90 or 100 million by the end of 1998. The Internet is currently growing at a rate of 10 percent to 14 percent a month as more businesses and institutions become connected (Pfaffenberger, 1997).

This growth is a far cry from the unenthusiastic reaction that state representative Al Gore received in the 1980s when he called for the creation of a national network of "information highways" (Laquey and Ryer, 1992). In 1994, Apple, Microsoft, and IBM began including connectivity to on-line services as part of their operating systems (Farber, 1994). In addition, software programs such as *ClarisWorks, The 1998 Grolier Multimedia Encyclopedia,* and *HyperStudio* incorporated Internet components into their programs. Electronic services such as CompuServe and America Online offered browsers or software programs so subscribers could more easily access the Internet, thus extending the Internet's influence even more.

Given the Internet's tremendous influence, we have to wonder, "Who pays the bill?" The answer is simple: University and research organizations pay to maintain their branches. Companies, organizations, and individuals who want direct access to the Internet also pay providers to connect. Finally, the government channels huge amounts of tax dollars through the National Science Foundation and various other governmental agencies such as NASA in order to help finance the Internet.

How the Internet Works

In the past, the Internet was difficult for the novice to use. However, Swiss researchers developed the World Wide Web, a system that lets the user move smoothly through the Internet, jumping from one document to another. Software tools were developed that made access to the Internet resources uncomplicated. In 1993, Marc Andreessen developed *Mosaic* at the University of Illinois's National Center for Supercomputing Applications. *Mosaic,* a software breakthrough, was a navigator tool for interactive material. This software browser allowed you to view pictures and documents by simply clicking on your mouse. A simple interface let you travel through the on-line world of electronic information along any path you wished in order to discover the wonders contained on the Internet. Figure 11.10 shows *Mosaic*'s introductory screen.

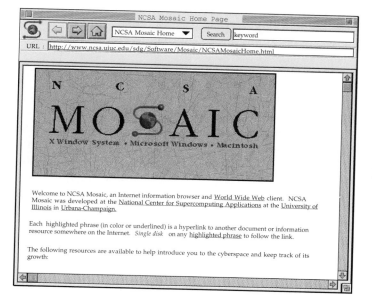

Figure 11.10
Mosaic
Mosaic™, NCSA Mosaic™, and the "spinning globe" logo are proprietary trademarks of the University of Illinois. These trademarks identify "Web" browser products developed and owned by the University of Illinois.

Some software houses purchased a nonexclusive license to sell and support *Mosaic.* At the time, Jim Clark, founder of Silicon Graphics Inc., decided not to license the source code but hired some of NCSA's programmers to reengineer a *Mosaic*-like browser. *Mosaic* author Marc Andreessen and Jim Clark formed a partnership they called Netscape Communications Corporation. They produced *Netscape,* which was a higher performance World Wide Web browser with multiple and simultaneous image loading. This browser was faster than *Mosaic* and much simpler to use. It also was more advanced than other browsers in the way it handled graphics (Morgenstern, 1995). In a short period of time, more browsers were developed, like Microsoft's *Internet Explorer;* these browsers made it unnecessary to learn the Unix commands that people used on the Internet. However, computers connected to the Internet presently still run some form of **UNIX,** the operating system that controls the computer. Some common UNIX commands follow:

Common UNIX Commands

Bye	Logs off from a program or system.
cd	Changes the directory.
cp	Copies a file or directory.
ed	Edits.
kill	Kills the process.
logout	Terminates the current session.
ls	Lists files.
mail	Displays mail.
rx	Receives XMODEM.
rz	Receives ZMODEM.
send	Sends text to user.

Logging onto the Internet

Every Internet user, whether an individual or numerous individuals using a single computer, has a unique electronic address. An address generally has the following information: the user's identification (or userid, the name of the account) followed by the *at* symbol, @, the name of the host, the subdomain, and the domain. The userid usually identifies the holder of the account. The **host** is the individual computer at a given location. A subdomain is the location of the computer. Finally, the domain is the broader location of the computer. The United States has six domains:

1. government (gov),
2. educational (edu),
3. military (mil),
4. network (net),
5. organization (org), and
6. commercial (com).

Here's an example of an Internet address:

vicki.sharp@huey.csun.edu

vicki.sharp represents the name of the user, Vicki Sharp; *huey* is the host computer; *csun* is California State University, Northridge; and *edu* means the computer is located at an educational institution. This format can vary.

Once you log onto the Internet, you can begin to use the tools that are available. You can look at a picture file of the Dead Sea Scrolls located in the Library of Congress. You can read an electronic copy of *Little Women,* obtain a weather satellite photograph, or chat with people around the world regarding a problem in physics. You can conduct legal research, consult job listings and career information, or download public domain software for your computer. Most of the computers that connect to the Internet have resources such as electronic mail, searchable databases, and file transfer capabilities.

Problems with the Internet

There are quite a few security drawbacks on the Internet. People have been known to steal information, and some companies have had clients' correspondence violated. It is for this reason that Chrysler, Chevrolet, and Ford will not send designs over the Internet. Even though data is encrypted or encoded, it is difficult to verify a user's identity. "The Internet still is not 100 percent secure," says Taso Devetzis, a Bellcore Lab researcher who is responsible for doing encryption work for the Internet (interview on Internet). Another controversial issue is advertising over the network. Many people do not want to see advertising on the Internet, and yet it is there. Despite these problems, the Internet continues to grow rapidly because of the vast array of information and activities possible. The following section provides synopses of some of the more popular Internet resources.

Internet Resources

Electronic Mail.   *Pine* (University of Washington), *mail,* and *mailx* are tools that send and receive mail communications. Figure 11.11 shows *Pine's* main screen. From this menu you can get

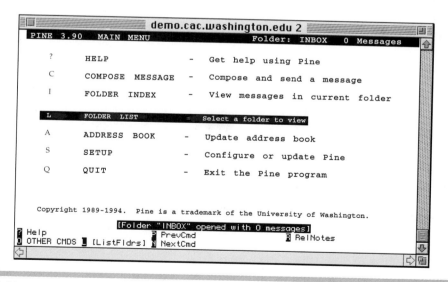

Figure 11.11
Pine's main screen
Pine is created, trademarked, and copyrighted by the University of Washington.

help, compose messages, and read your current mail. The mail sent can be text files, source programs, electronic magazines, or messages, and it can be sent anywhere on the Internet. In addition, you can read mail from and send mail to other mail systems, such as America Online, that are connected to the Internet.

Microsoft's *Internet Explorer* and *Netscape* have e-mail applications integrated into their respective programs. Furthermore, there are stand-alone commercial programs like *Eudora Pro* (Qualcomm) and Claris's *Email* that are feature ladened. Students who need fewer bells and whistles can download a freeware program like *Eudora Light* or *Pegasus* (David Harris, publisher) and use this program without restrictions. Both programs have basic components like sending and receiving messages, forwarding, replying, and setting up an address book.

Wide Area Information Service (WAIS).   WAIS accesses many databases that are distributed around the Internet. For example, you can use it to access ERIC (Education Resources Information Clearinghouse). When you use WAIS, you can tell it what databases to search by specifying a list of keywords to use in the search. WAIS searches every article in all the databases that you select. You can then view or print out the list of articles found in the search.

Telnet.   Telnet is a software utility that lets you log on to a remote computer. Telnet converts domain names to Internet addresses, and it uses these addresses to access the target computer.

File Transfer Protocol (FTP).   Internet users may copy files that are spread around the Internet in large and small archives. These files contain text, pictures, sounds, and computer programs. The standard tool for copying these files is called **FTP.** Using this tool, you can copy a file from the archive of a host computer to your own computer. If you do not have an account on the host computer, the Internet will recognize the special account name *anonymous.*

Archie Server.   The Archie server helps you find a file stored at an anonymous FTP site. Once you know the name of the site, it is easy to download the file using FTP.

Gopher.   **Gopher** displays a simple series of menus through which you can access any type of textual information on the Internet. Gopher systems, are locally administered and no longer as popular.

Internet Relay Chat (IRC).   IRC is a place at which you can take part in public discussions with a large group of people. These conversations address numerous and varied topics. You can also choose an individual with whom to have a private conversation.

Finger Service.   Finger service lets you find out information about another Internet user, including the name of the person behind the userid.

Usenet.   The User's Network (**Usenet**) is not really a network, but it is a place for discussion groups. Through this network, individual articles can be distributed throughout the world. There are thousands of these discussion groups.

Multiple User Dimension (MUD).   MUD, a program that involves virtual reality, is similar to *Dungeons and Dragons*. You participate by taking on a role and exploring it in interactions with others.

Bulletin Board Systems (BBSs).   A bulletin board is a central computer that stores messages from other computers. It is often set up in a person's home, and the individual who is in charge is called a system operator or **sysop**. The bulletin board has three individual parts: (1) a message board where the user reads or posts messages; (2) a library of files where an individual can access programs ranging from graphics to public domain software; and (3) electronic mail (e-mail) for private communication with friends or colleagues.

There are thousands of bulletin boards across the country. The Internet has bulletin board systems at which messages and files devoted to certain topics are stored. Local interests run these computers and you can easily connect to them.

An excellent bulletin board is BMUG, the Berkeley Macintosh Users Group. BMUG distributes information, gives help on Macintosh computer problems, and provides software for its members. The popularity of bulletin boards is declining because browsers like *Netscape* make it easier to navigate the Internet and download files. Lately, bulletin boards have come under attack for harboring adult-only material that is easily seen by minors. These types of bulletin boards encouraged the U.S. Congress to pass legislation criminalizing the distribution, creation, and availability of obscene material or communication that is indecent for minors. However, the U.S. Supreme Court upheld First Amendment protection for free speech and declared that this Communications Decency Act of 1996 was unconstitutional.

Newsgroups.   Different from e-mail, newsgroups are like public bulletin boards in which you can read messages that others have written and write your own thoughts. People discuss a range of topics from news to entertainment to grade-appropriate lesson plans.

World Wide Web (The Web).   The Web is defined as "a global hypertext system that uses the Internet as its transport mechanism" (Pfaffenberger, 1997). The Web is a connection of computers containing documents accessed with special software that allows one to view text, graphics, video, photos and to easily link to another document on The Web. (The World Wide Web will be discussed in chapter 12.)

This section has presented a small sample of the tools and resources that are available on the Internet.

On-Line Services

There are numerous commercial computer services such as CompuServe, America Online, Prodigy, Dialog/Classmate, National Geographic Kids Network, and Scholastic Network. In addition to providing access to information, many of these **on-line services** offer electronic mail and news and information about the weather, entertainment, sports, and finance. Furthermore, with such services you can download thousands of free programs, make contact with fellow computer users, obtain free help from experts, connect to the Internet, participate in conferences on a variety of topics, and obtain hardware and software support. When you join one of these services, you receive a starter kit with a subscriber identification number, a temporary password, and a manual explaining how to use the service. Most of the services initially give free on-line time, but after this initiation period, the charges range from $3.50 to $19.95 an hour, with an extra fee for special services such as printouts of journal articles. Currently, most services are charging a fixed monthly rate and additional charges only for special services. Most of these commercial networks also have bulletin boards. What follows are brief summaries of some of the more popular commercial services.

Dialog

Dialog was created in the 1960s to keep track of the many documents produced as part of the space program. It is a useful service for educators because it accesses technical and scientific information. In Dialog, the first service listed for access is ERIC (Educational Resources Information Clearinghouse), the basic educational resource for research information. DIALOG'S CLASS-MATE, one of the classroom instruction programs (CIP), was designed for kindergarten through college and contains databases that cover a range of information services. More than 1,200 full-text publications are available on-line through Dialog; it also offers coverage from national and international presses and regional and updated news wire services as well as special sources for technology, business, tax, and medicine.

National Geographic Kids Network

National Geographic Kids Network is an international telecommunications-based science and geography curriculum. The program allows elementary schools to conduct original scientific research and then share their data, as well as information about their communities and themselves, with other students all over the world.

In each of seven different curriculum units, students investigate real-world scientific issues such as acid rain, solar energy, nutrition, water quality, weather, and trash disposal. During each unit, students perform hands-on experiments, collect data, and, through telecommunications, compare their findings with those of their research teammates in ten to fifteen other classes worldwide. A professional scientist helps students trace geographic patterns in the data from all participants. At the end of each unit, student observations spark classroom debate on the social and economic implications of the issues.

America Online

America Online (AOL) features mini bulletin boards that are run by forum leaders. These leaders are responsible for message boards and libraries and for operating the forum's events. An AOL forum has a file library that contains software and articles related to the interest of the particular forum. AOL lets you point and click to find your way around the service. AOL also has a quick search function that can access the entire collection of files. It allows you to search all the databases with keywords. To download a file, simply select the file and click on the word *download*. When the file is finished, a voice says, "file done." Through AOL, you can track stocks, play games, access the encyclopedia, or obtain news and weather information. Let's use AOL to explore how an on-line service works.

Our assignment is to use the *Grolier Multimedia Encyclopedia* to learn about Charles Babbage, the father of computers. Before you can access this information, remember that you must match your computer's modem settings, baud rate, data size, stop bits, and parity with the service's modem settings. If the settings are not identical, communication will not take place. For example, if the service has a 56-Kbps baud rate, you must also set your modem at 56 Kbps.

We begin by opening up AOL and then following these steps:

1. The first screen (Fig. 11.12) shows a list of AOL General Services. Since we're searching for Charles Babbage, we'll click on Research and Learning.

Figure 11.12
America Online
general services page
Copyright 1997–98
America Online, Inc. All
Rights Reserved

2. For a reference, we click on Encyclopedia.
3. From the list of references, we'll select *Grolier Multimedia* (Fig. 11.13).

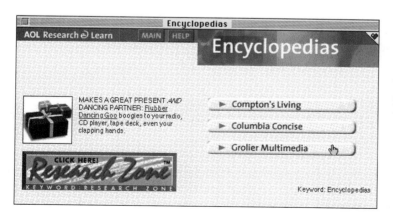

Figure 11.13
America Online
encyclopedia choices
Copyright 1997–98
America Online, Inc. All
Rights Reserved.

4. At the next menu, we type in "Charles Babbage" and click on Search (Fig. 11.14).

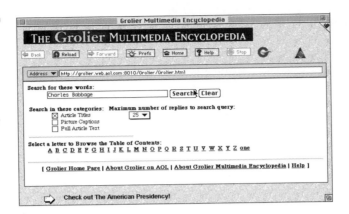

Figure 11.14
America Online's
*Grolier Multimedia
Encyclopedia*
Copyright 1997–98
America Online, Inc. All
Rights Reserved. © Grolier
Interactive, Inc. Reprinted
by permission.

5. AOL matches "Charles Babbage" to the headings of articles in the encyclopedia. If the search was unsuccessful, we would be notified that no articles were found. In this case there is only one match so we click on it (Fig. 11.15).

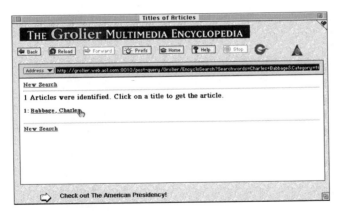

Figure 11.15
America Online
search results
Copyright 1997–98
America Online, Inc. All
Rights Reserved.

6. The article on Charles Babbage appears (Fig. 11.16).
7. We can now read, save, or print this information.
8. Finally, we disconnect from AOL and quit the telecommunications application software.

Scholastic Network

Scholastic Network is designed to help students explore the world around them. Using this network, students can send electronic mail, buy from the Scholastic store, chat on-line with other members, use the message boards, and download files. From the file libraries, students can obtain magazine articles, chapters of books, photographs, software demonstrations, digitized

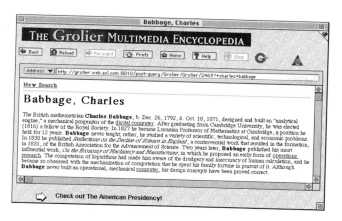

Figure 11.16
America Online's article about Charles Babbage
Copyright 1997–98 America Online, Inc. All Rights Reserved. © Grolier Interactive, Inc. Reprinted by permission.

video clips, maps, and charts. Students can locate a current news story related to search words or phrases typed into the computer, and can consult on-line weather reports, on-line encyclopedias, and on-line stock market reports. They can join professional conferences through the service, seek funding in the grant center, learn more about technology, and even advertise in the newspapers.

Prodigy

Prodigy (Fig. 11.17) has many of the same options that America Online has. It was the first service with a built-in Internet Web browser. One of its more popular services is home banking, which lets subscribers pay their bills electronically, transfer funds, and check their balances, all

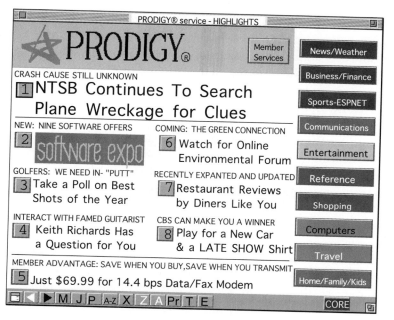

Figure 11.17
Prodigy
Courtesy of Prodigy Services Co.

from the comfort of their own homes. Prodigy's family-oriented computer service now offers a simpler interface.

CompuServe

CompuServe (CIS) is one of the oldest services and in the beginning was used mostly by businesspeople. At first, this service was very difficult to navigate, but it has changed its interface to resemble that of America Online. CompuServe provides services similar to the other commercial providers: Users can track stocks, play games, access encyclopedias, and obtain news and weather information.

Appendix F contains a list of commercial networks and databases.

The Internet has become a pervasive influence in our lives. As the number of individuals using the Internet increases, more people will be engaging in distant learning. In distant learning, the learners are physically separated from one another during class and instructors use audio and video conference and computer communication to teach.

Distant Education

Distant learning is an approach to education that is becoming popular throughout the world. It is being used in medicine, law, and business. For years, doctors, lawyers, and engineers have used it to continue their educational studies. Many of these professionals are too busy in their work to participate in classroom instruction. Recently, higher education institutions have used distance education to reach a diverse audience that would not be accessible through ordinary, traditional classroom instruction. Many universities are offering virtual degrees via the Internet. Duke University and the University of Maryland are offering master's degree programs entirely through the Internet (Molnar, 1997). Throughout the United States, professors are engaging in electronic instruction, and businesspeople are using electronic conferencing to conduct international meetings across the Pacific via satellite transmissions. Satellite communications are also being employed in the school and home. For instance, the University of Illinois at Champaign-Urbana (UICU) offers any student in the state the chance to take engineering courses without having to attend classes on campus. Presently, UICU students take exams, receive class assignments, are graded on their work, and engage in discussions with their teachers and classmates electronically, accomplished with conferencing software. Burks Oakley II, assistant department head of Electrical and Computer Engineering, developed the curriculum taught via electronic communications. For his pioneering work, he was awarded a two-year, $200,000 grant from the Alfred P. Sloan Foundation (T. H. E. November 1994). Thanks to the computer, students can more easily communicate with instructors, and instructors can be more accessible and responsive to the students' questions.

More and more schools and universities are developing two-way audio and video capabilities, hence, distant learning is expanding. Teachers and students at distant locations are easily communicating with each other. Students are interacting more with other students in different countries. Instructors are communicating more by e-mail, chat rooms, and video conferencing. As this trend continues, it suggests that the way we view the traditional school will change forever. At the very least, technology will change the way students learn and the time they spend in the school building.

For a more complete treatment of distance education, see *Compressed Video Operations and Applications* by Hakes et al. (Association for Educational Communications and Technology, 1993). See chapter 16 for additional information on teleconferencing.

Classroom Applications

Some invaluable telecommunications tutorials accompany products such as *Microsoft Works* and *ClarisWorks*. In addition to studying tutorials, students can engage in many activities that incorporate telecommunications into the classroom. What follows are three such activities.

▼   I. Language Arts   ▼

Materials
You will need a computer, a communications package, word processing software, a printer, a modem, and a telephone line.

Objective
Students will send a letter using a modem.

Procedure
1. Introduce the students to telecommunications.
2. Demonstrate how the computer, software, modem, and printer work.
3. Discuss the terms *bulletin boards, baud rates,* and *electronic mail.*
4. Show examples of completed pen pal letters.
5. Have students type and transmit letters to another school, using the modem.

▼   II. Science   ▼

Materials
You will need a computer, a communications package, a color monitor, a printer, a modem, a telephone line, and access to the Internet.

Objective
Students will identify and explain causes of chemical and physical weathering.

Procedure
1. Teach a unit on current environmental issues.
2. Have students measure local rainfall and its acidity level.

3. Access the Internet and have students use it to discover patterns of acidity in the rainwater across the continent.
4. Ask students to post their results on-line for other schools to use.
5. Have students download information from other students and draw maps and charts.

▼ III. General ▼

Materials

You will need a computer, a communications package, a color monitor, a printer, a modem, a telephone line, and access to the Internet.

Objective

Using the Internet, college students will find on-line activities or lessons.

Procedure

1. Have the students search the Internet looking for useful sites.
2. Choose a lesson plan for a specific topic in a subject area with an on-line interactive activity.
3. Print the lesson plan and discuss it with your class.

Summary

Telecommunications opens a new world of information. Students and teachers can lose themselves in the databases of information. However, what has been described in this chapter is just the tip of the iceberg. Numerous developments are on the horizon. (In chapter 16, we predict some future technological breakthroughs in this field.) We learned about telecommunications and its hardware and software. We discussed the Internet, the mother of networks, in detail, including its history and the many available Internet resources. Briefly, we examined the more popular on-line services. Using AOL as a model, we discovered how to use an on-line service to find information. Finally, we previewed suggestions for telecommunications activities in the classroom. A mastery test, classroom projects, and suggested readings and references follow.

Chapter Mastery Test

1. Define *networking*.
2. Discuss the advantages and disadvantages of using networking in the classroom.
3. Discuss the hardware and software involved in telecommunications.
4. Explain how a modem operates. Discuss three problems that a user can encounter when using a modem.
5. Identify and briefly describe one of the more popular on-line services, elaborating on some of its resources.
6. Describe the Internet and discuss three of its services.
7. What is the difference between e-mail and an electronic bulletin board?

8. Define the following modem terms: *baud rate, parity, data bit, stop bit,* and *handshake.*

9. What was *Mosaic* and why was it a technological breakthrough?

10. How could telecommunications improve learning in the classroom?

11. What distinguishes distance education from traditional classroom instruction?

Classroom Projects

1. Set up a modem in class and show how it works.

2. Take a field trip to a school that uses networking. Find out what type of network and software are being utilized and how the students are using networking in the classroom. Evaluate this school's program, listing its strengths and weaknesses.

3. Examine the different on-line services and compare their cost and benefits.

Suggested Reading and References

Anderson, Margaret D. "Using Computer Conferencing and Electronic Mail to Facilitate Group Projects." *Journal of Educational Technology Systems* 24, no. 2 (1995–96): 113–18.

Badgett, Tom, and Corey Sandler. *Welcome to Internet: From Mystery to Mastery.* New York: Miss Press, 1993.

Biehle, James T. "Four Keys to Putting Tomorrow's Technology in Yesterday's Buildings." *School Planning and Management* 36, no. 2 (February 1997): 27–28.

Bork, Alfred. "The Future of Computers and Learning." *T. H. E. Journal* 24, no. 11 (June 1997): 69–77.

Braun, Joseph A., Jr. "Past, Possibilities, and Potholes on the Information Superhighway." *Social Education* 61, no. 3 (March 1997): 149–53.

Bruder, Isabelle. "Schools of Education: Four Exemplary Programs." *Electronic Learning* 10, no 6. (March 1991): 21–24, 45.

Bull, Glen, Gina Bull, and Tim Sigmon. "Interactive Web Pages." *Learning & Leading with Technology,* 24, no. 6 (March 1997): 22–27.

"Conferencing Software Plays Key Role In Innovative University Project." *T. H. E. Journal* (November 1994): 79–80.

Cookson, Peter S., and Yu-Bi Chang. "The Multidimensional Audioconferencing Classification System (MACS)." *American Journal of Distance Education* 9, no. 3 (1995): 18–36.

Craig, Dorothy, and Jaci Stewart. "Mission to Mars." *Learning & Leading with Technology* 25, no. 2 (October 1997): 22–27.

Crawford, Walt. "Jargon That Computes: Today's PC Terminology." *Online* 21, no. 2 (March–April 1997): 36–41.

Crotty, Cameron. "Apple Automates Internet Addressing." *MacWeek* 11, no. 35 (September 15, 1997): 17.

Darrow, Barbara. "IBM Develops Prototype of Color Touch Screen for Laptops." *InfoWorld* 13, no. 16 (April 22, 1991): 6.

Dede, Chris. "The Evolution of Distance Education: Emerging Technologies and Distributed Learning." *American Journal of Distance Education* 10, no. 2 (1996): 4–36.

Desposito, Joseph. *Que's Computer Buyer's Guide.* Carmel, Ind.: Que Corporation, 1991.

Dewett-Elmer, Phillip. "The Battle for the Soul of Internet." *Time Magazine* (July 25, 1994): 50–53.

Duffy, Bob. "Buttoning Down the Content Explosion." *Electronic Library* 15, no. 3 (June 1997): 227–29.

Eklund, John, and Peter Eklund. "Collaboration and Networked Technology: A Case Study in Teaching Educational Computing." *Journal of*

Computing in Teachers Education 13, no. 3 (April 1997): 14–19.

Farber, Dan. "Are You Experienced with What Internet Participation Takes?" *PC Week* 11, no. 31 (August 8, 1994): 3.

Flanigan, James. "Tax Proposal to Meet the Future by Degrees." *Los Angeles Times* (December 18, 1994): D1.

Flanagan, Patrick. "The 10 Hottest Technologies in Telcom." *Telecommunications* 31, no. 5 (May 1997): 25–28, 30, 32.

Fraser, Bruce. "Digital Cameras Coming into Focus." *MacWeek* 11, no. 31 (August 8, 1997): 11.

Freedman, Alan. *The Computer Glossary.* New York: American Management Association, 1997.

Freedman, Debra. "Speech Students Learn through Computer Technology." *The Computing Teacher* 18, no. 8 (May 1991): 10–14.

Godin, Seth. *E-Mail Addresses of the Rich and Famous.* Boston, Mass.: Addison-Wesley, 1994.

Greenfield, Elizabeth. "At-Risk and Special Ed. Products: Tools for Special Learning." *T. H. E.* 18, no. 11 (June 1991): 6–14.

Grossman, Evan. "Tut Modem Boasts 2Mbps over Standard Phone Wire. *InfoWorld* 19, no. 40 (October 6, 1997): 74.

Hakes, Barbara and others. "Compressed Video: Operations and Applications," Washington DC, Publisher Association Educational Communication and Technology, 1993.

Hahn, Harley, and Rick Sout. *The Internet Complete Reference.* New York: Osborne McGraw Hill, 1994.

Harris, Judy. "Ridiculous Questions! The Issue of Scale in Netiquette." *Learning and Leading with Technology* 25, no. 2, (October 1997): 13–16.

Harris, Judy. *Way of the Ferret.* Eugene, Oreg.: ISTE, 1994.

Heinich, Robert, Michael Molenda, and James D. Russell. *Instructional Media and the New Technologies of Instruction,* 4th ed. New York: Macmillan, 1993.

Hiltzik, Michael Al. "Microsoft: Internet Explorer." *Los Angeles Times* (December 12, 1997): 1.

Holzberg, Carol S. "LCD Panels." *Electronic Learning* 10, no. 6 (March 1991): 46–49.

Keizer, Gregg. "In the Network Groove." *Incider A+* 9, no. 9 (September 1991): 40–45.

Kurland, Daniel, Richard Sharp, and Vicki Sharp. *Introduction to the Internet for Education.* Belmont, Calif.: Wadsworth, 1997.

Laquey, Tracy, and Jeanne Ryer (forward by Al Gore). *Internet Companion.* Boston, Mass.: Addison-Wesley, 1992.

Laurie, Peter. *The Joy of Computers.* Boston: Little, Brown, 1983.

Lindroth, Linda. "Internet Connections." *Teaching Pre K–8* 27, no. 4 (January 1997): 62–63.

Mageau, Therese. "Telecommunications in the Classroom." *Teaching and Computers* 7, no. 6 (May/June 1990): 18–24.

McCarthy, Robert. "The Advantages of Using A Network." *Electronic Learning* 9, no. 1 (September 1989): 32–38.

Molnar, Andrew R. " Computers in Education: A Brief History." *T.H.E Journal* 24, no. 11, (June 1997): 59–62.

Morgenstern, David. "Netscape to Add Tables." *MacWeek* 9, no. 10 (March 6, 1995): 1.

Morse, David. *Cyber Dictionary.* Boston Mass.: Knowledge Exchange, 1997.

Noack, David R. "Editor's Choice: Electronic Journals." *Online Access* 9, no. 1 (January/February 1994): 72–82.

Odvard, Dyrli. "The Internet Grows Up." *Technology & Learning* 17, no. 6 (March 1997): 42–47.

O'Leary, Mick. "Online Comes of Age." *Online* 21, no. 1 (January–February 1997): 10–14, 16–20.

Panepinto, Joe. "Family Parents' Guide to the Web." *FamilyPC* (February 1997): 42–60.

Peha, Jon M. "Debates via Computer Networks: Improving Writing and Bridging Classrooms." *T. H. E. Journal* 24, no. 9 (April 1997): 65–68.

Pfaffenberger, Bryan. *Que's Computer User's Dictionary,* 4th ed. Indianapolis, Ind.: Que, 1993.

Pfaffenberger, Bryan. Webster's New World Dictionary, sixth ed. New York, New York; Que, 1997.

Ralston, Anthon, and C. L. Meeks, eds. *Encyclopedia of Computer Science.* New York: Petrocelli, 1976.

Resick, Rosalind. "Pressing Mosaic." *Internet* (October 1994): 81–88.

Roberts, Nancy, George Blakeslee, Maureen Brown, and Cecilia Lenk. *Integrating Telecommunications into Education.* Englewood Cliffs, N.J.: Prentice Hall, 1990.

Roth, Cliff. "ISDN Modems Come to Town." *NewMedia* 6, no. 4 (March 11, 1996): 35–38.

Safir, Marty. "Getting the Bugs out of Digitizing Tablets." *MacValley Voice* 7, no. 6 (June 1991): 1, 5–7.

Salpeter, Judy. "Industrial Snapshot: Where Are We Headed." *Technology & Learning* 17 no. 6 (March 1997): 22–32.

Sharp, Vicki. *Netscape Navigator 3.0 in an Hour.* Eugene, Oreg.: ISTE, 1996.

Sharp, Vicki F. "Prospecting for Science Sites on the Internet." *CSTA Journal* (Fall 1996): 26–34.

Sharp, Vicki, Richard Sharp and Martin Levine. *Best Web Sites for Teachers.* Eugene, Oreg." ISTE, 1996.

Sharp, Richard, Vicki Sharp, and Martin Levine. *Best Math and Science Web Sites for Teachers.* Eugene, Oreg.: ISTE, 1997.

Simkin, Mark G., and Robert H. Dependahl. *Microcomputer Principles and Applications.* Dubuque, Iowa: Wm. C. Brown Publishers, 1987.

Sisneros, Roger. "Telecomputing Takes the Mystery out of On-Line Communication." *Telecomputing* (spring 1990): 15–22.

Solom, G. "Students Can Computer by Just Touching the Screen." *Electronic Learning* 7, no. 7 (April 1988): 50–51.

Staten, James. "CompuServe Planning New Internet Services." *MacWeek* 8, no. 36 (September 12, 1994): 14.

Taaffee, Joanne, and Elinor Mills. "Users Still Like Java Despite the Sun-Microsoft Dispute." *InfoWorld* 19, no. 48 (December 1, 1997): 77.

Trott, Bob. "Browser Wars Go Head to Head." *InfoWorld* 19, no. 40 (October 6, 1997): 77.

Turner, Sandra, and Michael Land. *Tools for Schools.* 2nd ed. Belmont, Calif.: Wadsworth, 1997.

Wiggins, Richard W. "Examining Mosaic." *Internet* (October 1994): 48–51.

Wiseman, Paul. "Internet Snares More Business." *USA Today* (July 7, 1994): money section B1.

Wilkerson, George J. "Teaching Composition via Computer and Modem." *Teaching English in the Two-Year College* 22, no. 3 (October 1995): 202–10.

Withrow, Frank B. "Technology in Education and the Next Twenty-Five Years." *T. H. E Journal* 24, no. 11 (June 1997): 59–62.

Wolf, Gary. "The Second Phase of the Revolutions Has Begun." *Wired* (October 1994): 116.

Wu, Kamyin, and Amy B. M. Tsui. "Teachers' Grammar on the Electronic Highway: Design Criteria for 'Telegram' " *System* 25, no. 2 (June 1997): 169–83.

The World Wide Web (WWW)

12

Objectives

Upon completing this chapter, you will be able to:

1. Explain why the World Wide Web is an invaluable resource;

2. Identify four criteria for selecting Web sites;

3. Talk about some unique World Wide Web sites; and

4. Elaborate on different effective classroom applications.

The World Wide Web and the Internet

The **World Wide Web** is an invaluable resource for people interested in knowledge. You are only a mouse click away from a vast reservoir of information. The web offers teachers a giant library with millions of sites that are increasing at a phenomenal rate each week. Almost 10 million children are online and it is predicted there will be 45 million online by 2002. The Software Publishers Association conducted a survey and found that the two leading uses of the Internet was Education and Research/Reference (Durli, 1998). The Web is the multimedia part of the Internet—that huge worldwide network of connected computer networks with no single master control center or authority. The Web consists of a collection of electronic documents, called **home pages** or **Web sites,** full of text, pictures, sounds, and even video. **Hypertext Markup Language (HTML)** is the language used to design these home pages. (This simple language is discussed in Chapter 14.)

There are thousands of Web sites that take advantage of the Web's multimedia capabilities. Web users can do such things as get information on any curriculum area, talk to an expert, explore the human brain, participate in on-line discussion groups, and download chapters from books or lecture notes.

Web sites, or home pages, have their own unique addresses called **URL**s (Uniform Resource Locators). These individual addresses make Web sites easy to find. URLs start with *http://*. As an example, the URL for the following Web site is a Web page created by my husband, Richard Malcom Sharp, and me.

http://www.csun.edu/~vceed009/

Once connected to a site, a reader will see that certain items on the Web pages are underlined. These underlined items, called *links,* are like threads in a spider's web and give the World Wide Web its name. Just by clicking on these links, the reader can jump from one page on the Web to another, be it a page on the same computer or a page on the other side of the world. One document is linked to another, which is linked to another, and so forth.

Connecting to the World Wide Web

To access the Web, you need a connection to the Internet. You can get an Internet connection through a commercial on-line service. The popular ones are America Online (800-827-6364), and CompuServe (800-848-8990). You can also get an Internet connection through an **Internet Service Provider (ISP)** like Earthlink (800-395-8410). Several places can help you find an ISP to fit your needs. If you already have access to the Internet through a commercial on-line service, you can check out a list of providers at

http://www.thelist.com/

Another place to find information about ISPs is in the local Yellow Pages or from a local computer user group. Web surfing also requires software called a **browser** that enables the user to take advantage of the Web's multimedia capabilities. *Netscape* and *Internet Explorer* are examples of Web browsers. Both the commercial on-line services and the ISPs provide users with the appropriate software.

To connect to the Web effectively, you need a computer running MS-DOS or Windows with at least a 386 processor and 8 MB of RAM or a Macintosh computer running System 7.1 or higher with at least 8 MB of memory. Because of the memory requirements for most browsers, you will be happier with at least 16 MB of RAM. You will also need a modem with a transfer speed of at least 28.8 **bps** or higher. The 56-Kbps modem is becoming the standard.

The power of your modem compared to your personal computer is still very antiquated. Using a modern modem with today's Power G3 Macintosh machines or Pentium II is like comparing a lawnmower with the fastest jet airplane. Modems are certainly faster then they used to be. Each improvement in speed seems fast at first, but eventually, due to larger downloading and more complexity, the modem seems slow again. The villain responsible is the **bandwidth,** or the amount of data that can be transmitted through the computer network in a certain time period. An analogy would be the amount of water than can flow through different size pipes. New technologies promise to change this situation and increase bandwidth capacity. Presently your choices are limited to the following: 56-Kbps modems, ISDN, digital subscriber line (DSL) modems, cable modems, and satellite data services.

The Future of Internet Access

The 56-Kbps modems achieve a faster speed using the regular phone line. These modems are probably the "Last of the Mohicans" or the last of their kind. Even though these modems are one-half as fast as the ISDN modem, the monthly charges for using the 56-Kbps service are less expensive. A drawback is that you need a good quality phone line in your house or you have to be within a mile or two of a phone company's switch, which means that rural areas will not see 56-Kbps. Furthermore, you need an ISP that has hardware support for this kind of modem.

The Integrated Services Digital Network (ISDN), designed in the early 1980s, as a replacement for analog telephone service, uses a single pair of wires. This service uses high-speed digital phone lines offered by the phone companies in most urban areas. The connection speed can range from 64 Kbps to 128 Kbps. When ISDN first burst on the scene, it was difficult to order and particularly difficult to install the hardware. Recently there has been renewed interest in this technology because of a demand for faster Internet access. The negative side, of course, is that ISDN is not universally available in the United States, and it is expensive because you have to pay per-call connect charges in addition to per-minute billing on data calls.

Digital Subscriber Line (DSL) modems provide a digital connection. Unlike ISDN, which is a dial-up service, DSL is point-to-point technology providing downloading at speeds up to 8 Mbps. DSL operates on high-speed leased lines over copper wiring. DSL has to produce affordable high-speed connections to make it a viable alternative to standard modems. Even though DSL and cable modems are different technologies, they both provide dedicated multimegabit connections to a service and they are always on, unlike a dial-up service.

A cable modem lets you connect to the Internet with the same cable that attaches to a standard television set. The cable modems, offered by many cable companies, provide shared point-to-point transmission up to 27 Mbps to a cable modem at the operator's site. In the next seven years, you will see faster cable modems. The cable company charges a fee for its content and faces the challenge of convincing customers this charge is worthwhile.

Satellite data service uses a satellite dish to connect to your computer. A satellite data service can give you 400 Kbps for downloading. However, you connect to this service via an analog modem, and the installation charges are expensive.

Of the technologies briefly described here, we can't be sure which will dominate in the years to come. However, we can be sure that the connection speed will run better than 2 Mbps (Brownstein, 1997).

Getting Started with Netscape

To take advantage of the Web, you need a software program called a browser. For our example, we will use *Netscape,* a popular browser. The following general instructions show you how to enter a URL to display a home page. When you first launch *Netscape* (Fig. 12.1), you see a toolbar at the top of its window. The toolbar has commands such as Print, Back, and Forward.

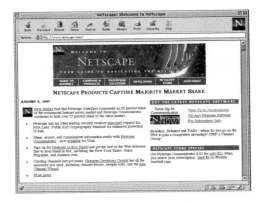

Figure 12.1
Netscape Communicator
Opening Screen
Portions Copyright Netscape
Communications Corporation,
1997. All Rights Reserved.
Netscape, Netscape Navigator
and the Netscape N logo are
registered trademarks of
Netscape in the United States
and other countries.

Next, you type the following URL in the dialog box and then Click Open (Fig. 12.2):

http://www.csun.edu/~vceed009/

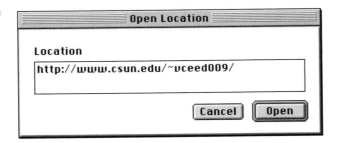

Figure 12.2
Netscape Commicator
Open Location
Portions Copyright Netscape
Communications Corporation,
1997. All Rights Reserved,
Netscape, Netscape Navigator
and the Netscape N logo are
registered trademarks of
Netscape in the United States
and other countries.

After a few seconds, the home page corresponding to the URL will appear (Fig. 12.3).

Figure 12.3
Vicki Sharp's Home Page
Portions Copyright Netscape
Communications Corporation,
1997. All Rights Reserved.
Netscape, Netscape Navigator
and the Netscape N logo are
registered trademarks of
Netscape in the United States
and other countries.

Wait until the page is fully loaded on your screen. Check for a message at the bottom of the screen that says Document: Done (Fig. 12.4).

Figure 12.4
Netscape Communicator
Portions Copyright Netscape Communications Corporation, 1997. All Rights Reserved. Netscape, Netscape Navigator and the Netscape N logo are registered trademarks of Netscape in the United States and other countries.

You are now ready to explore links, or connections, to other Web pages. Links are words that are underlined or displayed in a different color, (Fig. 12.5) or pictures that have a colored border around them (Fig. 12.6). *Note:* When you click on a live link, the pointer (or arrow) becomes a hand.

Figure 12.5
Word link on Richard and Vicki Sharp's Web site

Figure 12.6
Picture link on Richard and Vicki Sharp's Web site

All Web pages displayed in this chapter were opened using *Netscape.* Other browsers work in a similar way, although the display of the home page on your monitor may look different. If you cannot open a site with a given URL, use a search engine to find the site. Search engines are software programs that help you locate information in a database on the Internet (Morse, 1997). Well-known search engines are InfoSeek, Yahoo, Lycos, Magellan, and AltaVista. To use a search engine, type in the title of the site exactly as it appears, not its URL. All-In-One Search Page features a compilation of the various search tools that you can use to help you find things on the Internet. The URL is:

http://www.albany.net/allinone/

Finally, instead of looking through one search engine at a time, use a search engine that lets you use several search engines simultaneously. A good example is MetaCrawler, whose address is:

http:///www.metacrawler.com

Web Site Evaluation

Looking at sites on the Internet is an involved process; therefore it is important to be able to distinguish a good Web site from one that is mediocre. Users must be cautious, because anyone can place information on a Web page, information that can be true, false, or just someone's own creation. Use the following criteria to aid you in evaluating Web sites.

Download Time

Does the home page download fast enough to use during whole class instruction? Does this page download efficiently enough to keep the students focused during small group and independent group study? Does the page download too slowly because the site is graphic intensive?

Navigation Ease

Are your students able to easily move from page to page? Is the page designed in such a way that the students do not get confused or lost in cyberspace? Are the links and descriptions clearly labeled so the students have no trouble keeping on task? Do the majority of the links work, with few dead links?

Appearance

Is the home page's design attractive and appropriate for students? Is the students' first impression positive, and will they be motivated to return again and again? Is the design clear so that the students can explore the page effectively? Are the screens easy to read?

Graphics, Videos, and Sound

Do the graphics, video, and sound have a clear purpose, and are they appropriate for the intended students? Do the graphics, videos, and sounds help the students reach their objectives? Do the graphics enhance the content?

Content

Does the site offer information that covers the objective? Is this information clearly labeled and accurate? How is the site organized? Is the information at an appropriate grade level and can it easily be understood by the student? Are the related links worthwhile and appropriate? Is the content free of bias and stereotype? Does the site provide interactivity that increases its instructional value?

Currency

Is the site updated on a regular basis?

Contact Person

Is there a person available to answer the students' questions?

Now you have an idea of what is important when examining a Web site on the Internet. You might want to print out the evaluation form on page 300 and use these criteria to rate a site to see if it meets your curriculum objectives.

Web Sites

In the next part of the chapter, you will find Web sites that are particularly useful for teachers and students. They cover all curriculum areas and include an excellent collection of lesson plans, search engines, electronic HTML tutorials, and more.

The sites were chosen for their currency, ease of use, comprehensiveness, and organization. They met the criteria listed on the Web Site Rating evaluation form. The sites are updated frequently and have the latest information. Many of the sites are award winners and have been cited for being valuable for their authoritative and reliable information. To simplify, I have intentionally stayed away from long explanations. Each site description has an address and a brief description with navigational shortcuts, and a few have pictures. Many of these sites can be found in *The Best Web Sites for Teachers Second Edition* (Sharp, Sharp, and Levine, 1998).

Art/Music

ArtsEdNet

Courtesy Getty Education Institute for the Arts. Arts Ed Net URL: http://www.artsednet.getty.edu/ © 1998 J. Paul Getty Trust.

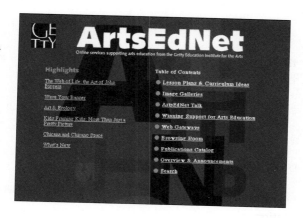

http://www.artsednet.getty.edu/

ArtsEdNet offers on-line services supporting arts education from the Getty Education Institute for the Arts.

WEB SITE RATING

Site Title: _____

Subject: _____

URL (address): _____

Grade Level & Class: _____

Objective: _____

URLs for individual site pages (addresses):

Evaluate the Web site according to the following criteria. Circle the number that you feel the site deserves, 5 being outstanding and 1 being the worst.

1.	**Download Speed**					
	Quickly loads text	5	4	3	2	1
	Quickly loads graphics	5	4	3	2	1
2.	**Navigation Ease**					
	Easy movement link to link	5	4	3	2	1
	Links clearly labeled	5	4	3	2	1
	Links to other sites operate effectively	5	4	3	2	1
	Links for backward and forward movement	5	4	3	2	1
	Adequate number of links	5	4	3	2	1
	Links are apropos and helpful	5	4	3	2	1
3.	**Appearance**					
	Visually Appealing	5	4	3	2	1
	Clarity	5	4	3	2	1
4.	**Content**					
	Information that meets objectives	5	4	3	2	1
	Clearly organized and labeled	5	4	3	2	1
	Linked to worthwhile sites	5	4	3	2	1
	Accurate and useful	5	4	3	2	1
	Provides interactivity	5	4	3	2	1
	Free of bias & stereotype	5	4	3	2	1
	Site author clearly identified	5	4	3	2	1
	Sufficient worthwhile information	5	4	3	2	1
	Authoritative source	5	4	3	2	1
	Readable by student at grade level	5	4	3	2	1
	Students collaborate with other sites	5	4	3	2	1
	Teachers share with others	5	4	3	2	1
5.	**Graphics, Videos, and Sound**					
	Use clearly identified	5	4	3	2	1
	Clear purpose and appropriate	5	4	3	2	1
	Aids students to achieve objectives	5	4	3	2	1
	Relevant for the site	5	4	3	2	1
	Graphics enhance content	5	4	3	2	1
6.	**Currency (Frequency of Updating)**	5	4	3	2	1
7.	**Contact Person**	5	4	3	2	1

Add the total number of points that the site earns to determine the overall rating.

Overall rating: _____

_____ Web site = (145–133 points) This site is of sound content, and I can let the students freely explore.

_____ Web site = (132–110 points) This site contains good instructional material, but the students will need very specific instructions to explore the site.

_____ Web site = (110–94 points) This site contains some worthwhile information, but students will need more specific links and a list of bookmarks along with frequent discussions to progress.

_____ Web site = (93–63) Although some useful information exists at this site, the best way to effectively use this site is through whole-class instruction and guiding the students.

_____ Web site = (62–52) This site contains some useful information, but other sites would be more appropriate and I must supervise the students.

ArtScene

http://artscenecal.com/

ArtScene is a comprehensive guide to art galleries and museums in Southern California.

World Wide School: Artwork Around the World

http://www.k12.wv.us/wschool/html/lesson/phyllis.htm

This site is a comprehensive index to art galleries, museums, and exhibits on the Internet and contains an inexhaustible source of pictures for kindergarten through twelfth-grade students. Click on the first letter of the name of the art museum you wish to visit.

Art Studio Chalkboard

http://www.saumag.edu/art/studio/chalkboard.html

Art Studio Chalkboard is a technical resource for artists and art students compiled and designed by Ralph Larmann. The focus is on the technical fundamentals of perspective, shading, color, and painting.

The Incredible Art Department

Reprinted by permission.

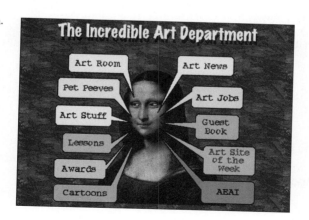

http://www.artswire.org/kenroar/

The Incredible Art Department includes, among its wealth of resources, creative art lesson ideas for all grade levels.

Music Resources on the Internet

http://www.skdesigns.com/internet/music/

Music Resources on the Internet provides a comprehensive guide to general, classical, and jazz music.

Classical Insites

Reprinted by permission.

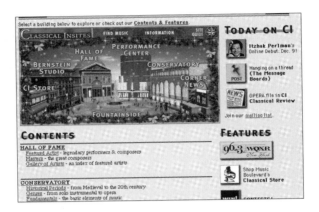

http://www.classicalinsites.com/

Classical Insites is a one-stop shop for everything you need to know about classical music.

RCA Victor's Beginner's Guide to Classical Music

http://www.rcavictor.com/rca/hits/guide/cover.html

Beginner's Guide to Classical Music contains historical information, composers, and famous musical compositions.

Music Education Online

http://www.geocities.com/Athens/2405/

Music Education Online is designed to aid music educators in connecting with a variety of music education resources located on the Internet as well as provide an interactive bulletin board for posting questions and comments on music.

American Music Conference (AMC)

http://www.amc-music.com/

AMC, based in Carlsbad, California, is a national nonprofit educational association founded in 1947. It is the only organization dedicated to promoting music, music making, and music education to the general public.

Computer History

Calculating Machines

http://www.webcom.com/calc/

This site is devoted to the historical development and classification of mechanical calculating machines.

The Virtual Museum of Computing

Reprinted with permission.

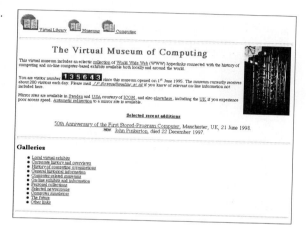

http://www.museums/museums.reading.ac.uk/vmoc/

This virtual museum includes an eclectic collection of World Wide Web sites connected with the history of computing and on-line computer-based exhibits available around the world.

The History of Computers

http://www-stall.rz.fht-esslingen.
de/studentisches/Computer_Geschichte/

The site shows the development of computers from the most primitive calculating aids to modern supercomputers.

Computer News

Yahoo's Tech News

http://www.yahoo.com/Computers/

You can read on-line up-to-date tech news from Reuters Wired and ZDNet news services.

Computer News Daily

Reprinted by permisson.

http://nytsyn.com/live/Latest/

This site features daily reports, provided by The New York Times Syndicate, on the fast-moving world of computer news, with highlights on industry issues, hardware, software, technology, and deal making.

USA Today Tech News

http://tech.usatoday.com/

© USA Today

This site presents the latest breaking tech news daily, an answer desk for your computer questions, and software and hardware reviews.

Electronic Lessons
Electronic HTML Lesson

Reprinted by permission.

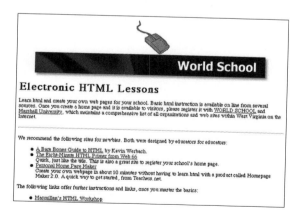

http://www.k12.wv.us/wschool/html/lesson/html.htm

Electronic HTML Lessons provides on-line tutorials for learning HTML and creating your school's Web page. The Eight-Minute HTML Primer from Web 66 is a quick and easy way to learn the basics and register your school's home page.

Learn the Net: An Internet Guide and Tutorial

http://www.learnthenet.com/english/

Learn the Net contains everything you want to learn about the Net, including guides and technology tips from Larry Magid's *LA Times* column.

Language Arts
SCORE Language Arts Resources

Reprinted by permission.

http://www.sdcoe.k12.ca.us/score/cla.html

SCORE Language Arts Resources, designed with the classroom teacher in mind, allows teachers to quickly identify and access resources that are classroom ready. The site includes Cyberguides for both students and teachers.

Project Bartleby Archive

http://www.columbia.edu/acis/bartleby/

Project Bartleby Archive, from Columbia University, is a well-indexed listing of famous authors and poets.

Center for the Study of Books in Spanish for Children and Adolescents

Reprinted by permission.

http://www.csusm.edu/campus_centers/csb/

Center for the Study of Books in Spanish for Children and Adolescents provides query access to a database of more than 3,000 recommended books published around the world in Spanish for children and adolescents.

The Complete Works of William Shakespeare

http://the-tech.mit.edu/Shakespeare/works.html

The Complete Works of William Shakespeare, among its features, includes a search of the complete works, both a chronological and an alphabetical listing of plays, and a discussion area.

Ethnologue: Languages of the World

http://www.sil.org/ethnologue/

Ethnologue: Languages of the World lets you look up languages by country or view an alphabetical list. Also available is a language family index and information on the number of speakers of the language worldwide.

Scholastic Central

http://www.scholastic.com/

Scholastic Central includes links to free stuff for kids and teachers, and the Scholastic directory contains many valuable links such as the *Instructor* magazine.

Merriam-Webster Online

http://www.m-w.com/

Merriam-Webster Online is a great place on the Internet to find authoritative information about the English language. This site includes a dictionary, word of the day, and word for the wise.

Lesson Plans and Teacher Resources

Collaborative Ideas

http://www.k12.wv.us/wschool/html/lesson/collab.htm

Collaborative Ideas provides a list of on-line projects in which your students can participate.

Big Sky Gopher Menu

gopher://bvsd.k12.co.us:70/11/Educational_Resources/Lesson_Plans/Big%20Sky

Big Sky Gopher Menu contains grades kindergarten through twelve lesson plans for math, language arts, science, and social studies.

AskERIC Virtual Library

Reprinted by permission.

http://ericir.syr.edu/Virtual/

AskERIC Virtual Library is one of the leading repositories of lesson plans on the Net, contributed by teachers.

Columbia Education Center Lesson Plans

http://www.col-ed.org/cur/

Columbia Education Center Lesson Plans includes lesson plans for grades kindergarten through twelve in language arts, mathematics, social studies, science, and a miscellaneous category. The lesson plans have been created by teachers for use in their own classrooms.

California Technology Assistance Project (CTAP)

http://ctap.fcoe.k12.ca.us/ctap/Lessons/CClesson.index.html

CTAP is a comprehensive lesson plan index for kindergarten through twelfth grade that covers all curriculum areas.

The Education Place

Screen capture from HOUGHTON MIFFLIN EDUCATION PLACE (http://www.eduplace.com). Copyright © 1998 by Houghton Mifflin Company. Reprinted by permission of Houghton Mifflin Company. All rights reserved.

http://www.eduplace.com/

The Education Place is a free Internet resource for grades kindergarten through eight that includes math, reading, social studies, and technology.

Educators Toolkit

http://www.eagle.ca/~matink/

Educators Toolkit offers many links of interest to teachers, including lesson plans.

Encarta Lesson Collection

http://encarta.msn.com/schoolhouse/lessons/

Encarta Lesson Collection is a growing collection of lesson plans and student activity sheets designed by teachers. Areas covered include fine arts, language arts, social studies, mathematics, computers and information technology, physical education, vocational education, and foreign language.

Grades

http://www2.classroom.net/Grades/

Global Resources And Educational Sites (GRADES) is a searchable database containing more than a thousand on-line links to high-quality educational sites reviewed by Classroom Connect.

Lacoe Teams' K–12 Lesson Plans

http://teams.lacoe.edu/documentation/places/lessons.html

LACOE TEAMS is a collection of lesson plans for language arts, mathematics, science, and history/social studies.

David Levin's Learning@Web.Sites

http://www.ecnet.net/users/gdlevin/home.html

This site is a comprehensive resource designed to assist high school educators in using the Internet to enhance their curriculum and instruction. Topics include language arts, science, math, social studies, music, art, physical education, home economics, nursing, vocational information, and careers.

Math

Activities Integrating Math and Science (AIMS)

Reprinted by permission.

http://www.aimsedu.org/

AIMS is the friend of every classroom teacher. The site contains math and science activities, puzzles, and other on-line materials to enrich your classroom.

SCORE California Mathematics Home Page

http://www.kings.k12.ca.us/math

SCORE, maintained by Kings County Office of Education for math teachers and students, includes a listing of math resources organized by grade level.

Ask Dr. Math

Reprinted by permission.

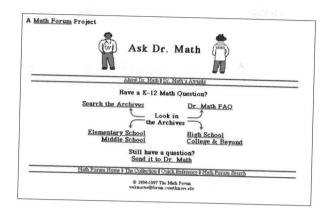

http://forum.swarthmore.edu/dr.math/dr-math.html

Ask Dr. Math has a team of experts providing you with an archive (by grade level) of answered questions. You can also submit your own math question via e-mail.

The Math Forum

http://forum.swarthmore.edu/

The Math Forum is a well-organized page with math resources by subject and by grade level and a student and teacher center. The site also includes a teacher's place, which is divided into two parts: "For Your Classroom," containing lesson plans, problems, software, and fun sites for kids; and "For Your Career," containing discussion groups, articles, and professional organizations.

Web Sites and Resources for Teachers

http://www.csun.edu/~vceed009/

Drs. Vicki and Richard Sharp, professors of education, California State University, Northridge (CSUN), have collected lesson plans and useful resources from the Internet for language arts, social studies, math, science, and other curricular areas.

Science

Athena, K–12 Curriculum Development

http://athena.wednet.edu/

Athena is developing curricular and resource material using geophysical and other data sets acquired via the Internet. Athena is preparing this material to form part of science, math, or technology curricula.

SCORE Science Home Page

http://intergate.humboldt.k12.ca.us/score/frames/

SCORE is maintained by the Humboldt County Office of Education, whose goal is to provide California kindergarten through twelfth-grade students and teachers with easy access to quality on-line science resources. The site includes "ask a scientist" and "science search," where you can locate quality sites by subject, grade level, and keywords.

Access Excellence

Reprinted by permission.

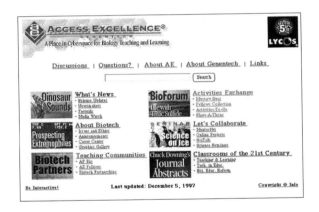

http://www.gene.com/ae/

Access Excellence is a place in cyberspace for biology teaching and learning. Among its wealth of resources are lesson plans, a collection of science sites, up-to-date science news, and a science mystery spot.

EcoQuest: Desert Edition

http://members.aol.com/QuestSite/1/

EcoQuest: Desert Edition is an interactive WebQuest designed for teachers in search of middle school science curricula. EcoQuest was structured to introduce students to Internet research and multimedia design.

Exploratorium ExploraNet

http://www.exploratorium.edu/

The Exploratorium is a museum of science, art, and human perception with more than 650 interactive hands-on exhibits.

The Franklin Institute Science Museum

Reprinted by permission.

http://sln.fi.edu/tfi/welcome.html

The science museum that never closes offers invaluable resources to teachers and students alike. The site contains exhibits and demonstrations that you can visit on your desktop.

Galileo

http://www-hpcc.astro.washington.edu/scied/galileo.html

Galileo offers kindergarten through twelfth grade science lesson plans including such topics as growing crystals on charcoal briquettes (grade 1), "mining" chocolate chip cookies (grades 3–4), and soup can races (grades 3–6). You can add your lesson plans to this site!

Nye Labs

http://nyelabs.kcts.org/

Nye Labs is the on-line laboratory of Bill Nye the Science Guy.

Science Education Gateway!

http://www.cea.berkeley.edu/Education/SII/SEGway/

Science Education Gateway! includes sections on space science, light, cycles, sun and earth, weather, and the solar system. Each section contains annotated lesson plan links that include grade levels and source of background information for the teacher.

ScienceWeb

http://www.sdcoe.k12.ca.us/iss/sciweb/

ScienceWeb is a collection of science sites for grades kindergarten through twelve.

Smithsonian Institute

http://www.si.edu/

Smithsonian Institute is America's treasure house for learning.

The Space Educators' Handbook

http://tommy.jsc.nasa.gov/~woodfill/SPACEED/SEHHTML/seh.html

The Space Educators' Handbook contains special NASA space education resources including space movies, science fiction as a space technology teaching tool, a space calendar, space comics, and other educational resources dealing with space exploration, math, and science.

StarChild

Reprinted by permission.

http://heasarc.gsfc.nasa.gov/docs/StarChild/

StarChild is a general astronomy learning center for young astronomers. Created by NASA, this site contains sections on the solar system, the universe, and "space stuff."

The Weather Underground

http://www.princeton.edu/Webweather/ww.html

The Weather Underground provides WebWeather information, where you can enter a city and state or zip code and view the current weather for that area. The site also provides a weather forecast.

Search Engines

All-In-One Search Page

http://www.albany.net/allinone/

If you need to find something on the Internet, this is the page for you. One of the most comprehensive lists of search engines available.

Social Studies

SCORE History–Social Studies Resources

http://www.rims.k12.ca.us/SCORE/

SCORE History–Social Studies Resources lists resources that have been selected and evaluated by a team of educators from across California. Resources were chosen for their accuracy, grade appropriateness, and richness.

American Memories

Reprinted by permission.

http://lcweb2.loc.gov/ammem/

American Memories provides historical collections for the American Digital Library. The site is a great on-line history resource that includes many film clips you can view right on your computer.

MayaQuest

http://mayaquest.classroom.com/

MayaQuest is an interactive expedition exploring the jungles of Mexico and Central America for clues to the collapse of the ancient Maya civilization.

Historical Documents

http://lcweb2.loc.gov.const.mdbquery.html

Historical Documents includes the Declaration of Independence, Gettysburg Address, Emancipation Proclamation, Martin Luther King's "I Have a Dream", and other U.S. historical documents.

Index of History Resources

http://kuhttp.cc.ukans.edu/history/

Index of History Resources, organized by subject area, contains a wealth of history resources for ancient Europe, African studies, and many others. The site can serve as a supplementary textbook for world history.

U.S. Civil War Center

http://www.cwc.lsu.edu/civlink.htm

U.S. Civil War Center is an organized index of more than 1,200 Civil War links.

Where on the Globe Is Roger?

http://www.gsn.org/roger/

Where on the Globe Is Roger? is an on-going Internet social studies project, part of the Global SchoolNet Foundation.

Special Education

Special Needs Education Network (SNE)

The Special Needs Education (SNE) website project is professionally managed by the Special Need Network (SNN), a grassroots charitable organization serving youth with developmental disabilities, based in Ottawa, Canada. The Special Needs Education initiative is made possible with the suport of the SchoolNet Project, a national progam provided by the Canadian Ministry of Industry in partnership with provincial and territorial governments.

http://www.schoolnet.ca/sne/index2.html

This site offers projects to aid parents and teachers of children with special needs as disparate as attention deficit disorder (ADD), autism, blindness, deafness, fetal alcohol syndrome, and many others. It is an invaluable "List of Lists" for links to services to aid these children, and it includes a SNEparentalk-L mailing list for you to discuss topics in the area of special needs education.

National Center to Improve Practice (NCIP)

http://www.edc.org/FSC/NCIP/

NCIP contains resources for students with disabilities. The site includes video clips illustrating how students with disabilities use a range of assistive and instructional technologies to improve their learning and more than 100 links to other sites dealing with technology and/or students with disabilities.

Arc Home Page

http://thearc.org/

Arc Home Page describes the nation's largest voluntary organization committed to the welfare of children and adults with mental retardation and to their families. The site offers many articles, especially with regard to advocacy, and related links.

Disability Resources, Inc.

http://www.geocities.com/~drm

Disability Resources is a nonprofit organization that publishes the on-line *Disability Resources Monthly* (DRM). The site includes the DRM WebWatcher, an easy-to-use guide to WWW resources, and Librarians' Connections, providing information about listservs, professional associations, and assistive technology to librarians who serve people with disabilities.

Special Education at The University of Kansas

http://www.sped.ukans.edu/

The Department of Special Education at The University of Kansas provides a variety of Internet resources on disabilities and special education research projects including thirty-seven thematic units developed by elementary teachers.

Reprinted by permission.

Special Education Resources on the Internet (SERI)

http://www.hood.edu/seri/serihome.htm

SERI is a collection of special education resources including information about general disabilities, legal and law issues, physical and health disorders, and learning disabilities.

Web Page Creation

Web Page creation has increased a hundredfold, and pages range from the informative to the ridiculous. Because of the popularity of Web pages, there are many programs that were designed to create them. Among these programs are *Web Workshop* (Vividus, distributed by Sunburst), *Claris Home Page, PageMill* (Adobe), and *HTML Editor* (Rick Giles). Working similar to a word processor, these programs generally have a menu bar and toolbar that lets users create the page as if they were viewing it through a Web browser. **Tags** are inserted automatically so no HTML (Hypertext Markup Language) knowledge is necessary.

Web Workshop (Fig. 12.7) is perfect for the beginning student grades three to eight. It contains clip art, familiar paint tools, and a simple interface that makes it easy for the student to create a Web page. All the student does is select backgrounds, add text, and place pictures with a click of the mouse. To create a link, students select an item and type in a World Wide Web address. This software is a perfect choice for the first-time Internet user and is open ended enough for the more advanced student.

Claris Home Page (Fig. 12.8) is a Web page authoring tool for a novice or the expert. It can be used by junior high students or the adult. Users can easily design and develop customized Web pages without a hassle because of its intuitive interface and extensive toolset.

In the same manner, *PageMill* lets you create full-featured Web pages without having to know anything about HTML or URLs. The software is a simple drag and drop operation with which you can quickly add frames and tables to your Web page.

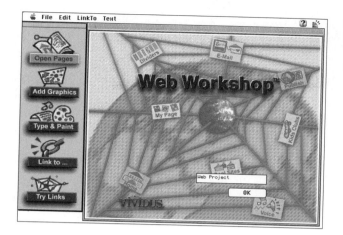

Figure 12.7
Web Workshop
Sunburst (800) 321-7511

Figure 12.8
Claris Home Page
Courtesy of FileMaker, Inc.

HTML Editor is less intuitive but is a very popular shareware program that can be purchased for a fraction of the cost of the others. Other programs of this kind are *Hot Dog* (Sausage Software) and *PageSpinner* (Jerry Aman, Optima System). In addition to these Web page creators, word processing programs like *WordPerfect* and *Microsoft Word* and Web browsers like *Netscape* and *Internet Explorer* have HTML features built into their programs.

Following is a list of sites that give tools for creating Web pages.

HTML Writer's Guild Tools and Utilities

http://www2.best.com/~wooldri/tools/tools.html

Web Developer's Virtual Library

http://www.wdvl.com/

Practical Guide to HTML Editors

http://members.aol.com/Rick1515/index.htm

Since Web page creation has become such a popular phenomenon, a whole cottage industry has developed around it. Some of the utilities that have become indispensable are bookmark managers, off-line browsers, web seekers, web printers, and security filters.

Web Utilities

DragNet (TikiSoft, Inc.) (http://www.tikisoft.com) is a necessary utility for anyone trying to manage more than ten bookmarks. This utility lets you organize these bookmarks into folders, creating an Internet database that can be used in conjunction with your Web browser. It automatically alphabetizes your bookmarks, lets you write descriptions about them, and imports them into your Web browser. It has an excellent search function to easily retrieve any bookmark you need (Figure 12.9).

Figure 12.9
DragNet
Reprinted by permission of TikiSoft Inc.
(www.tikisoft.com)
TikiSoft, Inc., 26041 Del Ray Street East, Mission Viejo, CA 92641, 714-829-8585

Web Wacker (Forest Technologies/ForeFront) lets you save Internet sites that include text, graphics, and HTML links to your computer hard drive. This utility is ideal for presentations and working with students off-line. You can use this off-line browsing tool to preselect the Web site you want and then have the students explore the sites later.

WebSeeker (Forest Technologies/ForeFront) gives you the power of more than twenty popular search engines. Using a single keystroke, you are able to run your information search through more than twenty different Internet search engines simultaneously.

WebPrinter (Forest Technologies/ForeFront) can turn your printer into a printing press. *WebPrinter* takes Web pages that are going to be printed and automatically reduces, rotates, and realigns the pages to print as booklets on any printer.

Cyber Patrol (Cyber Patrol) and *SurfWatch Venture* are internet management utilities that help teachers and parents control childrens' access to the Internet.

These utilities are only a few of the useful utilities that are available for Internet exploration. Besides having the proper utilities, users must follow the proper etiquette, or netiquette, when using the World Wide Web.

Netiquette

Getting along in the electronic environment (newsgroups and e-mail) is called **netiquette,** and here are a few suggestion for on-line usage:

1. Keep your messages to the point and brief.
2. Do not use ALL UPPERCASE LETTERS; this is considered shouting.
3. Never criticize a person's writing or spelling.
4. Don't overreact to items you see on-line.
5. Don't cross-post a message.
6. Don't post items that are offensive.
7. Use discretion by not getting too personal with anyone.

You can find further suggestions on netiquette at the following sites:

Welcome to Albion.com

http://www.albion.com/

Arlen Rinaldi's "The Net: User Guidelines and Netiquette"

http://www.fau.edu/rinaldi/netiquette.html

As you can see, the Web is becoming more of a pervasive influence on our lives. In 1994, only thirty-five percent of schools had access to the Internet, whereas in 1996 sixty-five percent of the schools have access to the Internet (Advanced Telecommunication in U.S. Public Elementary and Secondary Schools, Fall 1996, U.S. Department of Education, National Center for Education Statistics, 1997, Carr, 1997).

Classroom Applications

Many activities can incorporate the World Wide Web into the classroom. What follows are two such classroom activities.

▼   I. Preliminary Searching Exercises   ▼

Materials
You will need a computer, a communications package, a modem, and access to the Internet.

Objective
Students will find information using a search engine like Yahoo or InfoSeek.

Procedure
1. Introduce the students to searching on the Web using Yahoo or InfoSeek.
2. Have the students form small groups.

3. Using the following search questions, students will search to find answers.
4. When the students are finished, they will compare answers.

SEARCH QUESTIONS

1. Find an on-line museum about U.S. histroy for grades K–12.
   a. Write name of the site below.

   _____

   b. Write its address (URL) below.

   _____

2. Find a site with grammar activities for grades 2–12.
   a. Write name of the site below.

   _____

   b. Write its address (URL) below.

   _____

3. Find a site with math puzzles for grades 3–12.
   a. Write name of the site below.

   _____

   b. Write its address (URL) below.

   _____

4. Find a site about the planets for grades K–12.
   a. Write name of the site below.

   _____

   b. Write its address (URL) below.

   _____

5. Find a site about U.S. presidents for grades K–12.
   a. Write name of the site below.

   _____

   b. Write its address (URL) below.

   _____

6. Find a site for science experiments for grades K–12.
   a. Write name of the site below.

   _____

   b. Write its address (URL) below.

   _____

▼   II. Scavenger Hunt   ▼

Materials
You will need a computer, a communications package, a modem, and access to the Internet.

Objective
Students will find factual information about topics ranging from history to current events.

Procedure
1. Discuss different searching techniques with the students.
2. Have the students form small groups.
3. Using the Scavenger Hunt form on page 324, have the students find the answer to each question by searching the specific site.
4. When the students are finished, they will compare answers.

Variation: You can have students search for answers to the questions without giving them the Web sites.

The following three Web sites are excellent scavenger hunts:

World Wide Web Scavenger Hunt

http://www.crpc.rice.edu/CRPC/Women/GirlTECH/Materials/scavhunt.html

This site is a collection of educational Internet-based scavenger hunt sites.

Holy Redeemer Catholic School Scavenger Hunts

http://www.crcssb.edu.on.ca:1080/~red/htm/scaven.htm

These scavenger hunts can be printed and distributed to your students right from the Internet. They are based on elementary curriculum themes while incorporating the basics of internet navigation.

Internet-Based Scavenger Hunts for Students

http://www.best.com/~llipsick/CTN/treasure/treasure.htm

This site contains a collection of Internet-based scavenger hunt sites. Students must use the Internet to find the answers to questions. The hunt sites are listed with the appropriate grade levels. These are great activities for small groups of students.

SCAVENGER HUNT

1.   What is Michigan's state tree?

http://www.sos.state.mi.us/history/histroy.html

2.   What animal made Jane Goodall famous?

http://www.wic.org/bio/idex_bio.htm

3.   Why do leaves change color in the fall?

http://www.waterw.com/~science/kids.html

4.   Who was the first female to orbit the earth?

http://www.infinet.com/~iwasm/

5.   Which president served the shortest term in the White House?

http://www.whitehouse.gov/WH/kids/html/home/html

6.   What was the name of the Supreme Court decision that overturned legalized segregation?

http://www.mecca.org/~crights/

7.   What is the currency in Zambia?

http://www.cnnhotels.com/hotels/africa/zambia/zambia.htm

8.   In what year was the last star sewn on our present-day flag?

http://www.libertynet.org/iha/betsy/

9.   How many immigrants were processed at Ellis Island from 1872–1954?

http://165.90.42.35/features/ellis/

10. Starting from the foot of the pedestal, how many steps must you climb to reach the torch of the Statue of Liberty?

http://www.nationalparks.org/guide/parks/statue-of-li-1881.htm

Summary

We discussed the World Wide Web, described some worthwhile sites, and gave criteria for Web site evaluation. Finally, we discussed netiquette and ended with a preview of suggestions for World Wide Web activities in the classroom. A mastery test, classroom projects, and suggested readings and references follow.

Chapter Mastery Test

1. Define *netiquette* and give two examples.
2. Name three criteria for selecting a Web site.
3. Explain what a search engine is and give an example.
4. Define the following terms: *home page, URL, ISP,* and *HTML.*
5. What is the World Wide Web and why is it an invaluable resource?
6. Give an example of a browser and explain why you need to use one.
7. Distinguish between 56-Kbps modems and cable modems.
8. Name two ways you can use Web sites in the classroom.

Classroom Projects

1. Use the Web Site Rating evaluation form to rate five Web sites.
2. Investigate five different search engines and explain the advantages and disadvantages of each one.

Suggested Reading and References

Bond, Jill D., ed. *Internet Yellow Pages*, 6th ed. *Byte,* October 1997, pages 71–73: New Riders Publishing, Indianapolis, Ind.: 1997.

Brownstein, Mark. "Butter Up for Broadband. Byte, October 1997, pages 71–73: New Riders Publishing, Indianapolis, Ind.: 1997.

Cafolla, Ray, and Richard Knee. "Creating World Wide Web Sites." *Learning & Leading with Technology* 24, part I (November 1996): 3–9.

Carr, Stephen. "Putting it all together." *Education Week,* Vol. XVII, Number 11, November 10, 1997, pages 16–18.

Craig, Dorothy, and Jaci Stewart. "Mission to Mars." *Learning & Leading with Technology* 25, no. 2 (October 1997): 22–27.

Crotty, Cameron. "Apple Automates Internet Addressing." *MacWeek* 11, no. 35 (September 15, 1997): 17.

Dyril, Odvard, E. "Stats Making News." *Technology & Learning.* Volume 18, No. 7. March, 1998, page 64.

Grossman, Evan. "Tut Modem Boasts 2Mbps Over Standard Phone Wire." *Infoworld* 19, no. 40 (October 6, 1997): 74.

Hahn, Harley, and Rick Sout. *The Internet Complete Reference.* New York: Osborne McGraw Hill, 1994.

Harris, Judy. "Ridiculous Questions! The Issue of Scale in Netiquette." *Learning & Leading with Technology.* 25 no. 2 (October 1997): 13–16.

Hiltzik, Michael Al. "Microsoft: Internet Explorer." *Los Angeles Times* (December 12, 1997): 1.

Kobler, Ron, ed. *PC Novice Guide to the Web.* Lincoln, Nebr.: PC Novice, 1997.

Kurland, Daniel, Richard Sharp, and Vicki Sharp. *Introduction to the Internet for Education.* Belmont, Calif.: Wadsworth, 1997.

Laquey, Tracy, and Jeanne Ryer (forword by Al Gore). *Internet Companion.* Boston, Mass.: Addison-Wesley, 1992.

Levine, Martin G. "Social Studies Web Sites for Teachers and Students." *Social Studies Review* 36, no. 2 (Spring–Summer 1997): 95–98.

Luckman Interactive Editors. *Luckman's 1998 World Wide Web Guide.* New York: Barnes and Noble, 1998.

Metcalfe, Bob. "Cable TV modems are finally delivering the Net to homes and small offices." *InfoWorld* 20, no. 5 (February 2, 1998): 107.

Morse, David. *Cyber Dictionary.* Boston, Mass.: Knowledge Exchange, 1997.

Panepinto, Joe. "Family Parents' Guide to the Web." *FamilyPC* (February 1997): 42–60.

Pfaffenberger, Bryan. *Que's Computer User's Dictionary,* 4th ed. Indianapolis, Ind.: Que, 1993.

Reppert, Tracy. "Top 100 Web Sites." *Internet User* (summer 1997): 69–100.

Ryder, James Randall, and Tom Hughes. *Internet for Educators.* Columbus, Ohio: Merrill, 1997.

Salpeter, Judy. "Industrial Snapshot: Where Are We Headed." *Technology & Learning* 17, no. 6 (March 1997): 22–32.

Santo, Christine. "Ultimate Guide to the Web." *FamilyPC.* Ziff-Davis, New York (October 1997): 64–80.

Sharp, Vicki, *Netscape Navigator 3.0 in an Hour.* Eugene, Oreg.: ISTE, 1996.

Sharp, Vicki, Sharp, Richard, and Martin Levine. *Best Web Sites for Teachers, 2nd ed.* Eugene, Oreg.: ISTE, 1998.

Sharp, Vicki, Sharp, Richard, and Martin Levine. *Best Math and Science Web Sites for Teachers.* Eugene, Oreg.: ISTE, 1997

Slater, James, and Brian Beaudrie. "Doing the Real Science on the Web." *Learning & Leading with Technology* 25, no. 4 (December/January 1997–1998): 28–31.

Sosinsky, Barrie, and Elisabeth Parker. *The Web Page Recipe Book.* Prentice Hall, Upper Saddle River, N.J., 1996.

Staten, James. "CompuServe Planning New Internet Services." *MacWeek* 8, no. 36 (September 12, 1994): 14.

Stilborne, Linda, and Ann Heide. *The Teacher's Complete and Easy Guide to the Internet.* Ontario, Canada: Trifolium Books, 1996.

Taaffee, Joanne, and Elinor Mills. "Users Still Like Java Despite the Sun-Microsoft Dispute." *InfoWorld* 19, no. 48 (December 1, 1997): 77.

Trott, Bob. "Browser Wares Go Head to Head." *InfoWorld* 19, no. 40 (October 6, 1997): 77.

Turner, Sandra, and Michael Land. *Tools for Schools.* Belmont, Calif.: Wadsworth, 1997.

Williams, Robin, and Dave Mark. *Home Sweet Home Page.* Berkeley, Calif.: Peachpit Press, 1996.

Withrow, Frank B. "Technology in Education and the Next Twenty-Five Years." *T.H.E. Journal* 24, no. 11 (June 1997): 59–62.

Wolf, Gary. "The Second Phase of the Revolutions Has Begun." *Wired* (October 1994): 116.

Yahoo Editors. "Anatomy of a Web Site." *Yahoo Internet Life* 4, no. 2 (February 1998): 75–76.

Yahoo Editors. "Incredibly Useful Web Sites." *Yahoo Internet Life* 4, no. 2 (February 1998): 72–74.

Computer Hardware

13

Objectives

Upon completing this chapter, you will be able to:

1. Describe the major input devices and explain how each works;
2. Describe the major output devices and explain how each works;

3. List the salient features of the different printers, monitors, and storage devices; and
4. Choose the appropriate hardware in terms of established criteria.

Background

The **hardware** of a computer system includes the electronic components, boards, wires, and peripherals. The **software** instructs the computer hardware to perform various tasks. If you have only hardware, you are powerless to accomplish anything with the computer, much as if you had a car without fuel.

Buying hardware is a complicated and time-consuming job that requires an examination of many factors. You first should determine primary needs and then estimate future needs. For example, you might be satisfied initially with software such as *The Student Writing Center* but might soon require a sophisticated desktop package such as *PageMaker.* If you want to use an advanced spreadsheet or statistical software, you will need computer hardware with ample memory. You have to spend time learning about available hardware, its capabilities, and its functions. Current magazines (such as *MacWorld* or *PC Computing*) alert you to the latest hardware developments. You can save time and money by being prepared to ask appropriate questions. In the course of this chapter, we will look at some of the factors that most influence a buyer's decision and examine some of the basic hardware equipment available.

Input Devices

An input device gives information to the computer system so that it can perform its tasks. Years ago, the keypunch machine was the major means of input; today, it is the keyboard.

Keyboard

The computer **keyboard** is similar to that of a standard typewriter, but it includes extra keys such as the function keys and the numeric pad. Figure 13.1 shows a standard keyboard with a numeric pad on the right for quick data entry.

Although the keyboard is the primary way of entering data, it is not efficient for making screen selections. Furthermore, if you are an inexperienced typist, you are more likely to make mistakes when using the keyboard for screen selections. As a result, computer manufacturers created pointing devices that would lessen the need for a keyboard. Today, most computers use both a keyboard and supplemental pointing devices.

Figure 13.1
Computer keyboard
© Corel Draw 3.0

Pointing Devices

Light Pen

The **light pen,** one of the first pointing devices (Fig. 13.2), looks like a ballpoint pen connected to the computer by a cable. This instrument, used in conjunction with a video display, has a photoelectric cell in its tip that identifies its current location and sends this information via an

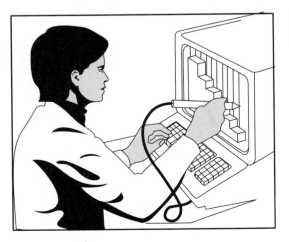

Figure 13.2
Light pen

electrical impulse to the computer. These pens are used frequently for drawing. The software traces the movement of the pen's light on the screen, filling in the lines you draw. You can then use the light pen to select items displayed on the screen by touching the pen to the items; however, as a selection device, the light pen is not as effective as the mouse.

Mouse

Originally designed by Xerox, the **mouse** (Fig. 13.3), was popularized by the Apple Macintosh computer. The original mouse was a palm-size box with a button on it. It was connected to the computer by either a cable or a wire. Today, mouses come in different shapes and sizes, some are cordless, and they can have from one to three buttons. They have two different internal mechanisms: mechanical and optical. The mechanical mouse has a rubber coated ball on the bottom of its case; when you move the mouse, the ball rotates. The optical mouse shows its position by detecting reflections from a light-emitting diode[1] that aims the beam downward. This mouse requires a special metal pad to reflect the beam correctly.

Figure 13.3
Computer mouse
© Dubl-Click Software, Inc.

The movement of the mouse is represented by a cursor or blinking light on the screen. If you move the mouse to the right, the cursor moves to the right. If you push the mouse's button, the cursor is positioned at that particular location. Furthermore, the mouse can be used to select items from a pull-down menu, to delete and insert text, and to draw or paint when used with paint or draw software such as *Corel Draw 7*. The mouse is easy to use and install; however, it is awkward for delicate drawing and it requires space. An alternative device that is stationary and requires less desk space is the trackball.

Trackball

The **trackball** (Fig. 13.4), which performs the same tasks as the mouse, operates with a rotating metal ball inset in a small, boxlike device and does not require a desktop. With your fingers, you roll the exposed part of the trackball, producing cursor movement on the screen. This device was very popular in portable computers until Apple's introduction of the trackpad.

---

[1]A diode, an electronic component that acts as a one-way valve, is used primarily as a temperature or a light sensor (A. Freedman, 1991).

Figure 13.4
Trackball

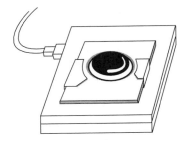

Trackpad

The **trackpad** is a pressure-sensitive pad that is smaller, more accurate, thinner, and less expensive to build than the trackball. It senses distortions in an electrical field caused by the positive charge of a fingertip. When you push your finger up on the pad, the cursor moves up on the screen. This device does not use absolute cursor positioning but relative cursor positioning, which means that a place on the pad's surface does not correspond to a relative location on the computer screen. The faster your fingers travel on the pad, the greater the distance you will cover on the computer screen.

MicroQue produces the QuePoint, a trackpad for desktop and portable systems (Fig. 13.5). This pad weighs 3.5 ounces, is encased in plastic, and measures 1.93 by 2.56 inches. The QuePoint is based on the same technology used in Apple's G3 model portable computers.

Figure 13.5
Trackpad
Photo courtesy MicroQue,
Inc. © 1994.

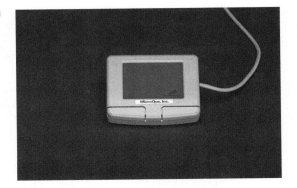

Joystick

The **joystick** (Fig. 13.6), a small box with a moving stick and buttons, is used primarily for games, educational software, and CAD systems. You manipulate the stick to position the cursor and click on a button to send impulses to the computer. The joystick does not interfere with your view of the screen (like a light pen) nor does it require the movement of an object (like a mouse). A joystick is fun to use because of the speed with which it moves the cursor on the screen, but it is awkward in selecting items from a menu, which is a strength of the touch screen.

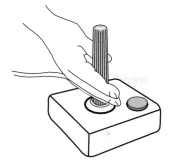

Figure 13.6
Joystick

Alternative Input Devices for Students with Disabilities

Many students have disabilities and cannot use a traditional input device such as a mouse, trackball, or keyboard. For these students, the computer industry has developed alternative devices such as touch screens, alternative keyboards, switches, touch tablets, voice controlled devices, and word prediction software systems.

Touch Screen

The touch screen is a pointing device on which users place their fingers to enter data or make selections. There are two types of touch screens: those designed with a pressure-sensitive panel mounted in front of the screen such as Touch Window (Edmark) and those that involve the use of a special, touch-sensitive monitor such as the IBM Info Window System. The software program for the touch screen displays different options on the screen in a graphic button format. For example, in a multiple choice exam, the student would touch the answer button on the screen, and the screen would change in response to this action.

The touch screen offers a real advantage to disabled students because it is a fast and natural way to enter data, to make selections, and to issue commands. Despite these benefits, a touch screen is not useful for inputting large amounts of data nor for pointing to a single character. Moreover, it is fatiguing to use for a long period of time, and the screen quickly gets finger marked. Lessons created on one variety of touch screen may not work on another because of software incompatibility. However, touch screen technology is still evolving, and in the future it may play a key role in the educational use of the computer. Touch screen are presently being used in airports, supermarkets, and museums.

Discover:Switch

The Discover:Switch is a talking computer switch for the classroom that attaches to the keyboard. With this switch, the computer user does everything that a standard keyboard and mouse can do. The Discover:Switch shows a keyboard on the computer screen that provides choices for writing, using the mouse, or clicking the graphics in multimedia programs such as *Just Grandma and Me* (Brøderbund). The choices are highlighted automatically, and students then press a switch to make their choice. In addition, Discover:Switch has an on-screen keyboard that can speak words, phrases, and even sentences, which offers nonspeaking students a way to communicate.

Intellikey

IntelliKey (IntelliTools) is for people with a wide range of disabilities who require a keyboard (Fig. 13.7) with a changing face. It can be used for Macintoshes, PC-compatibles, or the old Apple II computers. Each standard overlay has a bar code that IntelliKey recognizes. Students who use switches can choose from two built-in programmable switch jacks.

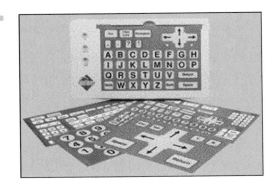

Figure 13.7
Intellikey
From IntelliTools, Inc.

Also available are talking keyboards for the classroom, like Discover:Board. The student presses Discover:Board keys for sounds and speech while doing work. Using this keyboard, the student can receive speech feedback with programs such as *ClarisWorks, Co:Writer,* or *Kid Pix* as well as with the Internet and on-line services. It can be used with pictures, text, or just letters.

In addition to pointing devices, many alternate input devices are used in the workplace. These devices include optical scanning devices that utilize laser capabilities. The laser searches for groups of dots that represent marks, characters, or lines. These input devices differ from each other in terms of the programs used and the way the computers massage the data.

Alternate Input Devices

Optical Mark Reader

The **optical mark reader (OMR)** was designed initially to read penciled or graphic information on exam answer sheets. Lamps furnish light that reflects from test paper. The amount of reflected light is measured by a photocell. When a mark is made on a sheet of paper, it blocks light from reflecting. The optical mark reader compares the pattern of marks on the test papers with the correct pattern stored in the computer's memory. Many schools and school districts use the optical mark reader to grade standardized tests. With the proper software, the OMR will also keep library records, attendance records, and report grades.

Optical Character Reader

The **optical character reader (OCR)** was devised with techniques developed from the optical mark reader. Ordinarily, this device uses laser technology or a light-sensing mechanism to interpret data. The OCR can read typed or printed characters directly from the original document, and advanced systems even can recognize handwriting. A common application of the optical character reader occurs at the neighborhood gas station, where the attendant uses an OCR imprinting device to process a credit card sale. The service attendant forwards the heavier credit card invoice to the company's center, where an optical character reader interprets it and prepares a bill. The advantage of this type of system is that the attendant can use a source document as direct input into the computer, avoiding the inaccuracies that occur from transcribing data. Today, there are many OCR devices that can be adapted to computers for less than $200.

Magnetic Ink Character Recognition Reader

The **magnetic ink character recognition reader (MICR)** recognizes characters that use a special magnetic ink developed by the American Banking Association. All the checks issued by a bank are coded with special ink and characters identifying a person's bank account number so that an MICR can read them. MICR sorts and processes these checks and creates a bank statement for the customer. The MICR reader is also used to read and process utility bills and stock proxy statements.

Bar Code Reader

The **bar code reader** was first devised by railroads to identify the location of railroad cars. This code's most popular application occurs in the supermarket, where the majority of the products sold are labeled with the Universal Product Code, or UPC (Fig. 13.8). At the supermarket, the clerk inputs the price of a product by passing a handheld optical wand over the price label or by passing the product's label over an optical reader. This reader is connected to computers that interpret the bar code, record the data, find the prices stored in their memory, and generate a sales receipt.

Figure 13.8
Universal Product Code (UPC)

The bar code reader also has many applications in a school setting. For example, library books are assigned bar code numbers, a database is created that contains the books' bar code number, and the students are issued library cards with bar code numbers. When a student checks out books, the librarian scans the student's library card as well as each book that the student wants, and the computer records the transactions. Another application of the bar code uses laser disc players and textbooks. Textbook publishers are now printing bar codes in the margins of their books so that students can wave the optical wand across the bar code that transmits a signal to the laser disc player to search and play the video portion correlating with the text.

Scanner

The **scanner** is now being rediscovered because of its affordability and its usefulness for desktop publishing, optical character recognition, and faxing. The scanner transforms images or printed text into electronic images or text. Figure 13.9 is a scanned line art image from The ScanMan user's manual. Figure 13.10 shows the results of using the scanner in conjunction with *TextBridge* (Xerox) a full-featured optical character recognition software, to input text. *TextBridge,* a relatively inexpensive product, eliminates the time, expense, and error of typing the material over again to input it.

Figure 13.9
A Sample scan
© 1988 Logitech

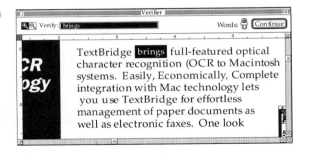

Figure 13.10
TextBridge
Reprinted by permission
of Xerox Imaging
Software.

Scanners digitize photographs or line art and store the image as a file that can be transferred into a paint program or directly into a word processor. If you create a newsletter and want to insert a picture into the text, you scan the picture, copy it, and then "paste" it into the document. Scanners used for this purpose come in a variety of forms: You could use a full-size flatbed scanner, a handheld scanner, an overhead scanner, a sheet-fed scanner, or a film scanner (Fig. 13.11).

A flatbed scanner easily scans documents, books, or periodicals. You simply open the lid of the scanner and place the materials on the "bed." It is more versatile than a hand scanner, but it is more expensive.

A handheld scanner fits in the palm of your hand. You slide it across the image or document slowly, at the rate of about an inch every ten seconds. It works well on four-inch columns, but it is not able to scan an entire line of text in a single pass. The only alternative is to stitch or paste the material together, which is time consuming but does produce acceptable results.

The overhead scanner scans large documents as a flatbed does. It also scans three-dimensional objects. The sheet-fed scanner can only scan paper rather than three dimensional objects or books. This scanner moves the paper across a stationery head. An example of this type of scanner is Visioneer's PaperPort Strobe.

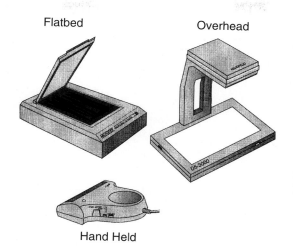

Flatbed

Overhead

Hand Held

Figure 13.11
Scanners
From the book *Que's Computer User's Dictionary.* Copyright © 1990. Published by Que Corporation, a division of Macmillan Computer Publishing. Used by permission of the publisher.

Finally, the film scanner is designed for scanning slides, negatives, or photographic prints. This scanner delivers resolutions that range from 1,000 to 4,096 dots per inch, and it can read 16.8 million colors.

Scanners differ in resolution; the more dots a scanned image contains, the sharper it is. An inexpensive scanner produces images at about 300 dots per inch. The more expensive scanners produce images at a higher resolution. In the past, most scanners produced black and white and half-tone images, and the color scanner was too expensive for the ordinary person. Today, however, an inexpensive color scanner can be purchased for under $500 through mail order.

Let us conclude this discussion with an examination of the digital camera, the graphics tablet, the handheld computer, and the voice recognition system.

Digital Camera

Digital cameras operate on the same fundamental principles as a basic camera, but they are better suited for desktop publishing. The primary difference between a basic camera and a digital one is that they employ different media for capturing images. The traditional camera uses film, while the digital camera uses a charged coupled device (CCD) that is readable by the computer.

One of the first digital cameras was FotoMan by Logitech. This camera delivered eight-bit, gray-scale photo images to a Macintosh computer without photo paper, scanner, chemicals, or film. This camera captured images in a 1 MB RAM buffer and transmitted these images by serial cable to the computer, where they could be saved in different formats. Apple's QuickTake 100 was one of the first digital cameras to offer good color-image quality for less than $1,000. Currently, the market is seeing a rash of digital cameras, and they are no longer exotic. A typical digital camera has a resolution of 640 by 480 and uses flash memory cards to store pictures. The Sony Digital Maverick MVC-FD7 (Fig. 13.12), an exception, uses standard floppy disks to transfer photos into your PC and has a 10X zoom lens. Other digital cameras are Epson PhotoPC 600, FujiFilm MX-700, and

Figure 13.12
Sony Digital
Maverick
From Sony

the QuickCam (Connectix). The QuickCam, with built-in microphone, offers an inexpensive (under $100) and easy way to capture gray-scale still pictures and moving images for your presentations. In addition, Connectix has a color QuickCam for under $200. On the more expensive side, Hitachi's High Performance MP-EGI digital camera can capture up to twenty minutes of full-motion video, up to 3,000 still images, and costs $2,000 plus. Digital cameras make picture taking easy, their image editing program gives you control over your pictures, and you don't have to work in a darkroom or drop film off at the local drugstore. The only trouble with digital cameras is that they cost as much or more than the 35mm single lens reflex film camera, and most have simple optics and limited abilities. Nevertheless, the digital camera is a quick way to get photos into computer readable form, which can be used for school reports, for quick security badges, or for shooting pictures for Web pages. Digital cameras are still in the process of evolving.

Graphics Tablet

The **graphics tablet** (Fig. 13.13) is a plotting tablet that you draw on to communicate with the computer. This device comes in different sizes and is accompanied by pens or styluses. As you draw, making contact with the surface of the plotting board, the computer detects a difference of electrical charges.

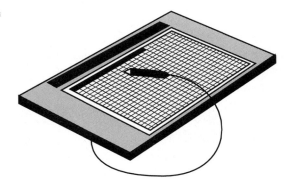

Figure 13.13
Graphics tablet

An early, well-known graphics tablet was the KoalaPad, a small seven-inch pad with a touch-sensitive surface and a stylus. This pad let the user easily design endless combinations of graphic pictures. The graphics tablet today is widely used in art production and CAD.

Handheld Personal Computers

The handheld computer or Personal Digital Assistant is a small mobile computer that accepts input through a penlike instrument called a stylus that you use to write on the computer's screen. This mobile computer lets you take fast notes, send and receive faxes, keep a calendar, and collect information from distant databases.

For example, the Psion Series 5 handheld computer (Psion) (Fig. 13.14) has a pen for easy screen navigation, a touch type keyboard and full page width touch-sensitive screen, and weighs less than 12.5 oz. The Psion offers the versatility of a laptop computer including e-mail, fax, Internet access capabilities, word processor, database, spreadsheet applications, and personal productivity software, all at a fraction of a laptop's weight and cost. The Psion connects to your personal computer, and exchange documents, spreadsheets and databases.

Figure 13.14
Psion Series 5
Psion

Sharp's, Mobilon HC-4500 is one of the most advanced of the handheld computers being the first in the United States to have a computer grade screen 640 by 240 resolution, 256 colors STN display that measures 6.5 diagonally. It has a built in 33.6Kbps modem, a voice record, and 8MB RAM ("Best of What's New," 1997). *Digital Video Magazine* (Fig. 13.15, page 338) envisions the handheld computers of the future as having picture capabilities so that users can see the person with whom they are communicating.

For the education market, Apple was the first to sell the eMate 300, an affordable mobile computer. Apple's eMate combines many of the features of a personal computer and the flexibility of a mobile computer with the ability to interact with a desktop computer, and the Internet. This machine was an important breakthrough that was unfortunately discontinued. However, there are machines that provide computer access for every student in the classroom and are quite inexpensive. For example the AlphaSmart 2000 (Fig. 13.16, page 338) works with virtually any Macintosh or PC running any application. This device prints directly to the printer and downloads files to the computer. The students can do most of their work wherever they happen to be in a classroom, lab, on a field trip, or at home. Weighing 2 pounds, this rugged unit has a word processor, and spelling checker. Furthermore, there are features for special needs: sticky keys, they stay down when you press them, key repeat control and four keyboard layouts.

Figure 13.15
Next Generation of
Computers
From the October 1994
cover of Digital Video
Magazine, "The definitive
source of information in
digital video creation and
production."

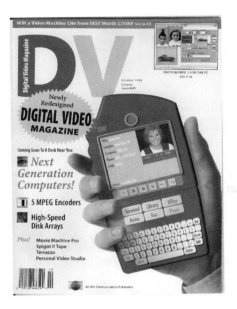

Figure 13.16
AlphaSmart 2000
Intelligent Peripheral
Devices, Inc.

Voice Recognition System

Everyone's computer fantasy is to be able to dictate a command to the computer through a microphone and have the computer execute the command on the screen. We have watched starship captains talking to their computers for years. Still in its infancy stage, the **voice recognition system** shows the most potential for growth in the computer industry. This system converts the spoken word into binary patterns that are computer recognizable; essentially, it understands human speech. You can enter data or issue simple commands through the system simply by speaking. The speech recognition systems require you to train the system to recognize your pronunciation of words by saying each of the words that will be used. The system develops a pattern for these words and then stores them. After training, the voice recognition system recognizes what you are saying and performs your commands.

Some voice recognition systems let you enter and store unlimited words. With this type of system, you can communicate with the computer without using a keyboard or any other input device. In the past, the prevailing type of computer speech recognition was discrete speech recognition in which the user spoke each word separately and clearly with a pause between each word so the system could transcribe the spoken language. This type of recognition was very cumbersome, and there was a need for programs that recognized normal speech. Continuous speech recognition programs that transcribed normal speech have always been available for highly specialized applications in medicine and other fields, but only recently have products appeared that make this system available to the ordinary person.

Recently, two companies—Dragon Systems with its NaturallySpeaking and IBM with its VoiceType—offer continuous speech recognition products at a reasonable price. You no longer have to pause between words; you can dictate directly to your computer as if it were your own personal secretary. You can talk at a natural pace and your words appear on the screen spelled correctly. Individuals who cannot type and disabled persons who cannot use handheld devices are able to easily operate such systems. Eventually, voice recognition could relegate the mouse and keyboard to the storage bin.

Output Devices

Printer

One of the most notable output devices is the **printer,** which gives you a permanent record of your work by producing a printout, or **hard copy.** Let us look at the five different types of printers currently used.

Daisy-Wheel Printer.   The **daisy-wheel printer** is an impact printer that produces a typewritten quality print. This printer has its type characters set around a daisy wheel (Fig. 13.17), similar to a wagon wheel minus the outer ring. When you type a character on the keyboard, the daisy wheel rotates until the required character is under the hammer. The hammer then strikes the character onto the ribbon, resulting in an imprint on the paper. The daisy wheel is mounted on the printer's frame, and the paper moves on a carriage similar to that of a typewriter. This printer can use many daisy wheels whose typefaces are interchangeable. Because it cannot print graphics, is noisier, and is less reliable than other printers, the daisy-wheel printer is just about obsolete.

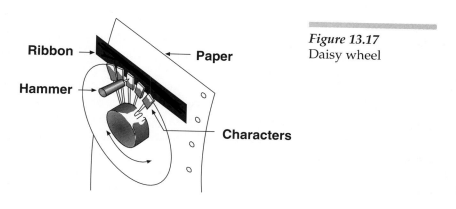

Ribbon → ← Paper

Hammer →

Characters

Figure 13.17
Daisy wheel

Dot-Matrix Printer.   For years, the **dot-matrix printer** was the most widely used printer. With the price reduction of laser printers and the advances in ink-jet technology, this situation has changed. The dot-matrix printer (Fig. 13.18) is an impact printer that produces characters and graphic images by striking an inked ribbon with tiny metal rods called *pins*. When the movable print head with its pins is pressed against ribbon and paper, it causes small dots to print on the paper (Fig. 13.19).

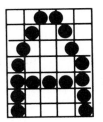

Figure 13.18
Dot-matrix printer
ClickArt Images ©
T/Maker Company.

Figure 13.19
Letter *A* on a dot-matrix printer

The print quality depends on the number of pins the printer has; that is, a twenty-four–pin printer produces better-looking characters than a nine-pin printer. The majority of dot-matrix printers have a draft mode that produces grainier, less dense characters and a near letter quality (NLQ) mode that produces print close to the quality of a typewriter.

When purchasing a printer, you must consider speed, especially for bulk mailing. Speed ratings for dot-matrix and ink-jet printers are measured in characters per second (**cps**), and each printing mode has a separate rating. For example, the ImageWriter II had three modes of print quality: a draft, high speed of 250 cps; a medium speed of 180 cps; and an NLQ speed of 45 cps. For dot-matrix printers, slow speed results in better print quality.

Ink-Jet Printer.   The **ink-jet printer** uses a nozzle to spray a jet of ink onto paper. These small, spherical bodies of ink are released through a matrix of holes to form characters. Ink-jet printers produce high quality output, have few moving parts, and are quiet because they do not strike the paper with metal parts. Ink-jet printers are still slower than good-quality laser printers, but they are faster than most low-cost laser printers.

Because of improvements in technology, color ink-jet printers have become very popular. These printers are very inexpensive, under $400, compared to color laser printers, which cost $3,000 plus. The ink-jet's color quality and speed are better than those of the old dot-matrix printers.

Laser Printer.   Producing near-professional quality print, the **laser printer** (Fig. 13.20) operates like a copying machine—with one important difference. The copying machine produces its image by focusing its lens on paper, while the laser printer traces an image by using a laser beam controlled by the computer. Laser printers produce text and graphics with high resolution; however, the print quality is not as high as that obtained by a phototype machine used by commercial textbook publishers. Many inexpensive laser printers that print in black and white are on the market today, and it is a sought-after printer because of its beautiful print and graphics capabilities. In the next few years you will see color laser printers at drastically reduced prices.

Figure 13.20
Laser printer
ClickArt Images ©
T/Maker Company.

Thermal Printer.   Thermal printing is the technology used in most fax machines. It is also widely used in bar code, point-of-sale, and desktop label printing applications. **Thermal printers** do not use toner cartridges or ribbons like conventional printers. Instead, they use specially treated paper that darkens when it passes over a heated print head. The advantage of thermal printing is that it is a fast, quiet, and reliable printing technology with few moving parts. The disadvantage is that it requires special thermal paper. The cost of the thermal paper is generally higher than plain paper, but this cost is offset by the fact that there is no toner or ribbon to replace. A good example of a thermal printer is the LabelWriter XL (Fig. 13.21), manufactured by CoStar Corporation. This tiny printer connects to any personal computer and prints laser-quality labels at an average speed of four seconds per label.

Figure 13.21
LabelWriter XL
© CoStar Corporation

Screen Displays

Cathode Ray Tube.   The **cathode ray tube (CRT)** (Fig. 13.22) is the basic element used in a video terminal or television. There are two types of CRT screens: the standard television screen and the monitor. As a permanent display for the computer, the TV screen is inadequate because the colors tend to run together, making the picture unclear and the speed of receiving the picture slow. The television receiver does not have the ability to handle all the data sent to it by the computer. However, in recent years, televisions have been designed to serve as video monitors.

Figure 13.22
Cathode-ray tube
(CRT)

Monitor.   As a display, the **monitor** is superior to the television. Although it looks like a television set, the monitor is designed to handle a wider and higher range of frequencies. There are three types of monitors: monochrome, composite, and RGB.

A *monochrome* monitor, the least expensive of the three, produces output that has one foreground color and one background color. Common examples are white against a black background, green against a black background, or amber against a black background. This monitor is best used for text in word processing and business applications.

The *composite* color screen is similar to a color television screen, but it can handle data more quickly and has a sharper picture. This monitor accepts a standard analog video signal that mixes red, blue, and green signals to produce a color picture.

Using three electronic guns, the red, green, and blue (*RGB*) monitor generates three colors. This monitor, the most expensive, produces the sharpest images because of the separate video signals used for each of these guns. In the past, RGB monitors came in digital and analog varieties.[2] Today, most monitors are digital, which means that every pixel is either on or off. Figure 13.23 shows an RGB monitor. Figure 13.24 represents a schematic of the inner workings of an RGB monitor.

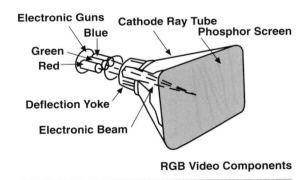

Figure 13.23
RGB (red, green,
blue) monitor
© Corel Draw 3.0

Figure 13.24
Inside an RGB monitor

---

[2]An analog display is a type of "video display capable of rendering a continuous range (an indefinite number) of colors of gray shades, as opposed to digital display, which is capable of rendering only a finite number of colors" (Woodcock, 1991).

Flat Panel Display.   The flat panel display will eventually replace the CRT. Found today in portable laptop computers, the flat panel display (Fig. 13.25) uses a number of technologies. The most common flat screen displays are the **liquid crystal displays (LCDs)** and the **plasma displays.**

Figure 13.25
Flat panel display
ClickArt Images ©
T/Maker Company.

Used for calculators, watches, and laptop computers, the LCD is created by positioning a liquid crystal material between two sheets of polarizing material squeezed between two glass panels. This display depends on reflected light, so the viewing angle is important; the image can disappear with the wrong angles and with inadequate adjustment of the contrast controls.

There are two types of LCDs: the active matrix and the passive matrix. In the active matrix display, each of the screen's tiny electrodes has its own transistor. The passive matrix display has only a single transistor that controls an entire column of the display's electrodes. The active matrix is superior in contrast and resolution, but it is much more expensive. LCD panels have always been available for laptops; now LCDs are being made for desktop computers (Fig.13.26). However, these thin screen panels are still very expensive; a 12" to 15" LCD sells for $1,500 to $3,000. LCDs are brighter and clearer than the CRT and are real space savers. In the next couple of years, these monitors will come down drastically in price and become a viable alternative. In fact, one of these days, you will probably have one hanging on your wall.

Figure 13.26
ViewSonic VP 140
From ViewSonic

The plasma display is produced by injecting a mixture of neon gases between two transparent panels, giving a very sharp, clean image with a wide viewing angle. The plasma display is found on higher end laptop computers and is very expensive.

LCD Projection Panel.   The **LCD projection panel** is important because it enables the classroom teacher to use the computer for the entire class. The LCD panel is a projector that receives computer output and displays it on a liquid crystal screen placed on top of an overhead projector. The overhead becomes the projector, displaying the programs that the computer generates on a larger screen for the whole class to see. The size of the panel varies depending on the manufacturer. The LCD projection panel is certainly an alternative to the more expensive computer projectors like Infocus.

Speech Synthesizer

Another output device, the **speech synthesizer,** is a computer chip that generates sound. This chip gives the computer the ability to search for words and their pronunciations in a database. The computer takes this data, converts it into codes, and delivers it audibly in a voice with a slight accent. The sound is clear enough for most people to understand. The speech quality is better if the computer has to speak only stock phrases rather than read items experimentally. Speech synthesis is very helpful for the visually impaired computer user.

Many products today use computer-generated speech. For example, automobile computers audibly remind drivers to shut the door or fill the tank.

Up to this point, input or output devices have been considered separate categories; now let's consider devices that perform a dual function.

Input/Output Devices

Magnetic Tape

At first, **magnetic tape** was a popular medium for storage (Fig. 13.27). A reel of tape usually was about 1/2 inch wide and could store roughly 25 MB of data. It lost favor as a medium because it was slow, unreliable, and hard to access. However, magnetic tape has made a comeback as a backup medium because of its high capacity for mass storage, improved speed, lower cost, reliability, and ease of access. It is ideal for long-term storage of large graphics files and for the transfer of data from computer to computer.

Figure 13.27
Magnetic tape

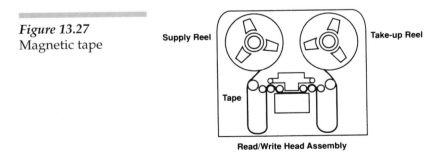

In the early 1980s, computer companies manufactured cassette tape drives for their less expensive personal computers and for the first laptops. Later, the floppy disk emerged as the most widely used secondary storage medium.

Floppy Disk

In the 1970s, IBM introduced the 8-inch **floppy disk** (diskette) for data storage. It consists of a circular piece of plastic, oxide-coated matter enclosed in a protective jacket, similar in appearance to an audiocassette tape. When the disk is placed in a disk drive, it rotates inside its jacket, thus allowing data to be stored on it and viewed later. The computer operator can randomly access the data from these disks.

Generally, disks are available in 5 1/4-inch and 3 1/2-inch sizes. The 3 1/2-inch floppy (Fig. 13.28) has completely replaced the 5 1/4-inch floppy as a storage medium.

3 1/2 inch Floppy Disk

3 1/2 inch Floppy Disk Drive

Figure 13.28
Disk and disk drive
(Disk drive) © Dubl-Click
Software, Inc., (floppy
disk) ClickArt Images ©
T/Maker Company.

The storage capacity for these disks varied, depending on the disk drive, which could be double density or high density. The high-density disk drive was designed to store more information on the floppy disk. Table 13.1 shows the disk storage capacity for some of the computer manufacturers.

Table 13.1

Floppy Disks	Size	Double Density	High Density
Apple	5 1/4	140K	280K
Apple	3 1/2	800K	NA*
Macintosh	3 1/2	800K	1.44 MB
IBM & compatible	5 1/4	360K	1.2 MB
IBM	3 1/2	720K	1.44 MB

Zip Drive

The Zip drive (Fig. 13.29) is a very popular removable storage device that is quickly replacing the floppy disk. Created by Iomega Corporation, the Zip drive provides 100MB of storage on inexpensive Zipdisks that are just a little larger than a floppy disk. Presently the Zip drives are becoming the number one portable backup storage devices for most personal computers (see chapter 2).

Figure 13.29
Zip drive
Iomega

Jazz Drive

The Jazz drive is a portable means of storage that provides 2 GB of disk space on each 3.5-inch cartridge. This device is invaluable for users who want to back up their hard drive or huge graphic files. However, the disks are expensive, about $189 apiece. The Jazz drive provides storage and has very quick access time, which makes moving files around a pleasure.

Hard Disk

The **hard disk** drive provides increased storage capabilities and faster access. Hard disks were developed by IBM in 1973. The early ones were extremely expensive; however, with mass production of the personal computer, a **hard disk drive** is now available for as little as $200, and it is incorporated into the computer system. A fixed, hard disk usually has one or more disk platters coated with a metal oxide substance that allows information to be magnetically stored on it. This storage system includes the disk, a read/write head assembly, and the connections between the drive and the computer (Fig. 13.30).

Figure 13.30
Hard disk & drive
components
From the book *Que's Computer User's Dictionary.*
Copyright © 1990.
Published by Que
Corporation, a division of
Macmillan Computer
Publishing. Used by
permission of the
publisher.

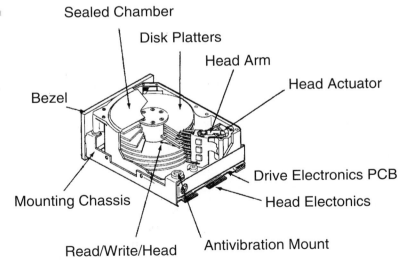

At first, these disk drives used 14-inch disks, but now they use 5 1/4-inch, 3 1/2-inch, 2-inch, and 1 4/5-inch diameters. In contrast to the floppy disk drive, hard disk drives hold from 80 megabytes to gigabytes and terabytes of information. When purchasing a hard disk, consider storage capacity and seek time, a measure of a hard disk's access speed. The smaller the numbers, the faster the disk. In the past, 65 milliseconds was the standard access time, but today the standard is less than 7 milliseconds.

Optical Disc

An **optical disc** has information recorded on it with a laser beam that burns pits into its surface. Another laser beam reads back information that it detects from these pits. There are three forms of optical storage: the WORM, the erasable optical disc, and the CD-ROM disc.

The write once, read many (WORM) is a disc with storage capabilities as high as one terabyte. You can write to this disc once and read from it many times. The WORM drives initially were used to store immense amounts of information for organizations that needed to publish large databases. However, with the advent of the erasable disk, the need for a WORM drive has diminished.

Erasable optical discs function like floppy disks and can be recorded on repeatedly. Since the laser beam scans the disc without physical contact, the optical disc does not wear out like a magnetic disk. The disks are small, 3 1/2-inch in diameter and lightweight; they are unaffected by dust or heat, and they hold huge amounts of data (Fig. 13.31).

Figure 13.31
Optical disc

Because of their expense and slower access time, these discs were used at first only by large companies. However, because of technological advances and ensuing cost reductions, erasable optical discs are becoming a viable alternative to the magnetic disk. This disc will play an important role as a storage medium in the future because it is removable and because it has immense storage capacity. Furthermore, the optical disc is a likely successor to the hard disk because it does not wear out in three to five years. Currently, there are special rewritable CDs that can be played on rewritable CD recorders. This specially formatted CD lets you record and erase as many times as you want. In addition, the CD recordable drive lets you burn a CD-ROM for permanent storage. This technology is now selling for $500 to $600, but the prices are getting lower (interview with Joe Krutsick, MacConnection).

Compact discs (CDs), compact disc read-only memory discs (CD-ROMs), and laser discs are optical discs that are recorded on when manufactured. They cannot be erased. CD-ROM discs store text, graphics, and hi-fi stereo sound in a digital format. The CD-ROM disc is similar to the music CD, but it uses a different tracking system. A CD-ROM disc handles at least 650 MB of data—the equivalent of 250,000 pages of text, of approximately 4,285 Apple 5 1/4-inch single-sided floppy disks, of four hundred 3 1/2-inch high-density floppy disks, or of fifteen 40 MB hard disks. This medium is invaluable for storing large volumes of data such as the *Grolier Electronic Encyclopedia.* Because of its digital signal, the CD-ROM does not handle moving pictures or a full spectrum of color as well as a laser disc does. This situation is changing for small video files according to Chris Saulpaugh (in an interview), a computer expert at Roger Wagner Inc.: "Because of the improvements in compression, MPEG Video can now compress a full-length feature film into CD-ROM so it can be played on your computer." With the advent of DVDs (digital versatile discs), CD-ROM and laser discs will probably disappear completely (Pfaffenberger, 1997).

DVD-ROM Drive

Digital Video Discs (DVD) are a CD-ROM format that is capable of playing a full-length movie and of storing up to 17 gigabytes of data (see chapter 8). Currently, DVD players are available in read-only single-sided disc drives, and they hold only 4.7 gigabytes. In the next two years these drives will probably have full read/write capabilities and store 17 gigabytes of data. The present CD-ROM disks are downward compatible[3] and can be played on the DVD players.

Laser Disc or Videodisc

Using an analog signal, a laser disc is a read-only optical disc that stores and retrieves still and moving pictures, sound, or color. This disc looks like a large CD and plays back high-quality digital audio files. Many laser disc systems were introduced in the 1970s, but only LaserVision optical disc technology survived. As of 1995, laser discs had not replaced the videotape format, but they were becoming extremely popular for instructional interactive purposes. A laser disc holds from thirty minutes to two hours of video data and provides direct access to any location on its disk.

Standard laser discs come in two formats: constant angular velocity (CAV) and constant linear velocity (CLV). The format you choose depends on how much video you need to store and how much you plan to access the laser contents. The CAV laser disc format uses concentric circles and every frame is uniquely addressable, but it can only hold thirty minutes of material per side. The CLV format uses a single spiral track that begins at the center of the circle and ends near the edge of the disc. This disc can hold sixty minutes of video per side, or a two-hour program. However, this format does not have as much versatility as the CAV because you cannot move through a program frame by frame, display a still frame, or search for a particular frame without special hardware.

Laser disc players have three application levels. At Level I, you have little control over the unit and it simply displays video on a monitor. This laser disc player is the one generally sold in

---

[3]"Hardware or software that runs without modification when using earlier computer components or files created with earlier software versions" (Pfaffenberger, 1997).

any electronics store. You access the video with a remote control unit. Level II has a built-in computer component added to the disc player. In this case, the software that controls the computer and laser disc is stored on the laser disc. Since the information can flow to the laser disc as well as to the central processing unit, you have more versatility and can stop and start at different locations on the disc and can branch to other locations. You control the unit with a remote control. Finally, at Level III, the highest level, a computer is connected to the laser disc player. At this level, the external computer controls the laser disc player operation. This level provides tremendous flexibility and is the most popular technology. You can start and stop the video, use a bookmark to return to a specific location, or review selected materials.

Using the TV to Search the Internet

A less expensive alternative to using the computer to search the Internet is to use the television set. Web TV Plus lets you surf the Internet painlessly. This product offers a television tuner that allows simultaneous Web browsing and TV watching. Web TV Plus has a 56 Kbps modem and a 1.08 GB hard drive. Furthermore, it has the ability to send video, still images, and audio via e-mail. You can also print out Internet material by connecting a printer to the back of the machine.

Fax Machine

Another input/output device, the facsimile (fax) machine, lets you transmit text and images between distance locations. Chapter 11 features a detailed discussion of the fax machine.

Modem

The modem lets two computers communicate with each other via the telephone lines. Detailed discussion of the modem can be found in Chapter 11.

Overview of Hardware

The following summary lists the devices discussed in this hardware chapter. After perusing this table, let's consider some criteria for selecting hardware.

HARDWARE SUMMARY

Input	Output	Input/Output
Keyboard	Printer	Magnetic tape
Light pen	Daisy-wheel	Disk drive
Mouse	Dot-matrix	Floppy disk
Trackball	Ink-jet	Zip disk
Trackpad	Laser	Iomega Jazz
Joystick	Thermal	Hard disk
IntelliKeys	Screen display	Optimal disk
Touch screen	Monitors	WORM
Optical mark reader	Monochrome	Erasable
Optical character reader	Composite	CD-ROM
MICR reader	RGB	DVD-ROM
Bar code reader	Flat panel	Laser disc
Scanner	LCD	Web TV
Flatbed	Plasma	Fax machine
Handheld	LCD projection panel	Modem
Overhead	Speech synthesizer	
Sheet-fed		
Film		
Graphic tablet		
Digital camera		
Handheld computers		
Voice recognition system		

Hardware Selection Criteria

Type of Computer

Is the computer compatible with other district computers? How easy is it to use the equipment? Is the documentation well written? Are the weight and size of the machine important considerations? How durable is the machine? Is it too delicate for classroom use? One of your main decisions is whether to buy a computer equipped with Windows 98 or Mac OS. The Macintosh is still easier to use and set up and expand than is a Windows computer. However, Windows computers outperform comparably priced Macintoshes. If you are interested in ease of use and expansion, graphics, multimedia, and video, buy a Macintosh; if you want the most value for your money and need spreadsheets and databases, buy a Windows system. Furthermore, the Windows systems offer a wider selection software and peripherals.

Memory

A very important consideration during the hardware selection process is the computer's random access memory, the working memory. (See chapter 2 for a complete discussion of RAM.) In the early 1980s, 64K of RAM was considered more than adequate for running educational software. Today, many applications need 8 MB or more of memory, and these memory requirements are continually increasing. For example, *HyperStudio* (Roger Wagner) requires 8 MB to effectively run, and *The Oregon Trail III* (Learning Company) needs 16 MB. Every time software publishers upgrade programs, they add more features requiring more memory. The amount of RAM memory a computer has affects the kind of software it is capable of running. Word processing, spreadsheet, and database programs require more memory to run than educational software generally does (except in the case of multimedia software). Any new system you are purchasing should have a minimum of 32 MB of RAM. Buy as much RAM as you can afford because you can never have too much.

Expandability

Consider these questions when your computer system is not powerful enough for your needs. Can you upgrade the processor chip? Can the memory of the computer be increased? Is the computer designed so that extra peripherals such as a scanner can be added easily? Can special equipment be added to the machine for the disabled student?

Speed

The speed at which the microcomputer accesses the instructions is another important consideration. Speed depends on clock speed and word size.

Clock speed is the number of electronic pulses per second, measured in **megahertz (MHz).** The more pulses the computer has per second, the faster it executes the instructions. The clock speed on a microcomputer can vary from 1 MHz to above 550 MHz. For example, the old Apple II had a clock speed of 1 MHz, the Macintosh LC and SE 30 have clock speeds of 16 MHz, and the Power Macintosh Minitower G3 has a clock speed of 266 MHz. Currently, there is a 480 MHz G3 prototype and the 1000 MHz machine is only a demo (Morgenstern, Feb. 6, 1998). Some programs, such as sophisticated spreadsheet programs, require more speed than others.

Keyboard

You should test out the keyboard feel by sitting at the computer and checking how comfortable it is to type on the keys. Keyboards today have many different ergonomic designs. One computer might have impressive specifications, but typing on the keyboard may be uncomfortable. See if an extended keyboard is available. Extended keyboards have additional keys that can be programmed to perform different functions and numeric pads that speed up number entry.

Hard Disk Space

Like everything else on computers, hard disk space has gotten larger and less expensive. Most new computers are being sold with a minimum of 6 gigabytes. You need a gigantic hard disk if you plan to store digitized photographs or edit videos; the bigger the better!

Video Output

When it comes to the computer monitor, a difficult choice is inevitable. The monochrome monitor works best for word processing and spreadsheets, while the color monitor is best for running educational software.

The higher the resolution of the screen, the clearer the screen display. Resolution is expressed as the number of linear dots, or pixels, that are displayed on the screen. The more pixels, the clearer the image or the better the resolution. The size of a monitor screen varies from 5 inches to 40 inches; usually, a screen displays twenty-four or twenty-five lines of text. The size of your monitor should not be smaller than 15 inches and for a few hundred dollars more you can buy a 17-inch monitor. The dot pitch, which is the smallest dot your monitor displays, should be no greater than .28. The refresh rate, the "rate at which a monitor and video adapter pass the electron guns of a cathode ray tube (CRT) from the top of the display to the bottom" (Pfaffenberger, 1997), should be 85 hertz at the resolution you use.

Video RAM (VRAM)

VRAM, or graphic memory, is "a type of memory in a video display board that holds the image that appears on the video screen" (Freedman, 1995). Make sure you have at least 2 MB of graphic memory. If you play multimedia software and video games, 4 MB is preferred.

Sound

The quality of sound is very important for playing musical compositions or educational games. Ask about the number of voices the system has. What are the octave ranges of the voices? Many computers offer speech synthesizers capable of pronouncing words.

Languages

Search for a computer that supports the language that your curriculum requires. BASIC and Logo are the most popular languages for education. Many computers used to have some dialect of BASIC built into the ROM.

Peripherals

Study the peripherals that you need and know the features that are available. Read magazines to determine which ones are best to purchase. Find out which peripherals have the lowest rate of repair and have the fastest access time.

Hardware Reliability and Dealer Support

There are some questions you should ask: Are the local dealers reputable? (Find a local store that can easily service the machine.) Does the store give free training on newly purchased machinery? Is there a service contract? Is the equipment warranted for a year, and is there quick turnaround on computer repair?

Ease of Operation

Ask these questions: Is the machine relatively easy to operate? Do you need hours to study its thick manuals? (For a young child or an easily frustrated adult, these considerations are important.) Is there quality documentation for the computer?

Cost

Prices that are quoted by manufacturers are discounted, so check the *Computer Shopper,* the local newspaper ads, and magazines to determine the price structure of a system. Is the machine too costly compared to similar machines? Does the manufacturer include free software? Is there a warranty on the product, on-site repair, or at the very least, a place to ship the machine for quick repair?

The hardware checklist on page 354 should serve as a handy guide in analyzing your hardware needs.

Summary

This chapter has explored the functions of the major input, output, and input/output devices. We considered the following examples of input devices: (1) keyboards, (2) mouse, (3) trackballs, (4) optical readers, (5) touch screens, and (6) voice input. The two most important output devices considered were the printer, which produces a hard copy of the work, and the screen display, which shows the information on the screen. Examples of the display screens discussed are the liquid crystal display (LCD) and the cathode ray tube (CRT). The major printers discussed were (1) dot-matrix, (2) ink-jet, (3) laser, and (4) daisy-wheel. The dot-matrix printer has a print head with wires to create its characters; the ink-jet printer sprays ink; the laser printer uses a process similar to photocopying; and the daisy-wheel printer uses a typing element.

We discussed and compared floppy disks, hard disks, and optical discs. Floppy disks and hard disks are still the most popular storage media, while optical discs are gaining in popularity. We also considered criteria for hardware selection.

A mastery test, projects, and suggested readings and references follow.

Chapter Mastery Test

1. Briefly explain the difference between a Level I and a Level III laser disc player.

2. What is a digital camera and how would you use it in the classroom?

3. Give two reasons why magnetic tape increased in popularity as a storage media.

4. Name two input and two output devices. Explain how each works.

5. Name four factors to consider when examining hardware.

6. Compare a laser printer with an ink-jet printer.

7. When is it advantageous to use a monochrome monitor, and when is it a good idea to use a color monitor?

8. Compare floppy disks and their storage capacities.

9. How are hard disks similar to and different from floppy disks?

10. What are optical discs? Why are they considered the wave of the future?

HARDWARE CHECKLIST

Directions: Examine the following items and determine which ones you feel are important for your particular class situation. Evaluate the hardware and place an X on each line where it meets your needs.

Computer Type _____   **Model** _____   **Manufacturer** _____

A. Features
— 1. Screen size
— 2. Text/graphics display
—   a. Number of lines
—   b. Characters per line
—   c. Resolution
—   d. Number of colors
— 3. Sound
—   a. Number of voices
—   b. Number of octaves
—   c. Loudness
— 4. Portability
— 5. Keyboard design
—   a. Number of keys
—   b. Numeric keypad
— 6. Ease of expansion
— 7. Color capabilities
— 8. Equipment compatibility
— 9. Networking
—10. Memory (RAM)
—11. Hard disk capacity
—13. CD-ROM drive (8x, 16x 24x 32x etc.)
—14. Zip Drive
—15. Other _____

B. Ease of Use
— 1. Easy program loading
— 2. Flexibility

— 3. Easy equipment setup
— 4. Tutorial manual

C. Consumer Value
— 1. Cost of basic unit
— 2. Cost of peripherals
—   a. Disk drive
—   b. Interfaces/cables
—   c. Memory expansion
—   d. Modem
—   e. Monitor
—   (1) Included in price
—   (2) Size
—   f. Printer
—   g. Other _____
—   h. Software included
—   i. Speech synthesizer
— 3. Total investment

D. Support
— 1. Service contract
— 2. Nearby dealer support
— 3. Readable manuals
—   a. Tutorial
—   b. Index
— 4. Money-back guarantee
— 5. Warranty period—carry in,
        on-site
— 6. Teacher training

Rating Scale

Rate the hardware by placing a check in the appropriate box.

Excellent _____   Very Good_____   Good_____   Fair_____   Poor_____

Comments

11. What is a speech synthesizer? What is the relationship between a speech synthesizer and voice input?

12. What is the difference between DVD and CD-ROM discs.

Classroom Projects

1. Visit a computer store to compare the output of laser and ink-jet printers. Report on the differences.

2. Take a field trip to a school that uses digital cameras and report how they are incorporated in student writing projects.

Suggested Readings and References

Bates, Allyson. "Apple's Next-Generation Systems." *Macworld* (January 1998): 69–73.

"The Best of What's New." *Popular Science* (December 1997): 44–81.

Brownsteing, Mark. "Batter Up for Broadband." *Byte* (October 1997): 71–73.

Bruder, Isabelle. "Schools of Education: Four Exemplary Programs." *Electronic Learning* 10, no. 6 (March 1991): 21–24, 45.

Crawford, Walt. "Jargon that Computes: Today's PC Terminology." *Online* 21, no. 2 (March–April 1997a): 36–41.

Crawford, Walt. "Faster, Better, Cheaper: A Decade of PC Progress." *Online* 21, no. 1 (January–February 1997b): 22–26, 28–29.

Darrow, Barbara. "IBM Develops Prototype of Color Touch Screen for Laptops." *InfoWorld* 13, no. 16 (April 22, 1991): 6.

Finck, David A., ed. *Computer Buyer's Guide and Handbook.* New York: Bedford Communications, 1997.

Flanagan, Patrick. "The 10 Hottest Technologies in Telecom." *Telecommunications* 31, no. 5 (May 1997): 25–28, 30, 32.

Freedman, Alan. *The Computer Glossary.* New York: American Management Association, 1991.

Freedman, Alan. *The Computer Glossary, 7th ed.* New York: American Management Association, 1995.

Freedman, Debra. "Speech Students Learn through Computer Technology." *The Computing Teacher* 18, no. 8 (May 1991): 10–14.

Fryer, Bronwyn. "What's Right for You?" *NewsWeek Extra: Computers and the Family* (winter 1997): 66–71.

Greenfield, Elizabeth. "At-Risk & Special Ed. Products: Tools for Special Learning." *T. H. E.* 18, no. 11 (June 1991): 6–14.

Grossman, Evan. "Tut Modem Boasts 2Mbps over Standard Phone Wire." *InfoWorld* 19, no. 40 (October 6, 1997): 74.

Harris, Stanley. *Computer Buyer's Guide and Handbook.* New York: Harris Publications, 1997.

Heid, Jim. "Photography Without Film." *MacWorld* (September 1994): 141–47.

Jessop, Deborah. "A Survey of Recent Advances in Optical and Multimedia Information Technologies." *Computers in Libraries* 17, no. 2 (February 1997): 53–59.

Mageau, Therese. "Telecommunications in the Classroom." *Teaching and Computers* 7, no. 6 (May/June 1990): 18–24.

Metcalfe, Bob. "Cable TV Modems Are Finally Delivering the Net to Homes and Small Offices." *InfoWorld* 20, no. 5 (February 2, 1998): 107.

Morgenstern, David. "IBM, Motorola Ready G4 Chips." *MacWeek* 12, no. 6 (February 9, 1998b): 1.

Morgenstern, David. "New Trackpad Uses PB 500 Technology." *MacWeek* 8, no. 41 (December 12, 1994): 8.

Morgenstern, David. "Vendors Speed Up CD-R, CD-RW Drives." *MacWeek* 12, no. 1 (January 5, 1998a): 41.

Norr, Henry. "Mini Windows Devices on Rise, But Apple Could Still Be Player." *MacWeek* (November 24, 1997): 2.

Pfaffenberger, Bryan. *Webster's New World Dictionary*. New York: Que, 1997.

Roberts, Nancy, George Blakeslee, Maureen Brown, and Cecilia Lenk. *Integrating Telecommunications into Education.* Englewood Cliffs, N.J.: Prentice Hall, 1990.

Robertson, S., et al. "The Use and Effectiveness of Palmtop Computers in Education." *British Journal of Educational Technology* 28 no. 3 (July 1997): 177–89.

Rooney, Paula. "Comdex/Fall Caps Banner Year in Voice Recognition." *Computer Retail Week* (November 10, 1997).

Ryer, Kelly. "Make Room for Zooms." *MacWeek* 11, no. 35 (September 15, 1997): 1.

Santoni, Andy. "Flat Panel Display Offers CRT Quality." *InfoWorld* 19, no. 29 (July 21, 1997a): 30.

Santoni, Andy. "Flat Panels Make Prime-Time Move." *InfoWorld* 19, no. 49 (December 8, 1997b): 32.

Schlack, Mark, ed. "Standing on a Moving Platform." *BYTE* (January 1998): 55.

Sisneros, Roger. "Telecomputing Takes the Mystery out of On-Line Communication." *Telecomputing* (spring 1990): 15–22.

Takezaki, Noriko. "Mobile Computing and the Internet." *Computing Japan* (October 1997): 31–33.

Trosko, Nancy. "Making Technology Work for Your Students." *Technology Connection* 4, no. 2 (April 1997): 20–22.

Trott, Bob. "Browser Wars Go Head to Head." *InfoWorld* 19, no. 40 (October 6, 1997): 77.

Turner, Sandra, and Michael Land. *Tools for Schools, 2d ed.* Belmont, Calif.: Wadsworth, 1996.

Vizard, Frank, ed. "Web TV Gets More Muscle." *Popular Science* (December 1997): 44–81.

Woodcock, Joanne, senior contributor. *Computer Dictionary.* Redmond, Wash.: Microsoft Press, 1991.

Programming Languages

14

Objectives

Upon completing this chapter, you will be able to:

1. Trace the major developments in the history of programming languages;
2. Discuss how a flowchart works;
3. differentiate a low-level language from a high-level one;
4. Be able to differentiate between a compiler and an interpreter;
5. Explain the advantages and disadvantages of the following programming languages:

BASIC
FORTRAN
COBOL
Pascal
C Language
Java

6. learn about JavaScript;
7. become familiar with HTML;
8. learn some guidelines for Web page design; and
9. discuss an authoring language and its feasibility for classroom use.

Programming

A controversy exists over whether teachers should be exposed to computer programming. Some authorities feel that programming teaches higher order thinking and it is the key to computer literacy (Jonassen, 1996, p. 228). The students should have the opportunity to learn about the computer by controlling it. If the teacher does not have the proper software the teacher can then write their own. The research has shown mixed results (Charlton and Birkett, 1994; Bernard and Morris, 1994). Other experts feel that teachers are afraid enough of the computer and programming is not necessary. Instead, the teachers should be shown how to integrate the computer in the classroom by using it as a tutor in subject areas such as language arts, math, and science. Furthermore, teachers should use the computer as a tool for word processing, databases, spreadsheets, drawing, and so on. Whatever position you take, it is important to learn what programming is and its origins. (See chapter 15 for the research results on programming).

What Is a Program?

A program is a sequence of instructions that informs the computer what tasks are to be performed. You must determine the order in which the computer is to perform these instructions. A flowchart helps you plan the order of a program more effectively.

Flowcharts

The **flowchart** uses symbols to help you describe or understand the process you will follow to solve a problem—it is a convenient, pictorial way of learning and communicating. Most program writers use the following symbols: oval, parallelogram, rectangle, diamond, and circle. The oval symbol represents the beginning or end of an operation:

The parallelogram can be used for input/output statements:

The rectangle defines variables and shows the arithmetic operations the computer will perform:

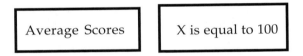

The diamond or decision symbol states a question and shows possible answers or choices:

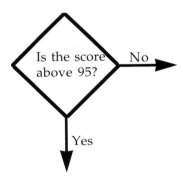

Arrows are used to indicate the direction of the flow, which is usually from the top of the page to the bottom. Figure 14.1 shows the top-down structure of a flowchart using an example from *MacFlow* (Mainstay). Step one, the oval, starts with your goal: draw a flowchart. Step 2 opens a document. Step 3 adds a symbol to the flowchart. Step 4 is a decision box and asks the question,

"Are you done?" If you are, you choose Yes, and follow the arrow to the rectangle process box that instructs you to save the flowchart and exit *MacFlow*. If you are not finished, choose No and follow the arrow to the rectangle process box that tells you to add another object. This procedure continues until you do answer Yes to the question, "Are you done?" After drawing a flowchart, you are ready to write a program following the flowchart's blueprint.

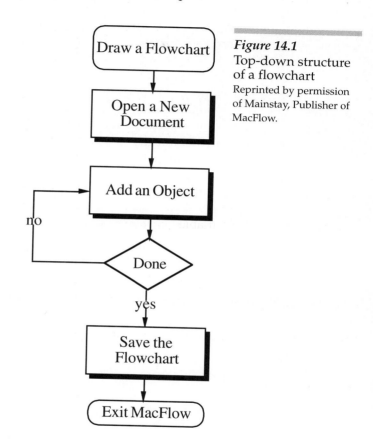

Figure 14.1
Top-down structure of a flowchart
Reprinted by permission of Mainstay, Publisher of MacFlow.

To write any program, you use programming languages that range from BASIC to C++.

Programming Languages

Programming is the sine qua non for computer operations. Programming languages are sequences of words, letters, numerals, and mnemonics that let you operate the computer. Each computer language has its own precise set of rules, syntax, and grammar that differ from those of ordinary language. Also, these rules and structures are rigid; in everyday language, a single word may have many meanings, but no ambiguity exists in a computer language. Each command can have only a single meaning.

Today, there are more than 400 computer languages including their many dialects. These languages perform a variety of tasks; no one language fits all situations. You determine the language needed by asking, Can I easily use the language? Is the language available on the computer that I am using? Is the language appropriate for the situation?

In some situations, more than one language is appropriate. As different as the languages are, they all have a common base of high and low voltages represented by the *0*s and *1*s of the binary code. One combination of *0*s and *1*s, in which the *0* acts as an off switch and the *1* as an on switch, tells the computer to process the data immediately, while another combination tells the central processing unit (CPU) to add. The computer circuitry responds to a group of these commands and performs a variety of assignments.

A machine language program composed of a pattern of *0*s and *1*s is far removed from the language understood by human beings. Figure 14.2 shows a small program written in machine language. This program instructs the computer to read the number stored in the memory address, to add it to the number already in the CPU, and to store the sum in a memory location. Since this abstract language involves a notational system for *0*s and *1*s, the programmer easily can err, preventing execution of the program.

Figure 14.2
Machine language

```
10100001 00000000 00000010
00000011 00000110 00000010 00000010
10100011 00000000 00000010
```

History of Computer Languages

In 1943, when Howard Aiken built the Mark I, machine language was the only language in existence. The Mark I received its instructions from punched-paper tape that technicians fed into the computer. Mauchly and Eckert's famous Univac was more difficult to program because a group of technicians had to set thousands of switches and insert cables into the machine. Whenever a user wanted to change a program, he or she had to rewire the entire machine.

Because of the difficulty in using machine language, John Mauchly directed his programmers to develop a language that would let the computer user enter problems in a derived algebraic form. This symbolic language was an improvement over machine language because the programmer could now write a problem in mathematical terms and then use a table to convert it into a two-character code. For example, a plus was coded as *07*. Another computer program would then convert this code into the machine language of *0*s and *1*s. This conversion program was a rudimentary interpreter that translated the program into machine code.

This intermediate code became outdated; nevertheless, it was the first step in a long series of advances that gave the computer user the tools to write programs in a language other than machine language. In 1949, at the University of Pennsylvania's Moore School of Engineering, Mauchly and Eckert delivered a series of lectures on a proposed computer that would store programs and data electronically in memory. Maurice Wilkes, an English mathematician who attended these lectures, returned home to England to design a computer, the EDSAC, based on this stored memory concept. The EDSAC did not use a machine code but rather a system of mnemonics. Each time the programmer issued an instruction, it was given in the form of a capital letter. For instance the letter *I* meant *read.* When the user typed this mnemonic on a special keyboard, the computer received the appropriate binary instruction.

Besides designing the symbols, the programmers devised a useful library of generalized subroutines for the EDSAC.[1] The programmers entered a short mnemonic command, and the computer would automatically place the subroutine in the program. Wilkes called the subroutines and mnemonics an assembly system because it assembled sequences of subroutines. The name *assembly system* still exists today: Any language in which a mnemonic represents one machine instruction is called an **assembly language.** An assembly language program or an **assembler** converts the mnemonics directly into the binary sequence of the machine language.

Figure 14.3 shows an example of an assembly program. The top line instructs the CPU to move the contents from main memory into a memory location named TOTAL and register AX. The next line tells the CPU to add the contents in memory to the contents of AX, and the bottom line instructs the CPU to move the contents to the main memory named TOTAL. This assembly language program produces the same output as the comparable machine language program in Figure 14.2.

```
MOV AX, TOTAL
ADD AX, VALUE
MOV TOTAL, AX
```

Figure 14.3
Assembly program
sample

Assembly language is cumbersome because of its mnemonic structure. Besides, assembly language is machine specific, and a program written for one machine does not make sense on a different machine. Because of these drawbacks, prominent mathematicians such as Alan Turning and scientific researchers such as Alick Glennie helped develop high-level languages. A high-level language is more removed from the machine's operation and approximates human language, whereas low-level language is nearer the machine's operation.

In 1951, Grace Hopper and a team of programmers leaped a step by establishing a system capable of translating a program written in a high-level language. This translating program was a "compiler" that Hopper named the A-O, for Autocode. The compiler was faster than the line-by-line interpreters, because it could convert an entire program in one step. This compiled program could be run immediately or saved for future use. Hopper's compiler was the first to be recognized throughout the world.

In 1956, Hopper and her colleagues devised another compiler called the FLOW-MATIC, which permitted businesspeople to program in a language close to English. The market was now ready for high-level language development because compilers could translate entire high-level programs into machine code.

---

[1]A subroutine is an independent program that the main program calls upon repeatedly.

FORTRAN

Shortly after Hopper's compiler, IBM researchers created the first high-level language, **FORTRAN**, an acronym for FORmula TRANslation, a language known for its ability to "crunch numbers." Eight men were assigned to the FORTRAN project and they were not familiar with computers. They were from universities, aircraft companies, and IBM's programming personnel. John Backus, a mathematician, headed the project with only a few years' experience. The FORTRAN team created their new language with basic notations, for example, assignment statements like M=100. In addition, they added subscripted variables, which told the computer which item in a list of variables was needed. For example, X(5) told the computer "the fifth item in X's list." The team had important DO statements that repeated a series of instructions a number of times. According to Backus, "what FORTRAN did primarily was to mechanize the organization of loops," which became important to scientific applications. FORTRAN was easy to use and learn compared to previous languages. The essence of language remained about the same over the years. Eventually, FORTRAN was adapted to a wide variety of computers. When this language was adapted to run on systems for which it had not been designed, changes led to confusion over what was really legal. Subsequently, computer manufacturers standardized the language in 1966 and again in 1977.

FORTRAN is found on minicomputers and mainframes, but it is not as common on a microcomputer. Today, FORTRAN, with its capacity for number manipulation and formulas, is still a popular language among scientists, engineers, and mathematicians. FORTRAN is the language of choice for intense mathematical applications. A standard exists for features that appear in all versions of the language. Adhering to these standards leads to high transportability of programs from one computer to another. On the negative side, FORTRAN was designed as a language that had great capacity for number manipulation and formulas and limited capacity for nonnumeric data. Because the education community deals mostly in nonnumeric data, schools see no reason to teach FORTRAN. This programming language is limited in file processing abilities, control over the format of the output, and clarity of expression. What follows is a program written in FORTRAN.

This program displays the average for the numbers entered. The user enters numbers and presses the return key or some other end-of-data indicator when finished (the particular characters used depend on the system). The program then displays the average.

Program

```
            INTEGER COUNT
            REAL SUM, NUM, AVERAGE
            SUM = 0
            COUNT = 0
    5       PRINT *, 'ENTER A NUMBER :'
            READ (* ,* , END = 10) NUM
            COUNT = COUNT + 1
            SUM = SUM + NUM
            GOTO 5
    10      AVERAGE = SUM / COUNT
            PRINT *, 'AVERAGE =', AVERAGE
            END
```

Output

This is what you will get when running the program:

```
ENTER A NUMBER :
19
ENTER A NUMBER :
87
ENTER A NUMBER :
25
ENTER A NUMBER :
36
ENTER A NUMBER :
86
ENTER A NUMBER :
90
AVERAGE = 57.167
```

Explanation

Lines 1 through 4 declare the types of variables and initialize them.

Line 5 asks to "ENTER A NUMBER"

Line 6 reads that number and stores it into the variable "NUM"; if the input is an end-of-data indicator (mentioned above) then the program is instructed to jump to line 10 and average the numbers.

Line 7 increases the count by 1 every time the program reads a number.

Line 8 adds up the SUM.

Line 9 instructs the program to jump back to line 5, it thus creates a loop that will keep asking for "ENTER A NUMBER" unless an end-of-data indicator is encountered.

Line 10 calculates the average.

Line 11 prints out the result.

Most subsequent languages were direct or indirect descendants of FORTRAN. After FOR-TRAN's introduction in 1957, **COBOL** (COmmon Business-Oriented Language), and **ALGOL** (ALGOrithmetic Language) were developed. COBOL was originally developed by the Department of Defense and later revised by Captain Grace Hopper. ALGOL, primarily used for mathematics and problem solving, was designed by members of the Association for Computing Machinery and European computer industry representatives. FORTRAN, COBOL, and ALGOL are considered classic high-level languages, and modern computer languages are variations of these three.

Table 14.1 (modified from *Current Major Programming Languages* by Pamela J. Milland) gives a thumbnail sketch of the major computer languages developed in the 1960s, 1970s, and 1980s.

Table 14.1   Summary Chart of Major Programming Languages

FORTRAN (1954) FORmula TRANslator. John Backus, with a team at IBM, developed FORTRAN, the first high-level language. This language, known for its number crunching, is widely used for science, engineering, and mathematical problems.

ALGOL 58 (1958) ALGOrithmetic Language. Designed by the members of the Association for Computing Machinery and European computer industry representatives, ALGOL 58 is used for mathematical problem solving.

COBOL (1959) COmmon Business-Oriented Language. The Defense Department developed this language and Captain Grace Hopper of the U.S. Navy perfected it. COBOL is primarily used for business applications.

LISP (1960) LISt Processing. John McCarthy created this language, which is used for special applications such as artificial intelligence.

RPG (1962) Report Program Generator. IBM created and used it to generate business reports.

APL (1962) Kenneth Iverson developed APL; it is used for scientific applications.

SNOBOL 4 (1963) StriNg-Oriented symBOlic Language. David Farber, Ralph Griswold, and Ivan Polonsky of Bell Labs devised the current version of SNOBOL, and it is still in use for text applications.

BASIC (1964) Beginner's All-Purpose Symbolic Instruction Code. T. E. Kurtz and J. G. Kemeny developed BASIC at Dartmouth College in order to teach students programming for educational and business applications.

PL/1 (1964) Programming Language 1. IBM created this language to replace COBOL and FORTRAN, which has not happened.

PROLOG (1970) PROgramming LOGic. Alain Colmerauer wrote this language at the University of Marseilles, France. It is used largely for artificial intelligence applications.

Pascal (1971) Niklaus Wirth invented Pascal, a structured programming language, to teach students how to program.

FORTH (1974) Charles Moore, the astronomer, developed this object-oriented language to control telescopes. This language is growing in popularity.

C (1975) Dennis Richie created C for the Unix operating system, and it is used for systems and general applications.

ADA (1979) Ada was named after Ada Augusta, the Countess of Lovelace, the first woman programmer. Jean Ichbiah headed a team of programmers that produced ADA, a language based on Pascal, used by the federal government for weapons system tracking.

Modula-2 (1979) MODUlar LAnguage 2. Niklaus Wirth, the author of Pascal, wrote Modula-2, a multipurpose scientific language.

Smalltalk 80 (1980) Alan Kay developed Smalltalk 80 at Xerox's Research Center. It is an object-oriented language, used for Xerox's original graphical windows system.

C++ (1983) Bjarn Stroustrup designed and implemented this object-oriented extension of C.

Source: Data from Pamela Milland, "Current Major Programming Languages" in *PC Magazine*, September 13, 1988, Ziff-Davis Publishing.

COBOL

As FORTRAN gained in popularity for engineering and science, the business world wanted a language to meet their needs. COBOL, released in 1964, was a high-level language designed for business applications. This language stored, retrieved, and processed accounting data and automated inventory control, payroll, and billing. COBOL is popular for several reasons. This language handles simple functions like addition, subtraction, and percentages and is machine independent; that is, programs written in COBOL can be moved from one computer to another. COBOL uses ordinary English words and syntax, which makes it easier to understand a typical program, find bugs, add or change features, and perform other functions. The beauty of the language became clear to Grace Hopper when she was left behind after a computer center tour in Japan. She and her hosts could not understand each other until she used two COBOL commands. "MOVE," she said, pointing to herself, "GOTO Osaka Hotel." The hosts understood her immediately and took her to her destination (Embrey, 1983). A sample COBOL program follows, which again calculates the sum and the average.

This COBOL program asks for six numbers, then calculates the sum and the average. For simplicity purposes, only the main portion of the program is shown here.

Program

```
*
00-MAIN-PROCESS.
DISPLAY " ".
DISPLAY "---> THIS PROGRAM ACCEPTS 6 NUMBERS, ACCUMULATES <---".
DISPLAY "---> THE TOTAL AND COMPUTES THEIR AVERAGE <---".
DISPLAY " ".

PERFORM 10-ACCEPT THRU 10-EXIT 6 TIMES.

COMPUTE AVERAGE-VALUE = (TOTAL-VALUE/IN-CNT).

DISPLAY "SUM OF THE SIX NUMBERS: " TOTAL_VALUE.
DISPLAY "AVERAGE OF THE SIX NUMBERS: " AVERAGE_VALUE.
*
STOP RUN.
*
10-ACCEPT.
ADD 1 TO IN-CNT.
DISPLAY "Please Enter Number #" IN-CNT.
ACCEPT IN-NUM FROM SCREEN-INPUT WITH CONVERSION.
ADD IN-NUM TO TOTAL-VALUE.

10-EXIT.
EXIT.
```

Output

```
Please Enter Number #
THIS PROGRAM ACCEPTS 6 NUMBERS, ACCUMULATES
THE TOTAL AND COMPUTES THEIR AVERAGE
SUM OF THE SIX NUMBERS: 343
AVERAGE OF THE SIX NUMBERS: 57.167
```

Explanation

Lines 2 through 4 display the objective of the program.

Line 5 instructs the program to execute the portion from "10-ACCEPT" through "10-EXIT" repeatedly six times in order to read six numbers entered by user.

Line 6 computes the average of those six numbers.

Lines 7 and 8 display the result of the calculation.

Line 9 stops the program when it finishes.

Lines 10 to the end are the two subroutines, "10-ACCEPT" and "10-EXIT," called by line 5.

Currently, COBOL is found in the corporate mainframe world. COBOL is rarely used in education. Even though COBOL is available for personal computers, most applications are created in C. In addition, COBOL requires great storage capacity. Unfortunately, many of the machines in the schools have limited hard disk space. Recently, funds have been spent on new computers with gigabyte hard drives.

ALGOL

ALGOL was an algebraic language similar to FORTRAN, used primarily for writing programs that solved numerical problems. This language was elegant, but it could not overcome FORTRAN's head start as a language. ALGOL is little used today; however, a number of languages were based in part on this language.

BASIC

In the 1960s, programmers designed languages such as LISP, RPG, APL, SNOBOL, and BASIC because academicians were looking for a way to make computers accessible to students. At this time, there was a scarcity of educational software, so teachers focused on computer programming. John Kemeny and Thomas Kurtz at Dartmouth College wanted a language that would require minimal instruction and that would be easy to learn in an academic setting. FORTRAN and ALGOL did not satisfy these requirements, so Kemeny and Kurtz designed **BASIC,** which was a blend of the best of these two languages. In 1964, students at Dartmouth College sat down at computer terminals and were greeted by the famous READY> prompt; thus began an era in which the novice computer user could write and quickly execute simple programs.

After BASIC's introduction, word spread about the new language designed for Dartmouth's time-sharing system. Time sharing permitted several students to interact with the machine at the same time. Students now had access to the computer. They no longer had to use punched-card machines and enlist the help of programmers who would process their programs only when convenient.

Robert L. Albrecht, a senior analyst for Control Data in Minneapolis, heard about the new language and lobbied successfully to make it the recommended language for secondary schools. In 1970, he started a company called Dymax that produced instruction books in BASIC, and he began circulating a bimonthly paper called *The People's Computer Company.* Albrecht wanted someone to write a similar version of BASIC called Tiny BASIC. He commissioned Dennis Allison, a skilled programmer, to write a series of articles with guidelines for the modified version. Dick Whipple and John Arnold responded with a 2,000-octal code of instructions. The Altair computer, the first affordable microcomputer, responded to commands entered in Tiny BASIC.

Albrecht's magazine continued publishing new versions of BASIC submitted by its readers, and some authors released these versions through public domain. In the mid-1970s, the authors of these programs began selling their versions of BASIC commercially.

Many variations appeared. For example, Tom Pittman wrote a Tiny BASIC interpreter, and Bill Gates and Paul Allen wrote a version of BASIC, using only 4K of memory. For their own versions of BASIC, manufacturers wired interpreters into their computers' ROM. By the mid-1980s, millions of people in the United States and abroad knew BASIC and had learned it on their own computers. The program's original designers, Kemeny and Kurtz, were upset about the compromises that had to be made in order to produce BASIC on the different incompatible machines. Computer scientists criticized the language because it lent itself mainly to short programs. Many high school teachers thought BASIC needed structure, so they abandoned it in favor of Pascal. An example of a BASIC program used to calculate the sum and average follows:

Program

The following program will ask for six integers; then it will find the sum and the average of those numbers.

A simple way of writing this program is:

```
10 PRINT "ENTER FIRST INTEGER:"
15 INPUT A
20 PRINT "ENTER SECOND INTEGER:"
25 INPUT B
30 PRINT "ENTER THIRD INTEGER:"
35 INPUT C
40 PRINT "ENTER FOURTH INTEGER:"
45 INPUT D
50 PRINT "ENTER FIFTH INTEGER:"
55 INPUT E
60 PRINT "ENTER SIXTH INTEGER:"
65 INPUT F
70 PRINT "THE SUM OF THESE NUMBERS IS:"
75 PRINT (A+B+C+D+E+F)
80 PRINT "THE AVERAGE OF THESE NUMBERS IS:"
85 PRINT (A+B+C+D+E+F) \ 6
END
```

This program can be rewritten, using the control-loop FOR, as follows:

Program

```
10 FOR I = 1 TO 6
15 PRINT "ENTER AN INTEGER:"
20 INPUT S
25 SUM = SUM + S
30 NEXT I
35 AVERAGE = SUM \ 6
40 PRINT "THE SUM IS :"; SUM; "; "
45 PRINT "THE AVERAGE IS :"; AVERAGE
END
```

Out put

```
ENTER AN INTEGER:
THE SUM IS: 343
THE AVERAGE IS: 57.167
```

Explanation

Lines 10 through 30 are a loop to repeat six times the routine of asking for an integer, reading the response from the user (line 20), then adding it up to value SUM.

Line 35 calculates the average of those six numbers.
Lines 40 and 45 print out the results.

Through the years, Kemeny and Kurtz made revisions, and in 1984, they collaborated on a microcomputer version of BASIC, *True BASIC*, that became the definitive version. BASIC was no longer a line-oriented language with little structure—it was a modern language. An example of a structured BASIC program is shown in Figure 14.4 (taken from *True BASIC* by John G. Kemeny and Thomas E. Kurtz).

Figure 14.4
A structured BASIC program
From *True BASIC Reference Manual*, by John G. Kemeny and Thomas E. Kurtz, 1988. Reprinted by permission.

Program Instructions	Explanations
READ x,y	Reads 3 and 4
PRINT x+y	Prints 7
READ x,y	Reads 2 and 3
READ a$,z	Reads The answer is and Reads 4
READ a$;(x+y)*z	Prints The answer is 20
DATA 3,4,2,3, The answer is, 4	The values read and manipulated
END	Ends the program

BASIC has improved in its sophistication, routines, and graphics. By adding statements such as Loop, Do, and Select Case, it has gained more structure. Today, BASIC has the ability to create data structures equal to Pascal or C and no longer has the memory limits of the earlier programs. BASIC programming has a built-in full-screen editor with automatic syntax editing and a built-in debugger, and it runs as fast as Pascal or C. BASIC has moved from an interpreter back to a compiler without sacrificing the instant feedback. The new compiler technology detects errors in programming and compiles thousands of lines of code in a few seconds. Popular commercial programs still are written in BASIC. Furthermore, new versions of BASIC such as *Future BASIC* (Zedcor) and Microsoft's *Visual BASIC* have been developed, and undoubtedly future versions of BASIC will emerge.

The language most often taught in the schools is BASIC because it is simple to use and has key words that resemble English. For a more in-depth discussion of BASIC, refer to the books listed at the end of the chapter.

Let's compare BASIC with two popular, high-level languages, COBOL and FORTRAN. In Figure 14.5, all three languages compute the average of five values. From this comparison, you might conclude that BASIC is a suitable language for the classroom teacher who wants to teach programming.

BASIC	FORTRAN	COBOL
10 INPUT A,B,C,D,E	READ(5,100) V1,V2,V3,V4,V5	ACCEPT Vs
20 LET S=A+B+C+D+E	100 FORMAT(5F3.0)	ADD V-1,V-2,V-3,V-4,V-5 GIVING T
30 LET AV=S/5	S=V1+V2+V3+V4+V5	DIVIDE T BY 5 GIVING AV-OF-ALL-Vs
40 PRINT"AVERAGE=";AV	AV=S/5	DISPLAY"AV="AV-OF-ALL-Vs
50 END	WRITE(6,200) AV	STOP RUN.
	200 FORMAT('AV=',F8.2)	
	STOP	
	END	

Figure 14.5
Comparison of three languages

Since BASIC's creation in 1964, many new high-level languages have been developed. The continued use of BASIC, a relatively old language, has sparked controversy. Within this context, let's examine some of the advantages and disadvantages of teaching BASIC.

Why Teach BASIC?

Until 1979, the computer's disk operating system was not a reality, so BASIC, built into the ROM chip for most computers, was a necessity. Today, the majority of computers no longer come with a programming language built into the ROM. However, you can purchase a program such as *True BASIC* or *Visual BASIC*. BASIC needs minimal memory and requires no special hardware, so schools do not have to make extra expenditures to teach it to their students. Many proponents maintain that BASIC is the easiest language to learn. Nevertheless, these arguments do not preclude it from having complexities that would sustain a student's interest. The enhanced BASIC versions have the ability to support graphics, color capabilities, and sound. Many teachers are familiar with BASIC, so teaching it requires no special retraining.

In spite of these attributes, BASIC has its opponents. Many feel that Pascal is superior to BASIC because of its structure, but they overlook the many versions of Pascal that do not support graphics.

Others prefer Logo over BASIC because of its better graphic capabilities, arguing that learning how to program graphics in BASIC is more complicated than programming in Logo. Logo advocates concede that BASIC is easy to learn; however, it does not serve the developmental needs of the young child. Because Logo is more prevalent in the schools, it is discussed separately in chapter 15.

Another criticism is that BASIC (Dartmouth version) teaches poor programming techniques because it does not follow the current structured programming principles. This argument does have some credence because it is more difficult for a teacher to learn a program in structured BASIC after having been using the older BASIC. A contingency of people are opposed to teaching any programming because they feel the emphasis should be on computer applications.

Whether you decide to teach BASIC really depends on your individual purpose. This language does give the students and teachers an introduction to computer programming. Many educators and students will not advance beyond writing a few simple programs; however, being able to program does give you self-confidence and a willingness to explore the computer's capabilities.

Many versions of BASIC, such as *True BASIC,* (True Basic) *Visual BASIC* (Microsoft), and *Future BASIC* (Zedcor), have made significant improvements on the older versions of BASIC. Teaching BASIC programming using an excellent, structured program such as *True BASIC* would be just as appropriate as using Pascal. Unfortunately, few books adequately teach this version of BASIC, and many of the books that do teach it begin with traditional methods and introduce structure later.

At the end of the chapter, you will find many articles and books on BASIC. Chapter 16 gives a synopsis of the recent research on BASIC.

Pascal

Pascal was named after Blaise Pascal, the seventeenth-century French mathematician. Niklaus Wirth, author of Pascal, began writing the language in 1968. He was professor of computer science at the Swiss Federal Technical University. Wirth wanted his students to have a language that followed sound programming practices. Because Wirth was dissatisfied with the major languages, he wrote a language that was more precise. At the beginning of a program the writer must define all variables and state each data type that is, whether the variable contents will be treated as integers or string characters. Pascal has a logical structure that divides a program into simple tasks. Using Pascal, the programmer has less freedom, but the programming style is more rigorous. This approach lessens the chance of committing errors, and makes it easier to read, correct bugs, and make changes. Pascal is great for teaching programming techniques and theory. However, it is not good for writing practical applications. For instance, Pascal lacks input and output statements; therefore, reading data from the keyboard or writing data to external storage is not important to this language. Pascal reduces the GOTO or unconditional loops that make it harder to detect errors, and it encourages rigorous organization. Pascal became very popular, and colleges on both sides of the Atlantic adopted it as a classroom aid for teaching programming. Pascal became the leader of a movement to teach structured programming. This movement wanted to change the way software was put together. Following is a PASCAL program that calculates the average of six numbers :

PROGRAM
Average (Input, Output);

```
        VAR
                In_Count,
                N,
                SUM:
                    Integer;
                AVERAGE:
                    Real;


        BEGIN
            Writeln('This program will ask for six integers');
            Writeln('then it will display the sum and the average');
            FOR In_Count := 1 TO 6 DO
                    BEGIN
                                    Writeln('Please enter an integer');
                                    Readln(N);
                                    SUM := SUM + N;
                    END
            AVERAGE := SUM/6;
            Writeln('Sum=', SUM, ',average =', AVERAGE:7:2);
        END
```

Output

This program will ask for six integers then it will display the sum and the average

```
                    Please enter an integer
                    19
                    Please enter an integer
                    87
                    Please enter an integer
                    25
                    Please enter an integer
                    36
                    Please enter an integer
                    86
                    Please enter an integer
                    90
                    Sum = 343.00, Average = 57.167
```

Explanation

The first seven lines are just declarations, that is, whether the numbers are integers and so on. We will focus on the main program. The main program starts from BEGIN. The two lines beginning with the Writeln command display the purpose of this program. The FOR loop, consisting of the line "FOR . . ." and the next five lines, will cause the program repeat six times asking the user for an integer, adding that integer to the SUM.

The line "AVERAGE . . ." calculates the average. The program then displays the result with the line "Writeln . . ."

Pascal has its advantages and disadvantages. Pascal follows structured programming principles, and it is hard to write a poor program. Teaching Pascal in high school is helpful for later college study of computer science. Pascal is available in both a compiler and interpreter version. On the negative side, the majority of teachers are prepared to teach BASIC or Logo because these languages are easier to learn. Pascal has no self-teaching materials and is a more difficult language. Finally, Wirth designed Pascal to teach college students, so it is not suitable for the younger child. The major concern is that most teachers are prepared to teach BASIC or Logo, and they have to take college or university courses to learn Pascal. Pascal has acceptance as a teaching language, but most professional programmers prefer to use C.

C Language

C was developed because programmers needed a way to let the UNIX operating system run on a variety of computers. C is a high-level language that was created at Bell labs in 1970. This language is able to handle the computer at a low level, just like assembly language. C became the language of choice for commercial program development during the mid-1980s. C can be compiled into machine language on almost all computers. C is modular, and it can take advantage of specific features of a specific computer. Programmers can write library routines that meet a particular programming need and use these routines in other programs. C is structured, which makes it more efficient and concise, and it runs faster than other high-level programming languages. The following C program will ask "how many numbers to enter" (let's say 6); then the program will find the sum and the average of those numbers.

Program

```
#include <stdio.h>
main()
{
float x, sum;
int i, n;
printf("How many numbers to enter ? ");
scanf("%d", &n);
printf("Please enter number 1: ");
scanf("%f", &x);
sum = x;
   for (i = 2; i <= n; i++)
   {
             printf("Please enter number %2d: ", i);
             scanf("%f", &x);
             sum += x;
   }
printf("Sum = %10.3f, average = %10.3f \n", sum, sum /n);
exit(0);
}
```

Output

```
How many numbers to enter ? 6
Please enter number 1: 19
Please enter number 2: 87
Please enter number 3: 25
Please enter number 4: 36
Please enter number 5: 86
Please enter number 6: 90
Sum = 343.000, average = 57.167
```

Explanation

For simplicity, we will skip the first four lines (mainly for headers and declarations) and start our discussion from line 5 (printf . . .). This line prompts for input from the keyboard: "How many numbers do you want to add up, and then find the average?" You will answer 6, for example.

Line 6 takes that answer into the program.
Line 7 prompts the user to enter the first value.
Line 8 takes that value.
Line 9 stores that value into a temporary space, called "x."
Lines 10 to 15 repeats the process of prompting the user's input and adding up into "x."
Line 16 prints the sum and the average.
Line 17 exits the program.

This is what you will get when running the program:
C became widespread, and a newer variation, C++, appeared. C++, created by Bjarne Stroustrup at Bell Laboratories, is also a high-level programming language. This language has

all the advantages of C and of object-oriented programming (OOP) languages. Apple has adopted C++ as its standard house programming language (Pfaffenberger, 1997).

Java

Java was developed in the early 1990's by a team at Sun Microsystems. They were looking for a way to write programs for consumer electronic gadgets, ranging from televisions to pagers. Java was modeled after C++ and is a cross-platform programming language. This uncomplicated language eliminates features that programmers find time consuming and tedious. Using Java, a person can write a program that will work on any computer that can run a Java interpreter, which is built into the majority of browsers today. The first browsers to run Java were *Netscape 2.0* and Sun's *HotJava* (Freedman, 1996). You find Java programs embedded in HTML documents on the World Wide Web. Java is typically used for creating games that run in a browser window, creating interactive Web graphics, and writing stand-alone applications. In 1996, Sun started selling stand-alone software applications written in Java. Using Java you can create applets, or small computer programs, that provide a specific function such as displaying a scolling, or ticker tape, message, a clock, or a calculator. These applets can be embedded in your Web page or in stand-alone applications. An example of a ticker tape applet follows:

Program

```
<APPLET CODE="TickerTape.class" HEIGHT=40 WIDTH=350>
<PARAM NAME="TEXT" VALUE=" This is a Java program. ">
<PARAM NAME="FONT" VALUE="Courier">
<PARAM NAME="FONTSIZE" VALUE=30>
<PARAM NAME="STYLE" VALUE="BOLD">
<PARAM NAME="FGCOLOR" VALUE="RED">
<PARAM NAME="BGCOLOR" VALUE="BLACK">
<PARAM NAME="DELAY" VALUE=50>
<PARAM NAME="CLICKURL"
VALUE="http://patriot.net/~gillette/applets/coffee.htm">
<PARAM NAME="SHADOWCOLOR" VALUE="BLUE">
<PARAM NAME="DEBUG" VALUE="">

</applet>
```

Explanation

This Java applet has the text scroll in a message box across the screen. The scrolling text's message is "This is a Java program." The font used is Courier, its style is bold, the font color red, and the background of the message box black. Each letter is shadowed in blue and there is a 50- second delay.

Java is important because it is a promising new software technology that could power a new generation of devices that might make today's desktop personal computers obsolete (Hiltzik, 1997).

JavaScript

JavaScript is a scripting language developed by Netscape Communications for publishing on the World Wide Web. Most people confuse Java with JavaScript even though their level of difficulty and use is quite different. Java is the full-blown programming language, while JavaScript is only a scripting language. According to Gesing and Scheider, 1997, "scripting languages combine tools from programming languages to make them more concise and usable." JavaScripting language has fewer features than Java, which makes this language less versatile. Nevertheless, it is easier for the novice or nonprogrammer to master. JavaScript's purpose is to expand the functionality of the Web pages, and it is written as part of the HTML document. Both languages share syntax and structure. JavaScript is able to control and share information with Java applets. By using JavaScript, you are able to customize a Web page, depending on your browser; check for mistakes in a form before it's submitted; get visual feedback on your actions; create animations; and have interactive features on your Web pages. An example of a JavaScript greeting message integrated into HTML code follows:

Program

```
<HTML><HEAD><TITLE>Scroll Example</Title>
<SCRIPT LANGUAGE=JavaScript">
<!—HIDE
var nspaces = 150
var timer
vr msg = ""
function scrollMaster() {
   clearTimeout(timer)
msg = "Welcome to Web Site for Teachers"
for (var i = 0; i <nspacs; i++) {
}
scrollMe()
}
function scrollMe() {
   window.status = msg
   msg = msg.substring(1, msg.length)+ msg.substring(0,1)
   timer = setTimeout("scrollMe()", 150)
}
//STOP HIDING—></SCRIPT.,/HEAD>
<BODY><FORM>
<INPUT TYPE="button" VALE-"Display" onClick="scrollMaster()">
</FORM></HTML>
```

Explanation

This script scrolls "Welcome to Web Sites for Teachers" in the menu bar from left to right.

There are pages on the Internet that give you a variety of free scripts. Here are a few addresses:

http://users.skynet.be/sky43465/index.html
http://www.bodo.com/javacool.htm
http://www.starlingtech.com/books/javascript/

The next language we discuss is a formatting language for publishing documents on the Web.

HyperText Markup Language (HTML)

HTML is "a declarative language for making the portions of a document (called elements) so that, when accessed by a program called a Web browser, each portion appears with a distinctive format" (Pfaffenberger, 1997). HTML is the formatting language behind the documents that you see on the World Wide Web. You use HTML tags to mark up text so that it can be read by your browser locally or over the network. This language lets authors insert tables, create forms that are used to get information from the user, style text, embed graphics, and create hyperlinks, which when clicked display another author's page. The *Beginner's Guide to HTML*, NASA's guide for home page makers, should further help you understand Web page creation. Here is its address:

http://www.ncsa.uiuc.edu/General/Internet/WWW/HTMLPrimer.html

The following brief guide will give you some of the basics for creating a HTML document. For our discussion, we will use *HTML Editor 1.14* by Rick Giles, an inexpensive shareware product. This example is not meant to teach you HTML but to give you an overview of how it operates and help you format the most basic Web pages. Refer to Figure 14.6 to follow the explanation.

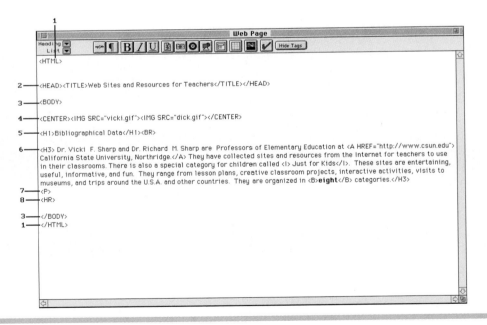

Figure 14.6
Example in *HTML Editor*
Courtesy of Richard Giles

HTML Explanation

An HTML document consists of two parts: the head and the body. All orders are enclosed in brackets, for example, <TITLE>. These brackets, or tags, can be used by themselves, like <P>, or together in pairs, like <H1> and </H1>. Notice that the closing tag is the same as the opening one except that it is preceded by a slash. Tags that create forms and link files require different parts or arguments to work. In addition, graphic tags require additional information, like the file name and alignment information.

1. Each document must begin with the <HTML> tag and end with an </HTML> tag.
2. The <HEAD> tag should be at the beginning of the document. Next comes the <TITLE> tag, the title "Web Sites and Resources for Teachers", and two ending tags: </TITLE> and </HEAD>.
3. Next type the document between two BODY tags: <BODY> and </BODY>.
4. To center a graphic, place the graphic between two Center tags: <CENTER> and </CENTER>.

   In this example we have two graphics so place the graphics by doing the following:
   a. Use a <CENTER> tag in front of the first graphic.
   b. To place a graphic on the page, type <IMG SRC= in front of the file name, which in this example is **vicki.gif.**
   c. Place the file name in quotes, "vicki.gif", and end with a bracket >.

   <IMG SRC="vicki.gif">

   d. Do same for the other graphic: **<IMG SRC="dick.gif">**
   e. End with a closing center tag: **</CENTER>**
   f. The result is:

   <CENTER <IMG SRC="vicki.gif"> <IMG SRC="dick.gif"></CENTER>

5. H# creates a header in large type. The type is largest when surrounded by H1 tags, it is smaller when surrounded by H2 tags, and even smaller when surrounded by H3 tags.
   a. The beginning and ending tags, <H1>and </H1>, make the text "Biographical Data" appear very large.
   b. The <BR> ends a line and inserts a space.

   <H1>Biographical Data </H1>

6. The next part of the document is made smaller and has a hypertext link as well as italicized and boldfaced words.
   a. The <H3> and </H3> tags make the print smaller.
   b. To create a hyptertext link, start with the opening tag, <A HREF=, which is placed in front of the URL, http://www.csun.edu/.
   c. The URL is enclosed in quotation marks and a bracket.

   <A HREF="http://www.csun.edu/">

d. A description for the URL is written as "California State University, Northridge." The end of the URL a closing tag has, </A>. The hyptertext link should look like the following:

<A HREF="http://www.csun.edu"<California State University, Northridge </A>

e. A beginning <I > tag and an ending </I> tag will format italic type, as in the following:

<I>*Just for Kids*</I>

f. A beginning <B> tag and the ending </B> tag will boldface whatever is between them. For example:

<B>eight</B>

7. The <P> tag indicates the end of a paragraph and adds a blank line.
8. The <HR> tag places a horizontal line on the page.

On the Web, this document would look like this:

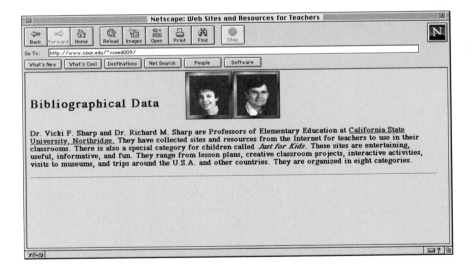

Before creating your own Web page, read through these guidelines.

Some Guidelines for Creating a Web Page

A good presentation, like a good Web page, has excellent overall design and well-chosen graphics. The following suggestions should help you generate an attractive Web page.

1. Plan ahead; that is, decide what type of information you want to put on the Web, then outline your ideas, write your text, and revise it. You need to present the information in a logical order and make every word count. Be sure to run your spelling checker and to carefully proofread.

2. You can make a good impression by paying close attention to how you organize your information. On a separate piece of paper, organize your Web page. Create a sketch so you can visually see where you will place your text and graphics. In other words, storyboard your ideas. You can use a drawing program like *ClarisDraw* for this purpose.

3. Create a map that shows your navigational buttons and where they will be placed. Your reader should not spend time scrolling, but be able to jump easily from one location to another.

4. Good first impresions count in Web pages as well as in life. See if your home page communicates well, sets a good tone, and catches people's attention.

5. Use your graphics wisely to enhance content. Don't overload your page with pictures so people have to wait too long for your graphics to load. Use an interlaced GIF image, which displays graphics with one set of alternative lines at a time.

6. The site should contain appropriate, relevant, timely, and engaging material.

7. The site must have authoritative and reliable information.

8. Be careful not to clutter the page with too many elements. Break up your text so it is more readable. At the same time, use a variety of items so as not to bore the audience.

9. Do not use too many typefaces because it detracts from the general feeling of the writing.

An example of a good Web site is Cells Alive.

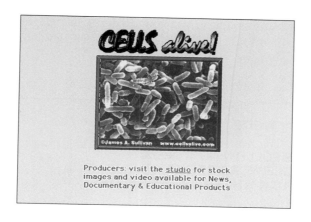

http://www.cellsalive.com/

This site is a primer on cellular biology featuring a fascinating collection of pictures and animations with clear explanations. You can actually see how penicillin destroys bacteria and can view microscopic parasites.

Learning a language is demanding, even though it gives you flexibility. Authoring languages provide an alternative for converting a lesson into a program.

Authoring Languages

An **authoring language** lets you design software to meet your curriculum needs. By learning only a few core commands, you can write interactive lessons and create new programs. You can design lessons without investing the countless hours of instruction necessary to learn a computer language. A single authoring language command conveys more instructions than a command in a high-level language.

In 1959, Donald Bitzer and a team of specialists developed PLATO for use on a mainframe computer. PLATO, one of the earliest computer systems for educational applications, had a special authoring language called TUTOR. Using the authoring language, Bitzer and his colleagues produced more than 200 lessons for the classroom. Expensive to produce, PLATO utilized a touch screen, and its terminal had a plasma screen that could display sophisticated graphics.

In 1969, John Starkweather and his associates at the University of California at San Francisco created what would prove to be one of the longest lasting authoring languages, Programmed Inquiry, Learning, or Training (PILOT). Their purpose was to make it easy for teachers to prepare tutorial or drill and practice lessons. This program, produced and developed by Apple Computer in the early 1970s, had only eight commands. The commands usually consisted of one letter with a colon; for example, the command J: meant to jump to a special place in the program, and the command E: meant to end the program.

A few years after PILOT's introduction, it was expanded by Apple into SuperPILOT with twenty-six commands, a graphics editor, and sound effects. In 1983, Earl L. Kyser Jr., a systems analyst, designed a simplified PILOT called *E-Z PILOT II* (Hartley). Figure 14.7 shows a simple program written in this language.

```
DEFINITION ********* WRITE ****** 0 LINES

 1  T:  DEFINE THE FOLLOWING WORDS:
 2  T:  GIVE A SINGLE WORD DEFINITION.
 3  T:  PRESS RETURN WHEN YOU ARE READY
 4  A:
 5  T:
 6  T:  WHAT DOES LOQUACIOUS MEAN
 7  A:
 8  M:  TALKATIVE, WORDY, GABBY, VERBOSE
 9  TY: EXCELLENT.  THAT IS CORRECT.
10  TN: SORRY, THIS IS THE WRONG CHOICE.
11  E:
```

Figure 14.7
Example of *E-Z PILOT II*
Courtesy of Hartley Courseware, a division of Jostens Learning.

Explanation

E-Z PILOT inserts line numbers automatically.
Lines 1, 2, 3: The letter T: prints the following lines:

DEFINE THE FOLLOWING WORDS:
GIVE A SINGLE WORD DEFINITION.
PRESS RETURN WHEN YOU ARE READY?

The computer will insert a question mark automatically after line 3.

Line 4: A: prepares the computer to accept an answer from the user.
Line 5: T: prints a blank line because there are no words after it.
Line 6: T: prints the following question and again the computer inserts a question mark:
"WHAT DOES LOQUACIOUS MEAN?"
Line 7: A: asks the user to type an answer.
Line 8: M: The command M: (match command) compares the student's answer with the following acceptable responses: **TALKATIVE, WORDY, GABBY, VERBOSE.**
Line 9: TY: tells the computer to display the following statement if the student's response is correct: **"EXCELLENT. THAT IS CORRECT."**
Line 10: TN: tells the computer to display the following statement if the student's response is wrong: **"SORRY, THIS IS THE WRONG CHOICE."**
Line 11: E: The command E: is an end statement.

There were numerous authoring languages designed for educational use (Barker, 1987) including *CourseWriter III* and *Course of Action. Coursewriter III*, a sophisticated language designed for the IBM family of computers, required considerable programming skill, whereas *Course of Action*, designed for the Macintosh, had an icon-based menu that was much easier to use. Authoring languages today are more powerful and flexible than before. They still are concerned with presenting interactive information to the user. Some authoring languages specialize in creating tutorial and drill and practice software, while others let teachers develop simulations for students. In chapter 10, we focused on authoring languages that produced multimedia presentations. These presentations create an exploratory environment for students.

Advantages

In many instances the authoring language, because of its simple command structure, is preferable to the programming language. The authoring language has flexibility, allowing for student spelling and spacing errors. Teachers can easily customize lessons for the gifted as well as for less academically talented students. With an authoring language, teachers can design interactive programs as independent learning activities. These lessons can include graphics, sound, animation, and rudimentary record-keeping capabilities. Authoring languages provide a simple way to access a wide range of peripherals such as CD-ROM and laser disc players; teachers can create multimedia environments with programs such as *HyperStudio, HyperCard,* or *Digital Chisel.* Advanced students can create presentations in computer format (see chapter 10). Finally, in the process of using an authoring language, teachers learn valuable information about computer programming.

Disadvantages

Although there are numerous benefits to using an authoring language, there are some drawbacks as well. An authoring language does not achieve the same sophistication that a general, all-purpose language such as BASIC does. An authoring language does not have full graphics capabilities nor the same flexibility in producing programs. If an authoring language is enhanced, it becomes more complicated to use than a general, all-purpose language. There are not as many books to help teachers master these languages, so they must rely almost solely on the user manual with whatever technical support is available. Learning a programming language is time consuming, but preparing a lesson using an authoring language also requires hours of diligent effort.

Another concern is the quality of the software that the teacher eventually creates. The instructor may not be competent enough to create an excellent product, or the authoring program may be limited. Furthermore, most authoring programs run more slowly than programming languages, so students experience more wait time.

From our discussion, you should have a clear picture of the pros and cons of an authoring language. Before leaving this topic completely, let's make a distinction between authoring *languages* and authoring *systems*.

Authoring Systems

In the literature, authoring *languages* and *systems* are used interchangeably. However, equating them is incorrect because an **authoring system,** designed for a special purpose, is a subset of an authoring language. The authoring system is easier to use because it offers a predesigned template, but it is not as flexible as an authoring language, which lets teachers customize their own lessons. An authoring system has prompts to lead you through the program. Like authoring languages, authoring systems do not limit themselves to drill and practice and tutorial programs; on the contrary, with them you can create simulations, databases for management, and adventure games. An example of an authoring system is *Test Designer Plus* (Superschool), which lets you design interactive tests.

Summary

We discussed the historical development of programming languages, which provided a background on languages ranging from BASIC to C. We became familiar with the basic principles used to create a Web page and reviewed guidelines for developing a good Web page. Next, we considered authoring languages, an alternative to the general, all-purpose programming language, as suitable tools for tailoring specific lessons to individual instructional needs.

Although authoring languages such as PILOT and E-Z PILOT II are easier to learn than BASIC, Java, or Pascal, they still require considerable time and effort to produce a quality product. The trend now is to produce more user-friendly and flexible authoring languages such as *HyperStudio, Digital Chisel,* and *HyperCard.* These hypermedia tools are discussed in chapter 10. We conclude this chapter with some questions, some teacher projects, and suggested readings and references.

Chapter Mastery Test

1. Trace the development of programming languages.

2. What are the strengths and weaknesses of an authoring language?

3. Distinguish among an authoring system, an authoring language, and a high-level programming language.

4. Explain what a programming language is.

5. Why were BASIC, Logo, and Pascal popular languages in the schools?

6. Give two cogent reasons why programming should and two reasons why it should not be taught in the schools.

7. What is the difference between an interpreter and a compiler?

8. What is structured programming? Explain the debate concerning it.

9. Give three general rules to follow when creating a Web page.

10. What is Java scripting and how is it different from Java?

11. What is HTML? Give an example of three tags and what they do.

12. Explain the main purpose of the following three languages: COBOL, FORTRAN, and Pascal.

Classroom Projects

1. Create a simple Web page that
   a. displays a graphic,
   b. has a link, and
   c. has text.

2. Research the history of a programming language. Prepare a two-page report that answers the following questions: (a) How did the language originate? (b) What are its features? (c) How is the language being used today?

3. Using an authoring language, design a lesson for your class's specific curriculum needs.

4. Using a flowchart, plan a lesson for the computer.

Suggested Readings and References

Abernathy, Joe. "Breaking the Programming Code: Part I." *Incider A+* (June 1990): 51-56.

Abernathy, Joe. "Programming Part I." *Incider A+* (July 1990): 56-62.

Agular, Hugh. "BASIC Recursive Techniques." *Computer Language* (May 1985): 45.

Anderson R., H. Bennett, and D. Walling. "Structured Programming Constructs in BASIC: Tried and Tested." *Computers in the Schools* (summer 1987): 135-39.

Athey, Thomas H. *Computers and End-User Software with BASIC.* Glenview, Ill.: Scott, Foresman, 1987.

Backus, John, "The History of FORTRAN I, II, AND III." *Annals of the History of Computing,* (July 1979).

Barker, P. *Author Languages for CAI.* London: Macmillan Education Ltd., 1987.

Bernardo, M. A., and Morris, J. D. "Transfer Effects of High School Computer Programming Course on Mathematical Modeling, Procedural Comprehension, and Verbal Problem Solving." *Journal of Research on Computing in Education,* 26, (no. 4) (Summer 1994): 523-36.

Campbell, Tom. "Programming Power." *Compute* 13, no. 6 (June 1, 1991): 73.

Castro, Elizabeth, *Html for the World Wide Web (Visual Quickstart Guide Series).* Berkeley, Calif.: Peachpit Press, 1997.

Chandler, Anthony. "Write Faster BASIC Programs." *Compute* 13, no. 4 (April 1, 1991): G-10.

Charlton, J. P., and Birkett, P. E. "Specificity Versus Nonspecificity of Cognitive Skills in Elementary Computer Programming." *Journal of Research on Computing in Education,* 26, no. 3 (spring 1994): 391-402.

Clements, Douglas H. et al. "Students' Development of Length Concepts in a Logo-Based Unit on Geometric Paths." *Journal for Research in Mathematics Education* 28 , no. 1 (Jan. 1997): 70-95.

Coburn, Edward J. *Visual Basic Made Easy.* Boston, Mass.: PNS Publishing, 1995.

Conlin, T. *PILOT: The Language and How to Use It Including Apple PILOT and SuperPILOT.* Englewood Cliffs, N.J.: Prentice-Hall, 1984.

Cooper, James W. *Microsoft QuickBASIC for Scientists: A Guide to Writing Better Programs.* New York: Wiley, 1988.

Cotton, Larry. "BASIC for Beginners: Keys to BASIC Programming." *Compute!'s Gazette* 7, no. 11 (November 1, 1989): 63.

Davis, William S. *True BASIC Primer.* Reading, Mass.: Addison-Wesley, 1986.

Dijkstra, Edgar W. *Selected Writings on Computer: A Personal Perspective.* New York: Springer-Verlag, 1982.

Dodd, Kenneth Nelson. *Computer Programming and Languages.* London: Butterworths, 1969.

Elson, Mark. *Concept of Programming Languages.* Science Research Associates, Chicago, Illinois, 1973.

Embrey, Glenn, "COBOL." *Popular Computing,* (September 1983).

Flanagan, David. *Java in a Nutshell: A Desktop Quick Reference (The Java Series),* 2d ed. O'Reilly & Associates, Cambridge, Massachusetts, 1997.

Freedman, Alan. *The Computer Desktop Encyclopedia.* New York: American Management Association, 1996.

Gates, Bill. "The 25th Birthday of BASIC." *Byte* (October 1989): 268-72.

Graham, Ian S. *Guide to Html 3.2 and Html Extensions,* 3d ed. New York: John Wiley & Sons, 1997.

Gesiny, Ted and Schneider, Jeremy. *Java Script for the World Wide Web.* Peachpit Press. Berkeley, California, 1997, p. 3.

Harter, Edward D. *BASIC-PLUS and VAX BASIC Structured Programming.* Englewood Cliffs, N.J.: Prentice Hall, 1988.

Heimler, Charles, Jim Cunningham, and Michael Nevard. *BASIC for Teachers.* Santa Cruz, Calif.: Mitchell Publishing, 1987.

Hiltzik, Michael, Leslie Helm, and Greg Miller. "Rival's Wave of Hot Java Has Microsoft Steaming." *Los Angeles Times* (October 1, 1997): 1.

Honeycutt, Jerry, Mark R. Brown, Jim O'Donnell, and Eric Ladds. *Using Html 3.2 : Special.* New York: Que, 1997.

Horowitz, Ellis. *Fundamentals of Programming Languages.* Rockville Md.: Computer Science Press, 1984.

Jonassen, D. H. Computers in the Classroom: Mind-Tools for Critical Thinking. Englewood Cliffs, New Jersey: Merrill (Prentice-Hall), 1996.

Kemeny, John G., and Thomas E. Kurtz. *True BASIC, Macintosh User's Guide,* West Lebanon, N.H.: True Basic, 1989.

Lemay, Laura. *Teach Yourself Web Publishing with Html 4 in 14 Days,* 2d ed. SAMS, 1998.

Levy, Steven. *Hackers: Heroes of the Computer Revolution.* Garden City, N.Y.: Doubleday, Author Press, 1984.

List, Peter. *Beginning Visual Basic 5.* Indianapolis, Ind.: Wrox Press, 1997.

Milland, Pamela J. "Current Major Programming Languages." *PC Magazine* (September 13, 1988): 96-97.

Morris, Mary E. S., and Randy J. Hinrichs. *Web Page Design: A Different Multimedia.* New York: Prentice Hall, 1996.

Nickerson, Robert C. *Fundamentals of Programming in BASIC: A Structured Approach*, 2d ed. Boston: Little, Brown, 1986.

Oliver, Dick. *Teach Yourself Html 3.2 in 24 Hours.* SAMS. New York, 1997.

Perminov, Oleg . *The Beginners Guide to Turbo Pascal.* Software Masters, 1994.

Pfaffenberger, Bryan. *Webster's New World Dictionary of Computer Terms,* 6th ed. New York: Que, 1997.

Poirot, J. L., and R. C. Adams. *40 Easy Steps to Programming BASIC and LOGO.* Austin, Texas.: Sterling Swift Publishing, 1983.

Ross, S. M. *BASIC Programming for Educators.* Englewood Cliffs, N.J.: Prentice-Hall, 1986.

Sharp, Richard, Vicki Sharp, and Martin Levine. *Best Math and Science Web Sites for Teachers 2nd Edition.* Eugene, Oreg.: ISTE, 1998.

Sharp, Vicki, Martin Levine, and Richard Sharp, *Best Web Sites for Teachers,* 2nd ed. Eugene, Oreg.: ISTE, 1998.

Spencer, Donald D. *Computer Mathematics with BASIC Programming.* Ormond Beach, Fla.: Camelot Publishing, 1990.

Starkweather, John. *A User's Guide to PILOT.* Englewood Cliffs, N.J.: Prentice-Hall, 1985.

Taaffee, Joanne, and Elinor Mills. "Users Still Like Java Despite the Sun-Microsoft Dispute." *InfoWorld* 19, no. 48 (December 1, 1997): 77.

Weinman, Lynda, and William E. Weinman, *Creative HTML Design.* Indianapolis, Indiana: New Riders Publishing, 1998.

Wexelblat, Richard L., ed. *History of Programming Language Design.* New York: Academic Press, 1981.

Williams, Robin, and Dave Mark. *Home Sweet Home Page.* Berkeley, Calif.: Peachpit Press, 1996.

Winer, Ethan. "BASIC, Yes; Feeble, No." *PC Magazine* 8, no. 18 (October 31, 1989): 187.

Yahoo Editors. "Incredibly Useful Web Sites." *Yahoo Internet Life,* 4, no. 2 (February 1998) 72–74.

Yahoo Editors. "Anatomy of a Web Site." *Yahoo Internet Life,* 4, no. 2 (February 1998): 75–76.

Logo

Objectives

Upon completing this chapter, you will be able to:

1. Trace the development of Logo;

2. Define *primitive, procedure, recursion,* and *variable;*

3. Draw simple geometric shapes and patterns with Logo; and

4. Give the key arguments for and against teaching Logo.

Background

When artificial intelligence (AI) began to be developed in the 1950s, researchers were looking for a language to express concepts in human words. Their first attempt was a family of languages called Information Processing Languages (IPL) whose central idea was the list. By putting data in lists, the programmers linked concepts in the computer's memory, similar to the way AI researchers think ideas are stored in the human brain. John McCarthy, a distinguished member of the artificial intelligence community, established an AI lab at Massachusetts Institute of Technology and in 1958 started working on a language that combined the use of lists with a set of symbols. He borrowed concepts from a branch of mathematics named lambda calculus and called his high-level language **LISP,** an abbreviation for LISt Processing.

LISP is simply a language of lists of symbols held within parentheses. A small section of a LISP program may include dozens of pairs of list-defining parentheses such as (PUT(QUOTE BOAT) (QUOTE LOC) (QUOTE(9 4))). In this list, the function PUT assigns the Cartesian coordinates 9 and 4 to a boat's location; the function QUOTE tells the computer that the user wants to see the name of a list, not its value; and the symbol LOC is the name of the location that belongs to the symbol boat. This language is difficult to read, but because of its structure you can use it to write programs that modify other computer programs. In addition, you can write programs or subroutines that can refer to themselves in a process known as *recursion,* which gives the program the ability to repeat itself.

Presently, LISP is the principal programming language for AI research in the United States, and it's the second oldest general purpose language in use. LISP has ease, speed, and the ability to write, run, and modify programs. Because of LISP's unique properties, it has many spin-off languages, with **Logo,** a high-level language designed for children, being the most popular. Logo contains many functions found in LISP; however, Logo is less cryptic and is user friendly.

Historical Background

Seymour Papert, his MIT colleagues, and members of Bolt, Beranek, and Newman created Logo. Papert, a mathematics professor, studied with Jean Piaget and worked in artificial intelligence. He felt that school-age children could learn to program, and he was convinced that BASIC was too abstract for the young child. This belief motivated him to create Logo. It was originally used on mainframe computers, but because of advances in computer technology, programs were eventually devised for the microcomputer.

In 1979, the first version of Logo was written for the Apple and the Texas Instruments 99/4 computers. Since then, there has been a proliferation of Logo versions, including *Apple Logo, Logo II,* and *LogoWriter* (Logo Computer Systems) and *Logo Plus, Terrapin,* and *Krell* (MIT versions). Along with these programs are simplified versions such as *Turtle Math* (Logo Computer Systems). Papert's clever innovation, the turtle, was first introduced in the form of a mechanical turtle that crawled on the floor and later as a graphic on the screen. Using simple commands, children were able to write programs that moved the triangular turtle across the screen. For example, if a child gives the commands Forward 50, Right 90, and Forward 50, the turtle will move as follows:

Why Teach Logo?

Why would you choose Logo over BASIC? What makes this investment in software worthwhile? Logo is a simple language that lets the novice learn logic and programming in a brief time frame. Because it is structured, Logo encourages children to develop good programming techniques. Most teachers who use Logo in classrooms create designs that can help children learn geometric concepts and develop an intuitive sense of logical patterning. The nature of Logo makes it a good introduction to other procedural languages such as Pascal. A tool for creative exploration, Logo is also an interactive programming language that helps individuals learn from their mistakes. Users receive instantaneous feedback, allowing them to revise the program immediately.

There are some drawbacks to this language. Since Logo handles the processing of lists and operates on numbers and words, it requires a large memory and file-handling capabilities that are appropriate for more difficult and sophisticated applications. According to research (Chapter 16), evidence that Logo can improve problem solving and skill development is inconclusive.

Philosophy and Psychology of Logo

In 1980, Seymour Papert discussed in *Mindstorms* his theories on how a computer should be used in the classroom. He felt a computer is best utilized to aid in the thinking process and not as a piece of hardware that dispenses information. He observed that CAI usually meant that the computer was being used to program the child and the child was the passive receiver of information:

> "In my vision, the child programs the computer and, in doing so, both acquires a sense of mastery over a piece of the most modern and powerful technology and establishes an intimate contact with some of the deepest ideas from science, from mathematics, and from the art of intellectual model building" (Papert, 1980, p. 5).

According to Papert, Logo creates an environment in which children are free to explore and discover. They can learn geometric concepts, actively test and retest their theories, and develop their intellect. Papert argued that the majority of schools' mathematics programs have nothing to do with reality because the students are taught in a rote, meaningless way. According to Papert, this rote instruction is the reason most children grow up hating and fearing mathematics. Logo combats this problem by letting the child experience a meaningful mathematics environment. Furthermore, Papert saw other ways that Logo could aid learning across all curriculum areas. For example, in his book he presented the case study of a student named Jenny who had difficulty with English grammar. When she used Logo to generate poetry, she discovered the necessity of knowing the difference between a noun and a verb in order to teach the computer how to write poetry. Because Jenny used Logo, she found a meaningless activity now meaningful.

Papert used the term *microworld* to describe the Logo environment in which the child freely experiments, tests, and revises his or her own theories in order to create a product. Using the microworld, the child better understands concepts in analytical geometry, physics, grammar, and composition. It is a playground of the mind in which the learner explores a concept from an intuitive to a formal level. The product can be one the child wants to create to fulfill his or her needs, so the creation of this product is meaningful.

Logo has been used in all areas of the curriculum, even though the majority of programs in schools have focused on it as a tool to teach mathematics. Using Logo, students can explore mathematical topics such as simple geometry concepts, estimation skills, and topology. Students can use Logo for problem solving, breaking down problems into smaller parts, and debugging programs. In language arts, students can utilize *LogoWriter* or *MicroWorlds Project Builder,* which combine word processing with graphics, to create text for describing their Logo graphics work. Using Logo's simple, list-processing capabilities, students can teach the computer the parts of speech, subject-verb agreement, or poetry. In science, students can use a program such as *Lego TC Logo,* (Lego Group) which combines Legos with Logo programming to build objects and control their movements, and in the process students learn about physics and develop problem solving skills. Furthermore, with commercial kits, students can use the computer as a measuring tool. They can write their own simple Logo programs and have the computer generate charts or graphs. For example, students might use a thermistor, a device whose resistance varies with temperature, and use Logo to write a chart-graphic procedure that produces a graph of temperature changes. In social studies, students can use *MicroWorlds Project Builder* to write about geographical concepts or use Logo to create interesting maps.

Working with Logo

This Logo introduction should familiarize you with the basic concepts of Logo programming. Use the following examples to understand the full potential of this language. Type the sample programs, run them, and save them on a disk. The programs and illustrations are created on the Macintosh in *Terrapin Logo*. Program variations will be indicated in boldface type, and the *Logo Computer Systems Incorporated* (LCSI) Apple II version will be shown. (Even though the Apple II series is dead, approximately 30 percent of schools still use these computers.) In general, all Logo programs including the IBM versions are quite similar, so you should be able to make the transition from the chapter examples to your own version.

Insert a copy of Logo in the disk drive, boot it, and when the Welcome message appears, **type ST for SHOWTURTLE. One of the following turtles will appear:***

Logo II Turtle   Terrapin Turtle
🪳   Δ

Background

Logo primitives are commands built into the language itself. More than 100 of these commands exist, but you need to use just a few to program. The following table shows the primitives that we'll discuss in this chapter:

Primitive	Abbreviation	Explanation
SHOWTURTLE	ST	Shows the turtle.
HIDETURTLE	HT	Hides the turtle.
FORWARD	FD	Moves forward.
BACK	BK	Moves backward.
RIGHT	RT	Turns right.
LEFT	LT	Turns left.
CLEARSCREEN or CLEARGRAPHICS	CS or CG depending on version	Clears the screen.
PENUP	PU	Does not leave trail.
PENDOWN	PD	Leaves trail.
HOME	HOME	Returns home.

Used with permission of Terrapin Software, Inc., Portland, ME and LCSI are trademarks of Logo Computer Systems Inc., (Logo II Turtle) used with permission. Available from Terrapin Software, Inc., 400 Riverside St., Portland, Maine 01403.

When you type in one of these commands, you give it a numerical value and the turtle responds. For example, if you assign the command Forward a value of 50, the turtle will move forward fifty steps. Using an abbreviation for the primitive, type in the following instructions. Be sure to put a **space** between the primitive and the number and then press Return or Enter after the number.

1. Forward Example

FD 40

Output

Explanation.   The turtle moves forward forty steps.

2. Right Example

RT 90

Output

Explanation.   The turtle turns 90 degrees, based on a 360-degree turning ratio.

3. Backward Example

BK 40

Output

Explanation.   The turtle moves forty steps backward.

4. Left Example

LT 270

Output

Explanation.   The turtle turns 270 degrees to the left, based on a 360-degree circle.

5. Combination Example

FD 40 LT 90 FD 40

Output

Explanation.   The directions tell the turtle to move forward forty steps, turn left 90 degrees, and move forward forty more. These instructions allow the turtle to complete a square.

The Total Turtle Trip Theorem states that the turtle must turn a total of 360 degrees to go around a closed figure in order to return to its original direction.

6. HIDETURTLE Example

HT

Output

Explanation.   The drawing remains, but the turtle has disappeared from the screen.

7. CLEARSCREEN or CLEARGRAPHICS Example

CS or CG (CS clears the screen for *Apple Logo* and CG clears the graphics for *LogoWriter* and *Terrapin*.)

Explanation.   The drawings are cleared from the screen.

8. PENUP Example

```
ST
PU
FD 40
```

Output

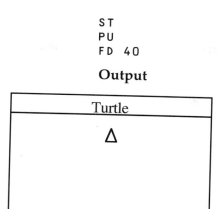

Explanation.   The ST command shows the turtle, and the PENUP command tells the computer to move the turtle without leaving a trail. FD 40 moves the turtle forward forty steps with no trail.

9. PENDOWN Example

```
PD
FD 20
```

Output

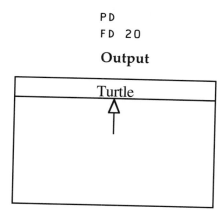

Explanation.   The PENDOWN command instructs the computer to reinstate the trail. After you type **PENDOWN,** every command that follows will leave a trail. FD 20 leaves a trail with twenty steps.

10. HOME Example

HOME

Output

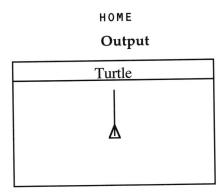

Explanation.   The HOME command returns the turtle to its original position.

11. REPEAT Example

After working awhile with Logo, you'll notice that you are reusing the same commands; the repeat command shortens this procedure.

Instructions.   Clear the screen by typing CS or CG.

REPEAT 4[FD 40 RT 90]

Output

Explanation.   This primitive tells the turtle to repeat the directions in the square brackets. In this example, the turtle repeats forty steps forward and a 90-degree right turn four times. When it stops, it has drawn a square. Using this repeat command, you can create interesting geometric patterns.

Procedures

So far, all the turtle can do is move forward or backward, turn right and left, and follow the REPEAT command to create a square. You have not taught it how to draw a square. Nevertheless, with the primitives you've learned, you can write a procedure, or set of instructions, to store in the computer's memory, essentially teaching the computer a new action. Let's teach the turtle how to draw a square.[1]

---

[1]Consult the owner's manual for the specific directions for getting into the editor and defining a procedure. Some versions execute the procedure outside the editor, while others execute the procedure inside the editor.

Square Procedure Example

Instructions.   Clear the screen and type the following procedure for creating a square. Be sure to leave a space between TO and SQUARE.

```
TO SQUARE
REPEAT 4[FD 40 RT 90]
HT
END
```

Instructions.   Type **SQUARE**. SQUARE is a new primitive that you have just added to Logo's vocabulary. Now you can use it whenever you want by simply typing the word.

Output

Explanation.   **TO** tells the computer that you are about to define a procedure and **SQUARE** is the name you've given to the procedure. (You just as easily could have called the procedure SQ or Box.) REPEAT 4 tells the computer to repeat four times what is in the brackets. FD 40, RT 90 creates a square. The HT hides the turtle, and END ends the program. Now let's create a design with the SQUARE procedure.

Design Subprocedure Example

Instructions.   Clear the screen and type the following procedure.

```
TO DESIGN
REPEAT 8 [SQUARE RT 45]
END
```

Instructions.   After the design has been defined, type DESIGN and press Return or Enter.

Output

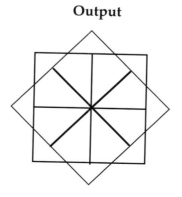

Explanation. The **TO** tells the computer that you are about to define a procedure and DE-SIGN is the name you've given to the procedure. The REPEAT command instructs the turtle to repeat eight times the procedure SQUARE and turn it 45 degrees each time. For practice, create a procedure for a star or a triangle.

Logo is a powerful language because you can use new words or procedures to define other words and can use a simple procedure to create a more complicated one. In the next example, we'll take two subprocedures that create circles and use them to create a Lazy 8 superprocedure.[2]

CIRCLE Example

Instructions. Clear the screen and type in the following procedure.

```
TO CIRCLE
REPEAT 36[FD 10 RT 10]
END
```

Instructions. After circle has been defined, type CIRCLE.

Output

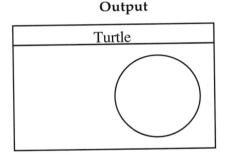

Explanation. The **TO** tells the computer that you are about to define a procedure and CIRCLE is the name you've given to the procedure. REPEAT 36 tells the computer to repeat thirty-six times what is in brackets [(FD 10, RT 10)], drawing a circle that is on the right side of the screen.

CIRCLEC Example

Instructions. Clear the screen and type in the following procedure.

```
TO CIRCLEC
REPEAT 36[FD 10 LT 10]
END
```

---

[2]A superprocedure is a procedure that uses other procedures, or subprocedures.

Instructions.   After CIRCLEC has been defined, type CIRCLEC and press Return or Enter.

Output

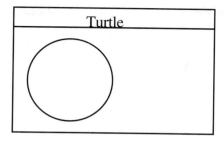

Explanation.   REPEAT tells the turtle to repeat thirty-six times what's inside the brackets, drawing a circle to the left.

LAZY 8 Example

Instructions.   The **TO** tells the computer that you are about to define a procedure and CIRCLEC is the name given to the procedure. Clear the screen and type the following procedure.

```
TO LAZY8
CIRCLE
CIRCLEC
END
```

Instructions.   After LAZY8 has been defined, type LAZY8 and press Return or Enter.

Output

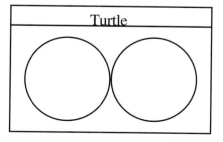

Explanation.   **TO** starts the Lazy 8 procedure. **CIRCLE** is the first subprocedure, and **CIRCLEC** is the second subprocedure. **END** finishes the new procedure.

As you work with Logo, you should experiment with more complicated projects such as designing a house. This task is not difficult if you break it into smaller components or subprocedures. Let us begin to create a house by first defining a procedure for the body.

Body Example

Instructions.   Clear the screen and show the turtle. Type in the following procedure.

```
TO BODY
REPEAT 4[FD 80 RT 90] FD 80
END
```

Instructions.   After the body is defined, type BODY.

Output

Explanation.   **TO** starts the procedure and **BODY** is its name. The repeat tells the computer to repeat what is inside the brackets, creating a square. FD 80 brings the turtle to the top, poised to draw a roof. Now you are ready to write a procedure for a roof.

Roof Example

Instructions.   Clear the screen and show the turtle. Type in the following procedure.

```
TO ROOF
RT 45 FD 57 RT 90 FD 57 RT 135 FD 81
END
```

Instructions.   After the roof is defined, type **ROOF.**

Output

Explanation.   Turn right 45 degrees (RT 45) and go forward 57 (FD 57) creates the left side of the roof. Turn right 90 degrees, which is two 45-degree angles (RT 90), and go forward 57 (FD 57) creates the right side of the roof. Turn right 135 degrees, which is three

45-degree angles (RT 135) and go forward 81 (FD 81) retraces the top side of the body, completing the roof.[3]

You now are able to write a superprocedure that will draw a house, using the subprocedures for body and roof.

House Example

Instructions.   Clear the screen, hide the turtle, and type the following procedure.

```
TO HOUSE
BODY
ROOF
HT
END
```

Instructions.   After the procedure for house is defined, type HOUSE and press Return or Enter.

Output

Explanation.   **TO** starts the procedure and **HOUSE** is its name. The first subprocedure executed is BODY, which uses the procedure it just learned. The second procedure executed is ROOF. HT hides the turtle, and the **END** statement ends the procedure.

When you write a procedure, you are using *modular programming,* which breaks the problem into separate components, each of which can be programmed as a separate unit. For this example, you separately created two components—a body and a roof—tested them to see if they ran, and then merged them into another procedure called HOUSE.

As you become experienced with Logo, you will create procedures for squares or circles of different sizes. These procedures are only applicable to the specified square or circle size. To avoid writing different procedures for each new circle or square, you can use variables.

Variables

Variables let you write only one procedure to cover all cases. A variable is a part of a procedure that changes when you tell it to change. Instead of typing FD 40 in the SQUARE procedure, type in :SIZE. In the following example, you can enter any size for the square.

---

[3]The roof is a right isosceles triangle whose hypotenuse (bottom side) is actually 80.6, but because of the screen's imperfections, 81 is used.

Square Variable Example

```
TO SQUARE :SIZE
REPEAT 4[FD :SIZE RT 90]
HT
END
```

Instructions.   After defining the procedure, type SQUARE followed by a number, for example, **SQUARE 10.**

Output

□

Explanation.   **TO** starts the procedure and **SQUARE** is the name of the new procedure. The colon is important because it tells the program you are naming a variable location. SIZE (**:SIZE**) is the name of the variable location for this procedure. There is no space between the colon and the word size. (You can use any name for the procedure as long as it is a letter or a word. For example, you can call it **:L** or **:INPUT.** Every time you run this procedure, you type the chosen name with a value.) The REPEAT command tells the turtle to repeat four times the set of actions inside the brackets. The HT command conceals the turtle and leaves the small square.

Recursion

Another powerful feature of Logo is recursion, which is the ability of a procedure to call itself as a subprocedure, using itself as part of its own definition. The program loops back and starts the procedure again, and this continues until you stop the program.

Pattern Recursion Example

Instructions.   Clear the screen. First create a square procedure such as the one enclosed in the following rectangle:

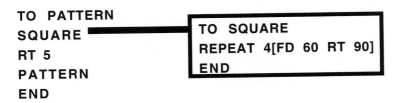

```
TO PATTERN
SQUARE
RT 5
PATTERN
END
```

```
TO SQUARE
REPEAT 4[FD 60 RT 90]
END
```

Instructions.   After you have defined the superprocedure pattern, type **PATTERN.**

Output

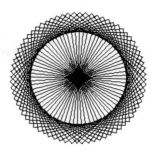

Explanation.   **TO** starts the procedure, and **PATTERN** is the name of the new procedure. The SQUARE procedure produces a square using FD 60 RT 90. The instructions for this subprocedure are enclosed in the box. The command RT 5 turns this square to the right 5 degrees. When the turtle reaches PATTERN, it repeats the same procedure, drawing a square and turning it 5 degrees to the right. The procedure reaches PATTERN again and repeats itself, continuing forever, if you want it to. Eventually the turtle will retrace its steps. If you hide the turtle, you can see its trail going around and around. The only way to stop this program in *Terrapin Logo* is to use Command G.[4] Let's work through another example using the same stop command.

EFFECT Example

```
TO EFFECT :SIZE
FD :SIZE RT 90
EFFECT :SIZE + 3
END
```

Instructions.   After defining **EFFECT,** type the name of the procedure with a value, such as EFFECT 3. Once the turtle has retraced many of its lines, use the stop command (Command **G**). Your output should look like this:

Output

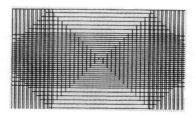

---

[4]Use the stop command that is appropriate for your version of Logo. *Terrapin Logo* (Macintosh version) uses Command G, *Logowriter* uses open Apple S, and *Apple Logo II* uses open Apple ESC.

Explanation.   **TO** starts the procedure and **EFFECT** is its name. The colon tells the program you are naming a variable location, and the word SIZE **(:SIZE)** is the name of the variable location for this procedure. FD :SIZE RT 90 tells the computer to go forward the number you enter (3) and turn right 90 degrees. **EFFECT :SIZE +3** tells the computer to run EFFECT with its present size (3) and increase it by three. The size will be increased by three every time this procedure is executed. Because of recursion, the **END** command is never reached. If you had not used the stop command, the program would have continued running forever.

You can halt a procedure within a program with a conditional statement such as IF S>50[STOP] or IF S>50 STOP. If the statement is true, the program ends; if the statement is false, the procedure continues until the statement becomes true. The following procedure shows the previous example with a conditional statement. Type the following procedure.

STOP Example

```
TO EFFECT :SIZE
IF :SIZE = 171 [STOP]
FD :SIZE RT 90
EFFECT :SIZE + 3
END
```

Instructions.   After EFFECT is defined, type EFFECT 3.

Output

Explanation.   **TO** starts the procedure and **EFFECT** is the name of the new procedure. The colon tells the program you are naming a variable location, and the word SIZE **(:SIZE)** is the name of the variable location for this procedure. **IF :SIZE=171[STOP]** tells the turtle to stop when it reaches a size of 171. The next line tells the turtle to go forward the number you enter (3) and turn 90 degrees. **EFFECT :SIZE + 3** tells the turtle to run EFFECT and increase the size by three. **END** ends the program once the value for SIZE is equal to 171.

Logo's Other Features

By now, you should be familiar with primitives, procedures, variables, and recursion. These powerful ideas apply to other parts of Logo, not just turtle graphics. Besides drawing pictures, Logo has many other capabilities; you can use it to work with numbers, words, and lists.

Logo knows how to add, subtract, multiply, and divide, using the symbols +, −, *, and /. You can instruct Logo to add three numbers by typing PRINT.

Add Example

```
PRINT 50+40+66
```

Output

```
156
```

Logo interprets a word as a series of characters with no blanks to separate them, so you can have Logo print out words by typing them.

Print Example

```
Print"Computer
```

Output

```
Computer
```

By working with lists, you can handle complex sets of information. A list is a set of words separated by blanks and enclosed in brackets: [computer monitor printer scanner]. Whenever you work with Logo in this capacity, you must use special commands that operate with lists of words. These commands can randomly pick out a name, a phrase, or a closing message. Besides working with words, numbers, and lists, many versions of Logo can produce music. You can then write sound effects to accompany graphics. For a more in-depth discussion of Logo, refer to the Logo books listed at the end of the chapter.

Other Versions of Logo

Originally, Logo lacked turtle graphics, ran only on mainframes, and used slow printers; however, there has been dramatic improvement in Logo. Logo now has sound graphics, excellent color, and telecommunication and database capabilities. Starting with *Turtle Math,* let us examine some other versions of Logo.

Turtle Math

Turtle Math (LCSI) is a popular program among teachers who want to introduce young children to the Logo language. An independent, simplified version of Logo, *Turtle Math* (Fig. 15.1) lets students explore such topics as probability, patterns, computation, and transformation.

Students use Logo commands to create lines, angles, and shapes. *Turtle Math* has three windows: the command window, the drawing window, and the teach window. When students type a command in the command window, they see the turtle move in response in the draw window.

Figure 15.1
Turtle Math
Turtle Math by Douglas H.
Clements & Julie Sarama
Meredith. Copyright 1994,
D. H. Clements, LCSI. All
rights reserved. *LogoWriter,
Turtle Math, MicroWorlds
Project Builder* and LSCI
are trademarks of Logo
Computer Systems, Inc.
Used with permission of
Terrapin Software, Inc.,
Portland, ME.

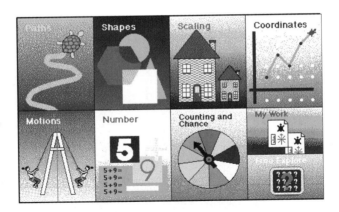

They are introduced to turtle commands and movement and learn to direct the turtle's motion on the screen. *Turtle Math* has a series of thirty-six built-in investigations and thirty activities organized according to topic. Using this program, children can create original drawings that can be saved as retrievable procedures.

LogoWriter

In 1986, LCSI released *LogoWriter,* a program that increased Logo's flexibility by combining programming capabilities with word processing. The programming part of *LogoWriter* is similar to that of *Logo II,* while the word processing component lets the *LogoWriter* user search and replace and copy, cut, and paste text. Programmers also can change the turtle into other objects such as helicopters, rabbits, or heads.

Besides using multiple turtle shapes, *LogoWriter* lets users print, save, and exit files. It creates animation, music, and sound effects and has a customized text editor. Students learn *LogoWriter* through a series of booklets and activity cards, covering all curriculum areas. Even with these positive features, *LogoWriter* is still a more difficult program to use than Logo because of its depth of features.

MicroWorlds Project Builder

MicroWorlds Project Builder (LCSI) introduces students to problem solving and creative thinking. Students use this Logo-based tool kit to create projects for any subject in the curriculum. It includes a projects book that takes students through the process of creating projects such as interactive newspapers or simple ecosystems. These projects can combine text, graphics, music, and animation (Fig. 15.2).

The program features drawing tools, predesigned background scenes, 140 colors, and an infinite number of turtles that can be set to any size or shape. Students can utilize a sound center to add their own musical creations to their projects. The program has a built-in word processor with features such as multiple text boxes; different fonts, sizes, styles, and colors; and the ability to place graphics. *MicroWorlds Proejct Builder* lets students create buttons, sliders, and hot spots to start and stop projects or hypermedia links. The program comes with a teacher's resource guide and a how-to book with a complete reference guide. If students run across a road block while using the program, there is comprehensive on-line help with built-in information balloons.

Figure 15.2
MicroWorlds Project Builder
LogoWriter and *MicroWorlds Project Builder.* Copyright 1994, LCSI. All rights reserved. *LogoWriter, Turtle Math, MicroWorlds Project Builder* and LCSI are trademarks of Logo Computer Systems, Inc.

Lego TC Logo

Using *Lego TC Logo,* students build machines in the form of cars, boats, towers, and trucks that include motors, sensors, and gears. After these machines are built, students connect them with wires and an interface box to a computer that speaks the proper dialect of Logo. Using a few simple commands, students write computer programs to control the machines. These commands turn the motors off and on and send them in various directions.

Lego TC Logo uses primitives such as ON, OFF, and RD (reverse directions), which are appropriate for machines. Because many students have built objects using Lego blocks, this program uses the already familiar Lego block as the main building tool. *Lego TC Logo* is really a relic of the early days of Logo programming when the experimenters with Logo used a "floor turtle," a mechanical robot connected to the computer by a cord. When video display terminals came along, the focus shifted to a "screen turtle" that was faster and more accurate than the floor turtle. Logo/Lego brings back the floor turtle with a few differences. Students are not restricted to turtles but can build all sorts of machines.

The Logo/Lego package includes an assortment of gears, wheels, motors, lights, and sensors. Students can send commands to Lego motors and lights and receive information from Lego sensors. The program can make a truck turn to the right or reverse direction when the truck touches a wall. Students can engage in all kinds of experimentation and they can learn the importance of changing only one variable at a time. They can use the scientific method as they invent their machines, and when they have problems with their inventions, they can develop hypotheses and test them out. When students use this computer-based system, they engage in data gathering, record keeping, and brainstorming.

Appendix A features an annotated list of Logo software programs that are useful for the classroom.

Summary

Logo has four powerful components: primitives, procedures, variables, and recursion. In 1970, Logo was derived from LISP by Seymour Papert and colleagues. Papert's orientation toward Logo grew out of Piaget's theories. According to Papert's theory, children learn best by constructing their own knowledge, building their own programs, and developing their own designs in meaningful interactions. Children control the computer instead of being controlled by the computer. Logo's intent is to make students analyze what has happened and what will happen in the future. Although Logo was designed with the child in mind, this programming language can be very sophisticated. There are cogent reasons for studying Logo: (1) It is a structured language that encourages good programming techniques; (2) It is a unique tool for exploration; and (3) It is a suitable introductory language.

Chapter Mastery Test

1. Describe briefly four characteristics of Logo.

2. Briefly define primitives, procedures, and recursion.

3. Give two key arguments for and two arguments against teaching Logo in the classroom.

4. Write a program that will draw a square, a rectangle, or a circle.

5. Briefly discuss Seymour Papert's philosophy.

6. Write a Logo program that produces the following design:

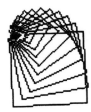

7. Write a simple procedure using a REPEAT command.

8. Sketch what the following procedures A and B will create:

PROCEDURE A	PROCEDURE B
TO A	TO B
RT 90	REPEAT 4[FD 10 PU FD 20 PD FD 10 RT 90]
REPEAT 6[FD 10 PU FD 10 PD]	END
END	

9. Explain what makes *Lego TC Logo* a good teaching tool.

10. What distinguishes *MicroWorld Project Builder* from *Logo?*

11. Explain The Total Turtle Trip Theorem.

12. Give two advantages that Logo has over another programming language.

Classroom Projects

1. Write a procedure that designs a house with windows and doors.

2. Produce the following graphic by writing out commands:

3. Copy a maze onto a transparency and then tape it to the monitor screen. Next, drive a Logo turtle through the maze.

4. Debug the following two programs. The first program produces a square; the second procedure draws a curved line.

   Program 1   TO SQUARE
                       REPEAT 4[FD 20 RT 60]
                       END

   Program 2   TO CURVE
                       REPEAT[FD 10 RT 10]
                       END

5. Experiment and create a design; then print it out for the class.

Suggested Readings and References

Abelson, H., and Andrea DiSessa. *Turtle Geometry.* Cambridge, Mass.: MIT Press, 1980.

Abelson, Harold. *Logo for the Apple II.* Peterborough, N.H.: Byte Books, McGraw-Hill, 1982.

Bitter, Gary G. *Apple Logo Primer.* Reston, Va.: Reston Publishing, 1983.

Cohen, Laura. *Logo Activity Cards: Problem Solving with a Turtle.* Compton, Calif.: Educational Insights, 1985.

Cohen, Rina S. "Computerized Learner Supports in Pre-Logo Programming Environments." *Journal of Research on Computing in Education* 22, no. 3 (spring 1990): 310.

Dunn, S., and V. Morgan. *The Impact of Computers on Education: A Course for Teachers.* Englewood Cliffs, N.J.: Prentice Hall, 1987.

A First Course in Programming in Terrapin Logo, LogoWriter, and PC Logo. Colorado Springs, Colo.: Logo Curriculum Publishers, 1991.

Goldenberg, Paul E. *Exploring Language with Logo.* Cambridge, Mass.: MIT Press, 1987.

Harper, Dennis. *Logo Theory & Practice.* Pacific Grove, Calif.: Brooks/Cole Publishing, 1989.

Heller, Rachelle S., and C. Dianne Martin. *Logoworlds.* Baltimore, Md.: Computer Science Press, 1985.

Hoyles, Celia. *Logo Mathematics in the Classroom.* New York: Routledge, 1989.

Jones, Linda. *Learning and Teaching with Logo II.* Northridge, Calif.: California State University Northridge, September 1990.

Kolodiy, George Oleh. "Science: Logo in the Science Laboratory." *The Computing Teacher* 18, no. 5 (February 1991): 41–43.

Labinowicz, Ed. *The Piaget Primer: Thinking, Learning, Teaching.* Menlo Park, Calif.: Addison Wesley, 1980.

Martin, Donald. *Apple Logo Programming Primer: Featuring Top-Down Structured Programming.* Indianapolis, Ind.: H.W. Sams, 1984.

Martin, Kathleen, and Donna Bearden. *Mathematics and Logo.* Reston, Va.: Reston Publishing, 1985.

Mathinos, Debra A. "Logo Programming and the Refinement of Problem Solving Skills in Disabled and Nondisabled Children." *Journal of Educational Computing Research* 6, no. 4 (1990): 429.

Muir, Michael. "Talk & Draw: Logo and Artificial Intelligence." *The Computing Teacher* 18, no. 7 (April 1991): 31–33.

Nastasi, Bonnie, K., Douglas H. Clements, and M. T. Battista. "Social-Cognitive Interactions, Motivation and Cognitive Growth in Logo Programming and CAI Problem-Solving Environments." *Journal of Educational Psychology* 82, no. 1 (March 1, 1990): 150.

Olive, John. "Logo Programming and Geometric Understanding: An In-Depth Study." *Journal for Research in Mathematics Education* 22, no. 2 (March 1, 1991): 90.

Ortiz, Enrique, and S. MacGregor. "Effects of Logo Programming on Understanding Variables." *Journal of Educational Computing Research* 7, no. 1 (1991): 37.

Papert, S. *The Children's Machine.* New York: Basic Books, 1993.

Papert, S. "Different Visions of Logo." *Computers in the School* (summer/fall 1985): 3–8.

Papert, S. "Educational Computing: How Are We Doing?" *T.H.E. Journal* 24, no. 11 (June 1997): 78–80.

Papert, S. *Mindstorms: Children, Computers and Powerful Ideas.* New York: Basic Books, 1980.

Papert, S. "The Next Step: LogoWriter." *Classroom Computer Learning* (April 1986): 38–40.

Piaget, J. *The Construction of Reality in the Child.* New York: Basic Books, 1954.

Reinhold, F. "An Interview with Seymour Papert." *Electronic Learning* (April 1986): 35–36.

Rosen, M. "Lego Meets Logo." *Classroom Computer Learning* (April 1988): 50–58.

Ruane, Pat. *Logo Activities for the Computer: A Beginner's Guide.* New York: Julian Messner, 1984.

Swan, Karen. "Programming Objects to Think With: Logo and the Teaching and Learning of Problem Solving." *Journal of Educational Computing Research* 7, no. 1 (1991): 89.

Watt, D. *Learning with Logo.* New York: McGraw-Hill, 1983.

Watt, M. "What Is Logo?" *Creative Computing* (October 1982): 121–26.

Weir, Sylvia. *Cultivating Minds: A Logo Casebook.* New York: Harper & Row, 1987.

Weston, Dan. *The Second Logo Book: Advanced Techniques in Logo.* Glenview, Ill.: Scott, Foresman, 1985.

Yoder, Sharon. "Logo for Teachers." *The Computing Teacher* 18, no. 8 (May 1991): 33–34.

Yoder, Sharon. "Mousing Around with Your Turtle . . . Or Turtling Around with Your Mouse?" *The Computing Teacher* 19, no. 12 (August/September 1991): 41–43.

Zaskis, Rina. "Implementing Powerful Ideas: The Case of RUN. Variation on a Simple Logo Task: Introduce Students to Advanced Programming." *The Computing Teacher* 17, no. 6 (March 1, 1990): 40.

Issues and Research: Present and Future

16

Objectives

Upon completing this chapter, you will be able to:

1. Identify and discuss major ethical issues regarding computers;
2. Describe three factors related to computer privacy;
3. Define the term *virus* and explain some precautions for preventing a virus from infecting a computer system;
4. Define *computer-assisted instruction* (CAI) and summarize general research findings about CAI;
5. Summarize the research findings on CAI and (a) gender differences, (b) science

simulations, (c) learning time, (d) word processing, (e) learning by disabled students, (f) motivation and attitude, (g) Logo and problem solving, and (h) programming;
6. explain what artificial intelligence is and describe its application in the classroom;
7. explain two ways the computer can help the disabled;
8. discuss how technology will change the traditional roles in education of the teacher, students, and parents; and
9. discuss three ways to lessen the chance of computer-related injuries.

Ethical Issues

Computers have benefited us in many ways. Computers have improved education, medical care, and business operations. Computers have also helped artists be more creative and allowed factories and businesses to operate more efficiently and effectively.

Unfortunately, no advance comes without disadvantages. In this section, we will examine some of the problems associated with computer technology, including invasion of privacy, computer crime, software piracy, computer viruses, and health risks.

Privacy

The concern for privacy is an issue that is not unique to computerized systems, but such systems increase the likelihood that an individual's privacy will be invaded. There are many different computerized systems, and these systems contain many different types of information. If a person lives in the United States, his or her name appears in federal, state, and local government data banks and in many private sector files.[1] The Internal Revenue Service keeps files on everyone who files tax returns. State and local governments maintain files concerning taxes and law enforcement, public and private institutions keep records on students' educational performance, and medical data banks store medical records. It is hard to determine exactly who has what information and how this information will be used. The Society for Human Resource Management (SHRM) did a research survey of more than 500 group members of primarily human resource professionals. They found that 36 percent of the organizations providing e-mail to customers look at their employee's e-mail records for business purposes or security, and 75 percent of those polled felt that employers should have the right to read company-provided e-mail. Personal information such as addresses, telephone numbers, and maps to homes is accessible through the Internet. A technology called a *cookie* keeps records of the on-line activities on your hard drive. "Cookies are data entries sent from a Web server to a special file on your machine" (Dyrli, 1997). A cookie gives the server the name of the site you visited and information about your choices, and when you return to the site, it requests information from your cookie file and gets even more data on your habits.

With so many different types of computerized systems, financial or academic indiscretions of ten years ago may return to haunt you. Information that you provided for one purpose may be used for another. The computer poses a threat to our privacy, and we should be concerned about the possibility of unauthorized persons or groups gaining access to personal information simply by entering a social security number into a system. By looking at statements of charges from the Cigar Warehouse, Ticketron, Kids Mart, Egghead Software, and Foreign Automotive, a "computer detective" can deduce that you like cigars, go to the theater, have children, and own a computer and a foreign automobile. If bills are examined over an extended period of time, a personal, psychological, and economic profile can be developed, and this information could be used to bilk you out of huge sums of money—or even to blackmail you.

Another concern regarding invasion of privacy is computer record matching, the comparison of files stored in different governmental agencies on the same individual. Law enforcement agencies use computer matching to find a criminal by comparing the Medicare files and Social Security benefits files to identify individuals who are believed deceased but still "receiving" Social Security checks. Supporters of this use of the computer argue that people who break the law should be punished and this procedure saves the taxpayers money. Opponents argue that it uses information for a purpose different from what was originally intended. If the people who supplied the information thought that it would be used against them, they might falsify data or not supply the needed information, impeding the operation of the asking agencies and costing the taxpayers money.

In the 1970s, a series of laws were enacted to protect privacy by controlling the collection and dissemination of information. The Freedom of Information Act (1970) gave individuals access to information about themselves collected by federal agencies. The Fair Credit Reporting Act (1970) gave citizens the right to access data about themselves, challenge it, and correct it. Under the

---

[1]A data bank is an electronic storehouse for data.

Privacy Act of 1974, people can decide what data would be recorded by a government agency and how it would be used. If the agency makes a mistake recording this data, people must be given a method for correcting it. This act required the organization or agency to make sure the data were correctly collected, thereby preventing unauthorized use of the data. The Privacy Act also stated that data collected for one purpose could not be used for another.

The Privacy Act of 1974 was sweeping in its changes, but unfortunately it did not reach beyond federal governmental abuses. The Family Education Rights and Privacy Act (1974) regulated access to public and private school grades and anecdotal records stored on computer. The Right to Financial Privacy Act (1978) limited how much access the government could have to a person's records stored at any financial institution, and it protected, to a small degree, the confidentiality of a person's financial records. The Comprehensive Crime Control Act (1984) prohibited unauthorized individuals from accessing a computer file to obtain information protected by the Right to Financial Privacy Act; it also protected any information found in a consumer agency file. The Comprehensive Crime Control Act made it illegal for private individuals to modify, destroy, disclose, or use information stored in a government computer. In the early 1980s there still were no clear laws to prevent individuals from accessing military computers or the White House computers. Ian Murphy, a twenty-four-year-old hacker[2] called "Captain Zap" changed this situation when he and three companions used a home computer and telephone lines to hack into electronic companies, merchandise order records, and government documents. The group was caught and indicted for receiving stolen property. Murphy was fined $1,000 and sentenced to a 2 1/2-year jail term. After this case, legislators spent several years in research and discussion. The culmination was the Computer Fraud and Abuse Act of 1986, "A U.S. federal law that criminalizes the abuse of U.S. government computers or networks that cross state boundaries" (Pfaffenberger, 1997). Fines and prison sentences are given for illegal access, theft of credit data, and spying. Herbert Zinn, a Cornell high school dropout, was the first case to test this law. He was convicted on January 23, 1989, under the Computer Fraud and Abuse Act of breaking into AT&T and Department of Defense systems. He destroyed $174,000 worth of files, copied programs worth millions of dollars, and published passwords and ways to circumvent computer security systems. Because Zinn was not eighteen, he was only sentenced to nine months in prison and fined $10,000. However, if Zinn had been eighteen, he would have received thirteen years in prison and a fine of $80,000.

Numerous states have adopted laws to address the privacy issue, but litigation of violations has been very limited (BloomBecker, 1998) compared to other computer crimes such as theft of time. The primary reason is that many people are unaware that their rights have been violated because the data is transferred electronically. The individuals who are aware hesitate to take claims to court because of the inevitable exposure of their private lives.

In the future, other laws will be enacted because, even though few computer crimes have been reported and fewer still prosecuted, computer crime in general has escalated. In 1989, Buck BloomBecker conducted a study of computer security professionals. He found that only

---

[2]A hacker is a computer programming expert, or someone who illegally accesses and tampers with computer files.

6 percent of the crimes were reported: "There is no direct relationship in the number of computers in use and the number of prosecutions" (BloomBecker, 1998). In 1994, BloomBecker reported the number of such prosecutions that occurred in California between 1986 and 1992 (Table 16.1).

Table 16.1

1986	1987	1988	1989	1990	1991	1992
29	53	27	16	13	13	31

BloomBecker, Jay J. Buck "View Point, My Three Computer Criminological Sins." *Communications of ACM*, November, 1994, vol 37, No. 11, pages 15–16.

From this data, you can see that computer crime is not a high priority in the legal system. As concerned citizens, we must continue to use computer technology for our benefit while remaining vigilant for abuses.

Crime

Earlier, we discussed the controversial use of computerized records by government agencies and private companies to fight crimes. Let's examine now the ways that criminals use computers to commit crimes such as embezzlement, accessing records without authorization, and software pirating.

Today, there are many examples of computer crime or abuse. The cost to the nation amounts to billions of dollars in lost time and services (BloomBecker, 1998). Criminals steal computers from people's homes and department stores, manipulate financial accounts, break into secret governmental computer files, and even use computer on-line services to lure young people to their homes.

Some criminal violations are perpetrated by hackers for simple amusement. Members of the 414 Club, a well-known hackers' organization,[3] made a game out of accessing private computer files. By the time the FBI apprehended them in 1983, they had broken into many different business and government computers.

Not all hackers are interested solely in the thrill of accessing files. The Stanley Rifkin case is a perfect example of a computer crime perpetrated for money. Stanley Rifkin, a bank consultant, posed as a Security Pacific Bank employee to enter the wire funds transfer room of the bank.[4] He used the password number that was taped to the wall of the computer terminal to dial the Federal Reserve Bank number and transfer $10.2 million into his private account. He then withdrew the money, took it to Switzerland, and bought diamonds with it. This crime would have gone undetected if Rifkin had not confided in an attorney he knew.

There are many reasons for the proliferation of these types of crimes today. A key reason is that more individuals are working with computers, so more people have become knowledgeable about computer operations. In addition, the disparity between existing computer technology

---

[3]These hackers were called the 414 Club by the FBI because their area code was 414.

[4]Security Pacific Bank was formerly known as Security Pacific National Bank.

and our ability to control it is widening. Finally, biased news coverage causes many people to be more accepting of computer crimes than other crimes.

Software Piracy

Thomas Jefferson (1743–1826) once said, "Some are born good, some make good, some are caught with the goods." Thousands of illegal copies of software are made each year. The Software Publishers Association (SPA) (1998) estimated that in the United States $7.5 billion per year in revenue is lost to software **piracy.** Software that is illegally copied and may be distributed worldwide. Software companies are suffering tremendous losses from software pirates—$11.3 billion globally in 1996 (Software Publishers Association, 1995). Software copies work as well as the original and sell for less money. Unfortunately, piracy is easy and only the large piracy rings are caught. Moreover, software pirates know they will not serve hard jail time because of the overcrowding of our prisons with people who commit more serious offenses (BloomBecker, 1998). Even the U.S. government's Department of Justice was involved in stealing copyrighted software. The University of Oregon was charged with using pirated software and had to pay restitution to the SPA's Copyright Protection Fund (Groner, 1992). An SPA report found many forms of software piracy on the Internet (SPA, 1996c). Internet sites have pirated software for free downloading, and bulletin boards give you these links. For example, a college student at the University of Puget Sound, Washington was caught illegally copying and distributing software via the Internet (Software Publishers Association Announces Settlement with College Student. (1997) http://www.spa.org/piracy/releases/puget.htm). In the 1980s one of the most popular computer programs was a copy program that was able to duplicate protected software. It is speculated that 30 percent to 50 percent of a typical school's software has been illegally copied. Some teachers have sent illegally copied software to the software manufacturer for repair when they had problems with it. People who would never think of stealing from a department store freely make illegal copies of software, justifying their dishonesty with the following rationalizations: (1) Software developers receive free publicity for their products through illegal copies; (2) software is grossly overpriced and, therefore, fair game for piracy; (3) teachers believe copying software is for the greater good of their students; and (4) the cost of copying software is borne by the developer and not the customer and developers have money to spare. The truth is that software developers never condone illegal copying; they expect buyers to use only a single copy of their products and make one backup. Software is very expensive to produce and market. The cost of copying software is borne initially by the developers, but it is ultimately paid for by the legitimate buyer (Guglielmo, 1992).

The unauthorized duplication of software violates the federal copyright law and deprives developers of the revenue they richly deserve. The law clearly states that "anyone who violates any of the rights of the copyright owner . . . is an infringer of the copyright" Federal Copyright Law (Section 501). Reproducing computer software without the proper authorization is a federal offense. The money paid for a piece of software represents a fee for one copy and does not give the user the right to copy freely. Civil damages for unauthorized copying can amount to as much as $100,000. Criminal penalties include jail and fines Federal Copyright Law (Title 18 Section 2319(b)). Many bills have been introduced in Congress to strengthen the copyright laws and increase the penalties for illegal copying. The software piracy issue is certain to receive continued legal attention. The SPA has tried to help the software industry by having a hotline for reporting software violations (1-800-388-7478). If the SPA finds a violation, they either work with the offending institution or petition the federal court for a seizure order. This organization represents the leading software publishers in education, business, and home use.

Software developers have produced elaborate copy protection schemes to combat the piracy problem. One method is to build instructions into the program that will override any command to copy the software. The problem with this method is the hackers can easily create a program that gets around this copy protection. Another method uses software fingerprints, an emerging protection method. Fingerprinting is a technique that examines a computer system's individual configuration to collect information that can be used as the system's unique identification. The data are selectively encrypted together to build a unique identifier that sets off a "time bomb" in the software program if the user does not pay. The program will erase itself along with any files that it created. Another method used is to program the software so it is linked to serial numbers inside the chips or logic board of the computer unit (Quinlan, 1991). Yet for every scheme that is devised, a copy buster program is developed to override it.

Unfortunately, schools are a major culprit in educational software piracy. Why do schools copy illegally? Many schools and districts are anxious to integrate the computer into the classroom. They have limited funds, and one copy for thirty-two students is not enough for group participation. Teachers want many copies so that they can have a group of students using the same software simultaneously. They view copying software as equivalent to photocopying teacher-made tests for their classrooms. In the end, the educator is the loser: Companies cannot make a profit selling educational software so they divert their money to manufacturing products that are more economically lucrative. Software pirates ultimately drive smaller companies out of business.

What can school districts do to dissuade teachers or students from illegally copying software? They can warn teachers about illegally duplicating software and institute some disciplinary action when violations occur. Furthermore, schools can keep software locked away in restricted areas and limit student and teacher access. They can appoint a person or committee to be responsible for keeping records on the software purchased and how it is being used. This group would maintain a log of the software purchased and the machine on which the software resides. In addition, districts can require that teachers supervise students when they use software.

In the classroom, teachers can discuss recent criminal cases or a movie such as *War Games* to make students aware of the problems involved. Teachers can explain the federal and state laws and the differences between a felony, a crime punishable by a year in prison, and a misdemeanor, a crime punishable by a fine or a prison term. After the students have an understanding of the seriousness of computer crimes, they can devise a computer break-in policy for the school. The teacher can give each student a copy of this policy to study and read. Using this break-in policy, the teacher can present hypothetical cases concerning computer ethic breaches and ask the students what punishment they would recommend for the offender.

Teachers should find better ways to combat their budget constraints. Buying lab packs or multiple copies of software is one answer. The district could be encouraged to buy on-site licenses for selected programs, allowing the schools to make legal multiple copies and do multiple loadings of a program.[5]

Schools should also move toward networking their machines, which would enable schools to run a networkable piece of software over multiple machines. Educators should buy software that includes a backup copy or that offers a backup at a reduced rate. Finally, teachers should involve students, parents, and the community in raising money for software. In the long term, it is better to purchase the software than to steal it because the buyer receives technical support and upgrades from the publisher. Most important, it is the honorable and ethical way to operate.

Viruses

Another harmful force in computing today is the **virus,** a set of instructions that infects computer files by duplicating itself. A malicious individual writes a code and buries it in an existing program. When the program is loaded into the computer, the virus attaches itself to other programs that are residing in the system. When a person inserts a disk thus infected into a computer's memory, the computer's files become infected. The reverse is also true; that is, a disk used in an infected computer becomes infected. Computers can be infected electronically when a hacker creates a virus and sends it over the phone lines to a local network. Since the network is connected to thousands of computers, the infection is carried to all the connected computers. When the virus arrives at each of these computers, it performs the assignment it was created to do.

A virus program can be somewhat harmless, simply producing an obscene or silly message unexpectedly on the computer screen. But it can be a very destructive force, wiping out huge amounts of data. For example, a recent version of a popular utility program contained a virus that destroyed all the data on the user's hard disk. Needless to say, the company rectified the situation by shipping a new version without the virus. A virus can also find bank accounts with certain names and give the owners large sums of money.

Viruses are very hard to detect because they can be programmed to wreak havoc immediately or to lie dormant until a given future date. Viruses that are programmed to go off at a certain time are called *time bombs.* They start doing the damage at a certain time on a certain date. For example, the famous Michelangelo virus, named after the artist, activated itself on Michelangelo's birthday. Another enemy of the computer user is the *worm,* which is sometimes confused with a virus. The virus is a piece of code that adds itself to other programs and cannot run independently. The worm is a program that can run by itself and replicate a full working version to other computers. The worm is "designated to find all data in memory or on disk and alter any data it encounters" (Pfaffenberger, 1997). After the worm is finished with its work, the data is usually corrupted and irretrievable. A famous example, called the Internet Worm, occurred on November 2, 1988. This program, authored by Robert T. Morris, a graduate student in Computer Science at Cornell, was responsible for disrupting the operations of more than 6,000 computers nationwide. A whole industry of virus protection software such as *Symantec's Norton AntiVirus,*

---

[5]Multiple loadings refers to loading a program from one disk onto several computers.

or *SAM* (Fig. 16.1), and *Virex* (Dr. Solomon's) has come into existence to combat the different types of viruses. The software scans for viruses, repairs damaged files, and prints status reports.

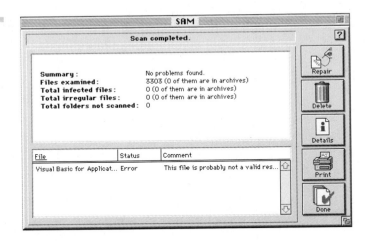

Figure 16.1
Symantec AntiVirus (SAM)
Reprinted by permission of Symantec Corporation.

Unfortunately, these antivirus programs are imperfect at best, because new undetectable viruses pop up all the time. According to Patricia Hoffman, antiviral researcher, "We are currently keeping track of about 3,732 computer viruses for MS-DOS computers" (Hoffman, 1997). Verna Knee, customer service specialist for *Symantec AntiVirus*, said, "Presently, there are over 32 viruses for the Macintosh computers and 12,793 for those with Windows installed." Furthermore, there are 1,467 macro viruses that affect Macintosh as well as Windows machines. Ten to fifteen new viruses are discovered every day (Symanics AntiVirus Research Center http://www.sarc.com).

The best protection against virus infection involves certain precautions, including the following: (1) frequently back up your hard disk; (2) download into a single computer as opposed to a networked system; (3) use virus protection programs to check every piece of software for a virus before loading it into the computer's memory; (4) do not store data on a program disk; and (5) always write protect program disks so that they cannot be destroyed.

Viruses certainly pose a threat to our computer systems, and this threat is increasing daily as we depend more and more on these technology wizards. However, some warnings about computer viruses are computer hoaxes. In 1997, a famous example, called Good Times, appeared. Many of us received a warning that said, "Beware of e-mail bearing the title Good Times." It went on to say, "Don't open this message; delete it immediately. If you read the message it will unleash a virus that will damage your computer hard drive and destroy your computer." The warning then tells you to e-mail your friends and tell them about this threat. Even some of the experts were scared, and big corporations fell for this hoax. In reality, simple e-mail cannot contain a virus; it has to be attached to an executable program. This hoax in effect is a self-replicating e-mail virus but not a computer virus. This hoax tricks individuals into replicating the e-mail message.

Security

Clearly, there is an urgent need for computer security. Computer owners must take steps to prevent theft and inappropriate use of their equipment. Computer users should be required to provide positive identification and computer access should be controlled. According to the insurance agency, Safeware, theft accounted for $1,011,000 of the estimated $2 billion in computer losses in the United States in 1993. In that year, computer-related losses were up approximately 53 percent, from $1.3 billion in 1992. "Theft of computers and intellectual property is a growing global problem costing an estimated 12 billion annually." (CANADEXPORT ON-LINE, January 31, 1997, http://www.dfait-maeci.gc.ca/english/news/newsletr/canex/97013lae.htm/)

Today, most computer facilities have some sort of security system. These facilities have means of confirming the identities of persons who want to use the system so that unauthorized users do not gain access. Usually, authorized users are issued special cards, keys, passwords, or account numbers. In elementary schools and high schools, this identification system may consist of a simple list of names. Each person on this list has a key that provides access to a computer room with bolted-down machines. Unfortunately, some users lend their keys and share their passwords. Often when computer users are allowed to choose their passwords, they choose easy-to-remember and easy-to-guess passwords.

One way to avert these problems is to assign access codes that are read by the computer from passcards. The user does not have to remember this number, so the number can be complex. Even if the card is stolen, the code can be changed when the theft is reported. Another way of increasing security is to require every individual to enter a special code with his or her card. Experts advise going a step further by checking people's personnel files for problems and restricting the number of people with access and the type of access they have to the computer. For instance, at most universities, students and professors use the same computer center, but they are not given the same access. Typically, the students have fewer privileges than the professors.

Another security problem concerns the protection of the operating system and data on the computer. It is essential that security measures protect all operating systems. Unscrupulous individuals have found ways to circumvent the system to print out a list of users' passwords, to give themselves access rights they are not officially assigned, and to spread viruses. For these reasons, all sensitive data should be stored and locked up when not in use. Some large companies use data encryption to store data in a scrambled form, meaningless to anyone without a special data item called a *key.*

Computer labs are prone to abuse by students who may unintentionally or deliberately alter computer files, trash programs, and create all sorts of havoc. Teachers can safeguard their computers from tampering by purchasing desktop security programs such as *FoolProof* created by SmartStuff Software (Fig. 16.2). This software protects the Macintosh desktop without covering it. Because of this protection, folders and files are impregnable and cannot be trashed or copied, and access to the control panels is restricted. *FoolProof* even limits file saving to a floppy disk or a specific folder on the desktop. Fool/Proof Security (SmartStuff Software), *Launch Pad* (Berkeley), *On Guard* (Power On Software), and *Kid Desk* (Edmark) are programs of the same ilk.

Computers should also be safeguarded against natural disasters such as power surges, fires, and earthquakes. At the fundamental level, a good surge protector will rule out most power

Figure 16.2
Foolproof
©SmartStuff Software. All
Rights Reserved.

surges. However, disks do wear out and fire destroys, so it is important to make backup disks and store them in a different location. Cartridge backup drives, such as SyQuest or the Zip drive, or Jazz drive are very popular as a storage medium because of their transportable cartridges.

From this discussion, it should be evident how important security is. How far one goes in implementing a system for security is related to its cost. Usually, the more complicated the system, the more costly it is to carry out. Security will continue to be a problem because the number of computers and users continues to grow. For example, in the period between 1983 and 1984, there were 92 students per computer in a school, but by the period 1991 to 1992 there were 19 students per computer, and in the period between 1996 and 1997 there were 7 students per computer (Fulton, Mary, 1997). Eventually, there will be a computer on each student's desk. The teacher's main job will be to determine how to use this technology as a powerful tool for education. The teacher will also have to provide appropriate security.

Health Risks Using Computers

There has been increased interest in ways to reduce the risks of injury caused by computers. Every computer store has a variety of injury-reducing equipment in the form of wrist pads, antiglare screens, and ergonomic keyboards and trackballs. Unfortunately, it is very easy to improperly use computer equipment to the point of damaging your body.

Repetitive strain injuries are a serious medical problem. According to Bureau of Labor statistics for 1992, Bureau of Labor Statistics http://www.bls.gov/, almost 11,000 cases of lost work time resulted from typing or key-entry job injuries. This data excludes other computer-related injuries and unreported injuries.

Computer monitors, like other electrical devices, generate electric and magnetic fields in a very low frequency. There is scientific debate over whether low-level electromagnetic emissions cause health problems such as cancer. Regardless, the computer industry has moved to reduce these emissions, and most manufacturers support the guidelines known as MPR-II, established in 1990 by the Swedish Board for Measurement and Testing, or the stricter TCO guidelines named after the Swedish office workers' union that developed them.

You can lessen the chances of computer-related injury by following these ten suggestions:

1. Position yourself in front of the screen like a concert pianist, relax your shoulders and keep your forearms and hands in a straight line. Make sure your lower back is supported and your thighs are horizontal. The top of the computer monitor should be slightly below eye level, and it should be positioned to avoid any type of glare. Finally, your feet should rest flat on the floor, and there should be clearance under the work area, between your legs and the desk (Fig. 16.3).

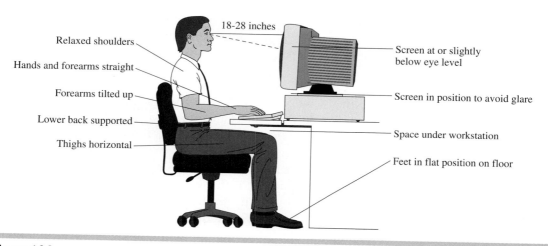

Figure 16.3
Correct posture for computer use

2. Always work 18 to 28 inches from the monitor. Electromagnetic emissions from the front of any display should be negligible at 28 inches. Furthermore, the left side of the computer and the back generate the strongest emissions, so try to stay clear of these areas.
3. Avoid unnecessarily turning up the brightness on the monitor because you may be exposing yourself to higher emissions than the MPR-II guidelines allow.
4. Do not overwork. Take frequent breaks from the computer, at least once an hour. Move around and exercise your legs, arms, and neck. Don't stare at the monitor continually, but look around every five or ten minutes. Remain relaxed.
5. Spend time finding a proper chair for your computer. Try it out and make sure you have ways of adjusting it to suit your individual needs.
6. The equipment you use the most often should be close enough that you don't have to stretch to reach it.
7. Check to make sure the keys on your keyboard are not too difficult to press. The keys should give some tactile feedback; do not press too hard on the keyboard. Use function keys to help cut down on keystrokes.

8. Do not grip the mouse too tightly because it will increase the risk of injury. Additionally, choose a mouse that is comfortable for your hands.
9. Never brace your wrists against mouse pads when you are typing because this will eventually cause injury.
10. Finally, if you continually work with graphics, buy an appropriate input device such as a drawing tablet.

Instructional Research

Because of increased access to computers, teachers are interested in the effects the computer has on instruction. The old instructional methods may not work with this new technology, or they may require modification. The research literature contains many computer studies related to teaching and learning. The major purpose of this section is to highlight some computer-assisted instruction research findings.

Computer-Assisted Instruction.   Computer-assisted instruction (CAI) refers to applications specifically designed to teach a variety of subject areas to children and adults (Freedman, 1990). In CAI, students receive feedback from the computer, which controls the sequencing of the subject matter.

Advocates of CAI have high expectations for the computer as an instrument for identifying and meeting individual needs. Many studies conclude that using CAI to supplement traditional instruction is better than the instructional program by itself. Tsai and Pohl (1977) studied the effectiveness of the lecture approach and CAI on college students learning how to program. They found a significant difference when achievement was measured by quizzes or final exam scores. The lecture approach supplemented by CAI was the most effective method of instruction. The lecture approach alone was the least effective. Burns and Bozeman's study (1981) showed evidence that a curriculum supplemented with CAI led to gains in achievement in some areas of the curriculum. Goode (1988) found that fifth and sixth grade pupils who used CAI scored significantly higher in mathematical concepts and computation than did a control group of students who used the traditional approach. Harrison and Van Devender (1993) found that students who received computer instruction showed greater increases in their achievement scores in multiplication and subtraction than did students who received traditional mathematical instruction. Kromhout and Butzin (1993) reported on Project CHILD, a computer-integrated instructional program for the elementary school. In their longitudinal evaluation of the effects of the program, they found that the effect on student achievement was positive and significant across grades and schools in math and reading. Chambless and Chambless (1994) compared effectiveness of computer-based instruction in grades kindergarten through second to traditional instruction in at risk second graders. They found a significant educational effect on the reading and writing achievement for the second graders. Using a meta-analytic technique (see footnote 6) over a twelve-year span, Christmann, Badgett, and Lucking (1997) compared the academic achievement of secondary students across academic areas. These students were instructed by CAI alone, by traditional methodology supplemented with CAI, or by traditional methodology alone. In addition, the study compared the recent results with earlier research findings. The results showed that the average student receiving traditional instruction supplemented with CAI achieved higher academic achievement than did 57.2 percent of the students receiving traditional instruction alone. However, the effect of CAI on academic achievement showed a decline during the twelve-year period; there was a $-.762$ correlation between the size of the effect and the number of years. Finally, Mann et al. (1997) did a study that was commissioned by participating New York school districts to see if computer technology made a difference for the region's students, teachers, and schools. The study involved 1,722 elementary and secondary school students and 4,041 teachers. The researchers found that student achievement was higher in schools in which teachers believed that technology had a positive impact on learning. Moreover, overall gain from increased use of computer-related technology for students and teachers was statistically significant.

Gene Glass (1976, 1977) introduced a technique called *meta-analysis*[6] in order to generate a clearer picture of the effects of computer-based treatments. Other researchers followed and compiled meta-analysis studies in the area of instructional computing. Kulik's series of meta-analysis studies were the most comprehensive (Kulik, Kulik, & Cohen, 1980; Kulik, Bangert, & Williams, 1983; Kulik, Kulik, et al., 1986; Kulik & Chen-Lin, 1987; Kulik & Kulik, 1991). The results of these studies showed that students who were taught using the computer scored higher on achievement tests than did those students who were taught using other methods. Kulik also showed that this analysis produced different results, depending on the grade, ability level, and type of instruction.

Richard E. Clark reviewed CAI in meta-analytical studies in 1985. He was critical of the research and suggested that studies by Kulik and others overestimated CAI's benefits because uncontrolled instructional methods were embedded in the instructional treatments. Clark (1991, 1994) feels that the existing evidence does not indicate that computers yield learning benefits.

Roblyer, Castine, and King (1988) summarized previous literature reviews on the educational effectiveness of instructional computing before they presented their meta-analysis of recent studies. Roblyer et al. noted that the studies from Kulik and his colleagues conducted during the early 1980s did not include microcomputer-based research studies. This fact affects the external validity and significance of Kulik's conclusions. Roblyer, et al. summarized twenty-six reviews of computer-based instruction. They also analyzed eighty-two research studies that they found had adequate internal validity and sufficient data to be included in their meta-analysis. Here is a brief rundown of their findings: (1) There are higher achievement results for college-age and adult students than for elementary and secondary students; (2) the computer produced the greatest achievement gains in science, with math, reading, and cognitive skills yielding about half the effect; (3) computer-assisted instruction software programs were all of approximately equal effectiveness; and (4) lower achieving students showed more gains with CAI than did students who were achieving at grade level, but these gains were not statistically significant.

George Bass Jr. (1990) cautioned researchers about generalizing from Roblyer's, Castine's, and King's conclusions. Bass felt that Roblyer et al. neglected to identify how many of the eighty-two

---

[6]Meta-analysis is a statistical technique that allows researchers to summarize the results of a large group of research studies and identify general effects.

studies involved the computer in a regular classroom situation. He said, "The independent variable in these eighty-two studies is not just the introduction of computer hardware, but rather the introduction of particular software on particular computers managed by particular educators. Physical equipment, instructional computer programs, and trained personnel are all factors that must be carefully described in order to generalize the research results to a specific school situation."[7]

Using a meta-analysis approach, Khalili and Shashaani (1994) reviewed thirty-six published studies to see how effective CAI was in improving students' academic achievement. They concluded that computers were very effective in improving academic performance and that duration of computer usage was an important factor.

As you can see from this discussion, recent research findings on CAI seem to point to CAI producing equal or greater achievement (Davidson, 1996; Harrison and Van Devender, 1993; Kromhout and Butzin, 1993; Khalili and Shashaani, 1994; Chambless and Chambless, 1994; Mann and Shakeshaft, 1997). CAI is still in its infancy stage, and there is still an urgent need for additional quality research.

Gender Differences.   Most gender studies try to get at the reasons for males using the computer more than females. Collis and Ollila (1986) examined the gender differences in secondary school students' attitudes toward writing on the computer. Females were significantly less positive than their male counterparts on every item that related to computers. Siann et al. (1988) studied gender stereotyping and computer involvement. They suggested there are some encouraging trends, but males still use computers more than females do.

Swadener and Hannafin (1987) studied the gender similarities and differences in sixth graders' attitudes toward the computer. They found that boys with higher achievement levels in mathematics also had high interest in computers. The boys with low scores had low interest in computers. This finding is completely opposite for females, with the low-achieving female students having the most interest in the computer.

Ware and Stuck's study (1985) explored the ways men, women, boys, and girls are pictured in computer magazines. Many stereotypic gender portrayals were cited in the 426 illustrations that were analyzed. Advertising portrayed computers as belonging to a male-dominated environment.

Sacks, Belilisimo, and Mergendoller (1993–1994) examined the relationship between alternative high school students' attitudes toward computers and computer use over a four-month time period. The results of the study showed that girls' attitudes toward computers improved over the course of the study, while boys' attitudes remained the same. Results also found that girls' attitudes toward computers with pre-post correlations were not stable, while boys' attitudes were. However, there were no overall gender differences in actual use of the computer nor did computer use increase across the course of the study. Sue Winkle Williams et al. (1994) examined the effects of factors such as past experience and sex typing on computer-interaction

---

[7]George M. Bass Jr. "Assessing the Impact of Computer-Based Instruction: A Review of Recent Research." *Educational Technology* (May 1990): 44.

tasks completed by 154 male and 223 female college students. The results of the study did support the pattern of male advantage, but they also highlighted the complex factors involved in computer interactions.

Makrakis and Sawada (1996) surveyed 773 ninth-grade students from Tokyo, Japan, to Stockholm, Sweden. They found that regardless of the country surveyed, males reported higher scores on computer aptitude and enjoyment than females did. Finally, Bernard E. Whitley Jr. (1997) did a meta-analysis of studies of gender differences in computer attitude and found that males showed greater sex-role stereotyping of computer use, higher computer self-efficacy, and more positive attitudes toward computers than did females. The largest differences were found in high school students; most other differences were small.

Science Simulations.   Generally, students learn very well with science simulation software. Linn (1986) conducted an experiment in which eight eighth-grade science classes used computers as lab partners for a semester. These students learned to use the computer to collect and display data and save and print out their reports. They used tools such as temperature and light probes that were attached to the computer, and the results were displayed on their computer screens. Linn found that the students instructed in the microcomputer-based labs outperformed seventeen-year-olds who took a standardized test on scientific knowledge. In addition, these computer-taught students demonstrated a very positive attitude toward experimentation. Farynaiarz and Lockwood (1992) examined the impact of microcomputer simulations on environmental problem solving using community college students. The students showed a highly significant improvement in problem-solving skills after being exposed to three simulation models on lake pollution. Finally, Kumar and Helgeson (1995) reviewed seven computer applications including simulation and found that simulation improved the quality and efficiency of record keeping and data analysis.

Moore, Smith, and Avner (1980) found higher student achievement with computer simulations when students had to interpret the results of the experiments to make decisions. If the students only had to follow directions and calculate the results, there was no difference between the experimental and control groups. Summerville (1984) and Fortner, Schar, and Mayer (1986) noted similar findings.

The results of the science simulation studies are very promising (Thomas and Hooper, 1991). Even a study that shows no significant difference between students who use the traditional method and students who use the computer is encouraging. Such a finding means that simulations can substitute for laboratory experiments, which is advantageous because science simulations are less dangerous, less time consuming, and less expensive than actual lab work.

Learning Time.   CAI research has generally been positive regarding the time it takes to learn concepts. Dence (1980) described several studies in which students learned more quickly with CAI than with traditional instruction. Gleason (1981) reviewed CAI research and interviewed researchers. His conclusion regarding CAI was that it results in a 20 percent to 40 percent savings in time as compared with the traditional methods of instruction. Fisher (1983) reported that students who used the computer completed their work 40 percent faster than when they did not have access to it. Krein and Mahollm (1990) found that CAI lessened by 25 percent the time it took students to learn the instructional material without computers.

Word Processing.   Many studies deal with word processing and its effect on the quantity and quality of student writing, but the evidence is contradictory. O'Brien (1984), Feldman (1984), Morehouse, Hoaglund, and Schmidt (1987), and (Jones, 1994) found evidence in favor of word processing. However, Daiute (1985) found that students wrote less with a word processor. Kurth (1987) found no differences in quality of writing or revisions between a secondary school group that used word processing for their writing and a secondary group that used pencil and paper. Lori Seaswel et al (1994) compared the effects of computer-based word processing and writing by hand on third and fourth graders' attitudes and performance in writing. The third graders made more revisions and edits when using word processors while the fourth graders made more changes in their hand-written drafts. Roblyer et al. (1988) summarized the research and said that word processing did not appear to improve the quality of writing. Hawisher (1986) reviewed the research on word processing and noted that implementation differences among the various studies could affect their outcomes. This criticism highlights the problem, not only for word processing studies, but also for other research concerning computer applications.

In the late 1990s, research turned to examining the use of computer-generated multimedia and video in combination with word processing to stimulate the quality of students' written composition. In a study completed in 1994, Jerry P. Galloway found that students who used hypermedia material for three years significantly outperformed members of their peer group who participated for the same length of time in control classroom situations using the traditional methods. Boone and Higgins (1992) felt that "through associative links, a hypermedia presentation system provides a reader access to related information in the form of additional text, pictures, and computer-generated voices. These enhancements to traditional text provide the reader with supplementary information, clarification, and elaboration, all within a familiar context and a single medium." Because of the improvement in technology and in multimedia software, the opportunities for using technology in reading and writing have increased. Along the same lines, Timothy Hays (1996) found that low spatial ability students increased their science comprehension with computer-animated presentations. However, further research in this area is warranted.

The Learning Disabled.   Most research indicates that the learning disabled (LD) benefit from involvement with CAI. For example, David McNaughton et al. (1997) investigated the impact of integrated proofreading strategy training on LD secondary students. This training consisted of using a computer spelling checker and student strategies on proofreading. Students showed an increase in strategy use and percentage of spelling errors corrected on student compositions and proofreading material. In 1995, Rwey-Lin Shiah et al. studied thirty elementary LD students and found that these students performed significantly better on mathematics tests by using a computer rather than using paper and pencil. The researchers found no differences among variations in computer-assisted instruction. Koseinski et al. (1993) conducted a study with six male LD elementary school students. They were taught multiplication facts using computer software programs with a five-second constant time delay procedure. The results of the study indicated that this computer-assisted program was very effective and that the learning generalized with varying degrees of success. Carman and Kosberg (1982) showed a significant positive influence on attention-to-task behavior for emotionally disabled children. Maser et al. (1979) investigated an alternative instructional approach to teaching basic skills to the educationally disadvantaged. At the end of a three-year period, they found CAI was effective in building basic skills.

Other studies also support positive effects of CAI with learning disabled (Hasselbring, 1982; Lally, 1980; Watkins and Webb, 1981). In 1987, MacArthur et al. used CAI with LD students. Their study of fifth and sixth grade students compared the effects of paper-and-pencil and computer-delivered independent drill and practice in spelling. This study was done over a four-week period with forty-four learning disabled students. The researchers found that the computer-practice students did significantly better than the traditional drill students did on spelling tests. The computer students spent more time on academic content and less time with their teachers than did the traditional drill students.

In the 1990s, two studies gave evidence of the potential of expert systems, laser discs, and hypermedia as educational tools for LD children. Garzella (1991) compared the effectiveness of an expert system for reading diagnosis and prescription to traditional methods of diagnosis. He found that LD students that had teachers who utilized the expert system significantly outperformed the students of teachers using traditional methods in word identification skills. Woodward and Gersten (1992) reported that when they taught LD high-school students with a laser disc program on fractions, about two-thirds of the students exceeded the performance criteria.

Motivation and Attitude.   Teachers face the challenge of motivating students and fostering in them a positive attitude to improve their chances for success in school. For example, an essential element for improving students' spelling is keeping interest high (Ruel, 1977). Many studies report students' positive attitudes toward the computer and how computers motivate students and help them maintain high interest (Hatfield, 1996; Westrom and Shaban 1992; Hatfield, 1991; Clement, 1981).

Hatfield (1996) examined the effective use of computer stations across the curriculum. The study's results showed overall increased computer use and increased student motivation and interest. Terrell and Rendulic (1996) did a comparative study of elementary school students and found evidence that the use of computer-managed instructional feedback can have a positive effect on student motivation and achievement. Richman's (1994) study showed how innovations in educational technology contributed to motivation and achievement of at-risk students in the New York's Berkshire Union Free School District. Robertson (1978) found that children who had experienced failure in the past responded positively to computer-assisted programs. She concluded that the children involved in the study did not experience a sense of failure over an incorrect response.

Some researchers have tried to find out if students prefer computer-based methods simply because a computer is involved. Other research has focused on the computer's influence on student attitudes toward school and curriculum. Bracey (1982) found that students reacted favorably to computer use for instructional tasks. He reported that students who worked on the computer had a more positive attitude toward the machine than did those students who had not used the computer. Kulik et al. (1983) reviewed studies on students' attitudes toward the curriculum after using CAI. In three of the studies reviewed, the results were statistically significant for the CAI classroom. In their meta-analysis, Roblyer et al. (1988) found that students do not seem to prefer the computer over other media. However, there were few studies with data measuring student preferences for computer media; thus, the results are unclear.

Generally, the CAI studies that focused on students' attitudes toward themselves and school learning were positive. However, the results are inconclusive on the effects on computer instruction as it relates to motivation and school achievement. One reason for this finding might be that achievement in school is not based on a simple set of variables but is the result of a complex set of factors.

Logo and Problem Solving.   There has been widespread interest among educators on the effects on students of Logo computer programming language. In a survey of instructional computer uses, Becker (1987) found that more than 9 percent of computer-using teachers in the United States use Logo. Numerous books have been written on Logo, and it has been the subject of many papers presented at conferences. However, it has been observed that only doctoral research has kept up with the interest in Logo (Pea, 1987). A number of studies attempted to determine the effects of Logo on students' self-esteem. Some of these studies found negative results and others found no statistically significant differences.

Keller (1990) completed a research review on the possible impact of Logo on cognitive development. She found that the teacher plays a critical role in the Logo environment. Some studies showed the difficulties that young children have in learning Logo (Horner and Maddux, 1985; Mayer and Fay, 1987). Grovier (1988) summarized a variety of American and British research related to Logo. She found one key factor: The studies with significant effects were the ones in which the teacher structured the learning.

The most frequent claim about Logo is that it promotes problem-solving skills or reasoning ability. Reeder and Leming (1994) studied the effect of Logo on the nonverbal reasoning ability of rural, disadvantaged third graders. The students were taught Logo for eight weeks and were then compared to a control group that remained in a traditional classroom setting to do homework. The investigators used the Matrix Analogies Test (MAT) to measure these groups. The results of the study showed that the Logo group scored significantly higher than the traditional group and that Logo did enhance the nonverbal reasoning ability of these children. Jyrki Suomala (1996) studied thirty-eight Finnish eight-year-olds using Logo. The results suggest that Logo promotes the development of problem-solving skills if each student receives sufficient support. Roblyer et al. (1988) did a meta-analysis on the effects of CAI on problem-solving and general thinking. Their findings indicated that Logo showed promise as a method for developing problem-solving skills, but this finding was not a statistical conclusion. Lu (1991) compared the problem-solving abilities of adolescents enrolled in a gifted program with experienced adolescent programmers. The students were given puzzles and problems to solve. The results demonstrated that the students with programming skill did solve the problems more efficiently, developed more highly structured plans, and systematically monitored their thinking processes better than the nonprogrammers did. Lu concluded that metacognitive skills gained through programming are transferable and do increase with programming experience.

Pea and Kurland's (1984) research results, however, did not support the connection between Logo and problem-solving skills. Dalton (1986) compared Logo to a curriculum created to improve problem solving and reported that the problem-solving group achieved significantly more than the Logo group or the control group at every level of student ability. Miller's 1993 article discusses Logo and that it is based on long periods of instruction, knowledgeable teachers, and numerous computers. He felt that recent research shows that Logo may confuse children's understanding of angles, not help it.

Clements et al. (1993) reviewed the research to discover the benefits of open-ended computer programs such as Logo. He discussed ways that the programs appear to develop problem-solving skill, socioemotional competencies, and subject-matter knowledge. In conclusion, numerous studies support the thesis that Logo improves problem-solving abilities; however, the research is not conclusive.

Programming.   Some studies discuss non-Logo programming languages, such as BASIC. These studies examine the impact that programming could have on different types of intellectual activities. The general conclusions from these studies are inconclusive and disappointing. Moreover, lately, there has been little additional research in this area.

There are proponents who want programming taught in the schools. Arthur Luehrmann, a well-known advocate, feels that persons who know programming can control and communicate better with the computer (Luehrmann, 1984). Many individuals argue that computer programming improves students' problem-solving ability (Soloway, Lockhead, and Palumbo, 1982; Clement and Reed, 1991). Still other supporters proclaim that programming should not be taught for the sake of programming, but instead to help children learn other subjects such as math (Papert, 1980; 1996).

A review of the research on such topics as the effects of programming on achievement, problem-solving, and transferability is inconclusive (Collis, 1990). Mayer, Dyck, and Vilberg (1986) concluded that there was no consistent evidence that learning to program had any positive impact on anything else: "There is no convincing evidence that learning to program enhances students' general intellectual ability, or that programming is any more successful than Latin for teaching "proper habits of mind.'"

Problems with the Research

Although a considerable amount of research has been done in the last twenty-two years, the research is problematic. Computer research is still in its infancy stage, and many CAI studies were conducted before microcomputers were readily available. In addition, many studies are not thoroughly reported in the literature, so it is impossible to tell if the conclusions drawn by the investigators are supported by the data. The meta-analysis that Roblyer et al. (1988) performed included thirty-eight studies and forty-four dissertations from a possible 200. The rest of the studies were eliminated because of reasons such as methodological flaws or insufficient data. A good portion of CAI research is anecdotal, based on experiences and not on experimental design. Educators are now beginning to understand what role the computer could play in educating students. However, we still don't know if computers are the answer. Studies have shown that students in most technologically advanced classrooms perform no better on standardized tests than their peers do (Trotler, 1997). There definitely is a need for higher quality computer research to get substantive answers to our many questions.

Research Generalizations

Even with these problems, some relevant generalizations can be made from the research:

1. In science, the computer is a useful tool for simulations. For example, the army and navy use war game simulations. Chemistry instructors can use computer-based simulations as substitutes for lab work. Flight instructors can use flight simulation software instead of putting novices at the controls of actual planes. A simulation program is generally less dangerous, less expensive, and less time consuming than the real experience.
2. The computer is helpful for individualization. Students working with computers can progress at their own pace. If they need help with math facts, they can turn to the computer for individualized tutoring, freeing the teacher to work with the same child in other academic areas. This type of individualization spreads the range of abilities in a class and allows some students to move ahead.
3. The computer changes attitudes toward the computer, school, and school subjects. The computer does motivate children, and there is speculation that it might improve the dropout rate.
4. The relationship between attitude and achievement is low. There is no strong body of evidence supporting the notion that a positive attitude toward the computer will result in improved achievement.
5. No substantial evidence supports the claim that studying programming improves problem-solving ability or enhances general intellectual development.
6. Research suggests that the computer is best used as a tool or resource rather than as a programming device.
7. Word processing motivates children to write. However, there is no difference between the quality of writing produced using a word processor and that generated with pencil and paper.
8. Gender studies have found that boys work more frequently with the computer than do girls. This finding appears to be a socially developed difference.

Future Trends

Examining the research leads to some natural questions: What will the future bring? What are the trends for microcomputer development? Will we have more artificial intelligence applications? Will there be more telecommunication and networking in the schools? Are there going to be further developments in multimedia technologies? How will this affect teaching? Let's try to answer some of these questions.

Computer Hardware

Recent developments such as the wireless computer and wireless computer network, flash memory chips, and the ever-changing laptop will play a more prominent role in the computer's future. The ultimate network is the IBM Almaden Research Center's prototype Personal Area Network, which uses the human body to transmit data ("Best of What's New," 1997). The wireless networks will eliminate expensive cabling and add flexibility, permitting users to move the machines freely around a room. Mainframes may be replaced by desktop computers resembling large laptops. The laptop will become smaller and more powerful and portable and in ten years, we will probably wear our computers (Hogan, 1998). The cathode ray tube (CRT) monitor will be replaced by a large active color matrix flat screen display or a plasma display. We will have poster-size screens as well as screens we can hang on the wall or unfold from our pocket. If we want to access the Internet, we can use the pocket Net computer, a computer that fits in our pocket, to log on anytime from anywhere. Computers will all have sophisticated voice recognition systems and be capable of running many applications simultaneously. We will be talking to our computer like Dave did in the classic movie *2001: A Space Odyssey*. The question is, Will the computer listen to us or will it be like HAL 9000, a murderous machine? Every computer will have built-in speech, and instead of typing commands, we will just tell our computer to launch an application or print that document. Improved color ink-jet printers will continue to figure prominently in the printing device market. Furthermore, color laser printers will become increasingly popular because of drastic price reductions and superior printing capabilities.

Another major computer trend is the development of equipment that is smaller, faster, and easier to use. Every time we turn around, someone has introduced a new computer that is quicker and can run more complex programs. The standard has quickly transformed 1 MHz machines to 500 MHz machines. Look for faster machines in the near future. The memory needed to run different applications has increased. In the early 1980s, most microcomputers needed only 16K of RAM memory to run the available educational software programs. Today, there are machines with 768 MB of RAM memory, and in three years, Mitsubishi will have one chip with 4 gigabytes of RAM memory.

Because of their large memory, the new microcomputers are much more powerful and can perform a myriad of tasks. The cost of the memory chip has decreased in price and will continue to do so in the next few years. In 1994, DEC's Alpha 21164 chip was the fastest microprocessor in the world. It could perform 600 transactions per second and there was a 300 MHz version of this chip (Ryan 1994). While these figures seem high by 2000, analysts say desktop PCs will hit speeds near 1000 MHz (Piller et al, 1998).

Not only has memory size increased, but storage devices have increased their capacity to store data. The 5 1/4-inch floppy disk faded into oblivion and the 3 1/2-inch disk is going in the same direction. Furthermore, the 100-MB Iomega removable Zip disk has become a popular option for storage. In addition, the Iomega's Jazz drive holds 2 gigabytes of information and has 2- gigabyte removable cartridges. The trend is toward smaller disks that hold more information, such as the 1.8-inch disks already available for some portables. Hard disks are still a viable alternative, with their ability to hold gigabytes of information and their inexpensive price.

CD-ROM discs and laser discs are being replaced by DVD. DVD is the same size as the CD-ROM, but it is capable of holding 17 gigabytes of data with digital images equal to laser discs (see chapter 13). With a reduction in price and faster access time, the erasable optical discs have emerged as a viable alternative to magnetic disks. These discs have the capacity to store gigabytes of information, and they do not wear out as floppy disks do. In addition to these features, optical discs offer the ability to reproduce high-quality color graphics, images, and animation. This technology holds promise for interactive video. These advances are just the tip of the iceberg—in the near future this huge amount of storage capacity will seem minimal.

Along with the changes in storage devices are changes in input devices. The movement is away from the keyboard as the primary input device. There are more touch screens, pens, and variations on the mouse. Of all the new developments, the voice recognition system seems to hold the greatest promise.

Voice Recognition Systems

The Optimum Resource Reading Program was the first interactive voice recognition reading program. It was designed for MS-DOS compatible computers for reading disabled children from ages eight to thirteen. The program was the result of a $500,000 grant awarded to Optimum Resource by the National Institute of Child Health and Human Development. The Optimum Resource Reading Program was tested for a year on children at six schools in Meriden, Connecticut. Research found that children using this program made significant reading gains compared to children using traditional methods.

With this program, the computer speaks to the student and the student responds. The speaking voice of the computer is clear, precise, and as understandable as a human voice. The computer is trained to recognize the student's voice. It corrects student errors and offers praise and encouragement for right answers. The program rewards the student with games, activities, color graphics, and animated sequences. It also keeps a record of each student's progress.

In 1991, Convox introduced a voice recognition system that allowed users to replace keystroke entries with spoken commands. The Voice Master Key System II worked on the IBM PC and PS/2 systems. This product could recognize sixty-four words and it could be branched to additional sets of words. Users typed in the words they wanted the system to listen for, repeated each only twice, and then typed in the desired keyboard responses. After this programming, users only needed to say a command to direct the computer to execute it.

Also in 1991, Emerson and Stern Associates, a research company, announced a breakthrough in speech recognition. Their voice recognition product, Soliloquy, differed radically from previous speech recognition technologies in the following ways: (1) It did not require special training and worked with a single speaker; (2) it could handle continuous speech; and (3) it did not require extra hardware. This software ran on the Macintosh's more powerful models.

A year later, David Nagel, senior vice president of Apple's Advanced Technology Group, used both voice and pen to pilot a high-end Macintosh, the Quadra 900. This system was programmed to recognize 100,000 words and, unlike other systems, it did not need to be trained to recognize the user's voice (Gore, 1992).

At the 1994 Comdex Convention, Kurzwell Applied Intelligence announced that it had formed an alliance with vendors such as WordPerfect to integrate speech recognition into applications. What this announcement means to users is that they would be able to use voice more smoothly in word processing or spreadsheet applications.

In 1997, Dragons Systems' *Naturally Speaking* and IBM's *Via Voice* software were released. These two continuous speech packages sold at reasonable prices. The user could now dictate a document into the computer, do the necessary editing, and spell check a finished product. These products are still not 100 percent accurate, but in the next two years, we will see more breakthroughs in speech recognition technologies. Many of these advances will be linked closely to artificial intelligence; the principles of AI are being used to improve the voice recognition system.

Artificial Intelligence

Artificial intelligence (AI) is a range of computer applications that are striving to simulate human intelligence and behavior. For instance, with AI, a machine or robot can recognize pictures and sounds. In the future, we may be able to walk up to any computer or robot, ask it for problem-solving help, and receive information useful in solving the problem.

In a short amount of time, the differences between the machine and an intelligent person will be reduced drastically. At UCLA and other universities, scientists are working on computer programs and, in some instances, on robots that will emulate conditions of life such as evolution. The computer ants program at UCLA is a product of an infant science called artificial life. David Jefferson, a computer scientist at UCLA, feels that the artificial ant colonies are a small step toward the creation of life itself. If these scientists are successful, electronic creatures capable of independent thought and action may emerge, which is both exciting and frightening. At Los Alamos National Laboratory, there exists a whole repertoire of self-reproducing computer codes. These are just variations of the computer viruses that have disrupted computer networks over the last few years.

AI systems are designed for particular fields to make evaluations, draw conclusions, and provide recommendations. They help doctors make diagnoses on diseases and treatments, they help drill oil wells, and they aid stockbrokers in making analyses.

This type of software will have a similar impact on education. Teachers are already demanding and using programs that have been made more interactive through artificial intelligence. The AI language will definitely increase the number of programs that respond in human ways. The software we will be using in the near future will tackle concepts and ideas. This software will accept a range of English language commands and be easier to use. In the future, you will be able talk and converse with your average computer and ask for help. The computer will automatically bring up the appropriate application to aid you in solving your problem. We will see real AI as Alan Turing, the famous mathematician, defined it when he said, "A machine has artificial intelligence when there is no discernible difference between the conversation generated by the machine and that of an intelligent person" (Hodges, Andrew, 1992).

Robots

A robot is a computer system that performs physical and computational activities. The robot can be created in a human form; however, industrial robots are not designed this way. The advantage of a robot is that it can perform many different human jobs often better than a person might perform them, or at least more efficiently or quickly. Robots are being designed with artificial intelligence features so they may respond more effectively to unusual situations. In the future, robots may be in the classroom serving as teacher's aides. Robots will spend time with the students, individually drilling them on math skills. In the chemistry lab, robots will handle dangerous chemicals. Robots will help the disabled student with homework.

As the average age of the population increases, the need and cost of assisted care will also increase. Under development are automated "smart apartments" that will help the old and disabled live more independently and comfortably. Bob Stark, the director of NASA's Far West Regional Technology Transfer Center, is building a model of a smart apartment (Kaplan, 1994). These apartments would have different types of machines to assist incapacitated individuals. Some possibilities are robots that dust, clean floors, reach items on top shelves, respond to voice commands, push wheelchairs, and walk dogs. The robots in such an apartment would differ from the industrial robots found on the factory floors; these service robots extend human abilities and help people rather than replace them. K. G. Engelhardt, a scientist at NASA, is doing pioneering work with robots in the home setting. Engelhardt has a few small robotics companies developing robots to perform different types of tasks. The Sidekick robot, developed by Robotic Assistance Corporation of Santa Ana, is a robot that gets a glass of water and picks clothes up off the floor. Jean-Claude Latombe, chairman of the computer science department at Stanford says, "One of the fastest-growing areas for robotics today is robot-assisted surgery." Stanford is doing brain surgery with robots. During radiation surgery for a brain tumor, the surgeon is not even in the same room with a patient. Instead, the doctor sits at a computer console in a nearby room and monitors what is happening during the operation (Kepler, 1994). Robots are also being used as targets in weapons training. Dan Fetterly's remote-controlled robot can move like a human, run up to 9 mph, carry 100 pounds and can spot any target (Dunn, 1998). In summation, people are using robots for jobs that range from working in an automobile plant or gathering things at the bottom of the ocean to mowing the lawn to brain surgery.

Computer Use by Disabled Persons

Many devices are currently available to aid the disabled pupil, including Braille keyboards and computer-operated telephone devices for the deaf. Hearing impaired people can learn to speak by matching words displayed on a screen with the sound waves for each word. Many speech programs that are now available help blind people use the computer. Digital Equipment Corporation has developed a portable speech synthesizer. The DECtalk Express Speech Synthesizer converts ASCII text into synthesized speech output that lets the individual hear computer screen contents. It weighs less than a pound, has a speaking rate of 75 to 650 words per minute, and features a user volume control, comprehensive pronunciation rules, and a large dictionary ("Portable Speech Synthesizers," 1994).

Desktop Videoconferencing

Videoconferencing lets you be in two places at the same time. Instead of moving large sums in an armored car, a bank can relay video messages on how much money it wants to pay. A teacher can confer with an ill student at home without leaving the classroom. A businessperson can attend a long-distance conference without leaving the office. Around 1992, videoconferencing equipment cost $100,000, filled a room, and required satellite hookups and expensive data lines (Leeds, 1994). Today the industry is expanding because of better compression of data, miniaturization, lower costs, wider availability of digital telephone lines, and faster processors. Nevertheless, videoconferencing is still difficult to configure, provides marginal video and audio quality, and lacks compatibility between systems, which means that videoconferencing can only be done with people who use the same system. In the schools, a multimedia-equipped computer with the proper audio/video cards, a modem, and a small video camera like a QuickCam (Connectix, Inc.) can transmit an image in color through the phone lines to another recipient's monitor instantly along with sound, so that two people can see and hear each other. This process lets individuals have two-way video conversations on the opposite ends of the globe. An inexpensive videoconferencing software package is *CU-SeeMe* (White Pine Software). This company recently released an update to its videoconferencing that will no longer restrict the users to conferencing only with other *CUSeeMe* users (Kahney, 1997).

Advanced Technology Labs

The *SmartLab,* the latest phase of the Technology Lab 2000 series of learning environments produced by Creative Learning Systems, represents the emergence of an ingeniously responsive instructional environment for young people and adults. In a studiolike setting, students engage in accomplishing real-world projects, integrating learning from many academic disciplines. The unique educational program incorporated into *SmartLab* uses a series of integrated curricular resources that challenge the student to discover the underlying principles of technology and apply them, through critical thinking, problem solving, and decision making. The scenario helps students acquire the skills and confidence needed to live and work in the technological environment of tomorrow.

In *SmartLab,* a computer-managed network gives students access to and control of content, applications, and information in many technologically oriented areas. Via the network, students import instructional modules and software applications to their workstation computers and receive supporting visual imagery on adjacent video monitors. Although the *SmartLab* incorporates an extensive collection of computers and peripherals, it is much more than just another version of the computer classroom. Rather than dominate the instructional program, computers serve as the tools by which students access the language and the images of a broader technological arena. The environment is a total, integrated system of furnishings, equipment, computer-mediated instruction, software, and hands-on computer-based learning.

The instructional resources are self-paced, interactive tutorials. The materials launch students into a variety of technological experiences and support self-designed projects that expand students' understanding of technological phenomena. The *SmartLab* gives students access to information in areas such as robotics, word processing, entertainment, engineering, multimedia production, satellite technology, and rocketry, to name just a few.

Figure 16.4 shows a sample floor plan of the Technology Lab 2000 SmartLab for Pre-Engineering Studies, one of numerous configurations available. Islandlike arrangements of versatile, leading-edge laboratory furnishings form a series of activity zones within which students work and learn collaboratively. Each station is also reconfigurable to accommodate new activities or advanced explorations.

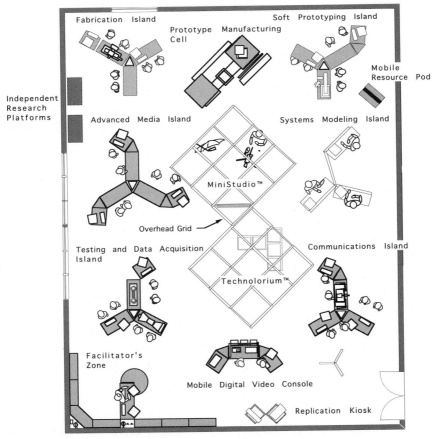

SmartLab™ for Technological, Pre-Engineering, and Entertainment Engineering Studies.
Reconfigurable, Integrated, Dynamic, Collaborative Learning Environment.
© Copyright 1994 Creative Learning Systems, Inc. All Rights Reserved

Figure 16.4
Sample configuration for a Technology Lab 2000 SmartLab for Pre-Engineering Studies, designed by Creative Learning Systems, Inc.
Technology Lab 2000/the SmartLab for Pre-Engineering Studies and the MiniStudio are trademarks of Creative Learning Systems, Inc., San Diego, California.

Student teams participate in computer-integrated enterprises in which all phases in the creation of a product—design, manufacture, production, and marketing—are linked and interdependent. Students work through the problems of taking an original idea and turning it into a tangible product by applying established guidelines of scientific analysis and engineering procedures used in research and development in the business community. The power of the Smart-Lab is realized when the vast array of activities are seen not as finite exercises but rather as open-ended investigations, each leading to the next, linked by the common thread of curiosity.

One of the greatest changes in this new mode of learning is the teacher's role. The teacher no longer needs to be an all-knowing instructor but rather a facilitator of learning. The teacher is freed to circulate among students studying individually or in groups; the teacher facilitates the creative contributions of all the students and coordinates those contributions so they evolve into a rich body of shared knowledge and skills.

Advanced Technology Classrooms

The Hueneme School District, located in Ventura County, California, has received international recognition for its leadership in developing technology. According to Superintendent Dr. Ron Rescigno, students have made marked improvement in their achievement.

The district offers technologically designed classrooms, called Smart Classrooms, organized by curriculum area. Each Smart Classroom is a state-of-the-art, completely furnished facility that follows unique design principles. The computer configuration of these classrooms allows for seamless exchange of data, voice, and video; total integration of equipment; computer instruction; and in-service training. Electronic connections are concealed under desks but are easily accessed with a simple command. Color monitors are recessed underneath desktops, and keyboards are housed in drawers that pull out for each student.

The Smart Classroom design emphasizes student interaction and academic success. Students learn to use different applications such as desktop publishing programs, word processing programs, and databases while gaining knowledge in all areas of the curriculum. Students engage in observations, explore different scientific phenomena, perform manipulation activities, and assume responsibility for their own learning with self-administered quizzes and answer checks.

Each student has an individual workstation with access to a CD-ROM disc drive, printer, and laser disc player. Each teacher has a work station with a color printer and color scanner. The teacher's workstation controls an overhead projection system mounted on the ceiling that projects to a motorized screen that can be used with a large group. Infrared electronic blackboards and conventional white boards are attached to the wall behind the teacher's desk. Furthermore, the lighting system is designed to eliminate glare.

Software

Software manufacturers are producing talking versions of their programs, and the majority of these are high-quality, multimedia programs that follow sound educational principles. For example, the *JumpStart* Series (Knowledge Adventure), designed especially for children in grades kindergarten through six, and *Body Voyage* (Times Warner Electronic Publishing), designed for junior high school students to adults, are innovative, multimedia programs. Prices for educational software and computers are now reduced, and parents are taking advantage of these lower prices by buying more computers and software.

Today, students interact with the computer programs in a more realistic fashion because of developments in artificial intelligence. Programs such as *CrossCountry California* (Didatech) and *Math Mind Benders* (Critical Thinking Books & Software) have elements of artificial intelligence. Publishing houses are moving in the direction of integrating software with the state-adopted texts. Lab packs and networkable products are now available as well. In the future, every textbook will come with a supplemental disk. Programs such as *Collier's Encyclopedia* (Sierra Home) that combine sound, still sequences, animations, and full-motion video, photographs, and simulations are becoming the norm. Virtual reality will be integrated into every software package along with *QuickTime VR* (See chapter 10 for a full discussion).

Concluding Thoughts

We would all like to see technologically advanced computer labs such as SmartLab 2000 and Smart Classrooms in our schools. Furthermore, we would want every student in our classrooms to have a computer and modem. If a robot aide could decrease our workload considerably, few of us would not order one tomorrow. Many of the items on our wonderful wish lists may never materialize. Unfortunately, schools do not have the money to buy the equipment to implement a technology-based program. The more sophisticated computer equipment will be found primarily at the college and university level. Elementary and secondary schools will not be able to afford this costly hardware. But there's another problem: the lack of teachers trained to manage this new technology. Still, many states now require that teachers complete a computer course for certification. Because of this requirement, there will be more trained teachers who can integrate the computer in the classroom.

What does the future hold? Computer use will increase, and the computers will be smaller, faster, more efficient, and less expensive. More emphasis will be placed on computer ethics, and the Internet will be available to all schools and children. Multimedia software will be more sophisticated and offer speech recognition, and it will be less expensive, more transparent, and menu and icon based. Computer storage capacity will be improved, and optical drives will allow teachers and students to access software more easily. More networkable machines will be available; advances in networking will lead to better communication between different classrooms, different schools, and different school districts. One classroom will be networked with another classroom on a national or state database. Eventually, classrooms will be networking with classrooms in other countries. Students and teachers will commonly use desktop publishing programs as well as scanners, cameras, and facsimile machines to import pictures and graphic images into their documents. The computer will be used with a DVD-ROM disc, and database.

Teachers will be "teaching" less because the computer will have a more prominent role in the classroom. Computers will allow teachers to assume the role of facilitators, designing learning experiences and individualizing instruction. There will be less drill and practice and more problem solving and real, meaningful learning activities. Many of our universities will have virtual degree programs, offering classes via the Internet. Books are still going to exist, but maybe as a supplement to technologies like the Internet. Ahead of his time, one Illinois state superintendent of schools wanted laptop computers instead of books. The time may come when the book will disappear forever.

The computer is a remarkable invention. Its possible impact on the curriculum is staggering, but it needs to be given a chance to show what it can do for children in the schools. It is up to educators to inspire, motivate, and excite students and colleagues about this remarkable instrument for learning. **Appendix A provides a list of useful software that you can employ in your quest to maximize the computer's potential in your classroom.**

Summary

Computers are not just a passing fancy; they will be with us for a long time. They have made life easier and more complicated. With the computer, we can accomplish a great deal more, but we have to work harder to keep up with the technology.

Computers are involved in new types of crime as well as some variations on the traditional ones. Computer embezzlement and unauthorized access to computer systems are two examples. Software piracy is a problem that computer companies are still trying to resolve. Software houses offer many alternatives to schools tempted to illegally duplicate software: onsite licensing, lab packs, and networkable disks. Many houses are dispensing with their copy protection schemes, hoping to reduce software piracy.

Computer security is a topic that is often in the news. A computer user must be concerned with protecting data from loss or unauthorized access. What is needed are proper identification of the user, authorizing passwords, equipment and disk protection, and proper backup of computer files. Backup copies should be kept at different sites to guard against data loss due to fire, theft, or failure of storage media.

There are many research studies on computer-assisted instruction (CAI). The synopsis of research findings presented in this chapter gives an overview of the successes and failures of this field.

In the end, we must consider the future of this exciting technology. We will definitely have smaller, faster, easier-to-use, and more powerful computers. Future software and hardware will be multimedia, be networkable, include voice recognition, be based on artificial intelligence, and involve robots. Education will integrate computers into the curriculum as much as possible, but problems with funding and lack of adequately trained teachers may limit what is accomplished in classrooms. We can only speculate on what will happen in the future. What we do know is that the coming years will be exciting!

Chapter Mastery Test

1. Discuss two issues related to computer privacy.

2. Describe the Security Pacific embezzlement case. Explain why computerized financial institutions are more susceptible to embezzlement than traditional ones are.

3. Explain the conflict between the computer user and the software publisher.

4. Why are computer viruses destructive? List some precautions you can take to prevent one from infecting your computer system.

5. What can ordinary persons do to protect their data from fire, theft, and storage media failure?

6. Discuss the findings of three research studies on CAI.

7. Does CAI research show that science simulations are more effective than laboratory experiences? Explain your answer.

8. Why are optical discs superior to floppy disks?

9. Why is the voice recognition system the wave of the future?

10. Define artificial intelligence and speculate on how it could be used in the classroom.

11. How can the computer help disabled children?

12. What has slowed the use of computers in the schools? How can these obstacles be overcome?

13. Explain how computers in the classroom will change the traditional roles of teachers, students, and parents.

14. What are some future directions for computer use in the classroom? Defend your choices.

15. Discuss three ways to reduce the risks of computer-related injuries.

Classroom Projects

1. Research an example of a recent computer crime and prepare a short report. In this report, tell (1) what happened, (2) how the crime was discovered, and (3) how the crime could have been prevented.

2. Research the software piracy problem. In spite of this problem, why is there a trend toward unprotected software?

3. Prepare a report on two types of computer viruses. Explain how they affect your computer and how they were discovered.

4. Compare two different surge protectors. Write a report detailing their battery life, cut-off time, and resistance to power failure. Which product is better and why?

5. Find three current examples of how computers were used to invade a person's privacy. How could these violations have been prevented?

6. Use research to argue that Logo improves problem solving.

Suggested Readings and References

Bass, George M., Jr. "Assessing the Impact of Computer Based Instruction: A Review of Recent Research." *Educational Technology* (May 1990).

Becker, H. J. *The Impact of Computer Use on Children's Learning: What Research Has Shown and What It Has Not.* Baltimore, Md.: The Johns Hopkins University, 1987.

Berkley, Hudson. "Go with the Flow." *Los Angeles Times* (November 15, 1994); 1E.

"The Best of What's New." *Popular Science* (December 1997): 44–81.

Blake, C. "Piracy: Everyone Loses." *Aldus Magazine* (July/August 1991): 10.

BloomBecker, Buck. "Commitment to Security." Santa Cruz, Calif.: National Center for Computer Crime Data, April 10, 1995.

BloomBecker, Buck. Interview by author. January 1998.

BloomBecker, Buck. *Spectacular Computer Crimes.* Homewood, Ill.: Dow Jones–Irwin, 1990.

BloomBecker, Buck. "Viewpoint: My Three Computer Criminological Sins." *Communication of ACM* 37, no. 11 (November, 1994): 15–16.

Boone, R., and K. Higgins. "Hypermedia Applications for Content Area Study Guides." *Reading and Writing Quarterly: Overcoming Learning Difficulties* 8 (1992): 379–93.

Bork, Alfred. "The Future of Computers and Learning." *T.H.E. Journal* 24, no. 11 (June 1997): 69–77.

Bossone, R. M., and I. H. Polishook, eds. "New Frontiers in Educational Technology: Trends and Issues." *Proceedings of the Conference of the University/Urban Schools National Task Force.* ERIC Document No. 281524 (November 1986).

Bowen, Ted. "Firewall Spec to Strengthen Web Security." *Info World* 19, no. 49 (December 8, 1997): 1.

Bracey, G. W. "Computers in Education: What the Research Shows." *Electronic Learning* 2, no. 3 (1982): 51–54.

Bramscum, Deborah. "Monitors and Health." *MacWorld* (December 1994): 175–76.

Brier, Steven E. "IBM Unveils Antivirus and Hotlinks Software." *InfoWorld* 19, no. 49 (December 8, 1997): 3.

Brown, Joan Marie. "Technology and Ethics." *Learning and Leading with Technology* 24, no. 6 (March 1997): 38–41.

Bruder, Isabelle. *"Visions of the Future."*Electronic Learning 9, no. 4 (January 1990): 24–30.

Bunderson, Eileen D., and Mary Elizabeth Christensen. "An Analysis of Retention Problems for Female Students in University Computer Programs." *Journal of Research on Computing in Education* 28, no. 1 (fall 1995): 1–18.

Burger, Ralf. *Computer Viruses: A High-Tech Disease.* Grand Rapids, Mich.: Abacus, 1988.

Burns, Patricia Knight, and William C. Bozeman. "Computer-Assisted Instruction and Mathematics Achievement: Is There a Relationship?" *Educational Technology* 21 (October 1981): 32–39.

Campbell, D. L., D. L. Peck, C. J. Horn, and R. K. Leigh. "CAI and Third Grade Mathematics." *Educational Communication and Technology Journal* 35, no. 2 (1987): 95–103.

Carman, Gary O., and Bernard Kosberg. "Research: Computer Technology and the Education of Emotionally Handicapped Children." *Educational Technology* (February 1982): 32–36.

Chambless, Jim R., and Martha S. Chambless. "The Impact of Instructional Technology on Reading/Writing Skills of 2nd Grade Students." *Reading Improvement* 31, no. 3 (fall 1994): 151–55.

Christmann, Edwin, John Badgett, and Robert Lucking. "Progressive Comparisons of the Effects of Computer-Assisted Instruction on the Academic Achievement of Secondary Students." *Journal of Research on Computing in Education* 29, no. 4 (summer 1997).

Clark, Richard E. "Evidence for Confounding in Computer-Based Instruction Studies: Analyzing the Meta-Analysis." *Educational Communication and Technology Journal* 33, no. 4 (winter 1985): 249–62.

Clark, Richard E. "When Researchers Swim Upstream: Reflections on an Unpopular Argument about Learning from Media", Educational Technology, v 31 n 31 (February 1991): 34–40.

Clement, Frank J. "Affective Considerations in Computer-Based Education." *Educational Technology* (April 1981): 228–32.

Clements, Douglas H. et al. "Students' Development of Length Concepts in a Logo-Based Unit on Geometric Paths." *Journal for Research in Mathematics Education* 28, no. 1 (January 1997): 70–95.

Clements, Douglas H., et al. "Young Children and Computers: Crossroads and Directions from Research. Research in Review." *Young Children* 48, no. 2 (June 1993): 56–64.

Collis, Betty. *The Best of Research Windows: Trends and Issues in Educational Computing.* Eugene, Oreg.: International Society of Technology in Education, 1990.

Collis, B., and L. Ollila. "An Examination of Sex Difference in Secondary School Students' Attitudes toward Writing and the Computer." *The Alberta Journal of Educational Research* 34, no. 4 (1986): 297–306.

Colvin, L. B. "An Overview of U.S. Trends in Educational Software Design." *The Computing Teacher* 16, no. 5 (February 1989): 24–28.

Crawford, Walt. "Faster, Better, Cheaper: A Decade of PC Progress." *Online* 21, no. 1 (January–February 1997): 22–26, 28–29.

Crawford, Walt. "Jargon that Computes: Today's PC Terminology." *Online* 21, no. 2 (March–April 1997):36–41.

Daiute, C. *Writing and Computers*. Reading, Mass.: Addison Wesley, 1985.

Dalton, D. W. "A Comparison of the Effects of Logo and Problem-Solving Strategy Instruction on Learning Achievement, Attitude, and Problem-Solving Skills." *Dissertation Abstracts International* 47, no. 2 (1986): 511a (University Microfilms No. 86–08596).

Davidson, Johan, et al. "A Preliminary Study of the Effect of Computer-Assisted Practice on Reading Attainment." *Journal of Research in Reading* 19, no. 2 (September 1996): 20.

Dence, M. "Toward Defining the Role of CAI: A Review." *Educational Technology* (November 1980): 50–54.

Dunn, Kate. "Inventor's Robot is a big hit on the Shooting Range. L.A. Times Business, D7. April 27, 1998.

Dvorak, John C. *Dvorak Predicts: An Insider Look at the Computer Industry*. Berkeley, Calif.: Osborne McGraw-Hill, 1994.

Dye, Lee. "Robots. . . Robots Who Need People." *Los Angeles Times*, (September 29, 1997): D 8.

Dyrlli, Odvard Egil. "Online Privacy and the Cookies Controversy." *Technology and Learning* (March 1997): 20.

Ediger, M. "Computers at the Crossroads." *Educational Technology* 28, no. 5 (May 1988):7–10.

Farynaiarz, Joseph V., and Linda G. Lockwood. "Effectiveness of Microcomputer Simulations in Stimulating Environmental Problem Solving by Community College Students." *Journal of Research in Science Teaching* 29, no. 5 (May 1992): 453–70.

Feigenbaum, E. A., and P. McCorduck. *The Fifth Generation: Artificial Intelligence and Japan's Computer Challenge to the World*. Reading, Mass.: Addison Wesley, 1983.

Feldman, P. R. "Personal Computers in a Writing Course." *Perspectives in Computing* (spring 1984): 4–9.

Fisher, G. "Where CAI Is Effective: A Summary of the Research." *Electronic Learning* 82 (November/December 1983): 84.

Fites, Philip E. *The Computer Virus Crisis*. New York: Van Nostrand Reinhold, 1989.

Flanagan, Patrick. "The 10 Hottest Technologies in Telecom." *Telecommunications* 31, no. 5 (May 1997): 25–28, 30, 32.

Fortner, R., W. Schar, and J. Mayer. *Effect of Microcomputer Simulations on Computer Awareness and Perception of Environmental Relationships among College Students*. Columbus: Ohio State University, Office of Learning Resources (ERIC Document Reproduction Service No. Ed. 270-311), 1986.

Freedman, Alan. The Computer Glossary. New York: American Management Association, 1990.

Freedman, Allan. *The Computer Glossary*, 5th ed. Point Pleasant, Penn.: American Management Association, 1990.

Freedman, Warren. *The Right of Privacy in the Computer Age*. New York: Quorum Books, 1987.

Fulton, Mary. "The Data may not be perfect. But if we don't start somewhere and have something to build on, we're never going anywhere." Education Week, Vol. XVII, Number 11, (November, 1997) pages 10–11.

Galloway, Jerry P. "The Effects of QuickTime Multimedia Tools on Writing Style and Content." In *Technology and Teacher Education Annual*, ed. J. Willis, B. Robin, and D. A. Willis. Charlottesville, Va.: Association for the Advancement of Computing in Education (AACE), 1994.

Garzella, M. F. "Using an Expert System to Diagnose Weaknesses and Prescribe Remedial Reading Strategies among Elementary Learning Disabled Students." *Dissertation Abstracts International* 52/09-A (Order No. AAD92-07011), 1991.

"Gender Bias: Recent Research and Interventions." *New Jersey Research Bulletin,* no. 22 (Spring 1996).

Glass, G. V. "Integrated Findings: The Meta-Analysis of Research." In *Review of Research in Education,* ed. L. Schulman. Itasca, Ill.: Peacock, 1977.

Glass, G. V. "Primary, Secondary, and Meta-Analysis of Research." *Educational Researchers* 5 (1976): 3–8.

Gleason, Gerald T. "Microcomputers in Education: The State of the Art." *Educational Technology* (March 1981): 7–18.

Goode, M. "Testing CAI Courseware in Fifth and Sixth Grade Math." *T.H.E.* (October 1988): 97–100.

Gore, Andrew. "Pen, Voice Will Shape Interface." *MacWeek* 6, no. 5 (February 3, 1992): 1, 98.

Grovier, H. *Microcomputers in Primary Education: A Survey of Recent Research* (Occasional Paper ITE/28a/88). Lancaster, U.K.: Economics and Social Research Council, 1988.

Groner, Jonathan. "Swatting Back at Software Pirates." *Legal Times* (June 1992.)

Guglielmo, Connie. "Managers Clamp Down on Software Piracy." *MacWeek* 6, no. 2 (January 13, 1992): 60–63.

Harmon, Amy. "Times Mirror Co. Launches On-Line Interactive Services." *Los Angeles Times* (October 27, 1994): 1D.

Harrison, Nancy, and Evelyn M. Van Devender. "The Effects of Drill-and-Practice Computer Instruction on Learning Basic Mathematics Facts." *Journal of Computing in Childhood Education* 3, no. 304 (May 1993): 349–56.

Hasselbring, Ted S. "Remediating Spelling Problems of Learning-Handicapped Students through the Use of Microcomputers." *Educational Technology* (April 1982): 31–32.

Hatfield, M. M. "The Effect of Problem-Solving Software on Student's Beliefs About Mathematics: A Qualitative Study." *Computers in the Schools* 8, no. 4 (1991): 21–40.

Hatfield, Susan. "Effective Use of Classroom Computer Stations across the Curriculum." (ERIC Document Reproduction Service

No. ERIC no-ED396704 RIENOV96, Dissertations/Theses, Research Technical), June 30, 1996.

Hawisher, G. E. "The Effects of Word Processing on the Revision Strategies of College Students." Paper presented at the annual meeting of the American Educational Research Association, San Francisco (ERIC Document Reproductions Service No. ED. 268–546), April 1986.

Haynes, Colin. *The Computer Virus Protection Handbook.* San Francisco: SYBEX, 1990.

Hays, Timothy A. "Spatial Abilities and the Effects of Computer Animation on Short-Term and Long-Term Comprehension." *Journal of Educational Computing Research* 14, no. 2 (1996) 139–55.

Hodges, Andrew. Alan Turning: The Enigma. Vintage Paper Back, Ranlon Century, London, 1992.

Hoffman, Patricia. VSUM Database, December 30, 1997. (VSUM, 3333 Bowers Avenue, Suite 130, Santa Clara, CA 95054. Telephone (408) 988-3773, BBS (408) 244-0813.)

Hogan, Mike. "PC of Tomorrow." IDG. (January 1998): 132–142.

Horner, C. M. and C. D. Maddux. "The Effect of Logo on Attributions toward Success." *Computers in the Schools* 2, no. 2/3 (1985): 45–54.

Jones, I. "The Effects of a Word Processor on the Written Composition of Second-Grade Pupils." Computers in the Schools, 1994, 11(2): 43–54.

Jerome, Marty. "The Fastest PCs in the World." *PC Computing* (August 1997): 183–88.

Jessop, Deborah. "A Survey of Recent Advances in Optical and Multimedia Information Technologies." *Computers in Libraries* 17 no. 2 (February 1997): 53–59.

Kahney, Leander "White Pine Brings CU-See Me to Version 3.1" *MacWeek,* Vol 11, no. 48, (December 9, 1997).

Kaplin, Karen. "Robots Roll Up Their Sleeves." *Los Angeles Times* (March 10, 1994): 1D.

Keller, Janet K. "Characteristics of Logo Instruction Promoting Transfer of Learning: A Research

Review." *Journal of Research on Computers in Education* 23, no. 1 (fall 1990): 3.

Khalili, A., and L. Shashaani. "The Effectiveness of Computer Applications: A Meta-analysis." *Journal of Research on Computing in Education* 27, no. 1 (fall 1994): 48–61.

Koseinski, Susan, et al. "Computer-Assisted Instruction with Constant Time Delay to Teach Multiplication Facts to Students with Learning Disabilities." *Learning Disabilities Research Practices* 8, no. 3 (summer 1993): 157–68.

Krein, T. J., and T. R. Mahollm. "CDT has the Edge in a Comparative Study." *Performance and Instruction* (August 1990): 22–24.

Kromhout, Ora M., and Sarah M. Butzin. "Integrating Computers into the Elementary School Curriculum: An Evaluation of Nine Project CHILD Model Schools." *Journal of Research on Computing in Education* 26, no. 1 (fall 1993): 5.

Kulik, Chen-Lin, and James A. Kulik. "Effectiveness of Computer-Based Instruction: An Updated Analysis." *Computers in Human Behavior* 7 (1991): 75–94.

Kulik, James A., R. Bangert, and G. Williams. "Effects of Computer-Based Teaching on Secondary School Students." *Journal of Educational Psychology* 75 (1983): 19–26.

Kulik, C. C., J. A. Kulik, and P. Cohen. "Instructional Technology and College Teaching." *Teaching of Psychology* 7 (1980): 199–205.

Kulik, C. C., J. A. Kulik, and B. J. Shwath. "Effectiveness of Computer-Based Adult Learning: A Meta-Analysis." *Journal of Educational Computing Research* 2 (1986): 235–52.

Kulik, James A., and C. Chen-Lin. "Review of Recent Literature on Computer-Based Instruction." *Contemporary Education Psychology* 12, no. 3 (July 1987): 222–30.

Kulik, J. A., and C. C. Kulik. "Timing of Feedback and Verbal Learning." *Review of Educational Research* 58, no. 1 (1988): 79–97.

Kumar, David D., and Stanley L. Helgeson. "Trends in Computer Applications in Science Assessment." *Journal of Science Education and Technology* 41, no. 1 (March 1995):29–36.

Kurth, R. J. "Using Word Processing to Enhance Revision Strategies during Student Writing Activities." *Educational Technology* 27 (1987): 13–19.

Lally, M. "Computer-Assisted Development of Number Conservation in Mentally Retarded Children." *Journal of Developmental Disabilities* (September 1980): 131–36.

Leeds, Matthew. "Desktop Videoconferencing." *MacWorld* (November 1994): 87–92.

Linn, C. "Learning More—with Computers as Lab Partners." Paper presented at the annual meeting of the American Educational Research Association, San Francisco, April 1986.

Lu, G. C. "Expert Adolescent Programmers: The Cognitive Consequences of Programming." Doctoral Dissertation, Columbia University Teachers College (Dissertation Abstracts Order Number DA9136407), 1991.

Luehrmann, A. "The Best Way to Teach Computer Literacy." *Electronic Learning* 3, no. 3 (April 1984): 37–42, 44.

Lundell, Allan. *Virus! The Secret World of Computer Invaders That Breed and Destroy.* Chicago: Contemporary Books, 1989.

MacArthur, C. A., J. A. Haynes, D. B. Melouf, and K. Harris. "Computer Assisted Instruction with Learning Disabled Students: Achievement, Engagement, and Other Factors Related to Achievement." Paper presented at the annual meeting of the American Educational Research Association, Washington, D.C., April 1987.

Makrakis, Vasilios, and Toshio Sawada. "Gender, Computers and Other School Subjects among Japanese and Swedish Students." *Computers & Education* 26, no. 4 (May 1996): 225–31.

Mann, Dale, and Carol Shakeshaft. "The Impact of Technology in the Schools of the Mohawk Regional Information Center Area." Technical Report, 1997. ERIC Document NO.-ED 405893 (800) 443-ERIC

Maser, Arthur L., et al. *Highline Public Schools Computer-Assisted Instruction Project: A Program* to Meet Disadvantaged Students' Individual Needs for Basic Skill Development: Final Report (July 1979): ED. 167–74.

Mayer, R. E., J. L. Dyck, and W. Vilberg. "Learning to Program and Learning to Think: What's the Connection?" *Communication of the ACM* 29, no. 7 (1986): 605–10.

Mayer, R. E., and A. L. Fay. "A Chain of Cognitive Changes with Learning to Program in Logo." *Journal of Educational Psychology* 79, no. 3 (1987): 21.

McAfee, John. *Computer Viruses, Worms, Data Diddlers, Killer Programs, and Others.* New York: St. Martin's Press, 1989.

McGrath, Diane, Chandima Cumaranatunge, Misook Ji, Huiping Chen, Winston Broce, and Kathleen Writh. "Multimedia Science Projects: Seven Case Studies." *Journal of Research on Computing in Education.* 30, No. 1 (fall 1997).

McNaughton, David, et al. "Proofreading for Students with Learning Disabilities." *Learning Disabilities Research and Practice,* 12, no. 1 (1997) 16–28.

McNeil, Barbara J., and Karyn R. Nelson. "Meta-Analysis of Interactive Video Instruction: A 10 Year Review of Achievement Effects." *Journal of Computer-Based Instruction* 18, no. 1 (1991): 1–6.

Milbrandt, George. "Using Problem Solving to Teach a Programming Language." *Learning and Leading with Technology* 23, no. 2 (October 1995): 27–31.

Miller, David. "Research into LOGO—What Are the Lessons for Primary Schools?" *Scottish Educational Review* 25, no. 2 (November 1993): 104–8.

Miller, Mark D., and William D. McInerney. "Effects on Achievement of a Home/School Computer Project." *Journal of Research on Computing in Education* 27 no. 2 (winter 1994–1995): 198–210.

Moore, C., S. Smith, and R. A. Avner. "Facilitation of Laboratory Performance through CAI." *Journal of Chemical Education* 57, no. 3 (1980): 196–98.

Morehouse, D. L., M. L. Hoaglund, and R. H. Schmidt. *Technology Demonstration Program Final Evaluation Report.* Menononie, Wis.: Quality Evaluation and Development, February 1987.

Nadeau, Michael, and Bram Vermeer. "Coming 'Soon': 3-GB CD-ROMs." *Byte* (October 1994): 4.

Norr, H. "Latest Mac Viral Infection Hits the Stacks." *MacWeek* (April 16, 1991): 17.

Norr, H. "Speech Recognizer Hears through the `Ums and Ers.'" *MacWeek* 4, no. 34 (October 9, 1990): 5.

Novice Editorial Staff. "Working at Home" *PC Novice* (September 1994): 61.

O'Brien, P. "Using Microcomputers in the Writing Class." *The Computing Teacher* (May 1984): 20–21.

Palumbo, David B., and Michael W. Reed. "The Effect of Basic Programming Language Instruction on High School Students's Problem Solving Ability and Computer Anxiety." *Journal of Research on Computing in Education* 23, no. 3 (spring 1991): 342–69.

Papert, S. *Mindstorms.* New York: Basic Books, 1980.

Papert, Seymour. "An Exploration in the Space of Mathematics Education." *International Journal of Computers for Mathematics Learning;* I (1996): 95–173.

Parker, Donn B. *Ethical Conflicts in Information and Computer Science Technology.* Wellesley, Mass.: QED Information Sciences, 1990.

Paul, Lawrence. "Keying Injuries Proliferate, Defying Clear Cut Remedies." *PC Magazine* (August 8, 1994): 81.

Pea, R. D., and D. M. Kurland. *Logo Programming and the Development of Planning Skills* (Technical Report No. 11). New York: Bank Street College of Education, March 1984.

Pea, R. D. "The Aims of Software Criticism: Reply to Professor Papert." *Educational Researcher* 16, no. 5 (June/July 1987): 4–8.

Pfaffenberger, Bryan. *Webster's New World Dictionary.* New York: Que, 1997.

Phelps, David. "SPA Reaches Settlement with Internet Software Pirates, Credits Teamwork with Internet Access Provider," 1997. (SPA Internet Address http://www.spa.org)

"Portable Speech Synthesizers." Byte (October 1994): 224.

Quinlan, Tom. "Apple Declares War on Software Piracy." *InfoWorld* 12 (August 1991): 8.

Richman, John A. "At-Risk Students: Innovative Technologies." *Media and Methods* 30, no. 5 (May–June 1994): 26–7.

Rizzo, J. "Erasable Optical Drives." *MacUser* (November 1990): 102–30.

Robertson G. *A Comparison of Meaningful and Nonmeaningful Content in Computer-Assisted Spelling Programs.* Saskatchewan, Canada: Saskatchewan School Trustees Association Research Center, 1978.

Robertson, S., et al. "The Use and Effectiveness of Palmtop Computers in Education." *British Journal of Educational Technology* 28, no. 3 (July 1997): 177–89.

Roblyer, M. D., W. H. Castine, and F. J. King. *Assessing the Impact of Computer-Based Instruction: A Review of Recent Research.* New York: Haworth Press, 1988.

Ruel, Alred A. *The Application of Research Findings.* Washington, D.C.: National Education Association, 1977.

Ryan, Bob. "Alpha Ride High." *Byte* (October 1994): 197–98.

Sacks, Colin H., Ylanda Belilisimo, and John Mergendoller. "Attitudes toward Computers and Computer Use: The Issue of Gender." *Journal of Research on Computing in Education* 26, no. 2 (winter 1993–1994): 256–69.

Salerno, Christopher A. "The Effect of Time on Computer-Assisted Instruction for At-Risk Students." *Journal of Research on Computing in Education* 28, no. 1 (fall 1995): 85–97.

Schroeder, Erica. "Voice Recognition Making Some Noise." *PC Week* 12, no. 20 (May 23, 1994): 7.

Shashaani, Lily. "Gender-Based Differences in Attitudes toward Computers." *Computers and Education* 20, no. 2 (March 1993): 169–81.

Shashaani, Lily. "Gender-Differences in Computer Experience and Its Influence on Computer Attitudes." *Journal of Educational Computing Research* 11, no. 4 (1994): 347–67.

Shashaani, Lily. "Gender Differences in Mathematics Experience and Attitude and Their Relation to Computer Attitude." *Educational Technology* 35, no. 3 (May–June 1995): 32–38.

Shashaani, Lily. "Socioeconomic Status, Parents' Sex-Role Stereotypes, and the Gender Gap in Computing." *Journal of Research on Computing in Education,* 26, no. 4 (summer 1994,): 433–51.

Shiah, Rwey-Lin, et al. "The Effects of Computer-Assisted Instruction on Mathematical Problem Solving of Students with Learning Disabilities." *Exceptionality* 5 (994–1995): 131–61.

Siann G., A. Durndell, H. Macleod, and P. Glissov. "Stereotyping in Relation to the Gender Gap in Participation in Computing." *Educational Research* 30, no. 2 (1988): 98–103.

"Software Piracy," Software Publishers Association, (White Paper). 1992.

Software Publishers Association Home Page, 1988.

Software Publishers Association News Release. 14 April 1992.

Software Publishers Association, News Release. October 1995, this URL on World Wide Web http://www.spa.org/Software Publishers Association. Reports published on the World Wide Web at URL http://www.spa/.org/ Fall 1996a–c.

Soloway, E., J. Lockhead, and J. Clement. "Does Computer Programming Enhance Problem Solving Ability? Some Positive Evidence on Algebra Word Problems." In *Computer Literacy: Issues and Directions for 1985,* ed. R. J. Seidel, R. Anderson and B. Hunter New York: Academic Press, 1982.

Stuart, Rory. *The Design of Virtual Environments.* Boston, Mass.: McGraw-Hill, 1996.

Summerville, L. J. "The Relationship between Computer-Assisted Instruction and Achievement Levels and Learning Rates of Secondary School Students in First Year Chemistry." *Dissertation Abstracts International* 46, no. 3 (1984): 603a (University Microfilms No. 85–10891).

Suomala, Jyrki. "Eight-Year-Old Pupils' Problem-Solving Process within a Logo Learning

Environment." *Scandinavian Journal of Educational Research* 40, no. 4 (December 1996): 291–309.

Swadener, M., and M. Hannafin. "Gender Similarities and Differences in Sixth Graders' Attitudes toward Computers: An Exploratory Study." *Educational Technology* 27, no. 1 (1987): 37–42.

Takahashi, Dean. "Which Disk Will Slip?" *Los Angeles Times* (March 14, 1995): 1D.

Teh, George P. L., and Barry Fraser. "Gender Differences in Achievement and Attitudes among Students Using Computer-Assisted Instruction." *International Journal of Instructional Media* 22, no. 2 (1995): 111.

Terrell, Steve, and Paul Rendulic. "Using Computer-Managed Instructional Software to Increase Motivation and Achievement in Elementary School Children." *Journal of Research on Computing in Education* 26, no. 3, (spring 1996): 403–14.

Tessler, Franklin N. "Safer Computing." *MacWorld* (December 1994): 96.

Thomas, Rex, and Elizabeth Hooper. "Simulations: An Opportunity We Are Missing." *Journal of Research on Computing in Education* 23, no. 4 (summer 1991): 497–513.

Thomas, Rex A., and Sylvester C. Upah Jr. "Give Programming Instruction a Chance." *Journal of Research on Computing in Education* 29, no. 1 (fall 1996): 96–108.

Tien, James M. *Electronic Fund Transfer Systems Fraud: Computer Crimes.* Washington, D.C.: U.S. Department of Justice, Bureau of Justice Statistics, 1985.

Trosko, Nancy. "Making Technology Work for Your Students." *Technology Connection* 4, no. 2 (April 1997): 20–22.

Trotler, Andrew. "Taking Technology's Measure." *Education Week* VolXVII, no. 11, (November 10, 1997): 6–13.

Tsai, San-Yun W., and Norval F. Pohl. "Student Achievement in Computer Programming: Lecture vs. Computer-Aided Instruction." *Journal of Experimental Education* (winter 1977): 66–70.

Viadero, Debra. "A Tool for Learning." *Education Week* 17 no. 11 (November 1997): 12–14.

Viscusi, Vance. "21st Century Classroom." *Computers in Education,* 8th ed., 31–33. Guilford, Conn.: Dushkin/McGraw-Hill.

Wanat, Thomas. "Internet-Savvy Students Help Track Down the Hacker of an NCAA Web Site." *Chronicle of Higher Education* 43, no. 29 (March 28, 1997): A30.

Ware, M. C., and M. F. Stuck. "Sex-Role Message Vis-a-Vis Microcomputer Use: A Look at the Pictures." *Sex Roles* 13, no. 34 (1985): 205–14.

Watkins, Marley W., and C. Webb. "Computer-Assisted Instruction with Learning-Disabled Students." *Educational Computer* (September/October 1981): 24–27.

Whitley, Bernard E., Jr. "Gender Differences in Computer-Related Attitudes and Behavior: A Meta-Analysis." *Computers in Human Behavior* 13, no. 1 (January 1997): 1–22.

Wiegner, Kathleen. "Software Predicts Radio Wave Action." *Los Angeles Times* (October 12, 1994): D4.

Williams, Sue Winkle, et al. "Gender Roles, Computer Attitudes, and Dyadic Computer Interaction Performance in College Students." *Sex Roles: A Journal of Research* 29, no. 7–8 (June 1994): 515–25.

Willis, William. "Speech Recognition: Instead of Typing and Clicking, Talk and Command." *T.H.E. Journal* 25, no. 6, (January 1998): 18–22.

Withrow, Frank B. "Technology in Education and the Next Twenty-Five Years." *T.H.E. Journal* 24, no. 11 (June 1997): 59–62.

Woodward, L., and R. Gersten. "Innovative Technology for Secondary Students with Learning Disabilities." *Exceptional Children* 58, no. 5 (March–April 1992): 407–21.

Wright, R. "Multimedia: What Is It?" *MacValley Voice* (October 1990): 2.

Zellermayer, M., G. Salomon, T. Globerson, and H. Givon. "Enhancing Writing-Related Metacognitions through a Computerized Writing Partner." *American Educational Research Journal* 28, no. 2 (1991): 373–91.

Appendix A
RECOMMENDED SOFTWARE

The majority of these programs are available in CD-ROM; a few still come on 3 1/2-inch diskettes.

ART UTILITIES PROGRAMS

Adobe PhotoDeluxe, **Adobe (Macintosh, Windows). Grades 7–Adult.**

Adobe PhotoDeluxe lets you personalize your photographs with special effects. This program has step-by-step directions that explain how to combine photos, add special effects, and remove red eye. Templates let you add your photos to calendars, greeting cards, and so on.

Adobe PhotoShop, **Adobe (Macintosh, Windows). Grades 10–Adult.**

This program is the standard for photo design and is a production tool for images that you can print and use on the Internet.

ArtDabbler 2.1, **Meta Creations (Macintosh, Windows). Grades 3–Adult.**

Art Dabbler 2.1 is an ideal art program for older students. It has a simple interface, visual tutorials, and a full array of natural-media painting tools. You can create animations and print them as flipbooks or save them as *QuickTime* or *AVI* movies.

Bricks, **Gryphon Software (Macintosh, Windows). Grades 2–Adult.**

Bricks is educational software that lets the user click on more than 300 brick styles to build objects that range from cars and boats to dinosaurs. There is an adult as well as child's version integrated into the program.

DeBabelizer, **Equilibrium (Macintosh, Windows). Grades 10–Adult.**

DeBabelizer is a high-powered automated application for students working with graphics, animations and digital video, the Web, and desktop products. This program can automatically perform an unlimited number of graphic processes on an unlimited number of images for any specification for an entire batch and output everything to more than ninety bit-mapped file formats.

Disney's Magic Artist, **Disney Interactive (Windows, Power Mac OS). Grades 3–up.**

Disney's Magic Artist is a drawing program that has realistic-looking tools such as whipped cream and bubbles, paints that smear, musical selections, and much more. The program includes a tutorial on how to draw Disney characters.

EA Kids Art Center, **EA Kids (Macintosh, Windows). Grades K–12.**

EA Kids Art Center is a paint program designed for K–12 students. The program features a paint box with colors, funny paint brushes, and various tools, each with its own sound. This program includes a talking alphabet, stickers, a coloring book, and block art.

Fine Artist, **Microsoft (Macintosh, Windows). Grades 3–8.**

Fine Artist has more than 100 animated clip art images with which students can create incredible multimedia projects. The program also makes stickers, posters, and comic strips.

Flying Colors, **Davidson (Macintosh, Windows). Grades 3–Adult.**

Flying Colors creates incredible masterpieces with exciting paint tools, patterns, and many other features. The program comes with 1,000 detailed images that you can rotate, shrink, and brighten. Included with this unique program is a color-cycling process for magical animation effects.

Kai's Power Goo, **Metatools (Macintosh, Windows). Grades 3–Adult.**

This program lets the user create liquid images and manipulate them by smearing, smudging, stretching, and fusing them. You can superimpose these images and blend parts of one image with another to create a third image.

Kid Culture, **Pierian Spring Publishing (Macintosh, Windows). Grades 3–6.**

This program lets students explore history, myth, art, tradition, and daily life in an interactive environment. Each culture offers printable art in which students can construct authentic headdresses, masks, castles, entire 3-D villages, skyscrapers, trains, cars, boats, animals, people, and more.

Kid Pix 2, **Brøderbund (Macintosh, DOS/Windows). Grades K–8.**

Kid Pix 2 combines the original *Kid Pix* with *Kid Pix Companion*. In doing so it creates an enhanced version that not only has a set of art tools, but has slide show capabilities.

Kid Pix Studio Deluxe, **Brøderbund (Macintosh, Windows). Grades K–8.**

Kid Pix Studio is an enhanced, CD-ROM version of *Kid Pix* that includes a compilation of multimedia features. With three new features—Moopies, Stampinator, and Digital Puppets—students can add animation, video, and sound effects to any picture or slide show.

Print Artist 4.0, **Sierra (Macintosh, Windows). Grades 2–6.**

An easy-to-use program, *Print Artist* lets students design posters, signs, greeting cards, and more in a matter of minutes. The program features more than 10,000 full-color graphics, 1,500 professionally designed layouts, and 600 spectacular photos.

The Print Shop Premier Edition **Brøderbund (Macintosh, Windows). Grades K–Adult.**

This classic program comes in different flavors, such as *Print Shop Ensemble* and *Print Shop Deluxe*. With *The Print Shop*'s clip art, borders, and fonts, you can create calendars, posters, signs, banners, greeting cards, personal stationery, and advertising material. In addition, *Print Shop Premiere Edition* lets you send on-line greetings and design professional-looking certificates using its 23,000 plus graphics and photos.

AUTHORING TOOLS/PRESENTATION SOFTWARE

Digital Chisel, **Pierian Spring Software (Macintosh, Windows). Grades 6–12.**

Digital Chisel is a multimedia authoring tool for teachers and students. With this program, you can create exciting interactive presentations, storybooks, lessons, tests, or reports. *Digital Chisel*'s strength is its ability to create tests in a variety of formats, including multiple choice, essay, fill-in, true/false, and matching.

HyperCard, **Apple Computer (Macintosh). Grades 8–Adult.**

Developed by Bill Atkinson, *HyperCard* is an authoring tool that lets you create on-screen "cards," or screens containing text, graphics, sound, and animation. You can design various card sizes; enhance drawings, sound, and animation; and open up stacks of cards simultaneously. *HyperCard* can be used to teach programming or to create lessons.

HyperStudio, Roger Wagner Publishing (Macintosh, Windows). Grades 7–12.

HyperStudio is an extremely popular authoring program that is used worldwide. It offers many built-in features and functions, including color, laser disc, and CD-ROM support, animation, scrolling, and exporting to the Web.

LinkWay Live! IBM (DOS). Grades 6–Adult.

LinkWay Live! lets teachers and students develop multimedia presentations that combine text, color graphics, picture images, music freeze-frames, and full-motion video. The program features pull-down menus, a paint program, a text editor, a font editor, and demonstration programs. *LinkWay Live!* organizes information into folders, much in the way that *HyperCard* organizes cards into stacks.

MicroWorlds Project Builder, Logo Computer Systems (Macintosh, DOS/Windows). Grades 4–8.

MicroWorlds Project Builder is a hypermedia tool with which students build projects in practically any curriculum area. Students use this Logo-based tool kit to create and combine graphics, text, animation, music, and sound in interactive books, playhouses, newsletters, maps, and other products.

mPower, Multimedia Design Corporation (Macintosh, Windows). Grades 7–Adult.

mPower is a multimedia presentation tool that uses a push-button interface. This product creates and edits *QuickTime* movies and links to the Internet, and it controls your hardware peripherals.

MP Express (Bytes of Learning) (Macintosh, Windows). Grades 2 and up.

This program is an easy-to-use multimedia presentation tool for children as well as adults. Its streamlined design and simplified user interface lets beginners and advanced users produce high quality presentations in minutes.

Multimedia Workshop, Davidson (Macintosh, Windows). Grades 5–Adult.

Multimedia Workshop helps students create printed documents and video presentations in three workshops: Writing Workshop, Paint Workshop, and Video Workshop. Students can view video presentations on a storyboard grid or on the computer screen.

PowerPoint, Microsoft (Macintosh, Windows). Grades 9–Adult.

PowerPoint is a presentation tool that lets high-school students turn ideas into powerful presentations. The program has instant layouts, on-screen directions, and tool tips that make compelling multimedia presentations. PowerPoint lets you create overheads for class presentations, slides for a meeting, or dazzling effects on-screen.

DATABASE PROGRAMS (SEE SPREADSHEETS/ INTEGRATED PROGRAMS)

FileMaker Pro, Claris (Macintosh, Windows). Grades 7–Adult.

An easy-to-use but still powerful and sophisticated piece of software, *FileMaker Pro* offers many layout possibilities to meet the varied needs of student and teacher without compromising output or performance.

TableTop Jr. (younger students) and TableTop Sr. (older students), Brøderbund/TERC (Macintosh, Windows). Grades 1–12.

Using these tools, students can sort, manipulate, and create data sets. Both programs provide databases for the students to explore.

DESKTOP PUBLISHING

Amazing Writing Machine, Brøderbund (Macintosh). Grades K–6.

This program inspires children to write and illustrate their own stories, journals, essays, letters, and poems. They can design pages from scratch or use predesigned templates. The program has a built-in spelling checker and a rebus tool that transforms words into pictures.

Easy Book Deluxe (home version) and *Chickadee Software* (school version), Tom Snyder Productions (Macintosh). Grades 2–6, Special Education.

With *Easy Book,* children create real books with a minimum of effort. They simply write their stories and illustrate them with simple paint tools. The program determines the page layout and is even able to print on both sides of the paper.

Imagination! Express, Edmark (Macintosh, Windows). Grades 1–6.

Edmark has reached a new plateau in education with this sensational multimedia desktop publishing program. Students create interactive books and print out beautifully illustrated stories. The program features a multitude of illustrated backgrounds, hundreds of character and prop "stickers," a text placement feature, a sound record option, and music capabilities.

Kid Works 2, Davidson (Macintosh, DOS/Windows). Grades K–4.

Kid Works 2 is a combination word processor, text to speech program, and paint program in a simple-to-use package. Students learn to express themselves in Spanish or English and listen to the computer read their own stories.

Microsoft Publisher, Microsoft (Windows). Grades 5–Adult.

Microsoft Publisher performs a wide variety of choices from creating a business card or flyer to producing a newspaper. The program requires less learning time than a program such as *QuarkXPress* or *PageMaker,* but it is more complicated than *The Children's Writing and Publishing Center* or *Imagination! Express.* You can work from scratch or work through a series of questions posed by the program to determine how to build your publication.

My Own Stories, MECC/Softkeys International (Macintosh, Windows). Grades 3–8.

In this charming program, students create stories by selecting scenes, objects, colors, sound effects, and music. They use a simple word processor with on-screen icons and graphics tools to write and illustrate. This creative writing process helps them develop their reading and writing skills.

PageMaker, Adobe Learning Systems (Macintosh, Windows). Grades 11–Adult.

The publishing package that launched the desktop publishing revolution, *PageMaker* gives advanced users the ability to produce professional documents quickly. The program uses an intuitive electronic pasteboard that enables you to lay out and view text and graphics easily on a page. Several templates and predesigned publications come with it.

Print Shop PressWriter, Brøderbund (Windows). Grades 4–up.

With this program, you can create newsletters, brochures, reports, letterhead, resumes, booklets, and flyers. You answer a series of questions; based on your answers, the program builds the publication.

QuarkXPress, XTensions (Macintosh, Windows). Grades 10–Adult.

This program is becoming the standard for desktop publishing, possessing a full range of features for the sophisticated user.

Stanley Sticker Stories, Edmark (Macintosh, Windows). Grades Pre-K–2.

Students create their own animated storybooks featuring the Edmark characters Sammy, Trudy, Millie, and Baily.

Storybook Weaver Deluxe, MECC/Softkeys International (Macintosh, Windows). Grades 1–4.

Storybook Weaver Deluxe gives young students a simple interface with which to create elaborate storybooks that combine graphics, sounds, and text. The easy-to-use word processor has a spelling checker, a thesaurus, and text-to-speech capabilities. This program operates in both English and Spanish and has drawing tools and an excellent collection of graphics.

Student Writing Center, Learning Company (Macintosh, Windows). Grades 4–10.

Student Writing Center is a quality word processor and desktop publishing program. This program comes packed with features, including a spelling checker, a bibliography maker, a thesaurus, process writing capabilities, and grammar tips. Included in this package are thirty predesigned letterheads and borders and more than 150 clip art pictures.

The Ultimate Writing and Creativity Center, Learning Company (Macintosh, Windows). Grades 2–6.

Students create reports, signs, journals, storybooks, and newsletters. This program has the ability to have documents read aloud and to add animation.

EARLY CHILDHOOD

Allie's Playhouse and *Allie's Activity Kit,* Opcode Interactive (Macintosh, Windows). Grades Pre-K–2.

Allie is an alien friend who plays sixteen different exciting learning games with the user. Students learn about counting, math, the alphabet, spelling, time, biology, music, art, and singing. The interactive activities feature children's voices, animation, music, and multimedia.

The Backyard, Brøderbund (Macintosh, DOS/Windows). Pre-K.

The Backyard is an interactive program with elements of strategic thinking, simulation, and discovery. Children are introduced to the fascinating world that exists in their own backyards through an assortment of educational games and activities. Children learn about animals, mapping, music, plants, and facial expressions.

JumpStart series, Knowledge Adventure (Macintosh, DOS/Windows) Pre-K–5.

Students learn to navigate through a schoolhouse full of interactive educational songs, puzzles, and games with a friendly host.

Kid's Zoo, Knowledge Adventure (Macintosh, DOS). Grades Pre-K–4.

Kid's Zoo introduces the younger child to science by exploring the world of zoo animals. The interactive zoo includes games, movies, an animal picture dictionary, and a talking storybook.

McGee, McGee Visits Katie's Farm, McGee at the Fun Fair, and *McGee's School Days,* Lawrence Productions (Macintosh, DOS/Windows). Pre-K.

When children click on various objects on the screen, the objects respond with speech and movement. In the first program, McGee completes the tasks that most children accomplish in the morning: He brushes his teeth and goes to the bathroom. In the second program, he visits Katie's farm to ride a horse, go fishing, pick raspberries, and gather eggs. In the third program, McGee and his best friend, Tony, attend the summer Fun Fair and enjoy a day of entertainment. In the fourth program, McGee visits the school and plays classic games such as duck-duck goose and hopscotch. These programs are engaging introductions to the computer for small children.

My Amazing Human Body, Dorling Kindersley Multimedia (Macintosh, DOS/Windows,). Grades K–4.

A 3-D skeleton teaches the students about topics that range from human anatomy to health. They engage in activities such as building a body and playing a "taking me apart" game.

Playroom, Brøderbund (Macintosh, DOS/Windows). Grades Pre-K–1.

Playroom is an interactive program with elements of strategic thinking, simulation, and discovery. By clicking on a clock, computer, mixed-up toy, mouse hole, ABC book, or spinner toy, children select activities in which they explore letters, numbers, and time. Every game, toy, and surprise has something to teach; the program skillfully uses animation, sound, music, and graphics.

Putt-Putt Joins the Parade, **Humongous Entertainment (Macintosh, DOS). Grades K–2.**

Putt-Putt is a car that takes students on a fun-filled adventure. Students play games in a toy store, chat with a fire engine, and collect items they need before joining a parade. Adults as well as children love this delightful talking program that requires them to learn directions, mapping skills, colors, and numbers. In *Putt-Putt Goes to the Moon,* another adventure by Humongous, Putt-Putt joins another vehicle and together they learn the benefits of cooperation and the value of friendship.

Reader Rabbit's Ready for Letters, **Learning Company (Macintosh, DOS/Windows). Grades Pre-K–1.**

This fun-filled program uses six activities with wonderful cartoon characters and lifelike speech and animation to help children learn letters, find shapes and colors, match words and letters, and spell.

Richard Scarry's Busytown, **Paramount Communications (Macintosh, DOS/Windows). Grades Pre-K–2.**

The adorable characters from Richard Scarry's books come alive in twelve original playgrounds. *Richard Scarry's Busytown* will keep young children busy for hours with activities that let them experiment with objects, manipulate real machines, and practice working behind a counter. Furthermore, they can build a house, become a doctor, or fight a fire. Another new title produced by Paramount is *How Things Work in Busytown.* In this program, the Busytown characters teach cause and effect relationships.

Stickybear's Early Learning Activities, **Optimum Resources (Macintosh). Grades Pre-K–1.**

This program offers the early learner six colorful and entertaining activities that teach basic skills including the alphabet, counting, shapes, and opposites.

The computer voice is delightful and converses in Spanish and English.

Zurk's Learning Safari, **Soleil (Macintosh, DOS/Windows). Grades Pre-K–2.**

Zurk's Learning Safari is a colorful content-rich multimedia experience that introduces children to skills in basic science, reading, and math. Engaging animated characters lead children on a safari through the African Serengeti. They swim in a bowl of alphabet soup and explore Zurk's activity-filled "magic shape box."

GRAPHICS

Claris CAD, **Claris (Macintosh). Grades 10–Adult.**

With this computer-assisted design program, students can create any two-dimensional geometric design as well as lines, arcs, spline curves, and more.

Cricket Graphics III, **Computer Associates (Macintosh). Grades 8–Adult.**

Cricket Graphics is a complete graphics program that offers a wide variety of chart types. In a relatively short period of time, users can produce magnificent three-dimensional color graphics for presentation. The program is relatively easy to use, and most high schoolers can master it.

DeltaGraph Pro 3.5, **DeltaPoint (Macintosh). Grades 10–Adult.**

DeltaGraph Pro is a high-power feature-laden charting program. The program has a built-in help function that advises users on the appropriate display for their data.

Kid CAD, **Davidson (Windows). Grades 2–8.**

Kid CAD is a clever three-dimensional kit with which students build houses with electronic building blocks and click them into position. Students can paint, decorate anything displayed on the screen, and fill the house with pets, furniture, and even a dinosaur. The program features a realistic environment that lets students customize the perspective they are viewing.

LANGUAGE ARTS/READING PROGRAMS

American Girls Premiere, **Learning Company (Macintosh, Windows). Grades 2–6.**

This program lets students create plays by choosing scenery, props, and characters and by adding narration and text. In addition, the program offers story starters and music from that time period.

Bailey's Book House, **Edmark (Macintosh, Windows). Grades Pre-K–1.**

When children enter the enchanting environment of *Bailey's Book House,* they learn the alphabet, make rhymes, and develop visual memory and discrimination. They create adventure stories filled with spaceships, flying carpets, and monsters.

Beginning Reading, **Sierra On-Line (Macintosh, Windows). Grades Pre-K–2.**

Beginning Reading is a creative program that teaches reading skills through a talking chimp named Bananas and a jack-in-the-box. These creatures talk to the students in authentic voices to help them arrange words in alphabetic order, learn sight vocabulary, and read stories. The chimp gives positive reinforcement for correct responses and keeps track of student progress.

Community Exploration, **Conter—a division of Josten Home Learning (Macintosh, Windows). All grades.**

Community Exploration is an interactive, language-building program that lets students explore fifty-two interesting places in a make-believe community. They see how people work, live, and play. This program is excellent for students learning English as a second language.

Deluxe! Reader Rabbit 1, 2, and 3, **Learning Company (Macintosh, DOS/Windows). Grades K–4.**

Reader Rabbit 1, 2, and 3 can be purchased on three separate disks or on a single CD-ROM. These primary programs are beautifully designed with lifelike speech and characters that mesmerize readers. The programs

use a game approach to teach phonics and reading skills, including word building, vowel sounds, word concepts, and beginning dictionary skills.

Corporate Climber, **JayKlein Productions (Macintosh, Windows). Grades 7-Adult.**

Corporate Climber helps you learn and master the English language. Users enter the corporation as a probationary employee and embark on an entertaining and educational journal through the company's ten divisions. In the process they learn about subject-verb disharmony, spelling, apostrophes, pronouns and much more.

English Express Deluxe, **Davidson and Associates (Macintosh, Windows, laser disc). Grades 5–Adult.**

This program is designed to teach English as a Second Language (ESL) students. Students hear standard pronunciations and make connections among spoken and written words and sentences and images representing the words' meanings to help them acquire language skills naturally.

Grammar Games, **Davidson (Macintosh, Windows). Grades 3–6.**

Grammar Games helps students build and practice grammar skills in areas such as subject-verb agreement, punctuation, and identification of sentence fragments. Set in a rain forest, the program features forty-two original stories, musical sound effects, and interesting rain forest facts.

Hollywood High, **Theatrix (Macintosh, Windows). Grades 7–12.**

Hollywood High encourages creative writing and provides an opportunity for students to listen to their own written work and make revisions. When students use *Hollywood High,* they choose characters, expressions, and scenery for their play. They write scripts, add actions, edit these scripts, and then listen to and watch the characters perform.

Inside the SAT, **Princeton Review (Macintosh, Windows). Grades 9–12.**

Inside the SAT is a tutorial program that uses a step-by-step approach to help students master the strategies for dealing with material found on the SAT in all pertinent subject areas. The program's instructor reviews basic skills using multimedia lesson topics. Furthermore, students can research more than 1,200 colleges, including financial aid information, and contact the home pages of these institutions on the World Wide Web.

Leap into Phonetics, **BrightStart/Distributed by FTC (Macintosh, Windows). Pre-K–1(ESL).**

Leap into Phonics teaches Pre-K through first graders the eight beginning phonemic awareness phonic skills including rhyming, auditory memory, sound segmentation, alphabet, sound substitution, blending sounds, identifying environmental sounds and nursery rhymes.

Living Book **Series, Living Books (Macintosh, Windows). Grades K–5.**

This excellent series of delightful interactive books comes in English and Spanish. The titles continue to grow in number. Five of the more popular books are *Arthur's Teacher Trouble, Just Grandma and Me, Little Monster at School, New Kid on the Block,* and *Ruff's Bone. Arthur's Teacher Trouble* tells of the grade school adventures of a shy aardvark. *Just Grandma and Me* is a story about a grandma's and grandson's adventures at the beach. *Little Monster at School* is a funny story about the trials and tribulations of a new kid at school. *New Kid on the Block* encourages students to learn the meanings of words by exploring a collection of poems with appealing topics and themes. *Green Eggs and Ham* has clickable games and is based on the classic Dr. Seuss tale. Finally, *Ruff's Bone* is a story of a brave dog's search in distant places for a missing bone.

Macbeth, **Hoffman + Associates (Macintosh, Windows). Grades 9–Adult.**

Students using this program are taken on a guided tour of the play *Macbeth.* They learn about the life and times of the characters and Shakespeare and about Scottish history.

Major League Reading, **Sanctuary Woods (Macintosh, Windows). Grades 2–11.**

Major League Reading contains 1,500 baseball articles and 2,500 questions. The articles are very interesting

because they contain the inside scoop on all the pro teams and players.

An Odyssey of Discovery: Writing for Readers, **Pierian Spring (Macintosh, Windows). Grades 4–9.**

This interactive program lets students brainstorm with the development of plot, characters, setting, dialogue, and other story elements. The options include portfolios, sticky notes, and features that encourage students and teachers to communicate with each other.

Reader Rabbit's Interactive Journey, **Learning Company (Macintosh, Windows). Grades Pre-K–3.**

Reader Rabbit's Interactive Journey is a comprehensive reading program that teaches beginning reading with lifelike speech. It guides children through forty gradually graded storybooks that lead to independent reading. This program is motivating and develops self-confidence. It supplements the storybooks and helps develop reading skills with 100 phonics and word lessons. Animation, exciting graphics, and sounds make this an inspiring product for children.

Reading Blaster: Invasion of the Word Snatchers, **Davidson (Macintosh, Windows). Grades 1–4.**

Reading Blaster is an exciting adventure game that builds reading and thinking skills. It includes five action-packed activities that teach children how to alphabetize, differentiate between antonyms and synonyms, read and follow directions, and spell correctly. In the process of playing the games, children apply deductive reasoning and critical reading skills.

Reading SEARCH: In Search of Lost Folk Tales. **Great Wave Software (Macintosh, Windows). Grades 1–6.**

Students are sent to one of four ancient sites to collect clues so that they can unscramble one of the seventy folktales. This program is good for comprehension practice. It has animated characters and keeps track of progress.

Research Paper Writing, Tom Snyder Productions (Macintosh, Windows). Grades 7–12.

Research Paper Writing is a comprehensive hands-on writing experience with accessible on-line library tools. Students learn and practice the techniques of research: reading-comprehension, note-taking, organization, and interviewing. This program eliminates haphazard topic selection and stimulates focused exploration.

Romeo and Juliet, Cambrix Publishing (Macintosh, Windows). Grades 8–Adult.

Students read and listen to the play, which is enhanced by synchronized on-screen text presented with hypertext study notes. This CD-ROM disk would be very helpful for the special needs student.

Sitting on the Farm, Sanctuary Woods (Macintosh, DOS/Windows). Grades K–3.

Sitting on the Farm integrates multimedia features such as animation and sound so that students can record and play back their voices, sing and read in three languages, or publish their own original stories. Sanctuary Woods produces many delightful programs for varying age groups; among them are *The Cat Came Back; Hawaii High: The Mystery of Tiki; Victor, Vector & Yondo: The Hypnotic Harp;* and *Oscar Wilde's The Selfish Giant.*

Stickybear's Reading Room, Optimum Resources (Macintosh, Windows). Grades Pre-K–5.

Stickybear's Reading Room is an entertaining program that teaches reading and critical thinking skills in Spanish and English. It features the wonderful Stickybear characters in animations and lifelike speech in four activities: Word Bop, Word Match, Word Find, and Sentence Builder.

Super Solvers Midnight Rescue! Learning Company (Macintosh, Windows). Grades 3–5.

In *Midnight Rescue,* students use deductive reasoning and critical reading to stop villain Morty Maxwell from erasing the school. This is an action-packed reading comprehension program that helps students pinpoint the main idea, recall relevant facts, and draw conclusions. It includes more than 200 selections and 500 on-screen definitions and pronunciations.

Ultimate Speed Reader, Davidson (Macintosh, Windows). Grades 5 and up.

Ultimate Speed Reader increases reading speed and comprehension. It has six activities, a training plan, graphics and charts, and more than 200 reading passages in a variety of formats.

Ultimate Word Attack, Davidson (Macintosh, Windows). Grades 4–Adult.

Ultimate Word Attack offers a rich variety of ways to learn vocabulary and spelling through five activities including a crossword puzzle and a maze game. The program is also helpful in decoding new words.

Wiggly Works, Scholastic (Macintosh, Windows). Grades Pre-K–2.

Wiggly Works is an inventive reading program that contains three amusing picture books and engaging activities. It includes a phonetics component as well as a practical management system for the teacher. Students hear stories, rewrite them, and read them aloud.

Word Smart, Princeton Review (Macintosh, Windows). Grades 7–Adult.

Students explore a movie studio, where they find new words in movie scripts. The program offers quizzes, eight levels of difficulty, 1,600 words, and movie clips from *The Producers.*

MATH PROGRAMS

Algebra Quest, Media Quest (Macintosh, Windows). Grades 9–Adult.

Algebra Quest teaches students how to master the challenges of algebra instruction. The program is powerful and easy to use, with a personal guide named Ali Gebra who motivates students with friendly, corrective feedback.

Algebra Smart, **Princeton Review (Macintosh, Windows). Grades 9–Adult.**

Algebra Smart is an interactive tutorial that covers a full year of Algebra I. It has more than 500 practice problems with step-by-step solutions, algebra games, and 130 videos that take you through twelve key lessons.

Algebra World, **Cognitive Technologies Corporation (Macintosh, Windows), Grades 7–Adult**

Algebra World teaches and reinforces Algebra concepts in a unique environment. Equations and their relationships to word problems are emphasized throughout the program. Areas covered include gears, proportional reasoning, spatial reasoning, math patterns, and developing operational sense.

Coordinate Geometry, **Ventura Educational Systems (Macintosh)., Grades 7–12.**

This tutorial introduces students to Cartesian plane geometry and leads them in an exploration of coordinate geometry. The program explores, among other topics, locating points on the Cartesian plane, defining a locus, using set notation, and the concept of a y-intercept.

Counting on Frank, **EA Kids (Macintosh, Windows/DOS). Grades 3–7.**

Counting on Frank presents students with real-life math problems about everything from bath water to dog food. The program is a near flawless balance of challenging problems and an entertaining story line. Students gain experience with word problems, estimations, compound equations, multiplication, and division.

Early Math, **EA Kids (Macintosh, Windows). Grades Pre-K–2.**

In *Early Math,* six fun-filled activities teach counting, shape recognition, addition, subtraction, and spatial concepts.

Fraction Munchers, **MECC/Softkeys International (Macintosh, Windows). Grades 4–6.**

Students practice their skills in fractions in a Pac Man–type game by directing the Muncher to eat fractional expressions that match target values, including factors, primes, multiples, equalities, and inequalities. Following the same game format, *Number Munchers,* also from MECC, helps the Munchers hunt for numbers or numerical expressions, such as factors, primes, multiples, equalities, and inequalities.

Geometer's Sketchpad, **Curriculum Press (Macintosh, Windows). Grades 9–Adult.**

Using *Sketchpad 3,* students manipulate and create geometric figures. They are able to explore freely or use the program as a tool to do assigned problems. The program comes with a user manual and sample activities.

The Geometry Supposer **Series, Sunburst Communications (Macintosh, DOS). Grades 8–Adult.**

The Geometry Supposer Series consists of three programs: quadrilaterals, triangles, and circles. This series gives older students the chance to explore Euclidean geometry freely and independently, forming mental models of geometric concepts, generating shapes, performing constructions, and taking measurements.

Grade Builder Algebra 1, **Learning Company (Macintosh, Windows). Grades 7–9.**

Using sixty interactive lessons, *Grade Builder Algebra I* covers an entire year of Algebra I. The students have fun mastering the topics with games and unlimited practice problems.

GraphPower, **Ventura Educational Systems (Macintosh). Grades K–8, Special Education.**

GraphPower develops students' ability to analyze and interpret data by teaching students how to create an array of graphics including pictographs, bar graphs, and circle graphs. An on-line tutorial helps users overcome graphing problems. Ventura Educational Systems produces two other excellent interactive programs for teaching math concepts visually: *Balancing Act* and *Probability Tool Kit.*

Hands-on-Math Series, Ventura Educational Systems (Macintosh, DOS). Grades K–8.

Hands-on-Math is a series of enjoyable simulation programs that use manipulative devices to meet the math requirements of most states. Each device lets students freely explore and discover important math concepts. Every program contains a data disk and a guide with a broad spectrum of teaching suggestions.

Inside the SAT and ACT Deluxe 1998 Edition, Princeton Review (Macintosh, Windows). Grades 9 and up.

This preparation software covers the PSAT, SAT, and ACT. It covers lessons on all subject areas including math. It contains four practice tests, with useful study tips and tutorials.

Interactive Math Journey, Learning Company (Macintosh, Windows). Grades 1–4.

This program has twenty-five math games that include interactive books, challenge games, and songs. Some of the games are multiple levels, and the record-keeping function tracks the student's progress.

KidsMath, Great Wave Software (Macintosh, Windows). Grades K–3.

In *Kid's Math,* eight entertaining activities teach a range of basic math skills, from counting and fractions to developing positive attitudes toward math. Great Wave Software has produced two other very useful programs: *NumberMaze* and *Decimal and Fraction Maze.*

Major League Math 2d Edition, Sanctuary Woods (Macintosh, Windows). Grades 3–6.

Major League Math contains more than 4,000 different math questions. Students play by picking a team, what kind of pitch, and what kind of hit. How they do is determined by how they answer the questions.

Math Ace Junior, Magic Quest (Macintosh, DOS/Windows). Grades K–3.

Math Ace Junior takes place on a submarine, where students learn about math in an undersea environment. Students try to win fish and treasures for an aquarium by successfully completing different math activities. There are four levels of difficulty and nine inventive activities with vivid graphics. *Math Ace,* a more advanced program by Magic Quest, even covers geometry.

Math Advantage, Aces Research (Macintosh, Windows). Grades 9–Adult.

This five-set CD-ROM covers algebra, geometry, calculus, trigonometry, and statistics.

Math Blaster : Algebra, Davidson (Macintosh, Windows). Grades 8–Adult.

This tutorial program reviews and gives practice in algebra basics. More than 670 problems cover different areas of algebra. New problems can be added with the editor feature.

Math Blaster 9–12, Davidson (Macintosh, Windows). Grades 4–6.

This version covers multi-operand equations, adding fractions, logic, and more. It has more than 50,000 problems and ten levels of difficulties. It includes an easy-to-use spreadsheet and graph program. The *Math Blaster* series covers the ages of 6 and up with programs such as *Math Blaster 6–9, Math Blaster 9–12, Math Blaster Pre-Algebra, Math Blaster Algebra,* and *Math Blaster Geometry.*

MathKeys, Unlocking Geometry, Volume I, MECC/Houghton/Mifflin (Macintosh, Windows). Grades K–6.

MathKeys offers a fresh hands-on approach to mathematics learning. The series spans eight major content areas including whole numbers, fractions, money, measurement, and probability. It provides grade-specific resource materials and helps children connect physical objects to abstract math concepts. This program has Spanish and English options and supports the NCTM goals.

Math Heads, Theatrix Interactive (Macintosh, Windows). Grades 3–7.

Students use TV channels to practice their prealgebra skills. They learn about such topics as multiple representations, proportions, and estimation.

Math Library, Learning Company (Macintosh, Windows). Grades 7–Adult.

This complete math collection contains hundreds of integrated lessons and thousands of practice problems. Topics include math review, Algebra I, Geometry, Algebra 2, Trigonometry and Calculus.

Math Munchers Deluxe, MECC/Softkeys International (Macintosh, Windows). Grades 2–12.

The students race through a grid to capture a solution to a math challenge while avoiding evil troggles. The program offers twenty topics that range from prime numbers to factors.

Math Rabbit Deluxe! Learning Company (Macintosh, Windows). Grades Pre-K–2.

In *Math Rabbit,* four captivating circus activities help students develop skills in areas such as counting, number patterns, adding, and subtracting. This program features lifelike digitized speech and delightful animated prizes for successful performance. Teachers may customize the program for students' needs.

Mathville, Ingenuity Works (Macintosh, Windows). Grades 7–Adult.

Mathville is a good basic program for the reluctant learner. This program covers the entire spectrum of basic mathematics in an engaging approach to learning math. *Mathville 1,2,3,* the earlier program in the sequence, is directed at grades 1, 2, and 3.

Math Workshop, Brøderbund (Macintosh, Windows). Grades K–8.

Math Workshop gives students an opportunity to practice critical math skills in a creative environment filled with games, music, and animated characters. By engaging in a variety of captivating math activities, students can build problem solving, critical thinking, and computational skills. There are seven activities including Bowling for Numbers, Puzzle Patterns, Sticklers, and Rhythm Generator.

Mighty Math Calculating Crew, Edmark (Macintosh, Windows). Grades 2–12.

Students are given practice in handling topics such as multiplication, division, number lines, money, and 3-D geometry. Many of the activities contain virtual manipulates, which help students make connections between concrete and abstract math configurations.

Millie's Math House, Edmark (Macintosh, Windows). Grades Pre-K–1.

Millie's Math House is an award-winning multimedia program that teaches beginning math skills. Children learn about numbers, patterns, sizes, and shapes in six interactive activities with animated characters, colorful graphics, and lively music.

Money Town, Davidson (Macintosh, Windows). Grades K–3.

Using the colorful Greenstreet characters, students learn about working, saving, making change, coin recognition, and more.

Probability Toolkit, Ventura Educational Systems (Macintosh, DOS). Grades K–8.

Probability Toolkit is an engaging program that helps students develop a basic understanding of probability and statistics. This educational tool has a variety of interesting simulated experiments involving marbles in a jar, colored spinners, colored chips, dice, and cards. The results of each experiment can be graphed in many different formats such as bar graphs, circle graphs, or line graphs. Furthermore, a detailed instructor's guide and activity sheets accompany the program.

Puzzle Logic, Ventura Educational Systems (Macintosh, Windows). Grades 6–Adult

Puzzle Logic consists of 17 challenging puzzles which build thinking skills. The puzzles are very different ranging from Magic Squares to the Tower of Stars. Students choose challenging puzzles and then find themselves in an interactive environment where they use a variety of Math and logic skills to find a solution.

The Quarter Mile, Barnum Software (Macintosh, DOS/Windows). Grades 1–9.

The Quarter Mile is an addictive drill and practice program. It covers whole numbers, fractions, decimals, percents, integers, equations, estimation, and math tricks. Students compete in a drag race against themselves. The program offers an excellent teacher management component and many additional features.

Real World Math: Adventures in Flight, Addison-Wesley/Sanctuary Woods (Macintosh, Windows). Grades 4–6.

Real World Math: Adventures in Flight is an exciting program that sets math problems in an airport—the problems involve everything from flight schedules to baggage claims. This program is very versatile in that it integrates math with other subject areas. A special feature lets students build and decorate their own airplanes.

Sesame Street Numbers, EA Kids (Macintosh, Windows). Grades Pre-K–1.

This program explores the world of numbers with the help of the Sesame Street characters. Children play four inventive math activities that focus on essential math readiness, number recognition, set classification, and counting and spatial relationships. The program includes more than an hour of interactive video and song from the Sesame Street series.

Stickybear's Math Town, Optimum Resources (Macintosh, Windows). Grades K–5.

Stickybear's Math Town uses animation to both verbally and visually reinforce student effort. The program has six levels of difficulty, covers the four basic operations, and features great graphics and lifelike speech. This is a bilingual package that develops math excellence in both English and Spanish.

TesselMania! MECC/Softkeys International (Macintosh). Grades 4–12.

TesselMania! inspired by the work of M.C. Escher, helps students explore transformational geometry while stretching their imaginations and developing spatial and visualization skills. Students create their own interlocking puzzlelike designs, connecting art and geometry.

Treasure Galaxy! Learning Company (Macintosh, DOS/Windows). Grades K–5.

Treasure Galaxy! is a math adventure that helps students develop an understanding of such topics as measurement, basic fractions, geometric shapes, and number patterns. Students engage in six interactive, realistic activities. Nonreaders can understand this program easily, because each activity has an on-line demo with animated directions. A companion to this program is *Treasure MathStorm!* an alpine adventure that builds math, money, counting, time-measurement, and thinking skills.

Troggle Trouble Math, MECC/Softkeys International (Macintosh, Windows). Grades 1–6.

Based on the NTM Framework, *Troggle Trouble Math* is an imaginative, arcadelike math game that offers a rich variety of activities. Using an on-screen calculator, children solve difficult math problems. In addition, they practice the various operations and perform mental computations and estimations in different problem settings.

MUSIC PROGRAMS

Anatomy of Music, Tom Snyder Productions (Macintosh, Windows). Grades 5–12.

This program explains the structure of classical music. Students access different musical passages by clicking on the mouse. Students listen to different musical selections and study their structure on the computer screen in order to analyze the different parts and their relationship to the whole piece.

Antonín Dvořák: Symphony Number 9, Voyager (Macintosh, Windows). Grades 8–Adult.

The *Antonín Dvořák* CD-ROM contains the entire score of the composer's Symphony Number 9, expert commentary and musical analysis, glossary definitions, and musical examples. It includes a special illustrated section on the instruments of the orchestra as well as an in-depth historical essay on Dvořák's life and the historical times. At any time during the program, students can choose to play a board game that tests their knowledge. Voyager produces a series of these discs including *Ludwig Van Beethoven: Symphony Number 9* and *Wolfgang Amadeus Mozart: "Dissonant" Quartet.*

ConcertWare Pro, Jump! Software (Macintosh, Windows). Grades 5–12, Adult.

ConcertWare Pro is one of the best programs for teaching students music notation. This theory program has a simple interface and professional capabilities. *ConcertWare Pro* supports editing, printing, and playback of musical pieces and arrangements.

Dr. T's Sing-A-Long Around the World, Dr. T's Music (Macintosh, Windows). Grades Pre-K–5.

Dr. T's Sing-A-Long Around the World has the students star in a sing-along adventure. This program exposes children to the music of different cultures around the world. Students visit animated characters from twenty-two different countries, reading and listening to the lyrics of the characters' songs in English or the original language. The program allows students to customize their own lists of songs.

Lenny's MusicToon, Paramount Interactive (Windows). Grades 3–8.

Lenny's MusicToon is another program that lets students make their own music videos. Students also develop skills in musical composition, harmony, and sound exploration. They direct stage performances, helping performers with note and sight reading, pitch recognition, and creative musical expression. This software program is filled with animated cartoon characters that talk, dance, and play instruments.

Making Music, Voyager/Learn Technologies (Macintosh, Windows). Pre-K–12, Adult.

This program allows children to experiment with the elements of music. It contains games and open-ended creativity activities.

Microsoft Multimedia Beethoven, Microsoft (Windows). Grades 7–Adult.

This program focuses on the life and times of Beethoven and does an in-depth analysis of his major works. In addition to this title, Microsoft offers *Multimedia Mozart, Schubert,* and *Stravinsky.*

Microsoft Musical Instruments, Dorling Kindersley Multimedia/Microsoft (Macintosh, Windows). Grades 3–Adult.

Microsoft Musical Instruments teaches about different musical instruments around the world. Students click on an instrument to see its description, learn about its components, or listen to its sound. This multimedia delight covers more than 200 musical instruments. The program has an impressive collection of more than 500 photographs of musical instruments and ensembles and more than 1,500 sound clips.

Music Ace, Harmonic Vision (Macintosh, Windows). Grades 3–Adult.

Music Ace illustrates essential music fundamentals with singing and musical notes that smile. This program is a series of twenty-four tutorials, each with a game and a Music Doodle Pad feature, which lets students use the on-screen piano keyboard to create and modify a library of musical pieces.

The Piano Discovery System, Jump! Music (Windows, Macintosh). Grades 1–12, Adult.

Based on the classic *Miracle Piano,* this program turns your computer into a piano and teaching machine. *Piano Discovery* comes with a MIDI keyboard and has arcade-style games and tutorials.

PROBLEM SOLVING AND LOGIC

Anno's Learning Games, Putman New Media (Macintosh, Windows). Grades 2–10.

Anno's Learning Games contains seven well-designed thinking activities, including a twenty-question guessing game, a weight with a spring scale, tangram puzzles, and Venn diagrams. This program is based on the puzzle book by the well-known Japanese author Anno.

The Incredible Machine 3, Sierra On Line (Macintosh, Windows). Grades 5–9.

This program has 160 mind-melting, unusual puzzles with 100 animated parts. Students build triplever contraptions by placing parts such as trampolines and monkey motors on the screen. When these parts are combined correctly, the machine is able to complete its task.

Myst, Brøderbund (Macintosh, Windows). Grades 7–Adult.

Myst is an advanced problem-solving program that involves students in reading for information. The program's *QuickTime* movies are quite unusual and the music has an eerie quality that draws users into a surrealistic setting. *Myst* is not linear, it is not shallow, and it has remarkable depth of detail.

Riven, Brøderbund (Macintosh, Windows). Grades 7–Adult.

Riven, the sequel to *Myst,* is the latest virtual reality program from Brøderbund. This program has greater graphic detail, full-motion video, and puzzles that are integrated into the story line.

Safari Search, Sunburst Communications (Macintosh, DOS/Windows). Grades 3–Adult.

Students work on twelve safari search activities that provide practice in drawing inferences and making complex judgments. The object is to develop a strategy for finding hidden animals in the least number of moves.

Secret Island of Dr. Quandary, MECC/Softkeys International (Macintosh, DOS). Grades 3–12.

Dr. Quandary, a mad genius, has trapped students on an island in order to turn them into mindless drones. To escape from this perilous situation, they have to solve any puzzles that the doctor gives them. The students exercise their abilities to formulate logical strategies, predict outcomes, and make decisions promptly.

Strategy Challenges 1 & 2, Edmark (Macintosh, Windows). Grades 3–Adult.

These programs help students build strategic thinking and problem-solving skills while playing games from around the world. The games include Mancala, Go-Moku, Nine Man Morris, Jungle Chess, Tablut, and Surakarata.

Thinkin' Things 1, Thinkin' Things 2 Collection, and *Thinkin' Things Collection 3,* Edmark (Macintosh, DOS/Windows). Grades Pre-K–3 and 1–6.

The *Thinkin' Things 1, Thinkin' Things 2 Collection* and *Thinkin' Things Collection 3* are programs that help students improve their problem-solving skills. With tools and gadgets, students explore rhythmic notation and develop their listening memory and powers of observation and spatial and logical thinking.

The Time Warp of Dr. Brain, Sierra On-Line (Macintosh, Windows). Grades 7–Adult.

The Time Warp of Dr. Brain is just one in a series of programs developed by Sierra On-Line that includes *The Island of Dr. Brain* and *The Lost Mind of Dr. Brain.* These programs have strong math and logical thinking elements. Students employ different strategies to solve puzzles that employ language, spatial reasoning memory, music, and so on.

What's My Logic? Critical Thinking Press and Software (Macintosh, DOS/Windows). Grades 5–Adult.

What's My Logic? is a series of mind-stretching games for older students and adults. Program users have to discover what the fundamental rule of logic is that will let them travel through a maze to the end. There are thirty different fascinating, very challenging mazes.

PROGRAMMING

FUNdaMental, KartoffelSoft (Macintosh, Windows). Grades 7 and up.

An advanced-user programming language that gives you more control over the computer than a program like *HyperStudio* or *Digital Chisel*.

LogoWriter, LCSI (Apple, Macintosh, DOS/Windows). Grades K–Adult.

LogoWriter comes in five versions: French, Spanish, primary, intermediate, and secondary. Combining word processing with Logo, students create animated graphics to accompany their writing.

MicroWorlds Project Builder, Logo Computer Systems (Macintosh, DOS/Windows). Grades 4–8.

See Authoring Tools section.

PcLogo for Windows, Harvard Associates (Windows). Grades 3–Adult.

PcLogo is a powerful programming language for Windows that is easy to comprehend. It features full-color on-line help, multiple turtles, turtle color, and speed and shape control.

Terrapin Logo, Terrapin Software (Apple II Family, Macintosh, DOS/Windows). Grades K–Adult.

Terrapin Logo is a full-featured computer language that can be used by the beginner and the experienced programmer alike. This program is a version of the language developed at MIT. The examples used throughout the Logo chapter in this book were generated with *Terrapin Logo*.

True BASIC Language System, True BASIC (Macintosh, Windows). Grades 8–Adult.

True BASIC is an easy-to-use and fully structured programming language. Students write less code to solve harder problems. This elegant program can be used to generate professional-looking graphs. The examples used in the BASIC section of this book were generated using *True BASIC*.

Turtle Math, LCSI (Macintosh). Grades 2–6.

Turtle Math is a popular program that introduces young children to Logo. An independent, simplified version of Logo, this program features a series of thirty-six built-in investigations and thirty activities organized according to topic.

Visual Basics, Microsoft (Windows). Grades 9–12, Adult.

The standard learning edition of this program is designed for the beginning programmer. It comes with *Visual Basic* as well as an interactive CD-ROM tutorial.

PUZZLE UTILITIES

Crossword Companion, Visions (Macintosh, Windows). Grades K–12.

A very easy-to-use crossword puzzle maker. You can write long clues, add graphics, mix numbers and letters, and much more.

Crossword Magic 4.0, Mindscape (Macintosh, Windows). Grades 4–Adult.

Crossword Magic is an extremely useful and popular product for all curriculum areas. This program shows the crossword puzzle on the screen and also prints it out.

Math Companion, Visions (Macintosh, Windows). Grades K–12.

A teacher tool that lets you create math activity sheets in four different formats with graphic capabilities. You choose from 110 NCTM math objects.

Puzzle Power 2.0, Centron (Macintosh, Windows). Grades 2–Adult.

This software program gives you a collection of puzzle-making software that includes Crossword Creator, Wordsearch Creator, Cryptos, Anagrams, Cross Sums, and more. You can have three types of multimedia themes, pictures, sounds, and movies.

Puzzle Logic, **Ventura Educational Systems (Macintosh, Windows). Grades 6-Adult.**

Puzzle Logic consists of 17 challenging puzzles which build thinking skills. The puzzles are very different ranging from Magic Squares to the Tower of Stars. Students choose challenging puzzles and then finds themselves in an interactive environment where they use a variety of Math and logic skills to find a solution.

Word Bingo, **Hi Tech (Macintosh). Grades 4–Adult.**

With this program, you can create a set of bingo cards on the vocabulary words that the students are currently learning. This easy-to-use program comes with Spanish capabilities, some very useful clip art, and excellent documentation.

Word Cross, **Hi Tech (Macintosh). Grades 3–Adult.**

This crossword puzzle maker is simple to use. It lets you create your own crossword puzzles and automatically generates a variety of puzzles from the same word list. You can customize *Word Cross* to help students learn new vocabulary words.

REFERENCE

3-D Atlas 98, **Creative Wonders (Macintosh, Windows). Grades 5–Adult.**

3-D Atlas is a first-rate atlas program that gives students a comprehensive view of the world with more than 800 photos, video, statistics, time-lapse photography, and nine different levels of detail. The students' journey is accompanied by a hauntingly beautiful soundtrack and exciting vocal narration.

Compton's Encyclopedia, **Compton's/Learning Company (Macintosh, Windows). Grades 2 and up.**

This encyclopedia is very comprehensive, and it lets students have easy access to 38,000 articles. In addition, it contains a thesaurus, dictionary, atlas, and timelines as well as an Internet directory with links to more than 4,000 Web sites.

First Connections: **The Golden Book Encyclopedia, Hartley—division of Josten Home Learning (Macintosh, Windows). Grades 1–6.**

First Connections is an interactive children's encyclopedia that contains more than 1,600 articles and 3,400 color images on topics that interest young children. Students can select a part of the text to be read aloud, they can use bookmarks so that they may return later to a particular article, and they can obtain on-line audio help. The browsing feature is excellent, enabling students to search for any article in a matter of seconds. A companion activity package includes such topics as conservation, dinosaurs, famous people, and the solar system.

Mayo Clinic Family Health Book, **IVI Publishing (Macintosh, Windows). Grades 7–Adult.**

Mayo Clinic Family Health Book is an exciting, interactive, comprehensive guide to family health and the human body. It contains information on more than a thousand medical conditions, first aid, and prevention. Three other excellent programs in the series are *The Total Heart, Family Pharmacist,* and *Mayo Clinic Sports Health and Fitness.* IVI Publishing has some very noteworthy programs for children including *Anatomy from Mayo Clinic* and *What Is a Belly Button.*

Merriam-Webster's College Dictionary, **Clearvue/eav (Macintosh, Windows). Grades 8 and up.**

Merriam-Webster's College Dictionary gives students access to reference information. It is combined with the *Merriam-Webster Collegiate Thesaurus* and the *American Concise Encyclopedia* and offers 214,000 definitions, 700 illustrations, and 6,500 biographical entries.

Microsoft Bookshelf, **Microsoft (Macintosh, Windows). Grades 7–12.**

Microsoft Bookshelf is a reference library that takes students beyond the limitations of the printed page with sound, illustration, animation, and fast search capabilities. This interactive tool features ten popular reference books including *The American Heritage Dictionary*, *The Columbia Dictionary of Quotations*, and *The World Almanac and Book of Facts*.

Microsoft Encarta, **Microsoft (Macintosh, Windows). Grades 7–12.**

Microsoft Encarta is a complete twenty-nine-volume encyclopedia that fits on one CD-ROM disk. It is based on Funk and Wagnall's new encyclopedia, and it contains more than 32,000 articles and 10,000 links to the World Wide Web. Furthermore, it has an excellent Mind Maze game to test students' knowledge.

My First Amazing Dictionary, **Dorling Kindersely (Windows). Grades Pre-K–2.**

My First Amazing Dictionary is an excellent reference tool for beginning readers. This program has four games that improve word recognition. The dictionary explains the meanings of 1,000 child-oriented words with clever animations, illustrations, and narrations.

The New Grolier Electronic Encyclopedia, **Grolier Publishing (Macintosh, Windows). Grades 4–Adult.**

With *The New Grolier Electronic Encyclopedia*, students are able to access audiovisual essays that combine photos, music, and narration to give a comprehensive overview of subjects such as the human body or space exploration. Thousands of pictures, sounds, full-color maps, updated encyclopedia text entries, and step-by-step animated sequences make it easy for students to understand the included topics.

SCIENCE

3-D Body Adventure, **Knowledge Adventure (Windows). Grades 3–Adult.**

The *3-D Body Adventure* program is a three-dimensional exploration of the inner workings of a "living" human body. Students can rotate this body, freeze it at any point, and examine any organ they want to. In the CD-ROM version, video clips present the inner workings of the human body; the program even includes clips from the award-winning movie *The Miracle of Life*.

3-D Dinosaur Adventure, **Knowledge Adventure (Macintosh, Windows). Grades Pre-K–6.**

3-D Dinosaur Adventure is a realistic interactive exploration of dinosaurs and paleontology. Students enter a virtual Dinosaur Park where they are exposed to more than twenty-five thrilling movies. The program features a dinosaur encyclopedia as well as an assortment of instructional activities.

ActivChemistry, **Salamander Interactive/Addison-Wesley (Macintosh, Windows). Grades 11–Adult.**

Using a multimedia approach, this program covers chemistry.

A.D.A.M. The Inside Story, 1997 Edition, Brøderbund (Macintosh, Windows). Grades 9–Adult.

A.D.A.M. is a dazzling multimedia exploration of the human body. The program merges an extensive database of biological and anatomical information with stunning imagery, sparkling animation, and brilliant sound. Students examine the twelve major body systems and learn the proper pronunciation of medical terms.

BodyScope, **MECC/Softkeys International (Macintosh, Windows). Grades 3–8.**

BodyScope teaches the names of the organs and bones, the organ functions, and the systems. This program features puzzles and on-screen diagrams of the human body systems and regions. The interactive nature of *BodyScope* lets students direct their own investigations and receive immediate reinforcement on their responses.

Body Voyage: A 3-D Tour of the Human Body, **Times Warner Electronic Publishing (Macintosh, Windows). Grades 9–Adult.**

The graphics for this program were created from a combination of computer imaging and medical photography and were based on a real human who donated his body to science.

BodyWorks, **SoftKeys International (Macintosh, DOS/Windows). Grades 6–Adult.**

With this program, students feel as if they are actually traveling in the human body and not just exploring a database. The program inspires students to learn the different functions of the systems of the human body. *BodyWorks* features a health section, colorful photographic graphics, 100 plus glossary entries, detailed movie clips, and sound. Additionally, lesson plans and quizzes improve the students' knowledge of human anatomy.

Bumptz Science Carnival, **Theatrix (Macintosh, Windows). Grades 3–6.**

This program has 200 different puzzles, and twelve short animated movies. Students apply the principles of gravity, light, and buoyancy as they explore an amusement park.

Coral Kingdom, **Sunburst Communications/Wings for Learning (Macintosh, Windows). Grades 8–College.**

Students investigate coral reef ecosystems through narrated slide shows and simulated underwater scuba dives. This multimedia program shows the grace, beauty, and mystery of coral reef life while giving students an extensive sea life database on the subject, which builds their understanding of the ecological concepts.

The Even More Incredible Machine, **Dyamix (Macintosh, Windows). Grades 7–Adult.**

The Even More Incredible Machine has 160 mind-liquefying and unusual puzzles with fifty-six animated parts. Students build trip-lever contraptions by placing parts such as trampolines and monkey motors on the screen. When these parts are combined correctly, the machine is able to complete its task.

Eyewitness Encyclopedia of Science, **Dorling Kindersley Multimedia (Macintosh, Windows). Grades 5–Adult.**

Students explore chemistry, math, physics, life sciences, and a who's who of science. This program contains 1,700 entries, 20 videos and 66 animations.

hip Physics, **Tom Snyder Productions/IPT (Macintosh). Grades 7–12.**

hip Physics is a powerful tool for exploring the physical world and learning how physics works. Students view images and animations that demonstrate concepts in science such as speed, velocity, acceleration, and electricity. The program includes a variety of ready-to-use activities and covers many of the science topics in the physical science curricula.

Life Story, **Sunburst Communications (Macintosh, Windows). Grades 3–Adult.**

Life Story is a high-quality example of interactive multimedia that recounts the discovery of DNA. Students can explore the book *The Race for the Double Helix* through film clips, on-screen text, and related exhibits.

Odell Down Under, **MECC/Softkeys International (Macintosh, Windows). Grades 4–10.**

Odell Down Under is a science simulation in which students develop their problem-solving abilities while learning about the predator/prey relationships and food chains of the Great Barrier Reef in Australia. Students assume the roles of the inhabitants of the reef, view life through their eyes, and make survival decisions.

Physics Explorer: Gravity, **Sunburst Communications (Macintosh). Grades 10–Adult.**

The physics explorer series provides students with hands-on physics experience and observation opportunity. The ten programs in this series enable students to manipulate visual models of waves and electrodynamics, AC/DC circuits, ripple tanks, and gravity. In the gravity program, students explore the motion of a body under the influence of a gravitating planet. They observe Kepler's Laws and apply these concepts to the sun, earth, planets, and satellites. This program features an on-screen tutorial, experiments, and constant visual information in the form of vector displays, bar charts, and histograms.

Sammy's Science House, Edmark (Macintosh, DOS/Windows). Grades Pre-K–2.

Sammy's Science House has five fun-filled activities that help children with sorting, sequencing, observing, predicting, and constructing. Students learn simple scientific classification and develop logical thinking skills painlessly by building toys and machines, classifying plants, and sequencing movies.

Science Court: Work and Simple Machines, Tom Snyder Productions (Macintosh, Windows). Grades 4–6.

Taking place in the courtroom, *Science Court* teaches students about work and simple machines. The program contains animated video clips with hands-on activities.

Science for Kids, Science for Kids Tools and Gadgets (Macintosh, Windows). Grades K–9.

The *Science for Kids* series creates a multimedia educational environment in science. The four programs in this bilingual series—"*Cell*"*ebration, Forces and Motions, Simple Machines,* and *Adventure with OSLO*—are based on NSTA guidelines. The series includes a complete package of science equipment, instructional material, and teacher suggestions. In the program *Adventure with OSLO,* engaging physical science explorations on simple machines incorporate fun-filled games and activities.

Science in Your Ear, MECC/Softkeys International (Macintosh, Windows). Grades 4–7.

Using these programs, students can collectively improve their critical thinking skills by taking notes, manipulating variables, analyzing the results, drawing conclusions, and offering solutions to problems. The program includes simulations, hands-on experiments, and lesson plans. Topics range from sound waves to musical instruments.

Science Smart, Princeton Review (Macintosh, Windows). Grades 7–Adult.

Science Smart reviews all major topics covered in high school science. It uses more than 70 animations to explain key concepts in biology, chemistry and physics and offers more than 600 practice problems.

Scholastic's Magic School Bus Explores the Solar System, Microsoft (Macintosh, Windows). Grades 1–5.

Children ride a school bus on an interplanetary adventure to investigate planets and moons. This program features realistic NASA and JPL videos and nine science experiments in which students make craters on the moon, put rings around Saturn, and see how big Jupiter is by filling it up with other planets. Another program in the same format explores the human body.

Where in Space Is Carmen Sandiego? Deluxe, Brøderbund (Macintosh, Windows). Grades 5–Adult.

In *Where in Space,* students explore the cosmos and human history, the mythology behind the constellations, and the science of planetary explorations. This astronomical learning game uses brilliant NASA photographs to teach the facts and features of thirty-two locations in the solar system.

The Wonders of Science, National Geographic (Macintosh, Windows). Grades Pre-K–3.

The Wonders of Science is an interactive primary level reading series of thirty-six books on eight CD-ROM disks. The books contain 600 stunning photos, word and syllable pronunciations, and explanations in English and Spanish. Thousands of interactive picture buttons invite exploration. Some of the CD-ROM titles are *A World of Animals, Our Earth, A World of Plants,* and *Seasons.* This program is good for teaching ESL students.

SOCIAL STUDIES PROGRAMS

Amazon Trail II: Rain Forest, MECC/Softkeys International (Macintosh, Windows). Grades 4–10.

In MECC/Softkeys International's *Amazon Trail II,* students travel through the jungles of South America, encountering five rain forest habitats and 100 animals. Students experience hardships, risk possible death, meet different creatures, and learn navigational skills and history.

Archibald's Guide to Mysteries of Ancient Egypt, Swifte International (Macintosh, Windows). Grades 2–8.

In this animated adventure, a young boy named Archibald explores Egypt, making discoveries about mummies and learning how to read hieroglyphics.

Crosscountry USA, Ingenuity Works (Macintosh, Windows). Grades 4–Adult.

Students play the role of truck drivers on a mission to pick up and deliver certain commodities. Students practice map reading, logical thinking, and record keeping as they deliver the products all over the United States. Other programs in the series are *Crosscountry California, Crosscountry Texas,* and *Crosscountry Canada.*

Cultural Debates, Tom Snyder (Macintosh, Windows). Grades 6–12.

Using this program, students view one of twelve short video clips together. The video clip acts as a springboard for discussion. Afterward, the students use a worksheet to construct their debate questions.

MayaQuest Trail, MECC/Softkeys International (Macintosh, Windows). Grades 4–11.

Students gain a better understanding of history, geography, archeology, and Central America. They can explore rain forests in Mexico, Belize, and Guatemala in search of a lost Maya city. With the additional classroom kit, students can connect to the Internet and aid in the expedition by communicating their ideas.

Microsoft Ancient Lands, Microsoft (Windows). Grades 3–Adult.

Microsoft Ancient Lands lets students explore the worlds of the past. It features 1,000 interactive articles on ancient civilizations and their legends, fascinating clips and videos on ancient toys, hands-on activities, and games.

The Oregon Trail III, MECC/Softkeys International (Macintosh, DOS). Grades 5–12.

The Oregon Trail III transports students to the 1850s, where as pioneers they must outfit their wagons for the journey west from Independence, Missouri. If students make the right decisions, they reach their destination. During the journey, students learn about the time period.

SimSafari, Maxis (Macintosh, Windows). Grades 3–Adult.

SimSafari puts students in charge of their own virtual African wilderness park and tourist camp. Students assume the role of a safari ranger and make all decisions from choosing plants, to selecting animals, and placing new buildings. They handle natural disasters, tackle wild missions, and deal with everyday problems like hiring staff.

SimTown, Maxis (Macintosh, Windows). Grades 3–7.

SimTown is a popular simulation program designed for younger students. Students build and manage a small town and influence the lives of the residents. This program's stunning animated graphics show people in houses and buildings, kids skate boarding, and cars driving down streets. Seeing the town grow gives students the opportunity to understand the basic concepts behind economics, ecology, and city planning. Other well-known programs in this series are *SimCity 2000, SimFarm, SimCity Classic, SimLife, SimEarth,* and *SimAnt.*

Where in America's Past Is Carmen Sandiego? Brøderbund (Macintosh, DOS/Windows). Grades 6–12.

Where in America's Past Is Carmen Sandiego? covers 400 years of American culture and regional history.

Students track down Carmen and her band of villains by looking up clues in *What Happened When*, a 1,300-page encyclopedia of American history and culture. This popular series also includes *Where in Europe Is Carmen Sandiego? Where in the World Is Carmen Sandiego? Where in the USA Is Carmen Sandiego? Where in Time Is Carmen Sandiego? Where in Space Is Carmen Sandiego?* and *Where in the World Is Carmen Sandiego? Jr. Detective Edition.* The new improved CD-ROM version of *Where in the World Is Carmen Sandiego? Deluxe* is exceptional!

World Discovery Deluxe, Great Wave (Macintosh, Windows). Grades 3–12.

World Discovery is an inventive drill and practice program that features nineteen highly detailed maps from around the globe and twelve games that teach political and historical places, people, and events.

World GeoGraph II, MECC/SoftKeys International (Macintosh). Grades 6–12.

World GeoGraph is an interactive database that allows students to manipulate 105 categories of information about 230 nations. Data can be printed in graph, spreadsheet, or chart format. Similar programs in the series are *USA GeoGraph II* (English and Spanish Editions) and *Canada GeoGraph II*.

The Yukon Trail, MECC/Softkeys International (Macintosh, DOS, Windows). Grades 10–Adult.

The Yukon Trail transports students to the year 1896, with all its trials and tribulations. In this adventure, students attempt to travel safely from Seattle to Alaska. In Seattle, they choose a partner, buy supplies, and head for northwestern Canada. On the trail, they make decisions on the basis of the information gleaned from conversations with historical figures.

Zip Zap Map! USA, National Geographic (Macintosh, Windows). Grades 4–Adult.

Zip Zap Map! USA is a fun-filled geography game that teaches locations of states, state name, state capitals, major cities, and prominent physical features.

It offers three levels of difficulty, three speeds of play, and exciting sound effects.

SPECIAL NEEDS

Blocks in Motion, Don Johnson (Macintosh, Windows). Grades 1–adult.

Blocks in Motion allows students to create, manipulate, and animate blocks. This paint and motion program has multiple tools, sound effects, and many programmable options to bring forth the student's creativity.

Simon Sounds It Out, Don Johnson (Macintosh, Windows). Grades Pre-K–2.

This program is a phonics tool that lets students practice letter sounds. It has a helpful on-line tutor that leads students through thirty-one sequenced sounds and words.

Words Around Me, Edmark (Macintosh, Windows). Grades K–12.

This program is useful for ESL and special education students. Using *Words Around Me*, students learn more than 275 common vocabulary words and 186 plurals. This is a step-by-step approach that lets users engage in five activities for practice.

Write: OutLoud 2.0, Don Johnson (Macintosh, Windows). Grades 2–8.

Write: OutLoud is an easy-to-use word processor that talks. Students can listen to their work as they type it. The spelling checker lets students hear and see suggested replacement words. The program features a handy on-screen ribbon that lets students quickly access the program's options.

SPREADSHEETS AND INTEGRATED PROGRAMS

ClarisWorks, Claris (Macintosh, Windows). Grades 7–Adult.

ClarisWorks combines a word processor, spreadsheet, database manager, and a communications, painting, and drawing module smoothly and flawlessly. The program incorporates macros that make it easy to perform repetitive tasks and offers special features such as footnoting and mail merge.

Corel WordPerfect Suite 7, Corel (Macintosh, Windows). Grades 9–Adult.

Corel WordPerfect Suite 7 includes the following software: *WordPerfect, Quattro Pro, Corel Presentations, Sidekick, Dashboard,* and *Envoy* as well as 150 fonts and 10,000 clip art images. You can install the entire suite or only the programs that you want.

The Cruncher, Davidson (Macintosh, Windows). Grades 5–Adult.

The Cruncher is an enjoyable and easy-to-use spreadsheet tool that teaches how a spreadsheet works, when to use one, and how to create one. The spreadsheet comes with ready-to-use templates and projects and an easy-to-use step-by-step tutorial.

Microsoft Excel 97, Microsoft (Macintosh, Windows). Grades 7–Adult.

Microsoft Excel is an award-winning spreadsheet for Windows and Macintosh. It combines its spreadsheet with graphics and a database. The program has more than 16,000 rows and 250 columns. *Excel*'s features include multiple fonts, auditing tools, a dialog editor, drag-drop cell operation, and 3-D chart types.

Microsoft Office 98, Microsoft (Macintosh). Grades 9–Adult.

This program includes five applications—*Microsoft Word, Microsoft Excel,* the *Microsoft PowerPoint Presentation* graphics program, the *Microsoft Outlook Express* e-mail, and *Microsoft Internet Explorer.* Microsoft also offers a Windows version with many of the same features and applications.

Microsoft Works, Microsoft (Macintosh, Windows). Grades 9–Adult.

Microsoft Works is a versatile and simple integrated software product for word processing, data management, spreadsheet charting, drawing, and telecommunications. Microsoft provides outstanding technical support and plenty of understandable documentation.

Spreadsheet 2000, Casady and Green (Macintosh, Windows). Grades 7–Adult.

Spreadsheet 2000 lets you use drag and drop almost every part of your spreadsheet, including cell tiles, formulas, and charts from floating palettes into your new document. Using your mouse, you connect these elements to create your calculation chain. The program contains forty-nine templates for school and home.

TEACHER UTILITIES

Easy Grade Pro, Orbis Software (Macintosh).

Easy Grade Pro is an award-winning program that is well regarded by all Macintosh users. This program has a wide range of tools including grading, attendance, seating, analysis, and reporting. Unlike other grading programs, *Easy Grade Pro* integrates all classes into a single file and at the same time lets each class be managed individually. The program has many options that range from multiple subjects in reports to adding and rotating furniture.

FullProof Desktop Security, SmartStuff Software (Macintosh).

FullProof prevents students from tampering with the desktop or hard drive. This program lets you lock the control panels and chooser. It has password protection, directs the file saving, and does not cover the desktop.

Gradebook Plus V6.1, E.M.A. (Macintosh).

Gradebook Plus V6.1 is an intuitive program that any novice can use. The program helps you with oral reminders such as "Don't forget to back up." With this program, you can create form letters, add any of fifteen user-definable comments to reports, and annotate sound to student reports. On-screen editing and a mini word processor allow you to create the reports and letters.

Grade Busters Mac: Making the Grade (Macintosh) and *Gradebusters: Record Breaker* (Windows), Jay Klein Productions.

Grade Busters is a complex and sophisticated electronic grade book and attendance program. You can keep records on eighty students per class, for 320 assignments, in ten assignment categories, with five grading scales per class; make seating charts; and display the results graphically. Furthermore, you can generate reports in English, German, French, and Spanish.

Grady's Profile, **Aurbach and Associates (Macintosh).**

Grady's Profile, a *HyperCard* application, stores student work samples with assessment and narration. With this tool, you can import scanned images of writing, math problems, and art and print these reports through any word processor. Furthermore, you can make recordings of students reading, talking, singing, and playing music and even can include *QuickTime* videos of performances.

Inspiration, **Inspiration Software (Macintosh, Windows). Grades K–12.**

This program is a visual learning tool that helps students develop ideas and organize their thinking. Students or teachers can create concept maps, story webs, semantic maps, storyboards, bubble diagrams, and outlines.

Learner Profile, **Sunburst Communications (Macintosh, Windows).**

The *Learner Profile* has the versatility to be used either with a bar code scanner or the Apple Newton Message Pad. You can use the program to record and organize data for student assessment portfolios. You can instantly record your observations of pupil learning; the observational information can be uploaded to the computer where it becomes part of the database. This program is very fast and easy to use, and it eliminates burdensome paperwork.

Lesson Plan Helper, **Visions (Macintosh, Windows).**

This helper provides the user with a database of more than 300 lesson plans in all elementary curriculum areas. All the lessons can be changed to meet the teacher's objectives.

Scholastic's Electronic Portfolio, **Scholastic (Macintosh).**

This program is a multimedia tool in which teachers can create, manage, and present multimedia student portfolios using scanned images, sounds, full-motion video, graphics, and textual data.

SPSS/PC, **SPSS (PC Version).**

SPSS/PC is a popular statistical package for the IBM and compatibles. It is menu driven and has interactive data analysis and an on-line glossary of statistical terms.

StatView, **Abacus (Macintosh).**

StatView is a state-of-the-art graphics and statistics program that includes some very advanced features, including outstanding documentation. You can use the program to import data from spreadsheets, databases, word processors, telecommunications programs, and text files.

Teacher Tool Kit, **Hi Tech (Macintosh, Windows).**

Teacher Tool Kit is simple to use and offers excellent on-line help. It includes four programs: word search, word scramble, word match, and multiple choice. This program lets you randomize questions and print out clean page layouts with answers.

Teacher's Helper Plus, **Vision (Macintosh, Windows).**

Teacher's Helper Plus has an elegant interface and easily imports graphics. You can use it to create tests, quizzes, activity sheets, and curriculum packages. There are twenty-three integrated formats including multiple choice, matching, true-false, and short essay.

TimeLiner 4.0, **Tom Snyder Productions (Macintosh, Windows).**

TimeLiner 4.0 lets you design and print out time lines of any length in Spanish or English. Data disks are available for the different curriculum areas.

TextBridge, **Xerox Imaging Systems (Macintosh).**

You can save time and effort and avoid typing errors with *TextBridge.* Using a scanner and this excellent OCR software, you can convert less-than-perfect documents into professional, electronic text.

Vital Links, **Davidson (Macintosh, Windows).**

This program comes with a CD-ROM, and the laser disc is optional. It contains six units, each unit lasting four to eight weeks. It contains a database of 300 primary source documents and tools for writing.

TYPING PROGRAMS

All the Right Type, **Ingenuity Works (Macintosh, Windows). Grades 2–Adult.**

All the Right Type is a simple-to-use typing program that links word processing to keyboarding. It includes a record-keeping feature and a boat race, and the lessons are customized for the student's use in a classroom setting.

Kid's Typing, **Bright Star (Macintosh, Windows). Grades 2–5.**

In *Kid's Typing,* a friendly ghost named Spooky teaches students necessary typing skills. The program has a library of actual stories for students to type and bonus rounds in which students help Spooky haunt a house.

Mario Teaches Typing 2.0, **Brainstorm (Macintosh, Windows). Grades K–5.**

Mario Teaches Typing is a fun-filled program with all the Mario characters and scenes. Students progress at their own pace through each adventure-filled level.

Mavis Beacon Teaches Typing 8.0, **Mindscape (Macintosh, Windows). Grades 5–Adult.**

Mavis Beacon Teaches Typing uses animated graphics, facts from the *New Grolier's Multimedia Encyclopedia* and *Newsweek* magazine, riddles, rhymes, and jokes to teach typing. Lessons range from 10 to 120 minutes. This new edition features a 3-D classroom, Internet access, audio spoken feedback, and six arcade games. The children's version is called *Mavis Beacon Teaches Typing! for Kids.*

Stickybear Typing, **Weekly Reader/Optimum Resources (Macintosh, DOS/Windows). Grades 1–6.**

Three activities, including an arcade game, sharpen students' typing and keyboarding skills. If the students are more advanced typists who need to review and brush up, this program can help. Pupils choose the level of difficulty and track their progress as they improve.

Typing Tutor 7, **Davidson (Macintosh, Windows). Grades 5–Adult.**

The new edition of *Typing Tutor* is loaded with video clips, games, animation, color, and graphics. The samples are from 100 well-known books.

WEB TOOLS

Claris Home Page, **Claris (Macintosh, Windows). Grades 7–Adult.**

Claris Home Page is a Web page authoring tool for a novice or the expert. You can easily design and develop customized Web pages without a hassle because of its intuitive interface and extensive toolset.

DragNet, **Tiki Software (Macintosh, Windows). Grades 7–Adult.**

This utility is necessary for anyone trying to manage more than ten bookmarks. It lets you organize these bookmarks into folders, creating an Internet database that can be used in conjunction with your Web browser. It automatically alphabetizes your bookmarks, lets you write descriptions about them, and imports them into your Web browser.

WebPrinter, **Forest Technologies/ForeFront (Macintosh, Windows). Grades 7–Adult.**

Using *WebPrinter,* you can turn your printer into a printing press. *WebPrinter* takes Web pages that you want to print out and automatically reduces, rotates, and realigns the type into booklet form. *WebPrinter* works with any printer.

WebSeeker, Forest Technologies/ForeFront (Macintosh, Windows). Grades 7–Adult.

This small program gives you the power of more than twenty popular search engines. Using a single keystroke, you are able to run your information search through more than twenty different Internet search engines simultaneously.

Web Wacker, Forest Technologies/ForeFront (Macintosh, Windows). Grades 7–Adult.

This program lets you save to your computer hard drive Internet sites that include text, graphics, and HTML links. This capability is ideal for presentations and working with students off-line.

Web Workshop, Vividus, distributed by Sunburst (Macintosh, Windows). Grades 2–8.

Web Workshop is perfect for the beginning student. It contains clip art, familiar paint tools, and a simple interface that makes it easy for the student to create a Web page.

WORD PROCESSING PROGRAMS

Bank Street Writer, Scholastic (Macintosh, DOS). Grades 4–Adult.

Bank Street Writer is an easy-to-use word processor with on-screen prompts and a tutorial. The Macintosh version has *HyperCard* and desktop capabilities.

Microsoft Word, Microsoft (Macintosh, DOS/Windows). Grades 12–Adult.

Word is a feature-laden word processor that first became popular in its Macintosh version. It lets students

generate tables, design forms, create newsletters, index, and outline. It is comparable to *WordPerfect*.

WordPerfect, Corel (Macintosh, DOS/Windows). Grades 12–Adult.

WordPerfect is a sophisticated, full-functioning word processor program. This best-selling word processor includes Grammatik, a grammar checker; advanced drawing features; and an equation editor. *WordPerfect* is well-known for its fast technical support.

RECOMMENDED LASER DISCS

The Age of Intelligent Machines, AIMS. Grades 7–Adult.

The Age of Intelligent Machines is a clever introduction to technology, covering topics such as artificial intelligence, computers, and expert systems. The program presents a new generation of machines that diagnose illness, create art, navigate jets, follow commands given in ordinary language, and even learn. The cinematography and music add to the desirability of this laser disc.

American Chronicles Series, AIMS. Grades 7–Adult.

Eric Sevareid, veteran news reporter, chronicles what he considers the most significant events in American history from 1918 to 1961. The ten disks in the series include *Between the Wars 1918–1931, The Turning Point 1941–1944,* and *The Fragile Balance, 1955–1961.*

Blue Planet, Lumivision. Grades 5–12.

This IMAX motion picture lets students see the earth as astronauts get to see it and experience the forces of nature that affect our existence.

Dinosaurs: Fantastic Creatures, **Lumivision.** **Grades 1–Adult.**

Students explore the world of dinosaurs and related topics such as the dinosaurs' extinction.

Dream Machine I, II, or III, **Voyager.** **Grades 9–Adult.**

Dream Machine shows the broad spectrum of computer graphics techniques and applications in areas such as space exploration, medicine, weather, and virtual reality.

The First National Kids Disc, **Voyager.** **Grades 2–8.**

This laser disc contains numerous activities, projects, and games for children. Students can learn to communicate in sign language, view hundreds of jokes, make movie flip books, and solve secret messages.

The Great Ocean Rescue, **Tom Snyder** **Productions. Grades 5–Adult.**

Students try to solve different types of problems affecting the ocean. The disc covers three areas: *Ocean Basics, The Living Seas,* and *Protecting Our Oceans.*

Great Solar System Rescue, **Tom Snyder** **Productions. Grades 5–8.**

This laser disc introduces concepts in geology, meteorology, chemistry, and numerous other scientific fields. Learning to be interdisciplinary thinkers, students use math, language arts, and social studies in their problem solving.

GTV: The American People, **National** **Geographic. Grades 1–12.**

Organized chronologically, *GTV: The American People* focuses on the nation's human history from the first

encounter between Native Americans and Europeans, to the importing of slaves, to the fight for civil rights, and more. The two laser discs feature more than thirty short videos and a bilingual format.

Habitats, **SVE. Grades K–3.**

Students observe how plants and animals live in different environments. The program includes short story excerpts, live photography, still frames, and teacher materials.

Interactive Nova: Animal Pathfinders, **Scholastic. Grades 5–12.**

Students learn about an animal's life through an hour-long NOVA program that includes fifteen short documentaries with accompanying text/graphic cards. Students can actually hear the animals breathing and moving. This disc is packaged with two other titles: *The Miracle of Life* and *Race to Save the Planet.*

In the Company of Whales, **Discovery** **Channel/Cornet/MTI. Grades 6–Adult.**

Students examine the biological features of a very misunderstood mammal, the whale. The bilingual presentation explores the relationship among whales, humans, and the global ecosystem.

The Miracle of Life, **Voyager.** **Grades 5–Adult.**

This laser disc takes students on a journey through the human body as new life begins. The journey begins with conception, follows the development of the fetus, and ends with the birth of a child.

The National Gallery of Art, **Voyager.** **Grades K–Adult.**

This program gives students access to 1,600 portraits and sculptures in the National Gallery of Art, features an interesting documentary on the museum's development, and offers a guided tour through the galleries. Students can view still photos and motion pictures organized by categories, such as artist, period, date, and subject.

Point of View 2.0 and *Community History Kit*, Scholastic. Grades 4–12.

This state and community history kit gives students the tools to put together a multimedia record of their state's culture, government, people, and environment. The program features outline maps; county maps; statistics on voting, income, and agriculture; flags; birds; and state symbols.

Regard for the Planet, Voyager. Grades K–Adult.

Regard for the Planet invites students to take a journey to distant cultures and continents. This disc features 50,000 photographs of world events and daily life.

The Visual Almanac, Voyager. Grades 3–Adult.

This disc is a classic, featuring 7,000 different images, resources, movies, picture sequences, still images, and sounds. It includes a 200-page guide and index along with a CD-ROM.

The Wonderful Problems of Fizz and Martina, Tom Snyder Productions. Grades 3–6.

In this math series, students are exposed to real-life math problems in a cooperative learning setting. This program meets the NCTM objectives, includes three volumes in English and Spanish, and is helpful for teaching ESL students.

A World Alive, Voyager. Grades K–12.

Actor James Earl Jones narrates this laser disc, which concerns the creatures that live on our planet. It features more than 120 animal species with sensational wildlife footage.

APPLE DOS 3.3

Initializing a Disk

1. Put the System Master Disk (DOS 3.3) in the disk drive and warm boot the computer (press control, open apple and then reset).

2. Remove the System Master Disk from the disk drive and insert a blank disk.

3. Type NEW and press the return key.

4. Type the following one-line greeting program, substituting your own name and the date, and press return. 10 PRINT "John Smith, 1/1/88"

5. Now type INIT HELLO and press return (no line number).

Running Different Programs

Applesoft Type RUN, one space, and the file name and press return.

I (Integer Basic) Type INT and press return. The prompt sign will change and look like this: >. Then type RUN, one space, and the file name and press return. When you want to return to Applesoft Basic, type FP and press return.

Binary files Type BRUN, space, and the file name and press return.

Running a program in memory Type RUN and press return.

System Commands

Catalog Type the word CATALOG and press return.
List Type the word LIST and press return.
Stop the program Press the control and reset keys simultaneously.

Saving Type SAVE and the program name and press return.
Load Type the word LOAD and the program name and press return.
Delete Type the word DELETE and the program name and press return.

Copying a File

1. Put the disk to be copied in Drive 1 and the formatted disk in Drive 2.

2. Type LOAD, a space, the file name, a comma, and D1 (Disk Drive 1) and press return.

3. Type SAVE, one space, the file name, a comma, and D2 (Disk Drive 2).

If you want to use the BRUN copy file program FILEM that is available, simply run BRUN FID or FILEM and follow the screen directions.

Copying a Disk

1. Put DOS 3.3 in the disk drive.

2. Warm boot the computer by pressing the control, open apple, and reset keys.

3. Type RUN COPYA (without a space) and press return.

4. Use the default settings by pressing return four times. To make a change, type a new number and press return.

5. The screen should say, "—PRESS 'RETURN' KEY TO BEGIN COPY—".

6. Now put the original disk in the other drive and press return for a two-drive copy.

PRODOS OPERATING SYSTEM FOR THE GS

System Utilities

1. Put the System Master Disk with the utilities on it in the disk drive.

2. Choose Sysutil.System and press return.

3. The next screen displays the utilities: Catalog, Format a Disk, Delete Files, Copying Files, Duplicating a Disk.

4. Once you have selected a utility, choose the location of the disk by slot and drive or by ProDOS pathname. (A pathname is the complete name of a file. It starts with a slash, and each element of the name is separated by a slash, for example, /Project/letters/Smith).

Formatting a Disk

1. Select the Format a Disk option.

2. At the first screen, press return.

3. The prompt asks for the disk's location. If it is already correct, accept the default by pressing return. If not, use the arrow keys to move and change one or both values.

4. Press return to accept the ProDOS default.

5. The prompt asks for a volume name. Use the delete key to erase the present name and type a new name that begins with a slash and then a letter. Do not exceed fifteen characters, do not add space, and use only letters, numbers, and periods, for example, /Computer1.

6. Press return and a prompt will direct you to insert the disk that you want formatted into the proper drive.

7. Insert the disk to be formatted and press return.

Cataloging a Disk

1. Select Catalog from the Utility menu and press return.

2. Accept the defaults and press return two times to view the catalog.

Duplicating a Disk

Instead of using this utility, it is faster and more efficient to use a program such as Diversi Copy (DSR).

1. Select Duplicate a Disk and press return.

2. The screen prompt asks, "Where is your Source Disk?" If the default is acceptable, press return; if not, change it.

3. The next screen prompt asks, "Where is your destination disk?" If this default is acceptable, press return; if not, change it.

4. The screen prompt asks you to put the destination disk and source disk into the correct drives and press return.

Copying Files

1. Select Copy Files and press return.

2. Accept the slot and drive default and press return.

3. If the source disk's slot and drive are correct, press return twice.

4. If the destination disk's slot and drive are correct, press return.

5. The screen prompt asks you to select some or all of the files on the disk. Make a selection and press return.

6. The next screen displays a list of files. Select the ones you want by pressing the space bar.

7. When you are ready to copy, press return.

The commands Run, Stop, Save, Load, and List are identical to those in DOS 3.3.

SYSTEM 8.1 FOR THE MACINTOSH

Formatting a Disk

1. When you insert an unformatted disk in the disk drive, a dialog box appears asking if you want to initialize the disk.

2. In the Name box, type a name for the disk.

3. This dialog box also has a drop-down menu that lets you choose the format to use, for example, Macintosh 1.4 MB. In the majority of cases, the default is fine.

4. Click on Initialize.

5. A dialog box appears with Continue or Cancel. Click Continue or press return.

Copying a Floppy Disk to a Hard Drive

1. Insert the floppy disk into the hard drive.

2. Using the mouse, drag the floppy disk icon so that its outline moves onto the hard disk icon, darkening it.

3. Release the mouse button.

Copying a File from the Hard Disk

1. Insert the floppy disk into the disk drive.

2. Find the file that is to be copied on the hard disk and place the cursor on top of it.

3. Click the mouse button and drag the file so that its outline goes onto the floppy disk and darkens it.

4. Release the mouse button.

Deleting a File

1. Select the file that you want to delete.

2. Click and drag the file onto the trash can, darkening it.

3. Release the mouse button. The trash can will bulge.

4. Open the Special Menu and select Empty Trash.

5. A dialog box appears telling how many files are in the trash and asking if you want to remove these items. Click OK. If you want to avoid this step, hold down the option key when you select Empty Trash from the Special Menu.

IBM PC/MS-DOS

Booting

1. Cold boot (computer off): Put the PC/MS-DOS in the machine and then turn on the computer. Warm boot (computer on): Put the PC/MS-

DOS floppy disk in the machine and boot the system by holding down the control and alt keys and pressing the del key. Release these keys simultaneously.

2. Press enter twice to accept the current date and time defaults.

3. When you see the prompt screen with the current drive, for example A >, DOS is loaded.

4. Insert the program disk and type the name that brings up this disk.

Turning Off the Computer

1. Save your work.

2. Exit the program and return the control to DOS A >.

Formatting a Disk

1. At the prompt, type FORMAT and a space and then type A: (for Drive A) or B: (for Drive B).

2. Press enter.

3. The screen prompts tell you to insert the new diskette in the drive specified and hit any key.

Viewing the Directory

At the DOS prompt, type DIR and press enter. This command lists all the files on the disk.

Making a Backup Copy

To copy a disk from Drive A to a disk in Drive B:

1. Type A: to make sure this drive is current and press enter.

2. At the DOS prompt, type DISKCOPY, a space, A:, a space, and B:. Press enter.

3. The screen will prompt you to insert the disk to be copied (the source) in Drive A and a blank disk (the target) in Drive B and then press any key to begin.

Copying a Selected File onto Another Disk

1. Type A: to make sure this drive is current and press enter.

2. At the DOS prompt, put a formatted disk in Drive B.

3. Type COPY, a space, the selected file name to copy, COMPUTERS.BAS, a space, the name of the directory that will receive the copy, a space, and B:. Press enter.

4. Type COPY COMPUTERS.BAS B: Press enter.

Deleting a File

1. Make the directory containing the file current by typing A: and press enter.

2. At the DOS prompt, type DEL, a space, and the file name to be deleted. Press enter. For example, type DEL COMPUTERS.BAS.

3. This will delete the file called *computers.bas* from Drive A.

WINDOWS 3.1 OPERATING SYSTEM

Formatting a Disk

1. Insert the blank disk in the drive.

2. In the File Manager window, click on Disk.

3. From the Disk Menu select Format Disk.

4. In the dialog box, select the following options.

   a. In the Disk In: box, select the drive that contains the disk to be formatted.

   b. Choose the correct Capacity and Density for the disk format. In most cases, use the defaults.

   c. In the Label box, click inside and type a name for the disk.

   d. Click OK.

   e. Another dialog box appears that gives you a final chance to cancel formatting.

   f. Click Yes.

Copying a Disk with a Single Drive

1. While in the File Manager window, insert into the disk drive the source disk with the files that are to be copied.

2. Click on Disk.

3. When the menu appears, click on Copy Disk.

4. When a dialog box appears, click on Yes.

5. When prompted, insert the disk that is to receive the files and swap disks as directed.

Copying a File

1. From the File Manager window, select the item or files that are to be copied.

2. Click on File and then click on Copy.

3. Type a destination path and/or a file name in the To: box (for example, A:) and then click OK to confirm and make a copy.

Deleting a File

1. From the File Manager window, select the directory containing the file you want to delete.

2. Click on File and then click on Delete.

3. When the dialog box appears to confirm deletion, click on OK.

4. When another dialog box appears, select All to delete all the files.

WINDOWS 95 OPERATING SYSTEM

Formatting a Disk

1. Insert the blank disk in the drive.

2. Double click on the My Computer icon.

3. Select the desired disk drive.

4. From the File Menu select Format.

5. In the dialog box, select the following options:

   a. Choose the correct Capacity and Density for the disk format. In most cases, use the defaults.

   b. Choose the Format Type.

   c. In the Label box, click inside and type a name for the disk.

   d. Click Start.

Copying a Disk

1. Double click on the My Computer icon.

2. Right click on the Floppy (A:) then click on Copy Disk.

3. When the pop-up dialog box appears, click on Start.

4. Insert your data disk (source disk), then click OK.

5. When prompted, remove your data disk (source disk) and insert your destination disk (target disk) in Drive A.

6. Click OK.

Copying a File using a Send To:

1. Start Windows Explorer.

2. Open the Windows folder containing the file you want to copy.

3. Right click on the file you want to copy.

4. A pop-up dialog box appears.

5. Move the pointer on Send To, then click on Floppy (A:).

6. A dialog box appears telling you the file is being sent to drive A:.

Deleting a File

1. Start Windows Explorer.

2. Select the file you want to delete by clicking on it.

3. Under the File menu, select Delete.

4. A dialog box appears, asking you if you want to delete the file.

5. Click Yes.

6. To complete this process, empty the Recycle Bin.

7. Right click on the Recycle Bin and choose Empty Recycle Bin from the menu.

Appendix C
DIRECTORY OF SELECTED
SOFTWARE PUBLISHERS

Abacus Concepts Inc.
1918 Bonita Avenue
Berkeley CA 94704
510/540-1949
510/540-0260 (fax)

A.D.A.M. Software Inc.
1600 RiverEdge Parkway, Ste. 800
Atlanta GA 30328
404/980-0888
800/755-2326
404/955-3088 (fax)

Addison-Wesley Publishing Co.
1 Jacob Way
Reading MA 01867
619/944-3700
800/358-4566
800/333-3328 (fax)
www.awl.com/sf-awl
www.addisonwesley.com

Adobe Systems Inc.
(formerly Aldus)
1585 Charleston Road, Box 7900
Mountain View CA 94039-7900
415/961-4400
800/833-6687
www.adobe.com

AIM Tech Corp.
20 Trafalgar Square
Nashua NH 03063
800/289-2884

AIMS Multimedia
9170 DeSoto Avenue
Chatsworth CA 91311
800/367-2467
818/773-4300
818/341-6700 (fax)

Apple Computer Inc.
20525 Mariani Ave.
Cupertino, CA 95014
408/996-1010
800/767-2775
www.apple.com

Aurbach & Associates, Inc.
9378 Olive Street Road, Suite 102
St. Louis MO 63132
800/77GRADY
314/432-7577
314/432-7072
www.thequartermile.com

Barnum Software
3450 Lake Shore Avenue, Ste. 200
Oakland CA 94610
800/553-9155
510/465-5070
510/465-5071 (fax)

Baudville Computer Products
5380 52nd St. S.E.
Grand Rapids MI 49512
800/728-0888
616/698-0888
616/698-0554 (fax)

Berkeley Systems Inc.
2095 Rose St.
Berkeley CA 94709
510/540-5535
800/877-5535
510/540-5115 (fax)

Bright Star Technology
1450 114th Ave. S.W., Ste. 200
Bellevue WA 98004
800/757-7707
206/451-3697

Brøderbund Software
500 Redwood Blvd.
P.O. Box 6121
Novata CA 94948
800/521-6263
415/382-4400
415/382-4419 (fax)
www.Broderbund.com

Chickadee Software Inc.
R.R.2, Box 79W
Center Harbor NH 03226
603/253-4600
603/253-4623 (fax)

Claris Clear Choice
5201 Patrick Henry Dr., P.O. Box 58168
Santa Clara CA 95052
408/987-7000
800/325-2747
415/513-0985 (fax)

Claris Corporation
5201 Patrick Henry Dr., P.O. Box 58168
Santa Clara CA 95052
408/727-8227
800/334-3535 (dealers)
www.claris.com

Classroom Connect
1866 Colonial Village Lane
Lancaster PA 17601
800/471-2248
717/393-5752 (fax)
www.classroom.net

Cognitive Technologies Corporation
5009 Cloister Drive
Rockville, MD 20852
800/335-0781

Compu-Teach
16541 Redmond Way, Ste. 137-C
Redmond WA 98052-4482
800/448-3224
203/883-9169 (fax)

Computer Associates International Inc.
One Computer Associates Plaza
Islandia NY 11788
800/225-5224
516/342-5224

Conduit
University of Iowa, Oakdale Campus
Iowa City IA 52242
319/335-4100
800/365-9774
319/395-4077 (fax)

Corel Corporation
1600 Carling Ave.
Ottawa ON
CANADA K1Z 8R7
800/772-6735
613/728-3733
613/761-9176 (fax)
www.corel.com

Critical Thinking Press
207 16th St.
Pacific Grove CA 93950
800/458-4849
408/375-2455
408/372-3230 (fax)

Davidson & Associates
19840 Pioneer Avenue
Torrance CA 90503
800/545-7677
310/793-0600
310/793-0601 (fax)
www.education.com

DeltaPoint Inc.
2 Harris Court, Ste. B-1
Monterey, CA 93940
408/648-4000
800/446-6955
408/648-4020 (fax)

Discis Inc.
45 Sheppard Ave. E#410
Toronto ON
CANADA M2N 5W9
800/567-4321
416/250-6540 (fax)
www.www.goodmedia.com/discis

Disney Interactive
500 S. Buena Vista St.
Burbank CA 91521-8178
800/900-9234
818/553-5010
818/553-6302 (fax)
www.disneyinteractive.com

DK Multimedia
95 Madison Ave.
New York NY 19916
800/567-4321
212/213-4800 x220
212/213-5240 (fax)
www.dk.com

Don Johnson Inc.
1000 N. Rand Rd.
Bldg. 115
Wauconda IL 60084
800/999-4660
708/526-4177 (fax)
www.donjohnson.com

Dr. T's Music Software Company
124 Crescent Road, Ste. 3
Needham MA 02194
617/455-1454
617/455-1460 (fax)

Dynamix
1600 Millrace Dr.
Eugene OR 97403
503/343-0772
503/344-1754 (fax)

EA Kids
A Division of Electronics Arts
1450 Fashion Island
San Mateo CA 94404
800/543-9778
415/571-7171
415/286-5556 (fax)

Edmark
6727 185th Ave. N.E., P.O. Box 3218
Redmond WA 98073-3218
206/556-8435
800/426-0856
206/556-8430 (fax)
www.edmark.com

Electronic Arts
Direct Sales
P.O. Box 7530
San Mateo CA 94403
800/245-4525
415/572-2787
www.ea.com

E.M.A.
P.O. Box 339
Los Altos CA 94023
415/969-4679

Evergreen Laser Disc
2819 Hamline Ave. N.
Saint Paul MN 55113
612/639-1418
612/639-0110 (fax)

Forest Technologies
514 Market Loop, Suite 103
West Dundee IL 60118
800/544-3356
847/428-2184
708/428-1310 (fax)

Fractical Design Corp.
335 Spreckels Drive
Aptos CA 95003
408/688-8800
408/688-8836 (fax)

FTC Group
P.O. Box 1361
Bloomington IL 61702
800/888-237-6740

Great Wave Software
5353 Scotts Valley Dr.
Scotts Valley CA 95066
408/438-1990
408/438-7171 (fax)
www.greatwave.com

Grolier Electronic Publishing
90 Sherman Turnpike
Danbury CT 06816
800/285-4534
203/797-3197 (fax)
www.gi.grolier.com

Gryphon Software Corporation
7220 Trade St., Ste. 120
San Diego CA 92121-2325
619/536-8815
800/795-0981
619/536-8932
www.gryphonsw.com

Hartley Courseware
A Division of Josten
9920 Pacific Heights Blvd #500
San Diego CA 92121-4331
800/247-1380
517/333-5300
517/333-5325 (fax)
www.jlc.com

Hi Tech of Santa Cruz
202 Pelton Ave.
Santa Cruz CA 95060
408/425-5654
408/425-8041

Houghton Mifflin Interactive
222 Berkeley Street
Boston MA 02116-3764
800/225-3362
www.hminet.com

IBM Corp.
3200 Windy Hills Road
Atlanta GA 30328
770/835-6881

IBM Multimedia Studio
590 Madison Avenue
New York NY 10022
800/426-7235
770/835-6262
212/745-7555
www.pc.ibm.com/multimedia

Ingenuity Works Software Ltd.
4250 Dawson St., Ste. 200
Burnaby BC
CANADA V5C 481
800/665-0667
604/299-4435

Inline Software
308 Main St.
Lakeville CT 06039
203/435-4995
203/435-1091

Inspiration Software, Inc.
7412 S.W. Beaverton Hillside Hwy., Suite 1
Portland OR 97225-2167
503/297-3004
503/297-4676
www.inspiration.com

Intelligent Peripheral Devices, Inc.
20380 Town Center Lane, Suite 270
Cupertino, CA 95014
408/252-9400
408/252-9409 (fax)
www.alphasmart.com

IVI Publishing Inc.
7500 Flying Cloud Dr., Ste. 400
Minneapolis MN 55344
800/432-1332
612/996-6001

Jackson Software
361 Park Avenue
Glencoe IL 60022
www.Jacksoncorp.com

Jay Klein Productions Inc.
2930 Austin Bluffs Parkway, Ste. 104
Colorado Springs CO 80918
719/599-8786
www.gradebusters.com

Jump! Music
201 San Antonio Circle, Suite 172
Mountain View CA 94040
800/289-5867
415/917-7460
415/917-7490 (fax)
www.jumpmusic.com

KartoffelSoft Inc.
3475 Edison Way, Suite H
Menlo Park CA 94024
415/306-0670
www.kartoffelsoft.com

Knowledge Adventure
1311 Grand Central Ave.
Glendale CA 91201
800/542-4240
818/246-5604 (fax)
www.adventure.com

Lawrence Productions
1800 S. 35th St.
Galesburg MI 49053
800/421-4157
616/665-7075
616/665-7060 (fax)
www.lpi.com

LCSI/Logo Computer Systems
3300 Cote Vertu Rd., Ste. 201
Montreal QC
CANADA H4R 2B7
800/321-5646

Learn Technologies Interactive/Voyager
361 Broadway, Suite 600
New York NY 10012
888/292-5584
212/334-2225
212/334-1211 (fax)
www.voyagerco.com

The Learning Company
6493 Kaiser Dr.
Fremont CA 94555
800/227-5609
510/792-2101
www.learningco.com

Lego Systems
555 Taylor Rd.
Enfield CT 06082
800/527-8339
203/749-2291
203/763-2466 (fax)

Living Books
500 Redwood Blvd.
Novato CA 94948
800/776-4724
415/382-4400
415/352-5238
www.livingbooks.com

Logo Computer Systems Inc.
PO Box 162
Highgate Springs VT 05460
800/321-5646
www.lcsi.ca

Magic Quest Inc.
2121 N. California Blvd., Suite 600
Walnut Creek CA 94596-3572
800/336-2947
510/933-5630
510/927-3736

Mainstay
5311-B Derry Ave.
Agoura Hills CA 91301
818/991-6540
818/991-4587 (fax)

Maxis
2 Theatre Square #230
Orinda CA 94563-3346
800/99-MAXIS
www.maxis.com

MECC/Softkey International
6160 Summit Dr.
Minneapolis MN 55430-4003
800/685-6322
612/569-1500

MetaTools, Inc.
6303 Carpinteria Ave.
Carpinteria CA 93013
805/566-6200
805/566-6385 (fax)
www.metatools.com

Microsoft Corp.
1 Microsoft Way
Redmond WA 98052-6399
800/426-9400
206/882-8080
www.microsoft.com

Milliken Publishing Co.
1100 Research Blvd., P.O. Box 21579
St. Louis MO 63132
800/643-0008
800/397-1947

MindPlay
160 W. Fort Lowell
Tucson AZ 85705
800/221-7911
520/888-1800
520/888-7904 (fax)
www.mindplay.com

Mindscape
(formerly Software Toolworks)
88 Rowland Way
Novato CA 94945
415/897-9900
415/897-9956 (fax)
www.mindscape.com

Multicom Publishing Inc.
1100 Olive Way, Ste. 1250
Seattle WA 98101
800/850-7272
206/622-5530
206/622-4380 (fax)

National Geographic Society
1145 17th Street N.W.
Washington DC 20036-4688
800/368-2728
301/921-1330 (in Maryland)
www.nationalgeographic.com

Opcode Systems Inc.
3950 Fabian Way, Ste. 100
Palo Alto CA 94303
415/856-3333
415/856-3332 (fax)

Optical Data Corp.
30 Technology Dr.
Warren NJ 07059
800/524-2481
908/668-0222
908/755-0577 (fax)

Optimal Learning Systems
1918 Orrington Ave.
Evanston IL 60201
708/475-9796

Optimum Resource Inc.
18 Hunter Road
Hilton Head Island SC 29926
888/784-2592
803/689-8000
809/689-8008 (fax)
www.stickybear.com

Paramount Interactive
700 Hansen Way
Palo Alto CA 94304
415/812-8200
415/813-8055 (fax)

Pierian
5200 S.W. Macadam Ave., Ste. 250
Portland OR 97201
800/472-8578
503/222-0771 (fax)
www.pierian.com

The Princeton Review
2315 Broadway, 3d Floor
New York NY 10024
800/955-3700
212/874-8282
212/874-0775 (fax)
www.review.com

Putman New Media
11490 Commerce Park Dr., Ste. 130
Reston VA 22091
703/860-3375
703/860-3620 (fax)

Queue Inc.
338 Commerce Dr.
Fairfield CT 06430
800/232-2224
203/336-2481 (fax)

Roger Wagner Publishing
1050 Pioneer Way, Ste. P
El Cajun CA 92020
800/421-6526
619/442-0522
619/442-0525 (fax)
www.hyperstudio.com

Sanctuary Woods/Theatrix Interactive
1825 South Grant St., Ste. 260
San Mateo CA 94402-9865
800/955-8749
510/678-2800
www.ah-hah.com

Scholastic Inc.
555 Broadway
New York NY 10012
800/541-5513
800/392-2179
800/724-6527
www.scholastic.com

Scott Foresman/Addison-Wesley
1900 E. Lake Ave.
Glenview IL 60025-9882
800/552-2259
www.sf.aw.com

Sierra On-Line Inc.
3380-146th Place S.E., Ste. 300
Bellevue WA 98007
800/757-7707
206/649-9800
206/649-0340 (fax)
www.sierra.com

Simon Schuster
1230 Avenue of the Americas
New York NY 10020
800/545-7677
212/698-7000
212/698-7555 (fax)
www.viacom.com

SmartStuff
PO Box 82284
Portland OR 97282
800/671-3999
503/231-4300
503/231-4334 (fax)
www.smartstuff.com

Society for Visual Education
1345 W. Diversey Parkway
Chicago IL 60614
800/829-1900
312/525-1500 (in Illinois)

SoftKey International Inc.
201 Broadway
Cambridge MA 02139
617/494-1200
800/227-5609
617/494-1219 (fax)

Software for Success
190 S. LaSalle Street
Chicago IL 60603
312/701-7257
312/701-7711

Storm Software
1861 Landings Dr.
Mountain View CA 94043
800/275-5734
415/691-9825 (fax)

Sunburst Communications
101 Castleton St.
Pleasantville NY 10570
800/321-7511
408/438-5502
914/747-4109
www.nysunburst.com

Superschool
1857 Josie Avenue
Long Beach CA 90815
213/594-8580

Symantec Corp.
10201 Torre Ave.
Cupertino CA 95014-2132
408/372-2041

Terrapin Software
10 Holworthy Street
Cambridge MA 02138
800/972-8200
617/547-5646
800/776-4610 (fax)

TikiSoft Inc.
26041 Del Rey, Suite E
Misson Viejo CA 92691
714/766-4852
www.tikisoft.com

Theatrix Interactive
1250 45th Street, Suite 150
Emeryville CA 94608-2924
800/955-8749
510/658-2800
510/658-2828
www.theatrix.com

Time Warner Interactive
2210 West Olive
Burbank CA 91506
800/482-3766
415/691-7734

Tom Snyder Productions
80 Coolidge Hill Road
Watertown MA 02172-0236
800/342-0236
617/926-6000
617/926-6222 (fax)
www.teachtsp.com

T/Maker Company
1390 Villa Street
Mountain View CA 94041
800/986-2537
415/691-7762
415/962-0201

True Basic Inc.
12 Commerce Ave.
West Lebanon NH 03784
800/872-2742
603/298-5655

Ventura Educational Systems
910 Ramona Ave.-E
Grover Beach CA 93433
800/336-1022
805/473-7382 (fax)

Videodiscovery
1700 Westlake Avenue North, Suite 600
Seattle WA 98109-3012
800/548-3472
206/285-5400
206/285-9245 (fax)
www.videodiscovery.com

Visions
11567 S.W. Sheffield Circle
Tigard OR 97223
800/385-6518

Vividus
378 Cambridge Ave., Suite 1
Palo Alto CA 94306
415/321-2221
www.vividus.com

Voyager Company
578 Broadway, Ste. 46
New York NY 10012
800/446-2001
212/431-5799 (fax)

Writing Tools Group
1 Harbor Dr., No. 111
Sausalito CA 94965
812/323-1740

Xerox Imaging System
Xerox Imaging Software
9 Centennial Dr.
Peabody MA 01960
800/248-6550

Appendix D
RECOMMENDED COMPUTER PUBLICATIONS

MAGAZINES AND JOURNALS

BYTE, McGraw-Hill Inc., 70 Main St., Peterborough NH 03458.

Club KidSoft, 718 University Ave., Ste. 112, Los Gatos CA 95030-9958.

Computer Science Education, Ablex Publishing Corp., 355 Chestnut St., Norwood NJ.

Computers and Composition, Michigan Technological University, Department of Humanities, Houghton MI 49931.

Computers, Reading, and Language Arts, Modern Learning Publisher Inc., 1308 E. 38th St., Oakland CA 94602.

The Computing Teacher, see *Learning and Leading with Technology*.

Digital Video Magazine, TechMedia Publishing Inc. and IDG Company, 80 Elms St., Peterborough NH 03458.

Educational Technology, 720 Palisade Ave., Englewood Cliffs NJ 07632.

Educational Technology Research and Development, Association for Educational Communications and Technology, 1025 Vermont Avenue N.W., Suite 820, Washington DC 20005.

Electronic Learning, Scholastic Inc., 555 Broadway, New York, NY 10012.

Family PC, PO Box 400451, Des Moines IA 50347-0541.

Future Generations Computer Systems, Journal Information Center, Elsevier Science Publishers, 52 Vanderbilt Ave., New York NY 10017.

Home PC, a CMP Publication, PO Box 420212, Palm Coast FL 32142-9468.

InfoWorld, InfoWorld Publishing Inc., 155 Bovet Rd., Ste. 800, San Mateo CA 94402.

Instruction Delivery Systems, Communicative Technology Corporation, 50 Culpepper St., Warrenton VA 22186.

Interact, International Interactive Communications Society, 2120 Steiner St., San Francisco CA 94115.

Interface: The Computer Education Quarterly, Mitchell Publishing Inc., 915 River St., Santa Cruz CA 95060.

Internet World, Mecklermedia Corp., 20 Ketchum St., Wesport CT 06880; http://www.iworld.com.

Journal of Artificial Intelligence in Education, AACE, Box 2966, Charlottesville VA 22902.

Journal of Computer-Based Instruction, ADCIS, Western Washington University, Miller Hall 409, Bellingham WA 98225.

Journal of Computers in Mathematics and Science Teaching, AACE, Box 2966, Charlottesville VA 22902.

Journal of Computing in Childhood Education, AACE, Box 2966, Charlottesville VA 22902.

Journal of Computing in Teacher Education, ISTE, 1787 Agate St., Eugene, OR 97403-1923.

Journal of Educational Computing Research, Baywood Publishing Inc., 26 Austin Ave, Box 337, Amityville, NY 11701.

Journal of Educational Technology Systems, Baywood Publishing Inc., Box D, Farmington NY 11735.

Journal of Interactive Instruction Development, Society for Applied Learning Technology, 50 Culpepper St., Warrenton VA 22186.

Journal of Research on Computing in Education, ISTE, 1787 Agate St., Eugene OR 97403-9905.

Learning, PO Box 2580, Boulder CO 80322.

Learning and Leading with Technology (formerly *The Computing Teacher*), ISTE, 1787 Agate St., Eugene OR 97403-1923.

Logo Exchange, ISTE, 1787 Agate St., Eugene OR 97403-9905.

MacWeek, Ziff-Davis Publishing Company, One Park Ave., New York NY 10016-5802.

MacWorld, Mac World Communications Inc., 501 2nd St., San Francisco CA 94107.

Media and Methods, American Society of Educators, 1429 Walnut St., Philadelphia, PA 19102.

Microcomputers in Education, Two Sequan Rd., Watch Hill RI 02891.

Online Access, Chicago Fine Print Inc., 900 N. Franklin, Ste. 310, Chicago IL 60610.

PC AI, Knowledge Technology Inc., 3310 West Bell Rd., Ste. 119, Phoenix AZ 85023.

PC Computing, Ziff-Davis Publishing Company, Computer Publications Division, One Park Ave., New York NY 10017.

PC Magazine, Ziff-Davis Publishing Company, Computer Publications Division, One Park Ave., New York NY 10017.

PC Novice, 120 W. Harvest Dr., Lincoln NE 68521.

PC Week, Ziff-Davis Publishing Company, One Park Ave., New York NY 10017.

PC World, PO Box 78270, San Francisco CA 94107-9991.

Personal Computing, Hayden Publishing Co. Inc., 10 Mulholland Dr., Hasbrouck Heights NJ 07604.

Technology & Learning, Peter Li Inc., 330 Progress Rd., Dayton OH 45499.

TechTrends, AECT, 1126 Sixteenth St. N.W., Washington DC 20036.

T.H.E. Journal, Information Synergy Inc., 150 El Camino Real, Tustin CA 92680.

Virtual Reality Special Report, Miller Freeman Inc., 600 Harrison St., San Francisco CA 94107.

Wired, PO Box 191826, San Francisco CA 94119-9866.

NEWSLETTERS

Classroom Computer News, International Education, 51 Spring St., Watertown MA 02172.

CUE Newsletter, Computer-Using Educators, Box 1854, San Jose CA 95158.

Education Computer News, BPI, 951 Pershing Dr., Silver Spring MD 20910-4464.

Educational Technology News, Business Publishers Inc., 951 Pershing Dr., Silver Spring, MD 20910-4464.

ISTE Update, ISTE, 1787 Agate St., Eugene OR 97403-1923.

Logo Update, The Logo Foundation, 250 West 57th St., Ste. 2603, New York NY 10107-2603.

Online Searcher, 14 Haddon Rd., Scarsdale NY 10583.

The Sloane Report, PO Box 561689, Miami FL 33256.

Syllabus—An Information Source on Computing in Higher Education, PO Box 2716, 1226 Mandarin Dr., Sunnyvale CA 94087.

Telecommunications in Education (T.I.E.) News, ISTE, 1787 Agate St., Eugene OR 97403-1923.

True BASIC Bulletin, 12 Commerce Ave., West Lebanon NH 03784-9758.

SOFTWARE REVIEW SOURCES

Children's Software Review, Active Learning Associates, Inc., 44 Main Street, Flemington NJ 08822.

Curriculum Products Reviews, 530 University Ave., Palo Alto CA 94301.

Educational Software Preview Guide, ICCE, University of Oregon, 1787 Agate St., Eugene OR 97403.

The Educational Software Selector, EPIE Institute, PO Box 839, Water Mill NY 11976.

Micro, Florida Center for Instructional Computing, University of South Florida, Tampa FL 33620.

MicroSIFT, Document Reproduction Services, Northwest Regional Educational Laboratory, 101 S.W. Main St., Ste. 500, Portland OR 97204.

Only the Best, Association for Supervision and Curriculum Development, 1250 N. Pitt St. Alexandria, VA 22314-1453.

Software Reviews on File, Facts on File Inc., 460 Park Ave. South, New York NY 10016.

Technology in the Curriculum, California State Department of Education, PO Box 271, Sacramento CA 95802-0271.

Appendix E
RECOMMENDED MAIL-ORDER
SOFTWARE SOURCES

Creative Computers' MacMall
2645 Maricopa St.
Torrance CA 90503-5144
800/222-2808
800/560-6800
310/222-5800 (fax)

Educational Resources
1550 Executive Dr.
Elgin IL 60123
800/624-2926
708/888-8300
708/888-8499

Educational Software Institute
4213 South 94th St.
Omaha NE 68127
800/955-5570

The Edutainment Catalog
932 Walnut St.
Louisville CO 80027
800/338-3844
303/661-9303

Egghead Software
22011 SE 51st St.
Issaquah WA 98027-7299
800/EGG-HEAD
800/949-3447 (fax)

Learning Services
P.O. Box 1036
Eugene OR 97440
800/877-9378
800/877-3278
508/937-5976
503/744-2056

Learning Zone
17411 Union Hill Rd.
Redmond WA 98052-6716
800/381-9663
800/417-1993 (fax)

MacWarehouse
47 Water St.
Norwalk CT 06854
800/255-6227
800/925-6227
908/905-9279 (fax)

MicroWarehouse
1690 Oak Street
Lakewood NJ 08701
800/367-7080
908/905-5245 (fax)

PC and MacConnection
14 Mill St.
Marlow NH 03456
800/800-1111
603/446-7711
603/446-7791 (fax)

PC and Mac Zone
15815 SE 37th St.
Bellevue WA 98006-1800
800/258-2088 (PC)
800/248-0800

Quality Computers
20200 Nine Mile Rd.
St. Clair Shores MI 48080
800/777-3642
810/774-7200
810/774-2698 (fax)

The Reading & Computing Place
14752 Beach Blvd. #200
La Mirada CA 90638
800/888-0553
310/943-2626
714/523-9000
714/523-1020 (fax)

TigerSoftware
9100 S. Dadeland Blvd., Ste. 1200
Miami FL 33156-7816
800/666-2562
800/888-4437
305/529-2990 (fax)

Appendix F
ON-LINE SERVICES AND BULLETIN BOARDS

America Online, 8619 Westwood Center Dr., Vienna VA 22182, 800/827-6364.

ARPANET, Stanford Research Institute, Menlo Park CA 94025, 800/235-3155.

AT&T Long-Distance Learning Network, 295 North Maple Ave., Rm. 6234S3, Basking Ridge NJ 07201, 201/221-8544.

BBS Channel 1, PO Box 338, Cambridge MA 02238, 617/864-0100 (voice), 617/354-3230 (modem).

BreadNET, Bread Loaf School of English, Middlebury College, Middlebury VT 05753, 802/388-3711.

BRS Information Technologies, 1200 Rte. 7, Lathan NY 12110, 800/227-5277.

Champlain Valley Union High School Electronic Bulletin Board, Champlain Valley Union High School, R.R.2 Box 160, Hinesburg VT 05461, 802/482-2101.

Classroom Prodigy, Prodigy Services Company, 800/PRODIGY (voice).

CompuServe Information Services, PO Box 20212, 50000 Arlington Centre Blvd., Columbus OH 43220, 800/848-8199.

Delphi Internet Services Corp., 1030 Massachusetts Ave., Cambridge MA 02139, 800/695-4005.

Dialog Classroom Instruction Program, 1901 N. Moore St., Ste. 500, Arlington VA 22209, 800/334-2564.

Dialog Information Services Inc., 3460 Hillview Ave., Palo Alto CA 94304, 415/858-2700.

Dow Jones News/Retrieval, PO Box 300, Princeton NJ 08540, 800/257-5114.

Educational Products Information Exchange Institute (EPIE), PO Box 839, Water Mill NY 11976, 515/283-4922.

Einstein, Addison-Wesley Publishing Co., Information Services Division, 2725 Sand Hill Rd., Menlo Park CA 94025, 800/227-1936.

ERIC (Educational Resource Information Center), National Institute of Education, Washington DC 20208.

FrEdMail Foundation, Box 243, Bonita CA 91908-0243, 619/475-4852.

GEnie Online Services, 401 N. Washington St., Rockville MD 20850, 800/638-9636.

Imagination Network, Fred D'Ignazio, Multi-Media Classrooms Inc., 1302 Beech St., East Lansing MI 48823, 517/337-1549.

Interchange Online Network, 800/595-8555, 617/252-5000.

LES-COM-net, George Willet, 3485 Miller St., Wheatridge CO 80033, 303/233-5824 (modem).

MeLink, Cathy Glaude, Maine Computer Consortium, PO Box 620, Auburn ME 04210, 207/783-9776.

NASA Spacelink, 202/895-0028 (modem).

National Geographic Kids Network, National Geographic, Washington DC 20036, 800/647-0710, 717/822-8226 (fax).

National Geographic Society BBS, Educational Media Division, 17th and M St. N.W., Washington DC 20036, 202/857-7378 (300 baud) or 202/775-6738 (1200 baud).

Online Journal of Distance Education and Communications, 11120 Glacer Highway, Juneau AK 99801, 907/789-4417.

Pals Across the World, 4974 S.W. Galen, Lake Oswego OR 97035, 503/697-4080 or 503/635-0338.

Prodigy, 445 Hamilton, White Plains NY 10601, 800/776-3449.

Scholastic Network/America Online, 740 Broadway, New York NY 10003, 800/246-2986.

Special Net, National Association of State Directors of Special Education, 2021 K St. N.W., Ste. 315, Washington DC 20006, 202/296-1800.

For the latest listings on bulletin boards, call Novation Inc., Tarzana CA, 213/881-6880.

Appendix G
GLOSSARY

Abacus An ancient calculating device consisting of beads strung on wires or rods that are set in a frame.

ABC An abbreviation for the Atanasoff-Berry-Computer, the first electronic digital computer.

Access time The time a computer needs from the instant it asks for information until it receives it.

Acoustic coupler A type of modem that lets the user insert the telephone handset into a built-in cradle that sends and receives computer signals through the telephone lines.

Active matrix A screen, generally used in portable computers, in which each pixel is controlled by its own transistor.

ADA A high-level programming language developed in the late 1970s and named after Augusta Ada Byron, Countess of Lovelace and daughter of Lord Byron.

Algorithm Generally a set of instructions for a person to follow in order to solve a problem. A computer program is an algorithm that tells the computer what to do in a step-by-step manner—in a language that it comprehends.

Analog device A mechanism that handles values in continuous variable quantities such as voltage fluctuations.

Analytical engine A sophisticated mechanical calculating machine designed by Charles Babbage in 1833. Conceived before the technology was available, it was to have been capable of storing instructions, performing mathematical operations, and using punched cards for storage.

Application program A program written for a certain purpose, such as word processing.

Arithmetic logic unit (ALU) The central processing unit component responsible for the execution of fundamental arithmetic and logical operations on data.

Artificial intelligence (AI) Use of the computer to simulate the thinking of human beings.

ASCII code The American Standard Code for Information Interchange, a standard computer character set that allows for efficient data communication and achieves compatibility among computer devices.

Assembler A computer program that converts assembly language programs into executable machine language programs.

Assembly language A low-level language that uses mnemonic words and in which each statement corresponds directly to a single machine instruction.

Authoring language A computer language used to create educational software, such as drill and practice lessons.

Authoring system A program requiring little knowledge, used to create computer-based lessons and tests.

Backup disk A second copy of a program or document.

Bandwidth The amount of data that can be transmitted through a communication network.

Bar code reader An input device that scans bar codes and converts the bar codes into numbers that are displayed on the screen.

BASIC Beginner's All-Purpose Symbolic Instruction Code, one of the most commonly used high-level languages.

Baud rate The speed at which a modem can transmit data.

Binary The number system a computer uses. It has only two digits, *1* and *0*.

Bit An abbreviation for binary digit, either *1* or *0* in the binary number system.

Boolean logic Devised by George Boole, a system of algebra that used the operations of informal logic.

Boot The process of starting the computer.

BPS An abbreviation for bits per second, the measurement of data transmission speed. Presently the fastest modem transfer over phone lines is 56 kilobits per second (kbps).

Browser Software that lets users surf the World Wide Web. *Netscape* and *Internet Explorer* are the two most popular browsers.

Bug A mistake or error in a computer program.

Bulletin board (BBS) A computer that serves as a center for exchange of information for various interest groups.

Bus Network has a single bi-directional cable or bus line that carries messages to and from devices. Each workstation can access the network independently.

Byte A unit of computer storage that consists of eight binary digits (bits). A byte holds the equivalent of one character, such as the letter *C*.

C A computer languaged developed by Bell Labs for the Unix operating system.

Cathode ray tube (CRT) The basis of the television screen and the typical microcomputer display screen.

CD-ROM (compact disc read-only memory) A means of high-capacity storage (more than 600 megabytes) that uses laser optics for reading data.

Cell In an electronic spreadsheet, the intersection of a row and column.

Central processing unit (CPU) The "brains of the computer," where the computing takes place. The CPU is also called the *processor*. It is made up of a control unit and the arithmetic logic unit.

Chip A piece of semiconducting material, such as silicon, with transistors and resistors etched on its surface.

Circuit board A board onto which the electrical components are mounted and interconnected to form a circuit.

COBOL (Common Business-Oriented Language) A high-level language used for business applications.

Compiler A program that translates the source code of a program written in a higher-level language such as BASIC into a machine-readable, executable program.

Composite color monitor A monitor that accepts an analog video signal and combines red, green, and blue signals to produce a color image.

Computer A machine that accepts information, processes it according to a set of instructions, and produces the results as output.

Computer-aided design (CAD) Use of the computer for industrial design and technical drawing.

Computer-assisted instruction (CAI) Use of the computer as an instructional tool.

Computer conferencing Communication between two or more computers in real time.

Computer-managed instruction (CMI) A computerized, record-keeping system that diagnoses a student's progress, provides instruction, and analyzes progress.

Connect time The time spent on-line from logging on to logging off.

CPS A term used to describe the number of characters printed per second by the printer.

Cursor The blinking light that shows the user where he or she is working on the computer screen.

Cyberspace The use of computer technology to create virtual space.

Daisy-wheel printer An impact printer that produces a typewriter-quality print. This printer has its type characters set around a daisy wheel, similar to a wagon wheel minus an outer ring.

Database A collection of information organized according to some structure or purpose.

Database management system Application software that controls the organization, storage, and retrieval of data that is in the database.

Debug Find the errors in the computer's hardware or software.

Demodulation Used in telecommunication, the process of receiving and transforming an analog signal into its digital equivalent, which can be used by the computer.

Desktop A computerized representation of a person's work as if he or she were looking at a desk cluttered with folders.

Desktop publishing The use of the personal computer in conjunction with specialized software to combine text and graphics to produce high-quality output on a laser printer or typesetting machine.

Digital camera A portable camera that records images in a digital format.

Digital computer A computer that operates by accepting and processing data that has been converted into binary numbers.

Digital video disc (DVD) Similar to CD-ROM in appearance, this disc format has the capacity to hold 17 gigabytes.

Digitizer A device that translates analog information into digital information for computer processing. Examples include scanners and digital cameras.

Direct-connect modem A modem that lets the user connect directly to the computer and plug into the phone jack, bypassing the telephone handset.

Disk operating system (DOS) A program that lets the computer control its own operation. This program's major task is to handle the transfer of data and programs to and from the computer's disks.

Display The representation of data on a screen in the form of a printed report, graph, or drawing.

Documentation The instructions, tutorial, or reference material that is required for the computer program to run effectively. Documentation can be on-line help or printed material.

Dot-matrix printer An impact printer that produces characters and graphic images by striking an inked ribbon with tiny metal rods called pins.

Dot pitch The smallest dot that a computer monitor can display. The smaller the dots, the higher the resolution.

Download The process of sending information from a larger computer to a smaller one by means of a modem or network.

Drill and practice A type of computer instruction that lets students practice information with which they are familiar in order to become proficient.

Electronic mail or **e-mail** A system of transmitting messages over a communication network via the computer. *Pine* is an e-mail service most commonly used at universities and *Eudora Lite* is a mail application used most often by the general public.

E-mail address A name and a computer location (often referred to as a host), for example, kberger@qmp.com, where *kberger* is the name and *qmp* the location.

Encryption The process of coding information so that it cannot be understood unless decoded.

Ergonomics The science of designing computers and furniture so that they are easy and healthful to use.

EtherNet One of the most popular types of local area network connections.

Execute Carry out the instructions given in machine language code.

FAQs (Frequently Asked Questions) Files found at Internet sites that answer frequently asked questions. It is a good idea to check for FAQs and read them.

Fax machine An input/output device that lets the user transmit text and images between distant locations.

Fiber optics A medium consisting of glass fibers that transmit data using light.

Field A record location in which a certain type of data is stored.

File A collection of related records.

Flame An argumentative posting of an e-mail message or newsgroup message in response to another posting.

Floppy disk Covered with magnetic coating, such as iron oxide, the mass storage device used primarily with microcomputers.

Flowchart A graphical representation of the flow of operations that is needed to finish a job. It uses rectangles, diamonds, ovals, parallelograms, arrows, circles, and words.

Format Prepare a disk so the user can store information on it. During the formatting process, the computer's disk drive encodes a magnetic pattern consisting of tracks and sectors.

FORTRAN (FORmula TRANslator) One of the oldest high-level languages, suited for scientific and mathematical applications.

FTP (File Transfer Protocol) The basic Internet function that lets files be transferred between computers. You can use it to download files from a remote host computer as well as upload files from your computer to a remote host computer.

Full-duplex A protocol that lets the user send data in both directions simultaneously.

Function key A key located on the keyboard that the user programs to perform a specific task.

Gigabyte A unit of measure that equals approximately 1 billion (1,073,741,824) bytes.

Gopher A program that lets the user browse the Internet using menus.

Graphical user interface (GUI) A graphical interface, as opposed to a character-based computer interface such as MS-DOS. An example of a popular graphical interface is the Macintosh operating system.

Graphics tablet A plotting tablet that the user draws on to communicate with the computer.

Hacker A computer expert; sometimes one who illegally accesses and tampers with computer programs and data.

Half-duplex Synonymous with local echo, a protocol that lets data be sent in both directions but only one at a time.

Handheld computer is a small mobile computer that lets the user write on-screen with a stylus. This device provides tools for everyday such as a notepad, word processor, appointment calendar, address book and a fax modem.

Handshake A method of controlling the flow of data between two devices.

Hard copy Computer output that is on paper, film, or other permanent media.

Hard disk One or more disk platters coated with a metal oxide substance that allows information to be magnetically stored.

Hard drive The computer's main storage device.

Hardware The physical components of the computer system, which include the computer, monitor, printer, and disk drives.

High-level language Language that is farther away from the machine's operation and approximates human language. Low-level language (like machine and assembly) is nearer the machine's operation.

Home Page The main page in a Web site, at which you find hyperlinks to other pages.

Host The computer that serves as the beginning point and ending point for data transfer when accessing the Internet.

Hypertext Markup Language (HTML) The basic language that people use to build hypertext electronic documents on the Web.

Hypercard An authoring tool that lets the user organize information and retrieve on-screen cards that contain text, graphics, sound, and animation.

Hyperlink A graphic, an icon, or a word in a file that when clicked automatically opens another file for viewing.

Hypermedia Nearly synonymous with *hypertext* (however, it emphasizes the nontextual components of hypertext), a system that uses the computer to input, manipulate, and output graphics, sound, text, and video in the presentation of ideas and information.

HyperTalk The programming language that is used with *HyperCard*.

Hypertext Nonsequential associations of images, sound, text, and actions through which the user can browse, regardless of the order. An example of hypertext is a computer glossary from which a user can select a word and retrieve its definition.

Initialize See *Format*.

Ink-jet printer A nonimpact printer that uses a nozzle to spray a jet of ink onto a page of paper. These small, spherical bodies of ink are released through a matrix of holes to form characters.

Integrated circuit chip (IC chip) See *Chip*.

Integrated learning system (ILS) A central computer with software consisting of planned lessons in various curriculum areas.

Integrated program An application program that combines several tasks such as word processing and database management in one package and allows for the free interchange of information among applications.

Interactive video A system consisting of a computer, videodisc player, videotape, and software that provides the student with immediate feedback. It includes management features so lessons can be customized to specific student needs.

Interface The place at which a connection is made between two elements so they can work harmoniously together. In computing, different interfaces occur, ranging from user interfaces, in which people communicate with programs, to hardware interfaces that connect devices and components in the computer.

Internet A system of worldwide networks that enable the user to send electronic mail, conduct research, chat, and participate in newsgroups.

Internet Service Provider (ISP) An organization that charges a fee for users to dial into its computer for an Internet connection.

Interpreter A high-level program translator that translates and then executes each statement in a computer program. It translates a statement into machine language, runs it, then proceeds to the next statement, translates it, runs it, and so on.

Java A programming language, designed by Sun Microsystems to write programs that can be downloaded from the Internet with a Java interpreter. Many World Wide Web pages on the Internet use small Java applications, or applets, to display animations.

Joystick A small, boxlike object with a moving stick and buttons used primarily for games, educational software, and CAD systems.

Kbps (KiloBits Per Second) A computer modem's speed rating, measured in units of 1,024 bits. This is the maximum number a device can transfer in one second under the best of conditions.

Keyboard An input device similar to a standard typewriter but with extra keys, such as the function keys and the numeric pad.

Kilobyte (K) A unit of measure for computers that is equal to 1,024 bytes or 2^{10}.

Laser discs Large-sized optical discs that utilize laser technology for the purpose of video.

Laser printer A printer that produces high-quality text and graphic output by tracing images with a laser beam controlled by the computer.

Light-emitting diode (LED) When charged with electricity, a semiconductor diode that gives off light.

Light pen An instrument, used in conjunction with a video display, with a light-sensitive, photoelectric cell in its tip that sends an electrical impulse to the computer, which identifies its current location.

Liquid crystal display (LCD) A display that uses a liquid compound, positioned between two sheets of polarizing material squeezed between two glass panels.

Liquid crystal display projection panel A projector that receives computer output and displays it on a liquid crystal screen placed on an overhead projector. The projector displays on a large screen the program that the computer generates.

LISP Acronym for list processing, a high-level programming language frequently used in artificial intelligence systems that combines the use of lists with sets of symbols.

Local area network (LAN) A network that provides communication within a local area, usually within 200 or 300 feet, as found in office buildings.

Logo A high-level language designed for children that contains many functions found in LISP.

Low-level language A programming language, like assembly language, that is close to the machine's language.

Machine language A programming language composed of a pattern of 0s and 1s that is far removed from the language understood by human beings. This is the *only* language that computers understand.

Magnetic disk A device that stores data magnetically in circular tracks that are divided into sectors.

Magnetic ink character recognition (MICR) A character recognition system that reads text printed with a special magnetic ink. All the checks issued by banks are coded with this special ink and characters so that an MICR unit can read them.

Magnetic tape A reel of tape that is usually around 1/2 inch wide that can store about twenty-five megabytes of data magnetically in a linear track.

Mail merge A utility usually found in a word processor that takes names and addresses from a database and merges them into another document.

Mainframe computer A high-level computer designed for sophisticated computational tasks.

Mark I An electromechanical calculating machine designed by Howard Aiken at Harvard University and built by IBM.

Megabyte (MB) A unit of measure that equals approximately 1,048,576 bytes.

Megahertz (MHz) A measure of frequency equal to one million cycles per second.

Memory The circuitry inside the computer that lets it store and retrieve information. Generally, memory refers to the semiconductor storage (RAM) that is directly connected to the microprocessor.

Microcomputer system A computer that uses a single chip microprocessor, one that is less powerful than that of a minicomputer.

Microprocessor A chip that contains the central processing unit of the computer.

Microworld The Logo environment in which a child freely experiments, tests, and revises his or her own theories in order to create a product.

Millisecond (ms) Equivalent to 1,000th of a second.

Minicomputer A mid-level computer whose capabilities are between those of a mainframe and a microcomputer.

Modem Short for MOdulator/DEModulator, a device that lets two computers communicate with each other via the telephone lines.

Modulation Used in telecommunication, the means that a modem uses to convert digital information sent by computer to its analog form, so that the information can be sent over the telephone lines.

Monitor A video display that resembles a television set, designed to handle a wider and higher range of frequencies.

Morphing A special effect that changes one image into another image.

Mouse A popular input device that is used instead of the keyboard to make menu selections.

Multimedia A subset of hypermedia that combines graphics, sound, animation, and video.

Nanosecond (ns) The value 10^9, or one billionth of a second.

Napier's rods A device used for multiplying large numbers, invented by John Napier, a Scottish mathematician, in 1617.

Netiquette The etiquette used in cyberspace.

Network Computers that share storage devices, peripherals, and applications. A network can be connected by telephone lines, satellites, or cables.

On-line When a computer is interacting with an on-line service or the Internet. For example, a person goes on-line to read his or her e-mail.

On-line Service Refers to a commercial service like American Online (AOL) that gives access to electronic mail, news services, and the Web.

Operating system See *Disk operating system.*

Optical character reader (OCR) A device that uses laser technology or a light-sensing mechanism to interpret data. Advanced OCR systems can recognize hand printing.

Optical disc A round platter that has information recorded on it with laser beam technology. It is capable of storing large amounts of information.

Optical mark reader (OMR) A device that reads penciled or graphic information on cards or pages. Lamps furnish light reflected from the card or paper; the amount of reflected light is measured by a photocell.

Output After processing, the information that is sent from the computer to a peripheral device.

Parity A modem-checking technique for memory or data communication errors.

Pascal A high-level, structured language, designed by Niklaus Wirth in the late 1960s.

Peripheral The devices that are connected to the computer under the microprocessor's control, such as disk drives, printers, and modems.

Personal data assistant (PDA) A small, handheld computer that accepts input on the screen from a stylus.

PILOT Acronym for Programmed Inquiry, Learning Or Teaching, a CAI authoring language developed by John Starkweather in 1969.

Piracy The act of copying software illegally.

Pixel Short for picture element, a linear dot on a display screen. When this dot is combined with other dots, it creates an image.

Plasma display A display produced by a mixture of neon gases between two transparent panels, giving a very sharp, clean image with a wide viewing angle.

Plug-ins Programs built to extend your browser's capabilities. Plug-ins let you see and hear video, audio, and other kinds of multimedia files.

Presentation graphics Combining text and images, software that produces and displays graphic screens.

Printer A device that produces computer output.

Program A series of instructions designed to make a computer do a given task.

Public domain software Software that is not copyrighted and can be freely copied and distributed without payment or permission.

Random-access memory (RAM) Volatile memory. Whenever an individual turns off the computer he or she loses whatever information is in RAM.

Read-only memory (ROM) Memory that retains its contents when the power supply is turned off. Often referred to as hardwired, internal memory, it cannot be altered or changed.

RealAudio A plug-in that lets you listen to live or prerecorded audio transmission on the World Wide Web.

Real time The immediate processing of data as it becomes available. In telecommunication, when you are on-line you can be connected to other people who are on-line at the same time. Real time is quite different from e-mail, in which the other user does not have to be on-line.

Record A collection of related fields that are treated as a single unit.

Resolution The clarity or degree of sharpness of a displayed character or image, expressed in linear dots per inch.

Ring network A group of computers that communicate with each other in a ring, without a file server.

Scanner A device that digitizes photographs or line art and stores the images as a file that can be transferred into a paint program or directly into a word processor.

Shareware Copyrighted software that is distributed free but must be paid for if the customer is satisfied.

Simplex Data transmission that works in one direction at a time.

Simulation Software that approximates the conditions of the real world in an environment in which the user changes the variables.

Site licensing A software licensing system in which a person or organization pays a set fee to run copies of a program on a large number of computers.

Software A program that instructs the computer to perform a specific job.

Speech synthesizer An output device that generates sound. This chip gives the computer the ability to search for words and their pronunciations in a database.

Spreadsheet A computerized version of a manual worksheet, with a matrix of numbers arranged in rows and columns, that facilitates calculations.

Star network A communications network in which all the computers are connected to a file server or host computer.

Structured programming Programming that uses a limited number of branching instructions and emphasizes modularity.

Supercomputers The largest and fastest of the mainframe computers with the most advanced processing abilities.

Surge suppressor Also known as a surge protector, a device that protects the computer from damaging electrical surges.

SYSOP Acronym for SYStem OPerator, the person who runs a bulletin board.

System disk The disk that contains operating software and can also be used to boot the computer.

Tag In HTML, a special code where words or letter, number combinations are enclosed in less than (<) and greater than (>) signs such as <H2>.

This tag tells the Web browser how to display the content.

Telecommunication The electronic transmission of information, including data, television pictures, sound, and facsimiles.

Terabyte A unit of measurement equal roughly to one trillion bytes (actually 1,099,511,627,776 bytes).

Thermal printer Using heated wires, a printer that burns dots into a costly special paper.

Time bomb A computer virus that is programmed to go off on a specific day and time.

Touch screen A display that has a pressure sensitive panel mounted in the front. The user makes choices by touching the screen in the correct location.

Trackball A moveable ball that moves the cursor on the screen as it is manipulated.

Trackpad A pressure-sensitive pad that is smaller and more accurate than the trackball.

Transistor An electronic gate that bridges the gap between two wires and lets the current flow.

Tutorial Similar to a tutor, a program that explains new material and then tests the student's progress.

UNIX Originally developed by AT&T Bell laboratories, an operating system used on different types of computers that supports multitasking.

Upload Transfer of information from one's computer to a remote computer.

URL (Uniform Resource Locator) A site address on the World Wide Web. For example, the URL for the California State University home page is http://www.csun.edu.

Usenet A leading network system of bulletin boards that services more than 1,500 newsgroups.

User friendly A term that means *easy to learn and use.*

User group A group of users of a specific type of computer who share experiences to improve their understanding of the product.

Utility programs Programs that perform a variety of housekeeping and control functions such as sorting, copying, searching, and file management.

Videoconferencing A multiuser chat in which the live images of the users are displayed on each participant's computer screen.

Videodisc A read-only, optical disc that uses an analog signal to store and retrieve still and moving pictures, sound, or color.

Video RAM (VRAM) and **Dynamic Random Access Memory (DRAM)** Chips that are used to transfer and hold an image on the computer screen.

Virtual reality A computer-generated world in which a person is able to manipulate the environment. The user generally wears a head-mounted device and special sensor gloves.

Virus A program that infects computer files by duplicating itself.

Voice recognition A system that converts the spoken word into binary patterns that are computer recognizable; it understands human speech.

Warping A process similar to morphing, involving the altering and manipulation of a single image.

Wide area network (WAN) A network that uses long-distance communication or satellites to connect computers over greater distances than a local area network does.

Windows A graphical interface developed by Microsoft Corporation for IBM and IBM compatible computers.

Word processor A software program designed to make the computer a useful electronic writing tool that can edit, store, and print documents.

World Wide Web (WWW) An Internet service that lets you navigate the Internet using hypertext documents.

Worm A program that can run by itself and replicate a full working version to other computers. After the worm is finished with its work, the data is usually corrupted and irretrievable.

Index